SIN

BOOKS BY G. C. BERKOUWER

MODERN UNCERTAINTY AND CHRISTIAN FAITH

RECENT DEVELOPMENTS IN ROMAN CATHOLIC THEOLOGY

THE TRIUMPH OF GRACE IN THE THEOLOGY OF KARL BARTH

THE SECOND VATICAN COUNCIL AND THE NEW CATHOLICISM

STUDIES IN DOGMATICS SERIES —

THE PROVIDENCE OF GOD

FAITH AND SANCTIFICATION

FAITH AND JUSTIFICATION

FAITH AND PERSEVERANCE

THE PERSON OF CHRIST

GENERAL REVELATION

DIVINE ELECTION

MAN: THE IMAGE OF GOD

THE WORK OF CHRIST

THE SACRAMENTS

SIN

Studies in Dogmatics

SIN

BY

G. C. BERKOUWER

PROFESSOR OF SYSTEMATIC THEOLOGY

FREE UNIVERSITY OF AMSTERDAM

WILLIAM B. EERDMANS PUBLISHING COMPANY
GRAND RAPIDS, MICHIGAN

Translated by Philip C. Holtrop
from the Dutch volumes,
De Zonde I: Oorsprong en Kennis der Zonde,
and *De Zonde II: Wezen en Verbreiding der Zonde,*
published by J. H. Kok N.V., Kampen, The Netherlands

TRANSLATOR'S NOTE

Biblical quotations in this volume are taken from the Revised Standard Version (RSV), except where otherwise indicated. Throughout the volume the author makes repeated reference to the creeds and and formularies as used by the Reformed Churches (Gereformeerd) of The Netherlands. English translations of these (the Heidelberg Catechism, Belgic Confession, and Canons of Dort) are taken from the *Psalter Hymnal,* published by the Publication Committee of the Christian Reformed Church, Grand Rapids, Michigan, 1959. Quotations from Calvin's *Institutes* are from the Library of Christian Classics edition (vols. XX-XXI), edited by J. T. McNeill (F. L. Battles, translator), and published by The Westminster Press, Philadelphia. Quotations from Barth's *Kirchliche Dogmatik (Church Dogmatics)* are from the authorized translations, published by T. and T. Clark, Edinburgh. All other translations, except where specifically indicated, are the translator's.

CONTENTS

ABBREVIATIONS

BC	— Belgic Confession
CD	— Canons of Dort
Comm. (Komm.)	— Commentary
Denz.	— *Enchiridion Symbolorum,* ed. H. Denzinger
ET	— English Translation
Ev.Theol.	— *Evangelische Theologie*
Geref. Dog.	— H. Bavinck, *Gereformeerde Dogmatiek*
G.T.T.	— *Gereformeerd Theologisch Tijdschrift*
HC	— Heidelberg Catechism
Inst.	— J. Calvin, *Institutes of the Christian Religion*
K.D.	— K. Barth, *Kirchliche Dogmatik*
K.u.D.	— Kerygma und Dogma
K.V.	— *Korte Verklaring*
LXX	— Septuagint
N.T.T.	— *Nederlands Theologisch Tijdschrift*
Phil.Ref.	— *Philosophia Reformata*
P.R.E.	— Hauck-Herzog, *Realencyklopädie für protestantische Theologie und Kirche*
TWNT	— *Theologisches Wörterbuch zum Neuen Testament,* ed. G. Kittel and G. Friedrich; ET, *Theological Dictionary of the New Testament,* trans. G. Bromiley
Z.N.T.W.	— *Zeitschrift für die Neutestamentliche Wissenschaft*
Z.S.Th.	— *Zeitschrift für systematische Theologie*
Z.Th.K.	— *Zeitschrift für Theologie und Kirche*
Zw.d.Z.	— *Zwischen den Zeiten*

7

PART I

THE ORIGIN AND KNOWLEDGE OF SIN

CHAPTER ONE

THE QUESTION OF ORIGIN

WHOEVER REFLECTS on the doctrine of sin in the light of God's Word is struck very early with the question of sin's origin. That question is very common in the history of the Church and her theology. It would seem to find a parallel in the more general concern of man to know the origin of "evil" in his world. No real genius is needed to see life's battered and mangled pieces before us, and no particular wisdom is required to appreciate how profoundly abnormal life can be. Therefore the question would seem to be completely reasonable: What is the origin of sin? The answers given in the course of the centuries are many.

Yet, before we consider a few of those answers, it is necessary to examine the *question of origin*. Some people may find this a rather strange procedure, the more so because the question itself would seem so utterly natural and self-evident. Is it not true that all men endeavor to penetrate to the *prima causa* of all things? Need it surprise us when they seek to know the origin of sin? It would seem to be obvious that man's inquisitiveness is only sated when he has laid out the objects of his interest and exposed their various constituents. Why should that be different in the case of man's sin? Man, it would seem, has a natural propensity for analyzing his sin and piecing together its various "components." His efforts here are of one piece with his other attempts to "know the origins." He wants to know the origins of himself, his world, his soul, and the critical events that have shaped his history. Thus he searches out the relevant features that gave rise to the Second World War; he fits together the origins of Germany's defeat. Men have reasoned that every last thing has its first and final cause. Why should that be different in the situation of man's sin? Our investigation here would seem to be as natural and self-evident and as *a priori* legitimate as any other investigation of any

11

other origin. Why should we consider this *question of origin*
when the fact would seem so patent that our only real concern
is to give an answer?

What we want to say in this first chapter is that the question of sin's origin, in itself, is peculiar and suggests a problematic all its own. If we grant that an issue cannot be resolved
unless it is rightly set forth, that certainly holds in the situation
of man's sin. In our asking of this question we presuppose that
sin is one of those phenomena that are knowable in their
origins and whose origins we also desire to know. From that
standpoint we may understand the wide variety of *answers* but
also of *questions* in what would otherwise seem to be a rather
simple and universal concern. Men have asked the question
in the form of the query, *Unde malum,* or *Whence evil?* Yet
obviously, if this is what we want to know, everything depends
on what we mean by *malum.* The issue takes on a certain color
if we see in *malum* a common and universal abnormality and
aberration, or a mere frustration in human affairs. It is different if we accept the term in its biblical sense of "trangression"
against God's holy command, or the forfeiting of communion
with God and the rebellion against his lordship. Here already
it is clear that the nature and content of this question predefine
the nature of the answers that are given. The complexity and
remarkable variety in this question are explainable, to some
extent, already now.

Possibly there is no one who is under the illusion that we
live in an ideal kind of world, or a world of serene communion
and beatitude. Our human experience is not a matter of constant blessings. Therefore every man must agree that there are
appalling evidences of disturbances around us which can only
call forth the question of *unde.* But we shall have to consider
the *nature* of that question and shall have to listen, with well-
cocked ears, to the great disparity of answers concerning the
"inexplicability" and "strangeness" of evil. When we do so
we shall observe the widely divergent spirits not only in the
answers that are given but also in the very manner in which
the question is raised. Here we are touching on something that
shall occupy us at greater length in the course of our study:
the question of the *knowledge* of sin, or the ways in which our
sin is made known and laid bare for what it *is.* For now, it is
well to remember that not only the answers but also the question itself must introduce us to problems of a very profound

nature. One has to be careful in seeing the question of sin's origin as a matter that is "natural" or "self-evident." Indeed, the answer to this question is already presupposed in our outlook on what "sin" and "evil" *are*. The false dialectic of question and answer can only confuse the issue and exhibit more fully the darkness of our sin.

Herman Bavinck has written that the origin of evil is second only to the origin of being as the greatest enigma in man's life; moreover, it is certainly the hardest cross for man's understanding to bear.[1] But the Christian Church has generally approached the problem of the origin of being by professing the goodness of God's creation of heaven and earth. The problem of the origin of evil has proved a more difficult issue. Here the question can only be seen as an inexplicable riddle, for the mere professing of God's good creation can provide us with no answers. The sin of man cannot be analyzed in terms of God's creative powers.

Therefore, it is small wonder that some have always regarded *Unde peccatum* as a more fundamental and urgent or compelling question than *Unde esse*. One thing is certain: We cannot say that this question of sin's origin has a right to our attention only *after* we have asked the question of the origin of being.[2] Both these questions have their own peculiar structures. The question of sin is *not* related to creaturely reality but to reality's destruction and disruption. Our concern here has nothing to do with the origin of "being" and everything to do with the so-called "privation" of being. At the same time, we are not involved in a *mera* but an *actuosa privatio*. He who looks at the "being" of things may rightly be filled with amazement and admiration; he who looks at his own sin can only be filled with consternation and dismay. Thus we stand vis-à-vis

1. Bavinck, *Geref. Dog.*, III, 29.
2. In our day philosophy gives much attention to this fascination of man with "being." Heidegger begins his *Sein und Zeit* by treating this as the "fundamental question"; note his comments on the "fascinating peculiarity of what exists" (the "Befremdlichkeit des Seienden"). On this matter of "fascination": "Why is there existence at all and not much rather nothing?" (*Was ist Metaphysik?*, 1929, pp. 27-29). Cf. the same question in H. Kuhn, *Begegnung mit dem Nichts*, 1954, p. 1: "Why is there something at all and not rather nothing?" In this same regard cf. Bavinck already, in *Wijsbegeerte der Openbaring*, 1908, p. 74, on the fact "that there *is* anything, that there is a *being*, for which we are incapable of demonstrating the ground."

a different problem, or a different riddle, from the origin of being. We can *never* assign this "reality" of sin, in any perspicuous sense, to the goodness of God's creation. It stands to reason that exactly *at this point* the Church has waged a perpetual warfare against any semblance of heresy. Her polemic has been necessary and has had far-reaching consequences for the whole issue of the origin of sin.

The question of *sin's origin* has a qualitatively different character from the question of any other kind of origin. It is this "qualitatively different character" which forms the theme of our first chapter. But obviously this question is not a subject for a merely theoretical dispute. The man who says that it *is* must certainly be standing on very dangerous grounds. Yet, throughout the course of history men have tried to construct abstract and causal answers to this question of sin's origin and have failed to realize that in so doing they have violated the very limits of objectivity. A remarkable relation exists between seeking for the origin of sin and an *exculpation or exoneration of one's own person*. Whoever reflects on the origin of sin cannot engage himself in a merely theoretical dispute; rather he is engaged, intimately and personally, in what can only be called the *problem of sin's guilt*.[3] As soon as he refers to a definite evil or a particular guilt he is no longer concerned about a purely logical or abstract theory. Factors of an entirely different sort come into play, and these influence his question of origin decisively. Any "causal" explanation we propose can only be seen, in the practice of living, as a means of fashioning an "indisputable" excuse.

Hence our contention that the investigation of *unde malum* can only take place within a structure of its own. It can only take place within a peculiar structure which underscores the invalidity of applying a "cool" and "scientific" logic to the problem of our sin. Man's feeble efforts to find the deepest "cause" of his guilt can only succeed in fabricating a self-excuse. Sometimes the excuse is crass and sometimes more refined, but it is always in line with other causal "explanations." These excuses give ample evidence of the deepest intentions in all too many efforts to give an answer to the question of sin's origin.

3. Cf., e.g., K. Jaspers, *Die Schuldfrage: ein Beitrag zur deutschen Frage,* 1946.

What we see in those who excuse themselves is the same thing as happens, all too frequently, in disputes among the nations and particularly in the forum of world opinion. National or individual incriminations make easy way for a national or personal self-excuse. Thus the noble art of self-analysis is supplanted by the vicious practice of accusing someone else and excusing oneself. In that way a "causal" line of thought ends up in making references to someone else as the *prima causa* of one's own misconduct. Even if we assume responsibility for a certain proportion of life's miseries and woes, the "causal" mode of thinking finds it difficult to see that portion as any more than the *causa secunda*. This must obviously root in a still deeper *prima causa*. We do well to cast a wary eye on that sort of thinking.

Thus, when we take interest in the causality of sin we are not engaged in an *a priori* innocent activity. We are not involved in something purely theoretical. Our interest is not analogous to the natural scientist's quest for the *causae* of new or strange phenomena. The man who looks for the *causa peccati* is engaged in the sphere of the human and personal, and his interest can only be "existential." But if that be the case, his logical and analytical capacities are not the only ones involved in that enterprise. For man himself — *the whole of man* — is involved in a very profound way. Any explanation for the "storm" in human nature or human relations can only be structured on a different model from the storm of inclement weather or violent rains. Kipling once said that all lines of communication are then broken down, between one person and the next, and men invoke lies "over oceans of misunderstandings."

The structure of causal thinking, as applied to the "discovery of sin's origin," can only be called a "referential" structure or a structure of "pointing one's finger." We see that already in the Paradise account. Fallen man, addressed by God, responded by pointing his finger at someone else and by trying to vindicate himself. His thinking went something like this: "the *woman* whom thou gavest to be with me, she gave me fruit of the tree" (Gen. 3:12); then "the *serpent* beguiled me"; and only then, "*I* ate" (3:13). Notice the *prima causa* and the *causa secunda* in this chapter. Consider that God did not ignore these various lines of connection in the process of man's sinning. Witness here the severe indictment of the serpent: "Because you have done this..." (3:14). But in all these connections there is nothing which diminishes the gravity of man's iniquity or the judgment that is *his*. In the *context* of the various connections man's guilt is underscored and his innocence is denied. Furthermore, in that same context, God's verdict is announced: "Because *you* have listened to the voice of your wife, ... cursed is the ground because of *you*" (3:17).

These observations suggest an *a priori* warning against approaching the problem of sin by means of the concept of causality.[4] Genesis 3 is an admonition against any "neutral" or "objective" investigation of sin's origin. It should be seen as a paradigmatic or illuminative warning against any further effort to explain away man's sin.[5] Any such effort can only lead us to disruptive aberrations in which the shadow of self-excuse is the theoretical and *existential* background for the query, *Unde peccatum?* The same connections as we have seen in Genesis 3 are as big as life in the reality of our everyday experience. They are obvious in the sinning and the lying which we ourselves do. We are aware of these relations in the loss of true joy and in situations of conflict and estrangement, and whenever the question of sin's origin is transformed into a "self-excuse." Our investigations of sin's origin are then the seedbed for our further estrangements. Thus we must guard ourselves against the false assumption that this question of *unde peccatum* can ever be integrated in the "obvious" or "self-evident" causal thinking to which our spirits so naturally incline. If anything is obvious it is certainly this: A different "naturalness" and "self-evidentness" are apparent, all too often, in man's efforts to explain away his sin. The very forms of causal thinking are peculiarly adaptable to our own self-excuse. They are congenial to papering over the deepest depths of our own guilt.

All this brings up an important question: *Must* a causal mode of thinking concerning our sin inevitably or inexorably lead us to such a consequence as this? Could the result of such

4. Cf. G. von Rad, *Das erste Buch Mose*, 1954, pp. 73f., concerning the "first cause of events." Von Rad observes that nothing is said about a questioning of the serpent (p. 74).
5. See especially W. Zimmerli, *Die Urgeschichte*, I, 1943, regarding Gen. 3:12. "Only at the very end, hidden under the subterfuge of the preceding words, is the confession made: Then I did eat" (210). Also concerning the disintegration of solidarity ("the woman ..., she gave me"!): "in the moment sin was uncovered there remained only the sordid misuse of one's neighbor for hiding one's own guilt."

a causal chain be anything but a senseless self-excuse? This question is important because, as we have said, the very mention of a number of "connections" or a *"prima" causa* for our sin would seem to land us, necessarily, in the effort to excuse ourselves. Is our guilt automatically divested of its guilt-character when we try to "explain" it? Bavinck was of the opinion that it is. This is what he wanted to say when he expressed himself in the following terms: "Whoever tries to comprehend or to explain our sin, or attempts to show that it must follow necessarily from what has gone before, does an injustice to sin's very nature. He obscures the boundaries of good and evil and derives our evil from something that is good."[6] The affinity of causal reflections on sin and this sort of self-excuse must render invalid the question of sin's origin. The very practice of making alibis is really the product of man's own blindness.

This is the point that Paul well made in his reference to the gravity of judgment when seen in the light of divine revelation. *There can be no self-excuse.* Here we reflect on the words of Romans 1:20: "So they are without excuse." Consider also the statement in Romans 2:1: "Therefore you have no excuse, O man, whoever you are, when you judge another." Any effort to excuse ourselves is really the best evidence of how lamentably much we already "deceive ourselves, and the truth is not in us" (I John 1:8; cf. v. 10) .

We can appreciate that Bavinck, in view of these considerations, contended for the impossibility of explaining sin's origin. In that assertion he found no recourse in an *asylum ignorantiae,* but he only made the necessary and candid acknowledgment that we stand, at this juncture, at the very limits of our understanding. He conceived of those limits as implying much more than an epistemological hiatus. He saw them as the border which holds in this particular case *alone.* Any explanation for the nature of sin is "illegal and irrational," according to Bavinck,[7] and this irrationality can never be integrated in rational-causal relations without bestowing upon it a new legitimacy. If we assume that a clear and conclusive "explanation" for sin is possible, it can only follow that Bavinck's reference to sin as an "illicit" incursion in our universe can have no validity at all.[8]

6. Bavinck, *op. cit.,* 47.
7. *Ibid.,* 48.
8. *Ibid.,* 53.

Thus the *legitimacy* of the question of sin's origin is itself a question of very great importance. Is it the case that as soon as we search for the "components" of sin we can only emasculate or amputate the *reality of our guilt?*[9] It is simply impossible, we should judge, to sever this bond between an "explanation" for sin's origin and an illegitimate excuse. Obviously an "explanation" softens down our guilt in the very process of pointing out its constituents. Many voices are heard saying today that sin's origin is genuinely inexplicable. We do well to listen. We must not be tempted, along some devious route, to give an explanation for our sin. When we stand face to face with sin we stand face to face with a different "reality" from any reality that permits a "causal analysis." Furthermore, what is true for sin is true in the case of sin alone. It shrivels up into nothingness when we try to explain its "constituents."

This was the insight that brought Bavinck to the remarkable statement that sin has no "origin" but only a "beginning." Therefore he saw the question of origin, or the attempt to analyze and to know the reasons why, as illegitimate. It is not illegitimate because it penetrates too far into that which can only be a secret for man. In that case, we could join hands with a species of irrationalism which despairs of finding an answer or deplores the weaknesses of human flesh. This question is illegitimate for the simple reason that a logical explanation assigns a sensibleness to that which is intrinsically nonsensical, a rationality to that which is irrational, and a certain order to that which is disorderly.[10] In that light it is obvious why Scripture makes no effort at all to explain the origin of sin in terms of its component parts. There is no allusion to an im-

---

9. Cf. A. G. Honig, *Handboek van de Gereformeerde Dogmatiek,* 1938, p. 379, concerning sin as "an insoluble riddle," or an inexplicable foolishness, absurdity, and illogic itself. "And how could the illogical ever permit an explanation?" But immediately after this Honig backtracks from his position: "We must not even try, therefore, to solve *entirely* the riddle of sin" (italics mine).

10. In this senselessness, irrationality and disorder there is certainly a *will* for self-rule and autonomy, but there is no autonomy *itself*. Senselessness is not an autonomous "opponent," as we find in dualism; rather, in its disruption of sense it utilizes creaturely reality, and precisely in so doing it finds its border. This non-autonomy, however, does not imply a giving of sense to the senseless. Cf. H. Dooyeweerd, "De Wijsbegeerte der Wetsidee en de Barthianen," in *Phil. Ref.,* 1951, p. 153.

penetrable darkness or an unfortunate gap in our knowledge. There is only the *confession of our guilt*. In the act of confession we do not, and we cannot, yearn for an "explanation" of our sins. We recognize our sin as our *very own*. But in that case we are concerned with a different "causality" from the causality that is usually meant in the question of sin's origin. Our attention is not held captive by theoretical causality or abstract reasoning. Our interest is not in factors other than *our guilt*.

There is, of course, a thinking or speaking in which a man keeps guilty silence, in relation to his guilt, and actually conceals his sin (Ps. 32:3). But there is also a kind of genuine understanding of sin's "causality" which pierces one to the quick and banishes all self-excuse. "I acknowledged my sin to thee, and I did not hide my iniquity" (32:5). "Against thee, thee only, have I sinned, and done that which is evil in thy sight" (51:4). The real *causa* of sinful activity is evident precisely here. Nor need this be "explained." If any "reference" is made, or pointing of our fingers, it should only be to that ugly self-guilt which stands directly and irrefutably before our very eyes. "For I know my transgressions, and my sin is ever before me" (51:3). "Connections" outside ourselves need not be denied, for no man is an island to himself. We should not deny the universality of guilt. Our confession must be the same as Isaiah's: "I am a man of unclean lips, and I dwell in the midst of a people of unclean lips" (6:5). Yet, in all these "connections" and all this solidarity, there can never be a self-excuse. We can only pray for God's renewal of our lives and his blessing on the lives of others. "Purge *me* with hyssop, and *I* shall be clean; wash *me,* and *I* shall be whiter than snow" (Ps. 51:7). "Do good to *Zion* in thy good pleasure; rebuild the walls of Jerusalem" (51:18).

When we stop thinking in referential terms or in terms extrinsic to ourselves it is soon apparent that there is no room for locating outside ourselves the first and deepest *causa* of our sin. We then find it impossible to "explain" our sin in terms of those circumstances which surround us. The essential hallmark of true confession is this rejection of an explanation for our sin in terms of its component factors. In such an explanation our sin can never be *confessed*.[11] "Connections" are very evident, but they are not in the effort to make a self-excuse. Rather they are seen as an *intensification of our guilt*. Thus the

11. Cf. K. Heim, *Jesus der Herr*, 1935, p. 143.

Apostle Paul, who spoke with boldness concerning the entrance of sin in the world, gave no shred of support for those who sought for an excuse. We cannot find the slightest explanation for what has always been, and shall ever be, the responsible act of man.[12]

The tendency to make an excuse or an explanation is part and parcel of the very nature of sin. Therefore it is illegitimate. We need not wonder why sinful living, estranged from God, confronts us with these questions of sin's origin. But the questions themselves are essentially the same as self-excuse. The various forms in which they appear show forth the problematic which we have already observed above. That fact is evident in both the asking and the answering of the question of *unde malum?* It is evident in periods of crisis and need, and whenever *malum* is seen as the evil of deficiency or emergency and we therefore inquire, *Unde malum?* Whence this dire calamity? Our question then is not strictly the same as *Unde peccatum?* Here the murmurings of Israel in the wilderness are the classic example. "Why does the Lord bring us into this land, to fall by the sword? Our wives and our little ones will become a prey; would it not be better for us to go back to Egypt?" (Num. 14:1). This was the question that Israel repeatedly asked in her wanderings (cf. 16:13f.; Ex. 17:1ff., 32:23). Thus it was not guilt but *need* which really prompted her to ask. It was not *unde peccatum* but *unde malum*.

In the book of Ezekiel we find a poignant example of causal thinking, as related to Israel's needs and distresses. In the emergency that confronted the people they found a "solution" or an "explanation" in the sins of their forefathers. "The fathers have eaten sour grapes, and the children's teeth are set on edge" (18:2). Israel's circumstances and the emergency that stared her in the face were now "explained" in the referential thinking which we have already seen above. Against that kind of thought the prophet Ezekiel inveighed. *"The soul that sins shall die"* (18:4). The adage that naively assigned a "causality" to

---

12. Far from giving us an explanation for our sin, Romans 5 speaks of "death." It speaks of "death through sin" (v. 12). The extent to which self-excuse is absent here appears from the confession of guilt in the section that comes before vv. 12ff.: cf. "ungodly" (v. 6), "sinners" (v. 8), "enemies" (v. 10). We shall consider Romans 5 more extensively in Part II of this volume.

the forefathers was now explicitly forbidden by God himself: "As I live, says the Lord God, this proverb shall no more be used by you in Israel" (18:3). The words of the prophet were very pungent and left no doubt that "the wickedness of the wicked shall be upon himself" (18:20). That very same accent is apparent in other passages (cf. Jer. 31:29-30). In Deuteronomy 24:16, for example, the matter is very plainly stated: "The fathers shall not be put to death for the children, nor shall the children be put to death for the fathers; every man shall be put to death for his own sin."

What we find in Ezekiel is a strong renunciation of the people's apparently innocent, causal proverb. That fact is all the more remarkable when we compare this proverb with the second commandment. It would seem that the commandment underscores a definite "relation" between guilt and consequent judgment, and that both of these are apparent in the transfer of the sins of one generation to generations which follow. But those connections which are apparent may never be transformed by sinful or apostate men into a "referential" or "explanatory" relation. Everything is then thrust into a wrong light. The meaning and reality of God's judgment are then metamorphosed into an "illuminative excuse."

Thus, the antithetical and polemical thrust of Ezekiel is misconstrued by such a critic as W. Staerk. According to Staerk, the prophet obscured a fundamental truism of life, with grievous consequences for religion and morality.[13] On the surface it would seem that there is at least a measure of truth in the suggestion that Staerk wants to make. For the "proverb" does have the appearance of a valid statement. Yet the appearance is only skin deep. The connections that Israel drew between guilt and judgment were now hardened into objective "magnitudes," and objective conclusions were drawn apart from the living God and man's own guilt. In short, the "connections" were depersonalized and were used by rebellious men for their own "ultimate excuse." In making use of that proverb, the people of Israel prostituted the very words of God. They distorted his threat of punishment and turned it into a concept of bleak causality. This idea was no longer distinguishable from a fatalistic complaint.[14]

13. Cf. Staerk's "Persönliche Schuld und Gesamtschuld," in *Z.S.Th.*, 1927, p. 413.
14. Both Noordtzij (*K.V., Ezechiël*) and Aalders (*Comm. op Ezechiël*, I, 296) relate the second commandment to this discussion and rightly

Scripture, with no exceptions, explodes this causal thinking and all such references to "explanatory" circumstances. It demonstrates that this thinking is really the subtle attempt to escape our own guilt and responsibility. When Saul was disobedient he offered the lame excuse, which he thought would make things "clear": "... the *people* took of the spoil, sheep and oxen, the best of the things devoted to destruction, to sacrifice to the Lord your God in Gilgal" (I Sam. 15:21). This sacrilegious causality was punctured through by the piercing indictment of Samuel: "*You* have rejected the word of the Lord" (15:23).

Nor does Scripture allow a causal or a simplistic explanation for the calamities of others. When the news of the sad lot of the Galileans reached Jesus he rejected such explanations with a sweeping admonition and warning: "Do you think that these Galileans were worse sinners than all the other Galileans, because they suffered thus? I tell you, No; but unless you repent you will all likewise perish" (Luke 13:2-3). The same message is the heart of the powerful ninth chapter of John. There we read the story of the man born blind. Nowhere do we find a clearer picture of the question of *unde malum?* Christ was challenged to give an answer: "Rabbi, who sinned, this man or his parents, that he was born blind?" (9:2). The answer came very loud and clear: "It was not that this man sinned, or his parents" (9:3). Notice that Christ transposed the entire *causa*-problematic into a teleology or a reference to a goal: "that the works of God might be made manifest in him" (9:3; cf. John 11:4).

The total confusion in causal thinking was very evident even after Christ performed his amazing cure. *How* did the man gain his sight (9:15)? *How* could Christ do these things (9:16)? Christ, according to the Pharisees, was obviously "not *from* God, for he does not keep the sabbath." Yet *how* can a mere sinner do such signs as these (9:16)? The parents of the man were interrogated: *How* could their son now see (9:19)? The man himself was asked: "*How* did he open your eyes?" (9:26; cf. v. 27).

But what a senseless confusion we see in all of this! Naive causal thinking concerning the *sins of others* is set in contrast

deny any contradiction with Ezekiel 18. Cf. also T. C. Vriezen, *De Theologie van het Oude Testament,* pp. 336f. Vriezen sees the prophecy of Ezekiel as a refutation of a tragic or melancholy outlook on life or a feeling sorry for oneself.

to the teleological depths of the thoughts of God![15] We have to recognize that the most obvious sign of true repentance is precisely this: that we no longer think in terms of such "connections" as these. We do not draw the relations between sin and misery, misery and sin, to excuse ourselves and deny our own responsibility.[16] Only when guilt is *not concealed* but is *openly confessed* is the Lord our "hiding place" in the time of need. Only then — no matter what our guilt — do we joyfully celebrate with "shouts of deliverance." For our lives are then preserved in the day of our despair (Ps. 32:7).

On the basis of what we have said it is obvious that this "question of origin" is not so "innocent" as it may have once appeared. The issue is not a theoretical or a practical curiosity regarding the connections and the origins of things. Indeed, this question itself is found in a very different setting, and when we ask it we are already engaged in the power and murkiness of sin. Therefore there is every reason to ask why the investigation of sin's origin is still so frequently made. Why the question of *Unde peccatum?* Even when the motive for asking that question is not a conscious self-excuse, and when *peccatum* is very carefully distinguished from *malum,* the obvious connections within our sins encourage us to ask the question of *Unde? Whence?*

If we agree that these connections are real — and Scripture nowhere denies that fact — then what could hinder us from drawing the logical conclusion that sin is "causally determined"? We might still speak of the "inexplicability" or the "enigmatic character" of sin, but is there reason why we should not explain or unravel our sin as best we can within its "total context"? Here it is significant that when we follow the avenues which men have taken in these attempts we can only discover how

15. Those asking the questions do not know from whence Christ came. In contrast to their confusion we should observe the words of the man who was cured. His words shed instant light on the whole drama of this chapter: "Why, this is a marvel! You do not know where he comes from, and yet he opened my eyes" (John 9:30). Cf. v. 33: "If this man were not from God, he could do nothing." On their inability to answer, see R. Bultmann, *Das Evangelium des Johannes,* pp. 253ff.

16. Note the poignant example of the negation of guilt in Proverbs 30:20: "This is the way of an adulteress: she eats, and wipes her mouth, and says, 'I have done no wrong.'"

relentlessly self-exculpation dogs the heels of any explanation for our sin. That fact is especially apparent when we see the efforts of men to derive their sins causally from *God himself*. Possibly they stretch to its ultimate limit the self-evident postulate that "everything comes from God." We shall observe, in our next chapter, that the Church has always rejected this "explanation." With a remarkable unanimity she has not hesitated to call it a *blasphemy*.

What about the other "explanations" for our sin? We might search for the origin of sin in the "originality" of evil set side by side with good in a dualistic fashion. Evil is then the eternal counterforce to God and the explanation of sinful phenomena in our world. Or we might reject the blasphemy of monism and dualism and seek an explanation for sin in the "demonic realm." Nevertheless, no matter *how* we come to an "explanation" it is obvious that sin — to some extent — is made "rational" or "perspicuous." Sin is then construed in terms of a number of component factors which shed light upon its reality. In this process of "unriddling" we come in contact with the real genius of sin, as evident in the lives of all of us and in this situation of every fallen man. For whenever we find ourselves "encompassed" by our sins (cf. Hos. 7:2) we naturally try, in diverse ways, to lay our fingers on the origin and processes of our own activities.

The biblical witness itself makes use of a kind of "causal" terminology, but its usage is very different from a causal explanation for our sins. We are referred to the *heart of man* as the wellspring from which his sins flow forth (Mark 7:21). When we listen to the Scripture we hear of the ways of sin which proceed from the "inside" to the "outside" (Mark 7:23; Matt. 23:25; Luke 11:39; Joel 2:13). Yet there is no trace of a self-excuse in this kind of a statement. There is no room for any. The reference to the "heart" eliminates a concept of an "origin" apart from man himself, for the heart *is man* in the center and the wholeness of his being. *Man* is designated as the "seat of sin."[17] Therefore when Scripture speaks of a "process" it does so in reference to this transition from man's corrupt heart to his own sinful activity. When it points to that which "defiles"

17. Cf. M. H. Bolkestein, *Het Verborgen Rijk: het Evangelie naar Marcus,* 1954, p. 146.

a man[18] it does not give a causal explanation for man's sin. The heart of man is seen as that which is most deeply *man*. Precisely the heart of man is the "seat of his sin" and the gateway for expressing what is externalized in man's own sinful activity.[19]

Nowhere in Scripture is this existential circle of human living overstepped for the sake of giving a causal explanation of man's sin. Nowhere is the *"causa" peccati* sought for in terms of inscrutable or self-evident "heights" or "depths." The process from the inner heart to the outer act of man[20] does not excuse a man in his sinning but only points to sin at the deepest level of man's entire existence. In any explanation (no matter of what sort) the borders of man's living are violated. This is the case when men fasten attention on the "origin" of their sinning in some other locus than their own hearts. When they realize that the pathway from their evil hearts runs directly to their evil acts they can only cease to take false comfort in the "riddle" of their sin. They then appreciate the true nature of sin's "self-evidentness." The "causality" we then encounter is the causality of an "evil tree" which bears "evil fruit" (Matt. 7:17). This is the causality which James had in mind when he wrote concerning our sinning with the tongue: "Does a spring pour forth from the same opening fresh water and brackish? Can a fig tree, my brethren, yield olives, or a grapevine figs? No more can salt water yield fresh" (3:11-12).

Yet there is another "process" which, when rightly seen, can only exclude all self-excuse or self-evidentness, all causality or transparency. This is the process from the original goodness of creation to the later senselessness of sin.[21] Confronted by that process, all those who have ever reflected on sin can only come to a fork in the road. Must we stop our inquiry at this point and remain standing with the "strangeness" or "inexplicability" of

18. Mark 7:15: *ho dýnatai koinôsai autón.* Cf. 7:23.

19. Bolkestein, *loc. cit.*

20. The juxtaposition of these is significant for understanding the nature of cultic impurity and the question of what *sin* (in its deepest dimension) is. Cf. J. Schniewind, *Das Evangelium nach Markus*, 1949, p. 104, concerning the "fundamental reconsideration" ("die grundsätzliche Neubesinnung"). Cf. further Matt. 15:11: "what comes out of the mouth, this defiles a man."

21. In Part II it will be necessary to examine extensively that "process" which is of one piece with the *universality* and the *spread* of sin: the doctrine of original sin. Bavinck has called this "one of the most difficult subjects of dogmatics" (*Geref. Dog.*, III, 78).

sin? Is there any way in which sin can be made "clear" in any degree at all? Is it the nature of sin that an explanation is *a priori* impossible? When we try to "explain" our sin, can we only cast long shadows on the true reality of guilt?

We are of the opinion that an explanation for sin is truly impossible. Furthermore, when we say this we are not implying a hiatus in our knowledge which may soon be overcome. For the riddle of sin is of an entirely different kind.[22] It is completely *sui generis*. The mere fact that many have not seen it as such is understandable in the light of their own fears that when we speak of the inexplicability of sin we must end up in a kind of dualism. What choice do we have but to see sin as the independent or original "antipode" of good? Yet the net result of these fears has often been an added passion for discovering a final "explanation." We try to find some sense in the senseless, some reason in the irrational, and some legitimacy in the illegitimacy of sin. The driving impulse in these efforts is so strong that we can hardly afford to ignore them. Yet when we examine these "explanations" we are far removed from an effort to find faint flickerings of light on the problem of sin's "origin." We wish only to be better warned.

We shall examine, first of all, a concept which the Christian Church of all ages has renounced with a very striking unanimity. We are referring to the idea that God himself is somehow the ultimate "source" of sin. We shall give a separate chapter to that topic and shall listen to the voice of the Church. For the Church's voice is only the echo of the warning which comes to us, with a vibrant intensity, in God's Word. We have in mind what might well be called the *a priori* of the Church's entire message: the biblical *a priori* of the goodness, holiness, and spotless majesty of God. "*This* is the message we have heard from him and proclaim to you, that *God is light and in him is no darkness at all*" (I John 1:5).

22. See Chap. 5.

CHAPTER TWO

THE BIBLICAL A PRIORI

WHEN WE TAKE stock of the explanations for the origin of sin it is necessary to remind ourselves of what might be called the biblical *a priori*. We are very aware of the danger of framing too lightly *"a priori"* and "central" biblical motives which are then exempted from any further discussion. But the biblical *a priori* we have in mind is no merely human prejudice which predefines what our approach to Scripture must be. It is rather the message that confronts us, inescapably, in the whole of the biblical witness. What concerns us at this point is the truth that the Church has confessed on the basis of this witness: that God is not the Source, or the Cause, or the Author of man's sin. *Deus non est causa, auctor peccati.*

There is every reason for us to give full attention to the *a priori* character of this cautioning witness. For this apriority can be seen in the fact that, in the light of God's revelation and faith oriented to that revelation, a decision has already been made of far-reaching and even normative significance. This is not a theoretical or a speculative decision but a thoroughly religious one. With it the purity of our doctrine of sin must stand or fall. The echo of the biblical *a priori* can be heard in the Church's stalwart and bold denunciation of every effort to soothe man's thinking by explaining or deriving sin causally from God. In our first chapter we already indicated that self-excuse must hasten at the heels of every explanation for man's sin; now, in this present chapter, that peril will confront us with an even more striking clarity. For whenever man's fancy makes room for the notion that sin originates in God, the way is paved for his own definitive and final excuse. Small wonder, then, that the Church and her theology have always been conscious of this strategy for emasculating man's sin of its very "guiltiness" before the face of God. Here there is more than the mere "danger" of developing a self-excuse. For this kind of explanation and self-excuse are actually identical.

If anything is clear it is certainly that the Church has addressed herself to this issue in unequivocal terms. She has appreciated the inscrutable riddle of sin's disruptive reality and God's good government of our world; yet, in acknowledging that riddle, she has not been remiss in rejecting radically and emphatically the heresy which sees God as the Origin of sin. This fact is all the more striking because, as we shall later observe, she has also rejected dualism equally as well. In renouncing both monism and dualism we observe a certain "tension in responsibility" which is evident in all of Christian thinking on this score. The Church's criticism of dualistic Manichaeism, which envisioned in evil the eternal, original, and independent "antipode" of God, did not lead her to the enticing conclusion that "everything" comes from God; thus also the origin of sin must find its ultimate "clue" in him. On the other hand, the rejection of dualism did not occasion the query of whether there could be an ascertainable "connection" between God and sin, even if that connection were "causal." Thus, at one and the same time the Church denounced as blasphemy the *Deus auctor et causa peccati* and also spoke of a certain "relation" between God and man's sin. This relation was manifest, for example, in God's wrath, condemnation, and hatred for the sins which men commit. Yet, the Church not only noted this negative relation but proceeded to give an even more precise description. She spoke of the *permissio* of sin by God. The latter term, of course, presupposes a well-defined and positive relation of God and man's sin. Moreover, when theologians became aware of the very unsatisfactory character of this concept, as an ultimate explanation,[1] they proceeded to propose that God "wills" sin in some way or other. Here, of course, the problem of the "relation" between God and man's sin became very acute, even more so than in the concept of *permissio*.

In this connection it is necessary to understand the real meaning of the Church's *Deus non causa et auctor peccati*. That phrase does not permit such heresies as we find, for example, in Boehme and Schelling's illusion of some dark "depth-dimension" in God's being, in terms of which man's sin can be ulti-

---

1. Cf. Bavinck, *Geref. Dog.*, III, 37, 39; also my *The Providence of God*, 1952, pp. 151f.

mately explained. All such notions are diametrically opposed to the biblical witness concerning God. Therefore the Church has never wavered in rejecting these ideas.[2] Nonetheless, within the confines of even an orthodox theology, we come in constant contact with the question of sin's relation to God's will. Though there is very little affinity here with Boehme and Schelling, it remains the case that the truth and clarity of the *Deus non auctor et causa peccati* must lead us to inquire what precisely the Church has meant by her verdict of "blasphemy." We might rightly assume that this scathing denunciation shares in the clarity that is necessary for discussing the "relation" of sin and God. Therefore it is not for nothing that the Church has laid hold on such a very strong term.[3]

We do well to listen to the Church's voice in her scripturally-oriented confessions. The Belgic Confession, for example, states in Article 13 that "nothing happens in this world" without God's appointment, but it also adds immediately: "nevertheless, God neither is the Author of nor can be charged with the sins which are committed." The Canons of Dort (I, 15) profess that God is "by no means . . . the Author of sin (the very thought of which is blasphemy)." In fact, "the cause or guilt of . . . unbelief as well as of all other sins is no wise in God, but in man himself" (I, 5). The Heidelberg Catechism, in Lord's Day 3 (Q. 7), asks what can only be called a "question of origin": "*Whence*, then, comes this depraved nature of man?" But the

2. Regarding Boehme, cf. especially his *Beschreybung der drey prinzipien göttlichen Wesens,* 1619 (*Samtl. Schr.,* Ausg. August Faust, II, 1942), concerning the origin of evil and the wrath of God in the "first principle." Evil is original, and through the "second principle" the power of evil becomes subservient to good (IV, 44, 47; V, 7). For Schelling, cf. *Philosophische Untersuchungen über das Wesen der menschlichen Freiheit und die damit zusammenhängenden Gegenstände,* 1809 (in *Schellings Werke,* IV, 1927, pp. 228-308): nothing is offered us as explanation of evil "except both these principles in God" (p. 267), and evil is *necessary* for the revelation of God. Cf. also Ch. Werner's chapter "Le fond obscure de l'essence divine: Boehme et Schelling," in *Le Problème du mal dans la pensée humaine,* 1944, pp. 99-106; and R. T. Sertillanges, *Le problème du mal,* I, 1948, pp. 255-257, on Schelling.

3. One thinks of the concept of *blasphemy* in Scripture (cf. *TWNT,* I, *s.v. blasphēmía*). Cf. the blasphemy of the heathen (LXX, Isa. 52:5); the blasphemy at the cross (Mark 15:29); and that against the Holy Spirit (the "eternal sin" of Mark 3:29).

answer is very direct: "From the fall. . . ."[4] Question 9 asserts
that "man . . . deprived himself" of his original gifts. So too,
the Confessio Gallicana declares that God has created all things
and rules them according to his will; yet he is not the author
of evil, and the guilt of evil cannot be imputed to him.[5] Elsewhere we read that "evil and wrong do not stem from God"
(*"mala pravaque ex Deo non sunt"*).[6] Rather, sin, as the Confessio Rhaetica asserts, is *"ex mundo"*[7] — it is from ourselves and
the devil, the liar, who sows weeds in the field (Matt. 13:39),
deceives the whole world (Rev. 12:9), and works in the sons of
disobedience (Eph. 2:2). Opposed here is the idea of all those
who insert both good and evil in one and the same schema of
divine "causality." By so doing they can only stumble into the
heresy of the *Deus auctor peccati*.[8] This is a heresy which the
confessions have constantly rejected and have refused to embrace
in even the *slightest way*.[9]

Various confessions refer to God's power in and over man's
sin. But this sovereign utilization of sin (or this divine reversal
of evil for good) in no way threatens the *Deus non causa peccati*.
God is not the Author of man's sin, but rather in his infinite
wisdom (to quote the Irish Articles) he turns it "to the manifestation of his glory and to the good of his elect."[10] This
activity of God through man's sin, or his taking it into his
service and deflecting its course *(Umlenkung)*, is a major consideration in a number of confessions; yet in no way does this
mitigate or tone down the seriousness with which the *Deus non
causa peccati* is confessed. Frequently the Church has disavowed

4. Cf. CD, III-IV, 1.
5. J. T. Müller, *Bekenntnisschriften*, p. 223. Cf. Waldenser Bekenntnis:
   "ni autheur ni cause du mal" *(ibid.,* p. 501).
6. Also: "peccata non esse ex Deo nec ipsum auctorem pravorum, sed enim
   peccata esse opera *nostra,* non Dei" *(ibid.,* p. 165).
7. *Ibid.*
8. Cf. the parallel: "Deum et virtutum et vitiorum auctorem esse, nec
   minus eum scelerate facta velle quam quae cum virtute et bene fiant"
   (ibid.). In this connection, cf. also the Canons of Trent (VI, Can. 6):
   "Si quis dixerit, non esse in potestate hominis suas malas facere, sed
   mala opera ita ut bona Deum operari, non permissive solum, sed etiam
   proprie et per se, adeo ut sit proprium eius opus non minus proditio
   Judae quam vocatio Pauli. A. S." (Denz., 816).
9. Cf.: "Deus nullius *omnino* peccati sit author vel particeps" (Müller,
   pp. 377-378).
10. *Ibid.,* p. 529; cf. Confessio Gallicana: God has "des moyens admirables
    de se servir tellement des diables et des meschans, qu'il scait *convertir*
    en bien le mal qu'ils font et duquel ilz sont coulpables."

every *causa*-concept whatever; she has opposed the efforts to make "fine distinctions" within that terminology.[11] The Consensus Bremensis of 1595, for example, professes that God "neither fashions nor works evil," and places itself in opposition to the idea which profligates and libertines have suggested: namely that God is responsible for unchastity and murder,[12] or that godless men "sin according to the will of God" and that "God works such sins in them."[13]

Furthermore, it is not only the Reformed confessions which reflect this biblical *a priori*. The Lutheran Confessio Augustana states in Article 19 that man's own will is the *"causa peccati."*[14] The Apology repeats that same idea.[15] In its section on election (in reference to Romans 9:22) the Formula Concordiae maintains that God, according to the Apostle Paul, has "endured" the vessels of wrath without actually *making* them as they are. It adds that God is by no means to blame.[16] The Lutheran confessions declare that the *"praescientia Dei"* is not the *causa* of evil[17] and that God is not the Author of hereditary sin.[18] All of this is seen as *"extra controversiam."*[19] God is not the *cause* of our sin, even in the state of our corruption, for our corrupt nature itself is the work of Satan.[20] Therefore, though Lutheran theology has contended for a certain "relation" between God and man's sin,[21] it has also stressed constantly the *Deus non causa peccati.*

11. "Deus *nec* efficiens *neque* propinqua est causa peccati" (Erlauth. Bekenntnis, *ibid.*, p. 269; cf. p. 450).
12. *Ibid.*, pp. 754, 756.
13. *Ibid.*, p. 756.
14. Confessio Augustana, Art. 19: "de causa peccati docent quod, tametsi Deus creat et conservat naturam, tamen causa peccati est voluntas malorum, videlicet diaboli et impiorum."
15. Müller, *op. cit.*, p. 219.
16. "Non autem dicit Deum *fecisse* vasa irae.... In culpa sunt diabolus et homines, *nullo* autem modo Deus" (*ibid.*, p. 721).
17. "Non est causa mali neque est causa peccati" (*Luth. Bekenntnisschriften, ibid.*, p. 554; cf. p. 555).
18. "Non est a Deo, neque originale peccatum est opus aut creatura Dei, sed est opus diaboli" (*ibid.*, p. 582).
19. "... Quod Deus non sit causa, creator vel auctor peccati, sed quod instinctu opera et machinationibus Satanae per unum hominem peccatum (quod est diaboli opus) in mundum intraverit" (*ibid.*, p. 575).
20. "... Originaliter et principaliter opus Satanae."
21. We recall the discussions concerning the words in the Confessio Augustana, Art. 19: "causa peccati est voluntas malorum, videlicet diaboli et impiorum, quae *non adjuvante Deo, avertit se a Deo.*" German

If we inquire into the reason for these frequent and emphatic utterances, the answer is not really hard to find. It is simply the unambiguous witness of Scripture concerning the goodness, holiness and glory of God. Though the *"mysterium iniquitatis"*[22] has often seemed to be an insoluble riddle, in the face of God's triumphant activity, the Church has persistently professed the *a priori* of God's holiness and majesty. The *omnino* and *nullus* of the confessions are based on the admonitions of Scripture which emphasize constantly that "God is light and in him is no darkness at all" (I John 1:5).

This single text could well serve as a preface or a superscription to any reflection on the biblical *a priori*. It is a fascinating reference to the light and glory of God. John sets down his thesis ("God is light") and follows with an equally radical antithesis. In other places he describes the reality of God as "Spirit" and "love" (John 4:24; I John 4:16), but here he delineates the reality of God as "light." (We think of I Timothy 6:16, where God is said to dwell in "unapproachable light.") In John's argument this term is by no means meant in a theoretical, speculative, or metaphysical sense. His usage here anticipates the whole train of thought concerning the life of God's children "in the light." Having "fellowship" with him who is light suggests the analogy of walking in the light as he is "in the light" (I John 1:7); for in him is "no darkness at all." Misgivings and doubts are now done away with in him. There are problems that remain for our darkened understandings, and yet beside and beyond these problems is always the *a priori* of this message and proclamation. John says clearly that his concern is for the message which "we have heard from him and proclaim to you" (1:5). This is the *angelia* which the apostles

translation: "so Gott die Hand abgethan" (Müller, *op. cit.*, p. 44). A very important question is what is meant (in this context!) by the words "non adjuvante Deo." Is this a relativizing of the *Deus non causa?* In the Augustana Variata Melanchthon changed these words to read "contra mandata, Dei," though as J. Müller has rightly indicated (*Die christliche Lehre von der Sünde*, 1849, I, 358), this was certainly no clarification. Schleiermacher saw in the German text a clear reference to the activity of God: "This removal of God's hand, as a special divine act, is the first condition for sin" (*Der christliche Glaube*, 1884, I, 432). E. Gerstenmaier (*Die Kirche und die Schöpfung*, 1938, p. 122) correctly asserts that these words form no obstacle "for affirming that the confessions of the Lutheran Church adamantly deny any authorization of God in regard to sin, be it of a positive or a negative kind."

22. Concerning this term, see Chap. 5.

themselves had heard, as apostles of Christ (4:12).[23] They had heard it from the lips of the only true and faithful Witness, who revealed to them that God whom no man had ever seen (John 1:18).

Here John did not have in mind a maxim that is rationally or logically deducible; nor was he concerned about a conclusion from a natural doctrine of God or the end-product of some merely human line of thought. Much rather, he was concerned about a *proclamation,* a *message,* which remains in force despite our own confusions and possible uncertainties. This message, as God's good news, has everything to do with an *a priori* which convincingly and "therapeutically" penetrates our doubts. Exactly this *a priori* precludes our self-conceit which accuses God or excuses ourselves by involving God in our own sin. In contrast to every such notion the *a priori* articulates the biblical witness which (once proclaimed and heard) arouses in man the unconditional confession: "The Lord is my light and my salvation" (Ps. 27:1). In these words the Israelite acknowledged the "shadowless light" which was seen as *God's light;* in other words, he acknowledged the light which illumined his way, even in temptations, and enabled him to enter God's sanctuary with praise.[24]

Not only the Israelites but especially the apostles of Jesus heard this same message; furthermore, in that message we too are set before the reality of *God as Light.* The proclamation of Christ is the proclamation of him who was "in the bosom of the Father" and who "made him known" to us (John 1:18). This message is not relativized by Christ's own self-designation: "*I* am the light of the world" (8:12).[25] For the claim of Jesus stands in harmony with the further statement: "He who has seen me has seen the Father" (14:9). Christ refers to the Father as the One who alone is good (Matt. 19:17), as the perfect and holy Father (Matt. 5:48; John 17:11); yet he himself, in his entire being, is the revelation of the Father and the reflection of his glory (Heb. 1:3).[26] As Christ is the Lamb "without blemish or spot" (I Pet. 1:19),[27] who committed no sin and has spoken no guile (I Pet. 2:22; cf. II Cor. 5:21), so too there is

---

23. Cf. R. Schnackenburg, *Die Johannesbriefe,* 1954, p. 64.
24. Cf. Ps. 36:8f.; 56:13; Job 33:28; Hab. 3:4.
25. Cf. John 9:5 (the connection between the light of the world and the healing of the man born blind); cf. also John 1:5 and 12:35.
26. Greek: *apaúgasma tês dóxēs autoú.*
27. *ámōmos* and *áspilos.*

no darkness in God. The greatest antidote to any temptation which detracts from the goodness, holiness, and glory of God cannot be found in an abstract notion of who God is; nor can it be found in a *summum bonum* idea, but only in the word-and-deed message of Jesus Christ himself. Jesus is the one who guarantees and attests to us the *Deus non causa peccati.* He, and he alone, assures us of the depths and permanence of this unshakable truth.

Once we have heard this message that "God is light," in whom is "no darkness at all," we will also recognize this proclamation throughout the pages of Scripture. In the framework of Scripture it is no exaggeration which the Church has expressed when she called this notion of *Deus causa et auctor peccati* a "blasphemy." Repeatedly, in warnings and admonitions, we hear this same scriptural message concerning the nature of God. The message was given voice whenever the peril of a wrong view of God seemed especially acute in the early Christian community. At such times we hear the cautioning words of James 1:13: "Let no one say when he is tempted, 'I am tempted by God'; for God cannot be tempted with evil and he himself tempts no one."[28]

"*Let no one. . . .*" What could possibly be more far-ranging or absolute than that? Here is a text that would seem to cover *every man and every case of temptation.* Therefore James concludes with these words: "but each person is tempted when he is lured and enticed by his own desire" (1:14). Thus we find ourselves before a question of origin and a certain "explanation." After a process "from which," a process "to which" is also pointed out (1:15). "Then desire when it has conceived gives birth to sin; and sin when it is full-grown brings forth death." Anyone who says, "I am tempted by God," is only making an excuse. His reasoning is then as follows: Sin comes "from God," which can only mean that it does not come "from me." But James wants nothing to do with such a profanity. The God that he proclaims is not a Tempter-God involved in man's own guilt. If we speak of God as the "Origin" we can only refer to him in a very different way: for "every *good* endowment and every *perfect* gift is from above, coming down from the *Father of lights*" (1:17; cf. 3:15, 17). Furthermore, before this

28. Note the "no one . . . no one."

reference to this Origin James already had sounded his warning: "Do not be deceived, my beloved brethren" (1:16) .[29] Here, then, is a very real peril. It is not a peril of a pagan cosmogony or theogony but a peril for "brethren." It is a peril for the Church.[30] "Do not be deceived, my ... brethren." James proposes a "question of origin" and gives an answer which eliminates any excuse: "What causes wars, and what causes fightings among you? Is it not *your passions* that are at war in *your members?*" (4:1) .

"*Let no one say....*" The very suggestion that we are "tempted by God" is certainly meant in an accusatory sense.[31] It implies a groping after relations which nowhere and never exist and a stumbling after alibis in the quagmire of our guilt.[32] A specious kind of. logic presumes that "everything comes from God," and therefore our temptations do too. But James wants nothing to do with that kind of logic. He indicates its impossibility. God himself "cannot be tempted with evil" (1:13) ,[33] and evil can have no hold on God. The absolute antithesis of God and evil excludes the possibility that evil could ever come from God.[34] Instead, there is a very different "explanation" for this process of sin and temptation, which can only end in man's own death. This is an "explanation" without the least room for excuse: *man's own desire and his own heart.*[35] Any other explanation is a mere travesty which can only cast a blight on the Father of lights. Therefore, "*let no one say....*"

The reason this error finds root in man's heart is not hard to understand. Ultimately, it is only the *projection of the dark problematic of sin to God himself.* In common parlance this concept of "projection" connotes a theory in which human re-

29. Also in other texts we see the gravity of this warning. Cf. I Cor. 15:33; Gal. 6:7.
30. This is the fallacious concept (the "wanbegrip," Grosheide, *Comm.*, 1955², p. 360) in which a right view of the Father of lights can only be lost.
31. *Ibid.*
32. *Ibid.*
33. *ho gár theós apeírastós estin kakõn.*
34. *Ibid.*, p. 359. H. Schamberger, *Die Einheitlichkeit des Jakobusbriefes im antignostischen Kampf*, 1939, wrongly sees in James 1 a polemic or correction of the Lord's Prayer. On the sixth petition, cf. my *Faith and Perseverance*, 1952, Chap. 6.
35. This is certainly not disputed in I Cor. 10:13 where we read that God, with temptation, will also make a way of escape. At stake in that text is not the *origin* of temptation; cf. *TWNT*, VI, *s.v. peirasmós.*

ligion is seen as the objectification or "projection" of man's own inner self. Therefore our idea of God is the sum-total of our spiritual or "projective" activity. It is not God who makes man after his image but man who makes his "god." Here we need not examine this idea of projection,[36] but we can certainly affirm that when man deduces from God his own temptation to do evil he is only projecting. His activity is full of darkness and roots in the disposition of his heart. His purpose (in line with the *analogia peccati*) is then to implicate God in his own sin. James admonishes his "brethren" to be on guard against such a temptation as this.

Many persons have denied that James' letter has the profundity of the other New Testament epistles. Yet, we hear in this letter a vibrant witness which has constantly maintained and restrained the Church in her reflections on man's sin. Here is a witness that renounces any notion that God shares in man's own guilt. Here too is a summary of the Old Testament message as found in such a text as Habakkuk 1:13. For God is of "purer eyes than to behold evil," and he cannot "look on wrong."

This biblical *a priori* is seen in all its absoluteness already in the Old Testament. There the message is very radically proclaimed that it is "far ... from God that he should do wickedness, and from the Almighty that he should do wrong" (Job 34:10). The echo of the holy and good deeds of God is very evident: there is no iniquity in the Lord our God. Time after time we hear Israel's paean of praise to God's goodness (Pss. 136:1; 92:15; 118:1, 29; 33:4). Because God was good it was good for the Israelite to draw near to him in praise (Pss. 73:28; 119:68). Nothing of the lividness of sin could linger round his throne; there could be no trace of evil in him. Therefore the Israelite contrasted God's goodness and holiness with what he saw to be the case among the nations. In God there was no "perversion of justice" or "partiality" or "taking of bribes" (II Chron. 19:7; cf. Ex. 23:6-8). In the revelation of God's activity the Israelite did not experience the prejudice of a merely human caprice or the arbitrariness of an "acceptance of persons." For God transcended all such attitudes and was not subject to the "necessity" of human fickleness.[37] The awareness of God's distance

---

36. Cf. my *Man: the Image of God*, 1961, Chap. 10.
37. Cf. also Acts 10:34. Grosheide in his *Comm.* on Acts brings to mind the partiality of oriental judges.

from evil is poignantly expressed in Habakkuk's imploring of God in the midst of adversity (1:12-13): "Art thou not from everlasting, O Lord my God, my Holy One? . . . Thou . . . art of purer eyes than to behold evil and canst not look on wrong. . . ." Here we find a very urgent appeal to God; yet God remains silent while "the wicked swallows up the man more righteous than he." God merely "looks" on those who are faithless (1:13). No wonder that Habakkuk stood before the ways of God which were inscrutable to him. Nevertheless, he spoke of God's "pure eyes" which could not look on evil.

Throughout the Old Testament we hear this same proclamation of God's goodness. Sometimes it is sounded in thetical terms and sometimes in terms antithetical to man's own sinful activity. God is regarded as "the Rock" whose "work is perfect," for all his ways are justice. "A God of faithfulness without iniquity, just and right is he" (Deut. 32:4; cf. Ps. 18:31). Any conceivable possibility of indicting God or implicating him in man's sin is now denounced as a nonsensical effort of man's own cunning. Any *analogia entis* of divine and human activity is simply contraband. "God is not a man, that he should lie, or a son of man, that he should repent. Has he said, and will he not do it? Or has he spoken, and will he not fulfil it?" (Num. 23:19). "And also the Glory of Israel will not lie or repent; for he is not a man, that he should repent" (I Sam. 15:29).

In looking at such texts as these we need not discuss, at this point, the scriptural references to God's repentance. For the thrust of these texts is obviously to exclude from God what is humanly sinful and changeable in the contexts of man's living. God does not change his mind or turn his back on his own word. The God of Israel is not of that sort, and none of his words can fall to the ground. In him we see only holiness and no blemish or shadow. Thus Job's mind was very clear when he attributed no wrong to God (1:22) and later returned to his confession with his hand upon his mouth (40:5): "I have spoken once, and I will not answer; twice, but I will proceed no further."

This chasm between God and man's own sinful activity, with all its consequences, was very obvious for ancient Israel. "For thou art not a God who delights in wickedness; evil may not sojourn with thee. The boastful may not stand before thy eyes; thou hatest all evildoers" (Ps. 5:4-5). So great was that chasm, and so sharp the antithesis, that Scripture speaks of God's "abhorrence" of bloodthirsty and deceitful men (5:6) and refers to God's "hatred" of diverse weights and measures (Prov. 20:10; cf. Zech. 8:16-17; Isa. 65:12). "There are six things which the Lord hates, seven which are an abomination to him" (or "an abomination of his soul"; Prov. 6:16).[38] This whole matter could hardly be stated more clearly and forcefully than in this pointing to the very depths of God's soul and in this use of the concept of *abomination*. We see here the full horridness of sin which evokes God's hatred and from which he revolts in a holy aversion.[39] The intensity of this repugnance is pictured in a very graphic way where God, because of Israel's own mutiny, refused to be entreated and forbade the prophets to pray their intercessory prayers, even though the plight of Israel was very desperate. Consider how he shut up his ears to the prayers of Jeremiah for Israel (7:16; 11:12; 14:11; and especially 15:1). Listen to the following words: "Though Moses and Samuel stood before me, yet my heart would not turn toward this people. Send them out of my sight, and let them go!" (15:1).[40] The curse of the Lord rested on "the house of the wicked" in contrast to his blessing on "the abode of the righteous" (Prov. 3:33).

In this vein the Scripture speaks of the "relation" of God and sin. Even the man who rejects a dualism radically can hardly have scruples against the strongest possible terms for describing this antithesis and chasm. The "relation" which we see here is the "relation" of abomination, detestation, and curse. This is the relation of God's *judgment*. In that light we observe the revelation of God's wrath against man's sin. The sin of man touches on God himself, since every transgression is, in essence, a

---

38. Gispen, *Spreuken*, I, 110. Gispen speaks of "disgust" ("walging") and "wholehearted aversion" ("hartgrondige afkeer").

39. One is reminded of the "abominable thing which the Lord hates" (Deut. 12:31), in the sacrificing of sons and daughters to honor pagan gods. Cf. K. Dronkert, *De Molochdienst in het O.T.*, 1953, Chaps. 3 and 4. It is well to reflect on such excesses of sin when we consider the question of causality.

40. Cf. the appointment of four kinds of destroyers because of the people's rejection of the Lord (15:3, 6). The seriousness of this repudiation of intercession is all the more apparent because such a prophetic intercession was actually essential (Jer. 27:18; 37:3; Amos 7:2; Ezek. 9:8; 11:13). For a more extensive treatment of intercession, cf. P. A. H. DeBoer, "De Voorbede in het O.T." (*O.T. Studien*, 1943), and F. Hesse, *Die Fürbitte im A.T.*, 1949, especially p. 53. Hesse also points to the limit for intercession in the *New Testament* (I John 5:16).

forsaking and rejecting of him (cf. Jer. 2:13) and a choosing of man's autonomy instead of his good and beneficent rule. Therefore the proclamation of God's wrath does not imply a dark or dubious aspect in the "original ground" of being, or a stricture upon the glory of God himself. Much rather, it sheds light upon his glory. With no qualms at all we can say that the reality of God's anger is the reverse side of the *Deus non auctor et causa peccati*. Here, then, is God's burning wrath which confronts a sinner on his way; here is his reaction which stems from his holiness and shadowless glory. In wrath we see the revelation of the *absolute distance* and the radical and clear antithesis between God and man's sin. "Far be it from God . . . !"

Exactly in this distance, and exactly because of it, the God of Israel was seen as the enemy of Israel's enemies (Ex. 23:22) and even of the people of God themselves. Because they "rebelled and grieved his holy Spirit . . . he turned to be their enemy, and himself fought against them" (Isa. 63:10). He "bent his bow like an enemy" (Lam. 2:4), and thus "brought to an end in Zion appointed feast and sabbath" (2:6). He "scorned his altar" and "disowned his sanctuary," and because he was an "enemy" he delivered his own people into the hands of their enemies (2:7; cf. 1:17). In a variety of ways his enmity and his wrath were manifest in his dealings with his people. He gave them kings in his anger (Hos. 13:11; cf. Jer. 15:14) and hid their repentance from his eyes (Hos. 13:14). Yet, it was always Israel herself who aroused his anger and provoked her God (Deut. 4:25). "Why have they provoked me to anger with their graven images, and with their foreign idols?" (Jer. 8:19). In reaction to that provocation we see God's curse and discomfiture of Israel. We observe his rebuke because of the evil of her doings and because she had forsaken him (Deut. 28:20). This is the "retribution"[41] which the Old Testament calls his

41. K. Koch, in an article "Gibt es ein Vergeltungsdogma im A.T.?" (*Z.Th.K.*, 1955, pp. 1-42), has tried to show that this question should be answered in the negative. The reason he adduces is that the Old Testament was still caught up in the notion of a "fatalizing act" ("schicksalwirkende Tat," pp. 32, 36, 37; cf. his terminology: "schicksalentscheidende Tatsphäre," a "fate-determining sphere of action," p. 39). This Old Testament accent, according to Koch, is quite different from the stress on the retributive act of God as we find in the LXX. How forced this contrast is drawn is evident, however, in Koch's own article, particularly in his discussion of the several texts from Proverbs. The fact that he finds the "age-old view" ("uralte Vorstellung")

activity "against his people." It is God's answer which impinges on their lives, an answer in which he takes very seriously that sin, as sin, is mutiny. Here is the revelation of the wrath of a "righteous judge, and a God who has indignation every day" (Ps. 7:11).

The only occasion for separation between God and man is *sin* (Isa. 59:2). Recall how Isaiah spoke of hands defiled with blood and lips that have spoken lies, and a tongue that mutters wickedness (59:3-8). There is only evil in man's sinning; but the eyes of the Lord see when there is no justice (v. 15). "He saw that there was no man, and wondered that there was no one to intervene" (v. 16). In the face of this evil "his own arm brought him victory, and his righteousness upheld him" (v. 16). The whole of Isaiah 59 is full of this glory of the Lord, which extends from the west to the east; it emphasizes his covenant and his Spirit, which cannot be nullified "from this time forth and for evermore" (vv. 19-21). There can be no doubt that Scripture, in its entirety, is very clear when it comes to this matter of God and man's sin. God only threatens his judgment against the mutilation of his gifts. The words of grace in Scripture do not tone down the seriousness of God's wrath. As a matter of fact, it is only in connection with the reality of wrath that the miracle of God's grace is fully understood.[42]

Therefore it is not the Gospels alone but the entire Word of God which exhibits how clear it is, and "beyond the shadow of any doubt, that God cannot be the Cause of sin, either directly or indirectly."[43] We can only see in him the lustre of an unapproachable light and the abundant fountain of every good thing.[44] We can only see the absolute antithesis of the *Deus causa peccati*.

The biblical *a priori* has always provided the most effective countercheck to any monistic system (whether pantheistic or

also in Paul's "sowing and reaping" (p. 36) cannot possibly support his conception. His construction is unsatisfying because of its exclusive emphasis on the "fatalizing act."

42. It would seem incontrovertible that anyone who denies the reality of God's wrath *must* be ensnared in one or another question of origin in regard to sin. This is apparent in Schleiermacher; also Ritschl. On Schleiermacher, cf. K. Barth's *K.D.*, III/3, 365ff. (ET, 319ff.).

43. J. Haas, *Die Stellung Jesu zu Sünde und Sündern nach den vier Evangelien*, 1953, p. 75.

44. Cf. BC, Art. 1: "Bonum omniumque bonarum *fontem* uberrimum."

non-pantheistic) which misconstrues as causal the relation between God and man's sin. Every effort in that direction is refuted by the message of the *kabod Jahwe* and the *trishagion* of
the angels in the vision of Isaiah 6. Yet it is nowhere more
obvious that the notion of God as *auctor et causa peccati* is an
utter blasphemy than in the revelation of God in Jesus Christ.
There we see the revelation of his wrath on "the Lamb of God,
who takes away the sin of the world" (John 1:29). There is the
revelation of him who was cursed and made to be sin on our
behalf (II Cor. 5:21). In this central event of all of history
we see definitively, and in clearest relief, how deep the antithesis
is and how wide the distance between God and man's sin, as
manifest in the God-forsakenness of the Man of Sorrows (Matt.
27:46). When we gaze on the face of him who died as one
accursed, "outside the camp," bearing his reproach (Heb. 13:
11-13), we are denied forever the privilege and the audacity
of thinking along the lines of the *Deus causa peccati*. This renunciation of blasphemy is tied up, indissolubly, with the reality
of God's wrath against man's sin. Therefore it is tied up with
the grace of God which delivers us from the wrath which is to
come (I Thess. 1:10).

We must remember that the Word of God summons us
to profess the glory of God and to assign all honor to him.[45] It
is he who is truly the "God of glory" (Ps. 29:3) and the "King
of glory" (Pss. 24:7, 10; 57:6; Isa. 42:8; Jer. 13:16) and who
shines forth "out of Zion, the perfection of beauty" (Ps. 50:2).
In this scriptural perspective there can be *no doubt* as to who
he is or what the disposition of his heart is in reference to man's
sin. The scriptural message is unambiguous in its speaking of
the eyes of the Lord which are turned against all that he hates
and all that confounds or makes misuse of the good life which
he gives. In holy wrath he condemns rebellion from his ways
and from himself; therefore he condemns the sin in all of sin
and the severing of communion with him. This conclusive answer of the Church to the question of the *Deus auctor et causa
peccati* is only a re-echo of the words of Isaiah concerning this
grieving of the Holy Spirit (63:10). Those words, though inscrutable, are tremendously powerful in their *very inscrutability*.
They refer to a grieving of the Spirit *because* of our own re-

45. Cf. *TWNT*, II, *s.v. dóxa*; Josh. 7:19.

belliousness. *This* God is certainly not the cause of *this* sin in which all of man's sin is manifest.

But how is it possible that despite the biblical *a priori* so much of our thinking on the "relation" of God and sin is unsettled and fraught with such difficulties? Are these concepts of *distance* and *antithesis* susceptible to misunderstandings? One can only answer that in large part these difficulties go hand in glove with what seems to be a contradiction: namely that sin is very real, though God is still sovereign in his government of our world. He who conceives of sin as completely *contra voluntatem Dei*, or the breaking of communion with God and the violation of his holy command, can still ask the question (where the possibility and actuality of sin are at stake) if these concepts of *distance* and *antithesis* are adequate. In reflecting on that problem we might possibly accentuate God's holiness and deny any "direct" relation between God and man's sin. By laying stress on God's holiness we might even conclude that there *could* be no such relation, since sin is an insubordination to that very law to which God (as the Law-giver) is not subject.[46]

Very clearly, this point of view reflects, in essence, the biblical *a priori* and the statements in the confessions which deny any "guilt" in God. But by making this academic distinction between "the law and the Law-giver" (or "under and above the law") we can scarcely gain a full perspective on God's glory. This is because the concept of "above the law" is frequently interpreted as a *Deus exlex* kind of arbitrariness which can only overshadow the majesty of God.[47] One speaks meaningfully, in this regard, only when he takes no recourse in a formal *exlex* idea but finds in the *majesty of God* the positive reverse side of the *Deus non causa peccati*. The majesty of God extends to all of his dealings, throughout the entire history of the world; for that very reason the name of God inspired such adoration in ancient Israel. "O Lord, our Lord, how majestic is thy name in all the earth!" (Ps. 8:1). Since God acts *within* this world he is no mere spectator, as it were, who peers down from an ossified transcendence. Rather, he is the mighty God of history. Therefore in our reflections on God and sin this question can only remain to tax our minds and to elicit our response: How can we still speak of

---

46. Cf. my *The Providence of God*, 1952, p. 148.
47. Cf. Calvin, *Inst.*, III, 23, 2, on the *exlex;* also my *Divine Election*, 1960, pp. 56ff.

a *distance* and *antithesis* and observe that God and man's sin are not two "parallel lines" which nowhere and never meet? In the biblical data we read that God's activities are manifest exactly *in and through man's sin*. Furthermore, man's sin is made subservient to the coming of his Kingdom. In that sense, in other words, we still speak of a "relation" and "connection," since sin is no independent power set over against our God. But the question of the *nature* of this relation is now the real issue at stake. If we say that it is "blasphemy" to speak of God as the *auctor et causa peccati,* can we continue to maintain his sovereign and holy activity *in and through our sin?*

We have said above that God hates man's sin. He unleashes his wrath against man's sin and condemns man's sin in no uncertain terms. The scriptural language sees him as the Archenemy or Antagonist (the "Anti-agonist") of sin. The idea of *anti* here is absolutely important. But one might ask if the *anti* is not minimized as soon as we introduce another relation: that is to say, a relation other than the radical *anti* itself. The man who reflects on God's activity in and through man's sin can still end up with a God who *is* the *causa peccati.* Loath as he may be to incriminate God in his own sin, he can still presume a "holy" *causa peccati* or a God whose incorporation of sin in his holy activity makes "sense."[48]

It is obvious, however, that the Church has not proceeded in this direction and has censored any such efforts. At the same time, we must notice how prevalent the idea is that Scripture itself speaks along these lines. Some people have made deductions from the omnipotence and sovereignty of God, and have fallaciously said that God is the compelling force in man's sin, and that this is so even though that force might still be used for

48. In this connection we should see the view of "incorporation" which is given expression in the famous "O felix culpa!"; cf. my *The Work of Christ*, 1965, p. 32; also *Divine Election*, 1960, pp. 275f. Cf. the view of Th. Haering, *Der christliche Glaube*, 1912, who discusses the "ordering" of sin with a view to redemption, alluding to Schleiermacher. Cf. the extended discussion of Schleiermacher in *Der christliche Glaube nach den Grundsätzen der evangelischen Kirche*, I, 1884, 423-433. Haering, in this context, wishes to maintain the "felix culpa" — rightly understood, he thinks, as the thanks to God "even for one's sin" (364). Such a "tolerance" is unacceptable, however, in terms of Haering's own views of this "teleology." Cf. E. Böhl, *Dogmatik*, 1887, p. 191; R. T. Sertillanges, *Le problème du mal*, II, 1951, 60; and J. Fruytier, "Gods Licht in het Kwaad," *Conf.*, II, 6.13 ("Bijdragen," *Tijdschrift voor Philosophie en Theologie*, 1956, pp. 270f.).

the victory of the good and the coming of his Kingdom. Many
people have averred that especially the Old Testament shows
traces in which we distinguish God and man's sin in *degrees
alone*. Frequently it ascribes the "causative" efficacy of evil to
God.

The appeal is not usually made, at this point, to such texts
as we find in Isaiah 45:7 ("I form light and create darkness,
I make weal and create woe") and Amos 3:6 ("Does evil befall a
city, unless the Lord has done it?"). There is a general agreement that these texts refer to the work of God's judgment and
punishment and not to his "effectuation" of man's sin. Furthermore, the calamity brought on by his anger is not incompatible
with his holy aversion against man's sin, but is rather the *revelation of that aversion*. God's activity of wrath is designed to
lead men to repentance and conversion and the forsaking of
their sin. Being subject to his condemnation and oppression,
his people must come to see the meaning of his wrath. "In the
path of thy judgments, O Lord, we wait for thee; ... for when
thy judgments are in the earth, the inhabitants of the world
learn righteousness" (Isa. 26:8-9). "Before I was afflicted I went
astray; but now I keep thy word" (Ps. 119:67). There is no
trace of an "antinomy" here; nor is there any suggestion that
the justice of God is different from a justice which leads sinners
down the most forbidding of paths. Rather, precisely because
the godlessness of godless men displeases him so much (Ps. 5:4),
he does not let sinners walk in their own ways (cf. Ps. 146:9;
5:6). As we read in Daniel: "Therefore the Lord has kept ready
the calamity and has brought it upon us; for the Lord our God
is *righteous in all the works which he has done,* and we have
not obeyed his voice" (9:14). Or as David has stated: "On the
wicked he will rain coals of fire and brimstone; a scorching wind
shall be the portion of their cup. For the Lord is righteous, he
loves righteous deeds; the upright shall behold his face" (Ps.
11:6-7).

All this, we repeat, is quite generally agreed. Yet there are
other passages in the Bible which appear, at least, to see
God as actively or efficiently engaged in man's evil. God is
the One who incites, or aggravates, or even causes man to sin.
God, we are told, does not only pass judgment but is actually
the *causa peccati*. Thus C. Clemen, for example, assumes that
he is leaning on a truly biblical support when he speaks of God

as the "disposer" or "contriver" ("*Veranstalter*") of man's sin.[49]
He takes exception to what we have called here the biblical
a priori and contends that we "need not regard a tracing back
of sin, in the Bible, as *a priori* impossible."[50] Clemen refers to
a number of Old Testament texts which suggest, in his judgment, a direct relation between man's sinful activity and God.
He cites the cases in which God hardens men's hearts or makes
them obdurate. He calls to mind the well-known examples of
Pharaoh and Sihon (Deut. 2:30; cf. Josh. 11:20; I Kings 12:15;
I Sam. 2:25). He refers to David, who thought it likely that the
Lord urged Shimei to curse him (II Sam. 16:10), or that God
stirred up Saul to be his enemy (I Sam. 26:19).[51]

Certainly we must recognize, in all justice to Clemen, that
this accent on God as "contriver" of man's sin does not eliminate
man's own responsibility. Clemen appreciates that the Israelite
did not experience, in this connection, an "antinomy" as such.
Yet God remains the contriver of man's sin. The ease with which
Clemen draws conclusions here is evident from the fact that he
still finds this standpoint throughout the New Testament. We
meet it, for example, in the sixth petition of the Lord's Prayer,
where God is seen as the "cause" of our temptations. We find
it in the hardening of men's hearts through the preaching of
Christ's parables. But the proof *par excellence,* as far as Clemen
is concerned, is the account of Christ's own redemptive activity.
Here, too, God's "contriving" of man's sin is seen in terms of
a deterministic motive in which the activity of God is named in
one and the same breath as man's own guilt.[52]

Clemen's real concern is the interrelation of divine and
human activity in the cross of Christ. In this regard he ventured

49. C. Clemen, *Die christliche Lehre von der Sünde,* 1897.
50. *Ibid.,* pp. 123-151. Here Clemen takes issue with orthodox *Lutheran*
dogmatics; but to *Reformed* theology he gives the dubious honor of
being sooner inclined to look into these matters and to think in the
direction he proposes.
51. It is striking that Clemen, in this connection, also cites Gen. 15:16,
on the measure of the iniquity of the Amorites, which was "not yet
complete." In this text he finds indicated a "prescribed *quantum* of
sins" which must be "filled up within a certain time" (*ibid.,* p. 126).
He later combines with this text Matt. 23:32f.: "Fill up, then, the
measure of your fathers. You serpents, you brood of vipers, how are
you to escape being sentenced to hell?" He asks if sin is not here
explicitly deduced from God.
52. *Ibid.,* p. 134.

into an area in which a good deal of attention has also been
given by other theologians. One thinks, for example, of Calvin.[53]
We have to face up to the undeniable biblical assertion that
God was engaged in the cross of Jesus Christ; at the same time
there are ample statements in Scripture concerning those human
actions against Jesus which betray *man's deepest guilt*. Jesus was
"crucified and killed by the hands of lawless men" (Acts 2:23).
As Christ himself put it, on the way to Emmaus, he was "delivered into the hands of sinful men" (Luke 24:7). *They* were
the ones who denied him before the face of Pontius Pilate (Acts
3:13; cf. 13:28; Luke 23:1f.). *They* were the ones who demanded that Barabbas be set free (Acts 3:14; Luke 23:25) and
that Jesus, the Author of Life, should now be put to death (Acts
3:15; cf. 10:39). Therefore Jesus was the "living stone, rejected
by men" (I Pet. 2:4; cf. I Thess. 2:15). He was rejected by
Jerusalem which killed the prophets. Nevertheless he was also
the prophet who could not "perish away from Jerusalem" (Luke
13:33ff.).

In Peter's Pentecost address we hear of God's *answer* to these
sinful acts of men. God "raised up" Christ, "having loosed the
pangs of death" (Acts 2:24), and exalted him at his right hand
(2:33; 10:39). Therefore the one whom *they* crucified was made
by *God himself* both "Lord and Christ" (2:36; cf. 5:30-31).[54]
And still it is an amazing fact that in the cross of Christ we
have to do with more than the sinful acts of men, to which
God's answer was appended in the raising of Jesus. In the cross
we see a very real relation between the divine and human
activity. Recall what Peter said: that Christ was "delivered up
according to the definite plan and foreknowledge of God"
(2:23). Or bear in mind that remarkable prayer which was
uttered "in one accord" in the early Church: "... both Herod
and Pontius Pilate, with the Gentiles and the peoples of Israel"
were gathered together "to do whatever *thy hand and thy plan
had predestined to take place*" (Acts 4:27-28). Therefore there
is every reason to speak of a "coincidence" between the divine
and human activity. When Peter referred to what *men* had done
he also reaffirmed that "what *God* foretold by the mouth of all

53. Cf. my *The Providence of God,* 1952, Chap. 5.
54. Cf. also the contrast seen in I Pet. 2:4: the "living stone, rejected by
   men but in God's sight chosen and precious"; also v. 7: "The very
   stone which the builders rejected has become the head of the
   corner." Cf. my *The Work of Christ,* 1965, Chap. 6.

the prophets, that his Christ should suffer, he thus fulfilled"
(Acts 3:18).

These, then, are the texts which have occasioned a view of
God, if not as the *causa peccati,* then somehow as willing man's
sin. The thought here is not merely, as Bavinck once put it,
that something so horrid could not have arisen entirely apart
from God's own counsel. Rather the thought is that man's sin,
in a "certain sense," was even *necessary* for God's purposes in
Christ.[55] In such a conception, however, we see how utterly
difficult it is to escape the idea of a "causality." For here the
necessity of man's sin (in God's plan) is simply forged as a
necessary link in a causal system. Though the *causa* itself is
given a soteriological aura, it is nevertheless impossible to see,
in such a view, precisely *why* the Church has so strongly condemned every *causa*-problematic. Why should she still have such
a guarded restraint as she has always seemed to show in the
past? Is there a valid reason to maintain the common distinction
between the *causa efficiens* and the *causa deficiens?* Do these
terms apply to the *origin of sin,* perhaps, while in the cross of
Christ we see the power and love of God's activity in such a
way that any such distinction is only inappropriate? Once we
start down that path of causality we can only use, it would seem,
a more moderate speech than the Church has always tended
to use. But has her intuition, in reference to God's honor, been
wrong? The Church has constantly denied God's "guilt"; yet
should she, perhaps, have spoken of God's "causing" of man's
sin with a view to his *own intent?* Is this "coincidence" of man's
and God's activities of such a sort that we are virtually constrained to use the concept of *causality?* When we entertain that
possibility we are led to inquire if we must still speak, in such
very serious tones, of the *Deus non causa peccati.*

Now it seems to us that these questions, concerning the
perspicuity of the biblical *a priori,* are simply unavoidable. In

55. This is very clearly expressed in E. Böhl, *op. cit.,* p. 191: God is "nowhere inactive, though it be good or evil that occurs." With a reference to Acts 2 and 4 he writes that "everywhere God's ordaining hand
is involved." Is it not he who works "all things according to the
counsel of his will" (Eph. 1:11)? Böhl reasons that this certainly has
implications for fallen man, for not even Adam's fall is "independent"
from God. "Only on a firm foundation that is not divorced from the
influence of God can one make such a statement. But that being the
case, the entire decree concerning Christ's mission was dependent on
the fact of Adam's fall" (*ibid.*).

answering them we must appreciate that the Church has had an open eye for God's activities in and through the sinful deeds of men. But she has also refused to conclude from this "coincidence" that God's "decree," in any sense at all, is the original *cause of man's sin*. This position of the Church cannot be dismissed as an inconsistency or a shrinking back from the final consequence. As a matter of fact, to draw this "consequence" is to misconstrue the relation of the divine and human activity in a totally illegitimate way. It is to conceive of a monistic synthesis in which man's sin is logically or causally integrated within God's total blueprint for our world. Therefore the senseless is assigned a full sense within the holy structure of God's plan. At this decisive point the Church has always been more aware of temptation than of "inconsistency." She has constantly shied away from blasphemy.

The biblical record of Acts 2-4 has frequently brought the Church to see the interconnection of divine and human activities in the cross. She has recognized in that nexus the very mystery of the atonement. Yet the confession that God employs the acts of sinful men has never enticed the Church to assign a sense to man's sin. The real reason for this refusal has always been the incontestable witness of Scripture that God, in the cross, does *not* regard the senseless, or the groundless, or the lawless as a meaningful "link" in his plan. Rather he condemns man's sin unconditionally, and curses it in a way that is nowhere else so clearly and absolutely manifest as here. What we see in the cross is not an awe-inspiring "coincidence" in which man's sin (in a teleological perspective) is given a "sense" within a divine-and-human dialectic. There is no such dialectic in the cross of Jesus Christ. There is no dialectic that is calculated to arouse our amazement or our sense of awe as we look at God's "omnipotence" in history. We agree, of course, that we see God's power in every process of the history of salvation when God turns apparent evil into good (cf. Gen. 50:20). But the *meaning* and *importance* of God's mighty acts are only fully manifest in his *condemnation of man's sin within the cross*. In the cross we see the way to God's grace and reconciliation.

We do well to recall the decisive and explicit statement of Paul that God, "sending his own Son in the likeness of sinful flesh and for sin, ... condemned sin in the flesh" (Rom. 8:3). "His death on the cross was God's judgment on sin in general;

his flesh was the sphere in which man's sin was condemned."[56] The activities of God and man do not coinhere, in the death of Christ, in a giving of sense to the senseless but only in God's own cursing of man's sin, in his radical condemnation of man's sin, and in Christ's bearing away man's sin and becoming a curse for us (Gal. 3:13).[57] In the cross we observe that sin is really (to use Melanchthon's term) a *horribilis destructio*. That is to say, sin is a "destruction" which cannot be included as a link in any cohesive whole. It can only be excluded, covered, forgiven, and blotted out. No sense can be given to that which is only idiotic. Therefore God, in the cross, is radically opposed to sin's inanity and radical senselessness. We cannot regard it as a "monistic synthesis" when the way of salvation is made visible within the darkness of Christ's death and when Paul glories in the "wisdom" and the "power" of the cross (I Cor. 1:18ff.; Gal. 6:14). What is demonstrated here is only the miracle of God in this disruptive and accursed coincidence. The senselessness of sin is completely *exposed in the cross*.

Acts 2-4 gives us no solitary reason for setting aside the clear confession of the *Deus non causa peccati*. That confession is not denied in the cross but is only fully confirmed. Our doubts and uncertainties, in this regard, are refuted in the cross. If we cannot see that in the bitter death of his Son, Jesus Christ, God is at war with our sin and condemns our sin with his curse and renunciation,[58] we have fallen victims already to a view which waters down and depersonalizes what is absolutely essential. We have then forsaken the vision of *God's love* and of *man's own guilt*. The man who points to these "relations" in the cross and sees *God* as the "real" Author of man's sin must be reminded

56. O. Michel, *Der Brief an die Römer*, 1955, p. 181.
57. Concerning this manner of curse as the way of salvation, cf. Gal. 3:13*a*: "Christ redeemed us from the curse of the law"; also v. 14 and 6:14; further Rom. 8:3 (the sending of God's own Son) in connection with John 3:16. Büchsel, in *TWNT*, I, *s.v. ará*, etc., gives what seems to us a caricature of "orthodoxy."
58. In the light of this *condemnation* of sin we can also understand the reference that Paul makes, in Rom. 3:25, to sins done in former times, under the forbearance of God. This *anoché* has as its purpose that God's righteousness (v. 26) might be shown at the present time, so that he himself is righteous. The "passing over" of sins (v. 25) is no tolerance of sin but is oriented to the demonstration of God's righteousness. Cf. Michel, *op. cit.*, p. 88 ("bisher ungestraft vorübergehen liess") and W. G. Kümmel, on *páresis* and *éndeixis*, in *Z.Th.K.*, 1952, pp. 154ff.

that the Church has always viewed the sacrifice of Christ as the fulfillment of Isaiah 53. There we hear of the Man of Sorrows who was wounded for our transgressions (vv. 5, 10) ; we also read of God's laying upon him the iniquity of us all (v. 6). *This,* then, is what God has done with our sin in the cross of Jesus Christ. So too, in Paul we hear the stirring witness that he "who knew no sin" was *made to be sin* on our behalf (II Cor. 5:21; Rom. 3:25; 5:8).

Therefore it is not the case that the senseless is dignified with sense. We can only guard ourselves against that conception. Reconciliation in the cross is the activity of God, for "God was in Christ reconciling the world to himself" (II Cor. 5:19) ; but this reconciliation reveals the guilt of man *in all its accursedness.* Thus the activity of God in the cross does not imply a diminishing of man's own guilt. Rather, as we see in Acts and the whole of the Scripture,[59] the activity of God only emphasizes man's guilt to the fullest extent. Knowing of God's purposes in Christ, the Apostle could restrain himself from any monistic-causal conclusions. He could point to the full reality of history and exclaim that the hidden wisdom of God is the wisdom which "none of the rulers of this age understood . . . ; for if they had, they would not have crucified the Lord of glory" (I Cor. 2:8).[60] Whoever speaks in this way[61] does not reduce the cross to an accidental and contingent event within the power of sinful man. He sees in man's guilt exactly the reality of sin which cannot be assimilated in causal systems of man's thinking. The reality of guilt calls for God's response precisely where guilt is most fully apparent.

In our discussion of God's providence we spoke of God's activity pervading and intervening all of man's activity. We referred to this "interlacement" and to Stauffer's "law of deflec-

---

59. Cf. the Gospel records on the sin of Judas; also John 19:11 concerning Pilate, and Luke 22:53, "But this is your hour, and the power of darkness." Further: H. Conzelmann, *Die Mitte der Zeit. Studien zur Theologie des Lukas,* 1954, pp. 75f.

60. In this text there is nothing of what Wendland infers; viz. that the rulers had indeed tried to hinder Christ's death on the cross, "seeing that Christ's crucifixion was God's means for their own destruction and the world's redemption from their dominion" (*Die Briefe an die Korinther,* 1954, p. 24).

61. Cf. Wendland *(ibid.)* concerning the *árchontes* as "the real authors of Jesus' crucifixion."

tion."[62] In that context we also referred to Acts 2-4. But here we should see that in the cross of Christ we are not confronted by a merely general idea of "intervention." Throughout the history of Israel we see the activity of God as an "interception"; we think, for example, of Israel's desire for a king. And yet, the *Umlenkung* or incursion in the cross is more than an intervening "guidance," no matter how miraculous that "guidance" may be. The intervention of God in which he condemns man's sin has its own completely *sui generis* character. All of God's intervention in the history of salvation is finally related to this definitive activity; moreover it acquires its deepest meaning therefrom. We are not concerned, however, with a philosophy of history which posits a "structure" in God's rule and proceeds everywhere to demonstrate that "structure." We are concerned about the once-and-for-all activity of God in the cross of Jesus Christ. Thus we are concerned about the great mystery "which was kept secret for long ages but now is disclosed" (Rom. 16: 25f.). What God has done, in the cross and resurrection, defies our generalized conclusions; therefore, whoever draws these must exclude forever the miracle of the cross. Such a man includes his sin within a "God-and-sin" schema in which a fully resonant *Deus non causa peccati* can no longer be heard.

Nothing could be further from the truth than that the cross itself might cause us to have second thoughts concerning the Church's verdict of "blasphemy." As a matter of fact there is every reason at this point, both now and forevermore, to join our voices with the Church in an unshakable certainty. For the Church has taken her stand in harmony with the reality of God's reconciliation and has recognized, as such, the ominous shadows of determinism. She has seen determinism as a very perilous danger.[63] This is because determinism can only lead,

---

62. *The Providence of God*, pp. 110f. and 105f.
63. We recall the meaning of *dei* in the New Testament as it relates to the sufferings of Christ. Cf. my *The Work of Christ*, 1965, pp. 146-147; also E. Fascher's article "Theologische Betrachtungen zu [*dei*]," in *N. T. Studien für R. Bultmann*, 1954, pp. 228-254. Fascher joins hands with Bultmann (*Das Evangelium des Johannes*, pp. 489ff.) in regard to the unity of Father and Son and the fullness of Christ's power which would exclude the *dei*. In a very confusing manner he contends that "for a fatalist neutral *dei* there is nowhere room" (p. 245); hence the exclusion of every *compulsion* (pp. 242-244). That this is also excluded in the Synoptics, however, would seem to be an indisputable fact. Cf. Bultmann, who thinks that it is "symptomatic" that Christ says *houtōs*

inexorably, to an equation of sin and God's activity. That is to say, it can only result in the making of alibis.

We return, at this point, to a topic discussed in the earlier pages of this chapter: the idea that we can speak of a relation of "willing" between God and man's sin, or a relation which *transcends* the attitude of wrath and abhorrence for man's sin. Those who speak of "permission," in connection with God's "willing" of sin, do not intend to detract from the sanctity and majesty of God. Nor do they wish to play down the vengeance of God against man's sin or his transcendence above its bleakness and confusion. In all these notions (more than the obvious heresies of Boehme and Schelling) the question is very real: How can we square this "relation of willing" with the Church's judgment of "blasphemy"? The tension in the problem of "willing," as seen in such persons,[64] is very evident from the fact that they themselves prefer, at one and the same time, to speak of both God's willing and "not willing" of man's sin. They are plagued by a certain indecisiveness and the inadequacy of their own position. How can we speak seriously of the Church's renunciation of blasphemy if we must also contend for this relation in God's "willing"? Can we ever do justice, in this way, to the biblical *a priori?* Or is the *a priori* compromised in our fear for a dualism?

One meets up with that problem, in a very striking manner, in the theology of Bavinck. There we read of "the unmistakable truth that a power so disruptive as sin could not have arisen accidentally, apart from God's will and counsel."[65] Yet, while Bavinck refers to the mysteriousness and unreasonableness, the lawlessness and illegality of sin,[66] he wants nothing to do with the idea of "fortuity." In some manner or other sin *must be*

poiō in John 14:31 and not *houtōs dei génesthai* (*op. cit.,* p. 490). As though Christ's activity in his omnipotence (which Bultmann calls his "real activity") could possibly be in opposition to the *dei (ibid.)*!

64. Regarding this "willing" of sin, cf. the statement of M. J. Arntzen: "God did not only know evil beforehand, but even *decreed it*" (italics mine). "De Leer der dubbele Praedestinatie bij Gottschalk van Orbis," *G.T.T.,* 1957, p. 171.

65. Bavinck, *op. cit.,* III, 33. One might ask what the word *accidental* (or *fortuitous;* "toevallig") really means in Bavinck; for in Vol. II (209) he speaks of a "creaturely, i.e. contingent character" *peculiar to the creature.*

66. *Ibid.,* III, 53.

related to God's will. We have noted already that Bavinck frequently maintained that sin is willed by God "in a certain sense." Those words — certainly when used so repeatedly — can only indicate his reluctance to speak unqualifiedly of God's willing of man's sin. Thus we see his hesitance to make sin a real object of God's will. Therefore these words can never be a solution to our problem but can only be a symptom of the complexities in the issue and a wholesome desire to be cautious. That desire is commendable on the part of anyone who faces up to this problem of God's will and man's sin. Yet the stresses and strains in Bavinck are apparent when he says that man's sin was not only "not accidental" but was also "not necessary." Sin is "not necessary for the creature's existence and even less so for God's."[67]

Therefore God's "willing" of man's sin, in Bavinck's conception, is surrounded by reservations and restrictions. God has "willed" evil in an entirely different way from his willing of the good.[68] His "willing" of sin is coupled with his divine hatred against man's sin and thus with a "not-willing" of man's sin. Bavinck stumbles for words to articulate this inexpressible idea. He guards himself against possible pitfalls and suggests that God's willing of sin amounts to saying that "God has willed that sin should be."[69] Thus he makes a distinction between God's willing of sin *in itself* and his willing of its *actual existence.* Actual sin is not *immediately,* and *as such,* the object of his will. Therefore the relation between God's will and man's sin is conceived in a very loose way, and room is made for God's "not-willing" of man's sin or the holy delight which he takes in good alone.[70] Yet in Bavinck's view there is always a "relation." In talking this way he is forced to consider the monistic motive of non-fortuity and non-contingency. Therefore the problematic of "relation" (despite the reservations which Bavinck has made) is finally set forth as a "relation of willing." Inevitably, "in a certain sense" can only lead to the question: *In what sense?*[71]

---

67. *Ibid.,* 35.
68. *Ibid.,* 39, 210.
69. *Ibid.,* 39.
70. *Ibid.*
71. Cf. Grosheide, *K.V.*, *Jakobus; Comm. op Jakobus,* 1955, p. 363: "in a certain sense, to a certain extent" *(tina),* with reference to James 1:18. Believers *become* first fruits; they *are* not that by nature. Zahn (Hauck),

The motive of self-excuse plays no role in this kind of halting formula. Self-excuse knows nothing of a hesitation but only
of an explanation for man's sin. Yet it remains a fact that once
we refer to a "relation of willing" (if only in a "certain sense")
we have opened the floodgates for the concept of causality. We
are then compelled to consider the relation of this "willing" and
man's sin and to re-evaluate the unity of God's will. In Bavinck
these problems re-emerge, despite his reservations. The extent to
which he remained entangled in the theme of *causality* is apparent in his contention that "sin does not have God as the *causa
efficiens* but only, at best, as the *causa deficiens*." Thus God is
"the negative cause or the *causa per accidens* of sin." The "real
cause must be sought in man himself."[72] It is obvious, however,
that such a distinction, within the *causa*-concept itself, sheds preciously little light and augurs no real solution at all. No matter
what the apparent advantage, the onus of the *causa*-concept is
back with us again. It is best to remember that the Church has
waged her polemic of defense and protest by confessing the *Deus
non causa peccati*. She has refused to draw any fine distinctions
within the *causa*-concept itself.

Certainly there is no *causa efficiens* in God. Nor, however,
is there a *causa negativa, per accidens,* or a *causa deficiens*.[73]
If we say that there is, we soften down the clear confession of
the Church. In any case, we see in such formulas a certain

    Comm., 71, expresses himself in a different vein and speaks of the
"modesty" of the statement in connection with the *factual situation*
of Christians. Obviously "in a certain sense" implies a defense against
misunderstanding; and to that extent this usage is an illustration of
what Bavinck means. It forms a warning against all too simple and
direct conclusions.

72. Bavinck, *op. cit.*, 40. In the *Synopsis Purioris Theologiae* (XIV, "de
lapsu Adami") we find the distinction between *causa externa* and
interna (XIV, XIX, and XXX), but here neither one nor the other
refers to *God;* what is more, the rejection of the "manifesta blasphemia"
is very clear (XIV, XXIV). Cf.: "Nec permissio causa istius peccati
statui potest" (XIV, XXV), "*nec* impulsio Dei" (XIV, XXVI). Cf. also
Wollebius (Heppe, p. 224): "causa transgressionis Adami et Evae nec
Deus est, *nec decretum Dei,* nec denegatio specialis gratiae, nec lapsus
permissio." Further, Witsius on the blasphemy that cannot enter into
any Christian's mind "sine horrore" (Heppe, *ibid.*); "Deum auctorem
peccati nec esse *nec quoque modo fieri posse*" (J. van Genderen, *Herman Witsius*, 1953, p. 141).

73. It seems to me completely illicit to introduce the notion of *causa* and
forthwith to point to the "mystery." A repudiation of the *causa*-concept
no longer permits of that appeal.

tension in resisting both monism and dualism. The theme of a contra-monism would urge us toward the *"non causa efficiens,"* while that of a contra-dualism would urge us toward the *"causa deficiens."* We might recall here, in passing, that this very same problem once occupied Turretin. He too reflected on the *"non sine Dei providentia"* and came to the same construction, and the same tensions, as Bavinck.[74]

We shall have to be very careful in criticizing these views. For often the motive has been far from establishing a causal relationship and has only intended to underscore the non-independence and non-autonomy of evil in the light of God's rule. Therefore the restrictions and the qualifications are very understandable. The purpose is frequently to demonstrate the triumphant nature of God's activity. Therefore in all of its bleakest depths, the sin of man is still subject to God's service and to those goals which he himself has set. Nevertheless, it is clear that any "willing" of sin by God is a very unsatisfactory idea. This is all the more apparent when we make an appeal to the concept of *causality*. It is very fortunate that the Church, in her confessions, has not embraced the distinction of the *causa efficiens et causa deficiens*. At the same time, our gratitude in that regard is not owing to the fact that these terms are unintelligible for the common layman. Much rather, the Church has refused to give a toe-hold for various forms of "causality" in discussing the relation of God and man's sin.

Surely the Church is very aware of what has always been an unfathomable problem for her. But she has also professed her faith by a strong renunciation of any effort to solve that problem by means of "causality." With Witsius[75] she has contended that we may never deny what is very manifest. Therefore she has continued to profess the biblical *a priori*.

74. Turretin stated that the "eventus tanti momenti" (sin) cannot possibly be said to have occurred "otioso tantum spectatore"; he referred to the "praescientia Dei," which however is not the "causa rerum." For, "nec ideo res fiunt quia praesciuntur, sed praesciuntur, quia futurae sunt," whereas it holds in regard to the decree of God that "decrevit quidem permittere, sed non efficere." Thus Turretin tried to keep the "peccati causalitas" far removed from God. *Institutio Theologiae Elencticae*, I, 1734, pp. 656ff.; especially 671, 673.
75. Cf. Heppe, p. 224: "Et etiamsi nobis difficile quin impossibile esset, veritates has secum invicem conciliare, non tamen propter id, quod obscurum est, negari debet id, quod manifestum est."

In the frequent allusions to Acts 2-4 we often see the whole-some intentions of those whose spirits are similar to Bavinck's. At the same time, it is unavoidable that this "relation of willing" calls forth the idea of causality. That remains the case unless, in an improper manner, we empty God's willing of its divine and efficacious character. This is what we tend to do when we speak of a "willing" of sin and add: *"causa non efficiens."* Thus we stand vis-à-vis the problem of the relation of God's twofold will — that is to say, his willing and his not-willing of man's sin.[76] Obviously we must examine the meaning of that paradox.

How can there be a union of "willing" and "not-willing" one and the same object (man's sin) and a binding together of "yes" and "no" in God's single, univocal will? Those who hold to Bavinck's view exclude the notion of a contradiction or antinomy in God's willing.[77] They indicate that we cannot really speak of "two wills."[78] They propose, therefore, that God's "actual" will is the will of his counsel and decree (the *voluntas decernens, beneplaciti, arcana*); nonetheless, the will revealed to us is not the "actual" or "proper" will of God but the will of his "norm," "command," and "precept" (the *voluntas signi, praecipiens,* or *revelata*). It is evident, however, that this "solution" only complicates the picture before us and only intensifies the problem of man's sin. For the proper will of God (or his only will) is then the will according to which "everything" takes place, including our sin. There can be no rationale for adding: "in a certain sense." We can only say: God has *willed* it thus and so, though his purpose is the one which he has ordained and his goal is unclear to us until the eschaton.

It is certainly obvious that this kind of thinking is very dangerous. Once we assume that the *voluntas revelata* is not God's actual will but is only in fact a "norm," we are left with an intolerable tension; furthermore, the very idea of *revelation* is then badly relativized. Revelation is then set in the shadow of a "factuality" in which "everything" happens (including man's sin) within God's hidden and actual will. But behind

---

76. In this world, according to Bavinck, there "is one thing that gives special difficulties for the doctrine of the will of God, and that is evil" (*op. cit.,* II, 210). "Evil may be ever so much under God's control but it still cannot be the object of his will in the same sense and the same way as good" *(ibid.).*
77. Cf. BC, Art. 1, on the simplicity of God.
78. On Bavinck, in this connection, see my *Divine Election,* 1960, pp. 115ff.

what is visible is still the relation of God and man's sin, and
that relation is seen as a "willing" of the *Deus decernens*. If,
however, this "willing" is more than a *voluntas inefficiens*, it
cannot be conceived of except in the schema of *causality*. Therefore the distinction of the *voluntas arcana et revelata* (or the
actual and inactual wills of God) cannot and does not solve a
thing. It exacerbates the problem in the new form of the relation between man's sin and God's will. The question, then, is
this: What is the relation between man's sin and the *real will* of
God, or the fullness and the glory of God's being?[79] When we
seek to unriddle that riddle by means of a distinction in God's
twofold will we can only follow a path in which nothing is
really unriddled at all.[80]

No wonder that Bavinck, while he wrestled with these problems, let loose his criticism of Maccovius at this crucial juncture
of God's will. Maccovius, the *enfant terrible* of supralapsari-
anism, had criticized the Reformed distinction of the will of
God's decree and the will of his command and had called the
latter no real will in any proper sense. God's proper will, he
said, is only the will of his decree. This alone is "the real will
of God."[81] Bavinck, however, took exception here and asserted
that sin, in Maccovius' view, was not only included in God's
counsel but "was definitely willed by him." Granting that this
view has a certain consistency, Bavinck wanted nothing to do

79. Cf. Bavinck, *op. cit.*, p. 213: "The actual will in God is the *voluntas
beneplaciti*, and this is one with God's essence, is unchangeable, and is
always fulfilled." We should keep in mind that the problems relating
to the distinction in the will of God have been considered also, and
even especially, in Lutheran theology; particularly the problem of what
is meant by the *voluntas revelata*. The Formula Concordiae (XI, Par.
34ff.) contests any contradiction in the will of God, since we would
then be without all comfort; it indicates that only from God's Word do
we know "what his will is for us." This problem is simply intensified
when the *voluntas revelata* is referred to as an "unactual" will. Cf. the
criticism of Vilmar, *Dogmatik*, I, 1874, 220, regarding the will of God
when seen "only as *significatio*." Bavinck denies that the issue here is a
"willing" or "not-willing" of sin on the part of God; he maintains the
usage of the term *voluntas signi*, in which God says "how and in what
way he does not will sin" (*ibid.*). It is far from clear, however, why
Bavinck refuses to formulate the *voluntas signi* by saying *simply that
God does not will sin*. He concludes, instead, that God "has willed sin
in a certain sense for his own wise reasons, even if these are hidden
from us" (*ibid.*, p. 213).
80. Cf. my *Divine Election*, 1960, p. 115.
81. Bavinck, *Roeping en Wedergeboorte*, 1903, p. 83.

with it.[82] He refused to accept the concentration of God's will
in the will of his decree, and reverted to the traditional Reformed distinction. There, at least, he thought, there is room
for conceiving of the will of God's command as a *viable will*.
At the same time, what Bavinck did with this distinction, within
his dogmatics, is of special importance for us to see. The Reformed conception, he suggested, has always been different from
the Arminian, Lutheran and Roman Catholic views. For all
these latter have the *voluntas signi* as God's "real will,"[83] while
the Reformed alone have proceeded from the *voluntas beneplaciti* and have regarded this as God's proper and essential
will.[84] Thus when Bavinck tried to show that the *voluntas signi*
and the *voluntas beneplaciti* are not inconsistent he proposed
that the former "is not really the will of God but only his command and precept, which applies as a rule for our conduct."[85]
Only in a "metaphorical sense" can this be seen as God's *will*.[86]

Thus we cannot escape the impression that Bavinck comes
very close to the thinking of Maccovius after all. As early as
1903 he had seen the "element of truth" in Maccovius' view;[87]
this, moreover, is all the more apparent in his dogmatics, when
he states that the *voluntas signi* is not God's will in any strictly
proper sense. If we look closely at that curious formula we find
that precisely what Scripture unceasingly calls the *will of God*
becomes (by means of this dogmatical distinction) no longer
his *actual will*. The result is that dogmatics is a far step removed from the biblical statement. One can certainly appreciate,
of course, what Bavinck was trying to say. Man, who violates
God's law, is "at no time independent from God"[88] but even
serves God's decree in the very moment that he sins. Furthermore, this way of seeing things was completely decisive for
Bavinck. His starting-point was not a "causality" (in terms of
the *voluntas beneplaciti*) but was rather the biblical witness that

82. "By this and similar arguments Maccovius earned for himself the name
    of an ardent Calvinist" *(ibid.)*. Cf. Bavinck on "the idle reasonings"
    and scholastic distinctions which got Maccovius nowhere.
83. Bavinck, *Geref. Dog.*, II, 212.
84. *Ibid.*, 213.
85. *Ibid.*, 214.
86. *Ibid.* Also cf. A. G. Honig, *Handboek van de Gereformeerde Dogmatiek*,
    1938, p. 212. Honig speaks, in the same sense as Bavinck, of the will of
    God's decree and refers to this as the "actual" will.
87. Bavinck, *Roeping en Wedergeboorte*, p. 83.
88. *Geref. Dog.*, II, 214.

God "magnifies his wisdom in men's foolishness, his strength in their weakness, and his justice and grace in their sinning."[89] Here we stand on a very biblical foundation — namely the "foolishness" and "wisdom," the "weakness" and "strength" which Paul sets forth in his first chapter of I Corinthians. In all of Bavinck's preoccupation with God and sin there remains a wholesome reluctance as soon as the concept of causality is broached. Thus, along with him, we repudiate the idea that God "causes" our sin. *Deus non est causa peccati.* At the same time, we speak with vigor and respect of the finality of God's activity.[90] We can speak of his goal and his rule and his omnipotence over our sin. Moreover, this attitude is not an escape from protology to eschatology.[91] It underscores the only manner in which this subject of God and sin can be spoken of legitimately without denying the biblical *a priori.*[92]

The fact that the Church, in the face of her critics, has always professed the *Deus non auctor et causa peccati* is an indication of how fruitful she has seen this shift in accent from protology to eschatology. In that perspective she has not regarded the eschaton as something purely *futurum.* She has been interested in eschatology in the sense of the "last days" which are ushered

89. *Ibid.,* 215.
90. Cf. Delling, "Zur Paulinischen Teleologie," *Theologische Literaturzeitung,* 1950, pp. 705f.
91. A strange attempt, which has nothing to do with Paul's "teleology" and is denied to us already by the perspective Paul draws in I Cor. 8:6: "Yet for us there is one God, the Father, *from whom* are all things and *for whom* we exist" *(ex hoú tá pánta kaí hēmeís eis autón);* cf. also Rom. 11:36.
92. Cf. the article of E. Stauffer in *TWNT,* III, *s.v. hína.* This orientation, this teleology of the activity of God, in no way obscures the reality of sin but excludes a causal explanation for sin. At the same time, we can see how far removed we are here from any "teleology" that regards the end as sanctifying the means. For this *telos* has nothing to do with a sanctifying or even a tolerating of sin, but only with sin's *condemnation.* Bradwardine is a case in point and illustrates the peril of systematizing sin in a teleology. Cf. G. Leff, *Bradwardine and the Pelagians,* 1957, pp. 63f. When this happens it ought not surprise us that the *Deus non causa peccati,* though not denied, is befogged in the mists of distinctions ("causa efficiens, formalis, finalis malae actionis, sed non materialis," *ibid.,* p. 64). Cf. H. A. Oberman, *Archbishop Thomas Bradwardine: a Fourteenth Century Augustinian,* 1957, pp. 123ff., especially p. 132, on the weakening of sin "by extenuating it as a constituent of harmony, so that it is made a final good." Cf. also *ibid.,* p. 227.

in by the outpouring of the Holy Spirit. She has been interested in that eschaton in which the finished salvation of reconciliation becomes a reality, no matter what the sins and guilt of men. Therefore the cross (or the reality of God's salvation-activity in and through man's sin) has never been interpreted as a relativizing of man's guilt. Rather it has been seen as the *removal and propitiation of his sins.* Therefore it has remained erect as the mid-point in all history and the center of the Church. The cross is the mystery of reconciliation. Thus it is the unveiling and manifestation of the love and justice of God. As such it is also the summons to repentance and conversion from sin and the invitation to enter into the splendor of God's glory.

That being the case, a man can never rightly construe a causal relation between the will of God and his own sin. The confusions apparent in this relation between the senseless and him who gave sense to the whole of creation are very obvious in those tensions that are introduced in the doctrine of the *voluntas Dei.* These tensions can only lead to a virtual denial of the *voluntas signi* as any "real" will of God. Though the *causa*-concept might not be applied to the *voluntas signi (revelata),* it can no longer be denied that God, in principle, *has willed sin.* The reservations that commonly accompany this concept do nothing to negate the concept itself. Therefore this concept is sometimes set forth with very few qualms at all.[93]

93. As seen, e.g., in the case of Böhl, *op. cit.,* Par. 37 ("Über den Ursprung der Sünde") and Par. 39 ("Das Geheimnis des Falles"). The *Deus non causa peccati* is rejected (pp. 183, 192) and the "relation" between God and sin is illumined in a "rational" manner. God "did not wish to obstruct sin" (p. 180); he permitted sin "in his knowledge and will" (*ibid.*); and there was a "cooperation of God in the fall," in that "he *denied* the presence of his Holy Spirit" for man's "definitive, absolute preservation" (p. 181). Cf. the *causa deficiens* (p. 182) — which Böhl translates as the "im Stich lassende causa"! God has "willingly" permitted sin "from a higher point of view" (p. 183). Though Böhl speaks of the "deep mystery of the fall" (p. 188), he affirms, nonetheless, that the fall could not have happened "apart from God" (p. 190). He even refers to "the directive activity of God, his cooperation in the realization of the fall," by withholding his measureless preservation. For to give a full measure of preservation would be "unwise" (*ibid.*). Man must always remain "not fully independent from God" (p. 191); cf. "O felix culpa" (*ibid.*). Moreover, to avoid blasphemy, all this is set in the framework of that statement "in which all Reformed dogmaticians are united: Deus agit circa malum ipsum" (p. 190). But only Böhl (it

In our thinking about God and sin it is best not merely to speak of "sin" in the abstract but to fill that word with a very concrete content. The more concrete the content, the more difficult it is to speak of God's *willing of man's sin*. The concept of *sin,* by itself, is far too comfortably vague. Thus it is easier to say that God wills "sin" than to say that he wills a particular murder, or promiscuity, or that he wants his people to defy his ways, or to break his communion, or to blaspheme his holy name. In the final analysis, of course, we are speaking of the same thing. For sin is never an abstraction but is only real *in concreto.* Therefore it is no solution to suggest, as some have, that alongside God's not-willing of sin in general we should speak of his willing of particular sins. We are not surprised when such thinking is surrounded by qualifications. One simply cannot speak of this "solution" and refuse to carry out his argument consistently. Furthermore, the problems that rise at this point do not have their root in our limited insight concerning God's ways. They root in the fact that we are talking about *man's sin.* The sin of man cannot be set forth in a transparent relation to God without diminishing God's glory.[94]

It is impossible to overcome a dualism by conceiving of sin in a causal relation to God or reducing it finally to God. Later we shall hope to show that dualism is untenable; but for now we should see that we cannot oppose it by a causal or structural schema. The *atonement* is what we need but not a rational *ordering* of that which is intrinsically disorderly.[95] God is the

would seem!) has given us the "key" to this "circa" in all its "reasonableness" and "necessity."

94. Clearly, the "appointment" referred to in the Belgic Confession, Art. 13, does not suggest a giving of order to disorder and sin; it only indicates God's power in and over everything. Precisely in this article the goodness of God and his government over all things are confessed, "so that nothing happens in this world without his appointment; nevertheless, God neither is the Author of nor can he be charged with the sins which are committed." Reference is made again to God's "power and goodness," which "are so great and incomprehensible that he orders and executes his work in the most excellent and just manner, even then when devils and wicked men act unjustly." Cf. Polman, *Onze Nederlandse Geloofsbelijdenis,* II, 83, on the concept of *appointment* ("ordinantie"); also his criticism of Thomas' "decree of ordering," as "key to the whole Roman system" (pp. 85ff.).

95. Cf. Polman's discussion of the idea of ordering or arrangement (*ibid.,* pp. 86f.), especially in reference to the "strong desire to demonstrate the *reasonableness* of God's providential plan in regard to evil" (p. 89).

Origin of all things (as the Church has constantly confessed),
but he is not the Origin of sin and its destructive tendencies.
For sin is only *contra* God, *contra* his work, and *contra* that
which owes its origin to him. Therefore the Church's faith-con-
clusion has always been that the *Deus non causa peccati* must
be thankfully professed, without the slightest hesitation or compromise. We must not hedge on the *"causa efficiens"* and the
"causa deficiens." Scripture shows that God rules over man's
sin and that sin is no autonomous counterforce to him. But it
also shows that God makes use of man's sin for his own purposes,
despite the intentions of man's sin. God intercepts man's sin —
and in the revelation of that profound mystery he both condemns and expiates his sin.

Therefore the mystery of God's good government (or his
reconciling the world to himself) cannot be fathomed in terms
of an "ordering" of man's sin within the totality of creation.
We may not proceed from the *gubernatio Dei* to the problematic of sin's origin, and in some way or other endow the
senseless with sense.[96] When the Church spoke of God as the
"Origin" of all things she certainly had in mind those things
with creaturely reality, whether visible or invisible. But no

Cf. also J. T. Bakker, *Coram Deo: Bijdrage tot het Onderzoek naar de
Structuur van Luthers Theologie*, 1956, pp. 132ff., with respect to the
bonitas Dei and the *bonitas* of creation. It is remarkable that Calvin
spoke of *"ordinatio"* and that Roman Catholic theology prefers to
speak of a *"positive permissio"* (Thomas); this latter concept is freight-
ed with more of a "structure" and systematization than we find in
Calvin. The main concern in Calvin is the omnipotence of God (as
also BC, Art. 13). On Thomas, cf. C. Friethoff, *De Praedestinatieleer
van Thomas en Calvijn*, 1925, pp. 33ff.; for Calvin, cf. especially his
Inst., II, 4, 2, on the "varietas in fine et modo," in reference to God's
activity and man's: e.g., Satan's activity in Job's life *and* the "Domini
opus" (*ibid.*). Calvin demonstrates, in this connection, how real he sees
the danger of speaking "irreverenter" concerning the works of God, and
how much he cherishes "sobrietas," though he rejects the notion of
"praescientia" (*ibid.*, 4, 3; cf. I, 18, 1). Cf. Polman, *De Praedestinatieleer van Augustinus, Thomas van Aquino en Calvijn*, 1936, p. 276, in
special reference to the "primum movens," "prima causa," and "mechanical causality."

96. Cf. H. Dooyeweerd, *A New Critique of Theoretical Thought*, I, 1953,
100 (also II, 30). The conjoining of meaning and reality implies no
actualistic abolishing of reality but the refutation of Husserl's attempt
"to abstract meaning from reality" (*ibid.*, II, 31). It is obvious that
Dooyeweerd, from this point of view, rightly affixes absolutely no
"meaning" to sin.

matter how sin burrows and burns in reality and seethes its
way into the deepest crannies of our hearts, it can never be
seen as part of that reality itself. Its goal is always the disruption and destruction of reality. Therefore it is simply impossible
to conclude, from the notion of God as the "Origin" of all
things, that he is also the "Origin" of evil. To see him in a
causal hierarchy, as the *Prima Causa* of creaturely reality, alongside or behind the *causae secundae*,[97] is a danger that is far more
factual than fictional. Furthermore, when we look at our own
sins we can only acknowledge that these allusions to causality
are illegal and completely untenable.

The issue of causality pivots finally on this question of the
"reality" of our sin. That is to say, it pivots on the problem
of sin's *nature and essence*. With a striking emphasis, Christian
thought has affirmed constantly that sin is no "substance"[98] or
"part" of creaturely reality. Were it a "part," we could only
conclude that there "would be a being that did not have God
as its author or that God must be its author."[99] Therefore
theologians, in examining this question if and to what extent
sin can be said to have "reality,"[100] have attempted to describe
man's sin by means of the negative concept of *privatio boni*.
Those who plead for this idea, however, expose themselves to
very serious perils. For *privatio*, as a concept, can only be maintained by conceiving of sin as something relative. Sin is then
a "hiatus" or "not yet." It is difficult, in this idea, to regard

---

97. We do not deny that God has often been called *"causa"* in a sense that
purports little more than *origin*. In that same spirit BC, Art. 1, refers
to him as an "overflowing fountain"; cf. Dooyeweerd, *Christelijke Encyclopaedie*, II, 1957, on "causaliteit" (126). Dooyeweerd here makes use
of the expression "first cause," interpreted in this way, but rejects the
idea that the theoretical aspect of the causal relation (the mechanical
aspect) is involved in God's activity in such a manner that God is the
First Cause in an abstract causal series.

98. Bavinck, *op. cit.*, III, 116: "Concerning this there has never been any
disagreement or dispute." One is reminded of Augustine's statement in
his *Confessions*, VII, that evil, whose origin he wished to know, is
nothing substantial ("non est substantia"), for if it were ("si substantia
esset") it would be good. Augustine inquired what wickedness is and
found it to be no "substance" ("non inveni substantiam"). Cf. A. Sizoo,
Toelichting op Augustinus' Belijdenissen, pp. 158f., in reference to the
privatio-concept.

99. Bavinck, *loc. cit.*; also p. 117.

100. Cf. O. Weber, *Grundlagen der Dogmatik*, I, 1955, 541, on the question
of the Scholastics: Does evil have reality?

our sin as that iniquitous and chaotic force which it most certainly is. Thus, when the Protestant Reformation spoke of
"privatio," to counteract the notion of sin's substantiality, it
also preferred to use the concept of *"actuosa privatio."* This latter term was employed to indicate the activeness and forceful-
ness of sin.[101]

Our purpose now is not to analyze the antithetical function
of the *privatio*-idea. Nor are we interested in those perils which
it breeds.[102] The concept was used to indicate that sin was not
created by God and that it did not have its origin in him. In
that same spirit Bavinck contended that sin can be called a
"nihil."[103] Thus another term is placed in the hopper for our
consideration. Furthermore, this term too has always given rise
to a number of misconceptions. By this "nihilizing" do we really
mean a "relativizing" of man's sin? At the same time, the very
idea of a *nihil "positivum"* has certainly been useful in indi-
cating the non-creaturely status of man's sin. Thus we set sin
apart from creaturely reality. Especially in this "non-creature-
liness," some have always seen the alien character of man's sin.
For precisely in sin we are not confronted by a creaturely reality;
nevertheless we are confronted by something which *is*. Sin works
and it manifests itself *in reality*. At this point, therefore, we join
our hands with Bavinck. "We do not know from whence it is
or what it is. It is here and has no right to be. It exists and
no one can possibly explain its origin. It has come into our

---

101. Bavinck, *op. cit.,* 125: "Abstractly seen, it is nothing but a privation,
     and yet *in concreto* it is a force that governs everyone and every-
     thing." Cf. 117: "... an active and perditious principle, a disruptive
     and destructive force." Bavinck also calls the concept *privatio* an
     inadequate description.

102. We hope to consider this important question more extensively in the
     second part of this volume. On the *privatio*-concept cf. Müller, *Die
     christliche Lehre von der Sünde,* I, 1849, 393ff., especially in regard to
     the difference between privation and negation in Thomas. Also cf.
     Bavinck, *op. cit.,* 118 and Weber, *op. cit.,* 541, 643f. On Augustine's
     concept of sin, as it relates to Neoplatonism, cf. especially J. Nörre-
     gaard, *Augustins Bekehrung,* 1923, p. 67. The central problem that
     constantly crops up in regard to *actuosa privatio* is the relation be-
     twen the creature and the intentionality or purposiveness of sinful
     acts. Oberman, with an eye to Bradwardine's theology, gives a fasci-
     nating account of this problem (*op. cit.,* p. 123); cf. also Leff, *op. cit.,*
     pp. 57ff.

103. Bavinck, *op. cit.,* 118; cf. the further explanation: *no* "nihil nega-
     tivum."

world without a motive and is nevertheless the motive for all men's thinking and doing."[104]

For that reason this "motivelessness" of sin cannot find its origin in God. This force, or this sin, "is nothing and has nothing and can do nothing apart from the beings and powers which God has created. And yet it organizes all these for rebellion against him."[105] It is the "biggest contradiction tolerated by God in his creation and is used by him, in the way of righteousness and justice, as an instrument for his glory."[106] But this "way of righteousness" is also the way in which God has not merely "tolerated" man's sin. Rather he condemns man's sin and thus atones for man's sin in the cross of Jesus Christ.

Therefore we see that the monistic motive has often been a threat to the biblical *a priori*. Only when we resist the temptations of monism can we hear very clearly the vibrant witness of Scripture. This witness impresses upon us that a right concern for this topic of sin cannot inspire us to speculate on sin's origin but only to confess our guilt. Confession is really the existential application of the *Deus non causa peccati*. It is the only "mood" in which we can rightly speak of the Creator of "all things." True confession entails an inescapable warning for every man whose thoughts and acts are caught up in the quagmire of his own sin. "When a man's folly brings his way to ruin, his heart rages against the Lord" (Prov. 19:3).[107]

Christian theology described man's sin as *privatio* and thus denied its "causal relation" to the Origin of all things. But does that mode of thinking involve us in a violation of the very boundaries of creaturely reality? Does it assign to sin a position apart from that reality in a manner that might possibly portend a *dualism?* We have said that this concern has constantly been the bugbear of all monisms. The only answer, however, is that the *Deus non causa peccati* is as far removed from dualism as it can ever be from any monistic thought. Therefore the Church has rejected both of these concepts with an equal fervor and with no sense of inconsistency at all. The question of how this was possible demands our attention at this point. Yet this one

104. *Ibid.,* 125.
105. *Ibid.,* 126.
106. *Ibid.*
107. Cf. Sirach 15:11f.

thing is very certain: a rejection of dualism in no way does violence to the authority and the witness of the *Deus non causa peccati*. At the same time, the warning against *blasphemy* must not darken our vision for those other hazards which are latent in any dualistic explanation for the origin of sin.

CHAPTER THREE

DUALISM

THE CHURCH has confessed the glory of God by repudiating the blasphemy that makes God the Author and the Cause of man's sin. In that way she has offered a resistance to the temptations of monism. In one sense or another, monism has always featured a bond of affinity between God and the evil of man's sin. It has so regarded that affinity that we no longer avoid seeing sin's origin in God. Monism is born of this passion for deducing all things causally from God. It subsumes sin, too, under the compass of that "everything."

But if we reject monism at this point we are compelled to consider another "solution" to the origin of sin: that of *dualism*. Dualism proposes a primordial antithesis between two original principles (viz., light and darkness) in terms of which every form of good and evil is ultimately deduced. Basic to that conception is always the fear that the sharp antithesis between good and evil might be finally obscured or eliminated in a monistic synthesis. In this light we understand why dualism has always had a very strong and suggestive influence. Recall, for example, that St. Augustine, while he wrestled with the problems of *unde malum*, came under the spell of a Manichaean dualism for a period of some nine years.[1] At that time Manichaeanism seemed to give him a satisfactory solution, and even a definitive answer, to the riddle of sin's origin. There he found

1. Cf. J. Nörregaard, *Augustins Bekehrung*, 1923, pp. 28f.; H. C. Puech, *Le Manicheisme, Son fondateur. Sa doctrine*, 1949; G. van der Leeuw, *Godsdiensten der Wereld*, II; A. Sizoo, *Toelichting op Augustinus' Belijdenissen*, pp. 71f.; also my *The Providence of God*, 1951, pp. 254ff. Many have commented on the influence of Manichaeism on Augustine's later ideas (e.g., his conception of man's total corruption). Cf. also A. Adam, "Der manichäische Ursprung der Lehre von den zwei Reichen bei Augustin," *Theologische Literaturzeitung*, 1952. On the question of how far this influence extended, cf. E. B. J. Postma, *Augustinus' De beata vita*, 1946, pp. 228ff.

a clue for positing the absolute antithesis of good and evil. Therefore he proceeded to posit that antithesis in the very "origin" of things.

We shall have to look closely at this dualism and shall have to inquire why it is that the Church has condemned this view with the very same fervency as the *Deus causa peccati*. Though dualism would seem to be quite reasonable and lucid, we must not be deceived. Dualism gives an answer to the question of the origin of evil by positing an eternal "contrariety" of good and evil — and beyond that we simply cannot go.[2] It appears to take this antithesis with an utmost seriousness; and this is the reason for the widespread influence which it has always had.[3] Here lies the great temptation for the Church. For the Church has never wished to minimize this antithesis; nevertheless, despite this apparent "point of contact," she has rejected all dualisms as heresy. The Church has protested the eternalizing of evil and has renounced the idea which assigns to evil an ur-reality apart from God's good creation. She has taken issue with any concept of an ur-darkness in opposition to God's light.

Therefore it is clear why the point at issue has always been the question of what is meant by confessing God's "good creation of all things." On this theme the Word of God lays a very

2. Puech, *op. cit.*, p. 74: "In any case, both have nothing in common but are entirely in opposition to each other. The problem of evil, therefore, received from the very outset the most realistic and extreme solution. One cannot deny evil, for it exists in itself and from all eternity; nor can one derogate from it, for it neither derives from good nor in any way depends on it."

3. Manichaeism aspired to be a *universal* religion and do away with the narrow confines of the earlier religions. Cf. *ibid.*, p. 63, on "this pretension of ecumenicity" and "its essential missionary character." In view of its success in various lands, the success and constructive force of Manichaeism can only be called amazing. Cf. H. Brink, *et al.*, *Theologisch Woordenboek*, II, 1952, 3069, which speaks of Manichaeism's spread into Palestine, Rome, and all sections of the Roman Empire, China, central and eastern Asia, and "among all peoples." Cf. also C. Werner, *Le problème du mal dans la pensée humaine*, 1944, especially p. 58, on France, "where it gave birth to the powerful sect of the Catharites or Albigenses, which flourished in the Thirteenth Century." Werner speaks of "the profound influence" of Manichaeism. In the *Woordenboek* (II, 2682, *s.v.* "Katharen"), it is pointed out that the historical contacts of this "Neo-Manichaeism" with Manichaeism are difficult to trace. Cf. Kramers, *Godsdiensten der Wereld*, p. 390, on Manichaeism's "unbelievable spread."

special accent.[4] The Church has never proposed, in a monistic fashion, that sin was "created" by God or originated in him; nevertheless she has denied any notion of a completely autonomous "counterforce" which has nothing to do with God's originally good creation. In the Nicene Creed she very early confessed that God is the almighty Father, the Creator "of all things visible and invisible."[5] Later, against the Priscillians, she drew the full consequences of that assertion and contested the idea which denies that the devil was originally a created angel. She opposed the concept which assumes that the devil was an autonomous principle sprung forth from darkness, or merely the substantiation of evil.[6] The Church rejected this crassly autarchical and "originaire" conception of evil as "substantial" and outside the realm of creaturely reality, with no "relation" to the Creator of heaven and earth. Thus she levelled her criticism against the notion that evil has simply "sprung forth" and "made its appearance" from darkness (in a very remote fashion) and that ever afterwards it simply *is*. The Church opposed the idea that, once having come, it has only itself to thank for its own final "principle" and its own peculiar "authority."[7]

These same protests can be heard in later times.[8] Therefore the Lutheran Confessio Augustana polemicizes against the Manichaeans and their acceptance of the two principles of good and evil.[9] The Belgic Confession raises its voice against those "who

4. In this connection Ps. 102:25; Amos 5:8, 9:6; Prov. 14:31, 22:2; Isa. 45:9ff.; etc. For New Testament references: Acts 4:24 ("the heaven and the earth and the sea and everything in them"), 7:50 ("all these things"), 14:15, 17:24; Rom. 1:20, 11:36; Rev. 4:11 ("all things"), 10:6, 14:7, etc.
5. Credo "Deum Patrem omnipotentem, omnium visibilium et invisibilium factorem" (Denz., 54; Nicea, 325).
6. "S.q.d. diabolum non fuisse prius bonum angelum *a Deo factum,* nec *Dei opificium* fuisse naturam eius, sed dicit eum *ex tenebris emersisse,* nec aliquem sui habere auctorem sed ipsum esse principium atque substantiam mali, sicut Manicheus et Priscillianus dixerunt, A.S." (Denz., 237).
7. Cf. all the anathemas against the Priscillians at the Concilium Bracarense of 561; also Calvin, *Inst.*, I, 14, 3, and I, 14, 16.
8. Cf. the Concilium Lateranense IV, 1215: "Contra Albigenses, Ioachim, Waldenses," etc.: "Diaboli enim et alii daemones a Deo quidem natura creati sunt boni, sed ipsi per se facti sunt mali" (Denz., 428); also the "Professio fidei Waldensibus praescripta" of 1208: "Diabolum non per conditionem sed per arbitrium malum esse factum credimus" (Denz., 427).
9. Confessio Augustana, Art. 1.

assert that the devils have their origin in themselves, and that they are wicked of their own nature, without having been corrupted."[10] As a matter of fact, the Church opposes all such ideas of "two original principles." At the same time, she has not disputed what is most frequently seen as the main ethical motive in dualism: she has continued to recognize the radical distantiation of good and evil.[11] The Church has opposed the autonomizing of evil and any pretensions that evil is self-subsistent, or has that quality by virtue of its *own peculiar ur-existence*. In rejecting this "eternal character" of evil, she has confessed the origin of all things in God. Thus she has viewed the antithesis as a contradiction which sprang forth and found its place within the structure of creaturely reality. Conscious of this absolute antithesis, she has refused to make evil an original or autonomous force.

In this conflict of the Church and dualism we stand before a very profound issue. Though the Church has confessed the holiness and glory of God, she has run up against a doctrine in dualism which is equally intent to show that God is not responsible for the reality of evil.[12] God has absolutely nothing to do with that reality. Therefore evil can only claim its own peculiar "principle" for its own peculiar existence. Here the fact that the Church did not embrace a dualism is a tribute to her insight concerning a very definite and acute danger — namely the danger that the origin of evil is dramatized, as a cosmic act, played out in the nebulae of mythological thinking and completely abstracted from man. If anywhere, certainly here, an explanation of evil can only be seen as an exculpation *from evil*. Dualism is only a cosmic excuse in metaphysical garb.

In dualism the man in darkness is called forth to light, and much still happens in this conflict between these magnitudes. Therefore we hear of the "fall" and the "intermingling" of good and evil; furthermore it is only in the eschaton that light shall triumph over darkness. Yet every dualism presupposes

---

10. BC, Art. 12. Mani is also mentioned in Art. 9.
11. Cf. J. Müller, *Die christliche Lehre von der Sünde*, 1849, I3, 562, concerning this ethical motive. Müller takes note "of the consciousness of the profound and unfathomable significance attaching to the antagonism between good and evil, and the impossibility of reconciling these two sides with each other."
12. Cf. Brink, *et al., op. cit. (s.v. "Manicheïsme")*, 3066.

a *fatal shadow* which falls upon our world. That shadow is the shadow of an original evil in cosmic form, apart from man and apart from the sphere of his own responsibility. Thus the origin of sin lies in a lethal attack from the original "kingdom of darkness." That kingdom is set in opposition to the Father of majesty and his "kingdom of light."[13] This, in other words, is what we see in all dualisms, despite their laudable intents and their dramatic and ethical appeal.[14] Dualism puts stress on man's *fate,* but not on his *guilt.*[15]

Because of those perilous accents, a dualistic tendency may crop up in our thinking despite our rejection of every formal "dualism." This happens whenever the antithesis of God and evil is unconsciously set forth or experienced in a dualistic way. The idea of an "antithesis" may cause us, involuntarily, to think in terms of two "powers." These may be conceived as unequal in theory but completely competitive in practice. Indeed, this tendency is present whenever we are struck by the apparent omnipotence or the infinite "scope" of the kingdom of darkness. It is clearly manifest whenever we are intrigued by the seeming independence or the infinite "power" of evil. Dualism is then a real option. The real danger of dualism is that its influence is not absent when we take our stand within the Church and repudiate all "dualisms of origin." As a matter of fact, the man

13. Redemption is the restitution of the original antithesis — after which, however, a new attack from the kingdom of darkness is no longer possible (Puech, *op. cit.,* p. 85).

14. In the literature on this subject the term *dualistic* (as opposed to *monistic)* is frequently used for pointing up the "chasm" or "break" in reality, without thereby implying an ur-dualism. K. H. Roessingh, for example, has spoken of "dualism" as a feature of right-wing modernism in contrast to the monistic old-modernism. Cf. also Gösta Lindeskog's use of this terminology in his *Studien zum N.T. Schöpfungsgedanken,* 1952, pp. 171ff., and his distinguishing this from Gnostic dualism (p. 175). He refers to this dualism as "not absolute" (p. 177).

15. In the situation after the separation of light and darkness (thus in the phase of "commingling"), guilt came to be inherent in the material world. Gnostic streams paved the way for this emphasis. Cf. G. Quispel, *Het Oudste Christendom en de Antieke Cultuur,* II, 1951, 447; also Brink, *et al., op. cit.,* 3070. Thus guilt was posited outside man's existence and responsibility, and salvation came to be seen (via asceticism) as the corollary of the "originality" of sin. Cf. further Puech-Quispel, *Op Zoek naar het Evangelie der Waarheid,* p. 47; for parallels within the problematic of dualism: Helmer Ringgren, *Fatalism in Persian Epics,* 1952, especially pp. 25f.

who analyzes evil from a purely "neutral" or phenomenological point of view (apart from creation and God's redemption in Christ) can only risk falling into a full-fledged dualism. The peril is then that we succumb to the hypnotic "powers" of evil and the curse of its ravages — the scourge of the "realm" and the "potency" of darkness. Thereby we forget that something absolutely decisive has already taken place in this struggle. At precisely this juncture the biblical witness refutes all dualisms and urges us away from the curse of its temptations.

Even in its reference to Satan's falling from heaven (Luke 10:18; Rev. 12) the Scripture removes us from the whole sphere of dualism. Similarly, the visions of the Apocalypse, with their breathtaking imagery and fearsome demonic events, are seen as a *comfort for the Church*. "Grace to you and peace from him who is and who was and who is to come" (Rev. 1:4), from "the Alpha and the Omega" (1:8; 22:13), "the first and the last" (1:17; 2:8; 22:13). How could a dualism be more convincingly excluded than here? One could say that this battle still has an impressive scope and is loaded with wide and cosmic implications; but we cannot assume that its contestants are coequal or that any indecision awaits its outcome. The battle is severe precisely because *God's decision in the history of salvation has already been made*. For that reason the demonology of the New Testament is radically different from a dirge on the demons or a "demonization" of our living; it has nothing to do with a lamentation concerning the "desolations of evil." Any such complaints are self-centered and call attention to themselves. The Apocalypse, however, bursts through all selfishness and centers attention on the song of Moses and the Lamb (15:3-4). Its eye is on the expectation of victory in creation and the eschaton (4:11). It does not play down the gravity of the conflict but it sings its song of victory precisely *in* the summons to the "battle of faith." The very idea of *apocalypse* does not suggest a dark or a sinister menace but the revelation of Jesus Christ as *King of kings and Lord of lords* (19:16).[16]

We get no better idea of the completely undualistic nature of the New Testament than by thinking through the biblical

16. Cf. K. H. Miskotte, *Hoofdsom der Historie*, 1945 (lectures given at the time of Nazi terrorism; see preface). Miskotte takes note, in these lectures, of the power of evil but also levels a relentless criticism against the subtle and dangerous temptation of dualistic thought. Cf. especially chapters 12 and 13 (Rev. 12).

witness concerning the Antichrist. The prefix *anti* might easily
deceive us, and certainly it will if we see it apart from the
name of *Christ*. But *anti* is not an independent word. It is tied
to someone or something against whom or what it stands inexorably opposed. Therefore the *anti* has to do with Jesus
Christ[17] — and as such it stands in the structure of the *heilshistorisch* activity of God. *Anti* is not a thesis but is only an
antithesis. Certainly this does not mean that we belittle its force
or significance. Paul himself could point the Church to the
"power" of the Antichrist and the "son of perdition" who is
still to come (II Thess. 2:3) and whose coming is "by the activity of Satan . . . with all power and with pretended signs and
wonders" (2:9). Yet, the Antichrist is defined by his name and
works in antithesis to him who is also included in his name
and sheds light upon his name. The *Christ* in the name of Antichrist is primary, and the *anti* is secondary. That is to say: the
anti stands in an antithetical relation to Christ. But if that
be the case, it is obvious that the concept of *Antichrist* is diametrically opposed to every form of dualism. Therefore we
understand why the scriptural warnings concerning the Antichrist anticipate the eschatological event of Christ's slaying the
"lawless one" and bringing him to nothing "by his appearing
and his coming" (II Thess. 2:8; cf. Rom. 16:20).

The prefix *anti* is negative and antithetical and therefore
has no room for a dualism. The same comment applies to the
epistles of John, where again the Antichrist has no thesis but
only antithesis. "Who is the liar but he who denies that Jesus
is the Christ? This is the antichrist, he who denies the Father
and the Son" (I John 2:22; cf. II John 1:7; I John 4:3). Only a
non-originality is manifest here. It is manifest in the telling
of lies concerning Jesus, or in lying against the truth, or in
positing the theme of darkness in contrast to the light. The
concept of *anti* implies an attempt to assume an original or
equivalent "counterbalance."[18] But that very effort is cancelled

17. Cf. K. Dijk, *Het Einde der Eeuwen,* 1952, Chap. 7; Miskotte, "In de
   Schaduw van de Antichrist," in *Feest in de Voorhof,* 1951, p. 244; also
   R. Schnackenburg, *Die Johannesbriefe,* 1953, pp. 128ff.; and B. Rigaux,
   Saint Paul, Les épitres aux Thessaloniens, 1956, pp. 259ff. and 654ff.
   Cf. the word *parousía* in reference to the Antichrist in II Thess. 2:9.
18. Cf. the "opponent" of II Thess. 2:4; *antikeimenos* is used in Zech.
   3:1 (LXX) for Satan. Cf. the many *antikeiménoi* in contrast to the "wide"
   and "effective" door of the Gospel (I Cor. 16:9).

out by the title of the Anti*christ*. Everything the Antichrist does
is also anti-God; yet his name is not the "Anti-God" but "Antichrist."[19] In that fact every trace of a dualism (whether theoretical or practical) is eliminated once and for all. The same
argument holds in regard to the term *ánomos,* where again there
is no thesis but only an antithesis to God's law (II Thess. 2:4).[20]

Therefore the Antichrist, in the New Testament, can only
be seen in the focus of Jesus Christ. His appearance is qualified
and temporally defined in terms of Christ, and it is simply impossible to think of him or to deal with him in isolation.[21] To
do so is to fall into a dualistic mode of thought. The shadow
of an independent, irresistible, and inexorable evil can only
then envelop our world again. In view of that fact it is strange
how prevalent the danger is of isolating the powers of darkness from their biblical setting and fashioning a general "phenomenology" of evil. That conception is either optimistic or
pessimistic according to the standpoint which we choose.

One can see the lines of this dualism in the theoretical views
of a Nineteenth Century theologian, Carl Daub. In his study,
Judas Ischariot oder das Böse im Verhältnis zum Guten,[22]
Daub reveals a number of dualistic strains. We might expect
that in such a topic, with its implied relation to Jesus Christ,
the dualistic conception would be held quite firmly in check.
As a matter of fact, it is exactly in that context that dualism
takes hold in Daub's thinking.[23] Daub raised his voice against

19. Cf. Daniel (7:25, 7:11), who makes reference to words spoken against
the Most High; G. Vos, *The Pauline Eschatology,* 1952, p. 105: "a
striking pre-analogy." The denial of the Son by the Antichrist also
involves the Father (I John 2:22).

20. Cf., in this discussion, Dan. 7:14, concerning the eternal dominion
which shall not pass away and the kingdom which shall not be destroyed; also the relation of the Antichrist to the temple of God (II
Thess. 2:4) and apostasy (2:3). For this antithesis to the law, cf. Dan.
7:25.

21. This "dating" of the Antichrist has reference to "the last hour" (I
John 2:18): the appearance of antichrists is the characteristic feature of
that particular time. See Schnackenburg, *op. cit.,* p. 125. For the limitation of the *anti* in terms of Christ, cf. also the "false Christs" with
their "signs and wonders" (Mark 13:22; *pseudóchristoi*), who make
pretensions of being Christ.

22. Heft I (1816); Heft II[1] (1818); Heft II[2] (1818); originally intended as
an introduction to a book on the origin of sin (cf. I, preface).

23. Cf. K. Barth on the poverty of German idealism in Daub, in whose
judgment Judas was a "sinner without equal" (*K.D.,* II/2, 559; ET, 502).

those who "deceptively locate the principle of evil in original good or even in the Deity."[24] He set forth his own conception of the *causa sui* of absolute and underived evil. His purpose was to develop this kind of thinking and to wage warfare against all monism. Yet his methodology is far from clear. What is absolutely unnatural, he suggests, is not that something is "self-generating" *(causa sui)* but that it is "self-inflammatory." It is not that it is *"ein sich selbst Erzeugendes"* but *"ein sich selbst Entzündendes."* Here Daub struggles with the age-old problem that is illegitimately "solved" in the monistic synthesis of God and evil. He ends up himself in a dualism which can only make Judas Iscariot the illustration of *absolute evil*.

It is obvious, of course, that the Gospels do not minimize the depths of Judas' sin. They are not reluctant to point to his guilt. But anyone who finds in Judas the epitome of evil in a dualistic fashion, and identifies him with evil in relation to God, and writes a book on "Judas Iscariot, or evil, in relation to the good," has badly misconstrued what the Scripture says concerning Judas.[25] Surely the relation of Judas and Jesus can give us no reason to think in dualistic terms. Exactly the betrayal of Judas is *used for the conquering of evil*. Therefore it is impossible to build a dualistic philosophy or theology of "good and evil" on the *anti* of Judas' activity. Why is it that Daub ignored the radical refutation of dualism in those events which center in the cross? Here we see the clearest proof of how deeply he took his starting-point in a general or a "neutral" phenomenology of evil. He merely exploited the scriptural data for the sake of finding in Judas the dehumanized "incarnation of evil."[26]

24. Daub, *op. cit.*, II2, 468.
25. According to Müller *(op. cit.,* I, 561), Daub later gave up his conception in this book.
26. How difficult it is to maintain this dualism consistently is evident in those tensions in Daub to which K. Lüthi has made reference *(Judas Iskarioth in der Geschichte der Auslegung von der Reformation bis zur Gegenwart,* 1955, pp. 89-93). Lüthi comments on the appreciative way in which Hengstenberg appraised Daub's work and questions: What does orthodoxy really mean in this connection? Hengstenberg's esteem for Daub is very difficult to comprehend. Exegetically, Daub's whole viewpoint rests on a misunderstanding of the scope of the New Testament witness on Judas, which certainly forms a contrast to any dualism. Cf. Barth, *K.D.,* II/2, 559. On the "Tendenzfrage," cf. Lüthi's article (against which several objections could be lodged):

The motives of dualism and monism have been in constant clash throughout the history of the world. It is necessary, however, that we take leave of both of these ideas. We may grant that the Church has been more adamant in condemning the monistic synthesis as a "heresy"; at the same time, we must not infer that dualism is a lesser peril. A strict dualism takes very seriously the antithesis of good and evil, but it does so in a way that is very highly objectionable. Moreover, this statement not only holds in regard to dualisms of origin but in regard to dualisms of every kind. Here we include those genres which are not particularly concerned about the immoral aspects of evil but about so-called "physical evil" in our world. We think of the calamities and catastrophes, the disasters and the death which everywhere surround us.

Many people have seen this "physical evil" as the evidence of a chaotic omnipotence. They have regarded it as an ominous and portentous threat to life. While rejecting the temptations of monism, they have preferred to adopt a form of dualism which sets limits on the power of God. In no sense do they wish to see a "chaotizing" of life in any relation to the Deity. Elsewhere we have drawn attention to the revival of Marcion's ideas concerning the independent force of chaotic and antithetical evil in our world.[27] When we speak of evil, Marcion maintained, we can only mean this: that God does not operate in and through, and is not present within, the forces of perdition. It stands to reason that the relation of tragedy and guilt has always been a matter of interest in such views. Yet the conviction is that tragedy incorporated within the bounds of man's own guilt can only lose its really "tragical character."

Consider the emotional protest which H. J. Heering has quite recently made.[28] Heering has referred to the "big and small Marcions" who wage guerilla warfare in the "hinterlands of the biblical proclamation" and by now have the sympathetic ear of many.[29] He has contended that the really "tragical" feature in Christian theology is covered over by the

"Das Problem des Judas Iskarioth — neu untersucht," *Ev. Theol.*, 1956, pp. 98-114.
27. Cf. my *The Providence of God*, pp. 240f. (discussion of W. Monod).
28. H. J. Heering, "De Categorie van het Tragische in de Theologie," *N.T.T.*, 1953, pp. 279ff.
29. *Ibid.*, p. 288.

doctrines of predestination, providence, and *sin*.[30] This same protest was sounded, at about the same time, in the discussions which followed the Dutch flood disaster in 1953.[31] Again it was argued that "dualism" is a fact which we must learn to live with.[32] The struggle of God against *tehom* is still incomplete.[33] Very remarkable in all these examples is that the attempted "solution" is made by way of eschatology. What is more, this eschatological perspective is now regarded, illegitimately, as the only real basis for rejecting Marcion.[34]

From Heering's own standpoint it is apparent that his conclusions cannot be acceptable to us. He charges that to link the truly "tragical" with man's own sin and guilt is to "gloss over" those tensions and conflicts which are evident in man's living, even at the very core. He calls this "gloss" a "Christian-sanctioned interpretation of life." Never does he realize that in that idea of a "sanction" he betrays his own and not the Church's error. In the disruption and the chaos of living, and the devastations which Jeremiah saw in his visions, we find no trace of a "sanction" or a "gloss." What we do see — precisely *in such tragedy* — is the inescapability of man's guilt. It is obvious that the concept of *chaos* is related to God's power and the goodness of the works of his hands. Therefore it is necessary for us to pause and to look more closely at what is meant by this term.

Our intention here is not to argue over terminology. We

30. *Ibid.,* pp. 279f.
31. Cf. H. Berkhof, "God en de Natuur," *Wending,* 1953, *contra* J. Sperna Weyland, "God en de Zee," *N.T.T.,* 1953.
32. Cf. Heering, *op. cit.,* p. 287.
33. *Ibid.*
34. Cf. *ibid.,* p. 290. Heering speaks of an eschatology "in which dualism will be satisfied." But one cannot dissolve any form of "dualism" in protology by referring to a transition to eschatology and hypothesizing that "God is more the Recreator than Creator." Even Manichaean dualism, as a matter of fact, had an eschatology. Cf. Heering's criticism of A. A. van Ruler's *De Vervulling van der Wet,* 1947, p. 472. When Heering and others champion the "metatragical," and find that this plays no part in an "eschatological ontology and theology," and when they envisage the threat to theology coming not from Marcion but Wodan, not from Bonhoeffer but Dort, not from a one-sided *vere homo* but a one-sided *vere deus* (p. 293), then there is every reason for us to take a hard look at the figure of Noordmans. Cf. my *Divine Election,* 1960, pp. 97ff.; also R. Niebuhr, *Beyond Tragedy,* 1946, especially pp. 20ff.

accept the fact that the terms *chaos* and *chaotic* refer in general to the confusions into which our lives and cosmos have been cast. They refer to disorder as opposed to order — to the "diabolical" in its etymological sense of "mixing together," in complete disharmony, those things that were once in harmony. But the main feature in all dualism is the absolutizing of the "chaotic." What results can only be a chaos apart from, or in opposition to, God's own creative powers. Certainly we should not close our eyes to the ruins and ravages, the devastation and destruction in our world. But an "absolutized chaos" can only mean a chaos that is lifted above the level of normativity. Thus it can only mean an *ur-chaos*. It is not the idea of an "antinormativity" to which we take exception here; for such an idea is really quite beyond dispute. It is rather the idea of a "super-normativity." We are arguing against a kind of thinking which sees this "super-normativity" as the natural conclusion from the empirical data in our world. We draw this conclusion on the basis of the tensions and antitheses, the light and the darkness, the goodness and the evil, the life and the death in our world.

One cannot contradict this idea of an "absolute chaos" with an optimism which finds harmonies where there really are none. We cannot ignore the difficult issues. Life *has* its chaotic threats and horrors, and the Bible never camouflages its "antinormativity." In the strongest of terms it speaks of this world as lying "in the power of the evil one" (I John 5:19). We read of "desolations in the earth" (Ps. 46:8) and a "desolation without inhabitant" (Jer. 34:22). We read of cities crumbled in heaps and gutted by fires; the "terror by night" and the "arrow that flies by day"; the "pestilence that stalks in darkness" and the "destruction that wastes at noonday" (Ps. 91:5-6). Yet, in the midst of all of this, we are encouraged *not to fear*. We are told the secret of a "fearlessness" which roots in the Most High as our hiding place and is the very opposite of a false harmony which shuts our eyes to true reality. Scripture inveighs, in the most passionate terms, against any facile synthesis which fails to take seriously how full of havoc life can be.

Our objection, in other words, applies to those cases in which good and evil, light and darkness are absolutized and are made into "original principles" by themselves. Chaos is then cut loose from the normativity implied, for example, in the judgment which Amos preached: "though they dig into Sheol" and "climb up to heaven" and "hide themselves on the top of Carmel" and "hide from my sight at the bottom of the sea" (9: 2-3). When we speak of chaos as an antithetical force the issue at stake is not the existence or non-existence of contrasts and real cleavages in life. It is rather the fact that men conceive of an anti-normative evil apart from the power, and thus from the eyes, of the Lord. All such foolishness can only meet with the response of the Lord in Amos 9: "And though they go into captivity before their enemies, there will I command the sword, and it shall slay them; and I will set my eyes upon them for evil and not for good" (v. 4).

This thought of an ur-chaos has frequently been linked up with the creation story. Many people have seen that story as the background of man's universal experience of an "ur-struggle" between chaos and the creative work of God. Especially Genesis 1:2 has suggested the idea of an original chaos which was presupposed in the formation of the cosmos. The shadow of an original darkness is then read into the statement: "the earth was without form and void, and darkness was upon the face of the deep." According to this argument the important thing is that original darkness is mentioned even before God's later separation of darkness and light (1:14, 18). Therefore the question is very obvious: Does this statement of Scripture permit us to take exception to all dualisms of origin and to find security in the Church's doctrine of God as the original Creator of "all things"? Can we still speak of the *creatio ex nihilo?*[35]

The answer we give depends on the relation we draw between verses 1, 2, and 3 of this chapter. What does it mean that after verse 1 ("In the beginning God created the heavens and the earth") it follows: "The earth was without form and void, and darkness was upon the face of the deep"? Especially the words "without form and void" have always given rise to a lively debate. Can those words mean anything but "chaos"? What do they have to say in the whole of this account? The

---

35. Cf. the "totality" of expression in the Apostolicum ("heaven and earth"); the Nicaeno-Constantinopolitan Creed ("by whom all things were made"); the Lateranum IV ("creator omnium visibilium et invisibilium, spiritualium et corporalium," Denz., 428); the Heidelberg Catechism ("who of nothing made heaven and earth with all that is in them," Q. 26; cf. QQ. 27, 28); and the Belgic Confession ("created of nothing the heaven, the earth, and all creatures," Art. 12).

traditional answer is that they in no way imply a "chaos" at all. They refer us to what was still unformed and unstructured *after* God's original creative activity (v. 1). Only in verse 3 does the further "formation" take place. Thus the implication in this view is the rejection of the so-called "restitution" hypothesis which envisions in Genesis 1:2 a fall within the angelic realm and which presupposes a certain interlude between the original creation and the later "restoration of order." This hypothesis wants to underscore the wasteness, voidness, and darkness of verse 2. It wants to speak of a "chaos" that was *really there.*

But nowadays practically no one embraces this hypothesis.[36] It is generally acknowledged that it is highly speculative and finds no support in the creation story. Yet other difficulties attach themselves to the more traditional view, especially when men accentuate the "chaotic" character of what was once formless and void. It is commonly said, in the traditional conception, that Genesis 1:2 must be seen, along with its surrounding context, in relation to the goodness of God's original creation. Therefore this text cannot imply a "chaos" as something threatening or contradictory and destructive and "set over against" creation. Bavinck has found in Genesis 1:2 a description of the unformed state in which the earth was originally constituted — that is to say, the state of "no light, no life, no organic being, and no form or shape to things."[37] In this traditional view God's creative work is conceived in a two-stage process. The first stage is the *creation* of heaven and earth and the second is the *formation.*[38] Thus *creatio prima* is followed by *creatio secunda.* The first stage is that of a formlessness and disorder. This is non-chaotic and non-destructive in its inchoateness. The process from creation to formation is a process of *distinctio* and *ornatus;* therefore it is a process of God's putting an end to the state of unformedness and *tohu wabohu.*[39] Such

36. Bavinck points out that Genesis does not say the earth *became* waste and void but that it *was (Geref. Dog.,* III, 49). Cf. G. von Rad, *Das erste Buch Mose,* I, 1953, 38, who refers to F. Delitzsch for this "colossal speculation" *(System einer biblischen Psychologie,* pp. 60f.).
37. Bavinck, *op. cit.,* II, 439; cf. the reference to "the empty space."
38. *Ibid.* Certainly there was "some time," no matter how short, according to Bavinck. He takes note of II Pet. 3:5 ("an earth formed out of water and by means of water"). Cf. Ps. 104:6.
39. *Ibid.,* 441.

a "distinction" or "ornation" is the work of the Holy Spirit who moves and broods on the face of the waters (v. 2).

Traditional exegesis understands this image as the hovering of a bird above that which already *was*. It is a giving of structure to that which was *already created but not yet formed*. The Spirit is regarded "as the principle of creaturely being and life"[40] who is busily engaged (as Aalders once put it) "in the already created world-substance."[41] Through the activity of the Spirit that which was originally without order becomes a well-ordered whole.[42] Thus the "waste" and "void" earth, in the traditional view, is the *materia informis* or God's good creation (of verse 1) in its unformed state. The essential point here is this process from creation to formation or from formlessness to form.

This view, of course, is unacceptable to those who conceive of Genesis 1:2 in a direct relation to the Babylonian mythology. These people conclude that God, according to Genesis, formed the world from the *chaos itself*.[43] They observe that the Babylonian creation story conceives of a mythical battle between God and original chaos, and they contend that similar traces of a mythical struggle can be found in Genesis and other Old Testament passages. Thus they refer us to Isaiah 51:9: "Awake, as in days of old, the generations of long ago. Was it not thou that didst cut Rahab in pieces, that didst pierce the dragon?" Obviously the mighty acts of Jahwe are here invoked on the basis of an analogy to the revelation of his power in ancient times. One thinks of a similar reminiscence in Psalm 89:10: "Thou didst crush Rahab like a carcass, thou didst scatter thy enemies with thy mighty arm."[44] Thus we find a poetic picture

---

40. *Ibid.*, 442.
41. G. Ch. Aalders, *Genesis (K.V.)*, I2, 82.
42. Aalders (*ibid.*, 73) translates: "enkel ledigheid en vormeloosheid en duisternis over een vloed." The word *vormeloosheid* (formlessness) deserves preference, he feels, to *woest* (waste), since the latter has misleading connotations. Cf. A. Kuyper, *Loci*, II (*De Creatione*), 84: "still no specific, no ordered creation." The danger was the "rudis indigestaque molis." The ordering and individuating principle had not yet penetrated all the way. We recall Kuyper's statement that "the notion of a God who must create only a finished product and no *tohu wabohu* is in conflict with the whole context" (*ibid.*).
43. H. Gunkel, *Schöpfung und Chaos in Urzeit und Endzeit*, 1895, pp. 29f.
44. See also Job 9:13, 26:12. Cf. A. Weiser, *Die Psalmen*, II, 389: "the subduing of the forces of chaos" which here (Ps. 89) "are thought of in

of Jahwe's victory over the forces of chaos, over Rahab and
Leviathan[45] and the threatening waters which are nonetheless
subject to him. "Thou dost rule the raging of the sea; when its
waves rise, thou stillest them" (Ps. 89:9; cf. 104:7). But such
references as these are no occasion for presuming, as H. Gunkel
has done, that there is an original power of chaos or that
underlying these references is the "myth of Rahab's being conquered in prehistoric times."[46] According to Gunkel, "Rahab"
is the power of chaos personified; therefore it is used as an
illustration in Israel's history or the means for enunciating God's
triumphant activity.[47] Nowhere does Gunkel deny the dissimi-
larities between the Babylonian mythology and Genesis 1.[48] At
the same time, he cannot view Genesis 1, historically, as "the
record of a special revelation."[49] Genesis merely changes the
Marduk and Tiamat myth into a Jahwe mythology.[50]

Bavinck, we have noted, contends that such Old Testament
words as these have nothing to do with "ur-chaotic powers."
They refer to "various natural forces which are fought and
conquered by God in past generations (especially in the redemption of Israel from Egypt and in the crossing of the Red
sea), or else they refer to a perpetual battle which is still with
us today."[51] Thus their poetic imagery says nothing about an
ur-chaos or an ur-antagonist of God. Genesis 1:2 has nothing to
do with an original chaotic power. Furthermore, when the

the form of ur-waters rearing up against God and personified in the
name of Rahab."

45. Cf. Ps. 74:14: "Thou didst crush the heads of Leviathan"; also Job
3:8, 26:13, and especially the often discussed words in Isa. 27:1: "In
that day the Lord with his hard and great and strong sword will
punish Leviathan the fleeing serpent, Leviathan the twisting serpent,
and he will slay the dragon that is in the sea." Cf. Brongers, *op. cit.*, p.
73; Weiser, *op. cit.*, p. 28; N. H. Ridderbos, *K.V.*, I, 184: "the annihilation of world powers described by ideas from folk-fantasy"; A. Noordtzij,
Gods Woord en der Eeuwen Getuigenis, 1924, pp. 92f.
46. Gunkel, *op. cit.*, p. 32.
47. Cf. the description of the uselessness and vanity of Egypt in Isa. 30:7:
"therefore I have called her 'Rahab who sits still.'" Gispen speaks of
"raging," "desolation" and "pride" *(Bijbelse Encyclopedie, s.v.* "Rahab"). In connection with Job 9:13 ("the helpers of Rahab") he speaks
of a mythical being: the *tiamat* of Babylonia or another Eastern sage-
hero.
48. Gunkel, *op. cit.*, p. 118.
49. *Ibid.*
50. *Ibid.*, p. 114.
51. Bavinck, *op. cit.*, 437f.

Bible makes use of these mythological images we are not obliged to believe in the actual reality of the powers which are described. Obviously, says Bavinck, we find such images in Scripture.[52] But these are not the evidence of how much Israel's poets and prophets adhered to a pagan mythology. Bavinck agrees that *tehom* in Genesis 1:2 is the same as the Babylonian *tiamat;* nevertheless the moving forces behind these two terms are far from identical. Thus the traditional conception re-emerges in Bavinck's thought. The *tehom* of Genesis 1:2 is the earth in its "unformed state."

We make no comment, for the moment, on whether this traditional view is right or not. The Old Testament does use a number of pagan imageries and conceptions without embracing a metaphysical dualism. Its purpose is clearly to point to the creative power of Jahwe.[53] Therefore to speak of mythological "elements" in the Old Testament is very confusing at best. There are no mythological "sections" that are "analyzable" as such. There is only a deliberate utilizing of a number of non-Jewish figures and images. All of this demonstrates "the anti-mythological tenor of the Jahwe-cult as well as the vital power of absorption in the Jahwist faith." It demonstrates a power "which, in terms of its own peculiar tradition of salvation-history, overcame every foreign element and made it subservient to its own ends."[54] Therefore the crucial question is not the existence or non-existence of "foreign material";[55] nor is it the question of whether Israel's faith was metaphysically conditioned. Rather, the very purpose of these images in the Old Testament was to give "forms of expression" to Israel's belief. For that reason Bavinck can rightly conclude that the Old Testament tells us nothing about a chaotic force which existed independently of or before God's creative activity. A very wide gap remains between the Babylonian and the biblical materials.[56]

52. *Ibid.,* 438.
53. Weiser, *op. cit.,* p. 28, sees a parallel in the manner in which the Old Testament treats of "gods"; cf. Von Rad, *Theologie des A. T.,* I, 1957.
54. Weiser, *op. cit.,* p. 34.
55. Cf. A. Noordtzij, *Psalmen (K.V.),* II, 73.
56. Bavinck, unexpectedly, has written that the *only* similarity between these lies in the fact that "a chaos, in both accounts, precedes the formation of heaven and earth" (*op. cit.,* 438). But this apparently represents no *new* perspective for Bavinck, since he states that the creation

With these considerations in mind we can make a better approach to the traditional concept of Genesis 1:2. The question is whether it is meaningful to say that the creative power of God is actually heightened by the use of the *chaos*-idea. We should say that it is. Furthermore, the concepts of *waste* and *void* and *darkness* are very chaotic and forbidding. But here our criticism of the traditional view does not imply a reversion to a dualistic mode of thought. Many people who find the evidences of chaotic force in Genesis 1:2 by no means regard these as inconsistent with the *creatio ex nihilo*. At first glance we might see these as inconsistent, but on closer reflection they certainly are not.

Take, for example, the illuminating study of N. H. Ridderbos. According to Ridderbos, the traditional exegesis of Genesis 1:2 is open to very serious dispute.[57] This is because the traditional *materia informis* cannot draw its support from *any other section of Scripture*. Nowhere else do the words "heavens and earth" (v. 1) refer us to an "unformed matter." Furthermore, the traditional concept is much too placid, naive, and "lifeless" in its interpretation of Genesis 1:2. Whenever the words *tohu wabohu* are used apart from this text they have reference to "wasteness" and even a "desolation." Though *tohu* can be translated "wilderness" (Deut. 32:10), in a number of contexts it has a much stronger and more onerous ring. It refers us to idols (the "vain things" of I Samuel 12:21) or unfounded assertions (the "snare" of Isaiah 29:21). It is used in the context of "darkness" and "waters" and other terms which imply an *inimical power* (Pss. 46:3f., 93:3f.). "When the waters rise, the cosmos is threatened again with chaos."[58] Moreover, the term *tehom*, when taken by itself, implies the most sinister of associations.

Nevertheless the question is important: Does all this suggest an inevitable dualism of origin? Ridderbos (quite rightly) affirms that it does not. He does not dispute the *creatio ex nihilo* and wants nothing to do with Brongers' notion that the data of Genesis 1 leave no room for the *ex nihilo* doctrine.[59] If there

story teaches *creatio ex nihilo* and knows nothing of a primeval matter (*op. cit.*, 439).

57. Ridderbos, *Beschouwingen over Genesis 1*, 1954, pp. 25-26; also, *Is There a Conflict Between Genesis 1 and Natural Science?*, 1957, pp. 48f.

58. Ridderbos, *Beschouwingen over Genesis 1*, p. 26.

59. Cf. Brongers, *De Scheppingstraditie bij de Profeten*, 1945, p. 18. Crea-

were a self-sufficient and autarchical force of chaos, which existed in pre-creation times, we should have to abandon, of course, the *creatio ex nihilo*. But Genesis 1 gives no hint of such a force. It merely offers us a non-scientific narration of the dynamic and creative activity of God.

Therefore Von Rad has judged that the real burden of this chapter cannot lead us to a dualism. This is a valid judgment, he holds, despite the fact that the biblical *tehom* shows definite lines of connection with the Babylonian *tiamat*. "It is false," he states, "to assert that the thought of *creatio ex nihilo* is entirely absent here."[60] Von Rad stresses the very dominant position of Genesis 1:1 and argues that it would be strange indeed if Genesis 1:2, quite in contrast, were to offer us a radically different view. It would be highly peculiar if verse 2 would revert suddenly to a mythical ur-dualism and confront us with an ur-struggle between God and original chaos. In that case, of course, we could only discard the *creatio ex nihilo*.

But if Genesis 1:2 cannot be brought into conflict with the *creatio ex nihilo,* the question is still pertinent: In what way does it shed light upon or describe the massive creative work of God?[61] To answer, we must appreciate that the whole idea is to illumine the majestic character of God's creative activity in contrast to everything that could possibly threaten or render impossible a structured cosmos. The point is that God's word of power knows no boundaries. Thus the "wasteness," "voidness," and "darkness" of this story are not seen as independent "forces of chaos." Rather, they form the dark background against which the creative activity of God is set forth. Therefore Ridderbos speaks of "life-impeding factors"[62] and regards God's work of the second day, and the initial activities of the third, as a bridling of the chaos or those "powers which make life impos-

tion, for him, means division and separation. "What is worked with is already-existing material; in the beginning there is chaos" (p. 17). God's work of creation, according to Genesis, is an "ordering" (p. 18); and thus *bara* must be understood less exclusively than is generally the case (p. 15). Cf. Ridderbos, *op. cit.,* pp. 24f.; also his "Genesis 1:1 and 2," *Oud-Testamentische Studiën,* 1958, pp. 252f.

60. G. von Rad, *Genesis,* I, 38-39.
61. Cf. Ridderbos' rendition of vv. 1 and 2 *(op. cit.,* p. 231): "Zu Anfang schuf Gott den Himmel und die Erde. Und [dabei ging es wie folgt zu]. . . ."
62. Ridderbos, *Beschouwingen over Genesis 1,* p. 27.

sible" (cf. Gen. 1:6-9). God, by acting in that way, has made the earth an inhabitable place for man.[63]

We finite men can hardly conceive of this world, as created and maintained by the infinite God, except by way of a "border concept." But that concept itself can easily give rise to the impression of another reality on the other "side" of that border. When such a "reality" is absolutized, a form of dualism easily results. Nonetheless we should not be deterred from speaking as the Scriptures speak — and the Scriptures, while they refuse to speculate on abstract borders, do make emphatic mention of those "borders" which God himself has set. We read in Psalm 148:6 that all things created by God have their "boundaries." "And he established them for ever and ever; he fixed their *bounds* which cannot be passed." Psalm 104:6-9 refers us to God's covering the earth "with the deep as with a garment; the waters stood above the mountains. At thy rebuke they fled; at the sound of thy thunder they took to flight. The mountains rose, the valleys sank down to the place which thou didst appoint for them. Thou didst set a *bound* which they should not pass, so that they might not again cover the earth."[64]

But all of this cannot impede God's mighty, creative activity. As a matter of fact, the real thrust of these texts is only to demonstrate the real *power of that act.* Therefore we do not read of a wearisome or a toilsome ur-struggle between God and "original chaos." We do read that God created all things "without having to wrestle with an obstinate stuff."[65] That fact does not mean that Israel was wrong in describing God's creative activity as the contradiction of everything that makes life impossible. It means that this act can only be defined in opposition to chaos, peril, wasteness, voidness and darkness, and the threat of the sea and the pride of her waves. In all these texts

---

63. *Ibid.,* p. 30.
64. Cf. Ps. 104:19: the fixed *times* for the moon and the *time* for setting, which the sun knows. Weiser has written concerning this psalm: "This hymn of nature has the appearance of a colorful, painted elaboration of the same creation story which in Genesis 1 has the rigid lines of a wood-carving" (*op. cit.,* II, 440). One thinks of Job 38:8: the "shutting in" of the sea "with doors, when it burst forth from the womb." Cf. vv. 10 and especially 11: "Thus far shall you come, and no farther, and here shall your proud waves be stayed."
65. Ridderbos, *op. cit.,* p. 25. Cf. H. Reinckens, *Israëls Visie op het Verleden,* 1956, p. 67: "the most awesome creations are a matter of a single day." Also Von Rad, *op. cit.,* 147.

there is no reference to a "substantialized chaos" or a "dualized ur-tension and chaotic menace." There is only a positive reference to the finiteness of creaturely reality which God has established and maintains in all its finitude and creatureliness, and in all its limitation and dependency. Therefore the poetic figure of "Rahab" is set before us. In that same spirit, Genesis 1:2 says nothing about a mythical ur-struggle, and Genesis 1:17 does not "mythologize" when it tells us that God put the two great lights "in the firmament of the heavens." No myth is implied in these words: " 'Let there be light'; and there was light" (1: 3; cf. 1:6, 14).

This conception of God as Creator is jealously preserved in the whole of the Old Testament. *Bara* (as distinguished from *asah*) has always God as its subject.[66] This holds true no matter whether it refers to "in the beginning" or to the majestic acts of God in the history and lives of men (Gen. 1:1, 6:7; Deut. 4:32; Isa. 45:12, 42:5). In the latter case God is said to "make" the wilderness into a "pool of water" (Isa. 41:18). He is also asked to "create" a new heart (Ps. 51:10) and is called the "Creator" of Jacob and Israel (Isa. 43:1, 15).[67] *This* is the God who is seen, in the focus of Genesis 1, as the mighty Creator and the God of the ends of the earth. He is the God who separates the light from the darkness and who sets his "boundaries" and "limits." Moreover, he does so not in some primeval struggle but rather in the positive act of his creative word. The fact that this mighty work is described against the background of a "wasteness" and "voidness" does not suggest that we h to do with a myth. Indeed, it repudiates every notion mythical or chaotic force which rivals the Creator God of its own "autonomous" and "antithetical" reality.[68]

Therefore, if we take leave of all such dualisms, in of Genesis 1:1, we cannot see the "chaos" of Genesis shrinking down of the biblical concept. We can onl term in its true setting and its clear reference to the

---

66. Cf. Ridderbos, *op. cit.*, p. 24, on *bara* as a word that alwa God as subject; also Von Rad, *op. cit.*, 146; F. M. Th. Böhl *Terminus technicus* der Weltschöpfung im A. T. Sprach A. T. Studiën für R. Kittel, 1913, p. 44; E. Jacob, *Théologie d Testament*, 1955, pp. 115f.
67. Cf. Rendtorff, "Die theologische Stellung der Schöpfungsg Deutero-Jesaja," *Z.Th.K.*, 1954, pp. 11, 13.
68. Cf. Th. C. Vriezen, *Hoofdlijnen der Theologie van het O.T.,* 193: "no antipode of God, as in the old Eastern mythologies.

God as Creator.[69] God's creation is not the product of a victory over the powers of an "ur-chaos." Rather, the categories of "wasteness" and "voidness" and "darkness" are used to accentuate his creative power.[70] Those concepts shed light on the greatness of that act which the Church has conceived under the heading of *creatio ex nihilo*.[71]

In this connection we shall have to take a good, hard look at Barth's interpretation of Genesis 1:2. Obviously he does not find the evidence here to support a dualistic conception. He considers the "mythological acceptance of a primeval reality independent of God" to be "excluded in practice by the general tenor of the passage as well as its position within the biblical

69. Artur Weiser, in discussing mythological conceptions, has spoken of "the historicizing of the myth" (see his *Glaube und Geschichte im A.T.*, 1931, pp. 23-32), alongside *other* historicizing. This "historicizing" of the myth implies that nothing is left over of the real myth at all; there is a "transformation of what used to be myth" into an historically-oriented mode of thought (*op. cit.*, p. 30). To describe this transformation Weiser utilizes such terms as "the taking over of the myth" (*Übernahme*) and "a particular form of appropriation (*Aneignung*) and, in large part, also, an inward overcoming of an alien good" (p. 32). Brongers justifiably criticizes the term *historicizing*: yet the issue here, it seems to me, is not of a material nature, since Weiser means about the same thing as Brongers does (cf. Weiser's reference to "making serviceable"). There is a terminological objection, however, to the term *historicizing*. For our concern here is not the introduction of myth *in history* but the overcoming of myth and mythical thinking, which cannot be regarded as "historicizing" without doing violence to the profoundness of the "transformation." We could better speak of "de-mythologizing" than of "historicizing," but this term too is obscure and cannot give the "transformation" its due.

70. Cf. P. ... and ... tion ... dem ... Schoonenberg, *Het Geloof van ons Doopsel*, I, 1955, 65. The question was: Why was the author of Genesis not more clear in his condemnation of every dualism? Cf. Ridderbos, "Genesis 1:1 und 2," p. 42: "... *nihilo* might be taught in the Old Testament as clearly as ... ct from the Old Testament, but that does not mean that ... ent teaches it as clearly as we might desire" (*ibid.*, p. ...ded as no relativizing (cf. pp. 38, 44, 45). Ridderbos ... on to what Genesis 1 wants to say about the omnip-
... 5).

...52f. Ridderbos' charge that it was an unhappy ...i's part to describe this *nihil* in such graphic ... it seems to me; it is attentive to the words of ... more careful and speaks of a "shriveling up ... to the concept of God). The motive of ... he *nihil* but to see it in relation to God's ...erbos, *ibid.*, p. 39; Vriezen, *op. cit.*, p. 193.

... *e l'Anc...* ... ...aube bei ... 1954[2], p.

context."[72] Therefore he is confronted by the main problem, as he sees it, in Genesis 1:2: What can be the solution of the apparent conflict (or "unbearable" tension) between the sovereign *bara* of Genesis 1:1 and the "mythologoumenon" of Genesis 1:2?[73] This is the *"crux interpretum"* which Barth has seen as "one of the most difficult in the whole Bible."[74]

Barth rejects, first of all, the exegesis which finds in Genesis 1:2 a primeval reality which anteceded creation. He regards that view as out of harmony with Genesis 1:1.[75] But he rejects, just as much, the traditional exegesis which continues to work with the concepts of *informitas materiae* and a "prior creation" (*creatio prima*). Here Barth asks his very critical question: *Tertium datur?* — Is there a third possibility? If we cannot accept an independent and original power or a "prior creation," then what can possibly be left? Barth answers that there is a third alternative, and he finds it in the idea of a "caricature."[76] The words *tohu wabohu,* in his judgment, signify what is vacuous or void and chaotic, while the concept of *water* ("in formal attachment to the Babylonian tradition") has reference to a principle opposed to the good creation of God.[77] *Tehom* can only mean peril. Genesis, by using such terms as these, does not propose to set before us the *ex tenebris lux* of the myth but a new conception of *post tenebras lux.*[78]

The idea of "post" might suggest a temporal order of chaos-to-cosmos — but such a sequence is not what Barth had in mind. The introduction of the *chaos*-idea in Genesis is not "for its own sake, to present it as a reality,"[79] but only to shed an important light on the creative act of God. Barth illustrates his point here by referring to the statement in Genesis 1:2. There the Spirit is said to "move" or to "brood" on the face of the waters. Barth sees the picture of a bird "hovering" or "brooding" on the face of the deep. But he hastens to add that this in no way implies (as tradition has said) a "preparation" for a later

72. Barth, *K.D.,* III/1, 113 (ET, 103).
73. Cf. K. Galling, "Der Charakter der Chaosschilderung in Gen. I, 2," *Z.Th.K.,* 1950, p. 145.
74. Barth, *op. cit.,* 112, 119 (ET, 102, 108).
75. *Ibid.,* 112 (ET, 102).
76. *Ibid.,* 114 (ET, 104).
77. *Ibid.,* 115 (ET, 105).
78. *Ibid.,* 117 (ET, 106).
79. *Ibid.*

"formation." Barth detects in this figure a "caricature" of the world's situation apart from God's creation and light.[80] Thus, in this *ruach* that passively and contemplatively "broods" on the face of the deep he sees exposed ("in a picture of devastating irony") the "spirit" that stands in stark contrast to the real Creator God.[81] The work of *that* "god" could never fashion a chaos into a cosmos. Therefore Genesis 1:2 presents the possibility which "God in his creative decision has ignored and despised, like a human builder when he chooses one specific work and rejects and ignores another, or it may be many others, leaving them unexecuted."[82] *God's* creation has nothing to do with this picture in Genesis 1:2. For the words of this text tell us that God passed by that dark "possibility" or that portentous threat.[83] They give us the comfort of knowing that *this myth can never be real.*[84]

Genesis 1:2, if we listen to Barth, would make the myth an "irony."[85] No wonder that Galling has challenged Barth to give "clarifying proof" of his hypothesis. He has challenged that Barth's irony-idea is by no means self-evident.[86] He has also called to mind the clear and explicit case of Elijah's irony in I Kings 18:27, and has pointed to the clarity of Psalm 96:5: "For all the gods of the peoples are idols; but the Lord made the heavens." Barth's irony-idea gives no insight for understanding Genesis 1:2. It finds no support at all in that passage. The whole purpose of Genesis 1:2 is to show that God's act of creation

---

80. Reference to Deut. 32:11; *ibid.*, 118 (ET, 107).
81. *Ibid.*, 119 (ET, 108).
82. *Ibid.*
83. *Ibid.*, 120 (ET, 109).
84. *Ibid.*, 121 (ET, 109-110).
85. Galling, *op. cit.*, p. 147. Cf. also the interpretation of J. T. Wiersma, *De Schepping: Hoe Lezen Wij het Scheppingsverhaal?*, 1948, pp. 17-18, who follows Barth in seeing the Spirit's hovering as the brooding of a bird which cannot find place for the sole of its foot. "In such a chaotic situation not even the Spirit of God can bring something to pass." The meaning here is clear: "so chaotic, so formless, hopeless, would our earth be, if it were not held in existence by the Word, the faithfulness, the forgiveness of God its Creator." Our present concern with Genesis 1 is only in relation to the problem of dualism, and therefore we defer to Ridderbos' exegesis of Genesis 1:2*b* ("the Spirit of God was moving over the face of the waters"). Ridderbos stresses the connection between the breath (*ruach*) and the speaking of God (*op. cit.*, p. 32).
86. Galling, *op. cit.*, p. 184.

takes place against the background of that which inhibits life and renders it impossible. This "inhibition," however, does not stem from an "ur-chaos" but from the reality of the created world which has no existence *in itself*. It is, in fact, wholly dependent on the mighty act of him who maintains its "boundaries."

We err badly if we find a dualism involved in this biblical "boundary"-idea. But if we guard ourselves against that notion we can take issue with the traditional exegesis and can do so without falling back into a dualistic conception. It is difficult to maintain the categories of a world "substance" or blank "space" that was once formless and has since been "filled" or given "form" in a process of "formation." Dooyeweerd has criticized this view and has said that it represents a false marriage of a Greek form-matter schema and Genesis.[87] In that marriage God's created reality is the *materia prima* which must still receive its "form."

Yet that very conception is loaded with dualistic tendencies.[88] Instead of this view we should find in Genesis 1 the description of God's creative activity in its religious significance. That is to say, we should see the placing of reality within the good "borders" which he himself has set. In that fact we should note the "goodness" of creation and observe that the door is forever shut to all dualisms. We are then confronted by the knowledge of the havoc and chaotic threat within our sinful reality and within our own hearts. We are made aware of the curse of God to which our earth is now subject. When we, in that spirit, seek to say something about God's creative activity, we do so with an eye to God's goodness alone — that goodness in which he has set the "boundaries" for his own creation. Therefore we make no references to a colossal ur-struggle of mythical and primitive powers but only to the mighty, creating Word of God.

We cannot speak of an "ur-struggle" between God and the power of "chaos" any more than we can speak of a relation between God and the "nothing" of the *creatio ex nihilo*. When we put the matter in that way, however, we do touch on an important point in the Church's confession concerning the

87. H. Dooyeweerd, "De Idee der Individualiteits-structuur en het Thomistisch Substantie-begrip." *Phil. Ref.*, 1943, p. 87.
88. Cf. Dooyeweerd on Thomas, *op. cit.*, p. 86, in connection with "form and *materia prima*."

creation of God. A full discussion of this point will have to wait until the doctrine of creation; at the same time, we are remiss if we say nothing here at all. This is especially the case in view of today's great interest in the subject of "nothing." That interest arouses a good many questions which also have bearing on the problems of dualism.

In the Church's formula of *creatio ex nihilo* the creation of God is qualified by the little word *ex*. Superficially viewed, we might think that there is still a reference here to a "source" or an "origin." In that case, of course, the word would function formally as the parallel to the scriptural concepts of "from," "of," and "out of." Recall, for example, the words in Romans 11:36: "For from him and through him and to him are all things." In that text we find a very clear reference to an *origin*. But the situation is very different in regard to the Church's use of *creatio ex nihilo*. By that concept the Church has not meant a causal or "genetical" origin, as though God created the world from an already-present *"nihil."* That sort of thinking ascribes a significance to *nihil* which Scripture nowhere and never endorses. As a matter of fact, the Scripture attaches no more value to *nihil* than in such a reference as Job 26:7: "he . . . hangs the earth upon nothing."

Surely this text does not presume a "relation" between the cosmos and "nothing." So too, in a similar manner, the issue in the *creatio ex nihilo* is God's free and creative activity, which in no way implies an already-existing reality. "For he spoke, and it came to be; he commanded, and it stood forth" (Ps. 33:9). Bavinck once said that the *ex nihilo* signifies a *"post nihilum"*[89] — but even that expression is inadequate, since it presupposes a temporal order and enables us to inquire (as much as ever) concerning the sense and meaning of *"nihil."* Yet the intention in this statement is very clear. God called the world into being without the presence of an antecedent "reality."[90] That is to say

---

89. Bavinck, *op. cit.*, 382. The expression itself cannot be found in Scripture. Cf. II Macc. 7:28: *hóti ex ouk óntōn epoíēsen autá ho theós;* Vulgate: "fecit ex nihilo."

90. Cf. the New Testament expression *katabolḗ kósmou:* John 17:24; I Pet. 1:20; Eph. 1:4. Frequently, in connection with the *creatio ex nihilo* idea, reference is made to Rom. 4:17 where Paul says that God "calls into existence the things that do not exist" *(tá mḕ ónta hōs ónta).* At stake here is God's free and unlimited power which simply "calls forth" and. does not presuppose something else: his independent

that the world was neither opposed to God nor was it part of his divine essence. It was created *out of nothing* by the Word of his power.[91]

Here we must see the fascination of contemporary philosophy in reference to this subject of "nothing." That fascination is really the opposite side of its interest in "being." Observe that even when contemporary philosophy has guarded against an absolutizing of "nothing" into a kind of "something,"[92] it has run the risk of treating "nothing" as an issue in itself or a problem with its own peculiar "content." Finally that preoccupation can only be explained in the light of its rejection of the Christian doctrine of creation. Therefore it is not by chance that Heidegger has referred to the *creatio ex nihilo* of Christian dogmatics. *"Ex nihilo fit — ens creatum."*[93] In this concept the word *nihil* can only mean "the absence of extra-divine being." The idea of "real being" and the idea of *nihil* are therefore completely opposed.[94]

But there is more to the story than that. In the Christian view, according to Heidegger, "nothing" cannot possibly be raised to the status of a "problem" since it is, at best, a reference to the positivity of God's calling all things into existence. Heidegger, however, wishes to see this *nihil* in a very peculiar fashion. In metaphysical discourse, he says, "nothing" is very much *more* than the "undefined antithesis of being."[95] Therefore when Job asserts that God hangs the earth on "nothing," it is precisely the nature of that "nothing" which calls for our attention. This, then, is Heidegger's main concern. He suggests the formula that "man's existence means his being held within the realm of the 'nothing.' It means his *"Hineingehaltenheit in das Nichts."*[96]

Thus the subject of "nothing," in Heidegger's philosophy, is a subject which demands attention *in itself*. It is raised to the status of a "problem" especially when we look upon man's

power. Cf. Heb. 11:3: "what is seen was made out of things which do not appear" but is brought into being "by the word of God."

91. Bavinck, *loc. cit.*
92. Heidegger, in *Was ist Metaphysik?*, 1929, p. 9, writes emphatically that the *nihil* (*das Nichts*) "is neither any object nor anything existent at all." Cf. his *Vom Wesen des Grundes*, 1949, p. 45.
93. Heidegger, *Was ist Metaphysik?*, p. 25.
94. *Ibid.*
95. *Ibid.*, p. 26.
96. *Ibid.*, pp. 20, 28, 29.

anguish. "Dread makes known what 'nothing' is."[97] "In the basic mood of dread we come to *the* event of existence in which 'nothing' is manifest and in terms of which it must also be examined."[98] Heidegger knows, of course, that Christian theology has also concerned itself with the phenomena of fear and anguish. Yet he feels that lacking in this theology is a full ontological awareness.[99] Christian theology analyzed anxiety "when the anthropological problem of 'man's being' gained a preference to that of 'God.' "[100] But the phenomena of dread and "nothing," in Heidegger's view, could hardly have captured the Christian's imagination. They could not for the simple reason that Christians proceeded from the *creatio ex nihilo* or from a concept in which *nihil* functions as a rebuttal category or an antithetical term which makes no claims for attention in itself. Therefore, within the presupposition of *creatio*, one *could* no longer entertain the *real problem at all*. If we grant that presupposition we have already answered the question of why there is "being" and not "nothing."[101]

It seems to us that we have to agree with Heidegger to a certain extent — namely to that extent that the Christian confession leaves no room for an abstract interest in this kind of "nothingness."[102] Heidegger speaks of the "defect" in Christian

97. *Ibid.*, p. 17.
98. *Ibid.* Cf. especially *Sein und Zeit*, 1935⁴, pp. 184f., and particularly p. 190.
99. This interest on the part of Christian theology he describes as "ontic and indeed, within very restricted limits, ontological." In this latter statement he refers to Augustine, Luther and Kierkegaard (*ibid.*).
100. *Ibid.*
101. "Those for whom the Bible, e.g., is divine revelation and truth have already given answer to the question before all questions: Why is there being at all, and not, much rather, nothing?, and have responded: All being other than God himself is created by him." Cf. Heidegger's view as represented by Roessingh, *De Godsdienstwijsbegeerte en Problematiek in het Denken van Martin Heidegger*, 1957, p. 151. Also: "Whoever stands on the basis of such a faith can surely ask this question in a certain sense, but he cannot properly ask it without surrendering himself as a believer, with all the consequences of such a step" (*ibid.*).
102. This holds, it seems to me, not only in regard to a general "being." Speculations concerning "being" and "nothing" are inextricably tied together. Cf. Roessingh's summary of Heidegger: "being" was never qua "Being," in its essence, the point at issue; nor was "Nothing" ever in dispute (*ibid.*, p. 160). Cf. A. Ehrhardt, "Creatio ex nihilo," *Studia Theologica*, 1951, pp. 31ff.

theology which refuses to meddle in ontology.[103] At this point he is entirely in line with the meaning which the Church and her theology have constantly given to the *ex nihilo creatio*. There is no possibility at all in the Church's confession for an abstract interest in *"nihil."* On the other hand, the confession of *creatio ex nihilo* can find no place in the ontological investigations of Heidegger.[104]

This kind of interest in "nothing" in no way implies that we must jettison the *creatio ex nihilo*. As a matter of fact, this problem of an abstract or absolutist thinking is no newcomer at all on the Christian theological scene. It was also found in much earlier times when the *ex nihilo creatio* was first defined in opposition to its critics.[105] And so it must ever be. Christian theology must blaze her own trail even in her terminology.[106] She must take her cues from the scriptural usages. When she does so she will find that Scripture, especially in this regard, keeps our attention firmly rooted in the creative work of God and holds our investigations within their creaturely borders. Within those borders not even the shadow of a dualism can possibly find room.

If the only dualism were the kind which roots consciously in two original principles, we could end our discussion at this point. But another kind of dualism does not envision an "original" evil in opposition to an "original" good. It sees a certain duality within the boundaries of a single created and creaturely

---

103. Roessingh, *loc. cit.*
104. All this, of course, has bearing on the way we view the concept of *dread*. Heidegger, illicitly, points to Luther as having not only an ontic but also an ontological interest in this matter. He cites Luther's commentary on Genesis (cf. *Sein und Zeit*, p. 190). But Luther's interest was man's relation with God, and was not what Heidegger calls the "ontological."
105. Cf. Bavinck, *op. cit.*, 382: "Theology has never taught that non-being was the father, the source, the principle of being." In opposition to that idea it has maintained the thought of *creatio ex nihilo*, "because it was particularly suited to extirpate all sorts of error" *(ibid.)*. Cf. Augustine's *Confessions*, XI, 5, 7 and XII, 7, 7: "et aliud praeter te non erat, unde faceres ea, deus...et ideo *de nihilo* fecisti coelum et terram"; also O. Weber, *Grundlagen der Dogmatik*, I, 553, concerning the *nihil negativum* as opposed to "a content-filled speculation on the *nihil* [das Nichts]." See further Th. Haecker, *Was ist der Mensch?*, 1949, p. 49.
106. Cf. Weber, *loc. cit.*

reality. Here it is important for us also to look at this kind
of dualism. The thinkers of this school do not find in Genesis
1:2 a mythical ur-struggle but a dualistic tension which has
always been in operation, ever since the "very beginning," in
creaturely reality. Stauffer represents such thinking in speaking
of a "primary antagonism" in creation,[107] or an antagonism
that is apparent in the separation of light and darkness already
in Genesis 1. Yet Bernhart, in particular, has given this notion
its most articulated form. He systematizes Stauffer's view in a
dualistic conception and refers to a tension (or "contra") within
original creation.[108] Though he rejects a metaphysical ur-
dualism[109] he propounds a dualism within the boundaries of
God's created universe.

Bernhart does not hesitate to speak of "the chaos of an innate demonism" or the Spirit who broods on "the chaotic
waters of the demonic."[110] Here everything in Genesis 1 is suddenly, as it were, calcified or substantialized, and the duality
that results is brought into an immediate relation to man's freedom. Therefore Bernhart speaks of the "demonic, schismatic
material of human freedom."[111] Man's freedom is "demonic" and
"schismatic" because it is also the "freedom to abuse that
freedom." Thus freedom is not able "to purify its demonic,
schismatic, and primeval vision for a likeness unto God."[112] It
is only the grace of God which determines that God "cannot
leave his demonic creation to its own fate."[113] What traditional
exegesis has referred to as "unformed matter" is conceived, in
Bernhart's view, as the "pre-cosmic chaos which is able to be
cosmos." In this light he sees the "chaotic" or "demonic" as a
"twofold possibility inherent in mankind's moral state."[114]
Therefore the "demonic" and "chaotic" are incorporated *within
creation* and sin is "explained" in that way. Meanwhile an ur-

107. E. Stauffer, *Die Theologie des N.T.*, 1948⁴, pp. 48, 246.
108. J. Bernhart, *Chaos und Dämonie. Von dem göttlichen Schatten der
      Schöpfung*, 1950, p. 55, with reference to 4 Ezra: "Gramen seminis
      mali seminatum est in corde Adami" (p. 60).
109. As also Stauffer: "These thoughts have absolutely nothing to do
      with a metaphysical ur-dualism. Light and darkness are both the
      creation of God" (p. 48; cf. Bernhart, *op. cit.*, p. 61).
110. Bernhart, *op. cit.*, p. 65. Cf. his reference to Gen. 1:2.
111. *Ibid.*, p. 62.
112. *Ibid.*, p. 72.
113. *Ibid.*
114. *Ibid.*, p. 25 (in connection with the *tohu wabohu!*).

dualism is denied. This relation between the "demonic" and man's freedom clearly indicates the divine shadow-side of creation.[115]

In short, the shadow of the "inferior" is given in man along with the "superior," from the "very beginning."[116] Nevertheless, all this is really a derived form of an ur-dualism. Though dualism is construed within the reality of creation, the structure of an "original evil" is still present. The situation of the "inferior" is the "cause, but not the result, of the fall." Evil is therefore seen as the "empowering of the inferior in man."[117] The final word is that there is a "demonic principle of sheer natural antagonism involved in all creaturehood."[118] *Angst* is really the same as an *"Urdämonie,"*[119] and Christ is the Light which removes our anxiety. Because of that Light we are enabled, "from out of our chaos, to distinguish the light from the darkness and to trace back the demonic, 'schismatic' drama of this existence to that part which was originally intended as 'better.' "[120] Therefore, in this view a dualism with demonic aspects is projected back into creation itself.

We cannot simply call this a case of Manichaeanism. Nevertheless the structure of that ancient heresy is still very much with us. The same kind of problematic is now manifest, and sin is once again dissolved in a very similar "explanation." Sin is dissolved, if not in reality, at least in possibility. Furthermore, we stand before the fact that a dualism within the boundaries of creaturely reality inclines us toward a monism again. The points of departure might be very different, and even antithetical, but given a place within a common reality these two

---

115. Bernhart does not hesitate to use strong terms: "Freedom itself is the distinctive feature of a world demonically structured, but its ineptitude for overcoming the demonic in favor of goodness and salvation is in turn the distinctive feature of our need for God's help and mercy" (*ibid.*, p. 101). He thinks his thoughts are in harmony with Roman Catholic ecclesiastical doctrine, though quite a different note is sounded by T. Haecker (also Catholic) in his *Was ist der Mensch?*, 1949, pp. 47ff.: "Der Mensch im Chaos." "The chaos of our day is the work of man." Haecker speaks of man's "guilt and misuse of freedom" (p. 51).
116. Bernhart, *op. cit.*, p. 103; cf. p. 116.
117. *Ibid.*, p. 103.
118. *Ibid.*, p. 110.
119. *Ibid.*, p. 124.
120. *Ibid.*, p. 125. Cf. the critique of A. Maceina, *Das Geheimnis der Bösheit*, 1955, p. 39.

views are very similar. When dualism looks for an "explanation" of man's sin, the shadows of the *Deus auctor peccati* are bound to fall again.

This is the case even when that concept is very emphatically denied. When we see the diversity of creation as the evidence of an "ur-antinomy," and the "ur-antinomy" as coming along with God's creation, we are bound to empty our sin of its enigmatic character and to fall back into the *Deus auctor peccati*.[121] It may *seem* that the thought of "creation" then overcomes the problems of ur-dualism and harmonizes with the Christian concept of *creatio ex nihilo*. But this false wedding of creation and dualism only emphasizes how easily an irreligious idea can creep into our thinking. Nowhere must the warning be more clearly sounded than here. For in no sense can we get beyond a monism by means of a dualism or a dualism by means of a monism. Very deep shadows surround the monism which the Church has condemned as heresy as well as the dualism which we have looked at in this chapter. The one as well as the other tries to *explain away our sin* and thus to *eliminate our guilt*.

---

121. We think also of the dualism between *sárx* and *pneúma* to which some have pointed for an explanation of sin. Cf. my *Man: the Image of God*, 1962, p. 341; also J. Müller, *Die christliche Lehre von der Sünde*, I, 407f. and Bavinck, *op. cit.*, III, 30f.

CHAPTER FOUR

SIN AND THE DEMONIC REALM

W E HAVE treated two fundamental conceptions, monism and dualism, in which the effort is made to explain man's sin and its origin. It remains for us to inquire into what might be called the demonological explanation for man's sin. In distinction from monism and dualism, this particular view might seem to approach what the Church and her theology have always meant by the relation of man's sin and the demonic realm. If we cast aside the *Deus causa peccati* and every ur-dualism, and constantly reaffirm that seductive, demonic, and satanic powers are the *causa* of our sin, do we shed any light on the *origin of sin?* Is this what the Catechism means when it tells us that man has "deprived himself and all his posterity" of God's gifts and when it also adds: "through the instigation of the Devil" (HC, Q. 9)? Here we are dealing with a matter that has always concerned the Church and her theology. We are dealing with the relation between man's sin and the demonic forces, or man's sin and the kingdom of darkness. We are concerned about the power of evil which tempts a man to sin.

The important question is whether we find, in this direction, a demonological "explanation" for our sin. Certainly a number of the Church's statements refer us to the power of darkness and those relations between this power and the sinning of man which are evident ever since the very "beginning" of man's sin. These relations are apparent in the transition from God's good creation to man's evil apostasy. But the ecclesiastical pronouncements say nothing about an "explanation" for man's sin. When Bavinck, for example, wrote that sin has no origin but only a "beginning,"[1] he was occupied with the same problem that concerns us now. The distinction between an "origin" and a "beginning" might seem to be a very subtle one at first,

---

1. H. Bavinck, *Geref. Dog.,* III, 48.

but it certainly is of real importance for the question of whether man's sin *is or is not explained*. A factual beginning is not "explained" when we merely call attention to the demonic and seditious forces of which Scripture so emphatically speaks. Indeed, we can only find an "explanation" here if our sinning is the inevitable result of the overriding activity of demonic forces. There is an "explanation" only if man is actually compelled to sin. If man is the victim (as an unarmed nation is the victim of some treacherous coup) we can speak of an "explanation" for our sin. As soon as we can refer to an "overwhelming force," or an irresistible *force majeure,* we can also point to the "origin" of this new situation which has come upon our world.

But it is not this sort of picture which the Scripture draws. We do read of sin in connection with demonic forces; yet we are nowhere referred to a fatal or a transcendent power which reveals the "origins" and explains the "beginnings" of man's sin. We are pointed, instead, to the reality of man's *guilt.* Man is guilty *in his subjection* to the realm of the demons. For that reason the Heidelberg Catechism speaks of something more than, or other than, a mere "instigation of the devil" (*"impulsore diabolo"*). It refers to man's "own willful disobedience" (*"sua ipsius contumacia"*). Man's sin is not a matter of his being only subdued but a matter of his being willfully conquered. The sinner is not a victim in his powerless passivity but is actively engaged. He is not innocently "caught" but is willingly seduced. Scripture leaves us no room to posit the origin of sin in a fatalistic or tragical intrigue. It tells us in Genesis of man's own temptation, fall and rebellion, and informs us of his breaking of communion with God and of God's revelation of himself to fallen man. Every concept of fatalism is absent, and we stand face to face with the original goodness of God's creature *man,* who once lived in a blessed fellowship with his Maker. The image of a hapless nation, overrun by a ruthless enemy, is very inappropriate for shedding light on the reason for man's fall. If we insist, therefore, on "explaining" the origin of sin, we shall get exactly nowhere by referring to the "kingdom of darkness" and man's "seduction." The more we see of the true nature of that kingdom, the more we observe the inexplicability of man's sin.

Only in this perspective can we understand that man was not the victim of a fatalistic power. Man hid himself "from

4 8 1 5 8

the presence of the Lord God among the trees of the garden"
(Gen. 3:8), and his lack of motive for sinning was reflected
in his trepidation when God inquired: "What is this that you
have done?" (3:13; cf. v. 10). That question makes no sense
at all in the situation of fate, and is only meaningful if we
notice the background of Adam's fall and rebellion: his own
act of sinning, which could only be met by God's curse and
judgment and the expulsion of Adam from Paradise (3:23-24).
In keeping with that fact we never find in Scripture an effort
to explain sin's origin by means of a catastrophic power of
darkness. Paul never mentions such a power but speaks of sin
which entered the world "through one man" (Rom. 5:12; cf.
5:17, 18). He refers to very obvious connections: "the serpent
deceived Eve by his cunning" (II Cor. 11:3),[2] and the woman,
once deceived, "became a transgressor" (I Tim. 2:14). But in
talking this way he does not see temptation as the explanatory
"origin of sin" and does not deduce sin causally from Satan's
beguilement.

We have seen that explanation and self-excuse are indissolubly wrapped up in a single package. It need not surprise
us, therefore, that every demonological "connection" in Scripture excludes radically this element of making alibis. This does
not mean that there is little reason to give full attention to
the demonic acts of temptation. It does mean, however, that
in this way we shall never *explain our sin*. No matter what the
strength of this temptation or beguilement, its effect on man,
and man's subjection to it, must always remain the *riddle and
the inexplicability of sin*.

There have always been those who say that Scripture speaks
causally, on repeated occasions, in describing this "relation" between the power of darkness and man's sin. They point us to the
demonological connections that loom large in the biblical
phrase, "from the devil." Here we concede immediately that
Jesus' argument with the Jews did center, frequently, in these
issues of "connection" and "origin." Take, for example, the
John 8 pericope, where the Jews make the claim of being
"Abraham's seed" (v. 33). Jesus did not deny their natural
pedigree but he did cite a still more important question of

2. The word *panourgia* in the New Testament is only negative and
means "cunning," "craftiness," and "able to go in any direction" ("zu
allem fähig"), in an amoral sense. Cf. *TWNT*, V, *s.v.*

origin. The Jews' natural descendance from Abraham was obviously worthless and ineffectual, for had they been Abraham's children *by faith* they would have done Abraham's works (vv. 39-40). When confronted by that indictment, the Jews took cover in a "deeper" origin: "We have one Father, even God" (v. 41). It was that origin that Jesus now denied. For if God had been their Father they would have loved his Christ, seeing that Christ is "from God." Where such love is lacking the conclusion is unavoidable: "You are of your father the devil, and your will is to do your father's desires" (v. 44). Here then is a definite relation and connection; we read of the "fatherhood" of the devil and the Jews' "origin" in him. "He who is *of God* hears the words of God; the reason why you do not hear them is that you are not *of God*" (v. 47).

Thus a "question of origin" is here proposed. At the same time, it is obvious that we do not stand before a causal explanation of sin. This appears from the fact that the reference to the Jews' "fatherhood" is made entirely in the context of an *accusation and rebuke*. There is no reference to a fate determined by "origin." When Christ charged that the Jews "could not believe" (John 12:39) it is clear that their incapacity was a matter of their own responsibility and guilt. It was not blind fate that determined that the devil was their father but only their own activity in the modus of their sinful lives. Therefore it was *their* sin that Christ now pointed out; and only in *that connection* did he indicate their relation to the devil. It was their *own plot* to kill the Christ (John 8:40), though *in* that plot their relation to their "father" was very evident. Their own lusts were the lusts of their "father" (8:41, 44) and *they surrendered themselves to him*.[3] This connection between the devil and *sinful men* illustrates the very nature of evil. When the devil lies "he speaks according to his own nature, for he is a liar and the *father of lies*" (8:44).

That same line of thought is found in I John, and a similar "origin" is there described. Those who are "born of God" are set in sharp contrast to the "children of the devil," and "whoever does not do right is not of God" (3:10; cf. 3:9; 4:8; 5:1, 4, 18). The little phrase, "of God," is now set squarely in opposition to the words, "of the evil one." Notice here the reference to Cain in chapter 3, verse 12. Observe, too, that the spirits must be "tested" to see if they are "of God" (4:1), and

3. Cf. F. W. Grosheide, *Comm., ad loc.*

"every spirit which does not confess Jesus is not *of God*" (4:3).
"For all that is in the world, the lust of the flesh and the lust
of the eyes and the pride of life, is not *of the Father* but is *of
the world*" (2:16; cf. 4:5).[4] Here the most decisive qualification
in all of human living is at stake, and yet there is nothing of
a simple parallel, or a dual metaphysical "origin" of two different "children" from two different "fathers." We find nothing
of a dualism that explains or deduces everything from the
original sources of God and the evil one. There is no suggestion of two different *causae* of good and evil men.

It is true that we read of a "being born" of God. The "origin"
of God's children lies in God's own activity or in a "being
born" from above and from the Spirit of God (John 3:3, 7; cf.
v. 5; I John 2:29; 3:9; 4:7; 5:13, 18). It lies in the act of God
concerning which we read in John 1:13: "not of blood nor of
the will of the flesh nor of the will of man, but of God." This is
the act of being "born anew, not of perishable seed but of
imperishable" (I Pet. 1:23; cf. v. 3). Yet the reference here
is not to the origin of man's creaturely existence *per se* but to
the decisive origin of his being a "son of God." "He saved us,
not because of deeds done by us in righteousness, but in virtue
of his own mercy, by the washing of regeneration and renewal
in the Holy Spirit" (Titus 3:5). "Of his own will he brought
us forth by the word of truth" (James 1:18). Here we find a
perspective on God's salvation from wrath and corruption, and
sin and guilt. The "origin" proposed only emphasizes the
depths and inviolability of God's salvation and the sonship that
believers possess in him. "No one born of God commits sin;
for God's nature abides in him, and he cannot sin because he
is born of God" (I John 3:9). "Blessed be the God and Father
of our Lord Jesus Christ! By his great mercy we have been
born anew to a living hope through the resurrection of Jesus
Christ from the dead" (I Pet. 1:3).

This whole picture changes when we come to the devil and
his "fatherhood." We can speak, with no hesitation at all, of the
origin of God's children in God; but never can we use that
same unqualified speech in describing the phrase, "of the evil
one." Those who are children "of the devil" owe their creaturely existence to God; therefore we cannot refer to Cain's metaphysical "origin" in the evil one. Scripture gives us no dualism

---

4. With this "of the world" cf. John 3:6 ("of the flesh") and 8:23 ("You
   are from below" and "of this world"). In both texts, *ek* is used.

but confronts us with the sin of man and the direction of his creaturely existence. We are told that certain men are "of the devil," but never is this a causal explanation of their sin. It is only an accusation of their guilt *within that relationship*. The fact that Cain was "of the evil one" does not presume an original *fatum* which once took hold of him. It is rather an indictment of his guilt. Recall that in this context of "being of the evil one" we still meet up with the question of *why*. "And why did he murder him? Because his own deeds were evil and his brother's righteous" (I John 3:12). Precisely where man is ensnared in this relation to the devil he stands naked in his guilt before the holy God.

Therefore Scripture does not give us a simple picture of two "fatherhoods." It speaks of God as father and the devil as father in very different ways. Nowhere do we read that man is "born of the devil."[5] The man who has God as his father stands in a different father-child relationship, both structurally and qualitatively, from the man who has the devil as his father. Being "of the devil" does not mean that one is bound by the categories of sheer fate; rather, the word *of* should be seen as a wholesale indictment of man's guilt. No satanic *force majeure* is apparent here in opposition to the good gift of God's sonship: for only *in and through one's guilt* does the power of the evil one take hold. A demonological explanation of sin's origin is therefore impossible.

Only when we deny outright the identity of these two father-child relationships and the "causalities" implied are we able to preserve a truly biblical accent on the relation of man's sin and the demonic realm. This relation is embraced in man's own guilt and apostasy, and only *then* takes hold in man's living. But once it does, it can best be described in such terms as *of* or *through*. It is best described in terms which shed light on the perniciousness of that power of which Scripture so persistently speaks. The power of darkness is a power that operates in the modus of man's guilt. When James 3:6 speaks of man's sinning with his tongue as a fire inflamed "by hell," we might possibly think that a "causative relation" of sin and hell is implied. At the same time, when James sees that connection *within* the bounds of man's own perversity he accentuates the depths of man's own guilt. He refers to the tongue as an "unrighteous world," a "restless evil," which "no human being can

5. Cf. Schnackenburg, *Die Johannesbriefe*, p. 171.

tame" — the tongue is full of "deadly poison" (v. 8). The stern
language, at this point, emphasizes the relations which James
wishes to draw: and yet we find nothing of an "explanation"
for the origin of sin. Evil is not seen as a "fatal force." Therefore
the Church, confronted by this "restless" and "untameable"
power, is still admonished: "My brethren, this ought not to
be . . ." (v. 10).

This demonological "explanation" of sin's origin presumes
that sin is explicable in terms of some "devilish intrigue." Yet,
as soon as we go in that direction we shall naturally want to
search out a still deeper "explanation" in some fall within
the angelic realm. It is absolutely inconceivable that anyone,
determined to find that explanation, could proceed in any other
direction. All his energies will then be spent on finding out the
prima causa of this angelic fall. How can we possibly explain
the incursion of that "first evil" within the boundaries of God's
good creation? Once we set foot on such a trail, however, it is
obvious in what kinds of errors we are almost certain to fall.
There can be no end to the speculation, and we cannot be
satisfied by a mere allusion to this "fall" in the angelic realm.
We shall want to penetrate the reason for that fall. Therefore
the man who travels this road must overstep immediately those
boundaries which the Scripture itself lays down.

When Scripture speaks of a fall in the angelic realm its
purpose is certainly not to give us an explanation of the kingdom of darkness. This is very apparent in the cases of II Peter
2:4 and Jude 6, the two most widely known references in this
regard. Consider the contexts in both cases. In Jude the "origin
of sin" is far from the center of interest; rather the theme is a
warning to the Church against false teachers who "secretly"
come in and "pervert the grace of our God into licentiousness
and deny our only Master and Lord, Jesus Christ" (v. 4).
Against such persons the Church must be on guard. It was to
emphasize this warning that Jude referred to God's righteous
judgment already exercised on Sodom and Gomorrah, which
still awaits the "angels that did not keep their own position
but left their proper dwelling" and are now kept in bonds
until that "great day" (v. 6). And so too in the case of Peter's
letter. Again, the main concern is God's judgment on lasciv-
iousness. Peter wanted to warn his readers that God did not
spare the angels when they sinned but preserved them for

judgment: so too he will know how to "keep the unrighteous under punishment . . ." (2:9). Therefore, in both of these cases, the issue has nothing to do with an "explanation" for the origin of sin. It is far removed from a causal answer to the question of *unde malum humanum*. Neither writer wishes to deduce man's sin from an angelic fall: yet neither would deny a "connection" between this sin ·and the realm of the demons. The remarkable fact is that in both Jude and Peter the only reference to an angelic fall is set in the context of an *urgent warning*. The analogy of what happened in the angelic realm only emphasizes how important this warning is. That point is very obvious when we see the "example" of the angels alongside the examples of Sodom and Gomorrah (II Pet. 2:6; Jude 7), and the references to "the ancient world" (II Pet. 2:5) and "the way of Balaam" (2:15).[6]

Recall the statement of Paul concerning man's sin and judgment in ancient times (I Cor. 10:11): "Now these things happened to them as a warning, but they were written down for our instruction, upon whom the end of the ages has come." The theme is once again the problem of *libertinism*, and the approach is the same as we find in II Peter and Jude. These latter references speak of a "fall" in the angelic realm and suggest nothing of a *causa*-problematic in regard to man's sin; they are merely illustrative of a very different kind of relation. They illustrate the relation of man's sin and God's judgment. Only incidentally, by way of example, is the reference made to an angelic fall. This same kind of incidental treatment is apparent in I Timothy 3:6, where Paul advises that a recent convert should not hold office, lest he be "puffed up with conceit and fall into the condemnation of the devil." Paul's interest was obviously in the qualifications for ecclesiastical office; yet in expressing himself as he did he laid hold on this very striking analogy. The analogy, however, has only an incidental or illustrative value, and amplifies the main point concerning man's pride and the judgment of God to come.[7]

We must be careful not to infer a causal explanation where

---

6. Cf. "the way of Cain" in Jude 11; also F. Hauck, *Die Kirchenbriefe*, 1953, p. 92, on the "three great examples of God's punishment." In a number of commentaries reference is made to Gen. 6:2ff. (among others, Hauck, p. 92, and Zahn-Wohlenberg, pp. 294f.). Cf. S. Greijdanus' commentary, *ad loc.*, contra A. Kuyper, *De Engelen Gods.*

7. *Krima* is used in this text as a judgment *upon* the devil. Cf. C. Bouma, *Comm.*, p. 137; also v. 7 on the "snare of the devil" as temptation.

the Scripture only makes a passing reference to this "fall."[8] This also holds in regard to another pericope which we have already noted — John 8. In that chapter a direct relation is drawn between man's sin and the devil, but no attempt is made to "explain." There is no effort to derive the Jews' sin from the fall among the angels. We may grant that Christ pictures the power of darkness in all its perversity and deceit: the devil has "nothing to do with the truth, because there is no truth in him" (8:44). As the King James Bible has translated: "he abode not in the truth." We may grant, too, that such a statement could give the impression of referring to the angelic "fall"; yet later translators have contented themselves with the idea of "not-standing in the truth."[9] Grosheide has written: "No mention is made of the fall but only the situation that followed."[10]

8. Barth contends, in reference to II Peter and Jude, that these statements are too "uncertain" and "obscure" to point in the direction of such an angelic fall. It seems to me, however, that these words are quite clear in themselves. For that reason already it is impossible to say that the idea of the fall of the angels "arises from the superfluous need to ground our knowledge of the fall of *man* upon the notion of a metaphysical prelude" (*K.D.*, III/3, 622-623; ET, 530-531). This point cannot be made to stick in reference to the "older dogmatics"; nor does it hold in reference to Peter and Jude, for whom there was no thought of such a "grounding" but only of analogy for the sake of warning. It stands to reason that Barth merely mentions in passing the exegesis which sees a connection here with Genesis 6 ("The remarkable passage in Gen. 6:1-14 was related to this verse"; 622; ET, 530). Such an exegesis cannot alter the situation, as far as Barth is concerned, since it *too* refers to a "fall" (cf. Wohlenberg, *op. cit.*, p. 295, who makes mention of a "previous enjoyment of freedom"). It might be said, in this connection, that dogmaticians have often given insufficient attention to the direction of these scriptural citations in Peter and Jude. But here we are touching on the profound issue of the *method* of dogmatics, which we cannot treat at this time. On Barth, cf. further my *The Triumph of Grace in the Theology of Karl Barth*, 1956, pp. 239ff., and "De Daemonen bij K. Barth," in *Op de Tweesprong*, pp. 209ff.

9. Cf. the arguments of Zahn, *Komm.*, p. 424.

10. Grosheide, *Comm.*, II, 49. In reference to John 8:44 Kuyper speaks, in *De Engelen Gods,* of a fall in the angelic realm; he contests the idea that this only signifies a "not-standing" in the truth (p. 212). "The form of the perfect tense expresses a state — but a state that is the consequence and result of an action." But the point at issue is exactly this: in this text nothing is told about this action. Kuyper's presupposition is seen in his exegesis: "Moreover, in the other concept Satan would have to be created evil, which could never be." See further on this question, C. Bouma, *K.V.*, I, 227: "The Lord says nothing here about the past but only about the present of the fallen angels."

John 8:44 speaks of the *de facto* character of the devil who sins "from the beginning" and is also the "father of lies." With all due gravity and warning the sin of the Jews is seen in the light of their concourse with the devil. Everything said about the devil is part of that warning. Thus John had no interest at all in analyzing the origin of sin or explaining man's sin in a rational manner.[11] He stressed the seriousness of resistance and the crassness of lies, but he did not draw a metaphysical conclusion from the concepts of "from the beginning" and "according to his own nature." There is no warrant here to adopt an ur-dualism.[12] The purpose of John 8 is to expose the nature of the devil and the deception of him who is always what he reveals himself to be "from the very beginning."

Yet, despite the existential urgency of these biblical statements, there are many who prefer the blind alleys of an idle speculation.[13] Vonier, for example, has argued that no *finite being* (not even an angel) is immune from an error in his understanding and will.[14] He proposes that this assertion is not a satisfactory "explanation" in itself, since angels too were originally good. The sin of the angels is understandable, according to Vonier, only when we consider that a spirit in its natural habitat cannot possibly err, but a rebellion against the God-ordained order *may take place* when a spirit is transposed to a supernatural sphere.[15] The spirit is then able to choose. He is able to choose in that process of being translated from his nat-

---

11. Barth points especially to John 8:44 (*K.D.*, III/3, 623; *ET*, 531) in connection with the words *ek tōn idiōn* and *ap' archēs*. Rightly he takes issue with an *explanation* for sin, but it remains unclear why he sees in the angelic fall an effort "not to allow nothingness to be what it is but to bring it into systematic connexion with God and the creature."

12. Cf. I John 3:8: "the devil has sinned *from the beginning*" (*ap' archēs*). Also Grosheide, *Comm. op Johannes*, I, 50, n. 2; Schnackenburg, *op. cit.*, p. 168; Zahn, *op. cit.*, p. 424.

13. These alleys are obviously difficult to avoid. A. Böhm has asserted emphatically that Scripture does not analyze the motives for apostasy and that we stand, thus, before an inscrutable mystery; yet he apparently finds satisfaction in the thought that God revealed the incarnation to the angels, as well as the resurrection and ascension, and thus disclosed to them the position of the glorified man Christ above themselves. "This offended the pride of a part of the angels" (*De Eeuw van de Duivel*, 1956, pp. 21f.).

14. A. Vonier, *De Engelen*, 1955, p. 93.

15. *Ibid.*, p. 94.

ural environment to a supernatural communion with the
family of God.[16] The spirit may choose if he prefers the isolation of his own natural glory or this new communion.[17] Therefore it is possible, at this point, for the spirit to be proud,
jealous, or rebellious against the holy ordinance and the supernatural order of God.[18] At the same time, it is obvious that
such a view as this cannot possibly explain the sin of the angels.
Vonier gives a line of reasoning deduced from quasi-possibilities
and calculated to "explain" the reality of sin. But sin's reality
cannot be explained. So too, when we hear of angels created
within the supernatural order but "free" to take it or to leave
it,[19] we can only conclude that this very thought betrays an
escape into an irreligious caricature of freedom. Imagine God's
granting this freedom to do evil! We can only dismiss this concept as impertinent.

The very same verdict holds for the view of Oswald,[20] who
speaks of a "testing" of the angels and refers to their being
created in a situation "in which they must freely decide."[21]
Oswald's purpose was to unravel the mystery of evil "in its
ultimate foundation," though he also seemed to sense that this
is a very thankless task.[22] The sin of the angels is no *"peccatum
carnale"* but the sin of pride: *"peccatum spirituale"* and *"su-
perbia."* It was the failure to appreciate the creature's own
creaturely dependence on God. But such a sin, in Oswald's
thinking, can only be explained in terms of a "freedom of
choice" which can easily lead to a diabolical apostasy. Once
again, it is clear that this gift of freedom cannot afford us an
explanation for our sin. Nor can the gift of freedom once
given to man. All these subtle analyses can only *describe* our

16. *Ibid.*, pp. 94-95.
17. *Ibid.*, p. 95.
18. *Ibid.*, p. 96. Cf. also the views of C. Friethoff, *Engelen en Duivelen*,
    1940, pp. 57ff., which run in the same direction: a disdain for a
    supernatural felicity, which was made possible by God's help (p. 62).
    In the light of that sphere in which the angels "could not sin" he
    concludes that the exposition of Justin and Clement, on Gen. 6:2, is
    untenable (p. 59; he also acknowledges his indebtedness). Cf., in con-
    nection with the entire doctrine of angels: Bavinck, *op. cit.*, II, 416-417.
19. Cf. Vonier, *op. cit.*, p. 99.
20. J. H. Oswald, *Angelologie, das ist die Lehre von den guten und bösen
    Engeln im Sinne der katholischen Kirche*, 1883, p. 89.
21. *Ibid.*, p. 92.
22. *Ibid.*, p. 93.

sinning at best,[23] and can never be an explanation of its "origin."[24]

Sin and its origin are inexplicable and cannot be seen as a fatality or an overarching "power" of evil. They cannot be regarded as a "force" that renders poor and helpless man its victim. But once we say that much we are not absolved from the responsibility of examining the biblical data and observing the emphasis on the power-aspects of the kingdom of darkness. We read of the "power of darkness" (Luke 22:53; cf. Col. 1:12, Acts 26:18, Luke 4:6), and of Satan as "the ruler of this world" (John 12:31; 16:11; 14:30) and "the prince of the power of the air" (Eph. 2:2). We hear of "principalities," "powers," "world rulers of this present darkness," and "spiritual hosts of wickedness in the heavenly places," against whom the man who lacks the "whole armor of God" cannot possibly stand (Eph. 6:12-13). There is an "hour" of darkness (Luke 22:53), a "god of this world" who has "blinded the minds of the unbelievers" (II Cor. 4:4), and a "murderer" (John 8:44) who has "the power of death" (Heb. 2:14) and who now "oppresses" (Acts 10:38). This is a power that is evident in very many ways. It obstructs the work of missions (I Thess. 2:18) and casts men into the most trying of circumstances. "Behold, the devil is about to throw some of you into prison, that you may be tested" (Rev. 2:10). In Satan's activity, power and seduction are tied up together, and the conspiracy that results is manifest on every hand. We see it in the temptation of him who is called "the evil one" (Matt. 6:13; 13:19; Eph. 6:16; I John 2:13-14; 5:18), "the deceiver" (Rev. 12:9), "the tempter" (Matt. 4:3), the one who sows weeds in the field (Matt. 13:25), and who "works in the sons of disobedience" (Eph. 2:2). His temptation comes to expression extensively and intensively. It foreshadows the "hour of trial which is coming

23. Cf. Bavinck, op. cit., 47f.
24. One feels strongly an appreciation for this inexplicability when Bavinck writes that the origin and nature of sin "differ profoundly with angels and with men," for angels have not been tempted: "they have fallen of themselves" (ibid., 46). Satan "has brought forth lies of himself" (reference to John 8:44). For the most fantastic speculations, see Giovanni Papini, De Duivel. Problematiek ener Toekomstige Diabologie, 1954, especially Chap. 2: "Oorsprong en Natuur van de Duivel." The governing thought of this book is the redemption of Satan by the voluntary cooperation of man (cf., e.g., p. 78).

on the *whole world"* (Rev. 3:10), and it also "deceives the nations" (Rev. 20:3, 8). It reaches to the very depths of man's heart and turns him aside to Satan (I Tim. 5:15). We read that Satan "put" it in Judas' heart to betray Christ (John 13:2) and "entered into" Judas (13:27). He "filled" Ananias' heart to lie against the Spirit (Acts 5:3).

Men have tried, in a variety of ways, to define this power of temptation.[25] But they have never succeeded in getting beyond the mere words of the Scripture. Oswald affirms that Scripture tells us nothing of the manner of this temptation; thus we are thrown back on "our own rational reflection."[26] To this we can only reply that reflection, too, can never furnish us with real insight. We are not "enlightened" when we hear of a *"primum agens"* that is capable of "causing even the beginnings of such impulses directly within us."[27] Nowhere does Scripture give the slightest explanation for making this transition from God's originally good creation to man's sinful exploitation a matter that is psychologically "explicable." The ineptitude of psychology in clarifying the origin of sin or the "connections" in temptation is no symptom of psychological "limits" which may someday be "overcome." It is rather implied in the *inexplicability of sin's origin.* For the origin of sin has a radical and all-pervasive impact on the deepest depths of man's heart. Therefore, when we speak of a certain psychological process in sinning, our analysis can only be restricted to the arena or the experiences of fallen man. Precisely because of man's *fall* his sin is *inexplicable.* Man's sin is unreasonable and unexplainable. Yet its reality is the consequence of man's own fallen heart. Thus James speaks of a "luring away" and "enticement" by one's own desire; he refers to a pregnant desire that "gives birth to sin" (1:14f.). Paul makes mention of a process of sinning which is intimately tied up with the en-

25. In the Lateranum IV we read that man sinned by the *suggestion* of the devil: "homo vero diaboli suggestione peccavit" (Denz., 428). Trent speaks of "serpens ille antiquus, humani generis perpetuus hostis," who confounds the Church and now — also in regard to original sin — "dissidia excitaverit" (787). In reference to extreme unction the devil is called "adversarius noster," who for all our lives looks for "occasiones" to devour ("devorare") us, but "vehementius" at the departure from life, when "ille omnes suae versutiae nervos intendat ad perdendos nos penitus" (907). Cf. HC, Q. 9: "impulsore diabolo."
26. Oswald, *op. cit.,* p. 166.
27. *Ibid.,* p. 167; cf. Vonier, *op. cit.,* pp. 102f.

trance of God's command (Rom. 7:9). But when we inquire
into the "origin" of sin, we can only grope in the dark. Furthermore, that darkness is not the emptiness of an epistemological gap but the bleakness of *our guilt*.

Once we see the obviousness of guilt we can only observe how
impossible it is to draw the relations between sin and the
demonic realm in exclusive terms of "power" and "brute force."
A *force majeure* or an inexorable fate is not the product of
those power-aspects to which we have already referred. Indeed,
the "power of darkness" can never be measured in the categories
of causality, and we can never say that sin is "determined" by
the *"prima causa peccati."* The examples of Judas and Ananias
(which we have noted above in connection with the "power"
of the evil one) are very important at this point. Consider that
Christ knew very well that the devil was active in Judas' heart;
but he did not regard that influence as an inexorable "fate" or
"lot" that Judas would have to endure. "Judas," he says, "would
you betray the Son of man with a kiss?" (Luke 22:48). So too
Peter, full of amazement and distress, inquired of Ananias:
"How is it that *you* have contrived this deed in your heart?"
(Acts 5:4). Ananias and Sapphira, we read, had *"agreed together* to tempt the Spirit of the Lord" (5:9).

Therefore, when Scripture speaks of the *power* of the evil
one we also hear (at the same time) of the "passions of our
flesh," and following the "desires of body and mind," and being
the "children of wrath" (Eph. 2:3). No power of darkness
causally "explains" our sin, and no inexorable force compels
us to do evil. There is no *ex opere operato "in malam partem."*
There is no unbounded power and work of the evil one; no
seduction that is unrelated to the guilt of man. There is no relentless force, except that which is actualized in the *modus* of
man's own culpability. Only *in* our guilt and capitulation to
the evil one is the power of evil irrepressible. Only *in* that way
does an evil man become the "slave" to sin. Only *within* that
situation do we find the *non posse non peccare*. Yet we find it
not as a *fate* but as *guilt*. On this path a man is more and more
the "object" of seduction and temptation; and in that same
frame of reference we understand the expressions of a brute
"power" in which an "objectified" man is miserably "ensnared."
The utter horror of that power is apparent in the limits of a
man's depersonalization. In this way we see the powerlessness,

captivity, and "objectification" of man. This is what is meant by being "possessed."[28]

Thus we can see a ruthless "power" or inexorable "force" which man no longer resists. In this light we read the reference to Satan's "binding" a woman for a period of eighteen years (Luke 13:16; cf. v. 11). We should also observe the disastrous working of the power of darkness which manifests itself, as an "unclean spirit," at the very limits of what it means to be a man. The spirit functions as the subject of speech in the man who is possessed (Luke 4:33-34).[29] Against that background we must recognize the extent of the blindness and dumbness, the self-destruction and complete perversion of humanity, so that a man becomes a mere travesty of what it means to be *man*. Here we must see the awful manifestation of *exousia* (Mark 5:5; cf. 9:18, 20, 22, 25-26; Matt. 12:22f.). When Peter speaks of the "power of Christ" he envisions Christ healing those who were "oppressed by the devil" (Acts 10:38).[30] The very language of Scripture calls forth the image of *terror*. Though Satan is obliged to surrender his "rights," he is still doggedly at work. Even Paul, as we read in II Corinthians 12:7, was "harassed" by Satan's messenger.[31]

A resistance to this "superlative force" cannot be expected from the side of sinful, bound, and weakened man. True freedom can only come from another power that seizes a man and reverses the course of his living. It must come from a "power" that is strong enough to cast out the evil spirits by command (Mark 9:25). Freedom must come from the Spirit of God (Matt. 12:28; cf. Luke 11:20). The evil spirits of the devil could only be exorcised by the disciples when the disciples cast them out in Christ's name (Luke 10:17). Because the Kingdom of Christ had come, the "strong man's house" was plundered (Matt. 12:22ff.); because the power of Christ was real, the evil spirits were "rebuked" (17:18).[32] But what happened when the dis-

---

28. Cf. *TWNT*, II, *s.v. daímōn*, esp. C. 4, regarding the "attack on the spiritual and physical life" of man.

29. *Ibid.*, 19: "The 'I' is so paralyzed that the spirits seem to be the subject that speaks."

30. Cf. also what Jesus says about entering into the house of "the strong man" *(ischyrós)* who must first be bound (Matt. 12:29).

31. The word Paul uses is *kolaphizein* (cf. Matt. 26:27; I Cor. 4:11; I Pet. 2:20), which has strong overtones of mishandling.

32. Cf. this power of Christ over the sevenfold demon (recorded in Luke 8:2; cf. 11:26) and the "many demons" (Luke 8:27, 30, 38). Especially

ciples could not rebuke an evil spirit and felt constrained to inquire: "Why could we not cast it out?" (Mark 9:28; cf. v. 18) ? The answer has nothing to do with an inexorable fate; instead, the *disciples themselves were rebuked.* "O faithless generation, how long am I to be with you? How long am I to bear with you?" (9:19; cf. Matt. 17:20). Then follows the revelation of the only way to cast out this "indomitable power." "This kind cannot be driven out by anything but prayer" (Mark 9:29).

"Not by anything but prayer...." We should notice especially two things. On the one hand, all rashness and pride are excluded, for here a real power of evil is referred to, which displays the earmarks of an "overpowering causality."[33] This is a power that "prompts" and "incites," "seduces," "binds," "blinds," and "ties" a sinner to his sin. But in the second place, we must see the full impact of these words, "not by anything but...." In that little phrase we observe the only manner to overcome the relentless power of the forces of evil. We can only appeal to God's salvation and redemption — for he alone is able to cast out the evil spirits. By following in the "way of Christ" the superior and irresistible power of God's grace is made evident, and every false interpretation of the power of evil is really quite senseless and even ridiculous.[34]

Therefore it is clear that the man who speaks of "demonological relations" in sin should not affirm an objective state of affairs in which a place is assigned to the power of demons. For

note the frenzied uncontrollability of these evil spirits (v. 29) in contrast to the calm and irrepressible power of Christ (v. 33). On the many facets of the New Testament message concerning Christ and the demons, see especially Bent Noack, *Satanas and Soteria. Untersuchungen zur N.T. Dämonologie,* 1948, and S. Eitrem, *Some Notes on the Demonology in the N.T.* (*Symbolae Osloensis fasc.,* Suppl. XII, 1950).

33. Cf. Thielicke's concept of "belongingness" or "oughtness" (Hörigkeit"), *Fragen des Christentums. Über die Wirklichkeit des Dämonischen,* 1948, pp. 207ff. In sin, says Thielicke, "one subjects himself to an *exousia,* a power."

34. We think of the Pharisee's interpretation, "It is only by Beelzebul, the prince of demons, that this man casts out demons" (Matt. 12:24), and Christ's answer concerning the impossibility that Satan should be divided against himself (vv. 25-26). The heated acrimony against Christ can be clearly seen in these words, which presuppose a certain connection between Christ and the demons (also in other scriptural references). Cf. Mark 3:22, "He is possessed by Beelzebul" (said the scribes); John 10:20, "He has a demon, and he is mad" (said many); John 7:20 and 8:48, "You have a demon!" (said the people and the Jews); Mark 3:21, "He is beside himself" (said his friends).

that power is only *relationally defined*. That is to say, everything
depends on how a man chooses to act in the face of that potency.
Man apart from Christ, and faith in Christ, is completely helpless when confronted by that power. "Not by anything but. . . ."
And yet, in faith and prayer this power is subdued. Believers
are enjoined not to fear; for assurance has already come. "Resist
the devil and he will flee from you" (James 4:7). The Church is
summoned to "give no opportunity to the devil" (Eph. 4:27).
She is charged to *resist* — and in that very charge she is called to
submit herself to God (James 4:7). Submission to God is the
way to avoid a submission to the devil. Therefore in that context in which the devil is depicted as an "adversary" who
"prowls around like a roaring lion," we are faced with this challenge: "Be sober, be watchful," and "resist him" with steadfast
faith (I Pet. 5:8, 9). That injunction is followed by paeans of
benediction and joy (vv. 10-11). The very presence or absence
of this devilish power is "correlationally defined." The "roaring
lion" can also "flee." In making our approach to God the great
God himself draws near to us (James 4:8).

When the New Testament speaks of the increase of these
powers of darkness (intensively and extensively) we also read
that this takes place by the manifestation of God's salvation. For
that reason the revelation of these powers is itself an indirect
witness of the majestic glory and salvation of God. The increase
in powers is not made known to us to disquiet the contrite hearts
of believers but only to fortify our resistance in faith. No "angels
or principalities" are able to separate us from the love of God in
Christ Jesus (Rom. 8:38). Precisely in the midst of augmented
powers[35] the faithful are summoned to take up the "shield of
faith" by which we are able to "quench all the flaming darts of
the evil one" (Eph. 6:16).

Therefore, the idea of a "fatal influence" of demonic powers

35. Cf. Thielicke, *op. cit.,* p. 183, on this intensification ("Potenzierung")
of demonic powers as opposed to the glory of the revelation of God
in Christ. Cf. Rev. 12:1ff.: over against the woman is the dragon who
seeks to devour; also Foerster, *TWNT,* II, *s.v. drákōn;* and K. Schilder,
Tussen Ja en Neen, 1929, pp. 53f. According to Foerster the dragon
is the image under which the Apocalypse views Satan. Cf. Rev. 13:4
("dragon" and "authority"); 13:11; 20:2 ("dragon," "serpent," "Devil,"
"Satan"). But all this is no sinister and enervating apocalyptic: it
represents the background against which the light comes all the clearer
into focus. Revelation is a book of *comfort* for the Church.

is an illegitimate abstraction. We may never trace back our guilt to causes other than *our guilt*. We may never point our fingers at an overwhelming demonic force or see in this a fatal conscription of our lives. Surely it is not the case that our only choice is a haggard surrender to these forces. When people speak today of a "demonization" of man's living it is hardly a sign of a revival of a genuinely religious motive. It represents a movement away from a giddy optimism and an idle self-confidence. But what we need is not an "analysis" of these powers but a conquering of the demonic realm. That alone can give us hope for the future. It is important that within that perspective the "forces of evil" are seen not only as the power of demons but also in the *light of the Gospel*. For the Gospel does away with all fatality.

The Scripture does not demand that we look at these power aspects in themselves. Rather it demands that we reach beyond them and observe that in them God *himself* is drawn into the battle. Here is the most spectacular proof of the completely undualistic character of the biblical message. The battle is not only a battle of "powers" but is also a *legal contest*. Satan is the one who accuses, and his weapons are the weapons of a legal strategy as well as of brute force. He wastes no time in wielding the "powers of darkness" and reveals himself as the *diábolos*. He is the one who corrupts and disrupts and who sends evil spirits to take possession of sinful men. He murders, destroys and blinds (John 8:44; II Cor. 4:4). In the battle of power the "works of the devil" are manifest (I John 3:8). Yet in the midst of those power-aspects we find a new and different role of Satan. For Satan is also an *accuser*. Nothing reveals more than this what is really at stake in the activity of Satan. What we see is not merely an exercise of power and its disastrous effects. For Satan must now reckon with the authority of *Someone Else,* who may not be ignored for even a moment.

The nature of Satan's accusation is very clear in Revelation 12:10. There we read that Michael and his angels are victorious over the power of the devil. Certainly the power of Satan deceives "the whole world" (v. 9), and there is no reason at all to dispute its enormity. Yet his power is a power that is "thrown down" before the dynamic salvation and kingship of God and his Anointed One. His power is subject to God's own *dýnamis* and *exousía*. The striking thing in this story is that the victory is proclaimed by a "loud voice in heaven" in such a way that

the "accuser of our brethren" (who "accuses them day and night
before our God") is once and for all "cast down" (v. 10). Thus
we see the inner connection and inherent synthesis of the devil's
power and accusation. We see that there is more than a "power"
that is overcome and more than an adversary in battle; more
than Satan himself and more than the *diábolos*. What is put to
nought is the power of an accusation, made incessantly, "day
and night." Therefore the analogy of an earthly power-struggle
is entirely inadequate for describing this strange contest in which
the devil makes his fierce charge "before the throne of God."
We are the witnesses in a trial in which the devil accuses believers before God's judgment seat.[36] We hear his legal charge
and we see him pointing his finger at the undeniable guilt of
believers. Yet we also see (in this dual role of "tempter" and
"accuser") how diabolical is this intrigue. Here we observe the
devilishness of the charge. For a very dark identity inheres in
these facts that Satan is both the accuser and the seducer of
"brethren." Thus the one who accuses is "less the attorney-gen-
eral than the Gestapo," and he makes his charge to gain his
own alibi.[37]

God's act of power and "throwing down" has reference to
this "accusation of our brethren." We hear a "loud voice in
heaven," or a divine and radical answer (v. 10), in the story of
the child who is suddenly "caught up to God and to his throne"
(v. 5). This, then, is God's response (full of power) to Satan's
devilish intrigue. Here is a power that insures the victory of
believers even upon the earth. "And *they* have conquered him
by the blood of the Lamb and by the word of their testimony,
for they loved not their lives even unto death" (v. 11). Those
looking to the death and resurrection of Jesus (looking, even in
the midst of martyrdom) now see that the devil's fierce charge
is "cast out." But why is that the case? Certainly not because of
the blamelessness of our "brethren" but only because of the redemptive power of that salvation of Christ which is *now revealed*. Thus the charge of Satan is refuted in a very unique

---

36. Cf. the accusers of the woman taken in adultery (John 8:10). The word
    in itself has no "demonic" connotation. Consider, for example, Jesus'
    statement in John 5:45: "Do not think that I shall accuse you to
    the Father; it is Moses who accuses you" (*ho katēgorōn*). Cf. the
    Jews as accusers, in Mark 3:2.
37. Thielicke, *op. cit.*, p. 185. Clearly we see Satan's initiative exercised
    with demonic intent in Luke 22:31f. Christ makes known the passion
    and desire of Satan to sift the disciples as wheat.

contest. The decision is made in a legal process. Though the fighting is still very fierce on earth, and though Satan shows "great wrath," we can say that the battle is over in "short time" (v. 12) .[38] If, however, it is over in "short time" we cannot suggest that Satan's power is "indomitable." The devil is an accuser who already is "thrown down." His power has already been condemned. Therefore there is now only a "short remaining time."[39]

The accuser of Revelation 12 is the same as the accuser of Job 1 and 2. Some have denied that these chapters in Job see Satan as God's antagonist, and have said that the book of Job regards him as a mere lackey in God's employment. Satan is then the one who reports what is "happening on the face of the earth." Only in later times, this argument runs, does the thought of an *antithesis* arise.[40] But even in these two chapters themselves we find a very different idea, especially in 2:3 where Satan tries to move God against Job to "destroy him without cause." We need not point to such a text as I Chronicles 21:1 ("Satan stood up against Israel, and incited David to number Israel") to find the element of an "anti" in Scripture. The very same antithesis is clear in the first two chapters of Job where we hear of the accusation of Satan. Yet, in Job's case the accusation does not concern an actual guilt but an interpretation of innocence. Satan casts a doubtful eye on Job and inquires: "Does Job fear God for nought?" (1:9) . As the accuser he anticipates a future

38. The text reads: "he knows that his time is short." E. Lohmeyer, *Die Offenbarung des Johannes,* 1926, p. 101, recalls the "little time" of rest in Rev. 6:11 and the serving of God "day and night" in 7:15.
39. In connection with this "accuser" we might consider the "adversary" of I Pet. 5:8 *(antídikos).* Schrenk points out correctly that here the original image of an adversary in a law case is no longer the picture in view (cf. *TWNT,* I, *s.v. antídikos);* he does see a relation to the accusing function of the *diábolos.* Cf. the "prowling around" in this text with Satan's conduct in Job 1:7.
40. For this idea of Satan's doing service for God and "reporting," cf. H. Torczyner, "How Satan Came into the World," *The Expository Times,* Vol. 48, 1937, pp. 563-566. In the light of this notion Torczyner explains why Satan does not appear again in the epilogue of Job; he had fulfilled "his duty; which is to report on every one of the Lord's subjects, who might perhaps harbour revolt" (p. 564). In that same spirit, cf. Von Rad, *Theologie des A.T.,* I, 1955, 406: "... no devilish opponent of God, but rather a functionary in Jahwe's royal estate." Also cf. Von Rad on the Old Testament idea of Satan, in *TWNT,* II, *s.v. diábolos,* where he contends that already in the Old Testament the elements are "implicitly" present which "later corrupted" the whole line of thought.

guilt, which will certainly appear the moment God stretches out his hand and touches what Satan assumes to be the presupposition of Job's piety: his own physical welfare (1:11; 2:5). In the contest that follows we see God's permission of Satan to manifest his power: "Behold, he is in your power; only spare his life" (2:6). Once again, the essential point is that the accusation of Satan takes place *before God's throne*. Thus the devil's indictment cannot possibly be viewed apart from this relation to God. If anywhere, it is certainly clear in these chapters that the power of the evil one is no "overwhelming force." Even the most dismal of human tragedies and emergencies are under God's control. "Only spare his life. . . ." The fact that Satan could *not touch Job's life* is an indication of that border beyond which he was not able to go.

Consider also the accuser of Zechariah 3. Again he levels his attack on an actual guilt and centers his attention on the person of Joshua the high priest. We find Joshua "standing before the angel of the Lord, and Satan standing at his right hand to accuse him" (v. 1). But this time there is every apparent reason for an accusation, for Joshua is "clothed with filthy garments" (v. 3) and we also read of his "iniquity" (v. 4).[41] Moreover, the charge is especially serious and critical for the entire nation, since its reference is to Joshua's "investiture as high priest."[42] Yet this charge too is thrown out of court, and the accuser himself is rebuked. "The Lord rebuke you, O Satan! The Lord who has chosen Jerusalem rebuke you! Is not this a brand plucked from the fire?" (v. 2). Here the reality of Joshua's guilt is not denied; but the trial is now cast in the light of the reality of God's electing love. Therefore there is no room for a neutral or objective statement of guilt. Joshua's investiture is confirmed by God's removal of his "iniquity"; and instead of his former "filthy gar-

41. On this accusation of Satan Von Rad maintains that "here, too, Satan is no evil power: the accused *is* guilty, but the accusation is thrown out" (*ibid.*, 72). But this is an unconvincing argument, since the presence of guilt and the accusation of the evil one by no means exclude each other. Von Rad's conception of Job and Zechariah 3 goes hand in glove with his vision of the evolution of the Satan-idea in the direction of an absolutizing of Satan. Though he does not exclude a Persian influence, he maintains that the Satan-concept has no analogy; only in post-canonical literature does the process advance to a "complete absolutizing of Satan in opposition to God." Von Rad sees the motive for this view of Satan as a "fallen angel" in the effort to escape a radical dualism (74).

42. J. Ridderbos, *ad loc.*, *K.V.*, III, 67.

ments" he is now clothed in "rich apparel" (v. 4). Satan's charge is answered by God's "rebuke," and in the focus of election it loses its meaning and legitimacy.

Once again we observe that the power of the demonic realm is limited. Zechariah 3, in distinction from Job 1 and 2, does not even mention that power, and the accent is on Satan's indictment. We do not read of a power *versus* power but the power of an *accusation* and its powerful *rebuke*. Therefore the qualities of *independentia* or *aseitas* are no attributes of the kingdom or the power of darkness. They cannot describe a single one of Satan's nefarious designs. The mere *fact* of Satan's accusations in the Apocalypse and Job and Zechariah, and the mere *fact* of God's response, can only demonstrate the subordination and the delimitation of Satan's power. The power of Satan is in contrast to God's boundless grace which removes man's guilt and *refutes this devilish charge.*[43]

Sinful man cannot take a casual view of Satan's power and complaint. Notice that the accusation of Zechariah 3 is not refuted by Joshua but rather by the word of Jahwe. So too in the case of the "accuser of our brethren" in Revelation 12. At the same time, the man who understands all this will find that there is no room for a sinister "fatalism," or a threatening tragedy, or an "inexorable force." There can be no thought of a "fatal origin" of sin which is now perpetuated throughout all history. The power of darkness and the accusation of the evil one are subject to God's own sovereignty. Therefore, we shall have to agree with Thielicke in calling the idea of "the satanic" a "relational concept."[44] Rightly understood, this term does not deny the reality but only emphasizes the non-autonomous character of

---

43. Rosa Schärf, *Die Gestalt des Satans im A.T.*, 1948, speaks erroneously of a "polarity" between Satan and the Angel of the Lord as "two sides of God's essence" which wage a contest over man (p. 156). In terms of Jung's thought, she too conceives the development and pivotal feature of the Old Testament God-concept in the notion of God's justice as a hindrance that makes way for his love. Concerning God's *punishment* of Satan she contends: "Here Jahwe has come to master his dark side" (p. 159); and thus the way is prepared for the New Testament idea of love. Schärf declares that we must thank the psychology of Jung (cf. her foreword) for "spiritual groundlines" in conceiving of this matter. This is especially apparent in the fact that the analysis does not concern "metaphysical entities" but "God and the devil as primitive pictures or archetypes of the human soul" (p. 10).

44. Thielicke, *op. cit.*, p. 183.

Satan's power. Scripture informs us that this non-autonomy is beyond all doubt and cannot be hidden or covered up by the "power of darkness" itself.[45] Any demonology that takes lightly this "subordination" of the demons to God[46] can only fail to appreciate the biblical message. It can only bring confusion to the Church.

Certainly we must insist on doing justice to the demonological relations in sinning. We must refuse to interpret a "short time" as though it were "no time at all." Yet we take real comfort in that light which even now shines over the kingdom of darkness. This is the light of him who was manifest "to destroy the works of the devil" (I John 3:8); it is the light of him who unbinds, destroys and breaks down the power of evil[47] and whose holy and healing activity is the very antithesis of the devil's *diabállein*. In this matter of "breaking down," the power of Satan cannot begin to match the power of Christ. Once again, it is necessary to observe that this battle is not a contest of mere

45. Along with the accusation before God's throne one thinks of James' statement concerning the demons who also believe that God is one and shudder (2:19). Cf. the evil spirits who were opposed to Christ and to the manifestation of Jesus as the "Holy One of God" (Luke 4:34; cf. Mark 5:7).

46. This "subordination" can never be disputed by appealing to the biblical description of Satan as "ruler of this world" (John 12:31; 14:30; 16:11). The word *árchōn* never implies an unlimited and autonomous rule. Especially three statements in John indicate that this "ruler" stands under judgment: he is "cast out" (12:31); "is judged" (16:11); and has "no power" over Christ (14:30). K. J. Popma rightly deplores the fact "that Satan's loss of the title 'prince of this world' is not generally recognized even by those acquainted seriously with Scripture" (*De Boodschap van het Boek Job*, 1957, ·p. 20). Cf. here the strong expression "god of this world" in II Cor. 4:4; this is no reinstatement of the title but a reference to its still-remaining power which — precisely in its being "still-remaining" — is revealed in its antithetical relatedness to the "gospel of the glory of Christ." Cf. the pretension of the devil in Luke 4:6 — a pretension of power over all kingdoms of the world; a pretension which, even in its forms of expression, can never transcend non-autonomy — for the authority was "delivered" to him (*hóti emoí paradédotai*).

47. One might think of the typical formulations of Christ's superior power as found, for example, in Mark 1:27: "with authority he commands even the unclean spirits, and they obey him." Cf. the account of the seventy: "even the demons are subject to us in your name" (Luke 10:17; also Christ's answer, 10:20). See further Matt. 8:16 ("he cast out the spirits with a word"); Mark 1:25 ("Jesus rebuked him"); Acts 16:18 ("I charge you in the name of Jesus Christ").

force against mere force. Rather the power of Satan is "broken down" by the power of him in whom salvation and power are bound together in a perfect unity. The unity is the unity of battle and sacrifice, victory and atonement; it is the unity in which the power of darkness is emptied and the devil's charge is refuted in man's own reconciliation to God.

Therefore we can never comprehend the witness of Scripture by laying an *exclusive accent* on the so-called "dramatic motive" of reconciliation. For both the battle and the victory are given their reality in the way of reconciliation *and sacrifice*. This is the unity that is insufficiently honored in such a figure as Aulén.[48] Our criticism, at this juncture, is certainly not that Aulén makes use of martial analogies; it is rather that he makes an *exclusive use of these*.[49] In so doing he obscures the true nature of Christ's victory. We must notice that the powerful conquest of Jesus was achieved through the lowly humiliation of the cross. In the cross of the "powerless Savior" the power of darkness was disempowered. It was emptied of its meaning by that power which is manifest in the way of his humility.

Nowhere are we given a clearer picture of this interrelation of reconciliation and sacrifice than in the words of Colossians 2:14-15. There we read of a "disarming" or a "public example" of "principalities and powers"; we also read of a "triumphing over them." But the revelation of Christ's power is only fully expressed in the way of God's pardon. God has forgiven "all our trespasses, having cancelled the bond which stood against us with its legal demands; this he set aside, nailing it to the cross" (vv. 13*b*, 14). There are aspects of genuine power that are certainly emphasized here. We read of a triumphal march; and we also find a use of martial analogies.[50] Yet the nature of that

48. Cf. my *The Work of Christ*, 1965, pp. 328ff.
49. Hillerdahl (*Gehorsam gegen Gott und Menschen. Luthers Lehre von der Obrigkeit und die moderne evangelische Staatsethik,* 1954, p. 271) takes issue with Barth, who, he alleges, sees "no reason for attributing to the work of Jesus Christ anything like a military outlook." Reference to Barth's *K.D.*, IV/1, 302 (ET, 274). One must object, however, that Barth says something different from what Hillerdahl seems to think; he merely asks "whether it is advisable to try to work out systematically our thinking in this direction." We must certainly note that he adds: "What is clear is that a place should be found for this group of images and the particular truth which it presents." This, however, is something very different from what the paraphrase of Hillerdahl suggests.
50. Despoilment and triumph are seen in the *apekdysámenos* and *thriam-*

triumph is very evident: it is grounded in the cross and resurrection. The victory does not take place in an isolated "religious"
sphere but stands, *in the spectre of the cross,* in cosmic dimensions. We read of "powers" and "disenthronement" (Heb. 2:14) ;
and life is now liberated from the "inexorable force" of principalities. The curse is now shattered for those who were "doomed
to slavery, throughout their entire lives, by their own fear of
death."[51]

We men are very susceptible to suggestions of "fatalism" and
"boundless powers." Indeed, we are so susceptible that it is difficult to give full weight to this New Testament message of "disenthronement" and "disarming." With a naive credulity we
sometimes nod assent to the increasing "recognition" of demonic
forces at work in our world. We find it difficult to understand
the irrefutable message of Scripture concerning the disarming,
unveiling, and unmasking of these "powers of the earth." Yet,
precisely *this* is the message which the Church is called upon to
proclaim. Furthermore, it is not a mere adjunct of that message,
but it *is* the very *message of the cross.* The despoilment of Satan
can only be seen in the reality of the *cross.*[52]

Therefore it is totally wrong to corrupt the proclamation of
that message by referring to a general "phenomenology" of evil.
We cannot regard this message as a frivolous optimism. For an
optimism could only result if we identified "disarming" and the
eschaton itself, or conceived of the present as the time in which
no one does *evil* any longer or "hurts or destroys in all God's
holy mountain" (Isa. 11:9). It is clear that the New Testament
does not see "disarming" in that way. It does know a certain
"phenomenology" of evil and speaks in a prophetic manner of
evil's extension until the "last of days." The tension between
what has happened and is still to come is not dissolved; as a
matter of fact, both of these are underscored in the New Testament with emphasis. There is no contradiction but only a unity
between what has happened in the past and is still to come in
the future.[53] Nowhere is there a vacillating tension in which

beúsas of 2:15. Cf. Paul's imagery in II Cor. 2:14; also on this whole
issue, H. Berkhof, *Christus en de Machten,* 1952, Chap. 9.

51. Cf. O. Michel, *Der Brief an die Hebräer,* p. 86: dread "must be removed as a curse that has come in from the outside."

52. Berkhof, *op. cit.,* p. 38.

53. On the one hand we think of Col. 2:14-15; also Heb. 2:14 and II Tim.
1:10 *(katargein).* Cf. *TWNT,* I, *s.v. katargéō* (under *argós*); also I Pet.
3:22, a description of Christ "at the right hand of God, with angels,

"unbending cosmic forces" can still find place; indeed, when we admit of such a thought we can only do violence to the message of the cross. The only tension is the tension which comes when the light of the cross falls on those "cosmic forces" and lays them bare in all their senselessness and impotence.[54]

All of these considerations are important for gaining a right insight into the demonological relations of the New Testament. It is simply impossible to construct an abstract "demonology" and thus to ignore these biblical accents.[55] The man who does so will find himself, sooner than he thinks, enmeshed in a hopeless speculation and a "metaphysical" fascination for the "demonic realm." When he returns to earth again he will proceed with fear and trembling and by raising his dirges on the works of the demons. Such a demonology is denied to us in Jesus Christ. Therefore we must be careful in speaking of a "phenomenology of evil." The most dismal blackness in the history of the world once found its limit in the revelation of God's *profound intention and grace. Jesus Christ was resurrected on the third day!* The emptying of Satan's power was then very manifest, and all the powers of this world were subjected to the fulfillment of God's plan.

Therefore, on the basis of what we have said, it is under-

authorities, and powers subject to him" *(hypotagéntōn autō̂ angélōn kai exousiōn kai dynámeōn).* On the other hand we read of an anticipated "destruction" *(katargeín)* of *archē̂, exousía,* and *dýnamis* (I Cor. 15:24), and of *death* (v. 26). Cf. v. 28: "When all things are subjected to him . . ." *(hótan dé hypotagē̂ autō̂ ta pánta);* also the expectation regarding Christ's enemies in Heb. 10:13, seen in the light of the *sessio Christi.*

54. The unity of the radical New Testament expressions on what has happened, and their clarity in regard to eschatological events, can only be seen in the light of the inviolability of Christ's victory. That inviolability must be fully honored, also in the "short time." The basis of this unity and clarity is the revelation of wisdom and power as only foolishness and weakness. Paul thus describes the structure of God's activity: God "chose what is low and despised in the world, even things that are not, to bring to nothing things that are" (I Cor. 1:28; *katargeín).* This is the tremendous message in Paul's letters, which points forward to a truly unimaginable unmasking and warns against all blindness in viewing world history. Note also the perspective in the Magnificat of Mary, Luke 1:51f.

55. It is certainly not accidental that the topics of the devil, Satan and the Fall of the angels are discussed in Bavinck's dogmatics only in Vol. III, and not in his earlier chapter on angels ("De Geestelijke Wereld," Vol. II).

standable that the disciples, in their ministry, enjoined the Church *not to fear*. The Church could know that the dualistic interpretation of a cosmic struggle was illegitimate. But this does not mean that she could speak, in an abstract sense, of the "impotence" of the power of darkness. It does mean that she had no reason at all to fear in this struggle, which was also the struggle of faith. Outside Christ there is no reason for speaking of this "impotence," and to do so is utterly precarious. It is very remarkable that the New Testament only mentions the "power" and the "impotence" of darkness in relation to the power of Jesus Christ. If we regard that reality of darkness *apart from him* we can only experience that it manifests its potency anew.

This is what we see when the Jewish exorcists attempted to imitate Paul and adjured an evil spirit by the Lord Jesus (Acts 19:13ff.). The spirit was not expelled but answered them: "Jesus I know, and Paul I know; but who are you?" (v. 15). The exorcists were overpowered by this superior potency, and "the man in whom the evil spirit was leaped on them, mastered all of them, and overpowered them" (v. 16).[56] This, however, was not a victory of the power of darkness over the triumphant progress of the Gospel; for precisely in that way the path was made clear for the "mighty growth" of the Word of God (v. 20). It is only in communion with Christ that the power of darkness is exposed in all its impotence. Therefore there is no room for any "magic." Only when victory over the demonic realm has its origin in the Lord himself can we speak of a transcendent and extraordinary force (cf. v. 11).[57] In *that power* miracles were performed at Ephesus "by the hands of Paul, so that handkerchiefs or aprons were carried away from his body to the sick, and diseases left them and evil spirits came out of them" (vv. 11-12).

Perhaps no reference has prompted more people to speak of a biblical "magic." But "magic" is only apparent when we stand outside the fellowship of the Lord and conceive of the expulsion of the "power of darkness" apart from his communion. Precisely because of that communion we read that Paul performed extraordinary and spectacular miracles,[58] while the sons of Sceva were

56. The phrase reads: *katakyrieúsas amphotérōn íschysen kat' autōn.*
57. Grosheide, *op. cit.*, II, 204: a surmounting of the usual apostolic power.
58. E. Haenchen, *Die Apostelgeschichte*, 1956, p. 503, speaks of the "uneasiness" of both liberals and orthodox, and the effort to "unburden Paul." Cf. his remarks on "sincere naivete" (Zahn), realistic theosophy,

overwhelmed when they attempted to do the same.[59] There is no inconsistency here between the impotence of the exorcists and the power of Christ's authority. For this very "duality" only demonstrates that one cannot speak meaningfully of the power of sin, or its "disempowerment," apart from the communion of Christ. In that communion it is the *battle of faith* to which believers are called. The New Testament can only be understood fully in this unity of *struggle* and not-fearing, *not-fearing* and struggle.[60] Here the problem of over-emphasizing the one and minimizing the other is entirely absent. For the dynamic of faith

and skepticism. Haenchen himself sees the picture of Paul, sketched in v. 11, as fulfilling the "demands of an ur-Christian pneumatism" (p. 504); he finds here the portrayal of a mighty, triumphant apostle. But that picture, he says, is incompatible with Paul's conception of apostleship, in which not glory but the shape of the cross of the Lord finds reflection. Haenchen appeals to E. Käsemann, "Die Legitimation des Apostels," *Z.N.T.W.*, 1942-1943. He sees in Luke a legend in which the apostle is regarded as suffused with divine *dýnamis*, as living no more in the sphere of the cross but glory. Haenchen's notion fails completely in comprehending what was true even of Christ's miracles: the miracle is a visible *sign* of God's dominion in the time of salvation, and is therefore never concealed, even if its true *meaning* cannot be understood and envisioned apart from faith.

59. On the use of magic, cf. Grosheide, *op. cit.*, II, *ad loc.* How much the exorcists imitated is apparent from their own words: "I adjure you by the Jesus whom Paul preaches" (v. 13). *Orkízō* is also an indication of this. Nowhere do the apostles make a similar use of this term (cf. I Thess. 5:27, in a very different context). We do find a similar usage on the part of the "unclean spirit," Mark 5:7 (cf. Grosheide, *ibid.*, 205).

60. Barth's strong accent on the triumph of grace and not-fearing has led him to a statement that also has a bearing on believers' *struggle*: "If the old aeon has been done away, as is the case according to the New Testament *kerygma*, we no longer need to fight against it" (*K.D.*, I/2, 118; ET, 107). But the thrust of the New Testament — so very clear at precisely this point — is apparent when Barth, as it were, corrects himself and adds: "Or rather, the armour in which it is combated has now become the purely spiritual kind described in Eph. 6." It is unfair when Hillerdahl (*op. cit.*, p. 271) ignores this correction ("or rather") and proceeds to discuss the "battle perspective" ("Kampfperspektive") in Luther and numerous New Testament references. This omission, apparently, should be seen in the light of Barth's own very strong statements (therefore his self-correction was necessary) — e.g. the following as cited by Hillerdahl: "The secularisation of nature, history and civilisation now ceases to present a problem as we look back upon the cross of Christ" (*ibid.*; Barth, *loc. cit.*). It seems to me that the issue here is not a matter of "no problem" but rather — in the light of Christ's triumph — the *nature of that problem*. Cf. Barth, *K.D.*, IV/2, 759ff.; ET, 671ff.

is only visible in the struggle of faith; and the Church is summoned to faith *on the basis of Christ's victory.*

Thus our summons to warfare is no less urgent because of Christ's victory, but is given its structure and receives its meaning in that light. Those who listen to John's "you have overcome the evil one" (I John 2:13-14), and who know that Christ appeared "to destroy the works of the devil" (3:8), must also hear this warning: "Little children, keep yourselves from idols" (5:21). The warfare of faith is the warfare of "abiding" in Christ's love (John 15:9-10) and "abiding" in his word (I John 2:14). Only in that battle is there protection against all the "flaming darts of the evil one" (Eph. 6:16; cf. II Thess. 3:3).

Therefore, the Church knows that Satan has been "thrown down" and his charge has been dismissed. But she also acknowledges another accuser in her confession: "though my *conscience* accuse me that I have grievously sinned against all the commandments of God and kept none of them..." (HC, Q. 60). The knowledge of *this accuser* cannot be acquired except (as the Catechism suggests) in the midst of confessing that we are justified in the sight of God. The Belgic Confession states that this accusation of ourselves is only set to rest because the crucified Christ frees our consciences from "fear, terror, and dread" and gives us "confidence in approaching to God" (Art. 23). Here is the echo of what we read in I John 3:20 concerning our hearts that "condemn us" and God who is "greater than our hearts."[61] This condemnation is totally different from the "accusation of our brethren" in Revelation 12 and is nothing but the confession of guilt on the part of the man who accuses himself in the light of God's forgiveness. It is very different from the satanic accusation "day and night." Therefore it must be taken with great seriousness.

We began this chapter by asking if a demonological explanation for sin's origin is possible, assuming that we first repudiate all monisms and dualisms. In considering that question we found ourselves in the midst of history and the New Testament. We have not strayed from the way in which we set out to go. But we have tried to suggest that a refutation of the demonological explanation for sin is only possible in the context of the message of Jesus Christ. That message does away with every false

61. Cf. my *Divine Election,* 1960, p. 298.

notion of "fatality" in the kingdom of darkness and envisions man in his guilt, slavery and bondage to the "powers of this world."[62] In this message we have no interest in man's dismal "fate" but only in the Gospel of *sinners who are saved.*

This is the message that excludes any trace of man's exculpation or explanation for his sin. The perfect prayer of the believer asks *first* for God's forgiveness and only *then* for deliverance from the evil one. In that perspective of a *real forgiveness of sins* the demonological explanation finds its definitive rebuttal. Only in the focus of forgiveness are we asked to give attention to those powers of the kingdom of darkness which are laid bare and are opened to a public display. Yet those powers command no interest in themselves. There is no reason for a believer to be disenchanted or skeptical as he finds himself confronted by them. For these are the powers that are vanquished in the single act of faith, struggle, and hope. Surely there were people in Thyatira who experienced "the deep things of Satan"; but they also had every reason to take courage in this word of the exalted Lord: "I do not lay upon you any other burden" (Rev. 2:24).[63] Being strengthened in their faith, they marched on to meet the coming Conqueror (v. 25).

Monism *(Deus causa peccati)* and dualism *(ex tenebris emersisse!)* and the demonological explanation for sin are all equally untenable. But the question, then, is this: Has the Church painted herself into a corner and assumed an impossible position? Is there any explanation at all that sets human reason to rest and gives us a measure of insight into the *"mysterium in-*

---

62. Cf. Ch. Moeller, "Dubbelzinnigheid van Satan," in *Satan (Etudes Carmélitaines)*, 1948, p. 4.

63. Concerning this "experience" or "learning to know" it is usually said that those who talked this way at Thyatira did not betray thereby their own practical amoralism. Precisely as *pneumatici*, it is suggested, they made the claim of having this knowledge (cf. Lohmeyer, *op. cit.*, p. 27). They had it as a "secret redemptive power" that raised them above all the temptations of heathendom (M. Kiddle, *The Revelation of St. John*, 1947, p. 40). It is not unlikely that this "learning to know" should be seen in conjunction, therefore, with an "initiation into an esoteric knowledge" *(ibid.;* cf. the *didachê* of v. 24). But the picture of Thyatira is of such a sort (see vv. 20-22) that this knowledge would seem to be linked intimately with an amoralism; and this fact is comprehensible in terms of that "esoteric" knowledge. The Church is called away from the "way" of such knowledge to the "way" of God (cf. v. 24 and Acts 15:28). She is enjoined to "hold fast" that which was given unto her (v. 25).

iquitatis"? Barth asked that question in reference to the theology of Julius Müller, after Müller had discarded a number of explanations as inappropriate for shedding light on the origin of sin. "Perplexed," wrote Barth, "he stands before a reality and has to reject as unsatisfactory every successive attempt to explain its possibility or to conceive it systematically. Will he be satisfied with that?"[64]

It is well known, of course, that Müller was not satisfied. Seeing the *aporia* in all such efforts to construct a "theodicy of sin,"[65] he proceeded to give his own "explanation" in terms of a pre-existent fall.[66] But it is vitally important to see *why*, in the face of the countless warnings of the Church in reference to the inexplicability of sin, we cannot and we may not come to such a desperate solution. In any event, we are not concerned about an "irrationality," or an *"asylum ignorantiae,"* or a *"docta ignorantia."* Nor are we proposing a tired distrust of human reason which must finally recognize its limits. Only in terms of the very *heart* of the Christian faith is it meaningful and legitimate to speak of the *inexplicability of sin.*

64. Barth, *Die protestantische Theologie im 19. Jahrhundert,* 1947, p. 541.
65. *Ibid.*
66. Cf. my *Man: the Image of God,* 1962, p. 338.

CHAPTER FIVE

THE RIDDLE OF SIN

I T IS WELL to pause here and take notice of what is often called the "enigmatic character" of sin. Since we cannot assume *a priori* that such a term is legitimate, it is important to ask what we mean when we speak of the "riddle" of man's sin. Those who have referred to sin as the *"mysterium iniquitatis"* have used a term that has overtones of something vague and ominous. Sin might even be seen as *"das Unheimliche."* But such a concept suggests a matter that is sinister and foreboding, and even evokes the image of a shadowy figure that is in and round about us and cannot be known in its inner intents. The "mystery" of man's sin is then seen as the "strangeness" of man's sin, at least for us here and now. Sin's "mystery" is the "unfathomableness" of sin for human and finite minds.

This sort of thinking makes it possible for us to conceive of the mystery of sin as a very difficult problem which finds place alongside other "mysteries" and "riddles" in life. But can the "mystery" of sin be "explained"? If we wait long enough and try hard enough will we ever be able to penetrate the fog and discover the "sense" and "harmony" of sin? Is this a riddle (like so many others) that temporarily baffles our minds and will ultimately be resolved? If we have more light and a greater vision, will this whole matter be cleared up? Is that what Scripture means when it tells us that that which was once "unknown" and "inconceivable" is later "fully revealed"? There is, indeed, a light in God's Word that enlightens what once was obscure: the "revelation of the mystery which was kept secret for long ages but is now disclosed and . . . made known to all nations" (Rom. 16:25-26) . Moreover, truth is the disclosure (the *alḗtheia*) of what once was hidden. There is a "disclosure" in the history of revelation; so too there is a "disclosure" in the unriddling of the eschaton. "For now we see in a mirror dimly, but then face to face. Now I know in part; then I shall understand fully, even as I have been fully understood" (I Cor. 13:12). "Beloved, we are God's children now; it does not yet appear what we shall be" (I John 3:2). "What I am doing you do not know now, but afterward you will understand" (John 13:7). "When you have lifted up the Son of man, then you will know that I am he" (8:28).

Clearly, there is a "disclosure" or "unriddling" in the course of revelation and the process of history. We read in Job: "I had heard of thee by the hearing of the ear, but now my eye sees thee" (42:5). In Acts we are made aware of the riddle that distressed the Ethiopian eunuch until Philip appeared and instructed him (8:31ff.; cf. Ps. 73:16-17). Yet there is not only a movement from riddle to unriddling but also the other way around. There is a process that turns revelation into a riddle because of man's own *guilty ignorance*. The two men on the way to Emmaus were reprimanded for being "foolish men, and slow of heart" (Luke 24:25); and the Gospels repeatedly call those who do not understand the meaning of Christ's words "foolish men." Listen to the judgment of Scripture: "Are you also still without understanding? Do you not see . . . ?" (Matt. 15:16-17; Mark 7:18). "Do you not yet perceive or understand?" (Mark 8:17). "Do you not remember?" (8:18). "Are your hearts hardened?" (8:17). "Having eyes do you not see, and having ears do you not hear?" (8:18). All kinds of historical and psychological factors may darken our understandings, and things may stand before us as a "riddle." Men's eyes were distracted and they were unable to see the significance of Christ's cross and resurrection (cf. John 2:19ff.). Similarly, the disciples only later recalled the words of Christ; and men were blind to seeing Christ as the Good Shepherd and Son of God (John 10:6; 8:27).

In all these references there is a riddle that *can* be dispelled and that *can* make way for a new and deeper understanding. But the riddle of sin is *not of this sort and lies on an entirely different plane*. It can never permit a greater or deeper insight into the nature and origin of sin. There is no insight to be gathered by a greater and deeper enlightenment and unriddling. In saying this, of course, we do not deny that there may be a clarification of those "motives" within the circle of fallen human life that led someone to a given act. The science of criminology presupposes that relative transparency of motives. But we do mean that sin itself, in its source and cause, can never be *explained*. We deny that anything, including faith, can shed a particle of light on the enigmatic character of sin. On the pathway of faith and repentance sin is only viewed as the more incomprehensible, inscrutable, and inexplicable. To the extent that a man comes more and more under the impression of God's goodness and majesty, his apostasy from God and his glory, and his holy law, can only take the shape of an enigma.

This, however, is not the "mystery" that was "hid" until the present time, nor the mystery of those "secret things" that "belong to the Lord our God" (Deut. 29:29). It is rather the enigma that confronts us more and more in faith and that stands in a greater and bolder relief as we contemplate the depths of man's rebelliousness against *that God* of whom it can only be said: it is good for us to be "near" to him (Ps. 73:28). For that reason we may never view man's sin as a riddle that has "not yet" been resolved, and that now remains to vex our troubled minds. The riddle of sin is of an entirely unique sort. For that same reason we should certainly be careful when we speak of the riddle of sin as the *"mysterium iniquitatis."*

It is well known that this term is the Latin equivalent of the New Testament word as used in II Thessalonians 2:7. There we read of the "mystery of lawlessness." Paul is speaking of the Antichrist (or the Antagonist) who "opposes and exalts himself against every so-called god or object of worship, so that he takes his seat in the temple of God, proclaiming himself to be God" (v. 4). He is referring to the man of lawlessness who is still restrained and will someday be revealed, "for the mystery of lawlessness is already at work" (v. 7). His coming manifestation, as it were, already casts forth long shadows and is clearly discernible. Therefore attention and resistance are enjoined. The coming storm is already brewing, and an ominous silence forespells its arrival. The energy of lawlessness is already at hand. But when Paul speaks, in this connection, of a "mystery," it is evident that he envisages something far different from what is enigmatic and inexplicable. Certainly he sees something "mysterious." There is something "already working" which is yet to be "revealed." And yet, his concern is to define this mystery in historical terms, and to conceive of it as the mystery which has *not yet been revealed.*

The terminology of *mysterium iniquitatis* is certainly derived from Scripture. At the same time, we cannot suggest that Paul intended the same thing by that term as other men have very frequently meant. Paul never dreamed of using *mystērion* without bearing constantly in mind that this would someday *be no more*. It would someday cease when "the lawless one" is revealed and the *kálymma*, or veil, is ripped away (v. 8). The concern of Paul was this "lawless one" who is still hidden; therefore the concept of "mystery" had nothing to do with the enigmatic or impenetrable, or a deficient insight into the "mysterious" nature of our sin. Paul was interested in something *not yet* revealed in history, though something which *will be revealed* when the "activity of Satan" expresses itself "with all power and with pretended signs and wonders, and with all wicked deception for those who are to perish" (vv. 9f.). This historical process was described by Paul as a process from "mystery" to revelation.[1]

We come across that same word, *mystery,* in the Revelation of John, where we read of the woman "sitting on a scarlet beast which was full of blasphemous names" (17:3). She has a golden cup in her hand, "full of abominations and the impurities of her fornication" (17:4). All of this is typified in her "name· of mystery," which is written on her forehead: "Babylon the great" (v. 5). Obviously, what John intended by this term is no vague or general concept. For very specific sins are now mentioned: fornication, blasphemy, abomination, impurity, and even the woman's drunkenness "with the blood of the saints and the blood of the martyrs of Jesus" (vv. 4, 6). It is also important that in this book of Revelation there is another rider who sits upon a white horse, and his name is "Faithful and True" (19:11; cf. v. 16). Moreover, this is a name "which no one knows but himself" (19:12). Again we find a reference to a "mystery" and something concealed. But the "mystery" of Revelation 17:5 is not of that sort. John says nothing there about a "mystery" that eludes our knowledge and is therefore enigmatic and secretive. In fact, when he "marvels greatly" at seeing the woman the angel confronts him with the question: "Why marvel? I will tell you the mystery of the woman" (17:7).

Therefore *this mystery* was not something ineffable or unfathomable but a mystery which could be *revealed.*[2] The name

---

1. Cf. II Thess. 2:2: "to the effect that the day of the Lord has come." Also Zahn-Wohlenberg, *Comm.,* p. 158, on *mystērion,* where the notion is contested that this term signifies an abandonment of "the conception of moral man," or that it ever presents man "as something incomprehensible, ineffable."

2. S. Greijdanus, *Comm.,* p. 343.

written on the woman's forehead characterized the woman herself: she was the "great Babylon." The word *mystery,* in other
words, has nothing to do with the connotations which we usually
assign to that term. It has nothing to do with something "mysterious"[3] but relates to that which, in the future, *will be revealed.* Thus it is used in the same sense as we have already
noted in II Thessalonians 2 (the "mystery of lawlessness"). It
stands to reason that the angel could explain this "mystery" and
open its meaning to a very puzzled John. The woman had made
the pretensions of grandeur and power and had sought to be-
wilder John by her name of "mystery": "Babylon the great."
Yet her mystery is now exposed in all of its depths. That which
her name had signified is met by God's judgment and condemnation. Therefore we see the final unmasking of what was only
shame and pomp and naked impotence in contrast to the glory
of him who was yet to be revealed.[4]

What men have usually meant by the "riddle of sin," or the
mysterium iniquitatis, has no shred of support in the New
Testament. For though the New Testament ties this word
mystery to the concept of revelation, in an indissoluble bond,
the *mysterium iniquitatis* refers commonly to the impenetrable-
ness and unfathomableness of sin. But here the idea of a "revelation" has *no place.* Against this background we assert that the
riddle of sin can only be set forth in a completely unique way.
One can only affirm that there is no *reason* and no sensible
motive for man's sin. Surely, if we maintain this position we are
on an entirely different track from any notion of an intangible
or "mysterious" evil in our world. No matter what the "mysteriousness" of evil, we shall never comprehend the *depths of
this great riddle.* For the riddle of sin is the same as the essence
of sin, with its anti-normative character and illegality. It is the
same as the senselessness of sin. Therefore, since every "unriddling" of sin implies a discovery of "sense" where no sense can
possibly be found, the very notion of an "unriddling" is impossible.[5] One cannot find sense in the senseless and meaning in
the meaningless.

3. *TWNT,* IV, *s.v. mystérion.*
4. *Ibid.;* cf. Rev. 10:7 on "the mystery of God."
5. L. vander Kerken, in "De Betekenis van het Geheimzinnige" *(Tijdschrift voor Philosophie en Theologie,* 1956, "Bijdragen," pp. 349-365),
   has proposed a "phenomenology of the mysterious." He does not, however, speak of the *"mysterium iniquitatis."*

All of this does not imply that sin is any less a power or an influence on reality, or any less "real."[6] What it does imply is that sin cannot be explained in terms of its component factors and cannot be made "explicable." We have seen that every initiative in that direction can only end up, unavoidably, in self-excuse. But we can also understand this "unavoidability" in connection with what Bavinck has called the "motivelessness" of sin. The senselessness of sin is the riddle of man's sin; and precisely that motivelessness *excludes* our sin from the arena of those mysteries which we penetrate and solve by way of analysis. Sin is enigmatic and inexplicable simply *because* it has no presuppositions and no cause and no real motive at all.

When the Preacher cried, "Who knows the interpretation of a thing?" (Eccl. 8:1), he was obviously wrestling with ineffable and impenetrable depths. He had wanted to gain wisdom but he found that wisdom eluded him. "I said, 'I will be wise'; but it was far from me. That which is, is far off, and deep, very deep; who can find it out?" (7:23-24).[7] A shroud of mystery was round about man. No one knows "what is to be, for who can tell him how it will be?" (8:7). The work of God was seen as something which no one can know, as no one can know the way of the wind or "how the spirit comes to the bones in the womb of a woman with child" (11:4, 5). Yet all these restrictions of human knowledge[8] are very different from the unfathomable riddle of man's sin. Here we see a riddle that is truly an "objective" and "essential" enigma. We find an "ineffableness" that has no analogue in the ineffableness of God's works. When we look at sin we observe an unfathomableness that cannot be compared to the unfathomableness of him whose ways are far beyond our own and whose thoughts are past tracing out (cf. Isa. 55:8f.). The riddle of sin is the riddle of the senselessness and motivelessness of sin.

6. Vander Kerken (*ibid.*, p. 354) writes: "In the experiencing of the enigmatic, as soon as it appears that a solution is improbable, the whole of what is enigmatic becomes enshrouded in a haze of improbability, and we slide back into the experience of the *unreal* or *inactual*." It is evident that this mode of thought is exactly what does *not* apply to the riddle of sin. Vander Kerken is obviously interested in "the mystery of being" (*ibid.*, p. 363) and makes no pretension of considering the dark problematic of evil.

7. Cf. Aalders, *Comm.*: "diep, ja diep"; LXX: *bathý báthos*.

8. Concerning the "sum of things" which the Preacher seeks without finding it, cf. Eccl. 7:25, 27 (v. 27 in LXX: *logismós*).

There are other references which call to mind this motive-lessness.[9] We think of that further statement of the Preacher: "God made man upright, but they have sought many devices" (7:29). It is obvious that the Preacher was not concerned about the mere deficiency of human knowledge and had no interest at all in an abstract enigma. His reference is to the groundlessness and motivelessness of sin. Man's activity is seen in contrast to the goodness of God's creation, and sin is regarded in all its *guilty estrangement* and inexplicability. There can be no reason for sin in God's creation and the gifts of God, or in anything that God has wished for man and has given to man. The Preacher recognized that "the guilt for the universal depravity in all of humanity does not lie in God."[10] No causal link can possibly join the act of God's creation and man's sinning. There-fore the reality of evil can only be called the "invention" of man and the product of his own depraved ingenuity.[11]

But what a miserable depravity is this! There can be no rationale for evil: yet precisely *"because* sentence against an evil deed is not executed speedily, the heart of the sons of men is fully set to do evil" (8:11). This word *because* does not explain man's sin but only points to sin's insanity. The Preacher wanted to "seek wisdom and the sum of things" and wished to "know the wickedness of folly and the foolishness which is madness" (7:25).[12] We do not know the result of his inquiry, for the Preacher himself remained standing, as it were, before the real-ity of an evil that manifests itself on every hand. But this we do know, that the "ingenuity" and "inventiveness" here are the same as we find in Romans 1:30. Those of a "base mind" are "inventors" of evil.[13] The evil that surrounds us can never find a motive in God's goodness or an excuse in God's creation. That is to say, it can never be rationally defined.

We recall, in this connection, the words of Christ in John 15:25: "They hated me without a cause." We meet with that text in a pericope that deals with the hate of the world for Christ's disciples. This is the same hate as the world has shown for Christ himself (v. 18; cf. v. 21). The coming of Christ into

9. Cf. my *Man: the Image of God*, 1962, pp. 344f.
10. Aalders, *op. cit.*, p. 169.
11. Cf. *ibid.*
12. Cf. *ibid.*, p. 162.
13. Greek: *epheuretás kakōn;* French: "ingénieux au mal"; Dutch Staten-vertaling: "vinders van kwade dingen."

the world is the decisive turning-point in history and the moment that *changes things*. "If I had not come and spoken to them, they would not have sin; but now they have no excuse for their sin" (v. 22). Now that the Light has come there is no more hiding and no more possibility of excuse.[14] Christ has come and has done his mighty works which no one else was able to do (v. 24). Yet one thing remains to be said: All this has come "to fulfill the word that is written in their law, 'They hated me without a cause'" (v. 25). Here Christ harks back to the statement in Psalm 69:4 and sees it fulfilled in himself. The psalmist, in the throes of a deep despair, had said of those who hated him: they "hate me without a cause." They hated with a dark and grim, a guilty and senseless hate.[15] Indeed, they hated with a hate that could never be deduced from a "cause" and that stemmed, instead, from their own vicious and hateful hearts.[16] Surely the psalmist did not mean that he himself was righteous and good. He readily confessed his sin (v. 5). But the hate which he experienced had no basis in his own sin and took root in a different source. In the face of that hate he could only pray that God would deliver him and would put his enemies to shame. He could only pray that God would deal with his enemies in a way that did justice to their own causeless and senseless hate.[17]

This is the phrase ("they hate me without a cause") which Christ now saw fulfilled in himself. We can sum up the factors that played a role and that prompted the Jews to hate. The Jews themselves gave their "reasons" and "motives" in the very clearest of terms. Christ had "broken their law" and "transgressed" their sabbath and "blasphemed" their God. But all these "motives" were notoriously false. They were senseless and illegitimate (cf. Luke 6:7).[18] The real motive for their accusation was their own self-excuse, and all other "motives" were contrived. The

14. Greek: *próphasis*. Cf. Grosheide: it can mean "self-exculpation" ("verontschuldiging").

15. The "irrational" element in this hate also comes to expression in Ps. 69:4: "What I did not steal must I now restore?" On this "without a cause," cf. also Ps. 35:19.

16. Cf. A. Weiser, *Die Psalmen*, II, 321: "ohne Grund."

17. One thinks of Ps. 129:5: "May all who hate Zion be put to shame and turned backward!" Also Ps. 34:21: "and those who hate the righteous will be condemned."

18. Cf. R. Bultmann, *Das Evangelium des Johannes*, p. 425, on the "groundlessness of this hate"; also the "groundlessness of their crime" (*TWNT*, IV, *s.v. miséō*).

Preacher, in Ecclesiastes 7, had seen that God made man "upright" and that no reason exists for man's sin. But by that same
token, there can be no reason to hate Christ. We would then be
hating him who is the Light of the world and who does not
break but *only fulfills the law*.[19]

Earlier, in connection with the senselessness and the irrationality of sin, we spoke of sin's *folly*. Now it is clear that the biblical concept of folly by no means implies a negation but only the
accentuation of man's guilt. The confusions in all of man's folly
can only emphasize the senselessness of sin. It is the fool who
says in his heart, "There is no God" (Ps. 14:1; 53:1). Folly is on
a single line with blaspheming God's name (Ps. 74:18, 22) and
despising wisdom and instruction (Prov. 1:7). The foolish man
thinks he has reasons for acting as he does, but "the folly of fools
is deceiving" (Prov. 14:8). A fool despises correction (15:5).
Thus the inner vanity and groundlessness of foolishness are pain-
fully evident: "Even when the fool walks on the road, he lacks
sense, and he says to every one that he is a fool" (Eccl. 10:3).
Therefore Isaiah spoke of the gravity and the guiltiness of foolishness: "For the fool speaks folly, and his mind plots iniquity:
to practise ungodliness, to utter error concerning the Lord"
(32:6). Moreover, the New Testament warns of the serious consequences for the man who is a fool. They were foolish men who
built their house on the sand (Matt. 7:26), foolish maidens who
"took no oil with them" (Matt. 25:3), and foolish scribes and
Pharisees who were really *blind* (Matt. 23:17, 18). The man
who had rich barns but a poor relation to God was called a
"Fool!" (Luke 12:20). The "wisdom of the world," according to
Scripture, is turned into mere "foolishness" by the activity of
God (I Cor. 1:20). In short, the concept of *folly* is no reason at
all for any self-excuse.

W. H. Gispen has asked why it is that the book of Proverbs
so rarely uses the Hebrew words for *fool* (*nabal*) and *folly*
(*nebalah*).[20] He concludes that this must be seen in the light

19. We recall here the words of Mark 6:6: "And he marvelled because of
their unbelief." This "marvelling" strikes us all the more because it
stands in a context in which Christ himself points out certain "reasons" for this unbelief: "A prophet is not without honor, except in his
own country, and among his own kin, and in his own house" (6:4).
In and *beyond* these "reasons," however, streams the glory of the light
of Christ: his *marvelling at their unbelief*.
20. W. H. Gispen, "De Stam NBL," *G.T.T.*, 1955, p. 16; cf. *K.V.*, I, 23.

of the writer's intent: to deal with "foolishness" in the general
sense of "stupidity." When the writer departs from this main
interest and speaks of hardened sinners and godless men, he
uses such words as *wicked* and *perverse*. *Nabal* and *nebalah* were
avoided, for the most part, because these terms refer primarily
to blatant and arrogant transgressions of the two tables of the
law.[21] They have to do with those sins which incur God's
greatest wrath and disfavor and with those calloused sinners
who deliberately break the covenant. It is not this sort of
"foolishness" that Proverbs has in mind. The intention is to
speak of that "foolishness" which characterizes a larger segment
of mankind: *stupidity*. Gispen's analysis points to *nebalah* as a
detestable and contemptible and completely objectionable trait.
But it is also a trait of which Proverbs very rarely speaks.[22]
This word was used so sparingly because the burden of the
book is to refer to foolishness as "stupidity" and to man's own
"lack of understanding."[23]

Of course, there is no radical disjunction between "foolishness" and "stupidity." But the fact that there is a difference
is quite beyond dispute. The stupid man in the gate "does
not open his mouth" (Prov. 24:7), but the foolish man, who
is thrust outside the gate, does not even have the *right* to open
his. Yet at the level of the *heart* these borders are easily obscured. The stupid man, who despises all knowledge, can also
dote on evil and take glee in doing wickedness (10:23).[24] Therefore the question comes: Is the man who is "stupid" obliged
to take this further step, if he has not already taken it?[25] In any
event, it is well to consider this element of "stupidity" and "unreasonableness." "Stupidity," in general, resists all urging toward
"wisdom" and persists in being stupid;[26] furthermore, in the
biblical concept of *folly* there is always this element of *stupidity*.

21. *Ibid.*, 163, 170.
22. *Ibid.*, 170, 162. Gispen translates *nabal* as "fool" ("dwaas") in Prov.
    17:7, 21; 30:22.
23. *Ibid.*, 170.
24. In his *K.V.*, I, 176, Gispen refers to Lev. 18:17 and other texts relating
    to gross sexual sins and incest. He speaks of "an indication of something
    that is very sinful."
25. Cf. *ibid.*, 170. The *kesilim* stand on one line with mockers and haters
    of knowledge (*ibid.*, 35).
26. Cf. Gispen's statement, *ibid.*, on "the spiritually indolent and dull man
    who hates knowledge and therefore comes to sinful thoughts, words,
    and deeds."

This is not apparent as an intellectual "hiatus" but as something that impedes all knowledge. For that reason we must see *folly* as objectively disqualifying and positively nonsensical. Folly and the groundlessness of sin are really one and the same. Therefore folly must never be given a rational answer: for folly has no use for reasoning (26:4).[27] It is far better to "answer a fool according to his folly, lest he be wise in his own eyes" (26:5). Here too we observe that folly is always opposed to wisdom, and to that fear of the Lord which is also the "beginning of knowledge" (1:7).[28]

All of this must lead us to a single conclusion. Sin may reveal itself in the foolishness of stupidity or in other ways in which stupidity is evident. Yet sin is always inexplicable precisely *in its senselessness*. All kinds of "motives" may play a role in any given act of sin. They may do so with such a force of conviction that we are tempted to speak of sin's "obviousness." A variety of "motives" is manifest in all of human life and the whole of human history; and there is always a tendency to hide behind a whole plethora of "motives." But the Word of God reveals to us the falseness, and speciousness, and stupidity of that act. It points us to the guilt and the groundlessness of our own self-alienation from God and our neighbors. The statement that sin is an inexplicable reality is really part and parcel of sin's *guilt*. Therefore, the more "motives" we adduce for our sin, the more we betray how *guilty we are*.[29]

The confession of guilt, in both the Old and New Testa-

---

27. Cf. *ibid.*, II, 243; besides Prov. 26:4 see also 9:8 and Asaph's confession of guilt, Ps. 73:22.

28. In connection with Gispen's views on "folly" and "stupidity," we might refer also to Barth's *K.D.*, IV/2, 463f. (ET, 411f.), where a sharp distinction is drawn between "stupidity" and intellectual deficiency. Barth rightly accentuates stupidity as guilt, as something very dangerous and humanly inconquerable. In that "stupidity" he sees "one of the most remarkable aspects" of sin (467; ET, 415) — precisely in this "folly" which is without meaning or ground (467-468; ET, 415-416). Cf. Barth's exposé on Proverbs, *ibid.*, 478f.; ET, 424f. Note that he does not draw the same terminological distinction as Gispen. Cf. also his discussion (463) of *"nabal oder chesil"* (ET, 411f.).

29. How sin confuses right insight is certainly in evidence, e.g., whenever one perverts the "second command" of the summary of the law by looking for "motives" in one's neighbor. In sharp contrast to this, cf. Matt. 5:44: "Love your enemies and pray for those who persecute you," and v. 46: "For if you love those who love you, what reward have you? Do not even the tax collectors do the same?" Revealing words for anyone who looks for "motives" in sinful reactions!

ments, can only be viewed against the background of this enigma and inexplicability of sin. So too, the light that God's revelation casts on this enigma can only prompt us *to confess*. Under the power and blessing of the Spirit, confession can be seen as the clearest confirmation of this biblical view of the inexplicability of sin. Confession entails a rejection of any meaningful explanation of sin and a recognition that sin is "without cause." Thus confession is the corollary of sin's senselessness. It affirms that there is no such thing as a universal "mystery" of evil and nothing that even vaguely suggests an abstract "evil" of dualism. The enigma of sin is a *sui generis* enigma, and can only be understood in the light of the goodness and majesty of God. That is to say, it can only be understood in the light in which every sin is seen as senseless. The meaninglessness of sin is set in sharp focus in the angelic joy over a single sinner who repents (Luke 15:7, 10).[30] There is joy in heaven when a sinner takes leave of those foolish ways in which all lights are extinguished and men "love darkness, rather than light" (John 3:19).

Now we are able to appreciate why the New Testament so persistently refers to sin as that which is "strange." It is especially strange when committed by a man who is *redeemed from sin* and who also knows and experiences, in thanksgiving, that Christ has made *atonement for him*. Certainly this word *strange* does not imply that sin is a vestige of the Christian's former self; for nowhere in the apostolic preaching do we read that sin is explainable in terms of our "old life." Instead, we are met by the apostles' remonstrance and genuine surprise. The apostles were full of *amazement* and *awe* because of this fact of *sin within the Church*. "Do you not know that your bodies are members of Christ? ... Do you not know that your body is a temple of the Holy Spirit within you, which you have from God?" (I Cor. 6:15, 19).[31] Paul's intention was not to inveigh against something which "should not be" and is therefore "improper." It was rather to condemn roundly that which is *absurd* and in diametrical *opposition* to communion with Christ and his indwelling Spirit.[32] Therefore Paul could only marvel at how

30. Greijdanus, *Comm.*, II, 740, explains *enōpion* as joy "before their face," viz. on the part of God. Cf. Zahn, *op. cit.*, p. 560. Note v. 7: joy *in heaven*.

31. Cf. also v. 15b and Paul's answer, "Never!" Grosheide speaks of an "absurdity" ("ongerijmdheid"); cf. his *Comm. op Corinthiers*, p. 173.

32. In sharp contrast to this absurdity, note the "self-evidentness" of Paul's

quickly the Galatians were seduced and came to believe a "different gospel" which was "no gospel" (1:6, 7).[33] He stood face to face with a reality which could not be denied but could only be affirmed with astonishment and dismay.

How could the Galatians be so easily "bewitched" and fall for a "different gospel" (3:1; 1:7)? Paul could not understand. His words do not explain a thing but only reveal to us the anguish of his heart. "O foolish Galatians! Who has bewitched you, before whose eyes Jesus Christ was publicly portrayed as crucified?" (3:1). The Galatians were caught in their own foolishness and were unable to distinguish the law from faith. Thus they were the victims of a bitter illusion which could only be dispelled for those who see the cross of Christ.[34] Paul was not amazed because of a theoretical lack of understanding but because of the utter incomprehensibility of the Galatians' attitude *in view of the cross*. Therefore he spoke of "bewitchment." How could anyone who gazes on the cross react in such a manner as this?[35] Certainly there were those who had led the Galatians astray; but that fact was no *explanation* for the confusion and bewitchment which Paul now saw. Here there was something diabolical at work[36] which could only be uprooted by the summons to repent. "Do not be deceived; God is not mocked" (Gal. 6:7; cf. II Thess. 2:11).

In all these apostolic warnings we observe the same amazement at the fact of sin which enters believers' lives and estranges them from the riches of salvation. We see the apostles' awe and dismay at this menacing and disastrous apostasy. For that apostasy was completely incomprehensible against the curtain of God's salvation once given and received. Apostasy cannot be explained or "systematized," but can only be denounced and confessed as *guilt*. Elsewhere we read of those who "are surprised that you do not now join them in the same wild profligacy" (I Pet. 4:4). But Paul's surprise was of a very different kind. For him it was not holiness but *sin* that was so

admonition: "If we live by the Spirit, let us also walk by the Spirit" (Gal. 5:25).

33. Cf. H. Schlier, *Der Brief an die Galater*, 1949, p. 79: "unconstrained amazement." Also Matt. 3:7 and Luke 3:7.
34. Cf. *ibid.*; in connection with Gal. 1:6: "astonishment" ("Erstaunen"), p. 11.
35. *Ibid.*, p. 79.
36. Schlier, *ibid.*, speaks of a "demonic compulsion" ("ein dämonischer Zwang"). Paul does not name the devil in this connection.

strange. "How can we who died to sin still live in it?" (Rom.
6:2). Sanctification and grace are certainly a miracle but just
as certainly no riddle; indeed the only riddle in the Church
of Christ is the *riddle of man's sin*. Moreover, this is no riddle
of theoretical thought but of *sin within the Church*. How can
there be sin in that Church which has passed "out of death"
and "into life" and has also been "bought with a price" (I Cor.
6:20)?[37] For the Church has been purchased by the death of
Jesus Christ.

On the basis of these accents, some people have said that
the Apostle Paul knew nothing of sin in the Christian's living. Wernle has written as follows: "The question of how a
Christian finds peace with God when he sins is very important
for us; yet it never entered the mind of Paul since he excluded
sin from his description of the Christian's life."[38] Wernle has
explained this phenomenon "in terms of the enthusiastic belief
that marked the outset of the Messianic period." He has pointed
emphatically to Paul's words in Galatians 5:24: "And those who
belong to Christ Jesus have crucified the flesh with its passions
and desires." This sort of thinking, of course, may strike us as
rather contrived: yet we must certainly notice that Wernle has
an open eye for important aspects in the Pauline theology.[39]
Furthermore, these aspects may not be ignored. Especially is that
the case when we think of the fact of sin in believers' living.
We tend to think of our sin in a matter-of-fact way, as the
product of our "old life" which remains with us until the
eschaton. Our criticism of perfectionism is then quite easy. But
Wernle has reminded us that Paul did not see sin in this way,
and specifically spoke of our "old man" as crucified with Christ
(Rom. 6:6). It is simply wrong to ascribe a "normalcy" to sin

37. Greek: *ēgorásthēte gár timḗs*. The much-discussed relation between
the indicative and imperative in Paul, rightly seen, can also be illuminating here. It is untenable to deny the real force of the imperative in
Paul's ethics; yet the imperative does not stand in isolation from the
indicative but is completely involved in it. See also H. Preisker, *Das
Ethos des Urchristentums*, 1949, p. 65, on the imperative. Preisker
speaks "of the continual, always new, struggling apprehension of the
already accomplished renewal; of man's 'yes' to the indicative."

38. P. Wernle, *Der Christ und die Sünde bei Paulus*, 1897, pp. 89f.; cf. p.
104.

39. Wernle notes that in Paul too the imperative has a place, but he
wrongly speaks of a contradiction of which Paul himself was not
aware (p. 89). Cf. P. Althaus, *Paulus und Luther über den Menschen*,
1938, pp. 6-7, 66f.

on the strength of our "old man." Therefore we must listen to Paul's words on becoming one with Christ in a resurrection like his own (Rom. 6:5). For this we know, "that our old self was crucified with him so that the sinful body might be destroyed, and we might no longer be enslaved to sin" (6:6).

Thus the thrust of this New Testament witness has everything to do with the radical transfer from death to life as we find it expressed especially in Paul and John.[40] When sin raises its head in the Christian's living the entire New Testament finds occasion for surprise. Even to say that sin remains in that place which was cleansed by the reconciliation, death, and resurrection of Christ is to speak in a "riddle." For sin is no "explainable" or "tolerable" magnitude which may someday be known. Rather, it is thoroughly out of joint with the reality described by John: "Any one born of God does not sin, but He who was born of God keeps him, and the evil one does not touch him" (I John 5:18). Here John does not show himself the mere pendant of the Apostle Paul (as Wernle has suggested), for John too was standing in an urgent and imperative situation and had just given his advice concerning a brother who had erred (v. 16). For both John and Paul, sin in a Christian's living can only be seen as a riddle. It cannot be "analyzed" but can only be announced and renounced as that which "ought not be."

Sin, for the Christian, is unreasonable, idiotic, and incomprehensible in the light of God's love as *now revealed*. For now the "darkness is passing away and the true light is already shining" (I John 2:8). Lying and murdering belong to the class of things which are no longer done in the Church of Jesus Christ. Therefore they cannot be seen in a matter-of-fact way. In warning and confession they are treated as "strange" and out of harmony with the radical change which has taken place from "death to life" (I John 3:14). In contrast to any legalizing of sin and self-excuse we must see the enigmatic character and utter senselessness of sin. These are more apparent and perilous in the life of the *Church*. "Little children, keep yourselves from idols" (5:21). On that high note of warning John ends his book. Thus he ends in a mood that is reminiscent of the warn-

---

40. We think of such texts as Rom. 6:11: "So you also must consider yourselves dead to sin and alive to God in Christ Jesus"; also 6:13: "as men who have been brought from death to life"; and Eph. 4:20f. Cf. I John 3:14.

ings of God to ancient Israel. As the people of God's electing love, the people of Israel had also been set apart for his own service (Ex. 20:3).

The early Church faced this problem of the possibility and reality of sin (and even gross sin) in the lives of those who are called and baptized in Christ's name. In a number of debates she concerned herself with this problem and tried to maintain the sanctity of the Church. She noted the wide gap between this transfer from death to life and believers' own activity. With a good deal of hesitation, and a number of distinctions, she groped to find her way. Especially "public" sins came up for an extended debate. The Church was interested in the problem of apostasy in connection with this question: Is there an unending opportunity for repentance, or is there a limit of *but one?*[41]

Battle-lines were drawn between the "stricter" and more "mellow" views,[42] and a whole variety of motives now entered these debates. Yet the Church has always run the risk of describing this relation of sin and penance in categories that do less than justice to such a chapter as Hebrews 6. The anomaly and incongruity of sin in the Christian's radically-altered life have always posed a very difficult problem. Advocates of the more "mild" view have leaned hard on the scriptural vision of God's mercy; but this does little to solve the issue of "gross" and "public" sins. A heavy haze has hung over the controversy in the notion of "second repentance." Meanwhile, the proponents of the "stricter" view have contended, quite rightly, that the Christian's life is not a self-evident and rather legitimate "synthesis" of sin and grace. This is the danger which, despite their good intents, has constantly harassed the advocates of "mild" views. For central to all these reflections on penance and the Christian's living must always be the apostolic attitude of *amazement when Christians sin.* But those who stress the communion of believers and their Lord have more room for genuine amazement than those who try to reconcile the sinner's old self and the Christian's new life.[43]

41. Cf. Harnack, *History of Dogma,* II, 109; Bavinck, *Geref. Dog.,* IV, 122f.; H. Brink, *et al., Theologisch Woordenboek,* I, 1952, *s.v.* "Biecht," especially 539.
42. Bavinck, *op. cit.,* 221.
43. May it be clear that this in no way is a plea for an ethical rigorism. In the vastly complicated development of the Church's practice of

Therefore the riddle of sin can never be dissolved in the fellowship of the Church. It is precisely in the *Church* that it is wholly known and confessed as *very real*. Faith and the communion in love are the context in which the senselessness and the irrationality of sin are more and more both seen and renounced. A love to God and our fellowmen is not a solution to this riddle. In fact it leads us to a confession of guilt and the elimination of *any explanation at all*. Every effort to view man's sin in a rational system is repudiated in this confession of guilt and communion of love. In love we understand rightly and fully how senseless our sin is. Where love is lacking sin knows no bounds and is evident in all its meaninglessness and sham. "If I speak in the tongues of men and of angels, but have not love, I am a noisy gong or a clanging cymbal" (I Cor. 13:1). The godless man is a loveless man, for only God is love (I John 4:16).

Therefore when the grace of Christ reveals the true meaning of our lives in a love for God and our neighbors, the riddle of sin is not resolved but is *only known and confessed*. Sin is more and more acknowledged as lawlessness as we grow in love for the commandments of God which are holy and right and good. For sin is then seen as rebellion against God's blessing and "new scepter." It is then recognized as a "falling into the abyss" in contrast to standing before the face of God. If we speak of a *"mysterium iniquitatis"* at all, we must certainly realize that sin is not a mysterious force which somehow holds us in its grasp. The mystery of our sin is the mystery of that dark evil which can never be explained but can only be forgiven and eternally blotted out.

There is a French proverb which reads, *Tout comprendre, c'est tout pardonner:* to understand all is to forgive all. We need not discuss the meaning of that proverb in human affairs, but the statement itself is certainly striking in its reference to the inexplicability and irrationality of sin. In this context of our sin, the easy synthesis of understanding and forgiveness can only be rejected. Surely we hear of many motives for sin, and man is said to be "impotent"; we are also aware of the con-

penance we are only concerned here with motives which must be seen no matter what one's further analysis might be. For a fuller discussion, cf. J. Pohle, *Lehrbuch der Dogmatik*, III, 1922, 355-359; especially B. Poschmann, *Busse und letzte Oelung*, 1951.

sequences of lovelessness and rebellion, and of man's heart as the seat of his sin. Yet, the sin of man remains, as Bavinck once said, the "incomprehensible riddle."[44]

We have said, in this chapter, that we may not take that riddle lightly. Therefore it is well, in conclusion, to consider briefly another question which has always had an important bearing on the unfathomableness of sin. Is the Church's confession of "original sin" an attempt to explain away our sin? Do we "unriddle" our sin finally, if not in its ultimate beginning then possibly in its universality and spread? Is there a "causal relation" which makes this problem of sin pellucid within the bounds of fallen humanity? All these questions suggest the area of criticism which has constantly been lodged against the Church in her confession of "original sin." The doctrine of "original sin" has been regarded as a causal notion of *sheer fate,* or a doctrine which (by very definition) precludes a personal responsibility. Many have seen here the attempt to explicate our guilt in terms of "someone else."[45]

Now this is not the place to discuss if the Church's language in this regard has been entirely felicitous. Possibly the Church herself has given rise to a number of problems.[46] Certainly she has if she has incorporated a kind of "fatal" interpretation in her confessions, or has spoken in terms of a "causal explanation." The slogan, *tout comprendre, c'est tout pardonner,* would then be a completely valid translation of the concept: Do your own sinning, yet be without guilt. Man's sin would then be metaphysically "explainable."

Nonetheless, it is important to see why this doctrine has been misunderstood, in our own day, at its most *central point.* For

44. Bavinck, *op. cit.,* III, 125.
45. We think of those pungent words of Marsman, in his "Tempel en Kruis": "Geen dragender, doodlijker wonde / Dan het knagend en slepend besef / Van een schuld, een erflijke zonde / Bedreven voordat wij bestonden / En waarmee ook het vlees is besmet...." (No more vicious or deadly an injury / Than the gnawing and lingering concern / Of a guilt and inherited sinning / Committed before we existed, / Though by it our flesh is besmirched....) S. Vestdijk has cited these lines and has spoken of the heritage of Christianity from the ancient world: the purging of guilt and sin in a rational and fittingly human way. To this he has appended that Christianity renounced this inheritance and exchanged for it, gradually, "a sterilizing theology of metaphysical guilt-projection and fruitless compunction." Cf. his *Kunst en Droom,* 1957, p. 116; also *De Toekomst der Religie,* 1947, pp. 276f.
46. Cf. Part II of this volume.

the spread of sin and the power of sin participate entirely in the senselessness and reasonlessness of sin. Therefore, if the biblical *a priori* must guard the Church against the chasms of monism and dualism (or any other "explanation"), it must also guard the Church against backsliding at this very crucial juncture of her faith. Faith must know that we are cautioned against integrating sin in a crystal-clear or rational mold. We cannot give sense to the senseless. Therefore we confess (in an anti-dualist way) that sin is *contra voluntatem* but never *praeter voluntatem Dei.*[47] At the same time, we understand that this *non praeter* does not give sense to sin. It does not rationalize the irrational or legitimize the illegitimate. It may never detract from the reality of the *contra* which underscores the senselessness and riddle of man's sin.

47. Cf. my *Divine Election*, 1960, pp. 117-118.

CHAPTER SIX

SIN AND THE LAW

NOW THAT WE have treated of the enigma and inexplicability of sin, another question is bound to rise: Does the enigma of sin preclude a valid *knowledge of our sin?* That would certainly be the case if the inexplicability were a "mystery" (the *"mysterium iniquitatis"*) in the usual meaning of that term. The search for sin's knowledge could only then be a groping amid question marks, and sin's obscure nature could only darken our knowledge. We could still retain a consciousness of life's abnormality, or the havoc, devastation and gloom that are wreaked upon our world; we might even be aware of a power which here and there captures men's thinking, including, perhaps, our own. We might spin out our theories on the nature of evil and concern ourselves with the ominous and imminent threat that evil always is. Yet we will then be miles removed from a penetrating *knowledge of our sin.* Once we assume that sin is a *"mysterium iniquitatis,"* we shall never pierce the shroud of that deep "mystery."

But we have seen that the riddle of sin cannot be construed as such a "mystery." It is not the case that the "meaning" of sin is only rationally inappropriable to our minds. The riddle of sin is the motivelessness and senselessness of our own estrangement from God and his glory and fellowship. It is the riddle of *our sinning.* It is the riddle of turning our backs on the Father of lights, and rebelling against the good Lord of all life; of breaking our fellowship with him, and distrusting the only trustworthy One, and resisting his love and righteousness. Even the "unpardonable sin" of Scripture runs true to this form. It is blasphemy against the *Holy Spirit.* But if that be the riddle of sin (and the only real riddle) [1] it remains a mean-

---

1. Which need not deny that sin can manifest itself as something "mysterious," also in the sense of having its own mysterious allure. But this mystery is a mystery of creaturely reality, which itself is full of mys-

ingful question to ask *how sin is known*. This question com-
ports with the fact that Scripture (though nowhere explaining
our sin) speaks frequently and emphatically of this *knowledge
of our sin*. It enjoins us to acquire that knowledge and even
regards it as "necessary." Nowhere does it insinuate that the
road to this knowledge is easy; and nowhere does it minimize
sin's ignorance and denial of guilt. But what Scripture does
do is to open our eyes to seeing that the essence of sin is
to lay roadblocks to all true knowledge of our sin. Furthermore, this is what happens in the life of every man. Our knowledge of sin is constantly thwarted by sin's own deception and
sham, and its own manner of presenting itself to us and
tempting us.

Many efforts have been made to describe this manner and
form of sin. We are told that sin comes *sub specie boni,* or
under the appearance and the form of good.[2] Those who talk
this way lean on a statement of Paul himself and reflect with
him that "even Satan disguises himself as an angel of light" (II
Cor. 11:14). That statement finds its place in a polemic against
false prophets (the *"pseudapóstoloi"* of 11:13) or men who
disguise themselves as apostles of Christ though they know very
well the sort of "deceitful workmen" that they are. Paul then
adds: No wonder, for in so doing they show themselves the
servants of him who uses this same method — Satan himself.

Thus we hear of an apostleship that makes the pretension
and appearance of being true but is fashioned in the same mold
as Israel's false prophets. Recall the words, "Thus says Jahwe!"
Here the single example of Hananiah, in Jeremiah 28:11, is
easily multiplied. Nothing original can be seen in these "servants of Satan" who masquerade as "servants of righteousness"
(II Cor. 11:14). In that sense the appearance of the "pseudo-
apostles" is "not strange" (11:15), for they merely follow someone else. They are the viziers of one who uses light that darkness may triumph. And yet their purpose leaves no room for

teries, of "heights and depths" impenetrable for us. The *real riddle* of
sin does not lie on this level. On the mysteriousness of sin, cf. E.
Reisner, *Der Dämon und sein Bild,* 1955. The demonic is evident also
in the suggestion of something intriguing and problematical, contrasting
to the simplicity and unity of God. Cf. *ibid.,* p. 275.
2. Cf. Bavinck, *Geref. Dog.,* III, 119: *"sub ratione boni"* in connection with
the liar who assumes the appearance of the truth. "Sin is always doomed
to borrow its activity and appearance, despite itself, from virtue."
Bavinck speaks here of subjection to an inexorable *fatality.*

an open viziership. Camouflage and deceit, treachery, masquerade, metamorphosis, and deliberately taking on another schema
or form:[3] these are the methods that suit the purposes of the
devil. They are the methods of him who presents himself as an
"angel of light" and holds before men the deeds that are only
God's for the doing and the gifts that are only God's for the
giving. By means of his sinister methods his ministers deceive
men and blind their eyes. They confuse their minds and "keep
them from seeing the light of the gospel of the glory of Christ,
who is the likeness of God" (II Cor. 4:4). In this way of *metamorphosis* they conceal their nefarious designs. They make no
plea for an open choice of darkness but only blind men's eyes
by their brilliant show of light.

This is a dominant element in all of temptation, and it brings
to mind a number of intriguing questions. We need not look at
the metamorphosis *per se* or the issue of why men actually fall
for this "light" or "schema" in their lives.[4] Satan tries to lure
men into temptation, and to do so at the very same moment
as he obstructs their knowledge of their sin. We cannot conclude, from sin's enigma, that this knowledge is impossible; but
we must certainly appreciate that sin's effect is to confuse and
suppress the knowledge that we have. It is an amazing fact that
despite this metamorphosis of Satan the knowledge of our sin
is not totally eclipsed. Indeed, every mention of this metamorphosis or these blinding powers, in Scripture, has only this one
end: to lead us to a true knowledge and to sharpen our per-
ception of our sin. This is what Paul had in mind when he
wrote that "we are not ignorant" of Satan's designs (II Cor.
2:11). For within the concrete life of the Church the subtleties

3. The *schēma* that conceals its true nature (Grosheide, *Komm.*); the
light-*schēma* or "acting as if."
4. On this point cf. A. Maceina, *Das Geheimnis der Bösheit: Versuch einer
Geschichtstheologie des Widersachers Christi als Deutung der "Erzäh-
lung vom Antichrist" Solowjews,* 1955, in the chapter "Verstellung als
Wirkungsweise" (pp. 83f.). Maceina attempts — with an allusion to
Heidegger (man as "Hirt des Seins") — to explain the metamorphosis in
terms of the idea that man is essentially "creative" and cannot bear
"pure negation." "As bearer and propagator of non-being the devil finds
no access to the human spirit"; hence he must assume a "quasi-form of
being," the appearance of positivity (p. 83). On this disguise cf. C. S.
Lewis's *The Screwtape Letters* and Denis de Rougemont's *Le part du
diable.*

of Satan are seen for what they are[5] and the way to true knowledge and insight is disclosed. This holds not only for sins of an
obvious "temptation" and "allure" but for sins of every kind. We
have a *knowledge* of the truth and a *knowledge* of our sin
through the "anointing by the Holy One." "But you have been
anointed by the Holy One, and you all know" (I John 2:20).[6]

Obviously, the inexplicability of sin does not exclude forever the knowledge which we have of sin. Here we do not mean
a knowledge that we gather from all kinds of contact with evil:
for the mere fact of that contact is far too obvious to be denied,
as is also the fact that there results therefrom a certain "knowledge." This kind of "knowledge" implies a general human propensity for distinguishing good and evil;[7] it suggests that sin
is no hidden magnitude in the inner chambers of our hearts.[8]
Rather it betrays itself in the fullness of our lives. It works its
havoc, and chaos, and disaster, and disruption in reality. Furthermore, it does so in a manner that we cannot but notice.
But our question of the knowledge of sin involves a very different kind of understanding of our sin. We are not concerned
merely with the disastrous and calamitous consequences but also
with the very *nature of sin itself*. In that question we touch on
the heart of our problem concerning the knowledge of our sin.
When we notice the deepest nature and intention of sin we
reject forever a mere "phenomenology of evil" which sees the
evil in others and merely acknowledges our own "chagrin."
At that level, of course, it is entirely too easy to observe the
splinter in our brother's eye and to ignore completely the
beam in our own.[9]

The sharpest criticism of Scripture is levelled against the
commonness and extent of this kind of knowledge. Scripture
does not deny the possibility of finding a splinter in someone
else; instead, it warns us against the distortion of that knowledge into a notion of "isolation" or "fragmentation," or a con-

5. Cf. Grosheide and F. J. Pop, commentaries, *ad loc.*
6. Cf. v. 21 on the contrast between lies and truth and the knowing of
   truth as opposed to the manifestations of Antichrist (vv. 18f.). These
   manifestations are revealed *as lies* in the light of the truth known.
7. Cf. my *General Revelation*, 1955, Chap. 8, and *Man: the Image of God*,
   1962, Chap. 5.
8. Cf. E. Brunner, *Der Mensch im Widerspruch*, 1937, p. 186. Even in the
   depths of man's heart evil is sometimes traced and indicated. One thinks
   of Camus's analysis of human egocentricity in *La Chute*.
9. Cf. my *Man: the Image of God*, pp. 26-27.

cept that fails to do justice to the solidarity of sin. The
"splitting up" in much of sin's "knowledge" can only emphasize the invalidity of this approach. For the very hallmark of
this "knowledge" is that, despite our moral sensitivities, we are
still far removed from applying to *ourselves* the scriptural statement that God *"searches our hearts"* (Ps. 139:1, 23). Thus even
in this real "knowledge" it is possible that sin reveals itself
with a stubborn pertinacity and manifests itself in our fleeing
from the knowledge of *our sins before the holy God.*

The prophet Jeremiah reminded us of the perversity of man's
heart and underscored its treacherous deceit. "Who can understand it?" (17:9). Similarly, the New Testament asserts that no
one among men "knows a man's thoughts except the spirit of
the man which is in him" (I Cor. 2:11). This reference permits
us to speak of a certain natural self-knowledge which men have
in and of themselves. But there is also a knowledge that Paul
points to by stressing that "so also no one comprehends the
thoughts of God except the Spirit of God" (2:11). In that same
light it is obvious that the knowledge of man's true nature
before God (in the deepest dimensions of his being) is by no
means natural or self-evident. There is no hint that man's
knowledge, in and of himself, has anything to do with a true
knowledge of his own sin. Rather, the criticism which we often
level against others can only betray the relativity and arbitrariness of our own criteria and norms. Surely when we look at
ourselves our vision is blind.

It is the Spirit, but not man, who "searches everything, even
the depths of God" (I Cor. 2:10). When a man (who knows
only a "man's thoughts") himself searches into these things his
viewpoint is naturally colored by the apostasy of his own
heart.[10] The result is that sin's blinding effect must rob a man
of any power to see rightly the life of someone else, to say nothing of his own. It deprives a man of the capacity to know life
in its inner nature and depths. The essence of sin is to blind and
to conceal; and therefore the sinner is unable to perceive and
to discover, or to measure the depths of his own life.[11] This is
the case also when he recognizes the faults and foibles of someone else and even (to a certain extent) himself. The mere
knowledge of life's teeming abnormalities or disruptions is a far
cry from acknowledging *our sin.* For sin is not an abstract or a

10. Cf. *ibid.,* Chap. 1.
11. Cf. K. Barth, *K.D.,* IV/1, 532 (ET, 479).

neutrally observable phenomenon. Sin is guilt. It is guilt before
the holy God and guilt in relation to God; and therefore it can
only be known and understood in relation *to God*. It can only
be known in the relation of man's own alienation and rejection. Because man's sin stands in this relation to God, we can
rightly speak of the "ignorance" of sin but never of sin's
"excuse." We are not excused because we "did not know."
Rather we must speak of the *guilt* of ignorance and self-alienation in which a man *does not recognize himself in sin*.[12]

This clouding of man's eyes is the natural product of his
self-alienation from God. It is implied in his own dreadful and
idiotic choice of disobedience, and his own arrogance in making his own distinctions of good and evil. The tempter, in the
paradise story, suggested that man's eyes would be opened in
the way of disobedience and autonomy, and that, "knowing
good and evil," man would be like God (Gen. 3:5).[13] What
actually happened is that by transgressing God's commandment
the eyes of man were closed.[14] The commandment became an
alien problem in the moment that man took leave of that
fellowship in which it was *no problem at all*. By choosing his
own way (and his own freedom) man proceeded to grope in
the dark. With all his distinctions of good and evil there was
only one way to escape the limitless caprice of his own judgments. That was *God's way,* in which the true knowledge of
sin and the true distinction of good and evil are revealed.
Only in the way of dependency is man attracted anew, in

12. When Scripture speaks of ignorance there is anything but a self-excuse
    implied. We read of ignorance, not-knowing, *ágnoia* in Acts 3:17
    ("And now, brethren, I know that you acted in ignorance, as did also
    your rulers"); but thereupon follows a call to repent and "turn again,
    that your sins may be blotted out" (3:19). So too, we read of the
    "ignorance that is in them" (*ágnoia;* Eph. 4:18), but also of the
    "futility of their minds," being "darkened in their understanding,"
    "alienated," having "given themselves up to licentiousness, greedy to
    practise every kind of uncleanness" (4:17ff.). Cf. Acts 17:30 ("the times
    of ignorance") and I Tim. 1:13: Paul persecuted the Church "ignorantly
    in unbelief" and calls himself, in this connection, a "blasphemer" and
    the "foremost of sinners" (vv. 13, 15). We shall return to this point in
    the second part of this volume, under the heading of "The Gravity
    and Gradation of Sin" (Chap. 9).
13. Cf. R. Schippers, *Levensvragen,* pp. 276f.
14. Cf. G. von Rad, *Das erste Buch Mose,* I, 1953, who finds it character-
    istic that the fall was not a matter of "moral evil" but of man's *hýbris*
    in not respecting his limits (p. 72).

childlike faith, to God's new command. Only by pursuing that way does he cease from abusing, in an autonomous fashion, the distinction of good and evil. Only then does he begin where he should: by seeing his own life in focus. "Let us test and examine our ways, and return to the Lord!" (Lam. 3:40).[15] In the light of God's revelation the earlier hiddenness is now radically altered.

Witness here the case of David, who first saw evil in detachment and then condemned it with a moral sensitivity. "As the Lord lives, the man who has done this deserves to die" (II Sam. 12:5).[16] Only thereafter, when confronted by Nathan's "You are the man," did he acknowledge his own guilt. "I have sinned against the Lord" (12:7, 13). In this uncovering of guilt the *kálymma* is torn away and the knowledge of our sin is transformed from an instrument of mere complacency to the open acknowledgment of guilt.[17] Only a confession before God's face can bring a pure recognition of ourselves in contrast to the foolishness of human self-knowledge.

And yet the question remains: In what *way* does this true knowledge of our sin arise? We can point (and we must) to divine revelation, but still we are prompted to ask: Along what *avenue* does revelation come in its exposure of our sin? The urgency of this question is obvious to anyone who appreciates the intimacy of the Scripture's conjoining man's knowledge and confession with the appropriation of God's salvation in *forgiveness of sins*. We do well to remember Christ's words that not the healthy but the sick are in need of a physician (Mark 2:17). So too, it is not the deniers but the *confessors of guilt who are forgiven*.

One must be on guard against recasting this scriptural correlation of confession-and-salvation into the common equation that "penance equals merit." But we should be just as wary of depreciating that correlation itself. In fervent tones the Scripture upholds the necessity of this bond. "If we confess our sins, he is faithful and just, and will forgive our sins and cleanse us from all unrighteousness" (I John 1:9). All such confessions stand in contrast to self-deception and the denial

15. LXX: *exēreunéthē*. Cf. I Cor. 2:10.
16. That the name of the Lord is invoked, as an oath, in no way alters the "objectivity" of guilt but only accentuates its blindness.
17. Cf. the confession of the publican in contrast to the self-deception of the Pharisee (Luke 18:11ff.).

of our sins, and thus to the exposure of how little the truth is in us (1:8). Scripturally viewed, confession is not the ground or the cause of God's pardon; but it does form the avenue or way along which salvation is received and experienced. The distance that separates those who think they are healthy from the physician only enunciates the importance of this confession-and-forgiveness correlate. No wonder that this correlate is frequently incorporated in biblical themes of warning and comfort: "He who conceals his transgressions will not prosper, but he who confesses and forsakes them will obtain mercy" (Prov. 28:13). Therefore Israel's prophets called her back constantly to this knowledge and acknowledgment: "Only acknowledge your guilt, that you rebelled against the Lord your God" (Jer. 3:13; cf. 2:23). Knowledge of sin and acknowledgment of guilt are indissolubly related to each other and are, at bottom, one. Making known our sins to God is only the reverse side, in the scriptural view, of God's forgiveness (cf. Ps. 32:3, 5; 51:5-6).

All of which suggests that the question we are now proposing is a very crucial one. What is the source of the knowledge of our sin? How is our sin *known?* This question is important for anyone engaged in pastoral work or preaching. At the same time, in the history of the Church and her theology, the question of the *modus* of divine revelation has always been a topic of dispute. Men have been at odds in the answers they have given. Though they have agreed that only divine revelation can make sin known, they have parted company on the issue of whether, within that revelation, the *law or the Gospel reveals.* But what can be the meaning of such a dilemma as that?

It is impossible to discuss the law, as the source of the knowledge of sin, apart from a continual reference to the Gospel. Therefore if we give a prior consideration to the law, we shall still be concerned with the Gospel throughout. At the same time, it is advisable to look first at the law, if only because so many have said that *not the Gospel but the law* teaches us our miseries. In their view a clear-cut choice can be made in this "dilemma." Not wanting to diminish from the Gospel, they assign to the law the exposure of our sin and reinforce their claims by appealing to such statements as we find in the Heidelberg Catechism (Q. and A. 3): "Whence do you know your misery? Out of the law of God." It is hard to think of anything that is more definitely stated than this. Moreover, the same "exclusiveness" would seem to be implied in Lord's Day 44. God's will, we read, is that the ten commandments be "strictly preached," in order that "all our life long we may learn more and more to know our sinful nature" (Q. and A. 115).

Thus the revealing function of the law is defined in its lasting significance for life. Furthermore, it is defined not only in the Catechism's section on misery (*usus elenchticus* or *paedagogicus*) but also in its chapter on gratitude (*usus normativus* or *didacticus*). Certainly we may say that the Catechism does not isolate the law to some corner of its own. The knowledge of misery in Lord's Day 2 is set deeply in the context of deliverance and thankfulness, and Lord's Day 44 is embedded in the theme of God's forgiveness. But the presence of this context in no way detracts from the fact that both these references point us incontrovertibly to *law*. They point us to the *sin-disclosing function of the law*. Not only confessionally but also dogma-historically, that fact is of great significance. For Lutherans especially have chided Reformed theology for demoting the law's function in the Christian's living to a merely informational role. In so doing, according to the Lutherans, the Reformed have conceived of the *tertius usus legis* as a normative "informing" of believers concerning the will of God.

Werner Elert, in particular, has followed this line of thought. He has pointed to Calvin's formulation of the law as the "rule of just and good living" and has also accused Calvin of having an open eye for only the law's "informational task."[18] Calvin regarded the law, according to Elert, not so much as the instrument for knowing *sin* as for knowing *God's command;* furthermore, the command of God was known as only a *Weisung* or a "rule of direction" for Christian living. Small wonder, then, that Calvin conceived of his third *usus* of the law as the law's "principal" function.[19] Though such terms as *praecipuus* and *tertius* do not permit us to speak of an "exclusive" function of the law, yet Elert finds in Calvin a tendency to view the law, in the Christian's living, as *informational instead of revela-*

18. W. Elert, "Gesetz und Evangelium," in *Zwischen Gnade und Ungnade,* pp. 136ff.
19. "The third and principal use, which pertains more closely to the proper purpose of the law, finds its place among believers in whose hearts the Spirit of God already lives and reigns" (*Inst.,* II, 7, 12). Cf. Bavinck on the "usus didacticus normativus" as the principal use (*Geref. Dog.,* IV, 435).

tional. Thus he regarded the law, according to Elert, as something regulative and legislative. Calvin inclined to recognize
the "possibility of a nomological existence in which the law
does not oppose those who fall in line with it."[20] But with that
conception, in Elert's judgment, he broke with both Luther[21]
and the Gospel itself. He ignored the fact that the law of
Scripture is given *not merely for information* (even for believers) *but also for judgment.* In this perspective of "not only
but also" there might have been a possibility for a further
discussion; but that very possibility shrivels up when Elert sees
Calvin in such a strongly legalistic scheme. In Calvin, according to Elert, we find "the decisive regulation of the human
relation to God" by means of *law.*[22]

Now we must certainly observe what is happening here. For
Calvin's intention was by no means to fashion a legalism but
only to understand the will of the Lord; furthermore, in that
concern the revealing function of the law was not excluded.
And yet, the issue is wider than a mere interpretation of Calvin
and has bearing on the entire function of the law in Reformed
Churches. That being the case, it is important to notice that the
revealing character of the law, in Lord's Day 44, is bound up
with the Catechism's preceding discussion of the Decalogue.
Obviously, the Catechism does not mean to set at loggerheads the
"revealing" and "instructional" functions of the law. It is not
true that Lord's Days 34 through 44*a* demarcate radically the
law as "informational" in contrast to the "revelational" function
which appears in Lord's Day 44*b*. For already in the discussion
of the Decalogue this "information" is interlaced with a demonstration and a revelation of sin. Therefore it is *in* seeing the
law as a rule of gratitude, and *while* analyzing the command
of God, that the Catechism adjures us to return from our sinful ways.[23] With no tension or inconsistency at all, it proceeds
from this analysis to enjoin a "strict preaching" of the law,
"that all our life long we may learn more and more to know

20. Elert, *op. cit.,* p. 166. Cf. also his *Das christliche Ethos: Grundlinien
    der lutherischen Ethik,* 1949, pp. 394f.
21. Elert sees in the *Inst.,* II, 7, 12 a conscious polemic against Luther,
    since Calvin there applied to the *tertius usus* the same expressions
    (*praecipuus* and *proprius*) that Luther, in his *Galater-Vorlesung,* re-
    served for the *usus elenchticus.*
22. Elert, "Gesetz und Evangelium," p. 168; *Das christliche Ethos,* p. 395.
23. Cf. its treatments of idolatry (Q. 95), image worship (Q. 96), swear-
    ing and cursing (Q. 100); also QQ. 105, 108, 114.

our sinful nature" (Q. 115). Thus our purpose must be to live "not only according to some but according to all the commandments of God" (114). Since the very nature of God's command transcends the "antithesis" of information *versus* revelation, there can be no incongruity here at all. Exactly *in* its command-character ("you shall not") the law discloses our sin and points the way to the will of God (cf. Rom. 12:1-2).

All of this, of course, has a very important bearing on the battle waged concerning the relation of the *tertius usus legis* to the so-called *usus elenchticus*. This has always been a big issue between the Lutheran and Reformed, to say nothing of the Lutheran factions themselves in the Sixteenth Century. It is well known that Luther, at odds with Melanchthon, admitted of no such thing as a *tertius usus legis*.[24] That very idea could not be integrated within his total theology.[25] But not for a moment can Luther be charged with inclining toward an antinomian position; he certainly exemplified (as Elert has said) a "joyfully obedient inquiring after God's will."[26] R. Bring has stated that he never entertained the idea "that the Christian is *not subject to the law*."[27] But where, then, is the real issue at stake? Bring concludes that "precisely the true believer stands

24. Elert, "Gesetz und Evangelium," pp. 161f., takes note of Luther's dispute with the Antinomians and argues — on good grounds — that it rests on a falsification, taken over from the later *Loci* of Melanchthon. G. Ebeling, in his own analysis, has come to the same conclusion; "Zur Lehre vom triplex usus legis in der reformatorischen Theologie," *Theologische Literaturzeitung*, 1950, pp. 235f. Cf. further O. Dittrich, *Luthers Ethik*, 1930, p. 76.

25. Cf. R. Bring, "Kennt die lutherische Theologie eine 'dritte Gebrauch des Gesetzes'?" in Thielicke-Schrey, *Glaube und Handeln*, p. 158; also G. Wingren, "Evangelium und Gesetz," in *Antwort*, 1956, p. 321. The differences among Lutheran theologians themselves, at this point, are frequently pronounced; think, for example, of Wingren's criticism of Barth's "gospel-law" order (*ibid.*, pp. 315f.), in contrast to N. H. Søe's *Christliche Ethik*, 1957², pp. 49f. Søe speaks of the "law of God as an aspect of the Gospel" and refers to the dependence of the law, "in every respect," upon the Gospel (p. 51). Cf. also his "Gedanken zur Auseinandersetzung zwischen K. Barth und der lutherischen Theologie," in *K.u.D.*, 1956, p. 228, where he indicates that already in 1933 he had set himself "against the traditional order of 'law and Gospel' " (p. 229).

26. Elert, *op. cit.*, p. 176. Elert adds that the Decalogue has no function in this regard, since it knows only *prohibitions*.

27. Bring, *op. cit.*, p. 165.

under the law."[28] And yet, if this be the case, then why do we still find such a sharp rejection of the *tertius usus?*

We are told that the relation between God and believers cannot be described in a "nomological" way. That is to say, it cannot be described in terms of the law and works.[29] It is only in the light of the Gospel that this relation is really set forth. Though the law has significance for the Christian's living, we may not refer to that function of the law as a *"tertius usus."* There is "no new usage over and beyond the other two forms of application." Rather, the *usus elenchticus* "has a full and complete validity for the Christian" which "no rebirth or conversion and no faith" are able to change.[30] Not a *"tertius usus"* but only the *usus elenchticus* holds valid for the lives of believers. There can be no separate function of the law for *"renati."* There can be no function that has nothing to do with the *usus elenchticus.*

This means that the *usus legis* is never, in the lives of the faithful, a mere "regulation by means of information." For the law discloses something and is still necessary so long as a believer is *peccator;* and a believer is *peccator* even though he is *simul justus.* The reality of the "old man" is still with us and must still be reckoned with.[31] Therefore the believer has not put the struggle "behind himself"; he is likewise in need of the disclosing and revealing function of the law. Being a sinner, he is still under the law; that is to say, he still stands under the *usus elenchticus.* For that reason it is wrong to lay on Lutherans the charge of an antinomianism.[32] The Lutheran concern is

---

28. *Ibid.*
29. Cf. the interpretation of Bring: "The law prescribes definite works in which obedience should be shown to God" (*Das Verhältnis von Glauben und Werken in der lutherischen Theologie,* 1955, p. 159). Such a statement is intended to counteract a legalistic peril and accentuate the antithesis of law and Gospel; the antithesis is between a fancied way of salvation through works and the true *via salutis.* In this connection we should also note the debate over the "necessity" of good works. Cf. Seeberg, *Dogmengeschichte,* IV, 2, 488, on the declaration of the Synod of Eisenach, 1556, and the statement of Otto: "summa ars Christianorum est: nescire legem, ignorare opera." The fact that he added "in hoc articulo" points out the background of the struggle. Cf. further O. Ritschl, *Dogmengeschichte des Protestantismus,* II, 417.
30. Bring, in *Glaube und Handeln,* p. 165.
31. Cf. *ibid.,* p. 159.
32. Cf. *ibid.,* pp. 165-166. Even the Lutherans who rejected the *tertius*

for the true (i.e., the elenchtic) function of the law within the
Christian's living.[33]

Yet if we reject the *tertius usus* we find ourselves before a
very difficult problem. It simply remains the case that believers
too are still called upon to obey and honor God's will. Moreover, this is true despite the dread which we might have for
a new works-legalism. Obviously, this is a point that is never
conceded by an antinomianism. But where, then, is the controversy? Are we involved in a merely terminological debate? Is
the whole issue here a logomachy, or a struggle in which all of
us are concerned to do justice to the "obedience of God's
command"?[34] Even if that were the case, it must still be said
that there is a strong reactionary tendency in the Lutheran
aversion to the *tertius usus*. Why should that be so? It is not by
chance that the Lutheran appeals for a "new obedience" have
shied away from speaking of the *"law."* They have given a
preference to such terms as *"Weisung," "Paraklese," "Paraenese,"*
even the *command of God, obedience to do his will,* and the like.
This very choice of words, however, in opposition to the concept
of *law,* is part of the Lutheran reaction against legalism. The
attempt is made to bolster this argument by enlisting the New
Testament itself. Therefore we hear of "the reluctance to describe the evangelical admonition as law" and the "avoidance
of the law-concept" within the New Testament.[35] One need
not add that such a terminological bias can never do justice to
the New Testament writings. In all of these efforts there is an
obvious attempt to get around the New Testament references
to *law.*[36]

---

usus *legis* in the Sixteenth Century did not deny the significance of the
usus *elenchticus* for Christian living. Otto, for example, saw the difference from Agricola's antinomianism at exactly this point. Cf. W.
Joest, *Gesetz und Freiheit: das Problem des tertius usus legis bei
Luther und die N.T. Paraenese,* 1951, p. 50; Ritschl, *op. cit.,* p. 416.

33. In the *tertius usus* Bring finds a tendency in the direction of "pietism"
(also seen in Melanchthon) — an inclination to speak of "converts"
and "regenerated" for whom the *tertius usus* was valid. For these
"renati" the usus *elenchticus* was discarded (*op. cit.,* p. 159).

34. Cf. Ritschl, *op. cit.,* p. 420, who contends that proponents and opponents of the *tertius usus* did not stand so far apart. Also the views
of H. Gollwitzer, in *Antwort,* 1956, and Søe in *Christliche Ethik,* pp.
106f.

35. E. Schlink, "Gesetz und Paraklese," in *Antwort,* p. 333.

36. Schlink points to *entolé,* as used by John, instead of *nómos.* When
James speaks of "law," Schlink sees the way paved for a "legaliz-

This reactionary strain is very apparent in the case of Bring. In opposition to Otto Ritschl, he contends that the old squabble between the proponents and opponents of the *tertius usus* is a matter of very great importance. This is because the proponents insist on viewing the Christian's life "fundamentally in terms of law."[37] We must be very clear, however, that the acceptance of the *tertius usus* was never meant to cancel out the *usus elenchticus*. Apparently the term *tertius* has caused an unfortunate misunderstanding. When taken by itself it might possibly suggest a new working of the law which has a special bearing on the Christian's life, or a function exclusive of the other two. It might also imply an "orientational" or "informational" role, or even the idea of a "supplanting." But once we see that this was never the intention of the *tertius usus,* we shall find it very difficult to understand precisely why the refutations have frequently blossomed into such acrimonious critiques. Especially Calvin has been misinterpreted in his statement that the *tertius usus* is the "principal use" of the law. Many regard that as a degradation of the *usus elenchticus*. But when Calvin spoke of the law's "principal use," or "proper purpose,"[38] he was by no means suggesting a legalistic outlook on the whole of Christian living. He wished to stress the significance of God's command for the lives of believers in God's new government of grace.

ing of the message" (*ibid.,* p. 334). He has to acknowledge that Paul "occasionally" includes commandments of the law in his *paraklese* (Rom. 13:9), and that he sees love as the fulfillment of the law (*nómos,* 13:10). Cf. Schlink (pp. 327, 333) on "the singular and paradoxical expressions" of Paul in Rom. 8:2, Gal. 6:2, and I Cor. 9:21 (*nómos* throughout). Note also the unsatisfying views of P. Althaus, *Gebot und Gesetz,* 1952 (*entolé* opposed to *nómos*), which betray the same difficulties with Paul. Althaus — curiously — attempts to find a way out in regard to Rom. 13:8 by qualifying: "where, however, the love-command, as the meaning of the law, comes into its place" (p. 9). His concern is for the will of God, what is well-pleasing to him, and the commandment of God; in Althaus, too, James represents an "exceptional case" (p. 10; "Sonderstellung"). Althaus even gives a separate chapter to discussing how "through the fall the commandment became law" (pp. 14ff.). It is clear, however, that *also* in regard to the *command* of God, one can think as much on what he *can* or possibly *has done,* as in reference to the *law.* For both of these (as they were in Paul) are identical. Thus a reaction against legalism should not lead one to oppose the *tertius usus;* for the thrust of that *usus,* too, is obedience to God's will.

37. Bring, *op. cit.,* p. 226.
38. *Inst.,* II, 7, 12. Cf. Søe, *op. cit.,* pp. 108ff.

This fact is obvious in his argument against those who simply
say that the law is "abrogated." We are free from the curse of
the law only because Christ, in fulfilling the law, came to earth
to heal us transgressors of the law.[39] For *that reason* (or because
of *that healing*) the doctrine of the law is unimpaired through
Christ. Therefore Calvin drew the conclusion that the *usus
elenchticus* and the *usus normativus* have everything to do with
each other and are virtually interfused. "By teaching, admonish-
ing, reproving, and correcting," the law "forms us and prepares
us for every good work."[40]

In short, the *tertius usus* has nothing to do with a vision of
believers which elevates them above all sin and strife. It is bound
up in an unbreakable union with the law's elenchtic function.
We have seen this already in Question 115 of the Heidelberg
Catechism. The dilemma of revelation *versus* information is
completely unacceptable, and Bring's argument against the
tertius usus (and his pains to show that the believer is *simul
justus et peccator* and needs the concrete *usus elenchticus*) is
really quite irrelevant. Bring has set up a straw man. All the
more is that apparent when we remember the injunction of
Lord's Day 44 that the ten commandments ought to be "strictly
preached."

Consider, too, that when Lutheran theology itself has spoken
of the *tertius usus,* its purpose has never been to supplant the
usus elenchticus by the *usus normativus.* This was obviously not
Melanchthon's intent, though we readily agree that problems
remain in his interpretation of the law.[41] When Melanchthon
spoke of the *tertius usus "in renatis"* he was constantly concerned
about the law's "normative" and "orienting" function. The will
of God was held before believers "that they might learn certain
works." Yet in discussing the *tertius usus,* he gave a prominent
place to the law's elenchtic element. Through the law we come
more and more to know our sin.[42] This same accent is sounded

---

39. *Inst.,* II, 7, 14.
40. *Ibid.: docendo, admonendo, obiurgando, corrigendo.*
41. We think especially of the problem of order or sequence as found in
    Melanchthon; also the relation of the law to the *"lex naturalis,"* which
    was obviously of influence in his total view of the law (including the
    tertius usus). Cf. W. H. Neuser, *Der Ansatz der Theologie Philipp
    Melanchthons,* 1957, especially pp. 85, 103f.
42. The faithful are freed from the curse of the law, but "interim tamen
    docenda est Lex, quae reliquias peccati indicat, *ut crescat agnitio pec-
    cati* et poenitentia et simul sonet Evangelium de Christo, ut crescat

in the final version of the Lutheran Formula Concordiae, where again the *tertius usus* is endorsed but with no supplanting of "revelation" and "disclosure" for the sake of "information." Rather, the place of the law is indicated in the midst of the still-imperfect lives of believers.[43]

What we have said will give us an adequate basis to reflect on the law of God as a source for the knowledge of our sin. Where both Lutheran and Reformed theologies have emphasized this function they have done so in direct relation to the *tertius usus*. Witness the Formula Concordiae and the Heidelberg Catechism. Both Churches have had an open eye for the accusatory character of the law which extends to the lives of believers. Therefore when Elert and others remind us that the law convicts "even Christians," we can only reply that not only Lutherans but also Reformed have never cast out the *usus elenchticus*. They have never made this attempt by appealing, for example, to such a text as I Timothy 1:9. There we read that "the law is not laid down for the just but for the lawless and disobedient, for the ungodly and sinners, for the unholy and profane."

The Formula Concordiae felt obliged to take up this text; but it did so in its reference to the *tertius usus*. It observed that Paul did not desire to say "that the righteous should live without law" or that such a conclusion is valid on the basis of this text.[44] Paul was responding to those "teachers of the law" who forgot that the law itself is a taskmaster for sinners. These people manipulated the law (by trying to make it more "legal") to such an extent that they understood neither "what they are saying" nor "the things about which they make assertions" (I

fides." So reads the often-quoted reference to the *tertius usus* in Melanchthon's *Loci praecipui theologiae*, 1559. Cf. H. Engelland, *Melanchthons Werke*, II, 1, 1952, 325-326.

43. The main example of this is in the *Epitome* (J. T. Müller, *Bekenntnisschriften*, pp. 536f.): believers are freed from the curse of the law but are not without law. Their renewal is still in its beginning-stage; they remain in the midst of strife. Thus they still have need of the perpetual illumination of the law ("opus est, ut homini lex Dei semper praeluceat," p. 537); so that the old Adam might not exercise his own will but follow the Spirit, being constrained "admonitionibus et minis legis." Cf. the *Solida Declaratio* (Müller, p. 640) where the law is cited, in reference to Psalms 1 and 119, as the *mirror* "in which the will of God, or what is pleasing to him, is actually portrayed" (*ibid.*).

44. *Ibid.*

Tim. 1:7). Paul's objection to this legalistic practice is evident from what he says about "the divine training that is in faith" as well as the *goal of admonition:* namely, a "love that issues from a pure heart and a good conscience and sincere faith" (1:4-5).[45] The interest is by no means the "antithesis" of spontaneity and God's law! For the only antithesis we find is that between faith and love, on the one hand, and the practice of legalism, on the other. The Pauline argument is that a "new law" could once again remove the Christian's living from God's grace.[46]

It is very important to see that there is no inconsistency here between the *usus elenchticus* and the *usus normativus.* This fact hangs together with the nature of the law itself. For the law, in exercising both these functions, exercises them *simultaneously* and conjoins them in the *single commandment of God.* Therefore, within that single commandment, the sin of man is announced and renounced, and the way of obedience is once again pointed out. God's law does not confront us as two isolated functions of "revelation" and "information" but only as a single commandment that both condemns and directs. It negatively prohibits and positively enjoins. Furthermore, it does so in a single act and time. In this spirit the Formula Concordiae underscores the "two-sidedness" of God's law. "But the law of God prescribes good works for believers in such a way that *at one and the same time,* as in a mirror, it both shows and teaches that these works are imperfect and unclean in us throughout this life."[47] The prohibition-character of most of the commandments in the Decalogue ("you shall not") illumines the path of

45. We think of Gal. 5:23, in this connection, where Paul, having summed up the fruits of the Spirit, continues: "against such there is no law." The intention is clear: there is no condemnation where the fruits of the Spirit are evident. If not in this text, then certainly in I Tim. 1:9, the men are named for whom the law is not set forth. Obviously, such references do not permit us to make a case for antinomianism; cf. Gal. 5:25, 6:2. On such conclusions, cf. Calvin, in his commentary on I Tim. 1:9, where he lays strong accent on Paul's polemic against those opponents who arm themselves with the law "adversus pios viros, veram legis regulam tota vita exprimentes." Concerning this "antithesis" between spontaneity and command it is instructive to note the contenders against the *tertius usus* in the Sixteenth Century (cf. Joest, *op. cit.,* pp. 50ff.). Otto, e.g., spoke of the "direct union of man's redeemed will and the will of God," in contrast to command. It is evident that here too the *usus elenchticus* is in peril.

46. Cf. P. A. van Stempvoort, *Oud en Nieuw,* 1951, p. 165.

47. Müller, p. 644.

disobedience and *(precisely in that way)* the path of obedience as well.[48] There can be no inconsistency between the law's disclosure and instruction, its revelation and its *Weisung,* its elenchtic and its normative usages.[49]

Surely the Reformers spoke, in a very emphatic way, of the revealing and disclosing function of the law. But what does it mean (as we find in Lord's Day 2) that we know the greatness of our misery from God's law? Obviously it does not mean that the law itself embraces an *objective* "knowability" or "clarity" apart from the question of how a man, through the law, comes to know his sin.[50] We are talking, at this point, of the *knowledge of sin* and how we come to have *that knowledge.* Is the law our only source, or can we also point to the Gospel? If we assume that we have that knowledge, have we come to have it by the *law alone?* Often this relation of the law and the knowledge of sin has been seen as a matter that is self-explanatory and even "exclusive." Men have regarded this knowledge as analogous to the knowledge we have of civil infractions as we study legal

48. This is obvious already in the first commandment: "You shall have no other gods before me" (Ex. 20:3). Cf. Deut. 6:4 and especially 6:13-14: "You shall fear the Lord your God; . . . you shall not go after other gods. . . ."

49. Cf. R. Schippers, *De Gereformeerde Zede,* 1954, p. 197. One can make distinction between a threefold use but there is "still always the same function of the one law of God."

50. Wingren (*op. cit.,* p. 319) takes issue with Barth's sequence of "Gospel-law" and contends that here everything is oriented to the problem of knowledge ("totale Dominanz der Wissensfrage"). In that way the law's demand (which actually precedes, and is independent of, knowledge) is watered down. This criticism is lodged, in particular, against Barth's judgment on the "Bürgergemeinde" in the light of the "Christengemeinde." Yet it is obvious that we cannot see the *central* question in the problem of order so long as we discuss the problems of the *usus civilis* in such a free and uncritical manner, as though a clear *isolating* of the *usus civilis* were possible. For reflections on the *usus civilis,* cf. Bonhoeffer, *Ethik,* 1949, pp. 237-239 ("Die Lehre vom *primus usus legis* nach den lutherischen Bekenntnisschriften"). Cf. the problem in the Formula Concordiae (*Solida Declaratio;* Müller, p. 635) concerning the "nuda legis praedicatio" ("sine mentione Christi"), which "hypocritas efficiat," and therefore: *"Christus* legem in manus suas sumit, eamque spiritualiter explicat."* The problem is much more complicated than is evident in Wingren ("demand," seen *apart from* "knowledge"). See also Søe, *op. cit.,* 1957, pp. 175ff., who is far removed from the "isolation" idea of Wingren, and comments (p. 177) on the "significant difficulties" and the "limitation" implicit in the "call to true humanity."

codes. Therefore the law of God is seen in its "disclosing" capacity. By means of its "revelation" *we have knowledge*. The purpose of the law is to arouse our receptivity for the comforts of the Gospel. Or to put the matter in another way: the disclosure of the law is a "primary phase" in a total process. It is the phase which *"must come first."* In this way the law creates the situation in which the Gospel (as God's good news) radiates its streams of light in the darkness with which a man is already familiar, thanks to the *working of the law*.

In this strictly temporal problematic the main conception is the relation between the knowledge of sin and forgiveness. The conclusion is that it is logical and necessary that the *usus elenchticus* must *first* disclose man's sin. Only in that way can the *meaning* of the Gospel of *forgiveness* be understood. The *usus elenchticus* must deposit us in the deepest "depths" of Psalm 130 and we must "cry out" from our miseries. In that light, however, the question is all the more urgent: Is the law the *exclusive* source for the knowledge of our sin? Here we must look more closely at the real *meaning* of the *usus elenchticus*.

Both in the Lutheran and Reformed communities men have discussed the law's disclosing and exposing function in connection with the explicit and lucid statements of Scripture.[51] One might ask, for example: Is anything more clear than that Lord's Day 2 reflects the spirit of Paul's own words in Romans and Galatians? Think of Romans 3:19-20, where we read that "whatever the law says it speaks to those who are under the law, so that every mouth may be stopped, and the whole world may be held accountable to God. For no human being will be justified in his sight by works of the law since *through the law comes knowledge of sin*." Lord's Day 2, Question 3, refers us to that text. Furthermore we are hardly surprised when Galatians 3:19 is cited so frequently. Paul there inquires concerning the "function" of the law and states that it "was added *because of transgressions*."

Calvin, of course, in discussing the law's "disclosing aspect,"

---

51. Calvin, before considering the *tertius usus*, speaks of the law's function in reminding man of his own unrighteousness (*Inst.*, II, 7, 6). There is an instruction the law gives against all insolence and arrogance. The law serves as a scale (7, 6) and mirror (7, 7), and through its testimony our iniquity is confirmed (7, 8). This is the first function or task of the law (7, 9).

appealed to Romans 3:20.[52] Indeed, it stands to reason that in treatments of the *usus elenchticus* (*theologicus, paedagogicus*) we frequently come across this text.[53] It is generally said that this *usus* of the law does not leave a man to his own ruin but convicts him of his guilt. It convicts him in such a way that he expects no more from his own powers and waits only for God's grace. In Calvin's words, the sinner flees "empty-handed" to God's mercy. Therefore Calvin emphasized the law's first task as a task of "preparation" and linked that task with Paul's description of the law as "our custodian" to bring us to Christ (Gal. 3:24).[54] Similarly, in this combination of Romans 3:20, Galatians 3:19, and Galatians 3:24, many theologians have found clear traces of the *usus elenchticus,* now introduced as the *usus paedagogicus.* Some scholars have said that Paul identified these two in Galatians: "So that the law was our custodian until Christ came, that we might be justified by faith. But now that faith has come, we are no longer under a custodian" (3:24-25).

We shall have to examine carefully this reference to Paul. Does he really approve this notion of the *usus elenchticus* or a concept of the law as a "preparatory stage" in a total process?[55] In the science of exegesis today it is not so easy to invoke these passages as a "proof" for the *usus elenchticus.* What we see is a shift in interpretation, which is especially apparent in connection with the function of the "pedagogue" in Galatians 3. Ridderbos, for example, does not find in this passage a positive preparation for Christ.[56] The pedagogue, in Paul's day, was a very *unpopular person.* He was a hired nurse for keeping immature youth in line, and his function had nothing to do with a positive training and everything to do with a negative *privation of freedom.*[57] *This,* in other words, is the background of the terms "confined" and kept "under restraint" (in verse 23)

52. *Inst.,* II, 7, 7: "There he notes only its first function...."
53. E.g., Bavinck, *Geref. Dog.,* III, 122.
54. Cf. Calvin, *Inst.,* II, 7, 11: "Therefore, through the recognition of their own misery, the law brings them down to humility in order *thus to prepare them* to seek what previously they did not realize they lacked."
55. On this "preparatory character" cf. Greijdanus' commentary, p. 264; also his *K.V.* on Gal. 3:24 ("heenleiden naar de Here Christus," p. 87).
56. H. N. Ridderbos, "Vrijheid en Wet volgens Paulus' Brief aan de Galaten," *Arcana Revelata,* 1951, pp. 90f. Ridderbos does see this function in Hebrews.
57. *Ibid.,* p. 91.

and "under the law" as our "custodian" (in verse 24). What is indicated is not the "rearing" or "preparing" of the law but the *destitution and impotence of being its subject.*[58] So too Schlier has denied that the pedagogue of Galatians 3 has anything to do with a "training unto Christ."[59] It is not the case that the law "brings us to recognize our sins, and shatters our confidence in our own selves, and thus finally awakens our longings for grace."[60] These words "until Christ" are not preparatory but indicate the *terminus ad quem.*[61] For *this long* the captivity under the law extended, and it only ended with the coming of Jesus Christ. Therefore the law is not a peaceful preparation for faith, but it sets a man under curse and death and servility.

This, then, is enough to show that a simple appeal to Galatians 3:24, to substantiate the *usus elenchticus,* can very easily lead us to difficulties. The matter is not so simple as that. Furthermore, the exegesis of Galatians 3:19 (even more clearly than Galatians 3:24) must point us in that same direction. Again the question is implied: What is the function of the law? Ridderbos opposes any translation which sees the law as "added to make

58. In *TWNT*, V, *s.v. paideúō,* D. 2, the pedagogue is discussed in its relationship opposite childhood. When Paul speaks of the pedagogue, his concern is not with the *nature* of the pedagogue but with "being shut up under sin and law" and the "servility of man under law and elements." Cf. the exegesis of Ridderbos (*loc. cit.*) in contrast to Greijdanus. The exegesis of "leading forth" and "preparing" is found in Calvin also; so too in K. L. Schmidt, *Ein Gang durch den Galaterbrief,* p. 125. In contrast, cf. Duncan, *The Epistle to the Galatians,* p. 121, and his criticism against the King James Version: "the law was our schoolmaster to bring us unto Christ." Such a translation leaves the impression that "the law's function was essentially educative."

59. H. Schlier, *Der Brief an die Galater,* p. 125.

60. Cf. also Ch. de Beus, *Paulus de Apostel,* p. 124, and P. A. van Stempvoort, *op. cit.,* pp. 102f.

61. De Beus, *loc. cit.;* Van Stempvoort, *op. cit.,* p. 193; Ridderbos, *op. cit.,* p. 92. In connection with this Ridderbos understands Rom. 10:4 (Christ as the end of the law, *télos*) not as goal but as actual end. This does not mean, to be sure, an end with no further context (as the end of a speech); rather there is an historical coming-to-an-end. H. Hellbardt has said that Christ is the *sense* of the law, and therefore can be its end. In this way an actual end and goal do not exclude each other, for the point at stake is not "the cessation of a matter" but the "end" in terms of and through a fulfillment ("Christus, das Telos des Gesetzes," *Ev. Theol.,* 1936, pp. 333, 345). Cf. Rom. 10:4*b*: "that every one who has faith may be justified" (ASV: *"unto* righteousness to every one that believeth"). A. Nygren, *Der Römerbrief,* p. 271: "In Christ, thus, the power of the law is ended."

transgressions manifest."[62] He observes that the whole thrust of this text is not concerned with man's acquiring a knowledge of sin but rather with *sin's being suddenly "emancipated" or "set free."*[63] Thus the picture is the same as we find in Romans 7:13. The law has been added in order that "sin might be shown to be sin, and through the commandment might become sinful beyond measure." Therefore Paul writes in Galatians 3:22 that Scripture has "consigned all things to sin." The law was added "because of transgressions" (3:19). It was not added in order that we might come to know our transgressions, by means of the mirror of the law, but rather that sin's lawless rebellion might be acutely *manifest in reality.*[64] Paul's intention, in all these references, is clearly to indicate that sin is intensified by means of the law. Therefore the law has a *negative effect.*[65] Through the law the full transgression-character of sin is made known; and therefore sin is sinful "beyond measure." But none of this implies a deeper *insight into the reality of sin.*

In Romans 3:20, however, we would seem to have a direct reference to the "knowledge of sin" which comes *"through the law."* Therefore the question is obvious: If the *usus elenchticus* finds little support in Galatians 3:19 and 24, does it find greater support in Romans 3:20? In answering that question, it

62. Ridderbos, *op. cit.*, p. 90; cf. also his *The Epistle of Paul to the Churches of Galatia*, 1953, pp. 183f.

63. *Ibid.*, p. 137: "to call forth the transgressions and make them manifest. This is to say more than that by means of the law sin should be acknowledged as transgression in its proper and terrible character." Cf. "call into existence," p. 138.

64. Cf. S. Greijdanus, *Comm. op Gal.*, p. 232, in reference to Zahn; also his statement, p. 233, "that sins must take on the character of transgressions, of conscious, intentional breakings of the law." See the article of O. Schultz, "[*Tí oún ho nómos*]," in *Theologische Studiën und Kritiken*, 1902, pp. 1-56. *Chárin* is here understood in connection with the intention that sin is "stamped" ("stempelen"), through the law, as conscious sin. But such an expression is certainly too weak. What happens is more than mere "stamping."

65. Cf. De Beus, *op. cit.*, p. 122. Read, too, what Paul says about the law "ordained by *angels* through an intermediary" (Gal. 3:19). This signalizes no disqualification of the law, but does indicate how "the lesser glory of the law compared with the promise becomes manifest" (Ridderbos, *op. cit.*, p. 138). Cf. Van Stempvoort, *op. cit.*, p. 97, who guards against calling the law "inferior," but does refer to its mediate and interim character (angels, mediator, viz. Moses). There is no notion here of a competition of law and promise. The law is no way of salvation but was added for this purpose: to increase sin.

is important to bear in mind what we read in Romans 5:20. For there, too, the point is made that the "law came in" to increase the trespass.[66] Paul does not speak of a greater and deeper *knowledge* of sin, but he does speak of sin's factual *increase*.[67] Moreover, where "sin increased," there "grace abounded all the more." With the law came the increase and intensification, and the accumulation of man's guilt.

And now we return to Romans 3:19 with that thought in mind. It stands to reason that through the law every mouth is "stopped" and the whole world is "held accountable to God." For the law brings no blessing to a man but *casts him into guilt.* Through the law it is inevitable that no one living is righteous before God (Ps. 143:2). Moreover, that very fact is apparent in the *increase of man's guilt.*[68] Paul's concern was not to observe the law as a "norm" or a "mirror" for measuring our shortcomings but only to notice that something *happens* by means of the law. It is the function of the law to increase the guilt of man.

Therefore, if we interpret the *usus elenchticus* in terms of the common "mirror-and-reflection" idea, we can find no support whatever in the entire book of Romans. Paul's thought was not structured in nomological categories which suggest that the only thing necessary for a knowledge of man's sin is a knowledge of God's law. It is not enough to know God's prohibition and command. Paul himself appreciated that fact as he looked on the history of Israel and his own life. For that reason he wished to see the law in its salvation-historical context as something "added" or "brought in." Possibly it is this point that perplexes us most, for we are all too inclined to conceive of the law in totally different terms. We tend to regard it as the "source-book" for the knowledge of our misery. We almost assume that the law has some latent powers for dispensing a "knowledge" of our sin. But if this is what we have thought, it is surely not what Paul had in mind. There was a sinning before the law, but its horrible guilt was only manifest *after the law "came in."* "When

---

66. Ridderbos, *Arcana Revelata, op. cit.,* p. 90.
67. Cf. Chr. Maurer, *Die Gesetzeslehre des Paulus nach ihrem Ursprung und in ihrer Entfaltung dargelegt,* 1941, pp. 48f. On Gal. 3:19, cf. p. 28: "The 'usus elenchticus' is not used here in the sense that the law makes man, through its exercise, ripe for grace."
68. The increase of wickedness is treated in still another context in Matt. 24:12: "And because wickedness is multiplied, most men's love will grow cold" (*plēthýnō*). On the "increase" in Rom. 5, cf. *TWNT,* II, *s.v. pleonázō.*

the commandment came, sin revived" (Rom. 7:9). Sin was completely revealed.[69] Moreover, because sin was now seen in full we can also say that "through the law comes knowledge of sin" (3:20).

Not for a moment does all this imply a degradation of the law. Paul knew very well that "the law is holy, and the commandment is holy and just and good" (7:12).[70] Yet through the law a *new situation has come:* "... for sin, finding opportunity in the commandment, deceived me and by it killed me. Apart from the law sin lies dead" (7:8). Therefore it is through the law that sin is *made to be alive.* Through the law sin is vitalized and actualized, agitated and inflamed. *This* is the issue that engaged the Apostle Paul: *the law and the increase of man's sin.* Certainly man's sin is made known by the law; but it is not made known in a placid or quiescent manner by merely "measuring" or "giving a reflection." It is made known in its opposition to the law and its *enlistment of the law for its own purposes. Therefore,* sin is now intensified and rebellion is seen in all its extremity. *For that reason* we see the judgment of God and the condemnation of sin from which the man of faith is set free (8:1).

This same vantage point is found in I Corinthians 15:26, where Paul again declares that "the power of sin is the law."[71] Sin is vivified in its confrontation with the law. In that way it is revealed and made manifest in reality. Thus the *kálymma* of sin is torn away. Sin was not known in the subjectivity of ancient Israel but was *manifest and made apparent in reality.* Israel and Pharisaism busied themselves with "law," but the law could not help them in coming to the knowledge of their sin. Most often they seized on the law to justify themselves and excuse their own works. But the result was that "the scripture consigned all things to sin" (Gal. 3:22; cf. Rom. 11:32). The law cast them into a guilt-generating guilt. Moreover, it did so not as a "bad law," or demonic force, but rather as the *holy law*

---

69. Barth, *K.D.,* IV/1, 653 (ET, 585f.).
70. Cf. I Tim. 1:8: "Now we know that the law is good, *if* any one uses it lawfully." A remarkable "if" here; — from which it becomes apparent that Paul never occupied himself with an abstract view of law but only with the law in correlation with its use or misuse.
71. "Here the thoughts that Paul develops in Romans 7:7ff. are tightly brought together" (H. D. Wendland, *Die Briefe an die Korinther,* 1954, p. 138). Cf. Grosheide, *Comm.,* p. 432, who likewise refers to Romans in illustrating sin's usage of the law.

of God. Because the law is *holy* it cannot be apprehended or interpreted as the means of salvation in itself. When this effort is made, the law can only show itself "weakened by the flesh" (Rom. 8:3).[72] Instead of life and salvation, it can only bring sin and death. *This,* then, is what the law "reveals" of sin. In contrast to what the law "could not do," Paul sees the salvation of Christ in whom the entire law is now fulfilled (8:4).

The law "reveals" because of what happens in this senseless and apostate manipulation of the law. "That, according to Paul, is the real relation between the law and Christ. But the law is not, in the first place, a 'guide' to Christ, which affords us an insight into our need for deliverance."[73] Paul does not point to such an insight but rather to the revelation of the full reality of guilt.

But *why* did Paul lay such stress on this "function" of the law and emphasize that the law causes us to know our sin *in this manner?* What did he mean by this "flaming up," or "vitalizing," or becoming "exceeding sinful" through the law? How should we understand this tremendous activity of sin in the face of God's command (Rom. 7:8)? It is clear, first of all, that sin takes its point of departure in the law. In the law it finds its "contact,"[74] or its "springboard," or its "base of operation" for its further activity.[75] Sin makes use of the law (or misuse) and through that relation to the law it becomes the extremely active force it is. Yet the law itself is not the "source" of this process. Paul confessed that the commandment which "promised life" proved to be "death" for him (7:10) and that sin, proceeding from the law, "deceived" him and "killed" him (7:11). But when he asked if God's "good" law in itself could possibly mean "death," he could only reply, "by no means!" (7:13).

Why, then, did sin get a new lease on life and break out with such ferocity?[76] This happened at the crucial moment in

---

72. Cf. the reference to this text in CD, III-IV, 5: because the law is *so weak,* it "leaves the transgressor under the curse."
73. O. Michel, *Der Brief an die Römer, ad loc.*
74. Michel (*ibid.,* p. 147) points in this connection to Gen. 3:1-7.
75. Cf. A. A. van Ruler, *De Vervulling der Wet,* 1947, p. 380; R. Schippers, *op. cit.,* p. 202, and *Levensvragen (Bijbels Dagboek),* p. 292 (on Rom. 7:11); Maurer, *op. cit.,* 1941, p. 49; E. Tobac, *Le problème de la justification dans Saint Paul,* 1941, pp. 60f.
76. This question is all the more sensible when we see that even before

the history of salvation when the law "came in" (Rom. 5:20) and "was added" (Gal. 3:19). The law came four hundred thirty years after the promise was made to Abraham (Gal. 3:17). It came as a salvation-historical incision. For when the law "came in" it became *apparent what sin in reality is, in opposition to this law*. Why did that happen? Why should there be a change in the manner of sin? Since there was surely a sinning before the law (Rom. 5:13), what *was* it that really *now began?* Whence do we find this dark relation between sin and the law, beguilement and death? Why did the law become the "power of sin"? Do we merely encounter, in all these questions, the general human rule that Ovid already articulated: When we see and approve the good, we do the bad, and all because of the secret inclination of our hearts?[77] Is *that* the kind of general psychology that Paul had in mind?

Bultmann has rightly said that such a "cheap insight" could never have been Paul's intent.[78] For Paul did much more than fit a general human "maxim" into his vision of sin and the law. He was not really interested in sin's mysterious conflagration, or in sin's natural aversion to any prohibition and command. He was concerned about sin's beguilement and seduction by means of *using the law* (Rom. 7:11).[79] It was not the common revulsion to the law that occupied the Apostle Paul (the *deteriora*

the coming of the law there was a process of growth in sin. We read of this especially in Gen. 6:5 ("the wickedness of man was great"); cf. 6:11 ("the earth was corrupt in God's sight"). G. von Rad has spoken of the "incursion of sin and its avalanche-like increase in Genesis 2-11" (*Theologie des Alten Testaments*, I, 1957, 159). Concerning the "deep estrangement," cf. p. 164. But even more striking is Paul's conjoining the multiplication of sin and the incursion of the law, thus pointing to a unique event that led to *this increase*.

77. "Video meliora probaque, deteriora sequor." This statement is cited by Calvin in his exegesis of Rom. 7:16, but not as an illustration of the "goading" or "inciting" of sin through law. He seeks rather to indicate the difference between this assertion and the "assenting" of God's law. Cf. D. J. DeGroot, *Comm. op Rom.*, pp. 218-219. This same statement *is* used as an illustration by C. H. Dodd, *The Epistle of Paul to the Romans*, 1949, p. 113. Cf. the criticisms of Barth on making associations between Rom. 7 and the notion of "nitimur in vetitum" (we hanker after what is forbidden); *De Levende God*, 1936; also *K.D.*, IV/1, 649 (ET, 581-582).

78. R. Bultmann, "Römer 7 und die Anthropologie des Paulus," in *Imago Dei*, 1932, p. 55.

79. *Exapatāō* is the same word as found in II Cor. 11:3: "as the serpent deceived Eve by his cunning." Cf. I Tim. 2:14.

sequor) but only the manipulation of the law for sin's own purposes and the transformation of the law into an essentially different law from what it *is*. Certainly the law was not "added" as a dualistic "counterforce" in opposition to the salvation already promised in Abraham; indeed, such a notion is opposed by Paul with the greatest emphasis. Nor did the law make useless the covenant already ratified (Gal. 3:17) or nullify the promises of God. Why, then, was the law "added" (3:15, 19, 21)? Why did the law "come in"?

The answer of Paul has everything to do on the one hand with the "transgression increased" by means of the law and, on the other hand, with the character of the law that was "added." The law was not a threat to the "promises of God" (3:21). "By no means!" What we see is no dualistic or Gnostic antinomy. In fact, if we think along those lines the law would be a *new means of salvation, or an "optional choice," and righteousness could then be gained by law* (cf. 3:21).[80] That, of course, was never God's intent! God's law was the law of his covenant and was also contracted with the people of his own electing love. "I am the Lord your God, who brought you out of the land of Egypt, out of the house of bondage" (Ex. 20:2). *This,* then, was the great occasion and the real reason for the law's "coming" when it did. The law must be seen as *God's* law in the uniqueness of this specific event which forms an incision in the history of salvation. It was no confusion or contradiction of God's former promise or manner of salvation. It was not the antinomy of his former manner of address. The law of God was rather that command which came to *Israel* in his gracious election.[81]

How *could* the people of his election stand *outside his command*? It was only *in* that command that election became concretely visible as the election of *this people*. God's election was not an abstract or an indefinite concern which found place outside the life of Israel. It was manifest *in his command*. "He declares his word to Jacob, his statutes and ordinances to Israel.

---

80. Cf. Gal. 3:12: "but the law does not rest on faith, for 'He who does them shall live by them.'" Paul sets himself against "the Jewish scheme of redemption" (Ridderbos, *The Epistle of Paul to the Churches of Galatia,* p. 125) and does not deny therefore a living according to law "out of the *grace* of God's covenant" (*ibid.*). Cf. Lev. 18:5 and 4*b*: "I am the Lord your God."

81. Cf. C. H. Dodd, *Gospel and Law: the Relation of Faith and Ethics in Early Christianity,* 1953[3], p. 11: "The commandments are a corollary to the facts."

He has not dealt thus with any other nation; they do not know his ordinances. Praise the Lord!" (Ps. 147:19-20) . Therefore the doxology of Psalm 147 has reference to both *election and command*: the history of Israel "reaches its zenith in election and the making known of God's will."[82] There is no antinomy between the *law* and the *promise;* for the law is no new means of salvation. It is only the obvious scepter which we expect to find raised over the people of God's choice.[83]

In opposition to *this* law, with *this* content, the sin of man is now "exceeding sinful." For sin misleads a man by radically reversing and confounding the meaning of that law which God has now "added." The issue here is not the general *"deteriora"* of Ovid but only the *deteriora* of a central and total transgression of God's most holy law. Therefore we see that sin, in fact, *did increase.* Sin completed itself within the realm of history and within the circle of God's activity in and over Israel. This increase resulted from Israel's antagonism to God's gracious election. For election was manifest in that command of God which was raised up for his own people. The law of God was seized and reinterpreted as a *new way of salvation* in opposition to the *promise of God.*[84] "While we were living in the flesh, our sinful passions, aroused by the law, were at work in our members to bear fruit for death" (Rom. 7:5) .[85] Then and then only did sin begin to "live." Only then began that fascinating history

82. A. Weiser, *Die Psalmen,* II, 1950, 559.
83. Cf. Von Rad, *op. cit.,* I, 193: "And there can be no doubt that with the proclamation of the decalogue over Israel election becomes a reality." One thinks of the characteristic statement: "This day you have become the people of the Lord your God. You shall therefore obey the voice of the Lord your God, keeping his commandments and his statutes, which I command you this day" (Deut. 27:9-10). Cf. Th. C. Vriezen, *Die Erwählung Israels nach dem A.T.,* 1953, pp. 80f., and Von Rad, *op. cit.,* 196, on the "fundamental negations." Recall, too, the introductory statement of the decalogue and first commandment; further Deut. 7:6 and 14:1f.; Lev. 26:1-13. Concerning the relation between covenant and election, on the one hand, and obedience in connection with conditionality, on the other, cf. Von Rad, *op. cit.,* 195, 228-229. Von Rad also refers to the New Testament relation between the indicative and imperative; cf. also A. de Quervain, *Gesetz und Freiheit,* 1930, pp. 127f.
84. Sin seeks "to cast us into disaster by mirroring before us that we must seek our salvation in the law" (Schippers, *Levensvragen,* p. 292). Cf. Van Ruler, *op. cit.,* p. 383, on this attempt to obtain salvation "by means of the law."
85. Cf. *ibid.,* p. 382.

of self-justification and sin's demonic proliferation which was brought on by profaning God's most holy law. And what is it that sin whispers concerning that law? "That I may perform its demands adequately of myself; that I may purge, justify and sanctify myself. It whispers to me that I am too good for the grace that is offered to me in the law, and that I should repel that grace. It whispers that instead of the faith recommended to me in the law of God I should impose my own works, my own piety, my own moralistic performance before God. In that way I shall make myself worthy of God."[86]

Thus the desire inflamed by the law must be seen as a passion for our own self-glory before the face of God. Here lies the real deception of man's sin. Proceeding from the law, it delivers a man to death. As a wife is redeemed from the law which has bound her to her husband as soon as her husband dies, so too we are now unshackled from the law of "sin and death" by the grace of God (Rom. 7:2-3). With a view to this law of "sin and death" (8:2) the believer himself has died (7:3, 6). Furthermore, he has died *not* because the law itself was a dubious agent of "sin and death" but only because it was misemployed, or misapplied, to the end of our own self-justification. Paul states this matter in the very clearest of terms. He indicates that "the law of the Spirit of life in Christ Jesus" has set us "free from the law of sin and death" (8:2). Therefore, we are "not under law but under grace" (6:14) and find our position again under the "law of the Spirit of life." In that law the goal we strive for is not a self-righteousness but the life under *grace*. Thus it is the life under God's *new command*. Apart from this perspective the law is deceptive and deadening. What else could happen when Israel's law was falsified and turned into the very opposite of its meaning?[87] For that reason we hear the words of Paul: "The very commandment which promises life proved to be death to me" (7:10).

It is now obvious that the thrust of Paul's argument can only be rightly grasped when we notice his distress at using the law for self-justifying ends. The law is no "point of departure" or "base of operation" for attaining our own righteousness. This is the way Israel had tended to regard it: but the quest for her own righteousness could only lead her to death. Paul observed

86. K. Barth, *Kurze Erklärung des Römerbriefs*, 1956, pp. 99, 100-103.
87. Bultmann, *Imago Dei*, p. 61, points out that Rom. 7:5 does not speak of transgressions.

this as he looked back on the example of Israel. For "Israel who pursued the righteousness which is based on law did not succeed in fulfilling that law"; on the other hand, the "Gentiles who did not pursue righteousness have attained it, that is, righteousness through faith" (Rom. 9:30-31). And why is it that Israel did not fulfill the law? "Because they did not pursue it through faith, but as it were based on works" (9:32).[88] In so doing they "stumbled over the stumbling stone" and the rock which gives offense, which was laid by God himself as a "stumbling block in Zion." For Israel refused to surrender her own righteousness and to live according to that faith in which no one shall be "put to shame" (9:32-33; 10:3).[89]

Paul Althaus has taken exception to this interpretation and has said that it "transforms all the essential concepts in Romans 7 into an obvious contradiction to their contexts and the other Pauline usages."[90] The point that Althaus is trying to make is that, according to Paul, the Jews not only "manipulated" the law for their own self-justification but also *"violated" the law*. Althaus refers us to such a passage as Romans 2:17ff., where the Jews are clearly guilty of *transgression*. Yet, in Althaus' view, the idea of *vainglory* (or the quest for one's own self-righteousness) is a theme that Paul only deals with for the first time in Romans 9-10. Thus in Romans 7 we find him limiting his charge to a transgression of the law.[91] It seems obvious that Bultmann paved the way for this criticism by drawing a sharp line between

88. Greek: *hōs ex érgōn*. On this lack of understanding for the spiritual sense of the law, cf. II Cor. 3:15 and Rom. 10:2-3 on the "zeal for God" which is "not enlightened": "for, being ignorant of the righteousness that comes from God, and seeking to establish their own, they did not submit to God's righteousness." Regarding this "zeal," cf. Phil. 3:6; Gal. 1:14; Acts 22:4. The lawyer who inquired after eternal life was referred to the law, and when he recited the law he got as his answer: "do this, and you will live" (Luke 10:28). But he continued to ask, "desiring to justify himself" (10:29).

89. Rengstorf has rightly seen the tensions apparent in every nomism in connection with "the problem of assurance of salvation." "It is grounded in the essence of every works-religion that its adherents cannot come to certainty on the question of whether they have attained the requisite measure of pious deeds or not" *(TWNT, II, s.v. elpis)*. This subjective uncertainty corresponds to the objective situation: "it is Moses who accuses you, on whom you set your hope" (John 5:45). On the Christian concept of hope, cf. *ibid.* (Bultmann), especially on the relation between faith and hope (Heb. 11:1).

90. P. Althaus, *Paulus und Luther über den Menschen*, 1938, p. 39.

91. *Ibid.*, p. 40.

"vainglorying" and "transgressing"; but it is just as obvious that this chasm is by no means necessary and certainly gives Althaus no right to make a new distinction. The "increase of sin" by means of the law and the quest for one's own self-righteousness are certainly not abstractions but are concretized in living. They are concretized in the estrangement from the covenant God and a disobedience which affects the whole of life. This fact need not be apparent in every concrete sin. We think of Paul who, "as to the righteousness under the law," was "blameless" (Phil. 3:6). At the same time, the Old Testament shows us that estrangement frequently does lead to the most grievous of transgressions.

It is clear by now that an abstract morality played no role in Paul's thinking. His concern was with the total and central relation of Israel to the law. He recognized that sin was present even in his own "blamelessness" and lured him on to death. For that very reason he was not able to exclude the theme of transgression (Romans 2, 7) from that of vainglorying in self-righteousness (Romans 9, 10). Romans 2 already includes both of these elements. Therefore we read of "relying upon the law" and "boasting of one's relation to God" (2:17); of "knowing his will" and "stealing" and "committing adultery" (2:18, 21f.). "You who boast in the law, do you dishonor God by breaking the law?" (2:23). This is what Israel did time after time in her history. So too, the "blamelessness" of Paul was tied up with his persecution of the Church (Phil. 3:6); also, in a similar way, men would later kill the disciples of Christ and think that they were pleasing God (cf. John 16:2). It is apparent, then, that Paul's argument in Romans has nothing to do at all with two divorceable problems of "vainglorying" and "transgressing." He was concerned about a vainglorying that *misuses the law* and results in an alienation of man from God, even in the concreteness of man's everyday living. Althaus' reference to transgression is no refutation of this view. As a matter of fact, we see the increase of sin in a *direct connection* with the misuse of God's law and the desire to *justify oneself*.

The most remarkable thing in all this deception of sin, in its contact with the law, is that God's final goals are not thwarted or denied. "On the contrary, in sin's misuse of the law the purpose of God is advanced."[92] *In this way* sin is made full and

92. Althaus, *Der Brief an die Römer*, p. 62.

manifest. By now it is evident that Paul's intention was not to define the law as a source or norm for our knowledge of sin in terms of which we simply deduce, by an intellectual activity, what is "good" or "evil." Paul was interested in the tremendous dynamic of redemption-history in which man's sin bursts forth as an open flame and reveals itself, and precisely in that way is made servile to God's purposes.[93] One does an injustice to Paul if he naively identifies this message on the law and sin with the *usus elenchticus* or indiscreetly claims the Apostle's support for Lord's Day 2. This is surely the case if we conceive of the *usus elenchticus* as a "disclosure" of God's will and the indictment of man which is thereby implied.

If we deduce the knowledge of sin from such a "disclosure" we are left with only the formal parallel to other "laws" which *also* have significance for the knowledge of "good" and "evil," or what is "legal" and "illegal." But the legal machinery we then have is by no means what Paul had in mind. There is no such law from which we derive the knowledge of our sin *apart from the Lawgiver*. In Paul's reference to the law of God he saw the Lawgiver himself who reveals himself as the living God. That is to say, the sense and purpose of this law can only be known when we know *God*. The knowledge of the law can never be "had" apart from the deepest intentions of the Lawgiver. When it is sought apart from him the law itself is transmogrified and is made into a legalistic ordinance. We might still sing our paeans concerning the law and regard it as "the embodiment of knowledge and truth," and a "light to those who are in darkness" (Rom. 2:19-20). But our alienation from God, or the falsehood of our act, will then be seen in the way in which we regard the law as the "source of knowledge" for the sins of *others* (2:21f.).

Thus the real *sense* of the law is only understood when we see the law as the law of the Lawgiver, or the God of the covenant and of gracious election. Only then is the key of knowledge (once lost) found again (cf. Luke 11:52).[94] There it is

---

93. In Rom. 7:7 Paul makes mention of the tenth commandment, which refers to coveting as sin. When he writes "if it had not been for the law, I should not have known sin," he is certainly not referring to an intellectual apprehension of knowledge. He has in mind, rather, "the practical recognition of evil: I 'acknowledge' my sin since it is activated in me" (*ibid.*, p. 61). In this connection, Althaus refers to Christ who "knew" no sin (II Cor. 5:21).

94. Cf. Schippers, *De Gereformeerde Zede,* p. 198.

clear that God, in the law, lays claim to man in fellowship. The
issue here is not an abstract morality but the relation of communion which is utterly concrete and can never be comprehended apart from *that fellowship*. In God's law the "good way"
is pointed out in which it is obvious that it is "good for us to
be near to him." Once we understand that fact, the commandment of God arouses our love and delight, and we turn our
backs on all efforts to misuse the law for our own self-righteousness.[95]

It is well to remember that in Lord's Day 2 the meaning of
knowing "out of the law of God" is immediately related to
Christ's own commandment to love.[96] Only in that way is Lord's
Day 2 really perspicuous. Thus it is obvious that what is meant
is no abstract or nomological interpretation apart from the fellowship and love of God. For in Lord's Day 2 the *believer* is
the one who is confessing — the believer who already had acknowledged, in Lord's Day 1, "three things" which we must
know in order to live and die *in comfort*.[97] The reference to the
law in Lord's Day 2 cannot possibly mean a retrogression from
this comfort to an abstractly legalistic relationship. It cannot
mean a relationship in which a legalistic standpoint is in any
way dominant. For *love* is the only meaning of the law:[98] therefore *obedience* to the law can only be an *echo or response to
God's love*. There is no abstractly "legal relationship," in Lord's
Day 2, apart from this "rule of gratitude." Indeed, as Schilder
has asserted, the purpose here is to enunciate already the rule of
gratitude as the primary character of God's law. In the fulfillment of that rule a man remains in the blessed presence of, and
in the communion with, his God.[99] This "rule" does not exclude
the *usus elenchticus* but rather *includes* it precisely within the

95. Consider what is said in Gal. 3, regarding the law, in connection with
    Gal. 4:21-32, where Paul argues precisely *in terms of the law:* "Tell
    me, you who desire to be under law, do you not hear the law?" Here
    the criticism of wanting to be "under law" casts no shadows on the law
    (meant in a wider sense than the decalogue). Paul's polemic against
    standing "under law" takes its point of departure in the old covenant
    and the meaning of that covenant. Cf. Van Stempvoort, *op. cit.*, pp. 131f.
96. Schippers, *op. cit.*, p. 204; *Levensvragen,* pp. 275f.
97. Cf. K. Schilder, *Heidelbergsche Catechismus,* I, 1947, 62ff., against any
    experiencing of these "three things" as "three biographically analyzable
    periods" (p. 63); also against any "abstracting" thought (p. 65).
98. Cf. A. Kuyper, *E Voto,* I, 25f. on love in relation to the knowledge of
    sin.
99. Schilder, *op. cit.,* I, 76.

meaning of the law. For rebellion is the very opposite of gratitude as lovelessness is the very opposite of love.

In the light of this *sense* or *meaning* it is understandable
that the law is never absent from a man but is binding on the
believer, too, as God's new commandment for those in fellowship
with him. Both in "leading" and in "watching," it shines as a
"lamp" whose "reproofs of discipline are the way of life" (Prov.
6:22-23). It both warns and preserves (6:24f.) and it must, as
such, be "bound upon the heart" (6:21; cf. 7:3). Precisely *as* a
rule of gratitude (and within this context) the law of love
should be seen as a "mirror." Only in that way is life both tested
and directed in all of its depths. Therefore all formalism and
moralism are laid aside. The performance of "good works,"
apart from love, is now seen as a threat and a vanity which
"profits me *nothing*" (I Cor. 13:1-3).

But we also recognize how impossible it is to derive from the
law, as a "source," a knowledge of our sin which anticipates the
Gospel. There can be no such knowledge derived from an "abstract legality." The law is the law of *love* and remains so also
when we speak of the *usus elenchticus.* This suggests that the
path of knowledge can only be trod in connection with, and in
terms of, the *Gospel.* Surely we are not saying that the law is on
a lesser plane than that of the Gospel. We are merely trying to
recognize the deepest meaning of the law. In precisely *this way*
the *usus elenchticus* is applied to every moment of our living.

We may still ask if Paul's use of the law has more than an
historical significance for us. What are the implications of the
fact that his usage was *"heilshistorisch"*-defined? Obviously this
question is far from meaningless when we consider what Paul
says about the increase of sin by means of the law which was
"added," or the period of slavery which has now "ended" in
Christ. That period has ended in that Christ who is also the
"end of the law."

This entire perspective (unmistakable as it is) must not
deter us from seeing the real significance of precisely this message: namely that the "end of the law" in Christ was the heart
and the driving impulse in all the apostolic *admonitions.* The
apostles warned in order to protect the Church from succumbing
again to the yoke of the law. Hence the urgency in Paul's letter
to the Galatians and his accent on glorying in the cross (6:14) in
contrast to a diminishing of this new light by performing the

"works of the law." Hence too the warning against the confusions of "another Gospel" (1:6) and the "bewitching" of those "before whose eyes Jesus Christ was publicly portrayed as crucified" (3:1). Here is the peril against which Paul admonished, *precisely in view of the "end of the law."* Paul was concerned about the threat that false teachers, who misunderstood the law's intent, might lead the Galatians astray by using the imperative of God's command as an impetus for man's own justification. In Paul's conception there is no antithesis of grace and law. Therefore he summoned believers to fulfill the law (6:2); and yet it was according to the "new rule" for "new creatures" that he enjoined the Church to act (6:15-16). Very obviously, this law (or this "rule") was no new way of salvation. It was only a signpost or a pointer to God's *one way of salvation: faith.*[100]

In other words, Paul's redemption-historical perspective, or his way of thinking concerning the law's "end," has a lasting significance for the New Testament Church. The preaching of the law (the "strict preaching" — HC, 115) is not a relativizing of the Gospel but the *proclamation of salvation.* Therefore the law is a "mirror" or a "source" for the knowledge of our sin. Therefore the *usus elenchticus* is valid. For here there is held before believers that sphere in which men no longer live when they live in the freedom of Jesus Christ. Furthermore, we see the consequences of this fact in the concrete practice of living. When the law of God is dissected into *many commands* the meaning of God's single command to have fellowship and love is no longer understood.

This use of the law is miles removed from a moralism which fails to appreciate the law's *heilshistorisch "end."* Moralism implies an eclipse of Christ's perfect work by the legalistic motive of self-righteousness. It does not see that the reality of Christ's passion and death interprets and also fulfills the law. Only because of that fact does the *usus elenchticus* have a really profound meaning. Now there remains no formal "mirror"-idea of the law with the correlative of a sheerly intellectual knowledge of the law's legal demands. Nor is there a *usus* that temporally precedes the Gospel and the *usus normativus.* For the *usus elenchticus* is nothing at all apart from this normativity of the law's meaning. The preaching of the *law of God* stands in the

---

100. The way of faith is the way of liberation from autonomy, even as the comfort of the Gospel is that we are no longer our own (HC, Lord's Day 1). Cf. I Cor. 6:19 (*ouk esté heautŏn*).

most intimate relation to the *end of the law,* and this is no paradox or mere play on words. There is only a single law of God
which accompanies the whole of man's living. It accompanies in
a convicting, restraining, and directing sense. Therefore that
single law (with its various sides and its unique *usus*) can only
be known in the context of, and from within, the love of contrition.

Any distinction that we impose upon this single *usus* will
run the risk of assigning an independence to the *usus elenchticus.* It will court the danger of a legal order anticipating, or
giving way to, the order of God's grace.[101] But once we see that
danger, we do well to consider that the Catechism instructs
believers in the *meaning of the law.* That is to say: it instructs
those who are taught by Christ and who understand their sin in
the *light of that law.* The *usus elenchticus* is applicable to us as
long as we are "in this life." Furthermore, that *usus* implies a
different "increase" from the increase of our sin. It implies an
increase in the *knowledge of our sin.* Here is the "more and
more" of the Heidelberg Catechism (Lord's Day 44) and the
Canons of Dort (III-IV, 5). Because of the law's "end" the sin
of believers is no longer increased and the law is no longer
manipulated for our own self-justification. Rather, we understand that the *usus elenchticus* is the usage of God's law which
enters our lives, also normatively, as *his scepter* (Gal. 6:2; cf.
5:4). Under this scepter we are led "more and more," and ir-
revocably, on the one way of life. We are led by the commandment of God and the law of Jesus Christ. *Therefore the law is a
source for the knowledge of our sin.*

There is no reason for us to deny the character of the law as
a "mirror," "norm," and "rule." But we go completely astray if
we legalistically absolutize that character. We cannot assume
that the path from the revelation of God's will to the true
knowledge of our sin lies within the limits of our own capacity.
We recall the pericope in which James compared the man who
is "a hearer of the word and not a doer" with a man who "observes his natural face in a mirror." He "observes himself and

---

101. We recall again the problems centering in the *usus civilis* or *politicus,*
concerning which the same danger is very real. One can study these
problems in the light of the complications of interpretation given the
usus politicus in relation to the *justitia civilis;* besides the Formula
Concordiae (Müller, p. 643), note the Smalkaldian Articles (p. 311).
The main problem is apparent in the relation of this *usus* to the
Gospel and the question of who the *subject* of this *usus* is.

goes away and at once forgets what he was like" (1:23-24). Here again we have the image of a "mirror." But the result of merely looking into *this mirror* is unfruitful and of no avail.[102]

Therefore a true knowledge of ourselves is not the product of merely holding up a mirror. We may talk about knowledge *only* when we immerse ourselves in the "perfect law of liberty." For this is the law which brings blessing to him who is "no hearer that forgets but a doer that acts" (1:25). When we do this we find that everything is suddenly changed. Every moralistic interpretation is thrust aside and the law is no longer abstracted from its God-ordained setting. With this perfect law of liberty we are now able to speak of the law as a "mirror," "norm," and "rule" for life. Moreover, we are able to do so without the slightest depreciation of the law. The man who speaks and who acts in this way is "blessed in his doing" (1:25).[103]

We have said that the *usus elenchticus* may never be divorced from the *meaning* of the law or the preaching of the Gospel in which the *end of the law* is set forth. By now it is clear why the dilemma of law-or-Gospel is false and inappropriate. The man who takes his point of departure in that dilemma and searches for the *knowledge of sin* by choosing for the *law* can never escape a legalistic absolutism. He may still see the law as the law of a "lawgiver" (in terms of a *lex naturalis* idea) [104] but the lawgiver will be very different from the God of the Gospels. The fact that men have frequently embarked on that kind of errant path is an evidence of the correlation they draw between confession of guilt and pardon, or the knowledge of sin and the knowledge of God's grace. All this we have already seen. The endeavor of men is then to avoid "cheap grace" and to give full vent to the accusing and convicting functions of the law. Therefore they lay all accent on the legal commandments which men have now broken. The conviction is that men, discomforted by their own guilt, must be comforted by the consolation of the Gospel. Law and Gospel are then seen together as two halves of one circle. But whoever reflects on what the

---

102. Cf. Grosheide, *op. cit.*, p. 365, on *katanoéō* (to consider attentively), which has, nevertheless, no use.

103. Cf. the entire exegesis of Grosheide, *ibid.*, pp. 365-366. The perfect law — in contrast to the yoke that oppresses — has its point of reference in the full will of the Lord, which is only "that we in gratitude act in accordance therewith" (p. 367).

104. On Melanchthon, in this regard, cf. Elert, *Das christliche Ethos*, p. 107.

Bible says on "sin and the law" is not forced to make a choice in this false "dilemma." When we bear in mind the relation between sin and the Gospel we can also appreciate why the *unity of the law and Gospel* is of decisive import for the knowledge of our sin.

CHAPTER SEVEN

SIN AND THE GOSPEL

WHEN WE MAKE a choice in this false dilemma of law or Gospel we will necessarily end up with insoluble problems. These arise when we abstract or misconstrue the law's *usus elenchticus* in relation to the Gospel and fall victim to a dualism of a *legal* order and the order of *love*. Historically and systematically, these two are then set at odds to each other. The preaching of the law is seen as "going before" the preaching of the Gospel. In this regard we should see that Lord's Day 2 does not imply a choice in this "dilemma" but only directs our attention to the normativity of God's will. This normativity does not cancel out the significance of the Gospel for coming to the knowledge of our sin. As a matter of fact, the Gospel retains its very vital significance.[1]

The Reformed Churches have recognized that significance in their formulary for celebrating the Lord's Supper. The formulary calls on believers to consider by themselves their own "sins and accursedness" and "abhor themselves," and to bear in mind "that the wrath of God against sin is so great that he, rather than to leave it unpunished, has punished it in his beloved Son, Jesus Christ, with the bitter and shameful death of the cross." Therefore, in the same breath as we are admonished to remember our sins and accursedness we are also referred to the evidence of God's wrath which rests on the "Lamb of God, who takes away the sin of the world" (John 1:29). In that fact the dreadfulness and awfulness of sin are very clearly apparent. At the same table at which we hear that our sins

1. Cf. K. Barth, *Die christliche Lehre nach dem Heidelberger Katechismus*, 1948, p. 34. In the Catechism itself, cf. Q. and A. 40: because of the "justice and truth of God, satisfaction for our sins could be made no otherwise than by the death of the Son of God." Also G. Brillenburg Wurth's rejection of this dilemma in *Het Christliche Leven*, I, 1949, 130: "Therefore no one should pose the dilemma, What enables us to make the discovery, God's law or God's love?"

187

are forgiven we are reminded of the revelation of sin in the
cross and the curse and condemnation of the Man of Sorrows.

Bavinck shows something of the obvious difficulties of trying
to break through this law-or-Gospel dilemma. With Schleiermacher and Ritschl he agrees that sin is manifest in its most
appalling dimension against the background of the Gospel of
God's grace in Christ. In this perspective sin is seen as man's
apostate answer to God's revelation, even to the point of blaspheming his Spirit. But for Bavinck it does not follow that
"not the law but the Gospel is the fountain for the knowledge
of sin."[2] He rejects any concept of exchanging the Gospel for
the law as the "wellspring" for the knowledge of our sin. He
takes issue with the notion that the Gospel presupposes the
law as forgiveness presupposes guilt; at the same time, he disputes the idea that the knowledge of sin is excluded from the
Gospel. In treating of faith and repentance, he explains "that
true repentance, true sorrow for sin, and a sincere return to
God and his service do not come from the law alone but just
as much, and even *more so,* from the Gospel."[3] When we say
that the knowledge of sin is arrived at by means of the law we
can only mean that every sin has its standard of measure in
God's command. But if we wish really to know our sin in its
true nature we shall have to turn to the Gospel. There is no
reason at all, Bavinck suggests, for a law-or-Gospel dilemma.
Therefore he finds nothing to criticize in Lord's Day 2. Sin can
only be regarded as *sin* in relation to the law, but the *way* in
which a sinner knows his sin is *first of all the way of the Gospel.*
Obviously we are touching already here on a number of questions that have a vital bearing on the nexus of the law and the
Gospel. On these we must come to a greater clarity.

Once we acknowledge, with Bavinck, that the Gospel has a
primary function in coming to the knowledge of our sin, we
shall also appreciate why it is impossible to make a clear-cut
principle that the preaching of the law must come "first" (as
usus elenchticus) and must "lead" men to the knowledge of
their sin. We cannot say that only on that basis can the Gospel
be preached as the message of "forgiven sins." That kind of
temporal problematic is far too simple and makes use of an
apparent logic that only a darkness can be illumined, and only

2. Bavinck, *Geref. Dog.,* III, 122.
3. Cf. *ibid.,* IV, 146.

an emptiness can be filled, and only a dead man can be made alive.

Similarly, the reality of pardoned sins would seem to point to the necessity of a twofold proclamation in which the preaching of the law is temporally antecedent to the preaching of the Gospel. If we accept that order we are hard put to escape the further conclusion that the preaching of the law has a special connection with the holiness and righteousness of God. We are then obliged to say that it is only in the law that these attributes clearly confront us. The law indicts us and functions (in its *usus elenchticus*) as a *lex accusans*. Though we are not compelled to deny the compassion of God, we are compelled to say that it comes only "later" into view. Other divine attributes are apparent in the law. The God of the law is a wrathful God whose honor, holiness, and majesty are trampled under foot. Thus the preaching of the law calls forth a pious dread. Man must see himself as a transgressor and must yearn for help and salvation, and only *then* will he find that these are given to him in the preaching of the Gospel.

It is cavalier to suggest that this whole notion of a temporal sequence opposes the law and Gospel in an antinomical relation. For both of these, of course, remain the Word of God. Yet they are seen, as the revelation of God, in a *temporal order* in which we first behold the wrathful God and only *then* the God of mercy. The law reveals God's vengeance and the Gospel proclaims his grace, and both of these "Words of God" find their common focus in the lostness of man which is manifest in the law and atoned for in the Gospel. Therefore the Gospel can never be the source of our knowledge of *sin* but can only be the source of our knowledge of *forgiveness*. God's forgiveness, as proclaimed in the Gospel, can only be a forgiveness of those sins which are revealed in the law. All this, of course, has a radical consequence for the structure of preaching, which is likewise defined by the same temporal sequence. Contrition must come before the joyful news of the Gospel. The lapse of time between the preaching of the law and the preaching of the Gospel may be ever so small and may even be infinitesimal. Yet the temporal problematic must still be maintained. Therefore the correlation of *guilt and forgiveness* is rigidly preserved.

Pietism especially has provided a case study for these kinds of conceptions. One thinks of the so-called *Busskampf* in which pietists were beleaguered by their horrors of the law until they

found a consolation in the righteousness of Christ.[4] It was sometimes assumed that a long period of preparation in misery
must anticipate this breakthrough of grace, and that such a
misery is an essential element in true conversion.[5] Moreover,
even when this was not assumed, it was felt that the preaching
of the law must prepare the soil for the good seed of the Gospel.
Here it is worthy of note that the problematic of a temporal
sequence gave birth to serious scruples within pietism itself.
It was frequently an occasion for doubts and suspicions. Zinzendorf, for example, though brought up on pietism, was thoroughly convinced that this is not the way in which a man
comes to have faith. The dread of the law and the pangs of sin
are not the essence of conversion. Therefore Zinzendorf concluded that true repentance springs up from the *Gospel*.[6]

Now obviously, these questions were disputed a long time
before the pietistic *Busskampf*.[7] The crucial issue of the relation
of the law and the Gospel has always been of interest in the
Church and her theology. Very early she rejected the dualistic
antithesis of Marcion. Therefore she was compelled to face the
question of the law-and-Gospel relationship.[8] It is especially
in Calvin's theology that these questions are set in a sharp focus.
Though Calvin was strongly under the impression of the holiness
of God's law and the gravity of man's sin, he affirmed that
repentance *follows* faith and is produced *by* faith. *Poenitentia,*
in his theology, does not anticipate the Christian life but finds
place *within that life*.[9]

4. Cf. *ibid.*, III, 535.
5. Cf. *ibid.*, IV, 140ff., where Bavinck describes Methodism as the effort to
   pull together the *Busskampf* in an acute crisis.
6. Cf. Bavinck on Zinzendorf (*ibid.*, III, 535). Zinzendorf saw more and
   more the peril of a works-sanctification and works-righteousness which
   views penance as the condition of salvation. He warned against "the
   doctrine of a serious demeanor in Christianity which anticipates pardon,
   and a necessary struggle of penitence (*Busskampf*) on the part of a man
   who seeks grace." Cf. F. Gartner, *Karl Barth und Zinzendorf. Die
   bleibende Bedeutung Zinzendorfs auf Grund der Beurteilung des Pietis-
   mus durch Karl Barth,* 1953, p. 17. Further, on Zinzendorf: Gösta Hök,
   Zinzendorfs Begriff der Religion, 1948, and Leiv Aalen, "Die Theologie
   des Grafen von Zinzendorf," *Gedenkschrift für W. Elert,* 1955, p. 220.
7. For the ancient Church, cf. V. E. Hasler, *Gesetz und Evangelium in der
   alten Kirche bis Origenes,* 1953.
8. On Marcion, cf. Hasler, *ibid.*, p. 44; also my *The Triumph of Grace in
   the Theology of Karl Barth,* 1956, Chap. 8.
9. Bavinck, in discussing this conception of Calvin, makes several comments on Luther which illuminate the problem. "Now Luther, also,

We let ride at this point the question of whether, and to what extent, Calvin himself *grew* in his doctrine of repentance.[10] We are only concerned with his final expression in his latest *Institutes*. We have in mind the chapter on repentance (III, 3) in which he viewed the entire substance of the Gospel in terms of repentance and forgiveness of sin. "It ought to be a fact beyond controversy," he states, "that repentance not only constantly follows faith, but is also born of faith" (III, 3, 1). How little this can be doubted, in his judgment, is evident from the use of the term *"extra controversiam."*[11] Calvin took issue with those who "suppose that repentance precedes faith, rather than flows from it, or is produced by it as fruit from a tree. Such persons have never known the power of repentance, and are moved to feel this way by an unduly slight argument" (3, 1).[12]

The appeal that such people make to Scripture confuses badly the whole point of the scriptural summons to repent (cf. III, 3, 2).[13] For when they read that summons, "do they not derive the reason for repenting from grace itself and the promise of salvation?" (3, 2). They fail to appreciate that the voice of the prophet "is bidden to begin with comfort and glad tidings" (cf. Isa. 40:1). What Calvin is concerned to show, in other words, is not a certain "space of time" in which faith produces repentance. Rather, in saying that faith "precedes" repentance his purpose is to demonstrate "that a man cannot apply himself seriously to repentance without knowing himself to belong to God" (3, 2). Calvin does not presume to dictate

certainly knew this *poenitentia*. He too was familiar with the fact that the true *contritio* presupposes *amor justitiae* and finds its origin in the benefits of Christ. But alongside this, he constantly held to the necessity of a preparatory preaching of the law and a so-called *contritio passiva*" (*op. cit.*, III, 523). This remark of Bavinck is certainly meant as a criticism — as is also his comment that in the Lutheran confessions and theology conversion is constantly subdivided in two parts, *contritio* and *fides*. These relate to the antithesis of "law and Gospel," whereas in Calvin penance is given a place *within the Christian life* (524).

10. Cf. the important article of H. Strathmann, "Die Entstehung der Lehre Calvins von der Busse," in *Calvinstudien*, 1909, pp. 187-245.

11. "Poenitentiam vero non modo fidem continuo subsequi, sed ex ea nasci, extra controversiam esse debet."

12. Cf. especially E. Blaser, "Vom Gesetz in Calvins Predigten über den 119. Psalm," *Festschrift für A. Schädelin*, 1950, pp. 67-78.

13. This centers mainly in the scriptural summons to repent: e.g., Matt. 3:2; 4:17; Acts 20:21.

how a man should be brought to faith; nor does he deny that some people have an "initial fear" (*"initialis timor"*) of conscience. But what Calvin does maintain is that there is no "semblance of reason" in the "madness" of those who, in order to begin with repentance, "prescribe to their new converts certain days during which they must practice penance, and when these at length are over, admit them into communion of the grace of the gospel" (3, 2). Calvin repudiates this claim in categorical terms. "Can true repentance stand, apart from faith? Not at all" (3, 5). There is always a fusion but never a confusion of faith and repentance; and "though they cannot be separated, they ought to be distinguished" (3, 5). Repentance, therefore, is true conversion to God with one's whole heart (3, 6), and comes forth "from an earnest fear of God" (3, 7). Taking its root in faith, it consists of mortification and vivification (3, 8), both of which are the effects of participation in Christ (3, 9). In other words, no case can be made for a repentance in terms of the law alone which antecedes one's faith. Though some persons speak of a "repentance of the law" and suggest that the "fear of God" is exemplified in Cain, Saul, and Judas (3, 4), the Scripture refers us to repentance as the gift of God (3, 21: *"singulare Dei donum"*). There is no such thing as an isolated "repentance of the law." Furthermore, we never hate our sin unless we have "previously been seized with a love of righteousness" (3, 20).

Karl Barth has noted with appreciation the fact that Calvin roots repentance in faith and derives both mortification and vivification from the concept of *ex Christi participatione* (3, 9). But he also inquires if Calvin was completely consistent at this point, and he replies in the negative. Barth finds in Calvin a dominant accent on the fear of God and impending judgment. He suggests that it was this strain which led to a onesided emphasis on *mortificatio*.[14] It seems to us, however, that this analysis does less than full justice to Calvin. Though it is not clear why Calvin took exception to a description of vivification as "happiness" (3, 3) and substituted "the desire to live in a holy and devoted manner," it remains the case that Barth goes too far in asking why Calvin, having once begun on the high note of *faith and repentance,* ends up in a "rather irrelevant discussion of the threatening sin against the Holy Ghost, and finally with a grim reminder of king Ahab and similar examples

14. *K.D.,* IV/2, 656 (ET, 581).

of a hypocritical and therefore useless repentance."[15] Barth fails to recognize that Calvin, in the light of this faith-and-repentance theme, was concerned to show the great difference between a merely artificial repentance and a true repentance which stems from faith (3, 25). Moreover, in demonstrating this difference he never wavered from his positive statements in regard to faith and repentance. No matter how he emphasized the significance of God's law, he did not conceive of that law in abstraction from the Gospel. Therefore he did not speak of the law as something which must "go before" on the way of repentance.

It is evident that the problematic of a law-and-Gospel sequence is completely untenable. Repentance does not come by the preaching of the law, to be followed by the preaching of the Gospel. And yet the function of the law is not ignored in the approach which we are now suggesting. It is not the case that the Gospel alone is important. As a matter of fact, repentance comes in view precisely *within* the preaching of the Gospel.

Therefore it is not by accident that Calvin, in order to show that repentance flows forth from faith, recalled the summons to repent in both John the Baptist and Christ. "Repent, for the kingdom of heaven is at hand" (Matt. 3:2; 4:17).[16] If we object that this imperative summons us to repent *first* before we enter the Kingdom, the answer of Calvin is that we little understand the "meaning that binds these words together" (III, 3, 2). For the summons to repent is motivated by the approach of the Kingdom and derives from "grace itself and the promise of salvation" (3, 2). There is no suggestion of a relativizing of repentance at this point; for the summons to repent is closely tied up with the message of the Kingdom. Therefore Christ upbraided "the cities where most of his mighty works had been

15. *Ibid.*, 657 (ET, 581).
16. Cf. also Acts 20:21: "testifying both to Jews and to Greeks of repentance to God and of faith in our Lord Jesus Christ." Cf. further W. G. Kümmel, *Das Bild des Menschen im N.T.*, 1948, p. 8, regarding the call to conversion "in view of this imminent kingdom of God"; H. N. Ridderbos, *De Komst van het Koninkrijk*, 1950, pp. 207f., on the riches of salvation, bound up with the coming of the Kingdom, which give structure to repentance; *TWNT*, I, *s.v. basileía;* III, *s.v. kērýssō*, D. 3. b, on John the Baptist, whose "preaching of repentance is also prophecy" (cf. Mark 1:7); IV, *s.v. metanoéō*, E. II. 1. The story of John's birth enunciates that his mission was prophetical and his call to repent bound up with the coming of Christ. Cf., e.g., Luke 1:76f.

done, because they did not repent" (Matt. 11:20; cf. v. 21). The concern in this passage is with that "way of righteousness" which was already pointed out by John and was followed not by the Pharisees but by tax collectors and harlots (Matt. 21: 31-32; cf. Luke 7:29). In other words, the concern was with "a baptism of repentance for the forgiveness of sins" (Mark 1:4). This repentance is the act of total and radical conversion[17] and never an isolated fact or a merely preparatory stage on the road to salvation. The focus is on those fruits that "befit repentance" unto God (Matt. 3:8).

For that reason the man who severs the bond between repentance and the Gospel can only lose both of these. "Some have understood John the Baptist as merely a gloomy preacher of repentance and have been deaf to the promising words of forgiveness of sins. Others have lost sight of the call to repentance in Jesus' words."[18] In that way they have forced a wedge between the law and the Gospel and have played off the one against the other. The only real defense against this danger is the Word of God itself. Surely the Gospel is for sinners, and Jesus is the "friend of tax collectors and sinners" (Matt. 11:19; Luke 7:47),[19] but precisely for that reason he calls sinners to repentance and conversion. Therefore there is "joy before the angels of God over one sinner who repents" (Luke 15:10). The proclamation of salvation *is* the summons to repent. Whatever we say about the *law* of God, or his *wrath* and *judgment,* cannot be said as a prefatory or a generalized truth; for we simply cannot comprehend the law until we have seen it in its unbreakable union with the Gospel of God's Kingdom and the forgiveness of our sins. Only then is repentance fathomed in its rightful relation to the Lord of the Kingdom (cf. Matt. 24:46; 25:1-13). Only then is every legalistic criterion for entering the Kingdom refuted in a very definitive way. "For I tell you, unless your righteousness exceeds that of the scribes and Pharisees, you will never enter the kingdom of heaven" (Matt. 5:20). Certainly the scribes and Pharisees knew the law. Yet the words of Christ were not a disqualification of the law (of which no

---

17. Cf. Ridderbos, *op. cit.,* p. 197.
18. J. Schniewind, *Die Freude der Busse,* 1956, p. 24; *TWNT,* III, *s.v.* *kērýssō,* D. 5.
19. The statement, though used opprobriously, was nonetheless true — the same as when the Pharisees murmured, "This man receives sinners and eats with them" (Luke 15:2). Unawares, they preached the Gospel.

iota or dot could perish) but a reminder that our password for entering the Kingdom is *true repentance*. In the light of this repentance the law of God was now extolled (Matt. 5:18).[20]

Therefore J. Schniewind rightly asserts that the "real sin of the Pharisees was impenitence."[21] In contrast to that sin we must see the repentance in which one takes up his cross and follows Jesus (Luke 9:23). Luther had a profound understanding of the *Gospel* when he posited as his *first thesis* in 1517: "When our Lord and Master Jesus Christ said 'Repent,' he called for the entire life of believers to be nothing but penitence." Certainly it is dangerous to lay hold on a single New Testament concept and to call it the "center" of Christian piety;[22] nevertheless, it is clear that the concept of *metánoia* is essential to the entire Gospel message. *Metánoia* (repentance, conversion)[23] has everything to do with both the law and the Gospel. We are not suggesting that the law is a "preface" to the Gospel. Nor is it something worthy of investigation in its own right in a so-called "psychology of conversion." But we do mean that repentance can only be viewed within the scope of the Kingdom of heaven and can only be preached within the message of that Kingdom, "not as its presupposition but as its consequence."[24] Conversion and repentance are not the *antici-*

---

20. Cf. especially L. Goppelt, *Christentum und Judentum im ersten und zweiten Jahrhundert*, 1954, particularly pp. 45ff.

21. Schniewind, *op. cit.*, p. 31.

22. Cf. H. Pohlmann, *Die Metanoia als Zentralbegriff der christlichen Frömmigkeit*, 1938.

23. It is clear that *metánoia* is not exhaustively defined by the term *repentance*. *Metánoia* is conversion, changing one's course of direction, contrition *in actu*, in which the direction of this activity is evident, as in the case of the Old Testament "turning to Jahwe." Cf. J. Bieneck, "Die Bekehrungspredigt," *Ev.Theol.*, 1957, p. 92.

24. O. Michel, "Die Umkehr nach der Verkündigung Jesu," *Ev.Theol.*, 1938, p. 11. The intention of Michel is obvious: *metánoia* cannot be seen as something isolated from the Kingdom. The way *to* the Kingdom *is* the way of conversion. "Unless you turn and become like children, you will never enter the kingdom of heaven" (Matt. 18:3). This turning is then a positive act — a turning *to* God (I Pet. 2:25; II Cor. 3:16; I Thess. 1:9; Luke 1:16; Rev. 16:9); at the same time, it is a turning *away from sin* (Acts 3:26; 8:22). There is grief (II Cor. 7:10) — but this *mortificatio* is not a "part" of conversion but an essential aspect; it is "godly grief" or a sorrow *toward God*. Cf. Acts 11:18 ("repentance unto life") and Lord's Day 22 on the "unity" of conversion ("heartfelt sorrow" and "heartfelt joy").

pation of the Kingdom "to come" but the decisive attestation that we have *already entered the Kingdom.*

With this message and this summons to repent the disciples went into their world. In these words Peter entreated the Jewish people to "repent, and be baptized every one of you in the name of Jesus Christ for the forgiveness of your sins" (Acts 2:38). As he set before them the *sufferings of Christ* he challenged them to repent. Repent *"therefore,* and turn again, that your sins may be blotted out" (Acts 3:19; cf. 8:22). This was the message that Paul proclaimed on the Areopagus. Though God has "overlooked" the times of ignorance he now commands that *all men everywhere should repent.* For now the righteous judgment is laid in the hands of him who is risen from the dead (Acts 17:30, 31). The cross of Jesus Christ motivates and defines the call to repent.[25] Therefore it is impossible that preaching should ignore, *for even a moment,* the reality of the Kingdom which has come. It is impossible that it should ignore the advent of salvation and fall back again into a situation in which salvation can still be left outside the limits of our attention.

All of this, we repeat, is not a disparagement of the law and the judgment. It is not a watering down of the condemnation and the wrath of God. For only in relation to these realities can the Gospel be understood at all. That fact is clear in the preaching of John the Baptist (cf. Matt. 3:2, 11). The *joy* of the Gospel is the correlate of man's own guilty, lost, and fallen estate; nevertheless the dreadfulness of the judgment is also manifest, now that salvation has come, in relation to the Gospel alone. There is no room for a preaching of "mere emptiness and lostness" which prepares the way for the message of Good News. "Today" is the time of fulfillment. That message gives us every reason to repent (cf. Luke 4:21, 18-19).

How little this diminishes from the importance of the law is apparent when we see that Christ's fulfillment of the law actually set the lives of believers under a "new law." Therefore we read of a repentance and conversion and a joyful subjection to this "new commandment" which is "not burdensome" (I John 5:3). This subjection is the clearest evidence of true repentance. *In* repentance God has every right to expect of believers that they fulfill his "new law." Therefore Paul (himself a convert; cf. Acts 26:18) knew that he continued to stand in

25. Michel, *op. cit.,* p. 412.

subjection to the law of Jesus Christ (cf. Gal. 6:2). His subjection to the law might seem, at first, to be quite complicated
and paradoxical; yet it was really a profound truth which he
uttered when he professed that he was personally not "under
law" and yet not "without law" (I Cor. 9:20-21). The commandment of God must be understood and obeyed as a "new
commandment" which calls for repentance (John 13:34; I John
2:8); nevertheless there *is* no repentance which stands apart
from, or which anticipates, the Gospel. Therefore Calvin intuitively conceived of the summons to repent *in relation to the
Kingdom*. He saw the intimate bond of faith and repentance
as *"extra controversiam"* for the members of the Church.

This appearing of salvation in the Kingdom which had
come must be seen as the main turning point in the history
of redemption. We cannot say, however, that a legalism was
prevalent in the early history of Israel. In the prophets' calls to
"return to Jahwe" there is no trace of a legalism at all. There
is no idea of an isolated concept of the law. Instead, the appeals
to a radical and constant conversion grew out of the situation
in which the God of the *covenant* "drew nigh." The appeals
were certainly "to obey," and yet they did not contain a legalistic
element. Obedience was seen as an essential feature of repentance.[26] Therefore the confrontation between Judaism and the
Gospel in Jesus' own day found place within the context
of the law. The issue was not the inner dialectic of the law and
the Gospel (both seen as the Word of God) but was rather the
repudiation of the law's misuse and the perversion of the rela-

---

26. Würthwein (*TWNT*, IV, *s.v. metanoéō*) contends that in later times
there was a "legalistic trait" ("ein gesetzlicher Zug") in the summons to repentance. He illustrates this by an appeal to Deuteronomy.
(We are not concerned here with the dating of this book.) Conversion,
in Deuteronomy, is seen as "obedience to the deuteronomic law" (cf.
30:2); also in Malachi (3:7), where the summons to repent is bound up
with the evil of robbing God of his tithe (3:8f.); also Nehemiah (9:29 —
turning back to the law). But to see a legalistic strain in these references is illegitimate; for in such a view we would presuppose that the
law is already abstracted from the living God. Since this, however, is
not the case, we cannot object to the manner in which Scripture speaks
in regard to repentance, for conversion is *to Jahwe* (*ibid.*, 985). To say
that in such utterances the prophetic thought of total repentance "could
not be held in its original grandeur and radicalness," is to fail to appreciate the meaning of radical repentance which makes such concrete
speaking possible. Cf. Ridderbos, *op. cit.*, pp. 274f.

tions in which the law was seen within the activity of God. True *metánoia* was lacking when men praised God with their lips though their hearts were far from him. It was idle worship in which they then engaged, for they taught as doctrines the "precepts of men" and misconceived the true meaning of the law (Matt. 15:8-9).

These persons must understand the words of Christ, who called *sinners* to himself and whose invitation was therefore seen as a *scandal*. "I desire mercy and not sacrifice" (Matt. 9:13). The course which Christ advised was to "go and learn what this means." The same words are found in a later context, in regard to the Sabbath: "And if you had known what this means, 'I desire mercy and not sacrifice,' you would not have condemned the guiltless" (12:7). The purpose of those statements is not to oppose the law but to *support the law;* and the reason why this was not seen is that the opponents of Christ had taken away the "key of knowledge" from the law (Luke 11:52). Certainly it is not difficult to understand the content of this accusation. Ridderbos speaks of the "proper temper" and "self-surrender," the "love" in which the whole substance of the law is fulfilled.[27] By forfeiting the "key of knowledge" the antagonists of Christ had misrepresented the law's meaning and had made a fatal caricature of the law. If ever they rediscovered that "key" and restored it to the lives of others, they would enter into the Kingdom. But as it was they had no access, and those who wished to enter were withstood. Without the "key" the bond between knowing and believing is broken. With the "key" one comes to know the *Father himself.*[28]

In all this it is evident why the demand to preach the law and repentance before or apart from the Gospel is so very objectionable. It is not because this notion overemphasizes the relations of forgiveness and guilt, life and death, God's grace and man's lostness, or the forgiveness and confession of sin. Whoever ignores those relations has failed to see the thrust of the biblical message and does injury to the essence and content of Gospel preaching. All this suggests why the problem of sequence has arisen in a false quest for an oversimplified preaching of the Gospel. In such a preaching rain and blessings come

27. *Ibid.*, p. 279.
28. Cf. Bultmann, in *TWNT*, I, *s.v. ginōskō*, E. 3. There is also, then, a harmony between knowing and keeping his commandments (I John 2:3-5). For his *new commandment* is the commandment of *love*.

down on a dry and thirsty land and even on souls who do *not thirst*. The Gospel must be preserved, it is said, for those who can rightly cry out: "O God, thou art my God, I seek thee, my soul thirsts for thee; my flesh faints for thee, as in a dry and weary land where no water is" (Ps. 63:1). Should not preaching give the prospect of a jubilee which comes when waters "break forth in the *wilderness,* and streams in the *desert*" (Isa. 35:6-7)? There must always be a concern lest we cut this implicit relation in God's comforting of those who truly *mourn* (Matt. 5:4), or satisfying those who *hunger and thirst* (Matt. 5:6; Rev. 22: 17), or opening the Kingdom to those who are *poor in spirit* (Matt. 5:3; 11:5).

Yet the harmony of Scripture is broken as soon as we conclude from this accent a temporal sequence of law-and-Gospel. Our legitimate concern for preserving the correlation of "guilt and forgiveness" is then reduced to an illegitimacy; furthermore, the law is then isolated from the Gospel, while the Gospel is seen as the answer to the state of dejection aroused by the law-in-itself. The only possible result in this kind of thinking is a dualism within our picture of God. We see a God whose wrath, holiness, and righteousness are opposed to (or juxtaposed with) his love and his mercy. Moreover, the cross, if not dualistically construed, is regarded on the side of his love, in opposition to his justice. God's justice has everything to do with law. The cross is then viewed as the source of our knowledge of forgiveness and the law is viewed as the source of our knowledge of sin. Already here, however, we observe the fallacy in this whole conception of the cross. For if anything is clear in the biblical revelation it is certainly that the cross is the revelation of God's love but *also, at the same time,* of his holiness and justice. In the cross we can see how futile it is to separate these attributes of God. Precisely *there* we find Christ as the "expiation" whom God "put forward" to exhibit his righteousness (Rom. 3:25f.). Therefore the cross does not display an inner dialectic of God's attributes which mutually restrict and relativize each other. Rather, it shows us that sin was atoned for precisely because *it was also condemned*. Thus the Gospel is a fountain of knowledge for our sins as well as our forgiveness.

Recall the Lord's Supper formulary which we have already referred to above. In the cross we see *how* God has acted in regard to our sin and what his *curse of sin involves*. For God

did not "blind himself" when he condemned our sin upon
the cross. As a matter of fact, the cross is the mirror which
enables us to see the reality of an utter God-forsakenness and
cursing of our sin. Christ became a *curse for us,* "for it is written, 'Cursed be every one who hangs on a tree'" (Gal. 3:13).
The *Gospel* reveals how God laid on him the iniquity of us all,
and how the punishment of our sin was *on him.* The *Gospel*
discloses how he was cut off from the land of the living for
the transgressions of others to whom the stroke was due (Isa.
53:6-8). How, then, could the Gospel *not* be the source of our
knowledge of sin when we read that God made him "who
knew no sin" to be sin for our sakes (II Cor. 5:21)? Sin is laid
bare in its deepest dimensions and ugliness in this fact that
God "did not spare his own Son but gave him up for us all"
(Rom. 8:32).[29]

So too, in the preaching of the cross we observe the utter
impossibility of this dilemma of the Gospel and the law. When
we look at the cross it is simply unthinkable that the preaching
of the law alone could lead us to repentance. Indeed, the man
who thinks that way can only do violence to the preaching of
the Gospel. He then draws a sharp dualism between the "orders"
of the law and grace and assigns the preaching of the law to
the former sphere alone.[30] It need not perplex us that this kind
of preaching ends up in a legalism or moralism which conceives of conversion as a preliminary "phase" or a meritorial
"condition." One comes to that position from a fear that the
preaching of the law may be eclipsed by the preaching of the
Gospel. He does not realize that the preaching of the law and
wrath of God is included within the fullness of the Gospel
proclamation. The man who knows that the law is fulfilled in
the Messiah and that God has condemned man's sin in the
flesh will also appreciate that the Gospel calls him to an obedience precisely in the perspective and the blackness of the
cross. At one and the same moment the Gospel declares to
us God's absolute judgment on our sin and the fullness and

---

29. Cf. Michel, *op. cit.,* p. 185, on this "delivering up" of Christ as a
    "judicial surrendering" ("richterliche Preisgabe"). So profound and so
    complete is this "delivering" that God will also freely give us, with him,
    "all things" (Rom. 8:32). The charge against God's elect falls away be-
    cause the judgment has already been passed on *Christ* (v. 33).
30. Cf. Blaser's references to the way in which Calvin combined the law
    with the promise of the Gospel (*op. cit.,* pp. 73f.).

depths of his grace. Here is the glad message which calls us away from the judgment and the condemnation of God, and which entreats us to share in his mercy. For sin is both revealed and condemned in the cross.

Therefore man's justification is not a mere "appearance" but is certainly *real*. The cross discloses our guilt and *forgiveness*. There are not two separable sources for knowing our sin but a single revelation of sin's reality in the cross. In the cross our sin is taken away and the justice of God's law is fulfilled. Those who ignore that fact have only a single alternative: to separate the Gospel and the law. They might not do so with the same boldness as Marcion, but their relating the law and Gospel to two very different divine attributes will bring them to a rather similar result.[31] We can get beyond this dichotomy only when we cease to isolate the law from the Gospel and resist the urge to conceive of the law in a static relationship. We must see the law as God's holy law which was given in communion and love but was violated by man's own transgression and sin.

Against *this* transgression God directs his holy wrath. He is revolted by this contempt for his love and his glory. We cannot conceive of the depths of man's *anomia* without seeing how *much* God despises this breaking of his law, and how *much* he refuses to let men walk in *this way*.

Therefore the man who preaches the Gospel must point to both guilt *and* forgiveness, both death *and* life, both judgment *and* grace, both being lost *and* being found again. The preaching of the Gospel is incompatible with superficial and sentimental platitudes. It can only lead to a confession of our guilt. Peter observed the brilliance of Christ's glory in contrast to the poverty of man. Therefore he cried out, "Depart from me, for I am a sinful man, O Lord" (Luke 5:8). But Peter did not need a preliminary reminder of his sinfulness.[32] In a similar way, the sinful woman who anointed Christ's feet from a very deep love was the special object of Christ's favor. "Her sins, which are *many*, are forgiven, for she loved *much*" (Luke 7:47). The Gospel, in other words, puts the final damper on any wrong notion that the message of the Church is a message of "cheap grace." The Gospel cautions us against trite and trifling

31. Cf. the statement of Tertullian: "Separatio legis et evangelii proprium et principale opus est Marcionis" (*Adversus Marcionem*, I, 19; 5, 16).
32. The context (Luke 5:1-11) is the story of the remarkable catch of fish.

phrases and any lack of esteem for the law and the wrath, the righteousness and holiness of God.[33]

This idea of "cheap grace" came into our theological vocabulary when Dietrich Bonhoeffer took his firm position against a certain kind of preaching. Bonhoeffer reacted against a preaching of grace apart from the law, or apart from the concreteness of God's addressing himself to sinful men, or apart from the marvel of forgiven *guilt*.[34] But certainly that protest was not against the "for nothing" of justification (cf. Rev. 22:17; Isa. 55:1). Bonhoeffer's criticism was against a preaching of the Gospel which fails to articulate the unspeakable value of the message of *joy* that God is Victor over man's sinfulness and lostness. Therefore he criticized a "grace" which fails to take account of the law and disrupts the relation between the law and the Gospel. Once that rupture is complete there is no room for a "new commandment" and preaching can only become shipwrecked on superficial clichés.

"Cheap grace," however, is precluded by the very meaning of *Good News*. The "for nothing" of grace can only make sense against the backdrop of the cross of *forsakenness and curse*. Therefore the reality of the cross closes the way to an isolation of the law in reference to the Gospel or the Gospel in reference to the law. Here we find the touchstone for any valid preaching of the Gospel. Such a preaching must understand and illumine this relation of the Gospel and the law.

Can we do justice to that relation when we say, with Barth, that the law is the "form of the Gospel"?[35] The discussion touched off by this formula has centered largely in the question of whether the "twoness" of the law and the Gospel is wrongly resolved by Barth into a false "unity." Does a reaction to legalism bring Barth to an antilegalistic extreme? Can he still give a valid function to the *law?*

If we call the law the "form" of the Gospel we would seem to imply that in the law it is really the *Gospel* which stands before us in a certain "formal dress." Therefore the distinction of form and content does not preclude the fact that it is really

33. It is wrong to see this resistance of the Gospel in terms of a "compensation" for the law which does violence to the full content of the Gospel. Any such notion of "balance" is certainly excluded.
34. Cf. H. Berkhof, *Crisis der Midden-orthodoxie*, pp. 31f.
35. K. Barth, *Evangelium und Gesetz*, 1935.

the *Gospel* — in this legal form — with which we have to do. Obviously Barth intended this distinction as the parallel to another expression which he frequently uses, namely that the wrath of God is the form (or *Gestalt*) of his grace.[36] Once again, the implication is that even in his wrath it is really the *gracious* God who stands before us.

Now certainly the intention of Barth is to steer clear of any legalism or dualism which isolates the law from the Gospel or divorces the wrath of God from his grace. Barth wants nothing to do with a law abstracted in a kind of legal hypostasis or having its own self-contained order, entirely apart from the order of God's grace. Here H. Gollwitzer has chosen sides with Barth. In an important article he has conceded that the distinction of law and Gospel was decisive for Luther's rediscovery of the Gospel's true meaning.[37] Yet that dogmahistorical fact, he says, does not mean that we have an easy objection to level against Barth. The whole issue in Luther's distinction presupposes a recognition of unity apart from which the distinction could not have been made at all.[38] Thus, if we want to avoid the pitfalls of Marcion we shall have no choice but to entertain this question of unity. Luther himself did that, as Gollwitzer affirms. In his distinction of law and Gospel he maintained the unity of the single Word of God.

Therefore the distinction does not imply a dualism in God's single address to man. It repudiates the law as a means of grace and refers us to the Gospel as the revelation of the only way of salvation. Nor can Luther's description of the law as an *opus alienum* and the Gospel as an *opus proprium* be seen in a dualistic way.[39] Rather, in this distinction God's acting and speaking in and through the law can be viewed in relation to man's own sinning and misuse of the law as an avenue of salvation. For that reason, in Luther too, the law was conceived as the Word of God and a summons to faith. Luther recognized that already in the first commandment man is called upon to make a decision and to surrender. Gollwitzer has therefore concluded that, according to Luther, both the law and the Gospel

36. Cf. my *The Triumph of Grace in the Theology of Karl Barth,* pp. 321f.; also Berkhof, *op. cit.*
37. H. Gollwitzer, "Zur Einheit von Gesetz und Evangelium," in *Antwort,* 1956, pp. 287f. Cf. his reference (p. 286) to Luther's statement: "Cum commiscetur legi promissio, mera fit lex."
38. *Ibid.*
39. *Ibid.,* p. 239; cf. especially J. T. Bakker, *Coram Deo,* 1956, pp. 74f.

come to us as a *demand*. "The will of God in the law and Gospel is therefore the same. It is precisely the unity of the law and the Gospel."[40] In that light, therefore, Gollwitzer endorses the statement of Barth: "The imperative is not alongside the Gospel but is the very form of the Gospel."[41] Gollwitzer does question if it is right to say, with Barth, that the law is "the necessary form of the Gospel whose content is grace."[42] For the concepts of *form* and *content* are philosophically loaded. At the same time, what Barth essentially meant is "not dependent on those terms."[43]

In that way Gollwitzer tries to shorten the distance between Luther and Barth. At the same time, Barth himself is very critical of Luther's statements concerning the relation of the law and the Gospel. He sees in Luther, as a rule, a "special revelation of divine Law, holiness and wrath, separate from the revelation of God's grace." Luther's concern was "the consciousness of sin, the fear of God's wrath, and penitence."[44] In opposing this interpretation of Luther (which Gollwitzer disputes), Barth contends that "in Scripture we do not find the Law alongside the Gospel but *in* the Gospel."[45] Therefore he reverses the usual order of "law and Gospel" and speaks of "the Gospel and the law." He recognizes that *within* this sequence there is room for reflecting on "the law and the Gospel." Nevertheless, the right accent is preserved only when we speak of the *Gospel first*.

This reversal of the sequence has everything to do with the inner structure of Barth's theology. Negatively, we find a radical antilegalism in Barth — for Barth is against the law as a means of salvation. Positively, we find the triumph and priority of grace. For our purposes, however, it is enough to say that a crucial problem is now exposed. The issue does not lie in the terminology of *form* and *content,* or the exactitude of the parallel which Barth draws between these terms and the wrath of God as the "form" of his grace.[46] That parallel follows from

40. Gollwitzer, *op. cit.,* p. 295.
41. Barth, *op. cit.,* p. 11.
42. Gollwitzer, *loc. cit.*
43. Cf. Barth, *K.D.,* II/1, 407 (ET, 362-363).
44. *Ibid.* "In this respect we do not follow Luther...." Barth's "usually" leaves room for other lines in Luther's thought (cf. pp. 407-408 and I/2, 340; ET, II/1, 363 and I/2, 311).
45. *Ibid.,* II/1, 407 (ET, 363).
46. Cf. *The Triumph of Grace, loc. cit.;* also H. Berkhof, *op. cit.,* espe-

his basic view of creation and redemption. Barth is adamant in rejecting the notion of creation as the ontic and noetic prestage, or the prior ordinance, of salvation. Here he touches on a problem that interested both Luther and Calvin.

We have observed that Calvin conceived of repentance as proceeding from faith and not from some "preparatory" preaching of the law.[47] This conception, we have said, must always determine the relation of the law and the Gospel. Yet one does injury to precisely *that relation* when he employs, with Barth, the terminology of *form* and *content*. For the preaching of the Gospel is the preaching of redemption from guilt and the brokenness of communion with God. It is the preaching of God's command. Therefore we can say that Gollwitzer has too easily brought Barth and Luther together.[48] As a matter of fact, Luther deliberately drove the distinction of "law and Gospel" to the very forefront of his theology. He did not conceive of these in the relation of form and content. He saw them as mutually related in the single preaching of salvation.[49] In this interlacedness the law was not swallowed up in the Gospel, and it did not emerge as a new way of salvation. Instead, the harmony of the single Word of God was preserved in both the Gospel and the law.

Therefore the crucial question is not if Luther and Calvin were consistently clear in discussing the *timor et terrores conscientiae*. The question is this: Did they tolerate a preaching of the law which could or should be isolated from the preaching of the Gospel? Did they try, in that way, to *anticipate God's grace?* If they did, they would have thrown out the "end" of

cially p. 40. In Barth's view, according to Berkhof, the law is nearly absorbed by the Gospel and the distinction between these is obscured.

47. Cf. Gollwitzer, *op. cit.*, p. 307.

48. Cf. *ibid.* Luther's thesis of "repentance from faith," Gollwitzer maintains, was amended under the influence of Melanchthon, who contended that one must first experience the threat of the law "so that the heart may be able to understand the Gospel as deliverance." This line of thought was then systematized in Lutheranism. It would seem to us, however, that Luther's interest was not in drawing conclusions from man's "independence" from God; he was concerned about the ambiguity of man's relation to God. There is nothing in Luther of what Gollwitzer finds in Melanchthon: the attempt "to gain a method of conversion from a psychological explanation of repentance" (*ibid.*). Cf. G. Spykman, *Attrition and Contrition at the Council of Trent*, 1955, pp. 90f., and K. Holl, *Gesammelte Aufsätze*, I, p. 82.

49. On this interrelationship, cf. especially Bakker, *op. cit.*, p. 74.

the law with all the "riches of salvation" implied. They would have discarded the very obvious sense of the summons of the cross to repent. They would have cancelled out the *heilshistorisch* significance of the cross. They would have substituted a temporal and *therefore an unhistorical sequence.* But if anything is obvious it is that the Reformers were well aware of these dangers. That fact is clear in their view of repentance. It is certainly borne out in their anti-legalist and anti-moralist polemic.[50]

While we differ from Barth, we shall have to face up to a further question: Does the interrelation of the law and the Gospel have only a "salvation-historical" aspect, or does it have reference to the "lapsarian" situation of man's own guilt and lostness? Can we speak of a prolapsarian state in which there was a "law"? Was there a "nomological" existence of man apart from and even prior to the distinction of the law and the Gospel? If there was, can we search there, perhaps, for the fundamental structure of what it means to be a "man"? R. Schippers, in weighing all of these questions, has affirmed that there was a law in man's "prolapsarian state," and that that law was there apart from the Gospel.[51] At the same time, we no longer may speak of this law in abstraction. Schippers' statement has reference to the creation of God which must certainly be distinguished from man's guilt and fallenness and therefore from the Gospel of God's grace which *saves.*

It stands to reason that we may not draw conclusions concerning the relation of the law and the Gospel or build a case for the "priority" of the law on such a basis as this. Man's original life under God's rule cannot be regarded, for even a moment, apart from God's love and communion. Within that communion man was subjected to God's holy and good commandment; furthermore, because of that communion the commandment was never an impersonal or a statutory rule. God's commandment expresses his lordship over *life.* Therefore, any discussion of the *usus legis,* in its various dimensions, is only conceivable in terms of this absolute goodness of God's commandment for creaturely man. The fact that this accent was sounded so frequently in Reformation and post-Reformation times is no evidence of the darkening of the Gospel, and is no recognition

50. Cf. Gollwitzer on Luther, *op. cit.,* p. 107, and Spykman on Calvin, *op. cit.,* pp. 245f.; also Blaser, *op. cit.,* p. 73.
51. R. Schippers, *De Gereformeerde Zede,* p. 197.

of a "legal order" above or before the "order of grace." What
we see in this accent is only the *enigmatic nature* of guilt in
the face of God's loving communion or the goodness of his rule.

Because of that fact we can never construe an antithesis between the covenants of "works" and "grace." We err if we interpret this distinction as though God's original covenant had
to do with *our* work or *our* achievement or *our* fulfillment of
his law, while the later covenant of grace has reference to the
pure gift of his *mercy* apart from all *our works.* If we assume
this we are compelled to say that God's original relation to
man was strictly "legal," or that the structure of that relation
was determined by man's merit. In that case, we lose sight of
the fact that man's obedience to God's command can never be
different from a thankful response to God's own fellowship.
Therefore S. G. DeGraaf has rightly said that the concept
which sees God's favor only at the *end* of man's way of obedience
is open to serious dispute. Man participates in God's favor,
communion and love already at the *very beginning.* In that
fact we see the awful reality of his guilt and apostasy.

There is good reason to ask if this terminological distinction of a "covenant of works" and a "covenant of grace" is
really so very happy. DeGraaf has rejected the concept of the
"covenant of works" and has said that it calls forth more problems than it can possibly solve.[52] If we view that term in contrast to the covenant of *grace,* he contends, we have no option
but to say that God preferred — at least at first — to hold himself aloof and not to commune with men. He wished to judge
men on the basis of their own merits and achievements. Here,
of course, DeGraaf's intention is very clear and incontestable.
He wanted to be done with the antithesis of merit and grace,

52. In "De Genade Gods en de Structuur der Ganse Schepping," *Phil. Ref.,*
I, p. 21. DeGraaf recalls in this connection that God threatens death in
the way of disobedience but does not promise life in the way of obedience. Cf. also his "Genade en Natuur," in *Christus en de Wereld,* 1939,
pp. 87f.; *Hoofdlijnen der Dogmatiek,* p. 61; *Openbaringsgeschiedenis,*
p. 18. All sorts of efforts have been made to clarify that the antithesis
merit-grace has not been meant in these two covenants; but it has
proved impossible, *de facto,* to eliminate this notion. This is evident in
the formulation of Kuyper, who suggested that there are two separate
"ways": that of the *worker* is by merit and that of the *believer* is by
grace. *Uit het Woord,* II, 209. Adam, as worker, followed the first way
and attempted to gain merit. Cf. what Kuyper says in *E Voto,* II, 389,
on the covenant partners in the covenant of works, who are "hired
servants" in contrast to the children of the household.

when seen as two possible "phases" in this one relation of
God and man. Even the obedience which men originally owed
to God could only be regarded as the product of God's own
love and graciousness, and could only root in God's own fellowship. If we drive a wedge between these concepts of *works* and
grace we interpose the notion of an impersonal legalism within
the original relation of God and man. In that way we convert
Schippers' statement, that the law could exist apart from the
Gospel, into a declaration that the law could exist apart from
the favor and fellowship of God.

Vainly do we search the Scriptures for any such antithesis
in the covenants of works and grace. Certainly there is a chasm
between *works* and *grace* as those two terms are used by the
Apostle Paul. But we find no indication that these terms point
to alternative paths which were once laid out by God. Rather
they point us to a much more radical antithesis. The way of
works is condemned by God because it is *not the way of God*.[53]

Therefore whoever burdens the so-called "covenant of works"
with the notion of achievement and presumes that we gain God's
favor in that way, must endorse the idea of a "nomological" ur-
existence of man and must cut asunder the law of God from
the fellowship of God. In that way he isolates and hypostatizes
the law. It is not clear how this infusion of *meritum* can leave
room for a genuine criticism of Rome concerning the question
of the meritoriousness of works.[54] Certainly it is better to say that

53. V. Hepp has wrongly opposed DeGraaf by alleging that this distinction
    finds place in Scripture in almost a literal sense; not terminologically
    but essentially. Hepp points to the contrast Scripture draws between
    "works of the law" and the grace of Christ (*Dreigende Deformatie*, I,
    1939, 41). His criticism is without any basis, however; for the desire to
    do the works of the law, as Paul saw it, is a *foolish* desire — a desire
    for one's own self-righteousness. We recall that Hepp accepted the
    word *merit* (*op. cit.*, 39) and solved the resulting problem by asserting
    that this term (as Paul used it) has no "economical" significance but
    only a "religious" one (39). But this is a clear indication of the kind
    of problem that rises when we identify the covenant of works with the
    way of works-righteousness. Hepp's appeal to the Westminster Confes-
    sion does nothing to substantiate his case; this confession speaks of
    "perfect and personal obedience" (cf. Müller, p. 558), though DeGraaf
    never challenged that. The issue was only the antithesis between *works*
    and *grace* — an antithesis that is incontrovertibly suggested by the
    terminology of these "two covenants" and can easily lead to serious
    consequences. Witness Hepp's own reference to the "works of the
    law" as a "proof" for the covenant of works.
54. We take note here of the views of Hans Küng. The idea of the meri-

God's commandment has always functioned exactly as it was
originally intended. That is, it has always functioned within
the situation of fellowship, where a man shares in God's favor
and is thus enjoined to abide in his love.

No fault of God's creation or communion has brought a
man to sever this fellowship with God. Furthermore, what remains after this break is not the law in its isolation but the
threatened judgment as prescribed by the law. Nonetheless, precisely this interrelatedness of sin and judgment must be seen
in the light of God's mercy. For God has turned in mercy toward
our world. In mercy his commandment is reinstated in all its
cogency and lucidity. In mercy it is seen as the sense and the
seal of his communion again.

We make a "problem" of God's commandment only when
we break this bond of communion between God and man and
empty the law of its meaning. In so doing we find that the
law is a *lex accusans* which kills and condemns and that God,
in the law, is our "enemy."[55] *Why* he is our enemy is clear to
anyone who fathoms the meaning and the depths of his command. When we understand that fact we appreciate the real
marvel in the harmony of the law and the Gospel. For God
does not confront us in a naked judgment but in the *preaching
of the Gospel*. He confronts us in the glad tidings proclaimed
within this situation of guilt and *despite* our disruption of

toriousness of good works is interpreted by Küng in terms of the New
Testament concept of reward. Cf. his *Rechtfertigung. Die Lehre Karl
Barths und die katholische Besinnung*, 1957, pp. 263ff. Trent, he says,
wished to regard merit as nothing but "an appeal to a sincere fear of
God and daily obedience, not a vain self-conceit" (p. 265). Cf. my
"De Kritische Functie van het 'Sola Fide,'" *G.T.T.*, 1957; and H.
Bouillard, *Karl Barth*, II, 1957, Chap. 5, 2 ("le partenaire de Dieu"),
and III, 285f.

55. The formulations of Erwin Reisner ("Bei den Verkehrten bist du
verkehrt," *K.u.D.*, I, 1955, pp. 321-329) are subject, it seems to me, to
serious criticism. He writes: "The thinking of fallen man is a perverse
thinking, and God accommodates himself in his judgment to this perversity; to the perverse he shows himself an equally perverse God."
Also: "He takes the order of disorder upon himself as though it were
really order" (324). But this is by no means the case, not even in the
Old Testament; it is far from supported in Ps. 18:26: "With the pure
thou dost show thyself pure; and with the crooked thou dost show
thyself perverse." It is evident that in Reisner's exegesis he goes far
beyond this text. For in God's attitude toward the perverse we see that
the eyes of the "haughty" are "brought down" (18:27). In reference to
this psalm Reisner also points to Rom. 1:18f. and Job 5:13.

communion. That is: he does not let us pine away in our lone-
liness or wither under the wilting judgments of the law. He
blesses us with salvation which is preached to the ends of the
earth. He implores all men everywhere to repent. Therefore
there is no dualism in the law and the Gospel. The one can
never be disjoined from the other. Therefore, too, it is no
depreciation of the law when the Church strives to do her only
task: namely, to *preach the Gospel.*

We have seen that this relation of the law and the Gospel
eliminates the problem of which of these is really the source
for the knowledge of our sin. The issue is not a matter of
priority but is rather the relation of the Gospel and man's
guilt. Yet once we have said that much, we should also observe
that the knowledge of our sin is not the self-evident result of
merely preaching the Gospel. As we have noted, the preaching
of the law of the covenant among the Israelites was not, in
itself, the assurance of a true repentance and obedience. Repeatedly it resulted in an actual increase of guilt and impenitence.

Furthermore, the advent of Christ's Kingdom did not guarantee that the Gospel of the crucified and risen Christ would meet
up with an automatic and positive response. The very factuality
and completeness of that salvation brought resistance on every
hand. Therefore Simeon foresaw that the Christ-child would be
"set for the fall and rising of many in Israel, and for a sign
that is spoken against" (Luke 2:34). Christ was the subject of
numerous disputes. He himself affirmed: ". . . blessed is he who
takes no offense at me" (Matt. 11:6). When Paul spoke of the
triumph of Christ and "the fragrance of the knowledge of him
everywhere," he also referred, in the same context, to "those
who are being saved" and "those who are perishing." Christians
are to one a "fragrance from death to death" and to the other
a "fragrance from life to life" (II Cor. 2:14f.). The Gospel came
into our world with an astonishing power and challenged men
everywhere to make a necessary choice. It impressed upon them
the urgency of Christ's words: "He who is not with me is against
me" (Matt. 12:30).

Therefore it is not the case that we pass *from* the law *to* the
Gospel as the source for the knowledge of our sin. Nor should
we see the Gospel as an easier or a quicker road to true repentance. One cannot say that the Gospel meets with less resistance

than the law. It does not automatically subdue our hearts. Paul knew the opposition which the Gospel of the cross elicited from both the Jews and the Gentiles. The Gospel was "a stumbling block" to the Jews and "folly" to the Gentiles (I Cor. 1:23; cf. Acts 7:51). Therefore Paul entreated his brethren to pray for him (II Thess. 3:1). He saw that the call to repentance and conversion must be urgent and real; yet he experienced that the herald, in himself, in no way assures a systematic or a uniform response. The question is very stubborn in the history of the Church and her theology: *Why* does the preaching of the Gospel bring forth such very different responses? The apostles were filled with the power of the salvation which they proclaimed, and they exalted in the glory of their message. Nevertheless, in the ministry of reconciliation they could only go forth as ambassadors with this very vital imperative: *"Be reconciled to God"* (II Cor. 5:20). They could not anticipate the results and could only wait prayerfully on God.

This message called for an answer and a choice, or an echo in man's heart. It is very remarkable that the apostles themselves did not expect to meet up, in an automatic sense, with willing responses. They knew that the Gospel is addressed to sinful, confused, and very stubborn men. Therefore those who preach must be supported by constant prayer. The apostles knew that they themselves did not have disposal over the fruits of their own preaching. God alone gives the increase.[56] Therefore *they* could pass no judgment on how the kingdom "comes" — for whenever the Gospel is heard and understood it is the evidence of the working of *God*. Therefore the disciples could only praise and magnify God. *He* was the One who gave the Gentiles repentance unto life (Acts 11:18; cf. 10:45; 14:27).

Certainly those who preached had to do with the unspeakable power of God's Word which "grew and multiplied" (Acts 12:24; 19:20). But they also experienced that the Gospel meets up with constant and relentless disdain (cf. Acts 28:24; 17:32f.). With joy and amazement the apostles observed the progress of the Gospel and carefully recorded the numbers that were added to the Church (Acts 2:41, 47). They could only be filled with

---

56. "I planted, Apollos watered, but God gave the growth" (I Cor. 3:6). Cf. v. 7: "So neither he who plants nor he who waters is anything, but only God who gives the growth." Yet it is striking that Paul says in this context: "For we are fellow workmen for God" (or "of God"); v. 9. Cf. Hillerdahl, *Gehorsam gegen Gott und Menschen,* 1955, p. 109.

awe. For the "way of the Gospel" is the "way of the Spirit," and the way of the Spirit (as Jesus told Nicodemus) is the way of the wind, which "blows where it wills, and you hear the sound of it, but you do not know whence it comes or whither it goes; so it is with every one who is born of the Spirit" (John 3:8). So too with every one who enters the Kingdom of heaven and who totally and radically repents.

Here we stand at the very limits of every human analysis of the depths of man's heart. We cannot know the "way" of this radical transition from unrepentance to repentance or "death to life." Only the symptoms are manifest in the confession of guilt and prayer (Luke 18:13; Acts 9:11), in humility and faith, and in actively doing the will of God (Matt. 7:21; 12:50). But the secret of this transition, in itself, can never be known. When the Canons refer to this process they rightly emphasize the miracle of the Spirit's regenerative work, which "pervades the inmost recesses of man." This is a work which "opens the closed and softens the hardened heart, and circumcises that which was uncircumcised; infuses new qualities into the will, which, though heretofore dead, he quickens; from being evil, disobedient, and refractory, he renders it good, obedient, and pliable" (CD, III-IV, 11). Nothing is explained in this statement — yet something is described. The miracle of a "new creation" is "not inferior in efficacy to creation or the resurrection from the dead" but is "evidently a supernatural work, most powerful, and at the same time most delightful, astonishing, mysterious, and ineffable" (III-IV, 12). Though this "ineffability" cannot be analyzed, it can be *confessed* as the mystery of the Holy Spirit. This is the same "ineffability" as we confront in the New Testament passages which speak of the progress of the Gospel in the early Church. For the message of the Gospel finds its center in the message of the end of all resistance and rebellion. It finds its center in the message of repentance and contrition *unto the forgiveness of our sins.*

It is striking that the focus on the Spirit in no way implies a watering down of the importance of preaching. The mystery of the Spirit did not detract from the dynamic of the Gospel but compelled the apostles to go out into their world. "Necessity" was laid upon them (I Cor. 9:16). They had no power to make or to break the Gospel but could only go forth in faith and in prayer. The mystery of the Spirit was evident in the very course of their mission. The early Church herself, once called from darkness, could only witness to the light. Therefore the miracle of the Spirit could not foster an "ecstatic mysticism" or an "eager passivism" but could only set the feet of messengers in motion with an élan which compelled them to circumscribe the earth with this one message: "Repent! and enter into the Kingdom of God!"[57]

The Church has been aware of this mystery of the Spirit and of her own mandate to preach the Gospel of Christ. She has recognized the urgency of her mandate and the impregnable barriers of man's heart when measured by the standards of men. The heart of man cannot repent and glories in the obstinacy of every sin. The Church has realized that she cannot eliminate preaching with a view to the Spirit or minimize the Spirit with a view to her preaching. Yet the question is very real: What is the "relation" between the *Word* and the *Spirit?* This is no theoretical or merely dogmatical question but a life-and-death issue in the preaching of the Church. How *can* both the mandate to preach and the stubbornness of man's own heart be *real?*

No rationally transparent solution can be given to explain this relation between the Word and the Spirit. At the same time, the Church has sought to *describe* that relation in terms of the Scripture. She has listened reverently to the Word and has tried to guard this mystery from the temptations of rationalism. She has heard, in the Pentecost story, how men were "cut to the heart" when the Word was preached. They were called upon to repent (Acts 2:37f.) .[58] Men were deeply moved; and something amazing and unexpected happened when Peter opened his mouth. *People repented.* But how can we "analyze" that miracle? How can we explain the manner in which we enter into the Kingdom of heaven? The Church has reflected on these questions and has seen that the relation between preaching and the Spirit's activity is very important. A number of "approaches" have been made to this problem, but a real *solution* has never been proposed.

The approaches to this problem have given rise to a good deal of debate. It is commonly said, in the history of dogma, that Lutherans have occupied a *per verbum* position, while the Reformed have spoken of *cum verbo* and the Spiritualists of *sine verbo*. It is important that we look at these distinctions

---

57. Cf. Matt. 28:19; Acts 1:8; Rom. 15:24.
58. *Katanýssō*. Cf. Grosheide, *Comm.*: "met een lans doorboren."

since the true knowledge of sin is not an isolated "subdivision" of faith but is knowledge *within* the radical transfer from death to life. Here we are touching on very critical questions. For the Church has always seen the knowledge of sin in direct relation to her preaching. Nevertheless, when we look at these rather scholastic-sounding terms, we discover that only the Spiritualists' *sine verbo* is immediately clear. In that position the power of the Spirit to reveal within man's heart cannot be cut loose from the *Word of preaching*. It is the "internal" as opposed to the merely "external" Word. The Word is no more than an illustration or a confirmation of the miracle wrought within us by the power of the Spirit alone. Furthermore, the Word itself has no essential role in bringing about that miracle.

Our interest, at this point, is in the apparent dilemma of *per verbum* and *cum verbo*. This very idea of "dilemma" has its difficulties when we read in the Heidelberg Catechism that the Holy Spirit works faith "in our hearts *by* the preaching of the holy Gospel" (*"per praedicationem evangelii"*; Q. 65).[59] Terminologically there is as little room for a "dilemma" here as in Bavinck's description of the Lutheran *per verbum* view. In the Lutheran position, according to Bavinck, the Spirit works *through the Word* as his instrument.[60] Therefore, in attempting to clarify the difference between the Lutherans and Reformed, Bavinck acknowledged, with the Lutherans, that the power of God's Word must certainly be seen in all of its dynamic

---

59. This statement comes as an answer to the question: "Whence comes this faith?" Cf. Art. 24 of the Belgic Confession: true faith is worked in man "by the hearing of the Word of God and the operation of the Holy Spirit"; also Canons III-IV, 12: not *merely* by the external preaching of the Gospel. In a declaration of 1905 it was stated that the Reformed Churches confess — in contrast to Lutheran and Roman Catholic — that regeneration "does not occur through the Word or sacraments *as such.*" But this formula makes nothing clear of the dogma-historical "dilemma" with which we are here concerned; and this fact is the more apparent in the added statement that the working of the Spirit "may not be separated from the preaching of the Word in the sense that both of them should be divorced from each other." The Gospel is later referred to as a power of God unto salvation, and mention is made of the activity of the Spirit which "accompanies" preaching. We might further note that we find *"per"* in the Lutheran Augustana ("per verbum et sacramenta tamquam per instrumenta"), whereas in the Formula Concordiae we read *"cum verbo"* (Müller, p. 729): "quod credimus Spiritum Sanctum cum verbo praedicato, audito et diligenter considerato praesentem atque efficacem esse et operari velle."

60. Bavinck, *op. cit.,* IV, 438.

reality. Certainly we must speak of the "power of the Gospel."[61] For that reason Spiritualism is a false philosophy,[62] while in large part the Lutherans are completely right. "The Word of God is always and everywhere a power of God and a sword of the Spirit,"[63] and in that Word we are concerned about the actual *presence of the Holy Spirit*.[64] The danger in the Lutheran view, says Bavinck, is that it tends to imprison the divine efficacy within the Word;[65] on the other hand, the advantage in the Reformed conception is its greater accent on the fact that the Word cannot be an impersonal or magical power but can only be seen in the service of the Spirit who maintains it and who *causes it to be efficacious*.[66] This alone is sufficient to show that Bavinck did not regard the Reformed *cum verbo* as a conception of two "parallel lines." He defined the Reformed view in terms almost identical to those he used in discussing the Lutheran conception. In either case the Holy Spirit works *through the Word as his instrument*.[67]

According to Bavinck, there is a subjective efficacy of the Spirit which must always *accompany* the objective Word.[68] That idea, of course, could give the impression of two neatly balanced or parallel lines. We could think of a subjective and objective "side," especially when we hear that this working of the Spirit "quite obviously cannot be enclosed in the Word. It is a different, accompanying and subjective activity. It is not a working *per verbum* but *cum verbo* — an opening of the heart."[69] Unfortunately, in all of this, *per verbum* and *cum verbo* are very

61. The analysis of Regin Prenter *(Spiritus Creator. Studien zu Luthers Theologie,* 1954, pp. 107-132) is important for an understanding of Luther at this point. Prenter discusses Luther's views on the opening of man's heart by the Spirit and the instrumental function of the Word. Rightly he denies any incongruity between these and affirms that the dilemma *"per or cum?"* is untenable. *Luther* and *Calvin,* at least, cannot be seen in opposition to each other. Cf. Prenter's reference (p. 108) to Luther's repeated citing of I Cor. 3:7 in this connection (it is God who gives the increase). Also on Luther: J. S. C. Locher, *De Leer van Luther over Gods Woord,* 1903, pp. 46f. and 155f.

62. Bavinck, *loc. cit.*

63. *Ibid.,* 439.

64. *Ibid.:* "semper huic adest praesens Spiritus Sanctus."

65. It is noteworthy that Bavinck does not speak of Luther but rather "the Lutherans" *(ibid.,* 437-439).

66. *Ibid.,* 440.

67. *Ibid.,* 437.

68. *Ibid.,* 440.

69. *Ibid.*

obscure terms. We think of the Lutheran struggle which centered in the figure of Rahtmann, a theologian who accentuated the "accompaniment" of the Spirit to such an extent that his fellow Lutherans accused him of weakening the power of the objective Word.[70] Thus Rahtmann spoke of two lines — the "external" Word and the power of the Spirit. As Ritschl has said, he was concerned about "the initiative of the Holy Spirit which must work apart from the scriptural Word if the Gospel is to be fruitful."[71] In so doing, says Ritschl, he came very "near to the Reformed conception."

But this kind of analysis oversimplifies our problem. Rahtmann built his entire standpoint on the *antithesis of internal and external,* while Bavinck rejected that antithesis. Rahtmann conceived of two parallel lines in coincidence and concomitance, while Bavinck spoke of the *instrumental* character of the Word along with the *cum verbo.*[72] When he referred to the Spirit's "accompaniment," Bavinck took his position against the *per verbum* and in favor of *cum verbo.* Nevertheless, he did so with the obvious intention of rejecting all *automatism or magic.* Bavinck professed the freedom of God in wielding the sword of his Spirit.

If we put all our accent on this "accompaniment" we will find it difficult to distinguish our position from that of the Spiritualists. Yet if we maintain, at the same time, that the Word is the instrument of the Spirit who alone makes it efficacious,[73] we can use the term *accompaniment* to avoid the

70. *Ibid.,* 437.
71. O. Ritschl, *Dogmengeschichte des Protestantismus,* IV, 159. On Raht-mann, cf. further, R. H. Grützmacher, *Wort und Geist,* 1902, pp. 220-245.
72. Grützmacher rightly asserts that Rahtmann dissociated himself from Luther at precisely this point of "the instrumental power of the Word" (*ibid.,* p. 240).
73. Luther, too, made frequent reference to this instrumental character of the Word. See Prenter, *op. cit.,* pp. 107f., and W. Koehler, *Dogmengeschichte,* I, 1951, 266f. He regarded the Word, according to Koehler, as the "bridge and pathway by which the Holy Spirit comes to us" (267). One should guard himself against proceeding too exclusively from the categories of "internal" and "external." These certainly played a role in both Luther and Calvin; but everything depends on *how* one operates with these and whether such concepts in themselves intend an antithesis that relativizes the power of the Word, in contrast to the Voice that speaks "internally." Cf. Grützmacher on Luther, *op. cit.,* p. 17.

inclusion of the Spirit *in the Word*.[74] Our difficulty, in this regard, only points to the fact that the nature of the preached Word, in relation to the power of the Spirit, precludes any final "systematization." The real reason why we shy away from these formulas is not that we recognize an unfortunate "gap" in our knowledge. Rather, we are aware of the limits within which we may neither minimize our calling nor ignore the dynamic of the Spirit. Therefore we need not be surprised when the Reformed confessions, while upholding the *cum verbo,* also use the Lutheran participle, *per.* Their whole intention is to do justice to the riches of God's Word.

Both the *cum* and the *per* have a very valid function. Also, it is necessary to respect the fullness in which the power of the Gospel goes forth in our world. *Per* suggests the meaningful function of the Word which is proclaimed, and agrees with those scriptural passages which point to the power of that Word.[75] *Cum* suggests that preaching in itself does not have an automatic effect. It emphasizes that the Word is appropriated in faith only by the power of the Spirit.[76] In that sense, of course,

74. We recall that Bavinck only refers to Rahtmann (IV, 437) in connection with the discussions within the Lutheran Church. In its essence, the difference between their positions is given expression in Bavinck's *Roeping en Wedergeboorte,* 1903, where he denies — in an anti-Spiritualist sense — that the Reformed have ever pleaded for a regeneration apart from the Word (p. 58). He refers especially to Lord's Day 25 and BC, Art. 24.

75. Think of Isa. 55:11: "So shall my word be that goes forth from my mouth; it shall not return to me empty, but it shall accomplish that which I purpose, and prosper in the thing for which I sent it"; also Heb. 4:12: "For the word of God is living and active, sharper than any two-edged sword, piercing to the division of soul and spirit, of joints and marrow, and discerning the thoughts and intentions of the heart"; and I Thess. 2:13: "... the word of God, which is at work (*energeitai*) in you believers." In Acts 4:33 we read that *"with great power* the apostles gave their testimony to the resurrection of the Lord Jesus"; cf. the *powerful weapons* of II Cor. 10:4. Paul received *strength* "to proclaim the word fully, that all the Gentiles might hear it" (II Tim. 4:17). All this indicates that the Word is much more than something merely "external," Moses received "living oracles to give to us" (Acts 7:38). One can solve no problem by saying that preaching affects the ear but not the heart; it touches *man* in his entirety and demands a decision in his *heart.* On the *"living* oracles" and the Spirit, cf. O. Noordmans, *Gestalte en Geest,* 1955, pp. 249f.

76. In a paragraph on "the working of the Word" (in *De Komst van het Koninkrijk,* pp. 136ff.), Ridderbos mentions the *automátē* of Mark 4:28 — "the earth produces *of itself,*" and even the one who sows is un-

the Scripture also speaks. We read that the *Lord* opened Lydia's heart to give heed to the things that were spoken by Paul (Acts 16:14).[77] Therefore the parallelism which would seem so unavoidable in the *cum verbo* should not be regarded as diminishing the power of the Word which is proclaimed. Certainly it should not degrade that power to something merely "external." It is possible to endorse the *cum verbo* to indicate that the correlation between preaching and appropriating the Word is by no means "automatic." A miracle is involved in the way in which that correlation appears. Though the acceptance of the Word would seem to be a matter of our own choice and activity, yet *in that choice* the power of the *Spirit* is at work.[78]

For that reason a merely theoretical solution can never do justice to this relation of the Word and the Spirit. Nor can we draw causal conclusions from such a formula. When we do so, we do violence to the dynamic and the mystery of preaching the Word. Our theological formulas must leave room for that mystery. Therefore there is something appealing in Rahtmann's accentuating the accompaniment of the Spirit, and something worthwhile in his criticism of the "objectification" of the Word. But his own views are far too simple and can easily lead to a dualistic parallel in which the function of the Word is downgraded as we seek to give the Holy Spirit his due.[79] No wonder that Barth has criticized both Rahtmann, on the one hand, and Hollaz and Quenstedt, on the other. Hollaz said that the Word is no *actio* but a power or potency, and Quenstedt took issue with the instrumental function of the Word.[80] Therefore the stress was laid on the immediacy of the *per verbum*, in such a way that the concept of the Word *as instrument* was thrown

aware of how the seed develops. Ridderbos sees in this an illustration of the working of the Word in our world (p. 138). It is not, of course, this working which we repudiate when we take issue with the "automatic" effect of the Word; we deny only that the Word leads automatically to faith. This "automatic-ness" is certainly denied by the parable of the sower itself; cf. Matt. 13:1f., 36f.

77. Cf. Grosheide, *Comm.*, II, 92 on the Word which does not find entrance "in itself" ("zonder meer"); also Luke 24:45 (the two men who went to Emmaus). Concerning Lydia we read that she both "heard" and "the Lord opened her heart" (Acts 16:14).

78. Cf. Calvin: "Inanis tantum sonitus aures feriet, nisi efficaciam habeat a spiritus doctrina." Cf. *Inst.*, IV, 1, 5f.

79. Ritschl spoke of the influence of Schwenckfeld on Rahtmann (*op. cit.*, IV, 160); cf. also O. Weber, *Grundlagen der Dogmatik*, I, 314f.

80. K. Barth, *K.D.*, I/1, 113 (ET, 124).

out. Thus a parallel emerges to Spiritualism which also (though in terms of the *sine verbo*) rejects the instrumental function of the Word.

In both these cases an abstract and causal mode of thinking has come to govern the course which the Gospel is seen to take in our world. The *sine verbo* of the Spiritualists and the *per verbum* of the "immediatists" have much in common. They both lose sight of the *mediacy of faith,* for both preacher and hearer, and conceive of the presence of the Spirit as the conclusion from a dialectical or rational thought. Neither view appreciates that the gracious presence of the Spirit is known only in the way of faith and prayer.[81] Therefore it is no accident when Reformed theology makes constant use of the concept of *instrument.* That concept does not make clear the relation between the Word and the Spirit; in fact it appeals to an analogy from a technical sphere which can easily be misunderstood. But the idea of an *instrument* does not *have to have* a "mechanical" or an "automatic" meaning. It enables us to see that the Word is both a "sword" and the "sword of the Spirit." Thus its reference is twofold. It excludes any concept of magic which ignores how necessary it is that *God opens our hearts.* Furthermore it eliminates any interpretation of *cum verbo* in which the function of *preaching* is no longer honored to the full.[82]

This relation of the Word and the Spirit is important for

81. Cf. H. N. Ridderbos, *Het Dogma der Kerk,* in opposition to both Spiritualism and a kind of Word-magicism (p. 519), as well as the possibility of a "conclusively logical system" which is acceptable "to our human comprehension." This rejection has nothing to do with irrationalism; it is enjoined by the free sovereignty of the *person of the Holy Spirit* (p. 523). Dogmatical reflection can never transcend this mystery but can only make us more *appreciative of it.*

82. By this same token, the antithesis between internal and external is eliminated. Calvin knew that "an inestimable treasure is given us in earthen vessels" and that "God breathes faith into us only by the instrument of his gospel" ("sed evangelio suo *organo*"; *Inst.,* IV, 1, 5). He speaks of God's consecrating the mouths and tongues of men "in order that his voice may resound in them" ("quod dignatur sibi consecrare, ut in illis sua vox personet"; *ibid.*). Cf. his view on the efficacy of the ministry, IV, 1, 6. Here Grützmacher's analysis of Calvin is inadequate; note his assertion that "often Calvin used the instrumental formula only under the strong influence of Romans 10:14" (*op. cit.,* p. 131). O. Weber (*Grundlagen,* I, 316) regards the "solution" as already present in Calvin; he points particularly to Calvin's commentary on Hebrews 4:2.

any right view of what it means to "know our sin." Therefore
we have treated of this matter at some length. We have said
that there are knotty problems in the *per verbum* and *cum
verbo* debates, and that the Spiritualist *sine verbo* is a threat
to any right conception of the knowledge of our sin. We agree
that it is necessary to warn against the "magic" of preaching
and any self-inflation on the part of the preacher who thinks
that he has ultimate destinies in his hands. Such attitudes are
wrong and inappropriate for those who entreat the world to
repent. Yet this should not detract from the fact that the summons to repent and to believe is made in the *message of salvation*.

Thus repentance is not a mystical or an abstract miracle
which is wrought in the "closedness" or the inner darkness of
man's heart. Rather, the radical and the decisive process from
death to life is tied up with the preaching of salvation and guilt.
A man must hear that he is a *sinner* and that Jesus has come
to seek and to save that which was *lost*. If someone says that the
"external" Word is inferior to the power of the Spirit, we can
only reply that he understands very little the "over-againstness"
of that Word which is proclaimed. He does not fathom how
lost men are confronted by the message of salvation. He does
not see God's way of knocking on doors that are closed. He does
not comprehend that this knocking has nothing to do with a
contrast of "internal" and "external." For the Word is preached
to recalcitrant and unrepentant men within the concreteness
of their living and the depths of their own hearts. Thus the
Spirit uses the Word as his holy "instrument." And yet, the
Word is always brought by ambassadors and the heralds of the
Kingdom (II Cor. 5:20).[83] It comes as a witness in men's lives.
The Word of *God* is the Word of salvation and the proclamation
of Good News — but it is also the Word which the *apostles*
preached with fervency and intensity.[84] The Canons of Dort
remind us that new birth is not effected by "moral suasion";[85]

83. *Presbeúomen*. Cf. Grosheide, *ad loc.*: "een officiële opdracht."
84. Cf. their zeal in speaking and teaching (Acts 18:25); their persistence
    (18:28); and the emphasis with which they testified concerning the
    Kingdom of God (28:23).
85. CD, III-IV, 12. This article is directed against the intellectual "suasio"
    which is also mentioned in the "rejection of errors," III-IV, 7, in con-
    nection with those who teach that "gratiam, qua convertimur ad Deum,
    nihil aliud esse quam *lenem suasionem*" — "or (as others explain it)
    that this is the noblest manner of working in the conversion of man,...
    and most in harmony with man's nature." This "sola moralis gratia,"

but that fact does not imply that all urgent advice and admonition, and all attempts to persuade and to convince, and all injunctions to take the necessary "step of faith" are simply superfluous.[86]

We must remember that the Holy Spirit is the Spirit of Christ, and as such he sent the apostles into their world and separated them for the task for which they had been called (Acts 13:2, 4). The message of the apostles was the message of the "riches" and the "depths" of those words which *they uttered as words of life* (Acts 5:20). It consisted of those words which could not be viewed, in themselves, as *flatus vocis*. As the *instrument* of the Spirit, the words participated in the content to which they referred and to which they bore witness. Therefore, when Paul spoke of the "foolishness of works" he also asked this question: "Does he who supplies the Spirit to you and works miracles among you do so by works of the law, or by *hearing with faith?*" (Gal. 3:5). So important was preaching that Paul could link it together with the activities of "hearing" and "believing" (Rom. 10:14) and could recall the Old Testament statement: "How beautiful are the feet of those who preach good news!" (10:15; cf. Isa. 52:7). Preaching, according to Paul, had a very *concrete content*. It was the message of good tidings, the publishing of salvation, and the comforting of God's people with the good news of redemption (cf. Isa. 52:7, 9).

Nowhere does Scripture give us an arbitrary illustration of what the Holy Spirit, *sine verbo,* can do. The scriptural concern is to give a clear and certain and trustworthy witness concerning Jesus Christ. In that witness we find comfort in the midst of life and death. The object of preaching is the full and concrete man, and its burden is to expound the Kingdom of God (Acts 28:23). By means of preaching Jesus was "publicly portrayed as crucified" before the eyes of the Galatians (3:1); by means of preaching the Gospel came into our world. The Gospel made use of the words of men, but it filled them with a content of judgment and grace and the necessity of repentance as the

some maintain, is sufficient to make the natural man spiritual, for the "consensus voluntatis" is worked by God "non aliter quam morali ratione." Against this position the Canons confess — with Scripture also — that the Holy Spirit works in conversion in a different, and more divine, and more powerful way than by any mere "suasio."

86. Cf. Acts 18:4 (*épeithen); also* 18:13 ("persuading") and 19:8 ("arguing and pleading about the kingdom of God").

way to life. The *word* of the cross is the power of God to those
who are being saved (I Cor. 1:18). That word is a word that
pierces to the bottom of man's heart and compels him to decide.
Thus the wide differences in the decisions that men make are
no denial of the gravity and the power of this witnessing Word
(cf. Acts 28:24f.). They only point to the urgency and the
cogency of warning.[87] Preaching does not imply the possibility
of speculating or prognosticating results. It is only the occasion
in which it is evident if a man is "blessed" and "takes no offense"
at Jesus or withdraws himself to a more rigid impenitence
(cf. Matt. 11:6).

The focal point in the message of salvation is that salvation
is in Jesus Christ. This is the content of preaching. We meet up
with that relation to Christ when we hear of the Comforter or
the Paraclete that Christ sends. He is "another Counsellor" who
will be with the Church "for ever" (John 14:16).[88] As the
"Spirit of truth" he will bear constant witness concerning Jesus
Christ — and in line with that witness the disciples too will
witness (15:26, 27). Yet the work of the Spirit, or the Comforter,
has reference to *this world.* The world cannot receive him because it does not know him, though his witness is still with us.
"When he comes, he will convince the world of sin and of
righteousness and of judgment" (John 16:8). He will convince
the world as a result of that salvation-historical event in which
Jesus came into the world and bore his cross and was resurrected
from the dead.

This "righteousness" of which the Spirit will convince (or
convict) the world has nothing to do with a common view of
"righteousness." It is rather a righteousness that is sharply defined in terms of salvation history. "... Because I go to the
Father, and you will see me no more" (16:10).[89] The way of the
cross is the way to the *Father,* and in that way "true righteousness" is revealed in contrast to the illusory and superficial
"righteousness" of men. Furthermore, when we read that the

---

87. Cf. my *Divine Election,* Chap. 7.
88. *Paráklētos.* He is the Comforter who is given to the Church,
"whom the world cannot receive, because it neither sees him nor knows
him; you know him, for he dwells with you, and will be in you" (John
14:17).
89. Cf. Nils Johansson, *Parakletoi,* 1940, p. 263. Johansson recalls that Jesus
is *díkaios* (cf. e.g., I John 2:1; 3:7), and in this word he sees "an echo
of Isaiah 53." Cf. Isa. 53:11.

Spirit convicts the world of *judgment* we find nothing of a general crisis but only a very concrete judgment that has an intimate relation to what the Messiah has already done. Therefore we read: "... because the ruler of this world *is judged*" (16:11). Similarly, when we see that the Spirit convicts the world of *sin* we are also given the reason: "because they do not believe in me" (16:9). Especially that text has demanded attention because of the intimate relation it draws between *sin and unbelief*. We are told that the Spirit convicts the world of sin — but he does so because of unbelief in Jesus Christ. We do not read of a variety of sins but only of a single, all-inclusive "unbelief." We have seen already how decisive this antithesis of "belief and unbelief" is in the teaching of Jesus. Now that he has come, salvation and condemnation can only be seen in relation to him. "He who believes in the Son has eternal life; he who does not obey the Son shall not see life, but the wrath of God rests upon him" (3:36).[90]

All of this does not deny the great *variety* of sin or the peculiar relation between man's sin and the *law*. But it does suggest that *from this time forth* all sins and aberrations from God will be focussed or centralized in this one decisive act of *un*belief or *dis*obedience to Jesus. "If I had not done among them the works which no one else did, they would not have sin; but now they have seen and hated both me and my Father" (15:24). This "concentration" of sin does not mean that sin is no longer "lawlessness," for lawlessness is manifest in the alienation from God's glory and the choosing of darkness now that Light has come. Therefore it makes sense that the Spirit *convicts* the world of sin because of its unbelief in Jesus (16:9).[91]

Zahn has challenged that we do not find in this passage the "untenable assertion that sin in general consists in unbelief in Jesus, or righteousness in general consists in praising Jesus, or judgment in general consists in the judgment over Satan which already now is complete."[92] But there is good reason to ask if this is not precisely what we read. Here we stand face to face with a concentration that is brought on by something new and decisive. *Jesus has come into our world.* From that

90. Cf. also 3:16, 18; 5:24; 12:48; also 8:24: "for you will die in your sins unless you believe that I am he."
91. Cf. the reference in Luther on unbelief as *the sin;* K. Barth, *K.D.,* IV/1, 461f.; cf. pp. 240, 434, 460. (ET, 415f.; cf. pp. 218f., 392f., 415.)
92. Zahn, *Das Evangelium des Johannes,* p. 589.

time forth, and down to the present, the entire activity of the Spirit's convicting and convincing can only be seen in conjunction with this all-important turning-point in the history of salvation. Therefore Zahn himself admits that "the sinfulness of man is fully manifest" in this act of unbelief in Jesus. He agrees that the convicting work of the Spirit has everything to do with this act. For in that act man's sin is laid bare and the indictment of the Comforter is seen as the index of man's guilt. Here, then, is the sin in all sin, not in a general moral sense or in the sense of a formal transgression of the law, but rather in the sense of the lawless reality of sin which is both defined and made known in this relation to Jesus.[93] The indictment of the Comforter has reference to that fact — for "the Spirit attacks at the central front."[94] Therefore the man who repudiates the Christ in unbelief is judged by the Word of Christ (12:48). Therefore, too, in the statement that the Spirit "convicts" or "convinces," we are not exposed to the usual meaning of that term. We do not *allow* ourselves to be "convinced," if we only wish to be. As a matter of fact the Spirit indicts us and warns, he admonishes and exhorts, and he reproves and points out the way from sin to repentance.[95]

This, then, is the reproof of the *Spirit of truth*[96] who makes the deepest intentions of man's heart indisputably manifest.[97] The reproof takes place in the proclamation of the Gospel.[98] Therefore the Spirit does not have a separate "punitive function" but reproves in connection with Jesus Christ. His reproof is the summons to believe and to take our leave of every vestige of self-centeredness and lawlessness. Knowing of this "con-

93. Barth, *op. cit.,* 460 (ET, 415), has referred to this idea that unbelief is *the* sin as "a specific feature of the Johannine witness." It is evident, however, that this same thought is *implicitly* central in other portions of the New Testament, wherever the seriousness of making a decision in regard to Christ is pointed out. Consider, e.g., Acts 2:38; 16:31; Rom. 10:9, 13; and the many Gospel references (Luke 2:34; Matt. 11:6, etc.).

94. C. Bouma, *K.V., Johannes, ad loc.* Cf. *TWNT,* II, *s.v. elénchō, 2, contra* Zahn: to regard *hóti* with Zahn, as causal, "is artificial."

95. Cf. *ibid.*

96. John 14:17; 15:26; 16:13; cf. I John 5:6 and 4:6, "the spirit of truth" in opposition to "the spirit of error."

97. In regard to Christ, cf. John 8:46: "Which of you convicts me of sin?" *(elénchei);* also the *perí hamartías* in John 8:46, 16:8.

98. Cf. R. Schippers, *Getuigen van Jesus Christus in het N.T.,* 1938, p. 168; Grosheide, *op. cit.,* II, 370.

centration," the apostles went into their world. They went as those who were separated and called and made subject to the witness of the Holy Spirit. Their ministry was qualified by the religious *clarity, simplicity,* and *concentration* of that message; as such, men were reconciled to God. The apostles were not concerned about a neutral imparting of "truth." They *were* concerned about the proclamation of salvation and the invitation to surrender and believe. This was a message that had no room for "cheap grace." It challenged men everywhere with a resonant summons to be saved. The Spirit of Christ witnessed, and the apostles of Christ witnessed, and *Christ was the content of their witness* (15:26) .[99]

Yet, in and with the witness of *sin,* it was *Christ himself who witnessed and reproved and who put men to shame.* The message of the apostles was a message of the Spirit of Christ and as such was wholly centered in the Christ. "For the love of Christ controls us, because we are convinced that one has died for all" (II Cor. 5:14). Within that ministry of reconciliation there was an admonition and a summons, and a certain "tension" was noticeable now that God was "in Christ reconciling the world to himself" (II Cor. 5:19). This is what Paul experienced as the "ambassador" of Christ. No wonder that he wrote as he did: "Therefore, knowing the *fear of the Lord, we persuade men*" (5:11).

There is no inconsistency here between love and fear or the Gospel and the law. Rather there is a perfect harmony. The fear that Paul had in mind was the fear of coming judgment which would come upon men because of their own failure to appreciate the love of Jesus Christ. The judgment seat of *Christ* is the judgment seat before which all men will appear (II Cor. 5:10). To *Christ* is given the judgment in that great day (cf. Acts 17:31). Therefore it is Christ's Gospel which must be proclaimed *now,* so that "all men everywhere" may come

99. *Peri emoú.* Cf. John 14:26: "he will teach you all things, and bring to your remembrance all that *I* have said to you." Also 16:13-14: "but whatever he hears he will speak.... He will glorify me, for he will take what is mine and declare it to you." The Spirit shall "guide ...into all the truth" (16:13), but he will do so *in* his witnessing of Christ. "The leading forth of the Paraklete is always, at the same time, a leading back to Jesus; the way into all truth is always the returning to him who is the way, the truth, and the life" (G. Bornkamm, "Der Paraklet im Johannes Evangelium," *Festschrift für R. Bultmann,* 1949, p. 27).

to repentance and conversion because of what God *has done*.
The content of this message defines the nature of the eschatological judgment. Furthermore, that fact does not imply a minimizing or a watering down of the Gospel but an "eschatological
exhortation,"[100] now that the time of God's "passing over former
sins" is gone forever (Rom. 3:25)[101] and the Gospel is proclaimed to all nations. This proclamation is not a negation of
the call to repentance in the law. It does not ignore man's
guilt. Rather it refers to the law of *God,* which is also the law
of *life*.[102]

The fact that it is necessary to preach the Gospel, therefore,
does not give us a reason to draw a conclusion in this untenable dilemma: Do we know our sin from the Gospel or the
law? Since the *Gospel* has to do with our *guilt,* the dilemma
itself is invalid. We can speak of a "dilemma" only if we see
the Gospel in contrast with a completely legalistic law. The
Gospel, however, enables us to fathom what the *meaning* of the
law is. It does so by speaking of the atonement and propitiation of our guilt. From that standpoint we can understand
and appreciate why Bavinck thought "primarily" of the Gospel
when he discussed this question: How do we *know our sin?*[103]
He did not see the word "primarily" in a quantitative sense, and
he never conceived of two independent "sources" for our knowledge. He did not criticize Lord's Day 2 but only the absolutizing of the knowledge which we gather from the law.

This sort of "absolutizing" presupposes that the law could
be known in its true depths apart from the Gospel. Thus the
depths of man's sin can be measured in terms of the law alone.
We then forget that the preaching of the Gospel has everything
to do with the impenitence in every single man. Preaching is
always geared toward the amazing, unfathomable and ever joyful
miracle of conversion and entrance into the Kingdom. For the
sake of conversion the Gospel puts men to shame, and reproves
and confounds them in the inner depths of their hearts. The
Gospel, like the Christ whose Gospel it is, has come into this
world *for judgment* (John 9:39) .

100. E. Haenchen, *Die Apostelgeschichte,* 1956, p. 465.
101. Cf. Grosheide, *De Handelingen der Apostelen,* II, 157.
102. In reference to II Cor. 5:11 ("we persuade men"), Zahn has rightly
       stated that Paul's terminology was "chosen with a view to the greatest
       possible generality and unrestrictedness" (*Comm., 2 Cor.,* p. 245).
103. Bavinck, *op. cit.,* IV, 146.

That fact does not alter the truth that God sent his Son into the world "not to condemn the world but that the world might be saved through him" (John 3:17). For these two terms, *judgment* and *condemnation*, are by no means the same. The biblical judgment is that in terms of which (or through which) "those who do not see may see, and . . . those who see may become blind" (John 9:39).[104] Therefore the message of salvation compels a man to make a choice.[105] As the message of *salvation,* it stands in opposition to all self-conceit and pride. It *is* that opposition *in itself.* The Gospel comes to sinners as a warning: "whoever does not receive the kingdom of God like a child shall not enter it" (Luke 18:17).

Here, then, is a text that is full of urgency and threat. Yet the threat is the threat of the Gospel, and it points the way (the only way) to repentance and humility. Luther once wrote that humility "saves," as faith itself also "saves" (cf. Luke 7:50; 8:48; 17:19; 18:42).[106] The way of humility is the surest evidence of true conversion[107]— for conversion can never be regarded by a humble man as the product of his own "achievement" or the "condition" for his gaining salvation. Conversion is only the echo of the proclamation of the law and the Gospel. It is only the response to the preaching of the Gospel of him who saves from the wrath which is to come. It is the answer to the Good News, which points us to him who "humbled himself" in the face of the curse of the law. Conversion is the reply to the message which enjoins us *therefore* to "have this mind among yourselves, which you have in Christ Jesus" (Phil. 2:8, 5). In the light of *his humility* we understand that God "comforts the downcast" (II Cor. 7:6). The mystery of Christ's humiliation in the crib of Bethlehem is the focal point for God's exalting "those of low degree" (Luke 1:52). For "God opposes

---

104. Cf. Grosheide on John 3:17 (*Comm.,* I, 235): "salvation comes in the way of [*krinein*], separation (John 9:39), but the purpose of this separation is salvation."

105. Cf. *TWNT,* III, *s.v. krinō,* esp. E. 8.

106. Cf. Luther's "humilitas sola salvat." See my *Faith and Justification,* 1952, pp. 180ff.

107. Lord's Day 33, in a twofold way, sees conversion in relation to man's heart: it speaks of "heartfelt sorrow" and "heartfelt joy." How little this sorrow can be thought of as negative is obvious from the fact that it stands in positive relation to God's will (it is "godly sorrow") and salvation itself (II Cor. 7:10; cf. v. 11). It is opposed to a "worldly grief" which "produces death." This worldly grief is "the sorrow of the man who sees his earthly well-being and caprices shattered."

the proud, but gives grace to the humble" (I Pet. 5:5; James 4:6).

The consolation of the lowly is the work of the Paraclete, who was sent by Christ for the purpose of giving us comfort. The comfort he gives is genuine and true. It is able to sustain us even in the midst of crises of judgment upon our own sin. Yet, precisely because of that comfort, the preaching of the Gospel is full of the Spirit's reproof. The criticism of the Spirit breaks us down — but it does so in order to build us up again. It leads us to the "more and more" of faith and love.

We have noted that the Lord's Supper form, where we celebrate the presence of the Spirit, gives an opportunity for repeated reference to the cross of Jesus Christ. It refers to his condemnation and his curse. We must remember that Christ has made atonement for our guilt. Therefore when Paul beseeches us "by the mercies of God" (Rom. 12:1) he also admonishes us not to be "haughty, but associate with the lowly; never be conceited" (12:16).[108] He encourages us to be joyful, loving, hospitable, and amicable in spirit (12:12-13). What he wants to say, at this point, has reference to more than the periphery of Christian living. It refers to the very center. True humility and repentance are the portion of those who live in the Kingdom of God and the very criterion of their entrance. But humility is not manifest in a cloistered aloofness or within the hidden depths of man's heart. Humility is lived in *concrete reality* and within the *totality of life*. Here Christ himself gave us the example. His entire life was a life of revelation, and in his life he was "gentle and lowly in heart" (Matt. 11:29).

In the mystery of the Spirit there is no greater gift than this gift of humility. Therefore it is identified with the gift of conversion itself. Only those who are humble can escape the judgment of which the *Gospel speaks*: "He has scattered the proud in the imagination of their hearts" (Luke 1:51). So decisive is that power of humility that it completely defines our attitudes toward other people as well as toward ourselves; it impinges on every act and decision in our lives. All our living is conditioned by this knowledge which we have of sin and the salvation which God has now revealed. Therefore when God's mercy is not fully seen (as all too often in the Church) there is room for the hardheartedness and cantankerousness of men. We then see how far we are from the gates of the Kingdom.

108. *Hypsēmá phronein* in 12:16 and 11:20; cf. Prov. 3:7.

Our efforts are then bent to conceal our sins and not to confess. In such efforts, of course, our sin is most flagrantly manifest. For sin is only *removed* when sin is fully *confessed*. In confession, before our God and our fellows, the new and unlimited powers of the Kingdom are made known (James 5:16) .[109]

Therefore in the act of confession we see those *fruits* which "go with" repentance (Matt. 3:8). Therefore the consequences of God's gracious justification and election are made manifest.[110] Confession enables us to "see things in a different light." It enables us to see things in the light of the "renewal of our minds." This light has nothing to do with an empty moralism, and permits us to recognize the will of God: "what is good and acceptable and perfect" (Rom. 12:2). Apart from that light and those fruits, our "repentance" is only a fraud and has nothing to do with the Kingdom, the law, and the Gospel of Jesus Christ. Our entrance into the Kingdom is manifest *in life*. Therefore we read: "Bless those who persecute you; bless and do not curse them. Rejoice with those who rejoice, weep with those who weep. Live in harmony with one another; do not be haughty, but associate with the lowly; never be conceited. Repay no man evil for evil, but take thought for what is noble in the sight of all" (Rom. 12:14-17).

In reproving and rebuking, in comforting and counselling, the Holy Spirit maintains a Christian *in humility*.[111] Therefore the law *and the Gospel,* the Gospel *and the law,* must be preached. The law may not be preached *apart from* but only *in relation to* the Gospel. As such it must be "strictly preached" (HC, Q. 115). Moreover, this preaching is no threat to the Gospel but is even *demanded* by the deepest motive of the *Gospel itself.* God's commandment has authority within a Christian's living. But his commandment is a "new command" which (precisely in its "novelty") retains its right to criticize and to censure, and thus to comfort and preserve.

For that reason a true knowledge of sin, in repentance, is far removed from a fruitless or a bootless pessimism. This

---

109. Note the connection this text draws between "confessing" and "praying for one another"; also the way both of these are brought into the context of "being forgiven" (5:15). Dibelius (*Der Brief des Jakobus,* 1956, p. 236) speaks of confession of guilt as "preparation for prayer."

110. Cf. Phil. 1:27: our manner of life must be "worthy (*axiōs*) of the gospel of Christ."

111. Note Grosheide's commentary, *Johannes,* II, 310, on the significance of *parakalein* as both warning and comfort.

knowledge has nothing to do with an accusation apart from the vision of him who searches our hearts. True knowledge of sin is concretized in a true confession of our guilt. *In* the act of confession the way is opened up for a man to live for others and not for himself. *Within* the act of pardon we are brought back again to the "new commandment of God." And how could that be different when men "awake" from their sleep and "arise from the dead" (Eph. 5:14)?[112] The law and the Gospel have everything to do with each other. Therefore there is no knowledge of sin apart from the purging or the sanctification of our living. "The night is far gone, the day is at hand. Let us then cast off the works of darkness and put on the armor of light" (Rom. 13:12).

We concluded our discussion of the origin of sin by pointing to the *riddle of man's sin*. We now see that the relation between the "riddle" and the "knowledge" of sin is by no means contradictory. Precisely this knowledge, as enlivened by the Spirit, obliges us to speak of the "enigma," or the "strangeness," or the "groundlessness" of sin. The "more and more" of our knowledge, as aroused by the "strict preaching" of the law, can only deepen our appreciation for the enigma and the riddle of our sin. This enigma is really the reverse side of a true confession of our guilt. In the light of God's grace communion is restored, and those motives which we once saw as our own "definitive excuse" are now recognized as empty and vain. This is the light in which we experience that it is "good to be near God" (Ps. 73:28). Though we were once "embittered" in our souls and "pricked" in our hearts (73:21), "stupid and ignorant" (73:22), there is only room now for a paean of joy: "Whom have I in heaven but thee? And there is nothing upon earth that I desire besides thee" (73:25).

Thus any compromise with darkness can only be met by the Spirit's unceasing rebuke. For now "the true light is already shining" (I John 2:8). Furthermore, when the power of the Spirit turns rebellion into worship, all the works of the Lord will be told (Ps. 73:28). When the commandment of the Lord is understood as a scepter which leads us to life, we shall

---

112. Read Eph. 5:14 in its context, vv. 15-21; also Rom. 13:11. Cf. C. H. Dodd, *Gospel and Law*, 1953, pp. 25f.; also H. Preisker, *Das Ethos des Urchristentums*, 1949, pp. 184f.

sing praises to him "seven times a day" (Ps. 119:164). We shall then love his commandments "above gold," yea, "above fine gold" (119:127).

PART II

THE ESSENCE AND
SPREAD OF SIN

CHAPTER EIGHT

THE QUESTION OF ESSENCE

W HEN WE PASS over to the topic of the essence of our sin it is well to remind ourselves again that we are not concerned with a theoretical or merely speculative riddle. We are not in search of a hidden "essence" which lurks behind the visible forms or the external manifestations of evil. Here we are concerned about the *nature* of sin or the evil consequences which corrode the whole of our living in the wake of every sin. We are involved again in the study of the *recognition* and the *knowledge* of our sin. As we have noted, this subject is a matter of the greatest importance.[1] For the man who misconstrues the nature of his sin cannot be excused by merely shrugging his shoulders. His error is much more than a merely intellectual deficiency. He is engaged in an urgent peril. Sin, as we shall see in this chapter, is a very vicious and mortal enemy, an irascible and persistent power, which must certainly be *known* in order to be *overcome*. Resistance to sin is the essential correlate of a recognition of sin's deepest motives. Therefore the book of Hebrews adjures believers to take a firmer stand against their sin and resist it to the point of "shedding their blood" (Heb. 12:4).[2]

Implied in that statement is the admonition that believers have, all too often, an inadequate awareness of their adversary or their arch-enemy who is "near by" and "couching at the door" (Gen. 4:7). The very presence of the adversary makes our attention and our recognition imperative. The summons to be alert is now coupled with a pointed description of sin as a seductive power. All illusions concerning the nature of sin are now banished.[3] This warning goes hand in hand with the

1. Cf. Part I, above, pp. 149ff.
2. Note the description of perils: "growing weary or faint-hearted" (12:3) and "failing to obtain the grace of God" (12:15).
3. We might reflect on the summons to sobriety and alertness in I Pet. 5:8,

fact that sin, on the one side, is described as one's very own, or as committed in one's *own responsibility;* on the other side, it is recognized as a constant *threat.* This second aspect especially has led to the biblical admonitions and injunctions. There can be no diminishing of man's responsibility but only a focussing and intensifying of his guilt. Sin is not seen in Scripture as an indomitable or an overarching force, or as that in terms of which we can regard ourselves as abject pawns. Any minimizing of sin is pointed out as a deadly peril which can only lure us to sleep.[4]

We should bear in mind at this point the famous statement of Anselm, concerning the relation of "necessity" which applies between the incarnation or atonement and the gravity of our sin. Because of that relation we may never play down the severity of sin.[5] Yet it is remarkable how common that act of "playing down" really is in our daily living. One can hardly overestimate its influence. Men try to conceal their own sinning, and in sin itself there is always an urge to "cover up." Thus sin manifests itself *sub specie boni* and obscures its true nature. Thus it obstructs our knowledge of what it is.[6] False prophets come and go — but they always come within the framework of a true apostolicity and present themselves as "apostles of Christ" (II Cor. 11:13). Furthermore their danger is no less real but is only intensified in that fact. Think of the Old Testament "false prophets." Their pseudo-character was hard to recognize because of their pretensions of the truth. Nevertheless the Apostle Paul was well aware of that strategy and knew that the "metamorphosis" of Satan (as an "angel of light") was the prime example of all such deceit.

That strategy of "covering up" is apparent not only in the

motivated by a reference to the power of temptation. Alertness is revealed in resistance (*antistēte*); sobriety (*nēpsate*) is opposed to drunkenness (which obscures one's vision) and is necessary for this struggle. Cf. I Pet. 4:7: "keep sane and sober for your prayers"; also I Thess. 5:8, concerning "the breastplate of faith and love."

4. We think of the situation that Peter considered quite harmless — a situation in which he distinguished himself from the other disciples (Matt. 26:33) and brought upon himself Christ's warning concerning his own imminent denial (26:34). Even after this warning Peter continued to have a fearless certainty (26:35). In Luke 22:31 this warning is coupled with a reference to Satan's desire to "sift you like wheat."

5. "Nondum considerasti, quanti ponderis sit peccatum" (*Cur Deus Homo,* I, 21).

6. Cf. above, pp. 149ff.

knowledge and recognition[7] but also in the essence and nature of man's sin. There is nothing so very "strange" in the pseudo-apostolate (cf. II Cor. 11:15). As a matter of fact, the goal of every sin is only to deceive. Therefore we read that the darkness deceives men and presents itself as light; that evil thrusts itself forward as that which is good; that slavery poses as that which is free; that irreligion takes on the form of religion. Sin, in short, seeks out its purposes *sub specie boni*.

Thus the forms of appearance are important for those who want to know the essence of our sin. Certainly we are interested in the backgrounds and the heart of our sin; yet in every sin there is always an *unclarity* which belongs to the forms of manifestation and the very nature of evil. There is always a *contra*-element in sin. Therefore there is always a certain strategy of deceit. We are not implying, at this point, that there can be no genuine disclosure of evil. As a matter of fact, the guise of sin is often seen as a gigantic hoax. How, indeed, could that be different? Yet we are suggesting that the New Testament picture of the Antichrist shows the clear traces of a pseudo-religiosity (cf. II Thess. 2:4). Furthermore, the *anti* forewarns us that the *contra* is complete in the sphere of false imitation and sham.[8] The opponent not only opposes but assumes the allure of a new and a *contra*-salvation.[9] Thus the *contra* of sin wraps itself in the vesture of the apostles and the toga of the Messiah himself.[10] This is the method of the devil's appeal. His invitation is accompanied by signs and wonders and by marvellous and astounding powers.[11] His deception reaches its goal in the attitude of bewilderment and amazement on the

7. See p. 150.
8. Quite rightly, reference has always been made in this connection to the "beast which rose out of the earth," which "had two horns like a lamb and it spoke like a dragon" (Rev. 13:11). Cf. Greijdanus, *Comm.*, p. 278.
9. Cf. K. H. Miskotte, "In de Schaduw van de Antichrist," *Feest in de Voorhof*, 1951, pp. 239ff. On the significance of the "anti" in *antichristos* see R. Schnackenburg, *Die Johannesbriefe*, 1953, pp. 127f. (the "Gegen-Christus," p. 128). One can certainly say that the reference to the pope as Antichrist, in Reformation times, had much to do with his title of *"vicarius Christi."*
10. In Matt. 24:26 Christ warns against the non-recognition of false Christs: "So, if they say to you, 'Lo, he is in the wilderness,' do not go out; if they say, 'Lo, he is in the inner rooms,' do not believe it."
11. Cf. II Thess. 2:9: "... with all power and with pretended signs and wonders." Cf. Rev. 13:2, 12, 13; and Mark 13:22, in close connection with "leading astray, if possible, the elect."

part of the man who is "bewitched" (Rev. 13:3; cf. v. 12). Sin discloses its true essence by *hiding its deepest intents*.[12]

Many have asked why it is that evil makes use of this form of good and encircles itself with the shroud of deception.[13] It has rightly been seen that the essence of seduction is apparent in this art of concealing. Here the aim of seduction is obviously to allure the sinful man, or the man who is lost, but the man who has not yet surrendered to the ultimate and demonic *contra*. That is to say, he has not yet chosen for the final consequences of darkness in contrast to light. Thus, in this metamorphosis of evil we see the power of seduction; but we also observe the profound impotency and dependency of sin. That situation is only thinkable in a world in which the ultimate *contra*-decisions are still held in check, or a world in which men are still called forth from the ominous ways of sin to the truth and the light of God's salvation. Evil has no thesis in itself but only antithesis. Precisely in that way it exhibits its impotent contingency.[14] The deception of the metamorphosis is therefore an indirect attestation of the light of God. For sin plays out its nefarious design in continual relation to that light. It covers its deepest intentions while it masquerades as good.

Therefore the real depth and the real danger of sin are apparent in its boasting of itself as a religious and not an antireligious force. We recall the hypocrisy and the false sanctimoniousness of Jesus' own day. "Woe to you, scribes and Pharisees, hypocrites!" (Matt. 23:14). For the sake of *appearance* the false leaders would utter long prayers; for that reason Christ referred to them as "white-washed tombs" (23:27). We might assume that their action had nothing to do with a *sub specie boni* idea, but the complicated phenomenon of Pharisaism

12. We see this disguise of sin even in the temptation of Christ in the wilderness (note the words, "It is written"). Even in the third temptation with its obvious "contra" (worshipping the devil), the "sub specie boni" plays a role. The devil assumes the authority of Christ over all the kingdoms of the world (Matt. 4:8ff.).
13. In reference to the Antichrist see further: Heinrich Schlier, *Vom Antichrist. Theologische Aufsätze für Karl Barth*, 1936, p. 120 (on the Antichrist as a "spiritual magnitude" — "eine geistige Grösze"). Also: Paul Schütz, "Metamorphose des Bösen," in *Macht und Wirklichkeit des Bösen*, 1958, pp. 73ff.; and above, pp. 150ff.
14. Cf. Bavinck on evil's making use of God's good creation and the demonic "parasitism" in regard to God's gifts (*Geref. Dog.*, III, 119).

should lead us to a different conclusion. In Christ's criticism the *contra*-character and deception of the Pharisees are evident. The Pharisees were despisers of the law (23:28), though ostensibly they intended a legal and religious piety. Therefore their duplicity, or insincerity, was the occasion for the strongest rebuke found anywhere in the Gospels. Christ inveighed against the *contra* and the religious sham in which that *contra* found its place. The subjective intentions of the Pharisees were now laid bare, and in that process the *contra* was manifest.[15] The Pharisees had a "form of religion" which was only skin deep and which lacked the power of true godliness (II Tim. 3:5). For that reason this process (as in the case of the "opponents of Moses") was now made "plain to all" (II Tim. 3:8-9).

When the Gospel is thus preached and exposes evil in a way that is "plain to all," there is always the tendency to conceal the seductive motives in our sin.[16] There is also a power which impels a man away from mere appearance to a more obvious *contra*.[17] This is what happens when the "light which has appeared" is preached. The Gospel is the laying bare of all make-believe and lies. In that way man's sin is exposed in all its seductiveness. Though man's sin promises a great reward its "wage" is only death (Rom. 6:23).[18]

Already in the Genesis account we find that man's sinning is described as seduction. Later we shall see what it was to which man was tempted, but for now it is sufficient to observe that the *contra* made use of the guise of being "like God" and opening man's eyes (Gen. 3:5; cf. II Cor. 11:3). Ever since that time seduction has been the form and the power of man's sin. Thus in the New Testament we are confronted by the final refinement of that strategy, and sin is seen as lawlessness *(anomia)* which utilizes the law and *by means of it* unleashes its deadening power (Rom. 7:11).

Only when we reflect on that concealment is it possible to understand why it is that sin is frequently not recognized or

15. Cf. John 16:2 on the inconsistency here: "They will put you out of the synagogues; indeed, the hour is coming when whoever kills you will think he is offering service to God."
16. One thinks of Paul's statement to Agrippa in Acts 26:26: "... none of these things has escaped his notice, for this was not done in a corner."
17. The folly of sin, we read in II Tim. 3:9, is really "plain to all."
18. Cf. the "wages of sin," referred to in Rom. 6:23. Heidland, *TWNT*, V, *s.v. opsōnion:* "sin is a deceiver; it promises life and gives death."

discerned in its true nature. Both in the practice of everyday living and especially in our theories on the essence of sin, we are tempted to see the *sub specie boni* in a way that waters down our sin and empties it of its evil. All kinds of particular sins may still be recognized and the abnormality of much of what we do may still be admitted. But the point remains that we are inclined to minimize the biblical witness concerning the truly *alarming character of our sin.* We then fancy our sin as "deficiency," or "lack," or "hiatus," or "mistake," or as something to be "regretted"; but sin is not a "disaster" or "catastrophe." Sin is no longer a disconcerting and ominous snare, to be resisted by "putting on the whole armor of God" (Eph. 6:11). It is not a damning power which holds our lives in peril. It is rather defined by a number of circumstances[19] and is always "not yet" in contrast to what "will be later."[20] Therefore, if we give enough time the restrictions on our present circumstances will be lifted away. Obviously, that standpoint is congenial to the notion that sin does not affect or pollute the deepest being of a man. It only impinges on the *periphery of our living.* Sin does not break down the harmony of life. Man retains his intrinsic powers to resist and to restore.[21]

Now it is clear that this concept (with every concept to water down sin) is opposed to the biblical witness concerning the nature, scope, and gravity of *sin.* Scripture refutes the essential and inner goodness of man and disputes the distinc-

19. Cf. E. Brunner, *Die Mystik und das Wort,* 1924, in the chapter on "Die Sünde als Atavismus und Schuld," pp. 228-247. On this qualification or restraint of sin, cf. p. 232 (on the concept of *Hemmung*).

20. This notion of a check or qualification, or obstacle, is not in itself unbiblical. Heb. 12:1 speaks of laying "aside every weight, and sin which clings so closely." One is reminded of a long garment which would be burdensome in a gymnastic event. Cf. O. Michel, *Der Brief an die Hebräer,* 1949, p. 289.

21. We recall the debate in Dutch liberalism, in which right-wing modernism cited as one of its main grievances against the old modernism the weakening of sin-consciousness. Roessingh spoke of "a different psychical disposition" in right-wing modernism and a different experience of the antithesis of sin and grace. Cf. K. H. Roessingh, "Rechts-modernisme," in *Verzamelde Werken,* I, 1926, 198. Opposition to this criticism was offered by A. Bruining in "De Kentering in het Modernisme," *Verzamelde Studiën,* III, 1923, 313ff. Even before Roessingh, G. J. Heering (*Zonde en Schuld naar Christelijk Besef,* 1912) distinguished himself from the old-modernist view of sin. According to Bruining, the difference between old-modernism and new ("rechts-modernisme") was more a matter of pedagogical method (*op. cit.,* 314).

tion of a "center and periphery." Man is viewed in terms of his total life-direction: man the sinner, the guilty one, the rebel against his God. In that biblical perspective there is no possibility of escape and no way out of man's guilty lostness. There is no return to a restoration or regeneration in man himself. Sin eliminates every alibi and is completely inimical to God and can only be called a *deadly force*. The inexorable consequences and dismal rewards of sin follow like a shadow. "For the wages of sin is death" (Rom. 6:23).

Those wages have nothing to do with a "vitalizing" of life but can only lead to destruction. Therefore the peril of sin is very obvious.[22] More than the "immanent consequences" of sin are apparent here; for we are also confronted with the wrath and the judgment of God. So grave is that judgment that the sinner himself can only be seen as hopeless and helpless. He has no possibility of escape from the demonic clutch and consequences of sin. Only divine mercy can pardon, and only the marvel of God's initiative can bring hope in the midst of this dire plight and dismal despair. But this kind of hope is the act of God's atonement. It is the "sweeping away" of transgressions (Isa. 44:42) and the "not counting" of our trespasses (II Cor. 5:19).

The fact that this is *exclusively* the work of God's grace accentuates the hopelessness and lostness of man. Therefore man is described in such terms as these: bondage, slavery, servitude, alienation from God, and a process of degeneracy which cannot be reversed, as far as man is concerned. Man is "dead in sin" and "lost" (John 8:34; Rom. 6:6; Eph. 4:18; 2:1, 5; Col. 2:13; Luke 19:10). The reality of sin brings down the wrath of God to such an extent that his judgments are manifest in the very midst of man's own sin. They are manifest *in* the intensification of sin and *in* "giving men up" to a further and a worse estate (Rom. 1:24, 26, 28). Here we see a remarkable feature in the holiness and wrath of God. The biblical witness concerning the gravity of sin, or the indictment against our sin, clearly shows us the true nature of sin and every effort to explain it or interpret it or explain it away. Sin is not a tragic lot which eliminates responsibility; it is not a pernicious plague which befalls a man apart from his own will. Therefore when we see our sin we must see ourselves as guilty. Every effort to soothe

---

22. On the end-result of sin, see further James 1:15: "sin when it is full-grown brings forth death."

away our guilt is vain. "Therefore you have no excuse, O man, whoever you are" (Rom. 2:1; cf. v. 3, 1:20). *This*, then, is the most distressing fact in the biblical indictment: *there simply is no excuse*. Sin can never be explained or causally interpreted but can only be *confessed*.

Scripture describes man's sin in a variety of ways. Yet nowhere do we find a theoretical conception of "sin's essence." Sin is seen in a living and a very existential manner, in connection with the foolhardiness of men. Surely man's sin is apparent in strange and diverse manifestations, within his daily living, in every cranny of his heart.[23] But it is obvious that in all the multiformity of sin there is always a common trait: sin is always *against God*. Never can we get at the "essence of sin" as long as we ignore this relation of sin and God and regard our sin as a mere "phenomenon" in human living. This fact is apparent when sin is described as enmity and rebellion, disobedience and alienation from God.

That kind of terminology is a far cry from the common view which leaves no room for the relational character of sin and implies that sin is a bothersome "deficiency." When we speak, for example, of the "sin" of lost time, or a wasted day, or a day that could have been better spent, our common view does violence to the biblical concept. Our popular view shows little sensitivity for the destructiveness and catastrophic character, the ominousness and the terror of our sin. It is merely an abstraction which is totally unrelated to the judgment and the wrath of God.

Where the biblical indictment is heard — that sin is sin *against God* — there is no suggestion that the relation of sin and our fellowman is of little importance. It is not that this relation contributes little to our understanding of evil. That fact is very apparent in the seriousness with which Scripture speaks of the judgment and wrath of God against all sinful disruptions in human affairs. The Scripture speaks emphatically concerning this sin of man against his fellowman: "If your brother sins against you . . ." (Luke 17:3ff.; cf. Matt. 18:15ff.). Therefore it is impossible, in a scriptural focus, to draw a line between a "real" sinning against God and an "unreal" sinning against our neighbors. Far better to profess that a love

---

23. On these diverse and strange manifestations, consider, e.g., Prov. 6:16-19: the sevenfold abomination which God hates.

for our neighbor is a God-given injunction; therefore an injury to our neighbor is a violation of his command. Consider the sin of Cain against his brother Abel. Here we would seem to have a clear example of a human infraction; but suddenly the matter is cast in a more serious light. "What have you done? The voice of your brother's blood is crying *to me* from the ground" (Gen. 4:10; cf. Matt. 23:35, Luke 11:50).

Nowhere does the Scripture take an easy view of our sin on the false presumption that it is merely a sin "against our fellowman." The anger of the Lord rests on that man who sheds an innocent man's blood. An unimaginable guilt may show its ugliness in human affairs: but just as unimaginable is the judgment against the man who spurns his neighbor and does injury to his fellowman who was made in the image of God. Recall the passage of Scripture which speaks of sin as "an unrighteous world" (James 3:5ff.) and calls attention to the world of "the tongue" which stains "the whole body, setting on fire the cycle of nature, and set on fire by hell." Why is it so unspeakably dreadful when the tongue of man "curses men" (3:9)? Simply because the tongue is a "restless evil, full of deadly poison" (3:8) and because, in reflecting on our sin against God and our neighbor, we have nothing to do with two separable "territories" or "realms" of sinning. For that reason David wrote as he did in Psalm 51:4: "Against thee, thee only have I sinned." He was not trying to eliminate his sin against his fellowman. Rather, he stood in all his naked guiltiness before the face of God. His guilt was described in the sphere of his fellowman in the parable which Nathan spoke (II Sam. 12:1f.).[24] At the same time we must remember, of course, that Nathan was the prophet *of God*.

Therefore this relation between a sinning against the "first" and a sinning against the "second" table of the law is very intimate. When we offend our neighbor we do injury in precisely *that way* to God. One of the greatest perils for Christians is the notion that these two "spheres" are really divorceable or that a discontinuity obtains between a love for God and a love for our neighbor. John points out the impossibility of that notion: "But if any one has the world's goods and sees his brother in need, yet closes his heart against him, how does God's love abide in him?" (I John 3:17).

24. Note the reference to the ewe lamb of the poor man, v. 4, and to acting without pity, v. 6.

Only a blatant illusion could hold these two "spheres" apart. Never is a sin against our fellowman any less serious than a sin against God. As a matter of fact, our relation to God can only compel us to take radically this relation to our fellowmen. Only in that light can we appreciate the passionate protest of the prophets against the social injustices of Israel. The notoriousness of Israel's crime was not toned down because of her religion and offerings and feasts. Quite to the contrary; her religion was exposed for what it was, in all its perversity and impurity. One cannot "desire the day of the Lord" while he sets his heels on the necks of those who are oppressed. As a matter of fact, an imminent woe awaits the man who sins against God in the act of sinning against his fellowman. "For I know how many are your transgressions, and how great are your sins — you who afflict the righteous, who take a bribe, and turn aside the needy in the gate" (Amos 5:12; cf. v. 15). As James has put it: "Behold, the wages of the laborers who mowed your fields, which you kept back by fraud, cry out; and the cries of the harvesters have reached the ears of the Lord of hosts" (5:4). Thus, alongside the "wages of the laborers" which "cry out" we hear of those cries which "reach to heaven"; and both are mentioned in one and the same breath. "You have condemned, you have killed the righteous man; he does not resist you" (5:6).

We may speak, with no hesitation at all, of a certain depth-dimension in the relations of human guilt. This is evident when apparently minor infractions are the occasions for the greatest condemnation on the part of God. Thus hate is identified with murder (I John 3:15). Therefore, too, we are forbidden to speak of two different levels: one against God and the other against our neighbors. When we sin against our neighbors we sin against our God.[25] Human relations are not compartmentalized or set off to a certain area of their own. They do not have their own relative norms and criteria. Rather, we are always concerned with the One who is God *in and over all things*. We are concerned with the God who directs and protects and who sees men as guilty in the midst of their daily affairs.

That being the case, it is impossible to suggest that a sin against God and a sin against our neighbor might stem from

25. The classic reference is Joseph's response to Potiphar's wife: "how then can I do this great wickedness, and sin against God?" (Gen. 39:9).

competing motives.[26] In God's work of redemption there is no exclusively private relation between the mercy of God and individual man. Instead, the mercy of God is manifest in the love of man for his neighbor. In a similar way, there is a relation between a sinning against our neighbor and a sinning against God. Our relation to God is validated and regarded as serious in the midst of our relation with our fellows.[27] Therefore the man who does violence to that intimate bond in whatever way (in theory or practice) must find himself confronted by this apostolic warning: "If any one says, 'I love God,' and hates his brother, he is a liar; for he who does not love his brother whom he has seen, cannot love God whom he has not seen" (I John 4:20; cf. v. 21).[28]

Both in love and in lovelessness, these relations to God and our neighbors are in no way set in competition with each other but are mutually implicative. That is to say, the one implies the other. Therefore Scripture opposes the effort to "isolate" our sin against our fellowman or to regard that sin on a lower rung than sin against God. This notion can only minimize the tremendous seriousness of the blood which "cries out" to the highest heavens from the lowest depths of the earth.

Now it is obvious that we can only speak in this vein in terms of the reality and relevance of what is often called the "double command to love." In that command we find the foundation for the unbreakable relation between sinning against God and sinning against our neighbors. When Christ spoke of a love for God and our neighbors he was not conceiving of a twofold command in the sense of two "parts" set next to each other. He did not affirm a "first" and a "second" command with no qualification. The first command required a total concentration of life in a love for God (love him "with all your heart, and with all your soul, and with all your mind"), and the second followed immediately and prescribed a love for our neighbors. But to this "second" it was then added that it is

26. There is no hint of such a competition in Peter's statement to Ananias: "You have not lied to men but to God" (Acts 5:4). The burden of this text is to underline that inter-human sins cannot be abstracted from a sinning against God.
27. Cf. K. Barth, *K.D.*, I/2, 1938, 442ff. (ET, 401ff.).
28. The theme of this unbreakable connection plays a major role in John's letter. Cf. 2:9-10; 3:15.

"like unto" the "first" (Matt. 22:39).[29] Here we do well to
pause and reflect on the total scope of this twofold commandment to love. In that way we may come to a better understanding of the character and reality of sin.[30]

Certainly this twofold prescription underscores the universal
significance of love. We know, of course, that love is the "canon
for the exposition of the entire Torah."[31] "On these two commandments depend all the law and the prophets" (Matt. 22:
40).[32] Yet in this twofold command there would seem to be a
problem. At first glance it is remarkable, and even strange, that
these two commandments are tied up with each other at all.
Is there possibly a contradiction? Christ refers us to the "great
and first commandment" and adds immediately a "second";
moreover, he then concludes that "there is no other commandment greater than these" (Mark 12:31). In other words, *both*
commands, when taken together, are exclusive and *may not be
broken.*[33] Yet it is obvious that Christ does speak of a "first"
and a "second." The "second," however, is not "secondary" in
the usual meaning of that term. It is no less important. It is
"second" within the context and comparison which Christ himself now draws. In that sense alone is it "second" in order.

Therefore we must guard ourselves against the fallacious
notion that Christ's twofold command can be pared down
to a single uniform injunction. For its *dual aspect* reveals the
real profundity of the law. Clearly, the "like"-character of the
second command eliminates the possibility of playing down the
importance of that command. Here "the command of neighbor-
love is set on an equality with the command of God-love, both
in significance and in binding force."[34] There is no parity of
God and man; nevertheless, there is a positing of the second

29. This addition is lacking in Mark (12:29f.) and Luke (10:27).
30. Cf. G. Bornkamm, G. Barth, H. J. Held, *Überlieferung und Auslegung
    im Matth. Evangelium*, 1960, pp. 70ff.
31. Bornkamm, "Das Doppelgebot der Liebe," in *Neutestamentliche Studien
    für R. Bultmann*, 1954, p. 93.
32. Cf. *TWNT*, III, *s.v. kremánnymi* ("abhängig sein"). The sense of
    the word here is "to hang on to." The meaning of the entire law
    (*hólos ho nómos*) is love.
33. It is not hard to understand why Bertram writes: "Only in Lk. can
    one really speak of a twofold command" (*TWNT*, III, *s.v. kremánnymi,*
    3). Luke sets these two commands next to each other with no further
    qualification (10:27), i.e., without reference to "first" and "second."
34. *TWNT*, V, *s.v. homoios.* This word is also used in connection with the
    parables: "the kingdom of heaven is like unto...." Cf. Matt. 13:33, etc.

command in the immediate and exalted context of the first. There is also a striving for a single "qualification of excellence."[35] Along with the first, the second command refers us to the exclusive and majestic government of God.

We should see that this New Testament focus on the twofold command is not really so new. In the Old Testament already we hear of a love for God with our whole hearts (Deut. 6:5), but we are also admonished to love our neighbors (Lev. 19:18). That *dual command* is now fulfilled by Christ in the reality of his messiahship. It is *Christ* who unites the new and the old commands (cf. I John 2:7, 8); furthermore it is now apparent how much he binds, and forever shall bind, a man to God and a man to his neighbor.[36] For all of that, however, the Old Testament sees the same sequence and unbreakable bond in this command. Thus the admonition to love our neighbors is set in the context of the statement: "I am the Lord" (Lev. 19:18).[37]

So close is that relation in the New Testament that the second commandment alone is frequently set forth as an illustration of the single commandment of love. Furthermore, there is no hint at all in such cases of a legalistic "honing down" of the single love-command. Therefore in his conversation with the rich young ruler, Christ reached back to the sixth, seventh, eighth, and fifth commands and concluded with these words: "You shall love your neighbor as yourself." He did not cite the *first table of the law* (Matt. 19:18-19). When he took leave of his disciples it was this new command which he gave them as a guide for their living: "A new commandment I give to you, that you love one another" (John 13:34). Their love for each other would be the *great evidence* of their disciple-

35. C. Spicq, *Agape dans le Nouveau Testament. Analyse des textes*, I, 1958, 41. The second command is analogous to the first "in this sense that, without being strictly equal, it is assimilated in it and constitutes, with it, one class, one special category of precepts, absolutely distinct from all the others."

36. For a better understanding of the love-command, see, further, Gutbrod, *TWNT*, IV, *s.v. nómos;* also Gerhard Barth (*op. cit.*, p. 70), who points to a number of illustrative passages in Matthew. One thinks, for example, of Matt. 5:44, in reference to the second commandment: "Love your enemies and pray for those who persecute you." Also Matt. 9:13: "I desire *mercy*, and not sacrifice." Cf. 12:7.

37. Notice how frequently this statement is added with reference to stealing (19:11), deceit (19:11), unrighteousness (19:15), murder (19:16), vengeance and hate (19:18).

ship. "By this all men will know that you are my disciples, if you have love for one another" (v. 35). This same note is sounded in Paul, where the fulfillment of the law is seen as a love for one's neighbor. Paul took note of the seventh, eighth, and ninth commandments, and concluded with a sweeping reference to "any other commandment" (Rom. 13:8f.).[38] He asserts that "the whole law is fulfilled in one word, 'You shall love your neighbor as yourself' " (Gal. 5:14).[39] In a similar way, James refers to the second table as the "royal law" (2:8).

Superficially, it may seem that the second table of the law is now the first and only commandment. Is the love for God deaccentuated in the framework of Paul's thought? How can it be that the "whole law" is fulfilled in this "one word"? Some people have drawn very radical conclusions, in this regard, concerning the "concreteness" of love. Ritschl, for example, has contended that there is no other way to love God than to love our neighbors. Obviously, he did not want to stifle the love-impulse for God. But he wished to say that this love reveals itself, and is realized *within,* a concrete love for our neighbors. In Ritschl's opinion it is wrong to speak of a direct or an immediate love for God. The love for God is fulfilled within, and by means of, our love for our neighbors.[40]

But that interpretation cannot be squared with Scripture's lucid *dual commandment of love.* The tendency now is to absorb the one aspect in the other and to misinterpret the heavy accent which the Scripture gives to loving our neighbors. We may grant that all attention is frequently centered, in certain passages, on the second table of the law. The "whole" law is "fulfilled" in this "one word."[41] But in the whole fabric of the New Testament this expression, or this "exclusive accent," is

---

38. There is no other command which could possibly possess its own structure and aim *alongside this one.* All commandments are brought under this — or, stated differently, they are seen in terms of it. They are "recapitulated" (*anakephalaioútai;* cf. Eph. 1:10) in this one command to love one's neighbor.

39. Cf. this *ho gár pás nómos* (fulfilled in the *second* command) with *hólos ho nómos* in Matt. 22:40 (first and second command: *en taútais taís dysín*).

40. See also the statement of Bultmann, as cited in N. H. Søe, *Christliche Ethik,* 1957, p. 447: there is no obedience "oriented directly to God." Cf. further (p. 134) the well-known assertion of Ritschl: "Love to God has no room for activity alongside that of love to one's brother."

41. Cf. Greeven, *TWNT,* VI, *s.v. plēsíon,* in reference to Jesus' word to the rich young ruler.

possible only *because* the second table of the law cannot be isolated from the first. The whole law must be seen in the unitary structure of love. Nowhere does the Scripture imply an autonomy or an independence of the second table. The fact is that Paul writes to believers that "you yourselves have been taught *by God* to love one another" (I Thess. 4:9). When Christ gave his "new command" he did so by referring to the love which he had shown to his disciples: ". . . even as I have loved you, that you also love one another" (John 13:34).

Within the purview of this "new" and unitary command, the entire law is now set forth under the heading of a love for our neighbors. If anywhere, certainly here it is evident that the relation of sin to God (all man's sin) by no means obscures but only intensifies the seriousness of sinning against our neighbors. In the fulfillment of the law, and our having love for each other, we are really concerned with the very hallmark of discipleship. Therefore the second table of the law is a matter of greatest importance. Therefore, too, the simple act of loving the least of Christ's brethren is tied up, within an eschatological perspective, with a great inheritance in the Kingdom of God (Matt. 25:34ff.).

Sin, by nature, is a violation of this commandment of God to love. But in making that statement we must bear in mind that this second table of the law appears in a very peculiar form: "You shall love your neighbor *as yourself*." There has always been much ado concerning those words. We might ask: Is there a warrant here to speak of a legitimate self-love or does Christ merely assume, so to speak, the factual and illegitimate reality of man's sinful and egotistical heart? In the latter case his purpose might well be to suggest that the concentration and direction of man's loving should not be toward oneself but *toward one's neighbor*.

We do well to take a hard look at that question. In so doing we shall fathom better the nature of love and the nature of our sin. We must see why some people have protested the exegesis that Christ in these words "as yourself" is really setting claim to a legitimate self-love. They have called to mind the further statement that "he who loves his life loses it" (John 12:25). Thus they have contended that self-love (or *amor sui*) is no true love but is rather the *revelation of man's sin*. Why should Christ have given a "new commandment of love" in

which the whole law is "fulfilled" and extol "self-love" as good
and exemplary when all the while that love is so very natural
and common to man? How, then, is the "new" man any different
from the "old"? Is it not better to say that the new command
is the termination of *amor sui*, and that self-love is the very
antithesis of Christ's new commandment to "deny ourselves"?
This, it would seem, is what the Golden Rule is really all
about. "So whatever you wish that men would do to you, do
so to them; for this is the law and the prophets" (Matt. 7:12).

Barth especially has denied that Christ's "new command"
implies a valid self-love.[42] Thus he takes issue with Kierkegaard
and makes a very proper appeal to Calvin, who also opposed
this idea of loving ourselves.[43] The burden of Christ's command,
according to Calvin, is not that self-love is good and right;[44]
for self-love is a *vitium*, an error, or a fallacy to be rectified.
Therefore Christ presumed the factual self-love of man in his
sinful state. By nature man is carnally-minded and disposed to
love himself. For that *reason* God commands us to love our
neighbors. Thus when the members of "the Sorbonne" assumed
that self-love receives a priority in Christ's command they
emptied his words of their meaning.[45] We can never have a
true love for our neighbors as long as our love for ourselves
is untransformed. "We have to admit that the Reformers were
right," says Barth.[46] "In spite of Augustine the invention of
a commandment to love oneself was a cardinal error."[47]

We should observe that both Augustine and Kierkegaard
saw this concept of self-love as no "fact" but as rather implied
in the command to love our neighbors. Certainly they did not
wish to have an egotism. They wished to have a "purified"
self-love, or a love that was ordered by and not in competition with a love for God and our neighbors. Yet, no matter

42. Barth, *K.D.*, I/2, 425ff. (ET, 386ff.).
43. Barth also appeals to Luther. In Luther's commentary on Romans he
    sees these words ("as yourself") as no command to love oneself, "sed
    ostendatur *vitiosus amor,* quo diligit se de facto" (Barth, *op. cit.*, 426;
    ET, 387).
44. The command does not mean "amorem nostri priore loco statuere, ut
    quisque se ipsum imprimis amet, deinde proximos" (*Comm. on Matt.*
    22:39).
45. "Evertunt enim, non interpretantur verba Domini" (*Comm. on Gal.*
    5:14).
46. *K.D.*, I/2, 427 (ET, 388).
47. *Ibid.*

how we twist and turn this self-love to integrate this "command" in the larger commandment to love, it is very difficult to imagine these words, "you shall love your neighbor," as the application of a more general dictum: "you shall love yourself"! This latter is all the more the case when we conceive of this rule as an "implicit command." It is far better to say that Christ, in the second table, takes note of the natural preoccupation of man with himself and uses it as an illustration of *how much* a man, in his new commandment, must be geared toward and bound up with his neighbor. Thus the authority of Augustine is very deceptive at this point, and the passionate protests of Luther and Calvin can lead us in the only rightful way.[48]

The second table of the law concerns a love for our neighbor. Therefore there is no reason at all to read into it a two-pronged injunction of *amor sui* and *amor proximi*. We need not deny, of course, the relation between loving someone else and preserving our own lives. After all, it is only in maintaining ourselves that we really serve our neighbors.[49] Nor should we ignore the gratitude that we must have for the lives which God has given to us. We can agree with Kierkegaard that self-

48. Anders Nygren has pointed to the complexity of Augustine's view of *amor Dei* and *amor sui*. On the one hand *amor sui* is the real sin and root of all evil; on the other, self-love is the presupposition and criterion of our love for our neighbor (*Eros und Agape*, II, 1937, 347f., 356f.). Cf., in this connection, the often-cited statement in *De Civitate Dei* (Lib. XIX, cap. xiv): "Iam vero quia duo praecipua praecepta, hoc est dilectionem Dei et dilectionem proximi docet magister Deus, in quibus tria invenit homo quae diligat, *Deum, se ipsum et proximum*" (Nygren, *op. cit.*, 356; Søe, *op. cit.*, p. 137; Barth, *op. cit.*, 416). On Kierkegaard, we might take special note of his *Liefdedaden*, 1919, p. 25, where he discusses the second table and writes that Christianity frees a man from his egotism and, at the same time, wrests open — as though it were a double key — the lock of self-love. The words "as yourself" pierce through to the deepest hidden chambers where man loves himself, and permit no excuse for the least trace of egotism. Here Kierkegaard seems, on the surface, to follow Luther and Calvin, but he breaks with them quite soon when he asserts that the way to true self-love is laid open when we do away with false self-love. He relates this comment to the meaning of the second table: one has to love himself in the proper manner. On the one hand, thus, the commandment aids a man to cut loose from selfishness (*op. cit.*, p. 30); on the other hand (according to the command) we must love our neighbors *as* we love ourselves (31). Kierkegaard combines, it would seem, these two aspects.

49. On the problem of self-love in Augustine, cf. further L. Binswanger, *Grundformen und Erkenntnis menschlichen Daseins*, 1935[2], pp. 387f.

denial, in the New Testament, is very different from self-annihilation, since obviously the man who annihilates himself is of no further service.[50] But the commandment of love, in the messianic Kingdom, was instituted by Christ in such a way that a man is set before his neighbor; furthermore, the factual direction of self-love is now dynamically changed within the borders of that Kingdom.[51] Think of Paul's words concerning a love which "does not insist on its own way" (I Cor. 13:5).[52] In those words we find the key for understanding the second table of the law. This kind of love is in contrast to Paul's description of the "last days" when men will be "haters of good" and "lovers of self" (II Tim. 3:2-3).[53]

Therefore every possibility is cut off for relativizing a love for our neighbors in the interest of a deeper love for God. Human affairs are seen as very vitally relevant when they are illumined by the light of the first table of the law. Consider the parable of the Good Samaritan. In the total context of that

50. In *K.D.*, I/2 (416ff.; ET, 378ff.), Barth takes his position resolutely on the side of Luther and Calvin, while in *K.D.*, III/4 (439ff., ET, 385ff.) he also speaks of willing in one's own living what God has promised and granted. Thus he speaks of "the affirmation of life as self-affirmation," which is, at root, an "act of obedience" (441; ET, 387).

51. Compare the second table ("as yourself") with the Golden Rule of Matt. 7:12: "So whatever you wish that men would do to you, do so to them; *for this is the law and the prophets.*" Cf. Grosheide, *Comm. op Mattheus*, 1954, pp. 116f.: "This command is diametrically opposed to all egoism." See also the "short summary of the second table of the law," p. 116. Further, cf. G. Barth, in *Überlieferung und Auslegung im Matth. Evangelium*, I, 1960, 74. On the second table and the theme of self-love, a more extensive classification of various views is found in V. Warnack, *Agape. Die Liebe als Grundmotiv der N.T. Theologie*, 1951, pp. 300-303.

52. It is remarkable that the New Testament speaks of self-love on a different level than the obligation to one's neighbor: the level of sinful factuality, and not of command. Cf. such well-known references as Eph. 5:28-29 and Matt. 10:39; Luke 17:33; John 12:25.

53. Think of Paul's word in I Cor. 10:24: "Let no one seek his own good, but the good of his neighbor"; also Phil. 2:3-4: "Do nothing from selfishness or conceit, but in humility count others better than yourselves. Let each of you look not only to his own interests, but also to the interests of others." It is questionable if this translation ("not only ... but also") is entirely accurate. Cf. Lohmeyer, *Komm.*, 1953[9], p. 80: "Look in humility the one upon the other, not thinking of your own things but the things of others." Greijdanus (*Komm.*, p. 178) observes that the term *mónon* is lacking here, since that which belongs to oneself may not be a proper object of striving and desiring.

story it is crystal clear how much Christ's teaching was concerned about our neighbors. For that reason Luke ties this story directly with the proclamation of the twofold commandment to love.[54] He couches it in the context of a "problem" concerning our "neighbor." "Who," we read, "is my neighbor?" That question was not asked with a theoretical or even a practical concern, but rather with the aim of the lawyer's justifying himself. "But he, desiring to justify himself . . ." (Luke 10:29). Nevertheless, the question takes a surprising turn at the end of the story when Christ responds: "Which of these three (the Levite, priest, or Samaritan) proved neighbor to the man who fell among the robbers?" (10:36). What kind of question is that! We might think, on the basis of the original issue, that the neighbor was the man who had need; yet even the lawyer had to concede that the neighbor was the *Good Samaritan*. Loath as he was to refer to him by nationality, he could only admit that "the one who showed mercy" was "the neighbor" (10:37).

Stauffer has rightly spoken of a "reversal" in the original question.[55] The original question had set the egocentric "I" in the foreground: "Who is *my* neighbor?" But Christ's answer exploded that order and fastened attention on the man who was robbed. "Who was neighbor *to this man?*" The Samaritan was seen as the true neighbor — as the one who "showed mercy" and was not concerned about *himself* but rather about *someone else*. Thus Jesus, having come to this point in his story, was ready for the final message: "Go and do likewise."[56]

The double command of love confronts us with an unexpected and unknown *world of love* in contrast to our own familiar *world of unrighteousness*. Within that world, or God's world, we men are snatched away from the world of demons and magic and *incurvatus in se*. We observe in our lives, before the face of God, a totally new direction and content.[57] The

54. Luke 10:25-28; 10:29-37. Greeven: "hineinkomponiert" (*TWNT*, VI, s.v. *plēsion*).
55. *TWNT*, I, s.v. *agápē*.
56. On the good Samaritan cf. the "christological" exegesis of Barth, *K.D.*, I/2, 460ff. (ET, 416ff.) and J. C. Schreuder, "De Naaste bij Karl Barth," in *G.T.T.*, vol. 44.
57. In Acts 20:35 Paul recalls a beatitude of Jesus which does not appear in the Gospels: "It is more blessed to give than to receive." Here we find a radical contradiction and explosion of the entire structure of sin,

spirit of I Corinthians 13 radiates within that new world, and the reality of love becomes the "down payment" and prophecy of the eschatological reality when men "shall not hurt or destroy" in all God's holy mountain (Isa. 11:9). The origin of that new reality is very evident. "For the earth shall be full of the knowledge of the Lord as the waters cover the sea." Because of that "knowledge of the Lord" the common features of our old world are no longer possible and eternal life takes their place. Therefore the sense and glory of our lives are understood anew.

We see very clearly the breaking of God's law and the nature of our sin in the light of this twofold commandment of love. That which was once "commonplace" and apparently "normal" is now laid bare as a disavowal of the glory of God. Yet we men are not left desolate, as it were, in the vanity of our own familiar world. Within our world of sin and guilt the commandment of love is proclaimed to us anew. Therefore it is not surprising that men, as they grope for a "definition" of sin, have constantly laid hold on this motive which underscores the deepest awfulness of sin. Man's sin is *lovelessness*. At the same time, we may ask if this term is really adequate. The man who reflects upon, and who understands, the profundity of this twofold command, than which "there is no ... greater" (Mark 12:31), will appreciate that no other description can possibly do better than saying that "sin is lovelessness." Therefore we read in John: "he who does not love does not know God; for God is love" (I John 4:8). The fulfillment of the commandments of God is set in contrast to "not loving" (5:3). That is to say, we keep the commandments of God when we keep his one command, *to love*.

Nevertheless, it is wrong to ignore the other descriptions of sin and to have an open eye for only this central, all-inclusive meaning of God's law. The man who does this is out of step with the various usages and descriptions of "sin" in Scripture. Certainly, every sin is a violation of God's single commandment to love. Yet in view of our concrete living it is possible to give other nuances of interpretation which are also concerned with the harsh reality of sin. Thus we find such Old Testament terms as *chapha'*, *pesha'*, and *'awon*:[58] "missing the mark," "rebellion,"

---

for the attitude of *giving* is now qualified as *blessed*. Literally: "It is blessed rather to give than to receive."

58. Cf. Th. C. Vriezen, *Hoofdlijnen der Theologie van het O.T.*, 1954², 225; *TWNT*, I, *s.v. hamartánō*.

and "moral corruptness."[59] These do not always imply, in an obvious and specific sense, a direct relationship to God. In fact the Old Testament usage of the word "sin" includes a whole variety of sin-relationships.[60] At the same time, the disruptive element in all these is constantly taken up in the religious description of sin as "sin against God."[61] Because of that relation to God our sin is viewed in a very urgent light. All the biblical descriptions of our sin have a single trait in common: *sin is always in relation to God*. Therefore our sin is not an apparent "deficiency" or the result of human, creaturely limitations and the relativities of our living. Nor is sin the phenomenon of a "shadow" set next to "light." Man's sin can only be *revealed*, since its origin can only be found in this disruption of the relation of man and God.

No one has ever defined our sin in a way that embraces the multiplicity of the biblical expressions. Such attempts have been made, of course, and have utilized a number of images to fill out our pictures of "sin." Bavinck once wrote that sin is "lawlessness,"[62] though in another place he has seen the essence of sin as *privatio*. Yet he further employed such biblical concepts as "rejection of God," "disobedience," "rebellion," "illegality," "anarchy," "pride," "selfishness," and "sensuality."[63] That very multiplicity in expressions should caution us against a preference for any single term.[64] For that kind of preference is bound to lead to a biased presentation and a failure to appreciate the richness of the biblical language. We agree that when Scripture describes our sin we sometimes get the impression that it gives a "definition." Nonetheless its descriptions are never meant in an exclusive sense. "Sin is lawlessness," we read in I John 3:4;[65] yet that same letter combines the terms *lawlessness* and *godlessness*, and both are viewed in close connection with *un-*

---

59. Cf. J. Pedersen, *Israel, Its Life and Culture*, I-II, 1926, 414.
60. Cf. Gen. 40:1; 41:9 (sin against the king of Egypt).
61. Thus, in all the various expressions, the "unity" of sin is not lost. Cf. *TWNT*, I, *s.v. hamartánō:* "It is evident that all variations mean, fundamentally, one and the same thing." Also Vriezen, *op. cit.*, p. 224, and Pedersen, *op. cit.*, p. 432: "All sin is a violation of God"; cf., "all sin is revolt and disobedience against Jahweh."
62. Bavinck, *Geref. Dog.*, III, 126.
63. *Ibid.*, 132f.
64. Cf., for the New Testament: *hamartía, hamartōlós, anomía, adikía, parábasis, parakoúein, píptein.*
65. Cf. I. de la Potterie, "Le péché, c'est l'iniquité," in *Nouv. Rev. Theol.*, 1956 (Tom. 48), pp. 785-797.

righteousness and *wrongdoing.* Therefore "all wrongdoing is sin" (5:17). It is incorrect to say that these biblical expressions "complete" each other. At the same time, they are mutually illuminating and ought to be seen as such.

Certainly when we say that sin is "lawlessness" we do· not mean that it is an infringement of an abstract law but only of *God's law.* The reality and the fullness of God are stamped on every description or every "definition" of our sin. That fact is clear enough when we see the many negative terms for sin: *disobedience, unfaithfulness, disbelief, lawlessness* and *loveless-ness.* These expressions imply that sin is something that is lacking, but they also point to the disconcerting and catastrophic character of sin. Thus they are more than merely negative, for that which is lacking bestows on them a certain positive ring. When we see that fact we understand why it is that men have always given special attention to one particular description of sin in which all the negatives of Scripture would seem to be combined. We are referring to the concept of *privatio.* Here we pass over the many connotations of that word in the history of theology. Our purpose is to hold at arms' length and examine the term itself, since it introduces a number of problems of real importance for the doctrine of our sin.

It might surprise us at first that this concept has played such a crucial role in the history of dogmatics. For *privatio,* when taken by itself, does not refer to something total or radical and catastrophic. No wonder that some have asked if this term makes any essential contribution to understanding the nature of our sin. Does it picture our sin, perhaps, as a relative deficiency, or a "mere privation," or a superficial evil? Is sin a surface corrosion which leaves untouched the inner being of a man? If that were the case we could refer to it as *privatio* but not *corruptio totalis.*

Therefore we shall have to agree that the term *privatio,* in itself, says very little. A man may be deprived of many things without losing anything really important.[66] Not every privation

---

66. The fact that this does not suggest, in itself, the illegitimacy of the *privatio*-concept is evident from the further fact that one could say exactly the same thing regarding the concept *lawlessness.* Anyone who describes sin by using this latter term has no guarantee that he really knows what sin is. No more classic example appears of this than Pharisaism. The Pharisee both acknowledged and utilized the notion of sin as lawlessness, but the "key of knowledge" (also the knowledge of sin) eluded him. Cf. Luke 11:52.

is a catastrophic calamity. Thus we err if we assume that this term is a full description of our sin. Nonetheless we cannot deny that this term has played an important role in the history of hamartiology. We shall have to ask why, precisely, that is. Is there a special motive here which we have not as yet seen?

In our day C. G. Jung has objected especially to the doctrine of *privatio*. We approach the problems here by taking note of his polemic, since exactly this criticism from a non-theological point of view has stimulated a critical reflection on the validity of our dogmatical language. Jung has regarded the *privatio*-idea as minimizing the true nature of evil. Though commonly the Church and her theology are censured for an over-accent on evil and a pessimistic outlook on man, the opposite is now the case. Jung regards the concept of *privatio boni* as ecclesiastical doctrine and he reads in this an "accidental deficiency in perfection."[67] He sees this "minimizing" of sin in *privatio* as a very serious occasion for the later denial and exclusion of the devil "in certain Protestant doctrines."[68] According to Jung, we must speak of sin in a much deeper and more penetrating way. "One has to conceive of evil in a more substantial way when he meets up with it on the level of empirical psychology. There it is simply the opposite of good."[69] For that reason Jung takes issue with what he sees as the effort of the early Church to speak of sin as something negative. The early Church embraced the concept of *privatio* by taking her point of departure in the goodness of the world, as created by God, and conceiving of evil as the negation of that goodness. But sin, in that view, had no "existence" or "reality" and was in no sense "substantial." "From these considerations it becomes apparent with what emphasis the reality of evil was already early denied."[70]

Jung appreciates the fact that *privatio* implies a polemic against the concept of sin as substance and especially against the doctrine of the Manichees.[71] But that fact does not soften down his opposition to the wide range of uses that Augustine gave to this concept. He objects to Augustine's reference to sin as *privatio boni*[72] and sees in this a weakening of the real power of

67. C. G. Jung, *Aion. Untersuchungen zur Symbolgeschichte*, 1951, p. 69.
68. *Ibid.*
69. *Ibid.*
70. *Ibid.*, p. 81.
71. *Ibid.*
72. "Non est ergo malum nisi privatio boni" (Jung, *ibid.*). It is noteworthy

evil. "One cannot describe what has happened and still happens
in the concentration camps of dictatorial states as a mere 'accidental deficiency in perfection.' That would seem to be an utter
mockery."[73] Does sin have only *privatio* and no "substance"?
Does it have no "reality"? Jung, as a *psychologist,* eschews every
concept which ignores what he sees as "empirical fact": that
within the empirical consciousness good is simply opposed to
the *reality of evil.* Granted that psychology knows nothing of
good and evil "in themselves," yet in the *subjective judgment*
both are seen as very *real.*[74]

Certainly Jung does not propose to mix the questions of
psychology and metaphysics. At the same time, metaphysics
must not soar above experience and interpret evil in a way
that is empirically irresponsible.[75] Precisely *this* is the error
of the *privatio boni.* This very concept, according to Jung, does
injustice to the empirical and psychological antithesis of good
and evil. It accentuates the good while it plays down the evil.[76]
Yet such a viewpoint cannot be harmonized with the psychological situation or the postulate of our own experience. There both
good and evil are *constantly opposed.*[77] Thus, Jung's criticism
is based entirely on the data of psychological experience. He
upholds the reality of evil and refuses any concept which regards
it as inconsequential or as even non-existent.[78]

How then should we answer this criticism of Jung? We must
bear in mind that it certainly contains an element of truth.
Jung has laid his finger on a real danger in the *privatio*-idea.
On the other hand, there are motives at work here which are
insufficiently recognized in this criticism. Thus there is nothing
in *privatio* of an automatic "undervaluing" of sin. We need not
give a full description of the Augustinian doctrine at this point,
but it is easy to see that even there the issues are much more

that Jung, in translating this statement of Augustine, renders *privatio*
by the German *Abwesenheit*: "Consequently evil is only an absence
(*Abwesenheit*) of good," p. 82. But this is doubtless a weakening of the
privatio-concept.

73. *Ibid.*, p. 86.
74. *Ibid.;* cf. p. 87. "My criticism of the *privatio boni* applies only in so
far as psychological experience extends."
75. *Ibid.*
76. *Ibid.*, p. 88.
77. *Ibid.* "The *privatio boni* may, thus, be metaphysically true. I make no
pretensions of being a judge on that matter."
78. *Ibid.*, p. 87.

complex than Jung would care to suggest. Augustine used the *privatio* as a polemical tool against the Manichees; at the same time, his Neoplatonism left a very clear imprint on that concept. Take, for example, the following statement concerning "the good" as we find it in the *Confessions*:[79] "Thus everything that exists is good and the evil whose origin I sought is not substantial (*non est substantia*), for if it were a substance (*si substantia esset*) it would be good." Augustine asks what evil is and responds that it is not substantial and has no reality.[80] Evil is the corruption of the will which has turned aside from the Highest Being and the Highest Substance. That is to say, it has turned aside from God.

Now everything depends on what we mean by this term *privatio*.[81] When the Reformers used that terms they were well aware of the latent perils, and especially this peril of relativizing our sin. To escape the danger of making sin a "mere privation" they conceived of sin as *privatio actuosa*. They acknowledged that sin is more than a "defect in general" and is always an active, dynamic and destructive force. Thus sin, for the Reformers, was not a *mera privatio*. Rather, precisely as privation it was seen as a *vitiositas*, despoilment, or *corruptio totalis*.[82] When we point to sin as *privatio* the full weight of this word is only felt if we add *what it is* of which a man is now deprived: *privatio justitiae*.[83] Therefore, despite the hazards in the term and the need for saying precisely what we mean, the term itself has always held a very honored place in the history of this doctrine. This fact is all the more remarkable when we see that the Reformation theology strongly rejected the Catholic view of sin as *carentia justitiae originalis*.

Obviously, there is nothing wrong in itself with that kind of terminology. Furthermore, the loss of original justice, when rightly viewed, is an utterly serious matter. So too is the *carentia amoris!* But the *carentia*-idea, as used in Catholic theology,

79. *Confessions*, VII, 8.
80. "... Et non inveni substantiam" (VII, 22).
81. Consider the query of Augustine: "Quid est autem aliud quod malum dicitur nisi privatio boni?" (*Enchiridion*, ed. O. Scheel, 1930, p. 6). Important, on Augustine's view, is Jens Nörregaard, *Augustins Bekehrung*, 1923, pp. 66ff.
82. Cf. Polanus: "non igitur est mera privatio, sed etiam mala qualitas animae inhaerens, contraria bonae qualitati conformi cum lege Dei" (Heppe, *Dogmatik*, 1861, p. 240).
83. *Ibid.*, p. 232.

had come to mean the loss of the *donum superadditum* and was
very different from the biblical *corruptio totalis*. Therefore that
concept came to have a certain *negative flavor*. In the Reformers
there remained a connection or identity between the *privatio*
and *corruptio* while in Catholic theology these two were held
apart.[84]

Therefore the Reformers continued to use the *privatio*-idea,
though mindful of its many dangers. The Heidelberg Catechism
(Q. 9) speaks in the following way: "Man, through the instigation of the devil, by his own willful disobedience, deprived himself and all his posterity of these gifts." Here we find an
appreciation for a certain motive or insight which is especially
profitable for understanding the essence of our sin; furthermore
it is not difficult to find out what that motive is. We can summarize the point as follows: The biblical witness precludes the
notion of sin as "substantial," since sin has no part in creaturely
reality. We confess that God is the Creator and Origin of all
things, but we do not allow that he is therefore the Author of
our sin.[85] This is the valid, biblical motive which influenced the
Reformers in their protest against the Manichees.[86] At this
point the Reformers and Augustine join hands. Therefore
Jung's interpretation of the *privatio* is entirely too simple.
It is not responsible to assert that *privatio,* in itself, must always
imply a minimizing of our sin.[87] Certainly there are dangers
in this term, but there is also a strongly religious motive which
runs like a thread throughout the polemical debates.

Now that we have come to this point, we can make a better

---

84. Important is the treatment of Calvin (*Inst.,* II, 1, 8), in his polemic
against those who view original sin as a lack of original righteousness
(carentia justitiae originalis). Calvin writes that, although "they comprehend in this definition the whole meaning of the term," they still
do not express effectively enough sin's "power and energy." "For our
nature is not only destitute and empty of good *(inops et vacua boni),*
but so fertile and fruitful of every evil that it cannot be idle." Therefore Calvin uses negative terms very consciously; he speaks of the
deficiency of integrity ("praecipua pars rectitudinis deficit"; II, 3, 4).
The legitimacy of the *privatio*-concept is evident in this context.
85. Cf. Part I, above, pp. 27ff.
86. Cf. BC, Art. 12.
87. Jung takes offense already at the terminology that Basilius used in
asserting that sin has no real substance *(idian hypóstasin toú kakoú
eínai);* he has no appreciation for the fact that such a statement *could*
at least signify a rejection of the independent status of evil (cf. Jung,
op. cit., p. 77).

approach to the concept of *privatio*. Many of the questions that
rise here are set in sharp relief by Bavinck. For Bavinck proceeds
on the premise that sin has no real or independent existence
but presents itself as a leech on what is "good" in creaturely
reality.[88] Sin has power only in and through the good which
God has given. Therefore man's sin is *privatio boni* and can
never be anything else.[89] Bavinck does not play down the real
power of man's sin, but he contends that *privatio boni* is an
"abstract and metaphysical" category. By this he means that
privatio, qua concept, is inadequate for describing what sin in
reality, and in all its destructive force, *is*. The issue, according to
Bavinck, is the meaning of *privatio*. He affirms that sin has no
"being," no "creaturehood" or "substance," but is only a *nihil*.
Sin is "nothing positive but is only privative. Whoever conceives
of it in a different way makes evil independent and eternal, in a
Manichaeist sense, and places the *summum malum* in opposition
to the *summum bonum*."[90]

Previously Bavinck had said that sin is insufficiently described in the *privatio*-concept.[91] This is because sin is no "mere
deficiency" or pure "not-being" but is rather a cataclysmic and
disruptive power. Yet in view of the specific intention of *privatio*, we may continue to see this term, he says, as "completely
accurate" and may even use it without reserve.[92] Sin is not
"material" but is parasitic on creaturely reality. Therefore we
call it a deformation or non-being, a *nihil*[93] and nothing but
privatio.[94] Therefore too the criticism of this concept can only
rest, according to Bavinck, on a misunderstanding.[95] Sin *may*
and *can* be understood, from a Christian standpoint, in no other
way.[96] For that reason Bavinck tries to summarize these negative
formulas in the following statement: "Sin *is* not but wants to
be; it has no true reality and never attains any. It is a lie in
its inception and a lie in its end."[97] Yet this kind of negative
statement can never exclude Calvin's accent on the *vis et energeia*

88. *Geref. Dog.*, III, 119.
89. *Ibid.*, 121.
90. *Ibid.*
91. *Ibid.*, p. 117.
92. *Ibid.*
93. *Ibid.*, p. 118.
94. *Ibid.*, p. 125.
95. *Ibid.*, p. 121.
96. *Ibid.*
97. *Ibid.*

of sin. For sin is always *privatio actio* and *privatio actuosa*. It is never a *mera* or *pura privatio*.[98]

This cautious handling of *privatio* only accentuates the real problems that crop up at this point. The issue is not the abridgment of the power and perniciousness of evil in our world but is rather the *nature of that "reality."* In Bavinck the fearfulness and destructiveness of sin are not denied but are even seen as the motive for all of man's thinking and doing.[99] Sin is a power that seeks to rule and to ruin everyone and everything.[100] "It is nothing and has nothing and can do nothing apart from the creatures and the powers which God has created; yet it organizes all these in open rebellion against him."[101] *Privatio* implies an apostate tendency in which all of privation is manifest.

Those who point to the reactionary, dependent, and parasitical character of sin have sometimes distinguished between the *forma* and *materia* of sinful activities. That distinction also finds place in the notion of concursus (the divine-human concurrence) in the doctrine of God's providence.[102] Granted, we can never make plain the relation between God's sovereignty and man's sin; yet there is a valid motive in this form-and-matter distinction. This motive goes hand in hand with the *privatio*-concept. The purpose, then, is to emphasize that sinful activity concerns the *forma,* or the trend and goal, of what we sinners do. Theologians have tried at times to shed light on that idea by introducing the word *intentionality.* They have tried to say that sin is no "reality" alongside other realities, and is certainly no substance or creature. Sin is the act in which we use, or abuse, the reality created by God.[103]

98. *Ibid.,* p. 118.
99. *Ibid.,* p. 125.
100. *Ibid.*
101. *Ibid.,* p. 126.
102. Cf. my *The Providence of God,* 1952, "A Third Aspect?"
103. In a fascinating account, H. A. Oberman has indicated the problem here as it comes to expression in Thomas Bradwardine: *Archbishop Thomas Bradwardine. A Fourteenth Century Augustinian,* 1957, especially pp. 123ff. Oberman, it seems to me, underestimates the importance of the polemical motive in *privatio* when he considers the notion "that evil has no real 'essence', but like a parasite lives on and consequently is dependent on that which really has 'essence,'" and when he refers to this as "the neo-Platonic-augustinian thought" (p. 123). Oberman speaks of the metaphysical optimism expressing itself in "the conception of evil as *privatio boni*" (p. 134), but adds that "this

Small wonder that everywhere in theology we run up against this question of the nature of man's sin when conceived as *privatio*. One might say that this is truly an *ecumenical problem* or a problem in which not only the Reformation but also Catholic theology has certainly had a stake. Sertillanges, for example, has contended that evil is no creaturely reality but is rather a "privation."[104] Yet on every hand the question comes: What then is the nature of our sin? Does the *privatio* soft-pedal the real reality of sin? Is not sin too virulent a force to be called a *negation*?[105]

Here we are touching on a new distinction. For *negatio* and *privatio* are sometimes set apart. The distinction is meaningful when we bear in mind that negation, in itself, does not entail an evil or "disharmony." If we say that a man is *not* a woman, or that human beings are *not* omnipresent and omniscient, we say nothing that implies an "evil" or a "sin." Thomas Aquinas already analyzed that question and concluded that sin, while *privatio,* is not *negatio*. The category of negation, he said, cannot help us in comprehending the nature of our sin. For not every not-having or not-doing is evil.[106] If there is something that a man is not, and does not have, and cannot be affirmed of man, this all might hang together with the nature of his *being a man*. But in that case we could hardly speak of *privatio,* either. The temptation of the devil ("you shall be as God")

need not yet lead to an un-biblical view of sin." But later he writes again of "Augustinian Platonism" in which Bradwardine "denies the real 'being' of evil" (227). When he indicts Bradwardine for "his undervaluing of sin" (134) he ties this together with his view of "carentia justitia originalis" — yet such an "undervaluing" is not necessarily implied in the usage of the concepts *privatio* and *intentionality*. Polemically, there is a valid motive in the *privatio*-idea; the concept of intentionality should also be seen in direct relation to a view of sin as the act of man in his entirety (— "out of the heart," as we read in the familiar words of Jesus). For a treatment of the problem of sin in the Middle Ages, cf. further R. Blomme, *Le doctrine du péché dans les écoles théologiques de la première moitié du XIIe siècle*, 1958, and A. M. Landgraf, *Dogmengeschichte der Früh-Scholastik*, I, 2, 1953, 204-281.

104. "Le mal n'est pas une réalité, mais une privation." Sertillanges, *Le problème du mal*, II, 5-6.

105. "The virulence of evil is all too evident"; and though it is important not to envision an "essence" in sin, "this does not diminish at all the gravity of the problem posed; nor does it make of sin a simple limit, a simple diminution of good, or a simple privation" (*op. cit.,* 6-7).

106. Thomas, *Summa Theologica*, I, Q. XLVIII, 5; cf. 3.

presumed that the negative of "not being as God" was a painful or a burdensome thing. The identification of negation and privation is implied in every temptation. Yet that identification can only fail to appreciate the goodness and the beatitude of being God's creature. We may speak of *privatio,* when rightly understood, but never of *negatio* as we seek to know the nature of our sin. For *privatio* (and not *negatio*) is open to a discussion of the catastrophic and destructive "reality" of sin.

In our everyday experience we are used to speaking of the "reality" of our sin. The sin of man cuts a wide path through all of human living and exercises its influence by exerting its powers and causing sensations in our lives. Sin manifests itself in the whole of reality and is so concrete that it can almost be "touched." So real is our sin in Scripture that it is sometimes personified. "Sin is couching at the door" (Gen. 4:7). Listen to the following words of Paul: "Sin ... wrought in me all kinds of covetousness" (Rom. 7:8); it "revived" (7:9) and "deceived me," and "finding opportunity in the commandment," it "killed me" (7:11-12).[107] So concretely is sin regarded that it is even allied with those organs through which it is expressed. Therefore Proverbs sounds a warning against "haughty eyes, a lying tongue, and hands that shed innocent blood, a heart that devises wicked plans, feet that make haste to run to evil" (Prov. 6:17-18).[108] Scripture regards it as impossible to conceive of sin in abstraction and apart from the fullness of reality.

Thus sin is seen as an abductor, an enemy, a power; as the blindness that comes with the setting of the sun; as the act of Cain who killed his brother Abel. In sin there is nothing "visionary." There are no chimeric shadows which permit us to "reach beyond" our concrete reality and to "get at" sin's essence. When Bavinck refers to sin as a *nihil* he does not suggest an idealistic category but something profoundly "real." Sin is *privatio actuosa.*[109] Exactly at this point — in sin's "reality" — we encounter what is most essential to sin in man's relation to God.

107. Cf. vv. 13 ("working death in me") and 14 ("sold under sin"). It is no longer Paul who works evil but "sin" (7:17). Cf. Ridderbos, *Comm.,* p. 150.
108. Cf. Ps. 12:4; also James 3:7ff., on slippery lips and a tongue which no man can tame.
109. Bavinck, *op. cit.,* III. Cf. Augustine's comment in reference to John 1:3: "Omnia per ipsum facta sunt et sine ipso factum est nihil. Peccatum quidem non per ipsum factum est ... quia peccatum nihil est" (Tract 1, cap. 13, *In Joannis Evangelium).*

As the Church has always professed, man's sin does not take root in God; nevertheless it is pictured in Scripture as very "real." We cannot do better than to use the language of Scripture itself. The demonic effrontery of sin is evident in its using the fullness of human life for the sake of its own malevolency. Thus its *nihil*-character (as Bavinck used that term) has nothing to do with a watered-down conception.[110] Rather, the dreadful horror of sin is evident in that it is both uncreaturely and *still finds place* in the central disposition of man's heart. Sin is not a peripheral phenomenon. Though it remains an "alien force" it is completely pervasive and wells up from the heart of man himself (Mark 7:21). In the heart of man are the "springs of life" (Prov. 4:23); and all of life is in the clutch of sin's pernicious power.

Therefore we see, from this vantage point, that it is completely possible to describe man's sin as *privatio,* providing that the real *contra*-character of sin is clearly set forth. ·Obviously *"privatio"* is not an adequate definition; but just as obviously there is a revealing reference here to the essence of man's sin, which can only be seen in terms of *that which has been lost.* Therefore we need not reject the *privatio* as a mere fiction or as too "negative" for our purposes. We can better reflect on the negative statements of the Decalogue ("you shall not"), which certainly exclude all that is inconsistent with the reality and riches of a covenantal fellowship with God.

It is always possible to moralize the concept of *not* and to turn it into a rigid set of *don'ts.* Yet the problem of moralism is not the product of negative statements *per se* but the manner in which these are utilized and applied.[111] Negative expressions can have a very positive meaning, and this is made clear in both the Old and New Testaments. The biblical "negativity" is a reference to the riches and salvation imparted by God, and enjoins us to stay within the good boundaries which he has set. Thus the purpose is to protect us and not to threaten us.[112]

110. Cf. Pedersen, *Israel,* I-II, 416. "It is not the external nature of the act which makes it sinful." Cf. p. 420.

111. We reflect here on the burdensome ordinances of which Paul so critically speaks in Col. 2:21: "Do not handle, Do not taste, Do not touch." Of *such* laws Christ is truly the absolute *end* (2:20). These are precepts and teachings of men and are the caricature of the Decalogue.

112. Cf. J. J. Stamm, *Der Dekalog im Lichte der neueren Forschung,* 1958; R. Schippers, "De Hermeneutiek van de Wet," *Bezinning,* 1958, p.

Therefore there is no dilemma between the positive and negative formulas in Scripture.[113] Positive expressions are made apparent in the light of the negative — that is to say, they are made apparent in the light of *that which is refused*. As in the case of the commandments of God, so too in regard to our sin. It is only when we insist on reading *privatio* as *"mera privatio"* that the issue before us is confused. The analogy to the negative statements of the Decalogue is then completely ignored and it is necessary to introduce new categories. This is what happened at the time of the Protestant Reformation. Therefore *privatio* was defined as *actuosa privatio,* or as enmity, iniquity, apostasy, antipathy, and the trespassing of God's command.

It is important for us to look at these negative descriptions of sin. Take, for example, the concept of *disobedience*. Since disobedience is the absence of obedience, as unthankfulness is the absence of thankfulness, the very absence or "privation" is a frightening reality which is also opposed to the whole *meaning of life*. For our lives have meaning only in obedience and thankfulness. Therefore disobedience (*parakoē*) is seen in Scripture in opposition to the original goal of obedience (*hypakoē*) or communion with God. Both these terms derive from a common root which means *to hear or to listen* (*akoúein*). The antithesis, in other words, is evident in the very heart of man. His hearing, listening, and obeying the commandment of God are set in opposition to *not-hearing, not-listening,* and *not-obeying*.[114] In its etymology the scriptural term *to disobey* (*parakoúein*) means simply *to hear alongside of* or *overhear*. Thus we recall what Scripture says concerning Jesus in Mark 5:36: he "listened alongside." That is, he "ignored" the news of Jairus' daughter (*parakoúsas*) and gave no heed. He turned a deaf ear and

125; G. von Rad, *Theologie des A.T.*, I, 1957, 196, on "this persistence in negations" and the "fundamental negations" which are full of *meaning;* also K. Barth, *K.D.*, II/2, 764 (ET, 684f.), on the "Abgrenzungen" ("delimitations") and the "Ortsangabe" ("definite sphere"); and M. Noth, *Gesammelte Studien zum A.T.*, 1958, p. 171.

113. Compare the "not" of the Decalogue with the "curse" in Deut. 27:15ff.; also the "not" in Lev. 19:9-19. On the fourth and fifth commandments, cf. Von Rad, *op. cit.*, p. 200; Stamm, *op. cit.*, pp. 9f. In Matt. 15:4 we find the positive and negative bound together: "For God commanded, 'Honor your father and your mother,' and, 'He who speaks evil of father or mother, let him surely die.'"

114. Cf. "obedience, which leads to righteousness" in Rom. 6:16; and "obedient children" in I Pet. 1:14.

went his way. For him death was not an overpowering, definitive or final reality.[115]

At the same time, the "hearing alongside" of disobedience (*parakoúein*) is the distinguishing feature in all of sin. When we turn a deaf ear in disobedience we do something desperately wrong. Our not-hearing and not-listening are the same as rebellion and transgression against God. Therefore *parakoḗ* and *parábasis* have everything to do with each other (cf. Rom. 5:14, Gal. 3:19). Transgression is identical with the refusal to listen or the plugging of our ears (Acts 7:57). Sin is the "stepping beyond" or "alongside" the border which is good and meaningful and which promises blessings and beatitude for life.

For that reason the negative expressions of Scripture point us clearly to a very dismal darkness. Consider the phrases "without God" or "without Christ," which leave us with "no hope . . . in the world" (Eph. 2:12) and which stand in contrast to the light which we have "in Christ" (2:13). Reflect on the meaning of "alienation from the life of God" (4:18) or the identity of sin and *privatio* in such a text as Romans 3:23: ". . . all have sinned and *fall short* of the glory of God." In the concepts of *alienation* and *falling short* the grief and despair of sin are very apparent.[116] We see in these terms the most dire of privations and the ominous non-presence of the deepest and best of everything that life can possibly afford. In short, we see the non-presence of *the life and glory of our God.*[117]

It is evident, by now, that there is no contradiction between these negative and positive descriptions of our sin. This is very obvious when Paul writes that "the mind that is set on the flesh is *hostile* to God; it does *not submit* to God's law" (Rom. 8:7). The destructive and tragic character of sin is seen in the very nature of these negative expressions. Sin is not an analyzable phenomenon, in and of itself, but is understandable in relation to the life and glory, the "day" and the "light" of God. Therefore we speak of sin as *un*thankfulness, *dis*obedience, *un*right-

115. Mark 5:35ff. Cf. *TWNT*, I, *s.v. hypakoḗ* (under *akoúō*).
116. For the content of this "alienation" (Eph. 4:18), note the scriptural reference to Gentiles "alienated from the commonwealth of Israel, and strangers to the covenants of promise" (2:12). In Col. 1:21 this alienation is bound up with an inimical disposition which is manifest in evil works (*apēllotriōménos kaí echthroús*). Cf. Eph. 4:18: "darkened in their understanding, alienated from the life of God."
117. Romans 3:23, *hysteroúntai:* fall short, come behind, be inferior to.

eousness, *un*belief, love*less*ness and faith*less*ness. *Sin* is darkness; and all the more so in contrast to that light which now has shone. Only when we see that light do we comprehend the darkness of our sin.

We come to that same conclusion when we reflect on the meaning of man's *fall*. This description of man's sinful life-direction refers to a passing from heights to depths or a falling *away*. The fall is an *apo*stasy, or standing *apart*, or *defection* from the fellowship of God.[118] Only when we observe where man once *stood* can we rightly contemplate the depths to which he fell. Thus the fall is in contrast to man's former *estate* or his former *stand*.[119] Even *within* the act of man's falling this relational aspect is very evident. Something is tragically lost. Privation comes in where life and glory *had been*. "The *crown* has fallen from our head; woe to us, for we have sinned" (Lam. 5:16).

Moreover, the decisive significance of Christ reveals the nature of this fall and the true nature of our sin. We hear that Christ "is set for the fall and rising of many in Israel" (Luke 2:34), and a blessing is pronounced on the man "who takes no offense at me" (Matt. 11:6). Salvation is seen as a light in contrast to "every one who falls on that stone" which is now "the head of the corner" (Luke 20:17-18). In that light the fall of Israel can also be understood (Rom. 11:11; cf. v. 22); for Israel's fall implied the background and the proclamation of salvation. In contrast to the covenant and the beatific life of God, it is obvious that Israel's fall occurred in the context of disobedience. "Let us therefore strive to enter that rest, that no one *fall* by the same sort of *disobedience*" (Heb. 4:11). Here we have a clear example of one description of sin which sheds light upon another. Yet both of these terms (*disobedience* and *fall*) refer to man's sin as a breaking *away, apostasy*, and *alienation from God*.

When we think of the fall we usually think of the story of Genesis 3. Nowhere do we read the word *fall* in that account, and yet it is obvious that sin is pictured as *apostasy from God*. This chapter is the background for all the negative descriptions

---

118. Thus we read of a falling away or departing *from faith* (I Tim. 4:1). Cf. Heb. 6:6 on "committing apostasy" after being enlightened and participating in the Holy Spirit (6:4).

119. Cf. I Cor. 10:12: "Therefore let any one who thinks that he *stands* take heed lest he fall." Also *TWNT*, VI, *s.v. piptō*.

of sin in Scripture. Once again we find that sin is no "human phenomenon" that is analyzable in itself apart from other relationships. Rather, man's sin is "loss," "destruction," and "severance," and presupposes the creation of man and his standing in fellowship with God. Therefore it is with very good reason that we meet with God's negative "You shall not!" (Gen. 3:17) .[120] No two ways are accessible to man but only one way. The first two chapters of Genesis describe the riches and fellowship of God. We hear him speaking and we see him acting (Gen. 1:3, 6, 9, 10, 14, 20, 22, 26, 27; 2:3, 7, 8, etc.) , and the fall of man is painted against the background of a beatific life. Only when we observe *that fact* are the depths and gravity of man's apostasy apparent.

Surely, the announcement of a divine punishment is always accompanied by a gracious promise for the future. Yet the perspective of an "enmity," established by God himself, does not blunt the tragedy of man's sin. Quite to the contrary, man's sin is now seen as very real. The story of Genesis sets forth the sin of man in a very urgent way. The writer tells us, "with a simplicity which even a child can understand, and therefore with an utterly convincing authority, how sin arose, and what sin is, and how it expresses itself."[121] Though the breadth of descriptions in the rest of the Old Testament is not found in this story, the chapter informs us, in the plainest of terms, what is really at stake when we speak of *man's sin*.[122] Furthermore it is easy to see the groundlines of those later descriptions. Therefore we find the aspects of temptation, disobedience, and transgression against the explicit commandment of God; we observe the loss of true innocence and the resulting disruption of human affairs. Man is cursed because of what he has *done* (3:11-13) . He is cursed because of his transgression and wrong listening (3:17). No definition is now given of sin, and yet our sin is laid bare in the reality of an act and the breaking of communion with God and the judgment of his wrath.

Remarkably, no mention is made of any excuse or escape from responsibility. Man bears the burden of what he has done. A grievous *privatio* is indicated in the devil's implication that man, as a creature, could rightly regard himself as deprived by God of his own legitimate divinity. The entire conversation

---

120. Cf. my *Man: the Image of God*, 1962, pp. 345ff.
121. *TWNT*, I, *s.v. hamartánō.*
122. *Ibid.*

of the serpent and Eve is steeped in this theme of *privatio*.
The writer sees the devil's intrigue as completely illegitimate
and sets his story against the background of that illegitimacy.
Man assumes that he is "deprived," and thus he forfeits the
gift of fellowship with God. Something *better* than he received
in his creaturehood was now set before him, and Satan asserted
that God's commandment stood in the way of man's attaining
his ideal. "For God knows that when you eat of it your eyes
will be opened, and you will be like God, knowing good and
evil" (Gen. 3:5). The alleged privation of sight and the implication that it is God who "keeps you blind" was now the very
center of Satan's appeal. Obviously the writer wanted to say
that in reaching for that "higher light" man lost the only light
he had. Therefore the consequence of temptation is apparent
in reality. The story of the fall is set in the context of a dispute
concerning man's *privatio*.

Thus Genesis 3 sees the sin of man as a "fall." It regards
man's sin as an infringement of the mystery of his creaturehood, the shattering of communion with God, and the transgression of God's command. Here some people have taken notice
of the sub-theme in this narrative in which the concept of
"evil" is referred to in very explicit terms. That concept, of
course, is found in the name for one of the trees in the Garden.
Genesis 2:9 tells us that in addition to the "tree of life" there
stood in the midst of the Garden the "tree of the knowledge
of good and evil." Genesis 2:17 relates the commandment concerning that tree: "you shall not eat." The commandment was
so serious that the threat of death was also attached: "for in
the day that you eat of it you shall die" (2:17). In Satan's
deception a reinterpretation of the commandment was now given
and the reality of punishment was denied (3:4). The man who
eats of the tree will be "like God, knowing good and evil" (3:5).
But when man *did eat* we hear again of the "knowledge of
good and evil," and this time the words are spoken by God
himself: "Behold, the man has become like one of us, knowing
good and evil" (3:22).

What must we make of these words, and how do they relate
to our understanding of the essence of man's sin? What are
the implications for man's apostasy from God and the judgment which must come? What do these words have to say about
the blindness and bleakness of our sin, the loss of God's glory,
and the estrangement from our Creator?

Elsewhere, in Scripture, we read of the "tree of life" (Prov. 3:18; 11:30; Rev. 2:7; 22:2); but this is not so in the case of the "tree of the knowledge of good and evil." The latter concept is found only in the story of the fall. Exegetes have said that this thread of the story is not concerned with a purely intellectual knowledge of good and evil but with a *deciding for oneself what good and evil are.* In that view the tempter seduces man to a self-determination and autonomy, which could then be exchanged for his own creaturely and dependent "listening" to the commandment of God. Kuyper, for example, regarded this passage in that way, in contrast to what he called the "contemporary" view.[123] This contemporary understanding he saw as an interpretation of these words and this "knowledge" as *cognitio experimentalis,* or a knowledge acquired by means of the act of apostasy. Kuyper judged that this was an impossible exegesis, especially because Genesis 3:22 tells us that God has a similar knowledge.[124]

Therefore, in Kuyper's judgment the point could not be an existential or experiential knowledge of a sinful act, or an active cognition of evil in contrast to the good. It could only be a hankering for the "right" to listen no longer and thus to decide for *oneself* what is really *good and evil.* " 'Knowledge of good and evil' signifies that a man knows himself to be independent and defines and decides *what* is good and *what* is evil for him."[125] In contrast to God's commandment and justice, he now substitutes his own decision or his own sovereignty and prerogative to choose.[126] In that act of sinning he makes this "knowledge" his own. Thus he chooses his *own* way and makes his *own* judgment on what pleases *himself.* Furthermore, in his "emancipation" he receives precisely what he desired. Therefore Genesis 3:22 is such a "dreadfully serious" text.[127]

A very different understanding of this text is found in G. von Rad.[128] Von Rad sees the "knowledge of good and evil" as a kind of omniscience and proposes that this phrase should

123. A. Kuyper, *De Gemeene Gratie,* I, 198.
124. Same argument found in Bavinck; *op. cit.,* III, 4.
125. Kuyper, *op. cit.,* I, 203; in a chapter on "knowledge as self-choice."
126. Cf. also G. Ch. Aalders on Gen. 3:22 (man's "emancipation," or becoming a law unto himself); also A. H. Edelkoort, *Bijbel met Aantekeningen,* 1954 (Genesis), p. 12, and Bavinck, *op. cit.,* III, 6, who wishes to follow Marti at this point.
127. *Ibid.,* 7.
128. Von Rad, *Genesis,* p. 65.

not be read in an exclusively moral sense. According to an Eastern mode of speaking, the term "good and evil" includes *everything,* and therefore this "knowledge of good and evil" implies an experiencing or being entrusted with all things. Against that exposition, however, we assert that the story, quite obviously, is not concerned with a universal "knowing" or insatiable lust for knowledge, but is rather concerned with the knowledge of a *distinction* or the ability to *decide* and to *discriminate.*[129] Therefore Von Rad, in his exegesis of Genesis 3:22, himself returns to the theme of man's autonomy. "Man has taken leave of the relation of dependence. He has refused to obey and has willed to make himself independent. No longer is obedience the guiding principle of his life, but his autonomous knowledge and will. Thereby he ceases, in effect, to understand himself as creature."[130]

It is common to link up these words concerning the "knowledge of good and evil" with the motive of autonomy. In disobeying God's command man burns his bridges behind him and abandons his own creatureliness and the glory of God. He proceeds forthwith to blaze his own trail. He misapprehends the nobility of his creaturehood, or the life of dependence, and regards his circumstances as *privatio.* He covets the prerogative of being like God and determining the knowledge of good and evil. He fails to appreciate that this "right" has been denied him for his own good and his own salvation. Therefore the threat of *punishment* must be read in that light. The "knowledge of good and evil" implies a lack of sympathy for *God's* exclusive privilege of determining right and wrong. In desiring to be "like God" man thrusts himself into a dismal and self-

---

129. Cf. H. Reinckens, *Israëls Visie op het Verleden. Over Gen. 1-3,* 1956, pp. 214ff. Reinckens does not deny that the expression "good and evil" has a frequent reference to "everything," but he sees this expression (also in the case of Gen. 3:22) as discerning or "discriminative," and not as all-inclusive. It is striking that Von Rad too points to I Kings 3:9, though that text only highlights the discriminative usage of this phrase: "Give thy servant therefore an understanding mind to govern thy people, that I may discern between good and evil."

130. G. von Rad, *op. cit.,* p. 78. Also Miloš Bic, *Vom Geheimnis und Wunder der Schöpfung. Eine Auslegung von 1 Mose 1-3,* 1959, p. 68, who takes sides with Von Rad and sees implied in this "everything" the judging capacity of man over good and evil — the *hýbris* of man, his titanism. Cf. also H. van der Bussche, *De godsdienstige Boodschap van de Oergeschiedenis. Israel Peilt naar de Zin van het Bestaan (Genesis 1-3),* p. 32: the "struggle for emancipation."

defeating privation. In so doing he forfeits the glory of his *creaturehood*.

We can only marvel at the profundity of Genesis 3 as we look at the history of this theme of autonomy. The chapter concerns the original problem of human existence which constantly recurs in the history of ancient Israel. There we observe the confusion which results when men call evil "good" and good "evil," darkness "light" and light "darkness," bitter "sweet" and sweet "bitter" (cf. Isa. 5:20).[131] God's answer to this "knowledge of good and evil" or being "like God" was to drive men away from the Paradise of his love and fellowship. Thus sin and judgment are linked together in the single theme of *privatio boni*. Man lost the grace and the smiling face of God.

In that way we see that the fall of man achieved the very opposite of what he intended. This theme, too, is very prominent in Genesis 3. The prophetic words, "your eyes will be opened," are re-echoed in the reality of man's sin. Man's eyes were opened to seeing his own shame (3:5, 7; cf. 2:25).[132] Reinckens has written in a poignant way of man's disenchantment. He had hoped for *more* and he ended up with *less*.[133] No longer did he appreciate the glory of his creaturehood. Therefore he no longer understood his fellowman. Alienation and frustration took hold where before there was only harmony. Therefore when men did try to find each other it was only *God* who was working in and through them and who also refused to let them go. Men themselves were strangers to themselves; yet God held them firmly in hand. He held them even while casting them from Paradise to till the accursed ground.

No other description or "definition" of sin can reach beyond the Paradise account. Israel knew her sin when she saw it, and she saw it in all its appalling negativity. She saw it as a fall and lostness and privation of all the good of creaturehood — as unbelief and disobedience, thanklessness and lovelessness.[134]

---

131. Cf. the reference in John 3:19 to men's preferring the darkness rather than light.

132. On the concept of *shame,* cf. the discussion between P. J. Roscam Abbing and G. C. van Niftrik in *Kerk en Theologie,* 1959.

133. Reinckens, *op. cit.,* p. 216. Cf. R. Guardini, *Het Begin van Alle Dingen,* 1957, p. 47.

134. The title of Reinckens' book *(Israëls Visie op het Verleden)* and the subtitle of van der Bussche's *(Israel Peilt naar de Zin van het Bestaan)* should not be understood subjectivistically — in the sense that a purely subjective vision is intended here. The "vision" does not lie

In Genesis we observe a sin whose essential traits return in *every sin*. Thus in the history of Israel the fall was apostasy from the fellowship of God and the assumption of man's own way. The fall was a misapprehension of God's love, a stubbornness in Israel's own heart, and a misconstruing of the whole purpose of her life. That pattern of degeneracy is not a denial of the historicity of the original fall and is certainly not a generalization of sin as a commonplace phenomenon. But it does indicate the nature of our sin, always and ever, and the character of sin in relation to God and his fellowship. Thus the later sinning of Israel follows the same lines as the breaking of the original "covenant" by Adam (Hos. 6:7).[135] Therefore the "lamentation over the king of Tyre" could be made by means of an analogy to the Garden of Eden (Ezek. 28:11ff.). In that way sin was seen in very bold relief.[136]

We should emphasize again that this manner of picturing the seductiveness of sin (as apparent throughout the Scripture) is not a "de-historicizing" of the Genesis story. The picture here refers to the real nature of our sin no matter where it appears. In differing situations but similar forms and structures, the sin of man finds an impetus in the acts of God himself and is manifest in the breaking of communion with him. In that unequivocally *relational sense* it shows itself in a large variety of ways. Only in the light of this relation is it *knowable*. We

outside the sphere of the inspiration of the Spirit. In saying this we do not deny the profound questions that emerge in connection with the intent and bearing of the Paradise account (especially the relation between kerygma and history). These questions play an important role in contemporary Roman Catholic theology and lead to difficult problems regarding the *status integritatus;* as also, in regard to this, the whole issue of monogenism, polygenism, etc. In contrast to earlier pronouncements of the Catholic Bible Commission (particularly 1909), the later developments are truly dramatic. We cite as examples: Charles Hauret, *Origines, Genèse I-III,* 1952; P. Schoonenberg, *Het Geloof van ons Doopsel,* I; and K. Rahner, *Fragen der Theologie heute.*

135. There has been much ado on this text, also in dogmatics, in reference to "scriptural proof" for the "covenant of works." Cf. C. van Gelderen for various translations *(Het Boek Hosea,* 1953, *ad hoc).* Van Gelderen sees a comparison here: Adam's paradise and Israel's promised land. Note p. 225.

136. God's verdict of judgment is the subject of Ezek. 28:11ff.: ". . . so I cast you as a profane thing from the mountain of God" (v. 16). There is also judgment on pride (v. 17) and the "multitude of iniquities" (v. 18).

have to appreciate *which* relation is now violated, and *whose* will is resisted, and *whose* honor and Kingdom are maligned. Thus, in view of these considerations it is evident that the nature of sin can *only* be seen within the depths and fullness of God's revelation. It is clear why the dilemma must be rejected that the knowledge of sin comes "either from the Gospel or the law."[137] That statement, of course, is no denial of the purity and majesty of God's law but is only the necessary recognition of the *Giver* of that law. Only by knowing *him* do we comprehend the nature of sin as unbelief and enmity, transgression and unrighteousness, disobedience and stubbornness. Without that knowledge every "definition" of sin is hollow and irrelevant, even though it may seem to be "exhaustive" and logically deduced from the data of Scripture.

Once again, this is no depreciation of Scripture and its importance for coming to the knowledge of our sin. We are only saying that we must know the true God if we are to know what sin in reality *is*. When John says that sin is "lawlessness" he is not giving us an abstract idea. His statement stands in the context of the message that God is light and love (I John 1:7; 4:8). Lawlessness and disobedience can *only* be contemplated when we appreciate how good the scepter is which God has raised over mankind. Lovelessness is conspicuous in contrast to the ardor of his love, and the depths of suspicion are apparent in contrast to his unbroken faithfulness.

This is what Bavinck meant when he wrote that the knowledge of sin comes through the Gospel in a "still stronger measure" than through the law.[138] We might think that these words ("still stronger") continue to smack of a false dilemma, and yet the intention is very plain. The message of God's grace streams into man's lost estate and removes the blinders from his eyes. Thus it enables him to see the glory of God. In that way (that is, the way of revelation) the great "mystery of sin" is both revealed and condemned. Here we see the seriousness of God's indictment as we hear it in the Old Testament prophets who spoke with a view to his covenant: man's sin is faithlessness and the failure to appreciate the grace of God. Therefore man, apart from that revealing light of grace and blinded by his sin, can only venture his own interpretation of the "defects" in his life and world. He can only spin out his own "phe-

137. See Chapters 6 and 7, above.
138. Bavinck, *op. cit.*, III, 122.

nomenology of evil." But true insight into the nature of *sin*
can only elude him, in that way, forever because of the blindness of his lies.[139] "If we say we have not sinned, we make
him a liar, and his word is not in us" (I John 1:10).

Therefore our lies are exposed in the searchlight of God's
truth and grace. In the Old Covenant the divine accusation is
rung out clearly against the background of what Jahwe had
done and the event of his electing grace. His love, compassion
and redemption are in strident contrast to the inflexibility and
rebellion of his people (Isa. 63:9-10; cf. Hos. 11:1-4). This is
very apparent in the account of the redemption from Egypt
and the blessing of Balaam (Mic. 6:3-5; cf. Hos. 11:1). What
was there that remained for Israel to do? "He has showed you,
O man, what is *good;* and what does the Lord require of you
but to . . . walk humbly with your God" (Mic. 6:8). In contrast
with his "good," man's evil was now made known. Therefore
Hosea refers to the spurned love of Jahwe, or the love which
went unrequited in the faithlessness and apostasy of his people.
"I would redeem them, but they speak lies against me. . . . They
have broken my covenant" (Hos. 7:13, 15; 8:1; 9:1).

When the grace of God is revealed, irresistibly, in the fullness
of times and the "end of the age" (Heb. 9:26) and is "made
known to all nations" (Rom. 16:26), there can still be only
a single valid knowledge of our sin. This is the knowledge which
comes in the *way of repentance* (cf. Acts 17:30). In that way
it is clear *what* sin is and against *whom* it is committed. In that
way our lies are laid bare and our darkness is known. For then
the "true light" already shines (I John 2:8). Yet it is also evident, in that way, how great the wrath of God *is* against the
sins of men. Rather than to leave those sins unpunished, he
has punished them "in his beloved Son, Jesus Christ, with the
bitter and shameful death of the cross." Thus the essence of
sin is revealed more and more, incontrovertibly, as the history
of redemption unfolds.

Among writers today, Karl Barth has given special attention to the significance of the knowledge of God revealed in

---

139. Note the blinding activity of the "god of this world" (II Cor. 4:4),
who has "blinded the minds of the unbelievers," and thus keeps them
"from seeing the light of the gospel of the glory of Christ." The context here is concerned with the nature of sin ("disgraceful, under-
handed ways," v. 2), which cannot see the light.

Christ for the knowledge of the essence of our sin. Barth opposes every formal and legalistic interpretation of sin and takes his point of departure in the Gospel itself. He sees the various scriptural words for sin as brimful of meaning (*K.D.*, IV/1, 140ff.; ET, 128ff.). Apart from that knowledge, as based on the Gospel, every insight into the nature of sin is bound to be confused. This is because the nature of sin is to render men blind. Therefore there is no access to the knowledge of sin if we merely look at "sin itself." Sin thrives on the strategy of exculpation and concealment. For that reason it opposes the revelation of our guilt. Only the light of God's revelation can make possible a knowledge of sin which is any more than "worldly grief" (II Cor. 7:10).[140]

How could men, in seeking the knowledge of sin, say anything about the will of God apart from Jesus Christ, "the biblical centre and substance" (IV/1, 406; ET, 367)? "What kind of knowledge will this be? What will be its basis? From what source will it draw its sustenance? What will be its content?" (427; ET, 387). Is no further mirror necessary for man to recognize himself as sinner (439; ET, 397)? Is it not *only* in the cross of Christ, indubitably and incontestably, that we come to know how *weighty is our sin* ("*quanti ponderis sit peccatum,*" 451; ET, 407)? Is not the cross of Christ the refutation of every theory which refuses to take seriously the depth and reality of sin? Is the wrath of God against our sin more clearly displayed than in the curse and God-forsakenness of the Son of Man (455; ET, 410f.)?

Barth sees the revelation of God in Christ as the only pathway to the knowledge of our sin. He is concerned to analyze sin's essence and true nature. In building his case, he is true to his all-decisive, christological standpoint (459f.; ET, 413f.). But he also proposes three categories which he wishes to define: the *pride,* the *sloth,* and the *falsehood* of sinful man.[141] At first

140. See Barth, *op. cit.,* IV/1, 399. Barth recalls the celebrated statement of Calvin on the impossibility of true self-knowledge without a true knowledge of God (405; ET, 366). In Barth's judgment this vantage point is insufficiently pervasive in Calvin's theology. Especially is that the case because the "confrontation" is not completed in the cross and resurrection of Jesus Christ, which are more than a general encounter of God and man. Cf. Barth on Torrance's interpretation of Calvin (406; ET, 367).

141. See *ibid.,* 459ff., 423ff. (ET, 414ff., 383ff.). Though Barth also sees the *fall* as included in the pride of man (531ff.; ET, 478ff.), and though

these categories may seem to be rather strange and even a bit arbitrary. On closer examination it is obvious that Barth is involved in a very competent and systematic analysis.

Barth does not regard these terms as fully exhaustive (IV/1, 459; ET, 414). He recognizes that such concepts as *disobedience* or *lawlessness* are certainly biblical, and he has no desire to eliminate those terms (460; ET, 414f.). At the same time, he wants a greater "concretizing," which is possible, he feels, by using other expressions. His christological model reveals that sin is *pride,* in contrast to the humility of the Son of God. Man's pride is laid bare in its ridiculousness and frightening rebellion as we peer into the mirror of the Son of Man's humility. In contrast to that "omnipotent act" of humility (465; ET, 419) man now strives to be "like God." In contrast to the Lord who was servant we find the sin of pride in all its futility and grotesqueness. Thus man tries to play the role of God. Barth's interest in sin as pride reminds us of the statement of Augustine: "God is already humble though man is still proud."[142]

So too the second category of sin, viz. *sloth,* might strike us at first as a novel description in contrast to the traditional concept where such an accent is hardly ever heard. As the pride of man is opposed to the condescension of God (IV/2, 453; ET, 403), so the sloth of man is in sharp antithesis to the kingly work of Christ (IV/3/1, 426; ET, 369). In contrast to the exalted Christ (as Son of Man in his office as Savior) we observe the man of sin in his "unnatural yet natural stupidity, inhumanity, dissipation and anxiety" *(ibid.).* When we bear in mind that sin cannot be seen *remoto Christi* or apart from the atonement, we now encounter the man of sin as a slothful laggard. We understand that sin is not revealed in only the heroic, dramatic form of "rash arrogance" or Promethean pride but is also made known in the non-spectacular form of slothfulness, stupidity, and foolishness. Sin is manifest in disobedience, unbelief, and ingratitude (454f.; ET, 404f.). In the specter of the true *humanitas Jesu* (459; ET, 409) we now discern the man of sin in his renunciation of God and his fellowman. The sinful man persists

he combines man's slothfulness with man's misery (IV/2, 423ff.; ET, 378ff.), and man's falsehood with condemnation (IV/3/1, 531ff.; ET, 461ff.), yet we can speak, in a summary way, of *pride, sloth,* and *falsehood* as the terms which Barth himself uses in IV/3/1, 426 (ET, 369).

142. *Sermo,* 142, 6. Motto of the book of F. van der Meer, *Augustinus de Zielzorger,* 1949.

in walking with his eyes closed, even in the light of full day. "We harden ourselves in our unreason, our ignorance of God, our lack of wisdom, our folly and stupidity" (460; ET, 410). Thus the turpitude of man is not innocent or innocuous but is an extremely dangerous attitude in man's living (465; ET, 414). Here Barth finds the primitive sin or "the primal phenomenon of sin in one of its most remarkable aspects" (467; ET, 415). *Man* is visible in the light of him who lives "wholly to God and his fellowman" (509; ET, 452); nevertheless the man who is visible is a wild and a savage man (524; ET, 464). The story of David and Bathsheba is not remarkable because of its spectacular or dramatic "pride" but because of its unbounded licentiousness and dissipation (524-527; ET, 464-467).

Finally, man's sin is evident in the form of his *falsehood.* This is apparent again in the full light of the atonement (IV/3/1, 426; ET, 369). As we contemplate the conquest of sin through Jesus Christ and reflect on the truth of God revealed in the incarnation, we can only conclude that man is a liar (429; ET, 371). Barth suggests the following formula: As pride and sloth are the *work* of sin, so falsehood is the *word* of sin. Falsehood is the negative reflection of the self-revelation of God or the darkness which is opposed to the brilliance of the light (426; ET, 369). In contrast to the truth of God, revealed in Christ, the man of sin appears in his wanton obstruction of the Mediator's prophetic work (430; ET, 372). Resistance to God's grace, which is obvious in pride and slothfulness, is here completed, as it were, in falsehood. Thus sin is the "caricature of the threefold office and work of Jesus Christ" (430; ET, 373). In falsehood it reaches its zenith. In opposition to the word of God in the Old Covenant, confirmed in the New, and the revelation of God in the *post Christum* world, the man of sin gives his answer of falsehood. Man is ensnared in guilt through pride and in slavery through sloth; and "what he chooses and draws down upon himself with his falsehood is his condemnation" (531; ET, 462). In that way we see "the man of sin in his fully developed form." In falsehood man takes his position against the message of redemption; yet beyond his lies is always the truthfulness of God's atoning and gracious act. *God* has acted in the Old Covenant, and in the witnesses of the Old Testament, and in the fulfillment of Jesus Christ (431; ET, 373). There is only one history of redemption, and it runs its course in this *post Christum* world which is also antagonistic to its purpose and its goal. Therefore, in the period of the promised Spirit, man answers his God with a lie. Falsehood is the consummation of his sin.

Later we shall notice that every sin has this same *contra*-structure, though certainly we should not conceive of every sin as equally severe.[143] There is an historical process within the *contra* which corresponds to the development of the acts of God and is only understandable in relation to not-believing in Jesus (John 16:9).[144] Within that process there is also an increase in man's sin. Therefore Barth sees falsehood, in our *post Christum* era, as a consummated or "potentiated" sin, or as sin in its "most highly developed form" (IV/3/1, 432; *"potenzierte Sünde"*; ET, 374). This *post Christum* development is necessary for bringing sin to its full revelation and fruition and for seeing it as "man's counter-revelation to the divine revelation of grace" *(ibid.)*. In that way man's lying is unmasked by the true witness and is branded as *false*. In pride and in sloth, and ultimately in falsehood, man's sin is unveiled in our *post Christum* era (545, 547; ET, 474f.).

Yet there is no reason for us to be pesssimistic in that fact, since lying cannot win the upper hand. "For the reality of God and man in Jesus Christ is superior to the pseudo-reality to which we are delivered by our falsehood. Nor is it idle in respect of it, but on the offensive against it" (549; ET, 477). In *this* light sin is revealed in its true character and essence as rebellion, unbelief, and disobedience. It is seen as pride, sloth, and falsehood, in opposition to the divine revelation, and as darkness in contrast to the light. Therefore sin is chaos and worthlessness and can only find its definitive qualification in reference to the Gospel.

When Barth referred to sin as "chaos" *("das Nichtige")* he opened a Pandora's box for all kinds of criticisms and misunderstandings. Certainly we can say that he did not mean a description of sin *in addition to* his categories of pride, sloth, and falsehood. By *das Nichtige* he tried to convey the senselessness, ridiculousness and worthlessness of sin; he also suggested a disqualification in contrast to the noble activity of God. He emphasized that he had no desire to describe man's sin as a matter of indifference or a mere "nothing." This would hardly be worthy of our consideration. *Das Nichtige* refers to the disas-

143. See Chap. 9.
144. Cf. above, pp. 222f.

trous and catastrophic character of sin because of which man's sin is the "condemnation of man" and arouses the wrath of God. Barth has written extensively on *das Nichtige* in his doctrine of providence (III/3, Par. 50), and he now reverts to that term, despite the protests of his critics (see IV/3/1, 202ff.; ET, 176ff.), in his doctrine of reconciliation. He reaffirms that this expression in no way suggests that "evil is nothing, that it does not exist, or that it has no reality" (203; ET, 178). Rather the point is that it has *no rightful existence and no ground.* It is "impossible, meaningless, illegitimate, valueless and without foundation" (204; ET, 178). Evil is "absolute inferiority."

But this impotence of sin can only be professed by the man who sees that *"Jesus* is Victor."[145] Sin is only understandable in the glow of the fullness and majesty of God's activity. It is always the answer and echo of ingratitude, disobedience, rebellion, and enmity. This is what sin was "in the beginning," and this is the "negativity" that is all the *more apparent* in the face of the ensuing acts of God.

We may ask, however: Do these rubrics of pride, sloth and falsehood give an adequate description of our sin? Could other expressions do just as well? This question is all the more mean-

---

145. Cf. the comments in IV/3/1, 203 (ET, 178): Evil "does not exist as God does, nor as His creatures, amongst which it is not to be numbered. It has no basis for its being. It has no right to the existence which to our sorrow we cannot deny to it. Its existence, significance and reality are not distinguished by any value nor positive strength." Barth gives an answer in this section to the questions and criticisms which I have set down in my book, *The Triumph of Grace in the Theology of Karl Barth* (ET, 1956). In response, it should be noted that I too have underscored the reality-character of sin in Barth's theology (e.g. in *The Triumph of Grace,* pp. 70ff.). But the real issue, which we cannot treat extensively here, is not whether Barth relativizes or minimizes sin and the essence of sin; rather it is the question of the relation between the power of sin and the grace of Christ *in preaching.* When Barth again, in his doctrine of the atonement, pictures "das Nichtige" as *reality,* we are struck anew by the parallel between his view and Bavinck's description of sin (*op. cit.,* III). Note the following concepts in Bavinck: *unlawfulness, unreasonableness, foolishness, absurdity* (p. 48); *illegality* (53); having *no proper principle* and *no independent existence* (119); the *annihilation* of all good as its purpose (*ibid.*); an *insoluble riddle* (125), which has come into the world with *no motive* (*ibid.*). Sin, says Bavinck, *is* not but only wishes to be; it has no proper reality and can never attain to any. Sin is a lie in its origin and a lie in its end (129). It has reality only as a deformation of being, and therefore can only be called *ouk ón* or *nihil.*

ingful when we notice that H. Vogel, for example, has centered attention on very different terms. He too has suggested that true knowledge of sin is only possible in the light of the Gospel of Christ, but the "Christian name for sin," so far as he is concerned, is *thanklessness.* Sin is revealed in its "hostility to grace."[146] In his dogmatics, Vogel goes beyond this point and treats of sin as *godlessness, unbelief,* and *selfishness.*[147]

Surely the difference between Barth and Vogel does not lie in a different choice in the dilemma of "law or Gospel." Barth, instead, wishes to see in sin a "reflection" of Christ's threefold office. At the same time, though he views man's sin in an antithetical relation to that office, he does not merely construe it in terms of that three-foldedness. He derives his concepts from all kinds of Old Testament and New Testament data. Therefore there is no real *essential* difference between the positions of Vogel and Barth.[148] *Both* desire to honor the concreteness and seriousness of sin, and to do so in the light that is *only available in Jesus Christ.* This agreement can be explained in terms of the fact that the scriptural references to sin are not made explicitly with a view to Christ's threefold office. Certainly Christ stands at the mid-point of the Gospels as the One who "committed no sin"; and "no guile was found on his lips" (I Pet. 2:22). Christ is seen in the Gospels as the Holy One whose meat was to do the will of his Father. Therefore when Barth refers to Christ's threefold office he makes use of a wide variety of biblical expressions and reworks these materials to set forth his threefold "antithesis."

In our own opinion we cannot and we should not steer clear of the multiplicity of the biblical usages. It would be very strange if we found in Scripture a clear "systematizing" of all of its various data. Nevertheless, the centrality of the concept of *sin in relation to God* sheds a powerful light on every biblical description of man's sin. In this perspective the various concepts of sin are rays of light which penetrate the darkness of

146. H. Vogel, "Die Sünde im biblischen Verständnis," in *Ev. Theol.,* 1959, p. 446.
147. Vogel, *Gott in Christo,* 1951, pp. 484ff.
148. We need not deny the nuances of difference here. One thinks especially of Barth's accent on sloth (IV/2, 452-546; ET, 403-483), as illustrated, e.g., in David and Bathsheba and the spies of Numbers 13-14 (542ff.; ET, 479ff.). It strikes us that Barth sees sloth, defined as "tardiness and failure" ("Versagen und Zurückbleiben"), under the general rubric of sin as disobedience (454; ET, 404).

our guilt. Many names and forms are given to these biblical references to sin, and any escape to a general or vague conception of sin is therefore impossible. Biblically speaking, we may not demarcate these terms too sharply. We must not see such concepts as *alienation, fall, hostility, unfaithfulness, lovelessness* and *thanklessness* in contrast to each other. As the glory of God's salvation is magnified in the many words which build upon each other[149] (for the wisdom of God is "manifold"; cf. Eph. 3:10),[150] so too in regard to the biblical references to our sin. These too are "manifold" and represent the sombre and antithetical parallel to the full glory of the salvation of God. That is to say: there are "unspeakable" depths in sin as there are also "unspeakable" depths in God (Rom. 8:39; Rev. 2:24; I Cor. 2:9; Rom. 11:33). Yet, whenever man's sin is described in any of its biblical forms there is always a single warning which can best be expressed in the statement of Vogel: "Sin cannot be defined but can only be opposed."[151]

Therefore, a description of our sin can only have meaning when it is useful to that task.[152] In man's sin the fall of man is visible, and borders are overstepped, and love is disavowed, and faith is denied, and the lie is proclaimed. All of this will continue until the truth of God incontrovertible, yet always controverted by sinful men, will come to its full light. "If *I* had not come and spoken to them, they would not have sin; but now they have no excuse for their sin" (John 15:22; cf. v. 24).

Thus we cannot reflect on the essence or the character of sin unless we do so in relation to God. But in our reflections the question must come with a very real urgency: Can we ever speak, within this arena of sin, of a certain *gradation?* Can the essence of man's sin (his fall, disobedience, faithless-

---

149. Cf. especially Paul's letter to the Ephesians.
150. Greek: *hē polypoíkilos sophía toú theoú.* H. Schlier, *Der Brief an die Epheser,* 1958, p. 156: "sehr mannigfaltig."
151. Vogel, *op. cit.,* p. 483.
152. One thinks of the *struggle* here which forms the very antithesis of sin and can be pictured in a single word: *faith* that overcomes the world (I John 5:4). This struggle can also be described in a number of different ways (consider the "whole armor of God" in Eph. 6:11, 13). Note also the various descriptions of the adversary in Eph. 6:12: principalities, powers, world rulers of this present darkness, and spiritual hosts of wickedness in heavenly places.

ness, enmity, unbelief, transgression, and alienation) ever permit
us to use such a concept? We grant immediately that there is
great diversity in the "forms" of man's sin and the times and
circumstances in which his sins are committed. But since all of
these forms are really expressions of the single genus of *sin,* may
we ever make such distinctions in degrees? Further, if there is
only one genre of sin and if only man is a sinner, then why
should we find nuances in the gravity and seriousness of sin?
On what basis do we draw the lines of distinction which are
clearly apparent in the history of theology? Obviously we do
well to pause and to look at that matter. If sin is sin against
God, then how can we speak of "many forms"? Our problem
here is the problem of the *gravity and gradation of sin.*

CHAPTER NINE

THE GRAVITY AND GRADATION OF SIN

THE WORD OF God sees sin as something radical and total, and regards it as a missing of the mark, apostasy, transgression, lovelessness, lawlessness, and an alienation from the life of God. In short, it sees man's sin as a denigration of God's glory. The man who appreciates this picture of sin will be inclined to say that every apparent "gradation" (or every "more so" or "less so" in sin) can only be *a priori* excluded. What could be the meaning of such a "gradation" when we contemplate the gravity of the scriptural word: "Cursed be every one who does not abide by all things written in the book of the law, and do them" (Gal. 3:10)?[1] Surely it was crystal clear for Paul that "no man is justified before God by the law" (Gal. 3:11). Is it not the case that "the righteousness which can stand before the tribunal of God must be absolutely perfect and wholly conformable to the divine law" (HC, Q. 62)? Does not the radical nature of sin, or the definition of being a sinner before the face of God, exclude every quantitative analysis of sin? In opposition to a sin-casuistic we could better recall that the "wages" of sin are death (Rom. 6:23). He who has ears to hear must understand the imperishable nature and the complete validity of the law. "Not an iota, not a dot, will pass from the law until all is accomplished" (Matt. 5:18).

As we examine these things it is necessary that we be circumspect. It is simply an undeniable fact that Scripture makes various distinctions and speaks of several "degrees" of sin. One thinks of the distinction which Christ himself drew between "every sin and blasphemy" which shall be forgiven and the great blasphemy against the Spirit which shall *not be*.[2] Many times, and in differing circumstances, the reference is made to the size and magnitude of sin. Christ says to Pilate that "he who de-

1. Cf. Deut. 27:26, 28:58, 30:10.
2. See the following chapter.

livered me to you has the *greater sin*" (John 18:11). Thus it is obvious that there is, in the scriptural parlance, a certain irrefutable "more" or "less" in reference to man's sin. Nowhere do we meet with an "egalitarian sin-idea." Certainly we hear that "there is *none* that does good, no *not one*," and that God looks down from heaven and finds that men have "all gone astray" (Ps. 14:1-3; cf. Rom. 2:1; 5:12; 11:32). But this sort of generalizing or universalizing does not preclude important distinctions and levels in regard to man's sin.

It is an incontestable and universal experience that there are obvious and profound gradations in sin. Here we do well to take account of these. At the same time, we are not concerned with a merely human "experience" which can only leave us with very shaky distinctions. We are concerned with the real sense of the *biblical* qualifications and gradations within the arena of God's *universal and serious complaint*. How can we speak of the "wrath of God" which man's sin evokes when man's sin itself is "qualified"? How can we speak of the righteous Judge "who has indignation *every day*" (Ps. 7:11)? What must we say about him who is "of purer eyes than to behold evil" and who cannot "look on wrong" (Hab. 1:13)?

These questions are meaningful when we observe that the biblical qualifications themselves are given a very specific form in Scripture. We recall the words of Christ in Matthew 5 as he enumerated various sins and built up to a climax in his argument. The sins of anger and insulting our brother and calling him "you fool" are balanced, so to speak, by the punishments of being "liable to judgment," "liable to the council," and "liable to the hell of fire" (v. 22). Surely Christ was serious about each and every sin. Nevertheless it is striking that in contrast to his isolated statement that "whoever kills shall be liable to judgment" (v. 21) he cites those sins which do not measure up, apparently, to the severity of murder but still call forth the *wrath and accusation of God*. In every instance, in the face of a superficial view of sin, he points to the real depth of man's guilt. Only in that perspective can we rightly see the gradations in man's sin.[3]

Nor is it necessary to limit ourselves here to the language of "more" and "greater" in Christ's polemic against the Phari-

3. On the polemic of Christ cf. Matt. 5:28 (concerning adultery and a lustful look). There is no relativizing of sin in Scripture, but there is a gradation. See Grosheide, *Comm. op Matth.*, p. 80.

sees. We also find that same language in connection with the *situation* in which our sins are committed. Therefore a comparison is drawn between Sodom and Gomorrah and the city which refuses to hear the words of the disciples. It is "more tolerable" for Sodom and Gomorrah in the day of judgment than for that city (Matt. 10:15).[4] Furthermore, this connection between sin and judgment is emphasized in the distinction between the slave who knew very well what his lord desired and did not do it and the slave who did not know and proceeded to do those things which deserved to be punished. The former slave received a severe beating and the latter did not (Luke 12:47-48).[5] Thus it is clear how completely impossible it is to regard man's sin as an objective or universal phenomenon in abstraction from the situation in which it is committed. Quite obviously, the situation has a profound impact on the gravity of judgment. This is the background in terms of which gradation can rightly be seen.

Any attempt to minimize our sin is radically opposed by the whole of the scriptural message. Yet time after time we read of a "greater" and "special" responsibility. This does not presume a measurable or objective act but man's own heart-disposition which gives rise to his act and in terms of which his act must be judged. The current debate against so-called "situation ethics" has pointed out the peril of a situation overshadowing or relativizing the absoluteness and universality of God's law. Nevertheless it is important to see that the Bible itself puts a stress on the varying character of different situations. Already in the Old Testament we find remarkable distinctions in the situations of man's sin and guilt. These distinctions suggest a definitely non-objective tendency.

There are a number of deeds which have, objectively speaking, an identical structure, and yet a distinction is nonetheless drawn. Consider, for example, the act of murder. The question is whether this act was purposeful or non-purposeful, deliberate or unintentional. We find nothing, in the Old Testament, of

4. Cf. Tyre and Sidon ("notorious cities": Grosheide, *op. cit.,* p. 81), in contrast to Chorazin, Bethsaida and Capernaum (Matt. 11:20-24).
5. Also the second slave "did what deserved a beating" (*poiēsas dé áxia plēgōn*). Yet it is striking that he receives a "light beating" (*darēsetai oligas*). Cf. v. 48: "Every one to whom much is given, of him will much be required; and of him to whom men commit much they will demand the more."

an objective criterion in terms of which every phenomenon of human experience is measured. We hear of the murderer who is put to death by the "avenger of blood" (Num. 35:16-19); on the other hand, there is a different verdict for the man who kills "without enmity" and forethought (Num. 35: 22, 24). In the latter case the manslayer is rescued from the hands of the avenger of blood (Num. 35:25) and is left to dwell in safety within the bounds of the city of refuge (Num. 35:28, 25). The very possibility of this city cancels out the simplistic and objectivistic condemnation of man's acts and emphasizes the subjective *intention* of his heart.

Thus Leviticus speaks of an "unwitting" sinning in one of those things which the Lord commanded "not to be done" (4:2). This does not diminish or tone down the force of man's sin or reduce it to a "nothingness." The "unwitting sin" of the anointed priest, we read, brings "guilt on the people" (4:3) and demands a "sin offering." If the entire congregation of Israel sins unawares against the commandment of God and does that which the Lord commands not to be done, the entire congregation is guilty (4:13) and a "sin offering" must be made.[6] Even an undeliberated sin of touching something unclean or uttering a rash oath is referred to, in Leviticus, as "guilt." Therefore it must be confessed and retribution must be made, to the end that atonement may be found (5:2-6). The "unwitting" or undeliberated sin is the evidence of unfaithfulness (Lev. 5:6; cf. Num. 15:22-31). When one does not *know* his sin he is nonetheless guilty and must bear his iniquity (Lev. 5:17). In such terms as these the Old Testament speaks of man's guilt in the context of every factual violation of God's command and every manifest departure from the rule of his scepter. In every such case the way of atonement is *specifically made clear*.

Yet the repeated reference to "unwitting" is not without its significance and deep meaning in Scripture. A distinction is made between this sin and a sin of deliberate intent and premeditated malice. The latter is called a "sin with a high hand." An undeliberated sin can be forgiven, "because it was an error" (Num. 15:25; cf. v. 26), but a "sin with a high hand" is a matter of a different kind (v. 30). This is the case whether that sin was committed by an Israelite or a sojourner (v. 29). The person who sins in this way "reviles the Lord"; therefore

6. On the unwitting sin of a ruler, cf. 4:22.

he "shall be cut off from among his people," for "he has despised the word of the Lord, and has broken his commandment" (Num. 15:30-31). For that reason no offering of atonement is possible. Gispen speaks of an "arrogant act" of open insurrection and contempt;[7] therefore the sabbath-breaker who openly defies the word of the Lord is put to death on God's command (15: 32-36). From this single example, and several others, it is clear that the intention and degree of consciousness in committing sin are important qualifications of sin. One might say that they are decisive for any proper measurement of punishment.

This distinction of motives and intentions is found not only in the Old Testament but also in the New. Especially in the book of Hebrews we read a strong warning concerning the danger of premeditated sin, particularly in the case of those who have received the "knowledge of the truth" (10:26). The warning is sounded for those who already have a certain level of knowledge, or already "know the truth"; and the curtain is raised on the real gravity of man's sin. What we see, in this passage, is not a specific act or objective phenomenon. Man's sin is qualified by a definite situation of recognition and knowledge. Furthermore the judgment is in harmony with sin's deliberateness. "There no longer remains a sacrifice for sins, but a fearful prospect of judgment, and a fury of fire which will consume the adversaries" (10:26-27).

At the same time, there is also a different accent here as compared with the Old Testament. Though the Old Testament stresses the concrete acts of sin (e.g., murder), the book of Hebrews emphasizes the apostasy and stubbornness of sin and the spurning of the Son of God (10:27-29). It warns us against outraging the Spirit of grace (10:29) and cautions against a "shrinking back" which leads to perdition (10:39). Everything is now seen against the background of *knowing the truth* or knowing that light which now has come in the atonement of Jesus Christ. "Deliberateness" is now seen in an undisguisedly *heilshistorisch* perspective. Moreover, that perspective implies an increase in man's responsibility.

Therefore we cannot generalize all sins or abstract them from their historical situations. The sequel in the Hebrews pericope suggests that fact with a very abundant clarity. The reference is made to setting aside the Mosaic law which had no mercy "at the testimony of two or three witnesses" (Heb.

7. Cf. Gispen, *Comm. Numeri*, I, pp. 247, 250.

10:28). Yet the statement is added that a *heavier penalty* is meted out to those who spurn and resist the Son of God and the Holy Spirit (10:29). That same perspective is repeated in chapter 12, where we hear of those who "did not escape" when they refused to listen to Moses, the spokesman of God on earth. Then the remarkable words follow: "much less shall *we* escape if we reject him who warns from heaven" (12:25). In this contrast of " 'how much more' are *we* accountable and 'how much less' shall *we* escape" we observe the modification which has come about by the process of God's activity in history. The situation in which Hebrews warns us is the situation of a growing or maturing illumination. It is the situation of the clarity and inescapability, the inviolateness and the irresistibility of God's revelation. In *that situation* there comes a *greater responsibility*. Within the crescendo of history it is more and more evident that sin can be called, in this new situation, a deliberate act against the light which has now arisen and the cross of God's atonement.[8] Only in that full knowledge of God's truth can we rightly speak of "greater sin." Thus the book of Hebrews is concerned with a sin whose gravity cannot be contemplated apart from designating its "date": *post Christum.* This kind of sin is committed in *full responsibility.* Therefore the latter state of *such a sinner* is worse than the first (II Pet. 2:20) and no sacrifice remains for sin.[9]

Obviously, all of this cannot imply a devaluation of man's sin. For the direction we have noted is not from more to less but from *less to more responsibility.* Within the process of God's saving activity the responsibility of man is *increased.*[10] There is a transition from "the first to the last," and within that transition the darkness of the last is very clearly seen. The "greater" responsibility is obvious when we hear that the "last state" is apparent in man's enslavement to the defilement of the world. This very contact with the world is a contact from which a man should be freed "through the knowledge of our

8. Cf. C. Spicq, *L'épitre aux Hébreux,* II, 1953, p. 322: "les péchés volontaires contra la lumière." Note Heb. 6:4: it is "impossible" to restore to repentance again "those who have once been enlightened."

9. Grosheide *(Comm. op Hebr.)* states that those who commit such a sin *recede behind* that which can be atoned for by the sacrifice of Christ (cf. the *ouketi* in Heb. 10:26).

10. This is the clear background of what Christ says concerning Chorazin and Bethsaida. His words stand in the context of the "mighty works" which had been done in those cities (Matt. 11:21, 23).

Lord and Savior Jesus Christ" (II Pet. 2:20). For that reason the last state is worse than the first. It is impossible to return to the earlier situation, since the advent of Christ prevents us from turning back.[11] Everything is now changed. So strongly is this "worsening" described that the statement is added: "It would have been *better* for them never to have known the way of righteousness than *after knowing it* to turn back from the holy commandment delivered to them" (2:21; cf. Luke 11:24-26). All of this remains despite the fact that the "defilements" are objectively the very same as before.

In this regard we should see that the theme of "ignorance" appears in the New Testament in a very profound light. Certainly ignorance is no small thing, and it brings a number of important consequences in its train. Yet Paul received mercy, we read, though he blasphemed and persecuted the Church of Christ, for he did so "ignorantly in unbelief" (I Tim. 1:13). The bond between ignorance and unbelief is all the more remarkable here because Paul, in the same context, refers to himself as a blasphemer, persecutor, and insulter of Jesus Christ. He goes so far as to call himself the "foremost of sinners" (1:15). Therefore we conclude that his reference to "ignorance" is not an attempt to excuse himself. It was precisely Paul who was "appointed" to Christ's service by an act of Christ's own *mercy* (1:12-13). That which was now entrusted to him must be seen in a strong contrast to his earlier state of living — viz., his ignorance. Certainly his ignorance was not a reason for his later appointment to Christ's ministry, and the sins which were done in ignorance were still sins.[12] Yet his ignorance is pointed out for a good reason, and is set in contrast to his later awareness. The inner axis of his earlier life was a false knowledge of God, and his earlier activity was certainly sinful. Yet he did not live in a conscious antagonism to God's light.[13]

Scripture speaks of this ignorance in other places. We read of the ignorance of the heathen and the "times of ignorance" which God "overlooked" (Acts 17:30). These times, however, are now past, and they are past because of what has happened in Jesus Christ. Therefore God now "commands all men every-

---

11. Thus the "turning back" or "repetition" in II Pet. 2:21 and Prov. 26:11 are of a very qualified sort. This can only be understood in terms of the situation of fleeing from God in whom we are saved.
12. Cf. Bouma, *Komm.*, pp. 86, 88.
13. Cf. *ibid.*, p. 88.

where to repent" (cf. Acts 17:31; I Pet. 1:14). Peter addresses himself to the Jews and adjures them: "As obedient children, do not be conformed to the passions of your former ignorance" (I Pet. 1:14). In ignorance they had crucified the Christ (Acts 3:17). This ignorance did not eliminate their guilt, but it did describe the *situation* in which they committed their sin. Paul also speaks of the ignorance of the Jews who were unknowing of "the righteousness that comes from God" (Rom. 10:3). Once again, there is no hint of self-excuse, for through this very ignorance they came to seek their own righteousness. In the act of crucifying Christ the guilt of man is very obviously present. Therefore Christ prayed for those who committed that sin, though they "knew not" what they did (Luke 23:34).

When Scripture speaks of man's ignorance in this way it refers to the dark night of unknowing that preceded Jesus Christ. Ignorance is opposed to the new situation which arose with the unveiling of Christ as the Revelation of God through the apostolic preaching. In this light we may speak of a certain gradation of sin. We may speak of an increase which is manifest in the history of redemption. Nevertheless, the question now comes: Does Scripture only speak in this *heilshistorisch* mood when it addresses the problem of the gradation of sin and the increase of man's responsibility? Needless to say, we encounter here an important biblical aspect in the "history of sin." At the same time, we must guard ourselves against ignoring other references to the growth and intensification of evil.

We see something of that intensification in the history of mankind, as described in the Scripture. We recall that the flood was occasioned by the obvious increase in man's corruption (Gen. 6:11-12). It grieved God that he had made man (vv. 6-7). The emphasis in this story is on that which was "full"; therefore we read of a "fullness" of violence in the earth (6:11). So too, in other scriptural references, we are made aware of a qualitative or quantitative "being full." There is a "fullness" in the increase of man's sin.[14] There is an evil which mounts up before the face of God (Jonah 1:2), and in the profluence of the ages there is a "filling up" of the measure of the fathers (Matt. 23:32). Nowhere do we encounter, in Scripture, a pellucid picture of the inner processes of man's sin. We do not

14. We think of Abraham's intercession for Sodom. Quantitative fullness can be seen in the number of "righteous" in that city (Gen. 18:22-33).

see in depth the psychology of evil. We read of a certain ripen-ing, or becoming full, or an increase in man's obduracy, which is more and more irresistible, until it is "full-grown" and leads a man to death (James 1:15).

Thus we hear of a hardness of heart, in both the Old and New Testaments, or a process in which it is evident that the last end of man is worse than the first.[15] The strong accent on the "last days" is certainly in line with that notion, and the intention is obviously to illumine the increase in man's evil. Therefore the "last days" are described by the fullness of sin and are referred to as "days of stress" (II Tim. 3:1).[16] Scripture is clear in underscoring the inner dynamics which are part and parcel of the essence of sin and which also reveal them-selves in very many ways. It does not attempt to see those dynamics in purely rational, historical, or psychological terms.[17] It indicates the growth of man's evil and the gravity of God's judgment on sin.

When we reflect on what we have said, it is evident that the problem of gradation is defined in terms of an obvious "process" in evil. Therefore it is wrong to speak of a "repeti-tion" of man's sin. We could better speak of "sinning anew." The scriptural accent is on the ongoing character and intensi-fication of God's revelation. Through that revelation sin is more and more made manifest and is fully seen *as sin*. The gradation of sin has nothing to do with a minimizing of evil

---

15. On this topic of hardening, cf. my *Divine Election*. Matt. 24:12 speaks emphatically of an increase or augmentation of wickedness: "And be-cause wickedness is multiplied, most men's love will grow cold." By way of contrast, consider the increase in faith and love as mentioned in II Thess. 1:3.

16. Especially Paul Althaus has made an extensive study of the increase of evil; cf. his *Die letzten Dinge*, 1933[4], pp. 277ff. Though he rejects the idea that one can formulate a specific theory here, he does speak of a "history of sin, the increase of sinful acts, the progressive and reciprocal effects of sin, and the development of a 'precipitate' of sin in customs and morality, as well as in the ordering of one's life." Althaus refers to "a history of consequences and reactions, of increasing disintegration and torpidity" (p. 282). It is not consistent when he adds: "The primi-tive sin has no history; here there is neither a forward nor a backward development" (p. 284).

17. Though the increase of sin is not explained, it is sometimes referred to *in a specific relation*. We are thinking of the coming of the law and the increase of sin (Rom. 5); also of God's judgment by means of sin (Rom 1:24, 26, 28).

and is only fully manifest in the light of God's countenance. Therefore the latter sin is worse than the first.

Up to this point we have treated of that which Scripture says very clearly concerning man's increasing responsibilities in the light of God's salvation revealed in Jesus Christ. We would do wrong if we said no more. Our attention is now focused on a different matter which cannot stand loose from what we have said but which does have its own peculiar genius. We have referred already to the book of Hebrews with its accent on the *heilshistorisch* perspective and man's deliberate or wanton sin. Now we should notice the fact that this same book presents us with a different kind of sin which is regarded by God in a different sort of way. A distinction is found in this book which is also calculated to give us great *comfort*. We are referring to Hebrews 5:2 where we read of a high priest who is able to "deal gently with the ignorant and wayward, since he himself is beset with weakness." He is able to make sacrifice for the sins of the people performed in ignorance (cf. Heb. 9:7). What we have, at this point, is by no means a duplication of the Old Testament situation. The writer's purpose is to comfort and to cheer *the Church*. His theme lies in the relation of the high priest and "our weaknesses" (4:14f.; 5:1f.).

Here, then, the picture of the Old Testament priestly "accommodation" is applied to Jesus and we see in him a priest who is aware of our weaknesses. "For we have not a high priest who is unable to sympathize with our weaknesses, but one who in every respect has been tempted as we are, yet without sinning" (4:15). The word *accommodation* is worthy of our consideration. Lightly weighed, it might seem to be a watering down of sins committed in ignorance or error. In any event, there is a very different divine reaction here from the reaction to sins with a "high hand." The Old Testament pictures a priest who deals "gently with the ignorant and wayward" and accommodates himself to those in error, since he himself "is beset with weakness." Therefore he is obliged "to offer sacrifice for his own sins as well as for those of the people" (5:3). *He* has no reason to stand on a pedestal and to treat with disdain those who are of a "lower estate."[18]

18. Cf. H. van Oyen, *Christus de Hogepriester,* p. 87. Cf. further Heb. 7:28: high priests who are troubled by weakness, in contrast to the perfection of the Son.

That fact is now borne in mind in the reference to the "true high priest" who does not act rigorously toward us, from some "height," but accommodates himself to us in commiseration and sympathy. His posture suggests that he is "reasonable" in regarding the weaknesses of his Church. He is moderate in his inner emotions and conduct.[19] He does not give vent to his displeasure as he looks at the infirmities of his Church.[20] Yet if we ask if this accommodation or commiseration is an empty view of sin we can only respond: By no means! This is evident from the entire burden of Hebrews, which is certainly not to give an empirical analysis of the Church in rosy terms. The message of the commiserating high priest is an incentive to the Church to proceed in boldness in mounting the *throne of God's grace*. Precisely *therefore* this boldness is not encouraged by a weakened description of our guilt. Man's guilt is not seen in relative terms which could better go ignored. We have boldness because of the mercy which we receive and the pardon we find at the "throne of grace" precisely in the "time of need" (4:16).

Whence come this "moderation" in judgment and this mercy which we now receive? The mood, at this juncture, is different from the old adage: "To understand all is to forgive all." Hebrews speaks not only of "weakness" but also of "waywardness" and "error" (cf. 5:2). Therefore it uses terms which the Scripture judges very harshly in other passages.[21] How is it possible that the Christ who addresses himself so sharply to the churches of Asia Minor (Rev. 3:14ff.) is now described as "sympathetic" or "accommodating" to those who are "wayward" and "in error"? The commiseration of Hebrews 5 is a commiseration in our "weakness"; therefore it is well to know what Scripture means by that term. We think of Paul's statement that "the Spirit helps us in our *weakness*" (Rom. 8:26). Nowhere does the New Testament minimize our infirmities. As a matter of fact, it warns us against that very attitude. Therefore Christ remonstrates with his disciples and girds them against that peril: "Watch and pray that you may not enter into temptation; the spirit indeed is willing, but the flesh is

---

19. Cf. *TWNT*, III, *s.v. archiereús*, E. 3. a.
20. Zahn, *Komm.*, p. 124. Van Oyen speaks of a "golden middle-way" between passion and apathy (*op. cit.*, p. 85). Cf. Spicq, *op. cit.*, II, 108.
21. Cf. *TWNT*, VI, *s.v. planáō*.

weak" (Matt. 26:41) .[22] In all such weakness we see the peril of stumbling. Our weakness may not be ignored. Yet we hear of the "accommodation" of our high priest, or his "commiseration" and act of mercy toward believers who are *weak* in the midst of their *new struggles.*

Thus we see a situation which apparently is of great significance for the judgment of our sin: the high priest and the weakness or the waywardness of believers. One might assume that believers are released from the most radical and total demands of sanctification, and one could wish that a more generous standard were applied to their infirmities. Yet the writer of Hebrews speaks of a special calling to sanctification and enjoins his readers to strive for sanctification, apart from which "no one will see the Lord" (12:14). He puts stress on the commandment of love, which is no less valid for believers than for non-believers. In fact it is even more valid. Nevertheless, there is a divine commiseration in the temptations of believers, for Christ himself "in every respect has been tempted as we are" (4:15). This entire pericope exalts the wonder of God's protection and underscores the revelation of Christ's mercy precisely where the struggle for Christians is still severe. Here we are touching on a problem which has always interested the Church throughout her long history: What about the possibility and the actuality of residual sins in the lives of those who believe? This is an area of concern for perfectionists especially but also for everyone who confesses the doctrine of the Church. How should we relate justification and sanctification in Christ with the Christian's practice of living? What must we say about the relation of "not yet" and our being crucified *already now* with Christ? What about our being *dead and buried with him?* This is the problem of the indicative and imperative. How do the two relate?[23] In the face of that problem the presence of the high priest in Hebrews 4 has always meant a comfort and a source of power in the lives of believers.

We hear the echo of Hebrews 4 in the Lord's Supper formu-

---

22. Cf. the connection between weakness and stumbling: *TWNT,* I, *s.v. asthéneia.* Stählin also recalls Rom. 5:6, where "helpless" is very close to "sinful." "Christ died for the ungòdly" (5:6), for "sinners" (5:8), for "enemies" (5:10), and for those who were "helpless" (5:6). Cf. H. N. Ridderbos, *Comm.,* p. 109.

23. Cf. Chap. 5, above; also my *Faith and Sanctification.* Further, Barth's chapter, in *K.D.,* IV/3/1, on "The Promise of the Spirit" (317ff.; ET, 274ff.). Cf. Chap. 17 below, on the "end of sin."

lary where reference is made to the sins which remain in believers. "... We find many shortcomings and miseries in ourselves, as namely, that we have not perfect faith, and that we do not give ourselves to serve God with that zeal as we are bound, but have to strive daily with the weakness of our faith and the evil lusts of our flesh." Yet all this is no obstacle for partaking of the Lord's Supper. For believers do not come to this meal "to testify thereby that we are perfect and righteous in ourselves, but on the contrary... we acknowledge thereby that we lie in the midst of death." Believers are "heartily sorry" for their shortcomings and "desirous to fight against" their unbelief and to "live according to all the commandments of God." This is a very remarkable declaration in view of the previous assertion that "all who know themselves to be defiled" with certain "gross sins" *should* "abstain from the table of the Lord." After that statement there follows a rather impressive roster of our sins, capped off by this very sweeping summary: "and all who lead offensive lives."

Therefore the formulary accentuates the seriousness of remaining sins in the lives of believers. A displeasure with ourselves plays a very important role here. We read of a "hearty sorrow" which roots in the grace of the Holy Spirit. The dynamic of the Christian's living is clearly set before our eyes. There is a restlessness and a sorrow along with a struggle for quiescence, and a confession of guilt along with a preparation for new sanctification and new fellowship with God from this time forth. We are sorry for our vestigial sins, and the whole future is opened up as we are *received again into favor.*

The essential point is the confession of guilt on the part of a starved and parched and hungry soul. The formulary makes the momentous judgment that sins that remain endure "against our will." But what sort of a psychology is involved in those words? Is self-excuse implicit here? Are we guilty if the remnant of sin is really "against our will"? Can the "self" be disjoined from the "will"? Are we weaklings delivered up to the monster of our sin and frustrated in helping ourselves? Surely the formulary does not intend a psychological analysis of our sinning. Its meaning is very obvious. There are those sins which remain and for these we must have sorrow.[24] There is also a

24. Besides the formulary for the Lord's Supper, cf. HC, Q. 56, concerning "my sinful nature, against which I have to struggle all my life long"; also Q. 62 — "even our best works in this life are all imperfect and

certain abhorrence of sin and a "distance" between ourselves and the evil that we do. Therefore the life of a believer cannot be defined in a single term. To be "heartily sorry" for our sin does not cancel the important fact that sin and infirmity *do* remain in us "against our will." There is no incompatibility on that score. Instead we see, as it were, a single frame of a moving picture which is taken during the believer's total life-struggle. Guilt is confessed at the same moment as we sin against our will, and we protest against our sin at the same moment as we struggle in the flesh. We stumble and are sad — but we also rise again.

Therefore the words "against our will" can never be seen as an explanation or an alibi for sins that remain. We make no "dissection" of our sin, and there is no explication of sin's components. We only observe the battle in which a believer thrusts all his life-energies against constantly recurring threats. This is the battle in which he repeatedly falls and comes to know real struggle as a persistent phenomenon in his living. Thus the believer is critically disposed toward himself in the focus of the light which God has sent. In that light (or in Jesus Christ) he cannot regard his daily sins as though they were mere trivia. Nonetheless he knows himself upgirded, weak and stumbling though he be, by that high priest who meets him "halfway." The structure of a believer's living is a "godly grief" which alone "produces a repentance" (II Cor. 7:10). For the Spirit himself leads him to sadness and remorse.[25]

One can illustrate all this by a short excursion on the Canons of Dort. Certainly the Canons do not hesitate to deal with this problem of residual sins. God delivers those who have faith "from the dominion and slavery of sin, though in this life he does not deliver them altogether from the body of sin and from the infirmities of the flesh" (V, 1). And "hence spring forth the daily sins of infirmity" (V, 2). *Quotidiana,* we read — there are no exceptions. What we read is no play on words. Yet we find this statement in the canon on *preservation.* The peace of God's preservation is related to a believer's disquietude and unrest. The Canons profess that "by reason of these remains of indwell-

defiled with sin"; Q. 114 — "even the holiest men, while in this life, have only a small beginning"; and Q. 115 — "that all our life long we may learn more and more to know our sinful nature." Also BC, Art. 23.
25. Cf. the "heartfelt sorrow" of HC, Lord's Day 33.

ing sin *("reliquiae")*, and because of the temptations of the world and of Satan *("tentationes")*, those who are converted could not persevere in that grace if left to their own strength" (V, 3). Thus there is every reason to take refuge in the crucified Lamb of God. The believer's life is pictured in the unmistakable lines of struggle. Peril is now indicated — the real peril of departing "from the guidance of divine grace" (V, 4). Watching and praying are enjoined, lest we fall into "heinous sins."[26] That possibility is not remote, and men cannot dismiss it lightly from their minds. For men are "drawn *into* these evils at times. Witness the "lamentable fall" (the *"tristes lapsus"*) of David and Peter.

Therefore we are far removed here from any minimizing of these "remains of indwelling sin." As a matter of fact, the spirit of the Canons is a far cry from any relativizing or quantitative vision of the weakness and the waywardness of believers. So much is that the case that we read of "heinous sins" or "enormous sins" by which believers "very highly offend God" and "grieve the Holy Spirit" and "very grievously wound their consciences" (V, 5). A way of escape is only possible in the faithfulness of God and his preservation (V, 3). Therefore believers are called to repent and to turn back to the way of faith which leads them to the face of God.

We can never understand what is meant here if we think of a casuistic compartmentalizing or a localizing of various sins. A warning is sounded against a real peril that continues to plague the lives of believers. This is the peril of "great and heinous sins." In the Lord's Supper form and the Canons we meet up with the same accents as we have already noted in the New Testament. In all of these we find an urgent warning against "grave sins." From the standpoint of logic it might seem that that warning is tautological. Are not all sins "grave"? At the same time, it is plain that the New Testament does *not* speak of all sins in identical terms. There is a general qualification which holds for each and every sin; Paul, for example, contends that "the unrighteous will not inherit the kingdom of God" (I Cor. 6:9; cf. Gal. 5:21 and Eph. 5:5). But there is no "equalizing" of sins. Therefore Paul draws attention to certain very special instances. "It is actually reported that there is immorality among you," he writes, "and of a kind that is not

26. Canons: "peccata gravia et atrocia."

found even among pagans" (I Cor. 5:1) .[27] In an earlier letter
he had addressed himself to this same problem (cf. I Cor.
5:9-10) , but now he gives it a fuller discussion. He does not
mean that believers should cease all contacts with "the immoral of this world, or the greedy and robbers, or idolaters,
since then you would need to go out of the world" (I Cor.
5:10) . But he does mean that believers should guard the
sanctity of the Church. Believers should avoid having fellowship with those (even in eating, v. 11) who are known as "brethren" in the Church but are nonetheless guilty of "immoralities."

Thus Paul was concerned about a *situation within the
Church*. He was concerned about a chasm which is always apparent, even among "brethren." Therefore he pointed to some
of the worst and most obvious sins.[28] He did not pass judgment
on those outside the Church; "for what have I to do with judging outsiders? Is it not those inside the church whom you are
to judge?" (I Cor. 5:12) . Paul's concern was for "brethren"
whose lives were caught in spectacular and self-evident sins.[29]
They were the ones who called themselves Christians even while
they continued to *live in their sins*. All the while the ambivalence
of this situation could only mean a *de facto* break with the
Church.

Thus the life of the flesh is in tension with the life of the
Spirit, "for these are opposed to each other, to prevent you from
doing what you would" (Gal. 5:17) . Two different modes of
existence, or radically different directions in life, are referred
to the *sárx* of man and the *Pneúma* of God. Paul is concerned about those who walk wrongly[30] and stand under the
power of Satan. He is not interested in what *we* commonly call
"immorality," but he mentions such sins as "enmity, strife, jealousy, anger, selfishness, dissension, and party spirit" (Gal. 5:20) .
His focus is on two "ways" in which men walk. Men walk
"worthy of the Lord" (Col. 1:10) , as "children of light" (Eph.
5:8) , or "according to the flesh" (Rom. 8:4) . If Christians walk
in this latter way the light in the Church is obfuscated. Therefore Paul warns against "times of stress" with all the concomitant and varying sins (II Tim. 3:1ff.) . He admonishes believers

27. Cf. H. von Campenhausen, *Die Begründung kirchlicher Entscheidungen
    beim Apostel Paulus,* 1957, pp. 15f.
28. H. D. Wendland, *Comm.,* p. 42.
29. Cf. Paul's warning in 1 Cor. 10:7: "Do not be idolaters." Cf. 10:14.
30. Cf. Schlier, *Galaterbrief,* p. 179.

to "shun" these things. "Avoid such people," he writes (3:5).
He gives a whole list of flagrant sins, but is not concerned with
a casuistic ethics. He stresses the emptiness and darkness of living in sin and sees in this a contrast to living in the light, or
living in the very presence of God. The book of Revelation
sets this contrast in an eschatological perspective.[31]

It is undeniable that the New Testament refers frequently
to alarming dangers and special threats. Therefore some people
have asked if we do not find, in these passages, a peculiar
casuistic tradition. How must we look at the New Testament
"catalog of offenses" and its concrete content of very specific
sins? Wubbing has quite rightly commented: "The catalog of
New Testament virtues and vices does not offer us, on the whole,
an exclusive picture."[32] We must bear in mind that the New
Testament summaries of sin do not contain, in any uniform
sense, *only* those sins which are violent or flagrant. The roster
of "sins of the flesh" includes unchastity and drunkenness, but
also strife, enmity and jealousy (Gal. 5:20). Thus, on the
grounds of the New Testament itself, it is impossible to come
to a casuistic "objectifying" of sin. In the contrast of the "works
of the flesh" and the "fruits of the Spirit" we find first one
and then another manifestation of life, each of which exempli-
fies man's alienation from God or estrangement from the world.
The "concretizing" of sin is pictured in variety and is only an
illustration of the sin in every Christian's living.[33] In this situation the fruits of the Spirit and the works of the flesh underscore the structure or direction of a Christian's living in his
world. Therefore the catalogs of virtues and vices are only
a manifestation of two different "walks" in two different "ways."

Paul, in this connection, has been seen in relation to a
dualism which crops up in Judaism and especially in the Qum-
ran texts. Wubbing has referred the "catalog of virtues and
vices" to a Qumran-oriented, dualistic anthropology.[34] He finds
this structure of dualism in Paul. But notice here that Wubbing

---

31. Cf. Rev. 22:15: "Outside are the dogs and sorcerers and fornicators and
murderers and idolaters, and every one who loves and practices falsehood." Cf. Greijdanus, *Komm.*, on the horror of sin, its baseness, and
its manifold exemplification.

32. S. Wubbing, *Die Tugend- und Lasterkataloge im N.T. und ihre Tradi-
tionsgeschichte unter besonderer Berücksichtigung der Qumran-Texte*,
1959; in *Beiträge zur N.T. Wissenschaft*, 25, p. 86.

33. *Ibid., passim.*

34. *Ibid.*, pp. 61f.

gives an ambiguous usage to the concept of *dualistic;* furthermore, the whole argument depends on the context in which
this "dualism" is described.[35] This is apparent when we see
that the Old Testament already spoke of "two ways" (e.g.,
Ps. 1:6), and the New Testament only elevates that image
to the well-known contrast of a broad and a narrow way (Matt.
7:13-14). There is, however, no dualistic anthropology or cos-
mology in Paul. Indeed, his discussion of "two ways" can *only*
be seen in an intimate relation to the revelation of Jesus Christ
and the newly found freedom which we have in him. Because
of that freedom the "duality" of the New Testament catalogs
is never "schematized." It is woven within the fabric of warning
and cheer.[36] The "ways" in which men walk are under the
verdict and the illumination which comes to us in Jesus Christ.
All of sin can only be seen as the refusal to live in the liberty
which he affords.

The lives of believers are lived within this kerygmatic context of warning and antithesis. They are not removed from
temptation, threat, or anxiety.[37] In the midst of struggle there
is comfort and encouragement; but there is also admonition.
All of this is under the merciful eye of the great high priest
who has "accommodated" himself to us and can sympathize with
us. The work of that high priest is accompanied by the evidence
of sanctification in our living or the fruit of the Holy Spirit.
"Against such," we read, "there is no law" (Gal. 5:23).[38]

We cannot examine this problem of gradation without considering the Roman Catholic distinction of "mortal" and "venial" sins. The very possibility of gradation, in the New Testament, would seem to indicate the importance of that matter.
Yet the Reformation Churches have recognized gradation in doctrine and practice but have strongly disavowed the Roman
Catholic conception. Significantly, they have done so precisely

35. Cf. *ibid.,* pp. 108f.
36. These "catalogs of works" are found especially in Paul (note Rom.
    1:29-31, I Cor. 5:10-11, 6:9-10, II Cor. 12:20-21, Gal. 5:19-21, etc.). Christ
    also speaks of those things which "come out of the heart" (Matt.
    15:19; Mark 7:21-22). Besides the work of Wubbing, cf. A. Vögtle, *Die
    Tugend- und Lasterkataloge im N.T.,* 1936 (*N.T. Abh.*), Bd. XVI.
37. Cf. Wubbing, *op. cit.,* p. 125.
38. It is striking that in contrast to the *works* of the flesh (Gal. 5:19), we
    read of the *fruit* of the Spirit (Gal. 5:22). Cf. Schlier on Gal. 5:22.

because of their appreciation for the *radical nature, totality and gravity of sin*. Here we come to the heart of our problem.

The Catholic distinction finds an honored place in Roman theology and especially in the Roman doctrine of the Church. That fact is obvious at the great Council of Trent. There the distinction was made between *mortal sins*, which we know by diligent self-scrutiny, and concerning which confession must be made, and *venial sins*, which plague us repeatedly but do not imply the forfeiture of the grace of God.[39] The latter sins *may* be confessed,[40] but Trent was especially concerned to say that *mortal sins must be confessed and pardoned*. When the *Christi fideles* fall into these sins they are children of wrath and the enemies of God. Therefore it is completely necessary that they solicit the grace of God in the way of confession.[41] While daily and frequent sins (venial sins) do not make a man a child of wrath, the situation is much more grave in regard to mortal sins. Thus the intention of Rome is to point to *two categories of sin*. The argument of Baius, namely that all sin is really unpardonable when taken by itself, was roundly rejected by Trent.[42] Furthermore even mortal sin was now described in terms of its disruptive effect — that is to say, in terms of the *loss of the grace of God*. Mortal sin deprives a man of sanctifying grace and other supernatural gifts and severs the bond of love between God and the man who sins. This, then, is the main feature in all of mortal sin and its main point of distinction from venial.[43]

That statement does not imply that venial sins are insignificant. The Catholic distinction is made within the arena of sin, and venial sins *are sin*.[44] They may call forth a temporal punishment, and they certainly display the confusions implied

39. In the decree on the sacrament of penance: "Ex his colligitur oportere a poenitentibus omnia *peccata mortalia*, quorum post diligentem sui discussionem conscientiam habent, in confessione recenseri." In distinction from this: "*venalia* quibus a gratia Dei non excludimur et in quae frequentius labimur." Denz., 899.
40. The strict necessity of confession is not taught here: "taceri tamen citra culpam multis aliis remediis expiari possunt." Denz., *loc. cit.*
41. Thus the "*juri divino*" does hold in the case of "peccata *mortalia*." Denz., 917.
42. Cf. the "Errores Michaelis du Bay," Denz., 1020: "Nullum est peccatum ex natura sua veniale, sed omne peccatum meretur poenam aeternam."
43. Cf. H. Brink, in *Theol. Woordenboek*, I, 1952, *s.v.* "doodzonde."
44. Cf. G. Thils, *Sainteté Chrétienne. Precis de théologie ascétique*, 1959, p. 494. "The struggle against venial sins is of primary importance."

in all of man's sinning. They cast long shadows in human relationships. At the same time, they cannot result (as mortal
sins) in a catastrophic apostasy from the fellowship with God.
They cannot issue in the *loss of his grace*. In short, they cannot
mean a radical break with God, for the supernatural life of
the soul is not destroyed. This latter *is* the case in regard to
man's mortal sin. When man sins mortally he *apostatizes* from
God and his sense of direction in regard to his own end is lost.
Therefore venial sins can be coupled with an abiding *caritas*
which orders a man's living toward his final goal. On the
other hand, mortal sin is the elimination of *caritas*.

Catholic theology has tried to make this distinction clear
by asserting that mortal sin is *simpliciter contra legem* while
venial sin is *praeter legem*. Here we see the real issue at stake.
For the question then cries for an answer: Is not *contra* the
very essence of man's sin? Can we even begin to talk about
praeter legem ("beyond" or "beside" the law) without involving ourselves in the *contra legem* of *all sin*? Assuming that we
retain the *sin*-character of venial sin, can we refuse to assert
its *contra*-character as well? What remains then to be "expiated"?[45] Catholic theology, however, insists that only mortal
sins display the *contra*-character of sin. Therefore the *contra*-
structure of venial sins can only be played down. What, then,
is the need for confession, if only man's mortal sins are "like
scarlet" or "red like crimson" (Isa. 1:18)?[46] Venial sins are not
entirely ignored since in any case we continue to deal with *sin*.
But now a curious thing happens. Stealing may be called a mortal sin, but petty thievery is venial; at the same time, even the
mildest venial sin may be a hindrance to full love and may
thus *dispose a man to mortal sin*. This means that the distinction
between these two is not so very clear-cut. The judgment upon
a mortal sin is very complex.[47] Nevertheless, despite these complications, Catholic theology continues to distinguish between the
disruptive forces of daily venial sins and the more calamitous
dissolution of the relation of God and man, as we find it, for

45. Cf. Denz., 899 ("multisque aliis remediis expiari possunt").
46. Cf. the words "ex parvitate materiae."
47. P. Anciaux, in *Het Sakrament der Boetvaardigheid*, 1957, p. 41, refers
    to the Catholic judgment on concrete deeds as not only complicated,
    but also, in many cases, "practically impossible." From the Catholic
    side, an appeal is often made to the statement of Augustine, taken
    from his *Enchiridion:* "What are 'light' and what are 'grievous' sins
    cannot be weighed by human but only by divine judgment."

example, in blasphemy, murder, robbery and open rebellion.

One cannot dismiss this Roman Catholic view. Scripture too, as we have noted, speaks of gradations in sin in a great variety of ways. But we have to ask if the Catholic distinction has the *same purpose in mind as Scripture*. Is it really an acknowledgment of the diversity of motives, responsibilities and degrees in the sins of Christians and non-Christians? To answer that question we shall have to look at the stern criticism of the Catholic view at the time of the Protestant Reformation. To this we now turn.[48]

We begin by noticing the criticism of Calvin. His argument is especially important for our purposes since he maintained the gradation of sin and refused to see all sin on one level. In his *Institutes* (IV, 12, 3) he distinguished between private and public sins, "concealed" and "open" sins, light and grave sins or "faults" and "shameful acts" (IV, 12, 4). While admonition and rebuke were enough for "light" sins, excommunication was necessary for sins that were more "grave." Thus lighter sins do not demand the severity of grave sins. They call for a "verbal chastisement," "mild and fatherly," which will not embitter the sinner and will bring him back to his senses (IV, 12, 6). On the other hand, "shameful acts need to be chastised with harsher remedy," as we learn from the Apostle Paul himself. Paul not only rebuked the shameful Corinthian but wished to see him banished from the Church (*ibid.;* I Cor. 5:1-5).

Thus it is clear that Calvin had an open eye for gradations in sin and spoke of various levels of discipline. Nevertheless he refused to accept the Roman Catholic distinction. It is important that he considered "venial sins" in the context of covetousness (II, 8, 58). He harked back to the command of love and stated that all powers of the soul must be mobilized with the end of love in view. Where evil desires take hold of us we are already transgressors of the law. The faintest of false desires cannot be disconnected from the judgment of death. Very explicitly

---

48. We should note already here that the debate did not involve the legitimacy of the term "peccatum *mortale*." The Canons of Dort also speak of the "deadly guilt" of sin (V, 5): "By such enormous sins, however, they very highly offend God, incur a deadly guilt, grieve the Holy Spirit . . . ," etc. Nor was the issue at stake the concept of "peccata *venalia*," for the Reformation did not regard man's sin as "unpardonable." The issue was the *nature* of this categorial distinction. Cf. H. Bavinck, *Geref. Dog.*, III, 134.

Calvin condemned the Scholastics for calling a direct violation
of the last commandment a "venial" sin. (Notice that this idea
was also rejected by Trent.) [49] At the same time, his disenchantment with the Roman view did not grow out of a concept of
the relation of sin and covetousness but bore a character more
firmly rooted in principle. Calvin recalled the words of Augustine concerning "false balances to weigh what we please and
as we please, according to our own opinion, saying, 'This is
heavy'; 'This is light' " (ibid.). Our concern must rather be with
the divine scales as we find them in Scripture, and we must
weigh our sins by God's own measure. Better stated, we must
"recognize what the Lord has already weighed" (ibid.). When
Paul calls death "the wages of sin," according to Calvin, he
shows that this "loathsome distinction" of Rome was totally
"unknown to him" (ibid.). Therefore Calvin sees little more
in the Catholic view than a false palliative "to soothe our sluggish consciences" (ibid.). Appreciating gradation and its implications for discipline, he regards the Roman Catholic view as
a "foolish distinction" which "plays with God" (III, 4, 28). He
remembers the word of Christ concerning the man who trans-
gresses "one of the least of these commandments." Such a man
shall be "least in the kingdom of heaven" (II, 8, 59).

The question is therefore this: Can we ever play down our
transgression of the law and contend that our sin does *not merit
death?*[50] *Every* sin is rebellion and deserving of the penalty of
death. Thus Calvin urged full attention for the radical and
total character of sin as an insurrection against God. His interest
was not only in *what is commanded* but in *who the Commander
is (ibid.).* Only from that standpoint can our sin be understood
in its full depths. Certainly sins are forgiven; but pardon is
granted not because of the "nature" of sins that are pardoned

---

49. Trent relates the following words to mortal sin: "occultissima illa et
   tantum adversus duo ultima decalogi praecepta commissa" (cf. Ex.
   20:17; Matt. 5:28). According to the Catholic numbering, both ninth
   and tenth commandments concern covetousness. It is added that also
   these "nonnunquam animum gravius sauciant et *periculosiora* sunt iis,
   quae in manifesto admittuntur" (Denz., 899). Also cf. canon 7 (Denz.,
   917): "etiam occulta et quae sunt contra duo ultima decalogi praecepta."
   Apparently the *concupiscentia*-problematic played a role in Calvin's
   thinking at this point.
50. Calvin, *Inst.,* II, 8, 59: "Omne peccatum mortale est, quia est adversus
   Dei voluntatem rebellio quae eius iram necessario provocat."

"but because they obtain pardon from God's mercy" *(ibid.)*.[51] Any different idea can only lose sight of God's gratuitous forgiveness. Here, then, we stand before Calvin's main objection. Pardon can never be *derived from the nature of sin* but can only be seen in the light of God's merciful forgiveness.

We cannot say that Calvin's conception is entirely clear. On the one hand he speaks of God's own "scales" and "balances"; on the other hand, he speaks with no further qualification of "lighter" sins. But the manifest "folly" of the Catholic distinction lies, in his judgment, in the misapprehension of the nature of *all of man's sin (ibid.)*.[52] Here his argument has won strong support in every quarter of Reformed theology. Everywhere we find reference to this organic character of God's commandment. There is a staunch protest against a quantitative, categorial, atomistic and abstract view of man's sin; furthermore the Roman Catholic view is opposed because it *isolates* "venial" sins from "mortal" sins and regards the former apart from the persons who commit them.[53] Heppe has observed that Reformed dogmatics was inclined at first to follow this distinction of mortal and venial sins but that the struggle with Rome led to a different and more careful analysis.[54] Reformed dogmatics came to emphasize, along with Calvin, that every sin in itself has a *mortal character*.[55]

In the confessions the attempt is made to combine the concept of *nullum peccatum sua natura veniale* and the obvious gradations in man's sin.[56] The fact that the Reformers rejected

51. "Non ex suapte natura, sed quia ex Dei misericordia veniam consequuntur."
52. Cf. *ibid.*: "si delirare perseverant."
53. Cf. Bavinck, *op. cit.*, 136.
54. Heppe cites Bullinger at considerable length. Bullinger spoke of "peccata venalia et quotidiana" which "concorditer vero omnibus seculis tradiderunt pii ex scripturis," and which are distinguished from "scelera quaedam clamantia nominantur" — e.g., those of Cain and Sodom (*Dogmatik*, 1861, p. 257). Bullinger speaks of "lapsus atque errores, qui ex ignorantia imbecillitateque magis quam malitia destinata fiunt ac a sanctis alioqui hominibus committuntur."
55. E.g., Wollebius (cited in Heppe, p. 257): "nullum peccatum *sua natura* veniale est seu tam leve, ut damnationem non mereatur."
56. In the Confessio Helvetica Posterior (1562) mention is made of "peccata actualia": "sive mortalia, sive venalia" (Müller, 178), and the words are added: "fatemur etiam peccata non esse aequalia." Note the Irish Articles (1615): "All sins are not equal, but some far more heynous than others; yet the very least is *of its nature* mortal, and without God's mercy makes the offender liable unto everlasting damna-

the Catholic view with such force can only indicate that they found something else in that distinction than the mere idea of gradation. Catholics have charged that Protestant theology itself maintains materially the same distinction. Thus they point to the Lord's Supper formulary, for example, where those who committed "grave" sins are commanded to abstain from the holy food while those who have committed lesser faults are allowed to partake.[57] But is there any real basis for agreement here? Were Calvin and others merely shadowboxing when they argued against the Roman Catholic view? Does Rome say what the Bible says when it refers to the idea of gradation? Does she merely apply this concept to man's concrete or daily living? Is there a parallel between her use of *venial* and the Reformed liturgy which points to those sins "which still remain in us against our will"? Catholic theologians have suggested that this is, indeed, the case. Anciaux, for example, finds a parallel between the words "against our will" and the Roman Catholic view. He contrasts those acts which stem from a deep voluntary resolution of a man and those which do not.[58]

What should we say about this view and its interpretation of the Reformed confession? Anciaux fastens attention on what belongs to man's activity and does not stand apart from his own responsibility but cannot be seen, nevertheless, as welling forth from the inner heart of his person. Is, then, the difference between Rome's view and the Reformation a mere difference in nuance? Is there anything really essential at stake? Are we dealing with sins which can rightly be called "peripheral"? Is self-excuse in any way implied?[59]

Certainly Reformation theology has never assumed that the differences at this point are irrelevant or unimportant. The unanimous conclusion, in former times and now, is that something lurks in the Catholic *peccata venalia* which Protestants have been either unable or unwilling to integrate in their conception of gradation. That something has everything to do with the distinction of mortal and venial sins. The bone of contention has always been these words *venial* and *pardonable*. Are we,

tion" (Müller, 529). Cf. the Westminster Confession (1647): "As there is no sin so small, but it deserves damnation" (Müller, 573).
57. H. B. Visser, *Het rechtzinnig Protestantisme feitelijk Katholiek gebleven*, 1959, pp. 104ff.
58. Anciaux, *op. cit.*, pp. 37f.
59. This is not implied in Anciaux. Cf. *ibid.*, p. 38.

however, involved in a mere logomachy, or a subtle and academic dispute? If we are merely concerned with the possibility of "being pardoned," the sense of these distinctions must fall by the boards. Obviously, mortal sins too, in Rome's conception, can be forgiven in the sacrament of penance. Therefore when Rome maintains her distinction, the definition she gives is on a different level from popular parlance. Popular opinion might say that "pardonable" and "venial" sins are less grave than "mortal" sins and are therefore less "serious." There is, of course, always a tendency to minimize these sins, and it is sometimes very difficult to distinguish between being "pardoned" and being "excused." Rome, however, has not interpreted the concept of *venial* in that sense. She has certainly spoken of sin, confession, and penance. On the other hand, the Reformers have seen a certain tendency to minimize. What, then, is the real issue at stake?[60]

Let us look, for example, at the following Roman Catholic statement. "Since venial sin is not fully *aversio a Deo* it does not alter the friendship of God and eternal destiny of man, and it can exist along with grace. It cannot affect or weaken grace directly, in its essence, but can only be an indirect threat."[61] In this remarkable definition, the alleged idea of "not-so-serious" is bound up tightly with a *threat*. Therefore it would seem that the common Protestant criticism is misplaced. Rome does not dismiss the importance of venial sins. She recognizes an indirect danger for the life of grace, and she contends that "venial sins," if prolonged, can lead a person to commit a "mortal sin." This is no concession to a Reformation criticism. As a matter of fact, the Scholastics already were very concerned

---

60. How little inclination there is, from the Protestant side, to stop the polemic at this point, is evident from only a few examples. Barth (*K.D.*, IV/2, 557; ET, 493) contends that the Catholic distinction finds root in a quantitative concept of sin. "It can serve only to veil the depth of human misery and therefore the depth of the free grace of God." Barth calls this distinction "quite irrelevant" ("tief uninteressant"; 558; ET, 493). It has a "dangerous tendency," he contends, in the direction of what Scripture calls the sin against the Holy Spirit. This is the sin in which one denies the "need of forgiveness in the case of some . . . sins." "The older Reformed teachers rejected this whole distinction. As they saw it, there can be no resting-place even for the regenerate" (557; ET, 493). Cf. further O. Weber, *Grundlagen*, I, 1955, pp. 682ff., and K. Schilder, *Heidelbergsche Catechismus*, I, pp. 457ff.

61. B. Bartmann, *Dogmatik*, II, 104.

about this same question and spent long hours discussing whether a venial sin *could become mortal.* The answer they gave was that this danger is very real. If we persist in our everyday sinning a habit is formed in which mortal sin can very easily take root.[62] Yet, despite that "indirect peril," the main accent in Catholic theology is certainly on the side of "light," "daily," or "venial" sins.[63]

This fact is very significant. All the more is that so when we see how closely these descriptions of "light," "daily" and "frequent" sins are drawn together in the Catholic conception. Is it possible to have an objective yardstick for differentiating these two categories of "common" and "uncommon" sins? In the newer Catholic theologies of penance (Anciaux, e.g.) a strong accent is placed on the great difficulty of maintaining that distinction. It is even said to be "practically impossible."[64] Yet the distinction *is* upheld and the question is *very real*: What is the correlation of *sin and forgiveness?*

We have said that Trent denied the necessity of confessing our "venial sins."[65] We have also said that this was a concept which the Reformation could not tolerate. While they recognized the degrees of sin, the Reformers were very eager to point to the correlation of guilt and forgiveness. With Rome the appearance of this correlation was maintained in the terminology of *peccatum veniale* but the concept of pardon (in the background of "venial sin") lost its meaning of *God's forgiveness.* In line with that change and a different conception of God's pardon, it was only natural that a view arose in which *peccata mortalia* were emphasized and *peccata venalia (levia et quotidiana)* were minimized. The term *levia* could lead to a "popularizing" of the concept of *pardon.* Yet, once we set foot on that course it is quite impossible to stop the consequences by merely asserting that *peccata levia* are still *peccata* and cannot

---

62. Cf. the extensive discussion by A. M. Landgraf, *Dogmengeschichte der Früh-Scholastik,* IV (Band II), 1956, 1-47, on the question: "Utrum veniale peccatum possit fieri mortale."

63. In addition to the penance-decree of Trent, the question of "peccata venalia" is treated already in the decree on justification. "Licet enim in hac mortali vita quantumvis sancti et justi in *levia* saltem et *quotidiana, quae etiam* venalia dicuntur, peccata quandoque cadant, non propterea desinunt esse justi" (Denz., 804; cf. 833).

64. Anciaux, *op. cit.,* p. 41.

65. Cf. *Dic. Théol. Cath.,* XII, I, 225-226, on Gerson. On Luther, cf. Denz., 775.

be seen as commonplace. Furthermore, our whole picture is only further confused by the non-necessity of *confessio*.

There is an unbiblical contrast at work in this Roman Catholic distinction. Catholic theology starts out with the *peccata mortalia* and ends up with the *peccata venalia* on a lower and less serious plane. As we have seen, there is also a contrast in Scripture, but the contrast is of an entirely different sort and points us in an *opposite direction*. With the increase of light and responsibility, or the process of God's salvation-activity, we hear of this comparison: "How much more" are we responsible and "how much worse" will our judgment be! This, as we have said, is the message of the book of Hebrews. There the greatest accent is placed on the moral category of sin. Rome, on the other hand, maintains a number of moral distinctions but the religious-moral aspect in all of man's sinning is insufficiently honored in the concept of "mortal" and "venial" sins. When we put proper stress on that aspect we cannot really speak of two categories of sin, of which the one is characterized by the concept of *levia*. Here the *contra*-structure in all of man's sin and the illicitness of using such terms as "small" and "great" are really the issues at stake. The Roman view loses all basis when Jesus warns of the judgment for speaking a single wrong word (Matt. 5:22) and when we rightly hear the statement: "I tell you, on the day of judgment men will render account for every careless word they utter; for by your words you will be justified, and by your words you will be condemned" (Matt. 12:36-37).

Thus the nub of the controversy does not concern the concept of *gradation* at all. It does not concern the recognition of various phases of man's sin, as the deterioration of evil, the hardening of man's heart and the callousness of his activity. This whole controversy centers in the biblical keywords of *grace* and *pardon*. A neat "compartmentalizing" of our sin, implied in the Roman distinction, is rendered impossible in Jesus' criticism of the pharisaical casuistry. Heaven and earth will pass away before a single iota perishes from the law (Matt. 5:18). Furthermore, whoever "relaxes one of the *least* of these commandments and teaches men so, shall be called least in the kingdom of heaven; but he who does them and teaches them shall be called great in the kingdom of heaven" (5:19).[66] We remember, in

66. It is evident that the words "one of the least of these commandments"

this connection, the words of the Apostle Paul: "Cursed be every one who does not abide by *all* things written in the book of the law, and do them" (Gal. 3:10). In a similar way James points to the unity and integrity of God's law: "For whoever keeps the whole law but fails in *one point* has become guilty of all of it" (2:10).

We pause to take notice of these very remarkable words. It would seem that James is at odds with the whole of human "morality" where distinctions are sharply applied between the various "levels" of sin. How can we square his words with responsible moral judgment? Yet the motivation in James' statement is very obvious. His reference is to the One who has given each and every commandment — "for he who said, 'Do not commit adultery,' said also, 'Do not kill' " (2:11). We can hardly suggest that James is proposing (as Dibelius has said) a "dispositional ethics" (*Gesinnungsethik*). Rather, he is concerned to recognize the living God *within* his command and in *all* of his commands. The law is not a mere collection of impersonal maxims which must simply be obeyed. God himself comes to us in his command. Therefore James adds: "If you do not commit adultery but do kill, you have become a transgressor of the law" (2:11). If we were dealing with a disjointed series of commands, the breaking of the one would not entail automatically a breaking of the other, to say nothing of the entire law. But because the living and personal God binds us to him by law, and because the law encompasses the whole of our living, we have no right to separate or to isolate the various commands.[67]

James had in mind this "atomizing" of the law. Therefore his statement is the very opposite of an abstract view which hypostatizes the various commandments or divorces them from

do not imply a "columnizing" or a "compartmentalizing" of sins. Cf. Schilder, *op. cit.*, I, 130.

67. Dibelius (*Der Brief des Jakobus*, 1956, p. 137) finds Jewish parallels to James' words (p. 135) and warns against a dangerous tendency in every nomistic religion, which darkens one's vision "for the value distinctions between the individual demands." But the charge here does not hold for James. Dibelius himself recognizes the "inner power and grandeur" of James' words (p. 136). Cf. E. L. Smelik: "The law is *a whole*, which receives its meaning from the center of God's purpose in it. Whoever abides by the entire law, but stumbles on one apparently peripheral point, stands guilty before the whole law. It is impossible to 'isolate' such a sin" (*De Stiefapostel. De Brief van Jacobus*, 1960, p. 48).

the Commander himself. Therefore his view deserves more attention than it commonly receives. Too many people have seen James as a kind of "step-apostle." If we learn, however, from Paul that there is "no one who does good," we learn from James the unity and coherence of *God's law*. Nowhere is a nomistic understanding of religion so forcefully excluded as here. The thrust of James' argument does not deny the importance of "value distinctions" (*"Wertunterschiede,"* Dibelius) but gives evidence of an appreciation of the sinner's place before God's face. Reformational theology has sometimes been criticized, from the Catholic side, for its pessimism concerning the *corruptio totalis* of fallen man. Even Protestants have sometimes seen an unbiblical "innovation" at this point. But in the light of Paul, *as well as of James,* we shall have to reject that criticism. One of the great ironies in the history of doctrine is that Luther's view was *vindicated by James.*[68] Nowhere does James propose a moralistic "equalizing" of man's sin; rather he conceives of man as a *sinner before the face of God.* Luther took that concept with real seriousness when he spoke of the personal nature of sin and appealed constantly to Christ's words concerning the "tree" and its "fruits"[69] or the real *being of man and his works.* James says this same thing in his admonitions concerning the unity of God's command. All of this does not imply a "levelling off" of God's commandments but stresses man's being guilty before God. The Reformation, in opposition to its critics, pointed to man as a *sinner* and contended that all of man must be seen in that illuminating light. Here, then, is the deepest objection to the concept of *peccata mortalia* in distinction from other "kinds" of sin.

Are we still left, then, with a concept of *gradation?* Does the book of Hebrews work with that concept at all? We run into real difficulties here if the sins to which the merciful high priest "accommodated" himself are *peccata levia.* Yet that notion cannot find a shred of support in the entire book of Hebrews. Believers are enjoined to "draw near to the throne of grace, that we may receive mercy and find grace to help in

68. In addition to those books cited, from the Protestant side, we refer to two works of Schlatter: *Luthers Deutung des Römerbriefs,* 1917, and *Gottes Gerechtigkeit,* 1935. In this same line, cf. M. Lackmann, *Sola Fide. Eine exegetische Studie über Jakobus 2 zur reformatorischen Rechtfertigungslehre,* 1949; also my own article, "De Kritische Functie van het *Sola Fide,*" in *G.T.T.,* 57.

69. Cf. P. Althaus, *Die christliche Wahrheit,* II, 1948, 121.

time of need" (4:16) . Therefore it is obvious why the Catholic
distinction cannot be identified with the Reformed conception
in the Lord's Supper, as noted earlier.[70] The weakness of the
Christian is bound up with his sorrow, which is quickened by
the Holy Spirit. We need not deny those sins which are "commonplace," but we cannot accept the distinction which Rome
has suggested. The words "against our will," in the Reformed
formulary, cannot be used as a basis for excuse. In no way do
these words imply a "fatalizing" of the Christian's living. They
merely point to the mysterious conjunction of sorrow and joy
(see the Heidelberg Catechism, Lord's Day 33) . This conjunction is the hallmark of Christian living.[71] Therefore we conclude that the Reformation's verdict of the Roman distinction
must certainly be upheld. For the Roman view obscures the
biblical indictment against man's sin and the meaning of God's
pardon.

At several points above we have suggested that sin is not
a "part" of creaturely reality but is rather an act of man
which proceeds from his heart and the totality of his being-
a-sinner. Here, too, we must see the importance of the problem
of gradation. Attention has often been centered on the relation
of a disposition and an act, and the crucial question is posed
as follows: Is man's sin defined primarily in terms of his overt
act or in terms of the disposition of his heart? This question
is frequently asked with a view to the problem of gradation.

Now surely the disposition of our hearts is decisive for a
right verdict on our concrete activities. It is always man himself,
or man in his entirety, who is present in every one of his sins.
Thus the sinning of man cannot be seen apart from man-the-
sinner. But there is also a certain "objectification" in sinful
activity. That is to say, man's sins, when once committed, are
removed from every power of decision or disposition and can
never be undone. Sin has an irrevocable character. Simone de
Beauvoir has taken issue with the statement of Dostoyevsky
that "if God does not exist, everything is permitted." She has
tried to maintain the urgency of an existentialist ethics by saying that although pardon, or the ignoring of sins, or meting out
punishment, does not presuppose the existence of God, never-

70. See H. B. Visser, *op. cit.*
71. Questions 89 and 90: "heartfelt sorrow" and "heartfelt joy."

theless "if God does not exist, man's faults are inexpiable."[72] This kind of reasoning, however, follows the line of a secular conception of forgiveness and cannot be the foundation for even an existentialist ethics. Forgiveness does not annihilate the irrevocable or irreparable character of a human act and its consequences. It only presupposes and accentuates the importance of that act. The effects of man's sinning are often much larger than the disposition which motivated his sins. Therefore, even if a man is sorry for his sins and confesses his guilt he cannot obliterate the consequences of his deeds.[73] The influences of sin remain. Though we compensate for our sorrows, it is evident how little the idea of a "reparation" can solve our real ethical problems. Furthermore, what *God* does with the sinner and his sin cannot detract from the guilt of *man's own sin*. The acknowledgment of that fact is the heart of all true confession.

Thus, our sin has a temporal dimension which cannot be undone and is frequently seen in the procession of the following generations. It is manifest in the grief which we bear for our own sins. Think only of the Apostle Paul. Though he experienced God's pardon he continued to call himself the "least of the apostles" because he had "persecuted the church of God" (I Cor. 15:9; cf. Phil. 3:6 and I Tim. 1:13). There is, in other words, an objective misery in evil which is not qualified by other factors which play upon it. Therefore Jeroboam lost control over the people of Israel, whom he himself had caused to sin (I Kings 14:16; cf. 13:34). Sin takes hold, as it were, in reality. For that reason it is impossible to speak of man's *subjective disposition alone*. When Hosea pointed to the seriousness of unrighteousness he did so by using the words of God himself: "I remember all their evil works. Now their deeds encompass them, they are before my face" (7:2). Evil-doers, so to speak, are hemmed in by the effects of their own sinful reality. "The wicked man conceives evil, and is pregnant with mischief.... His mischief returns upon his own head, and on his own pate his violence descends" (Ps. 7:14-16).

None of this detracts from the fact that sin takes root in

72. S. de Beauvoir, *Ethics of Ambiguity*, 1958, pp. 15f.
73. Cf. the valuable observations of Althaus (*Die letzten Dinge*, pp. 191ff.) on the "dreadfully far-reaching consequences" of untruth ("die furchtbaren Fernwirkungen eigener Untreue"). Also the pervasive effects of our acts in "indissoluble factuality" (unauslöschbarer Tatsächlichkeit"; p. 196).

man's heart and finds its expression in man's being-a-sinner. *Therefore* his disposition is very important for understanding the nature of his sin. The New Testament warns against a shallow view of sin in which the only sinful disposition is that which manifests itself *in activity*. It refers to the background or the source of our sins in which our sinful activity is given birth. Here it is important that not every disposition toward evil is translated into an act; nevertheless when our sins are condemned in Scripture it is obviously meant to include our dispositions as well as our acts. Christ was not satisfied to condemn the act of adultery which disrupted relations in human living. He pointed to the lust in man's own heart. "Every one who looks at a woman lustfully has already committed adultery with her in his heart" (Matt. 5:28). What is most striking in this warning is not the reference to the source of man's sin, or his heart in which his act is conceived, but the statement that that which remains in his heart is *itself an act of adultery*. What we keep within us is itself a deed in the confines of our hearts. That same identification is found in John: "Any one who hates his brother is a murderer, and you know that no murderer has eternal life abiding in him" (I John 3:15).

In the context of this text an overt act of murder is pointed out, as exemplified by Cain (I John 3:12). Yet the real message has to do with the disposition of hate, which is strongly condemned. Obviously, the awful consequences of an overt act are by no means ignored. The blood of Abel cries out to God (Gen. 4:10). But even when an outward act is not performed a man is not excused, for in that case God looks on the inner act of man's heart.[74] Therefore Christ warned against separating a man's inner intents from his external activities. He was not merely concerned about the legality of an external obedience[75] but about the entire man before and during his acts. Never can an act be judged on the basis of a formal analogy to the law. For in every act the critical moment, or the only reliable criterion, can be seen in an examination of one's heart. Only a penetrating self-analysis can uncover the real depths of man's sinning. Therefore, despite an external conformity to the law, the rich young ruler lacked that "one thing needful." He

---

74. Cf. the scriptural admonition against cursing the king "even in your thought," Eccl. 10:20.
75. Cf. L. Goppelt, *Christentum und Judentum im ersten und zweiten Jahrhundert*, 1954, p. 43.

suffered from a deficiency of love. No wonder the Pharisees sinned in what they did *not do* as well as in what they *did*. Nothing in their legalistic conformity could insure the result of returning from the temple justified (Luke 18:14). An alienation from the true sense of the law finds place in man's heart when the "weightier matters" are neglected: "justice and mercy and faith" (Matt. 23:23; cf. Mark 7:8). Thus, when we look at man himself there can be no break between his inner and his outer acts. Both good and bad deeds come forth from his heart. But the break is apparent in the act of his sinning when the real harmony of man is split.

Whenever the Gospel is preached man's sin is exposed and every excuse is laid bare. There can be no "dilemma" of disposition and act, for man himself is tested in his entirety. The law of God concerns his total and concrete deed. "Whoever does the will of my Father in heaven is my brother, and sister, and mother" (Matt. 12:50; cf. Mark 3:35). Scripture commands us to hear and to do the words of Jesus (Luke 6:46; cf. 8:21), and to perform works of mercy. "Go and do likewise" (Luke 10:37). Thus Scripture is concerned with *man in all of his acts*. It has to do with the *esse* of his *operari,* or the *tree* which bears *fruits* (Matt. 7:17ff.). It refers to the good man who brings forth good "out of his good treasure" and the evil man who brings forth evil "out of his evil treasure" (Matt. 12:35).

Goppelt has seen that these words of Jesus reveal what is frequently an unconscious state of affairs.[76] For the superficiality of man is never so plain as when he measures himself by his overt acts and ignores his being-a-sinner at heart. This kind of shallow examination can lead to the deepest kind of self-deceit. We then honor God with our lips while our hearts are far from him (Matt. 15:8; Isa. 29:13; cf. Mark 7:6).

As we have said, the biblical reference to man's heart, as the center of his disposition, is not a reference to a localized "part" of man. The idea is rather to point to the whole of man in the issues of his living and the explicit acts which he performs (cf. Prov. 4:23). We have in mind the unbreakable coherence of man's disposition and act. Thus all moralism is precluded. Man's act of deception, or his trying to justify himself, is laid bare and is seen for what it is. So too is the tremendous difference between God's looking on a man, in the

76. *Ibid.,* p. 44.

depths of his guilt, and man's looking upon himself (cf. Mark 7:8, 10-13). We get some feeling for this difference when we read in the Apocalypse that the "books" are opened in judgment (Rev. 20:12). Some people have thought this term refers to the consciences of men; thus our consciences are stamped with the things that we do wrong. The Belgic Confession, in Article 37, speaks along those lines: "Then the books (that is to say, the consciences) shall be opened, and the dead judged according to what they shall have done in this world, whether it be good or evil." But there is no exegetical warrant for making that identification between the books and the consciences of men.[77] Instead, the reference to "books" would seem to suggest a *totality and universal scope*.[78] It is clearly a warning against any superficial self-examination or any tendencies to deceive ourselves.

These statements on man's wholeness have given rise to the question: Does the Old Testament also make a similar kind of judgment? Does it speak of the disposition and totality of man, or is it only concerned with man's concrete activity? Does it lay stress on the good and bad intentions of man, in terms of which his acts are performed? Especially Eerdmans has answered that question in the negative. He contends that the Old Testament never gets around to this problem of sin's disposition. "It is the act that is sinful and not the underlying reasons from which that act flows forth."[79]

We can understand why discussions on this theme have centered so largely in the tenth commandment. The Decalogue, it would seem, is not concerned at that point with man's overt activity alone but is rather concerned with man's heart and intentions and motives, apart from the question of whether man's

---

77. Article 37 cites II Cor. 5:10, in addition to Rev. 20:12. This is a meaningful reference for the disclosure of *all* good and evil. On the thought of sins recorded in a book, cf. Dan. 7:10. Cf. J. Behm, *Die Offenbarung des Johannes*, 1949, p. 106.

78. Cf. Eccl. 3:15: "God seeks what has been driven away." This word underscores the irrevocability of evil, though sunken away in human forgetfulness.

79. B. D. Eerdmans, "Oorsprong en Betekenis van de 'Tien Woorden'" (in *Theologisch Tijdschrift*, 1903); cf. also his *Godsdienst van Israël*, I, 1930, 44. In 1905 Eerdmans defended his view in a new article, prompted by the attacks of Wildeboer, Bleeker, Matthes and Stade ("De Gedachte-zonde in het O.T.," *Theol. Tijdschrift*, 1905, pp. 307ff.).

desires are "realized."[80] But Eerdmans reads the words "you shall not covet" in a very different light. There is no injunction here, he says, for man's conduct in anticipation of his act. The tenth commandment, he states, refers to a "coveting and possessing at the same time." Therefore our desires and our deeds are one, and the real sin is illicitly taking for oneself what belongs to someone else.[81] Thus again, the act is forbidden, and man's disposition is not at all in view. Therefore the so-called dilemma of disposition or act must be answered, according to Eerdmans, in favor of act. By "coveting" is meant a "taking of something covetously."[82]

Yet, even on Eerdmans' own terms it is difficult to deny that the Old Testament embraces the same conception as the New.[83] When we speak of the relation between "coveting" and "taking covetously" we see the same view of sin as we have already referred to above. The Old Testament regards man, with all his motives, as present in sin and takes a dim view of an externalizing of his activity or any notion that a man can serve God with his lips while his heart is far from him. Time after time, the Old Testament accentuates the promptings or pre-

---

80. Cf. L. H. K. Bleeker, *De Zonde der Gezindheid in het O.T.*, p. 17. Eerdmans thinks it is wrong to suggest a number of references in the Old Testament which hold a "deeper" view of sin, or a view in accord with Matt. 5:28. Not even in the Psalms, he avers, do we find this situation (*Theol. Tijdschrift*, 1905, p. 321). Rather we find appeals to God because of a *lack* of guilt. Cf. *De Godsdienst van Israël*, II, 88.

81. Cf. Bleeker, *loc. cit.* Eerdmans refers to Ex. 34:24: "For I will cast out nations before you, and enlarge your borders; neither shall any man desire your land." This latter was seen as a concrete threat.

82. Note further, in this connection, J. J. Stamm, *Der Dekalog im Lichte der neueren Forschung*, 1958, pp. 46-50. Stamm asks: "Might the Decalogue really have forbidden, in its original antiquity, the false thought or the covetous impulse of the heart? This is not likely" (p. 47). Vriezen contests the position of Eerdmans, and takes sides with J. Herrmann ("Das zehnte Gebot," in *Sellin-Festschrift*, 1927). *Chamad*, according to Vriezen, implied not only taking something as one's own but "casting an eye on something" and "hankering after it" (*Hoofdlijnen der Theologie van het O.T.*, 1954², pp. 342ff.).

83. On the difficulty of distinguishing between the eighth and tenth commandments, according to Eerdmans, see Stamm, *op. cit.*, p. 49. Some writers have judged that the eighth commandment originally referred to kidnapping and slave-trade, but in time this significance was obscured. Stamm concludes that the "meaning adduced in the Septuagint, and the accepted interpretation of Christian exegesis, concerning the tenth commandment, have their beginnings already in the Old Testament itself" (p. 50). Cf. Deut. 5:21, in distinction from Ex. 5:27.

considerations which gave rise to a particular activity (cf. also
Mark 12:41ff.; Luke 21:1-4). The motives of men are pointed
to in the accounts which anticipate the building of the taber-
nacle, and we read of the willingness of men's hearts to give
to the Lord (Ex. 35:5, 21, 22, 29). Though the work of building is the main matter of interest, there is no report of that
apart from the spiritual attitude in which the work was done.
And why is that the case? Simply because man's disposition is
regarded by God as an act in which man reveals *himself*. Man's
disposition is the motivating force which results in a "freewill
offering" and makes his offering the offering of a willing heart
(cf. Ex. 35:29, 21).[84] The biblical account lays stress on the
concrete product of what was given "willingly." When thus
qualified, the money of the people was more than just money
in the eyes of God. The story reminds us of the words of Christ:
the pittance of the widow was worth far more to God than
all the treasures of the rich (Luke 21:3).

This awareness of man's intention does not mean, for either
the Old or New Testament, a priority of man's heart over
his act. It illustrates the relation of these two and examines
one's activity in the light of his deepest intents. In every man's
life or heart there are thoughts and intentions which fully
expose the whole of man to the omniscient gaze of God (Gen.
6:6; 8:21).

Therefore there is no reason to refer to the Christian ethic
as a "dispositional ethic." When we use that term we too
easily conceive of man's disposition and act apart from each
other and call forth the idea that the disposition is more important than the act. Thus the terminology itself cannot do
justice to the intention of God in his commandment. For God
was always concerned about man's *act* and the *fulfillment of his
law*. He warned that man's activity must come from the heart,
but in no sense did he ignore the importance of man's *act* (cf.
Col. 3:23). In contrast to legalism the disposition of man's
heart is emphasized in Scripture; nevertheless, this does not
imply a "dispositional ethic." The man who is called to have
the "disposition" or "mind" which was also in Christ Jesus
knows very well that his calling is not to a mere attitude alone.
His calling is a calling to activity, surrender, humiliation, and
obedience (Phil. 2:5-8). Therefore N. H. Søe has rejected the

84. Cf. Gispen, *Exodus*, II, 217.

concept of a *dispositional ethic* as entirely too confusing.[85] The term can only find support in the biblical rejection of legalism and moralism, and the criticism of many acts as "nothing" because of their one great deficiency: namely the lack of true love (I Cor. 13:1-3). Yet this very concept obscures the concreteness of the divine commandment concerning the way in which we must *walk*. Thus when Thielicke says that the specifically Christian nature of a given act can only be known in the motivation for that act,[86] he adds a proper "qualification against dispositional ethics."[87] He points to Jesus' debate with the Pharisees and comments that a human act cannot be known apart from considering its motives. Nevertheless, a proper motive, he says, already concerns the *act of man's love*.

When we see this unity of disposition and act we also appreciate the meaning of those words in Scripture which cancel out all superficial views concerning ourselves: "And before him no creature is hidden, but all are open and laid bare to the eyes of him with whom we have to do" (Heb. 4:13). That text follows a reference to the Word of God, which is "sharper than any two-edged sword, piercing to the division of soul and spirit, of joints and marrow, and discerning the thoughts and intentions of the heart" (4:12). Man's life is revealed before the eyes of God, and man is known in the inner depths of his thoughts. He is known in the wholeness of his existence, and his heart is manifest in every concrete act. His heart is crystal clear in the smallest details — in giving a glass of cold water to the least of Christ's disciples or in refusing to do the same (Matt. 25:35ff., 42ff.). Thus our entrance into the Kingdom is brought into the context of warning and admonition. We have to take seriously the New Testament eschatological preaching. For critical self-knowledge must necessarily imply the knowledge of our sins. That knowledge, of course, can be obscured in a large variety of ways. Yet when we hide ourselves we are always opposed to the disclosure of ourselves before the face of God.

We cannot escape from the "radicalness" of sin to the "gradation" of sin when we walk in the way of true confession. Thus we cannot have a quantitative yardstick for measuring the severity of our sins. Self-deception can only intensify our

85. S⌀e, *Ethik*, pp. 102f.
86. H. Thielicke, *Theologische Ethik*, I[2], 1958, 20, 22.
87. *Ibid.*, 23f.

guilt (cf. Ps. 32:3-4). In fellowship with him who is light, and in whom is no darkness at all (I John 1:5), we have the pattern for a Christian's living which leads us from hidden faults to a genuine confession of our guilt. Therefore the distance between God and man must always be presupposed. ". . . Who can discern his errors? Clear thou me from hidden faults. Keep back thy servant also from presumptuous sins; let them not have dominion over me" (Ps. 19:12-13). The psalmist feared a merely partial knowledge of himself and entreated God for his divine scrutiny of his heart in order that *he might be protected on his way.* "Search me, O God, and know my heart! Try me and know my thoughts! And see if there be any wicked way in me, and lead me in the way everlasting" (Ps. 139:23-24).

In our discussion of the gravity and gradation of sin we have not treated, up to this point, a question which must still be answered. Do we find a certain juncture in Scripture where sin is exceptionally severe and cannot be forgiven? Here we are referring to the scriptural witness concerning the "unpardonable sin" or the "sin against the Holy Spirit." We are touching on a biblical thought which, in different times and circumstances, has often led people to crises in their living and even to despair. We are not reverting to the Catholic doctrine of "mortal sin." For that doctrine, of course, does not imply an unforgiveableness. The whole sacrament of penance would seem to suggest the possibility of pardon. Rather we are concerned about a unique problem which has constantly disturbed the Church and has vexed her in her listening to the scriptural witness. Is this problem shrouded in "mystery"? Certainly there is every reason for us to pause and listen to the biblical warning concerning this sin against the Spirit.

CHAPTER TEN

THE SIN AGAINST THE HOLY SPIRIT

THROUGHOUT the history of the Church there has always been an interest in this problem: How should we understand the sin against the Holy Spirit? That interest, of course, has everything to do with the peculiar way in which this sin is set forth in Scripture. It is painted in the most somber tones, and its verdict is "unpardonable." No wonder that the Christian pastor meets frequently with people who are deathly afraid that they have committed this sin. Their anxiety can lead to the hopeless and hapless conviction that they are lost forever from the salvation of God.

Men have tried to find some clear and unmistakable definition of this sin, and have also assumed that we must guard against it with a special watchfulness and prayer. But what should we pray for? How is it that we guard against *this sin?* How do we really *know* what we are doing? There is a lack of clarity and a widespread lack of unanimity in this regard; and despite the efforts to clarify these issues there has always remained a veil of mystery. Furthermore, the greater the mystery the more perilous would seem to be this sin. Do we simply lack the necessary data to speak with any confidence? Why, then, does Scripture warn us in such urgent tones? Does this sin imply a special sin among the roster of sins which we commit? Is it related to a single commandment in the Decalogue? Does a single commandment receive an accent which the others are lacking? Does a violation remove us immediately from the grace of God's pardon?

We might think of the discussion of the third commandment in the Heidelberg Catechism (Q. 100) : "No sin is greater or more provoking to God than the profaning of His name." This statement takes on real significance when we consider that profanity is also seen in the blasphemy of the Holy Spirit. The Gospels make that clear enough. Is, then, the sin against the Spirit the same as the sin against the third commandment? One might possibly object that the definition of "no greater sin" is a *human* qualification and is also the product of man's own interpretations. Moreover, the Gospels point us to a special mode of blasphemy — a blasphemy "against the Holy Spirit." This latter point is not explicitly found in the third commandment.

But what, then, about the seventh commandment? Is there a special relation between this commandment and the sin against the Spirit? We cannot laugh out of court the advocates of a moralistic tradition who see a very easy relationship here. For Paul himself very clearly warns against the sin of sexual immorality: "Every other sin which a man commits is outside the body; but the immoral man sins against his own body" (I Cor. 6:18).[1] Moreover, Paul then adds a statement which gives even greater weight to this sin: "Do you not know that your body is a *temple of the Holy Spirit* within you, which you have from God? You are not your own" (I Cor. 6:19).[2] There is no question at all that Paul gives a special exhortation here; he underlines the importance and the destiny of the human body by pointing to the resurrection from the dead (I Cor. 6:14).[3] Yet we find nothing to suggest that this is *the* sin against the Spirit.[4] Paul's admonitions were simply a part of the New Testament paraenesis.[5] Furthermore, in those passages where

1. Wendland, in *Die Briefe an die Korinthiër*, 1954, p. 47, raises the question of whether a "sinning against one's own body" does not hold for other sinning as well. He points to the antithesis between unchastity in personal relations (v. 16) and communion with Christ. *Joining oneself* to a prostitute (*pórnē*) is the sin that Paul denounces here; and in contrast to this he sees "every other sin which a man commits ... outside the body" (*ektós toú sómatos;* v. 18). Cf. Grosheide, *Comm., ad loc.,* p. 175; also C. H. Lindyer, *Het Begrip Sarx bij Paulus,* 1952, pp. 121ff.
2. Consider the statement of Paul concerning our calling not to uncleanness but to holiness. "Therefore whoever disregards this, disregards not man but God, *who gives his Holy Spirit to you*" (I Thess. 4:7-8).
3. On Paul's frequent caution here, see *TWNT,* VI, *s.v. pórnē,* and H. von Campenhausen, *Die Begründung kirchlicher Entscheidungen beim Apostel Paulus,* 1957, pp. 16-17.
4. In the article in *TWNT* it is noted that sexual immorality is mentioned in I Cor. 6, and that yet we read (v. 11), "But you were washed."
5. This is the case not only in Paul but also, e.g., in James, though the latter puts an accent on other sins — unmercifulness, sins of the tongue, pride, and a contentious spirit. Concerning "adultery" or infidelity, in our relations with the world, cf. James 4:4; also Grosheide, *ad loc.* The sin of unchastity was not set apart in the decisions of the Synod of

we do read of the sin against the Spirit we find no reference at all to the seventh commandment. Therefore it is very profitable for us to search out what the Scripture does say, *expressis verbis,* on this sin.

When we turn to the Scripture another question confronts us. Apart from what this sin *is,* do we ever meet a definite limit beyond which it is *not forgiven?* Is that limit obvious in the case of this one sin *alone?* But why, then, should this single sin, *qua talis,* be outside the confines of redeeming grace? Where must we draw the line between those other sins that evoke God's wrath, but still are pardoned, and *this sin?* What must we say about the word of John: "the blood of Jesus ... cleanses us from *all sin*" (I John 1:7)? Should we cordon off the limits of that statement? How should we read the reference in Isaiah: "Though your sins are like scarlet, they shall be as white as snow; though they are red like crimson, they shall become like wool" (1:18)? The hallmark of divine forgiveness would seem to be its unrestricted scope; but how then can we speak of a *limit?* *May* we isolate this single sin? We read in the Scripture that God is "good and forgiving, abounding in steadfast love to all who call on him" (Ps. 86:5). What sense does it make to curb his steadfast love which "extends to the heavens" and his faithfulness which reaches "to the clouds" (Ps. 36:6)? The saints of the Old Testament knew that although their transgressions prevailed against them, yet God forgave (Ps. 65:3). "For I am ready to fall, and my pain is ever with me" (Ps. 38:17); "if thou, O Lord, shouldst mark iniquities, Lord, who could stand? But there is forgiveness with thee" (Ps. 130:3-4). "Thou wilt cast all our sins into the depths of the sea" (Mic. 7:19).

Is not *this* the glory of the Gospel, that there is forgiveness with God no matter what our guilt? Christ, it would seem, revealed the only true God when he came to seek and to save that which was lost, and to eat with publicans and sinners. Should we apply to ourselves the plaintive words of Cain: "My punishment is greater than I can bear" (Gen. 4:13)?[6] Is there no pardon where a man is most helpless and hopeless and lost?

Jerusálem; cf. Acts 15:20, 29; 21:25. (This point holds no matter how we answer the textual questions here involved.) Cf. Grosheide on Acts 15:20.

6. Some translations read: "Mine iniquity is greater than can be forgiven." See the footnote, ASV.

The Apostle Paul conceived of himself as the very evidence of the "perfect patience" of Christ. And why was he an example to those who believe in Christ for eternal life (I Tim. 1:16)? Simply because he "formerly blasphemed and persecuted and insulted" Christ himself (I Tim. 1:13); and yet he found mercy. This is the message of good news: the man who loves much is forgiven much, though his sins are *many* (Luke 7:47). Thus *seven* demons were cast out of Mary Magdalene (Luke 8:2).

Certainly we cannot say that all these questions are illegitimate. They rise from the context of the Gospel and the message of forgiveness, and are therefore important not only for the man obsessed with this particular sin (which he takes to be "mysterious") but also for anyone who listens to God's proclamation of salvation on earth: the glad tidings for *all creatures*.[7] How can we ignore what the Gospels say about God's pardon? Therefore we shall have to ask if this sin against the Spirit is shrouded in undeniable "mystery."[8]

Often men have emphasized the element of deliberateness in this sin, or a willful enmity against God. It is a fact that the Gospels accentuate that point; and therefore some have seen in this the keystone for understanding the nature of this sin.[9] We might note in passing that Karl Barth has given an

---

7. The questions involved here are obviously important for any theology of "universalism." Cf., e.g., W. Michaelis, *Versöhnung des Alls. Die frohe Botschaft von der Gnade Gottes,* 1950, pp. 49-53. "Is there no hope left whatsoever?" (p. 51). In connection with Mark 3:29 (*ouk échei áphesin eis tón aiōna*), Michaelis wishes to distinguish between *aeon* and *eternity;* he understands the reference in this text as "forever" (für immer"). The present tense (*ouk échei*) is related to the present life; and the *aiōnios* of v. 30 does not mean "endless." Thus sin remains "subordinate to an eschatological rule" (p. 53).

8. We think of the words of Augustine, e.g., on this sin as "grande secretum." Note: "forte in omnibus scripturis nulla maior quaestio, nulla difficilior invenitur." This is a frequently cited statement from *Sermo* 71. Cf. G. Fitzer, "Die Sünde wider den Heiligen Geist," in *Theol. Zeitschrift,* 13, 1957, p. 161; H. Leisegang, *Pneuma hagion. Der Ursprung des Geistesbegriff der synoptischen Evangeliën aus der griechischen Mystik,* 1922, p. 96; C. Clemen, *Die christliche Lehre von der Sünde,* 1897. The meaning of this sin, according to Clemen, especially interested theologians of the Seventeenth and Eighteenth Centuries. Cf., finally, A. Fridrichsen, "Le péché contre le Saint Esprit," *Rich. de ph. rel.,* 1923, p. 369: "a strange and bizarre severity."

9. Cf., e.g., G. Wisse, *De Onvergefelijke Zonde,* 1927, pp. 9-10. Wisse sees this sin as self-conscious, deliberate, and purposeful; it is the willful declaration that the Holy Spirit is the spirit of perdition. In Wisse's judgment, this sin is the "sin of our century" (p. 12). Cf. A. D. R. Polman,

alternative conception, though his viewpoint also lacks an exegetical foundation. Already in 1935 he asserted that works-righteousness is the one and only and ultimately unforgivable sin. *This,* then, is the sin against the Spirit.[10] Miskotte has called these words "difficult to comprehend," and has ventured that what Barth meant was something like a "persevering in one's own salvation by works."[11] Barth's words, he felt, are exegetically ungrounded and are void of any scriptural support, for Scripture does not combine this "sin against the Spirit" with the notion of salvation by works. Presumably Barth came to this view (which he never elaborated) as a result of his strong conviction that works-righteousness is the *enemy of grace.* In line with this thought we should read his later assertion that *antisemitism* is the sin against the Spirit. "Antisemitism is the sin against the Holy Spirit, for antisemitism is the rejection of God's grace."[12] In Barth's conception this sin against the Spirit is not a special sin against a particular command; therefore Barth escapes the bugbear of moralism. And yet the question remains: What are the grounds for this very definite and peculiar view of the sin against the Spirit? We shall have to have better support than Barth can give.

In looking at the scriptural data we find a sharp distinction between "all other sins" and this "one sin" against the Spirit. Matthew quotes Jesus as follows: "Therefore I tell you, every sin and blasphemy will be forgiven men, but the blasphemy against the Spirit will not be forgiven" (Matt. 12:31). This entire disjunction is defined by the specific relation between

De Zonde tegen de Heilige Geest, 1938, who sees this sin as deliberate willfulness, against one's better knowledge (p. 11).

10. Barth, *De apostolische Geloofsbelijdenis,* ed. K. H. Miskotte, 1935, p. 150.

11. Miskotte, *op. cit.,* p. 324.

12. Barth, "Die Kirche und die politische Frage von Heute," in *Eine schweizer Stimme,* 1938-1945, p. 90. After 1935 and 1945 Barth again came back to this sin in *K.D.,* IV/2, 558 (ET, 493) in connection with the distinction between lethal (mortal) and venial sins. Barth asks if the man who does not recognize his "need for forgiveness" for all his sins does not make himself "guilty of what is indicated in Mk. 3:28 and par. as a limiting concept, the sin against the Holy Ghost." The Roman Catholic distinction has a "dangerous tendency in the direction of this terrible limiting concept." Here too we see a return of the essential lines of Barth's earlier insight on the nature of this sin. Cf. the reference to the witness of the Gospels and the Pharisees (*ibid.,* 177; ET, 159).

this sin and the Spirit; yet something further is also added. "Every sin" which is forgiven is set in a close relation to the *Son.* Therefore we read: "And whoever says a word against the Son of man will be forgiven; but whoever speaks against the Holy Spirit will not be forgiven, either in this age or in the age to come" (12:32). The speaking against the Spirit is set in contrast to a speaking against the Son. In this way another distinction is introduced within the *single concept of sin,* which can only be a sin against *God.* Apparently within that single arena of sin there are important nuances and even a contrast. Thus, the Gospel of Luke makes very plain that "speaking a word against the Son" is set in contrast to blaspheming the Spirit (Luke 12:10).[13]

But when we come to the Gospel of Mark we find the following statement: "Truly, I say to you, all sins will be forgiven the sons of men, and *whatever blasphemies they utter;* but whoever blasphemes against the Holy Spirit never has forgiveness, but is guilty of an eternal sin" (3:28-29). Obviously it is wrong, then, to take blasphemy in itself as the characteristic feature of this sin against the Spirit; for blasphemy *also* falls under the heading of those sins which "will be forgiven."[14] Therefore we read in Matthew and Luke that the "words against the Son" are forgiven. The conclusion is that these texts are not only concerned about "sin and blasphemy" but more particularly about the sin and blasphemy "against the Holy Spirit." That fact is evident in the contexts of Matthew and Mark. We read of Jesus casting out demons; and the coming of the Kingdom is manifest in this act of the Son, as performed through the Spirit of God (Matt. 12:28). Christ's admonition comes after the flagrant denial and spiteful misinterpretation of obvious facts; for the power of the Spirit, so evident in the exorcising of demons, was assigned by the Pharisees to the devil himself: "It is only by Beelzebul, the prince of the demons, that this man casts out demons" (Matt. 12:24).[15] Mark then adds: "For they had said, 'He has an unclean spirit'" (3:30). The sin

13. This reference in Luke does stand in a very different context: namely, the confessing or denying of the Son of man (Luke 12:8-9). The Matthean and Markan setting of this text (the reference to Beelzebul, etc.) is found in Luke, but appears in a different place (Luke 11:14-23).
14. Cf. Matt. 12:31: *pása hamartía kaí blasphēmía.*
15. This statement is also found in Luke 11:15, but in that passage no reference is made to a sinning against the Spirit.

against the Holy Spirit must be seen, therefore, in *this context* of an obvious perversion and denial of the facts: *this antipathy* against the acts of Christ by means of the Spirit and the finger of God (Matt. 12:28; Luke 11:20) .

As we examine these passages we can certainly see important differences. Therefore some have asked: Is it really possible to come to the words of Jesus himself? G. Fitzer, for example, has denied the rhyme and reason and consistency of the various readings as we have them before us.[16] The text as we have it now, he feels, is not explainable. These passages present us with insoluble problems, especially the distinction between the one unpardonable and the many pardonable sins. "Does it make much difference," Fitzer asks, "if a man blasphemes the Son of man or the Holy Spirit?"[17] But surely we cannot plead for a textual emendation on such a basis as *this;* nor is· it wise to dismiss these problems as "insoluble." Fitzer is led to his conclusions on the basis of his own bias. He proceeds from the priority of Mark (as do Bultmann, Herman Ridderbos and others) but is led to think that Matthew supplements the Markan text and gives a *different meaning* to the sin against the Spirit.[18] In Mark we find a single motive (the charge that Jesus' power is from Beelzebul) , but in Matthew the story is more complicated, and relations are drawn between Jesus and the Kingdom of God and Jesus and the Holy Spirit. Certainly the Markan text gives us a statement on the sin against the Holy Spirit which can "never" be forgiven; but in Fitzer's judgment this already is an accretion.[19] Here Fitzer lays hold on the totally speculative conclusion that the original Markan text did not speak in general terms of "sons of men" but only in the singular: the "Son of man" (3:28) . The reference is to the *Son of man himself*. All sins will be forgiven *him,* but if *he* blasphemes against the Spirit he has no forgiveness in eternity but stands guilty of an eternal sin — for they said, "He has an unclean spirit."[20] Fitzer contends that Mark's original concern was the defense of Christ against the false accusation of bystanders. The outlandish charge that "he has an unclean spirit" was so preposterous that it demanded an answer. It was a slur against

16. Fitzer,· *op. cit.,* p. 168.
17. *Ibid.,* p. 164.
18. *Ibid.,* p. 170.
19. *Ibid.,* p. 175.
20. *Ibid.,* p. 176.

the fundamental fact of Christ's existence: that he always did
the deeds of the Spirit of God. Therefore, it would be an unpardonable sin for *him* if he ever did the deeds of an "unclean
spirit." It could only be called an "eternal sin."

Thus Jesus, according to Fitzer, was concerned about what
could or *could not* be forgiven him; and the issue here is the
issue of Christ's sinlessness. Fitzer proposes that his argument
is "completely plausible."[21] Though the original Markan text
was only a defense of Christ against his adversaries, and the
reference was to *his* conflict and a distinction in *his* life, the
recension of the text (and *a fortiori* Matthew) must lead us
necessarily to a very different meaning in Christ's words. For
now the reference is to men in general and *their sin*. To borrow
a thought from Augustine: the great *secretum* has become a
real "problem."

Fitzer's purpose was "to search out the clarity of obscure
passages by the aid of methodical work."[22] The problem, as
he saw it, is solved by historical analysis of the "originally modified text." But Fitzer proceeded from the *a priori* premise that
there is indeed an insoluble problem: namely this disparity between a sin against *Christ* and a sin against the *Spirit*. All anxiety on this score, according to Fitzer, may now be dismissed
as "misunderstanding." Therefore it is reasonable that this view
of Fitzer may be regarded by some as a certain "solution," or
an omen of hope in the ocean of uncertainty. But the objections against this "literary analysis" are so profound that we
cannot possibly see it as a solution to a difficult problem. Fitzer,
with an irresponsible ease, disposes of the whole problem of the
sinlessness of Jesus. Recall here that Mark speaks of "sins" as
well as "blasphemies." And more than that, the basis of this
analysis is *not* a literary and critical activity. A priority is given
to the Markan text; but we also read of a "change" that took
place within that text, for it too refers to the sins of *men in
general* and not of Christ *alone*. Therefore Mark "must have"
complicated the issue already, since the generalized reference
is not only a Matthean but also a Markan trait. Therefore, too,

---

21. Note Fitzer's words, *ibid.*, p. 179: "Even if one — only for the sake of
    the argument — takes account of the bare possibility that 'all will
    be forgiven' the Son of man, this position is still totally different from
    the common dogmatical view of the 'sinlessness of Jesus.'" It seems to
    me that Fitzer's appeal to H. Vogel, at this point, is completely unjust.
    But this can also be set aside for our purposes.
22. *Ibid.*, p. 182.

in the Markan text there "must have been" a change which makes it "unintelligible."[23]

Here Fitzer tries to plead his case at the really essential point. The plural number in Mark, he alleges, is very uncommon and must surely have been a singular number until the change was made.[24] This, then, is the "analysis" on which he rests his case; for this reason the "Son of man" must have been changed to "sons of men." Thus we are led to an exegesis which dismisses the whole line of ecclesiastical and historical problems concerning this "unpardonable sin." But we cannot find clarity in that way. We have nothing at all against Fitzer's opting for the priority of Mark. But we do have objections when the Markan text itself is regarded as untenable because of an *a priori* concept of this "insoluble problem."

Those who take issue with Fitzer's view must still face up to this question: What is the meaning of Christ's words? A glance at the Gospels (already Mark) would seem to convince us that the unpardonable sin has something to do with a conscious and radical renunciation of the Holy Spirit and his work. Many have therefore said that this sin is a sinning against one's better judgment and the revelation of a total recalcitrance in one's heart. Some have made this conclusion on the basis of the *situation* in which the words of Christ are recorded in Matthew and Mark.[25] They remind us that the issue here is the act of Christ by means of the Spirit, the coming of the Kingdom of God, and the brute denial of that Kingdom by an insensitive interpretation which is now exposed by Christ (cf. Matt. 12:26; Mark 3:24; Luke 11:17). This is the common view on the essence of this sin against the Spirit.

But if we only point to such matters as recalcitrance and deliberation, or notice that these are present in the sin of

23. *Ibid.*, p. 172.
24. *Ibid.*, pp. 174-175. On the word-usage of Mark, cf. Mark 1:17; 7:21; 9:13; also O. Cullmann, *Die Christologie des N.T.*, 1957, p. 156.
25. We lay aside the question of why Luke's reference is found in an entirely different context. Note, however, that the setting in Luke 12 is the setting of denying the Son of man; and whoever does this will be "denied before the angels of God" (Luke 12:9). It is striking, however, that *after this severe warning* we still read of the contrast between "speaking a word against the Son" and "blaspheming against the Holy Spirit." Cf. Fitzer, *op. cit.*, p. 171, and Greijdanus, *Komm. op Lukas*, I, 592f.

blasphemy, or underscore the purposeful intention of this sin, we have still not answered the vital questions at this point. For in *all* our sins, and certainly the "words" and "blasphemies" against the *Son,* we find these same traits of obduracy and deliberateness. Moreover, how can we account for the radical and total character of *this sin* if we merely take this approach? What then makes *this* blasphemy against the Spirit a *special blasphemy?* Nowhere else in the Scripture do obstinacy of heart and a radicalness of sin bring down the curses of God with no glimmerings of hope. Though a hardness of heart is a hopeless ailment apart from God's grace, we do read of God's breakthrough and transforming powers in the adamantine hearts of men. Hearts of stone are turned to flesh. The Heidelberg Catechism refers to blasphemy or profanity as a "heinous" sin and adds: "no sin is greater or more provoking to God than the profaning of his name" (Q. 100). Yet the Scripture also states that "all sins will be forgiven the sons of men," including this sin of blasphemy against God (Mark 3:28). Therefore the issue is what is specifically *pneumatological about this sin.* What distinguishes this sin as a sin against the *Spirit,* and why is it different from a sin against the *Son of man?*

We need more light from the rest of the Scripture before we can answer these questions. From the Gospels we clearly deduce the importance of the deliberateness and radicalness of this sin, but we find very little on the pneumatological aspect which distinguishes *this sin.* It is small wonder that men have turned to a statement in I John on "mortal sin" and a "sin unto death" — a reference that comes unexpectedly in the midst of an exposition on *prayer.* Here all emphasis is on the great significance of intercession; but suddenly we come to a limit or border beyond which all intercession is profitless. "If any one sees his brother committing what is *not a mortal sin,* he will ask, and God will give him life for those whose sin is not mortal. There is sin which is mortal; I do not say that one is to pray for that. All wrongdoing is sin, but there is sin which is not mortal" (I John 5:16-17).[26] What are we to make of such words?

There is no hint in this context concerning the meaning of a "mortal sin." Apparently it was presumed that the readers

---

26. There is a textual-critical problem in the last part of this text; but the problem is not of significance for our purposes here. On the relation between this text and intercessory prayer, cf. W. Nauck, *Die Tradition und der Charakter des ersten Johannesbriefes,* 1957, pp. 145-146.

knew what was meant. We are hard put to escape the impression of a concrete and tangible measure applied here in the practice of intercessory prayer.[27] But the question comes: What is that yardstick? How can we have certainty in exegeting this text? If we identify this sin with the sin against the Spirit, as is commonly done, we must notice that John says nothing about that *pneumatological aspect* which is so prominent in the Gospels. Thus the line of connection depends entirely on the use of the words "mortal sin" or a "sin unto death." Surely a distinction is drawn here between this sin and other sins. "If any one sees his brother committing what is *not* a mortal sin, he will ask, and God will give him (that is to say, his brother) life" (5:16). Some scholars have seen a close tie-up between the forgiving-and-not-forgiving motive in the Gospels and this life-and-death motive in John. But we can only ask if these two are really the same.[28]

In any case, a specific relation cannot be construed between this sinning unto death and the Gospel references to a sinning "against the Holy Spirit." Certain writers have assumed, for that reason, that John's reference has in mind an *apostasy in general,*[29] and yet an apostasy which can also be linked up with a sin against the Spirit. Interpreters have hesitated on the meaning of the words "I do not say that one is to pray for that" (5:16).

27. Cf. Calvin, *ad loc.*: "Nisi enim certa eius rei esset cognitio, frustra exciperet apostolus non esse pro hoc peccati genere orandum."
28. Cf. F. Hauck, *Die Kirchenbriefe,* 1953, p. 153: "What our author calls 'sin unto death,' in any event, is rather similar, essentially, to what Jesus calls the unpardonable sin." Greijdanus affirms, with no reservations at all, that the reference here is the same as the Old Testament reference to sinning "with a high hand" (Num. 15:30-31); it is also the same, he feels, as the Gospel reference to the sin against the Holy Spirit. It is "a fully conscious, deliberate sinning for the sake of sinning, in order to deny the Lord" (*Komm., ad loc.,* p. 529). R. Schnackenburg (*Die Johannesbriefe,* 1953, p. 249) does not wish "simply" ("ohne weiteres") to identify this sin with the sin against the Holy Spirit, "as many exegetes do." Cf. K. Schilder, *Heidelbergsche Catechismus,* I, pp. 486f.
29. E.g., Jos. Chaine, *Les épîtres catholiques. Études bibliques,* 1939, p. 219: "the sin of apostasy which causes a return from the light to the darkness." Also A. Charne, *La Sainte Bible,* XII, 1946, 533 ("l'Apostasie des Antichrists"); O. Baumgarten, *Die Schriften des N.T.,* IV, 1918, 222; and Calvin, *ad loc.:* "non esse partialem lapsum, nec praecepti unius transgressionem, *sed apostasiam,* qua penitus homines a Deo se alienant." Recall the strong relation in John between the Antichrist and the denial of the Christ: I John 2:22; II John 7.

Here there is no specific prohibition to pray for those who "sin unto death";[30] yet it is also the case that there is no clarification of the pneumatological aspect of this "sinning against the Spirit." As Calvin has said, we find a certain "border" in this text, and that fact alone should warn us against a too-simple analysis.[31]

Hebrews 10:26-29 is more germane to our purpose here. Moreover, apart from the Gospels this passage is also the most frequently cited reference on the sin against the Holy Spirit. We have already seen, in Chapter 9 above, that the main thrust of these words is to emphasize a deliberated sin "after receiving the knowledge of the truth." If the transgressor of the Mosaic law died without mercy "at the testimony of two or three witnesses," how much worse the punishment deserved "by the man who has spurned the Son of God, and profaned the blood of the covenant by which he was sanctified, and outraged the Spirit of grace" (Heb. 10:29). The close alliance here with the sin against the Spirit hangs together with the purposiveness or deliberation of this sin and the specific reference to an "outraging of the Spirit." That alliance is supported by the further reference which we find in Hebrews 6:4-8, the classic passage on those who apostatize from God having once been "partakers of the Holy Spirit."

But there are a number of important questions in these references. Notice that the letter to the Hebrews (both in chapters 6 and 10) makes mention of the Spirit of God, but *not in an exclusive sense*. The matter may be formulated as follows: Whereas the Gospels isolate the sin against the Spirit and see it in *distinction* from the sins against the Son of man, and thus assign a certain exclusiveness to the pneumatological aspect, the book of Hebrews, in contrast, *combines* the pneuma-

---

30. Cf. S. Greijdanus, *Komm.*, p. 531: "The apostle neither commands this, nor does he formally forbid it. In a certain sense, he lets the matter rest." Also J. L. Koole, *De Bijbel in Nieuwe Vertaling*, 1959, *ad loc.*: "in that case there is no certainty of an answer."

31. "Non temere in quendam ferendum est mortis aeternae judicium, potius nos caritas ad bene sperandum flectat" (*ad loc.*). Cf. Bucanus (Heppe, 262). This hesitation leads Heidegger to recall the words of Romans 14:4: "Who are you to pass judgment on the servant of another? It is before his own master that he stands or falls" (*ibid.*). In reference to I John 5:16 he speaks of an apostolic knowledge "ex speciali revelatione."

tological and christological elements. This is apparent in Hebrews 6, where the reference is first made to "partaking" of the Holy Spirit and immediately to committing "apostasy" by "crucifying the Son of God" on one's own account and holding him up to "contempt" (6:6). Or take the citation in Hebrews 10: with the "spurning" of the Son of God and the "profaning" of the blood of the covenant (by which he was sanctified) the Spirit of God is "enraged" (10:29). Spurning the Son of God is an act of primary offense and provides the condition for a radical apostasy. The author of Hebrews is speaking of the *Son of God,* and he does so with the deepest feeling; for the Son and the Spirit are conjoined.[32]

The denial of the Son of God is manifest in the profaning or defaming of the blood of the covenant. This is the blood of Jesus, which is held by his despisers as *koinós* — as profane, unholy, unworthy and useless. Think of such an attitude toward *that blood* which was shed for the pardon of our sins! Therefore the book of Hebrews speaks of "crucifying the Son of God on their own account" (6:6). The profaners of Jesus participate anew in the same act of enmity as the Jews who crucified the Christ. Only now the story is much worse; for they do it with a consciousness and full intent, and they know right well what they do.[33] Hebrews 6 speaks of those who take their stand on the side of the crucifiers of Jesus. This indictment does not render the cross a "timeless event"[34] but enables us to see what happens to those who thus apostatize. The definition of their apostasy is *christological.* Christ prayed for those who crucified him on Golgotha — "Father, forgive them; for they know not what they do" (Luke 23:34). But now there is a knowledge of the truth and therefore a greater responsibility. Hence the warning against apostasy and the admonition against this *ultimate sin* or this *final despising* of the Son of God.

There is no trace of a distinction here between a sinning

---

32. Cf. Zahn, *Comm.,* p. 327; *TWNT,* V, *s.v. patéō,* C. 2.

33. "Apostasy is a criminal act, responsible for the death of Jesus" (Spicq, II, 153). Spicq understands *anastauróō* not in the sense of "to crucify again," but "to raise up on the cross" ("élever sur la croix"). Here Grosheide (p. 146) takes a different view — "to crucify again." So too the early Fathers and various older translations. But Spicq's conception is essentially the same at this point.

34. Spicq goes too far when he declares: "The passion is not only an historical fact but a contemporary drama of all men who have to take sides, for or against the Savior" (*op. cit.,* II, 153).

against Christ and a sinning against the Holy Spirit; further-more, where the Spirit is referred to, in Hebrews 6 and 10, he stands in relation to Christ. Therefore despising Christ is the equivalent of *outraging the Spirit of grace* (10:29). The Spirit is introduced as a delineation of what it means to sin against the Christ, and his introduction is far from arbitrary. "Spirit of grace," we read; or the "Spirit of compassion." We are reminded of Zechariah 12:10, where God makes the prom-ise to "pour out on the house of David and the inhabitants of Jerusalem a spirit of compassion and supplication."[35] It is the Spirit of grace — the Spirit who grants and works his *grace* — who is also maligned when Christ is despised. This liaison between the christological and pneumatological aspects in apostasy or wanton sin is typical of the book of Hebrews. For that reason O. Michel is far from clear when he comments on Hebrews 10:28: "When Hebrews regards apostasy as an outright flaunt-ing of God's judgment we may see this as a form of the 'sin against the Holy Spirit,' in the tradition of Mark 3:29."[36] What Hebrews emphasizes is this *falling away* of the distinction between the christological and pneumatological aspects, even though that distinction is very real in the Gospels. In Hebrews the *exclusiveness of the pneumatological* is no longer apparent.

Therefore we can hardly escape the impression that men have too simply identified the apostasy of Hebrews with the "sin against the Spirit" in the Gospels. Indeed, the peculiarity of the Gospels is not found in Hebrews at all, and there is *no reference* to a specific sin against the Spirit. Bavinck has averred that these words in Hebrews are "factually and materially" identical to the sin of blaspheming the Spirit. He has defined that sin as a "conscious, insolent, and deliberate blaspheming of what is plainly recognized as the revelation of God's grace in Christ, by the Holy Spirit, but is nonetheless assigned, in hate and vengeance, to the devil himself."[37] But this description comes closer to the Hebrews 6 and 10 passages (with their accent on the christological *and* pneumatological) than it does to the Gospel references. Also in Schilder we find an insufficient rec-

---

35. Michel (*Der Brief an die Hebräer*, p. 236) says that Zech. 12:10 had an established place in the Johannine tradition; he points to John 19:37 and Rev. 1:7. But these texts only refer to a beholding of him who was pierced (Zech. 12:10*b*).
36. *Ibid.*, p. 237.
37. Bavinck, *Geref. Dog.*, III, 138.

ognition of this distinction in the Gospel accounts: a sinning against the Spirit in contrast to a sinning against the Christ.[38] It strikes us that this is what happens when we lay special stress on the motive of blatant and insolent, wanton and deliberated sin, and *proceed to define the sin against the Spirit in terms of that attitude.* This "conscious insolence" then becomes the *trait d'union* between Hebrews and the Gospel accounts, and we fail to recognize that this wantonness is strongly *qualified.* For many sins are committed in insolence and wantonness, or deliberated and intentional spite; indeed, Lord's Day 4 reminds us that the fall of Adam deprives all men of this capacity to do God's will aright. Through our brazen insolence we are now the victims of our sin.[39]

Surely, we have no desire to undervalue the notion of deliberate and willful sin. The man who reads Hebrews 10 will see how close this comes to the heart of that chapter. But we are dealing with a *special kind* of deliberateness and stubbornness, and not merely with a *psychological* attitude which characterizes our sin. This stubbornness is a wanton sinning which comes "after receiving the knowledge of the truth" (Heb. 10:26). So too in Hebrews 6 we meet only with that qualified arrogance in which a man curses his God and commits apostasy *even though he was "once enlightened."* The concern here is with those who sin in this way flagrantly, who have "tasted the heavenly gift" and are now "partakers of the Holy Spirit," and have "tasted the goodness of the word of God and the powers of the age to come" (6:4-5).

Nor do we wish to detract from the monstrous sin of blasphemy. But blasphemy in itself cannot be what is meant by the sin against the Spirit. In the Old Testament we read of a man who curses God, and immediately we are told: "Whoever curses his God shall bear his sin. He who blasphemes the name of the Lord shall be put to death." This astringent verdict held for "the sojourner as well as the native, when he blasphemes the Name" (Lev. 24:15-16). Gispen has spoken in this connection of a blatant and open blasphemy[40] and has suggested

---

38. Schilder, "De Lastering tegen de Heilige Geest," *Om Woord en Kerk,* I, 1948, 218ff. Cf. *Heidelbergsche Catechismus,* I, 462, where Schilder refers to this article as the product of his youth and makes certain corrections. These have no bearing on the judgment which we have made here.

39. HC, Q. 9, "sua ipsius contumacia."

40. W. H. Gispen, *Comm.,* p. 343.

that the purport of this passage is to throw light on a sin of special gravity: the sin of the desecration or degradation of God's name. That sin meets with an immediate and decisive penalty.[41] In all blasphemy there is something flagrant and brutal. There is an unsavory arrogance toward other people and things, a disrespect for God, a vitriolic use of terms, and a deliberated *contra*.[42] Every blasphemy is a prostitution of God's majesty[43] and the very nadir of all man's speaking *in malam partem*. It is the apex of man's superciliousness. All of this is described in graphic terms in the last book of the Bible (Rev. 13:6; 16:9).[44]

But though Scripture is serious in its portrayal of this blasphemy against God's name there is no key here for what is meant, finally, by the sin against the Spirit. The fact remains: "... whoever says a word against the Son of man *will be forgiven*," but whoever "speaks against the Holy Spirit *will not be forgiven*" (Matt. 12:32).[45] Whoever blasphemes in general is pardoned, but "whoever blasphemes against the Holy Spirit *never has forgiveness*" (Mark 3:28). Therefore the concept of *blasphemy*, in itself, should not be equated with the sin against the Spirit.

How then should we define this distinction between the Spirit and Jesus Christ? Should we conceive of a form of subordinationism and regard the Spirit as outranking the Son? Even if we reject that idea we can only conclude that the distinction here is tied up with the revelation of the incarnate Word and the uniqueness of the Son of man in his *humiliation and hiddenness*. Grosheide seeks for the meaning of this distinction in the idea that the sin against the Spirit (as *Jesus*

41. Cf. Lev. 24:15: "Whoever curses *his God* shall bear his sin." V. 16, however: "He who blasphemes the name of *Jahwe* shall be put to death." Cf. Gispen, p. 345. Also A. Noordtzij, *Leviticus (K.V.)*, p. 241.
42. Cf. the blasphemy of God's name by the heathen, Isa. 52:5; cf. Ezek. 35:12.
43. Cf. *TWNT*, I, s.v. *blasphēmía*.
44. On this blasphemy against God's glory, cf. Jude 8-10 and II Pet. 2:10-12; on "speaking words against the Most High," in the Old Testament, cf. Dan. 7:25.
45. "Already the fathers had difficulty in expounding Mt. 12:32. It was seriously discussed how blasphemies against Christ could be forgiven, but not against the Spirit" (*TWNT*, I, s.v. *blasphēmía*).

referred to it) cannot be excused.[46] He sees this in regard to a *possible uncertainty* with reference to the Son of man. The appearance of Jesus gave rise to contradictory sentiments. There was widespread ignorance among his enemies (cf. Luke 23:34) but also among his friends and disciples. He was viewed as the fulfillment of Daniel's prophecy (a man with a messianic dignity; cf. Dan. 7:13),[47] and yet he was the humiliated Messiah. He came as the King of Zion (cf. Zech. 9:9) but he did so in humility and upon an ass. He had no place to lay his weary head. His words seemed frequently out of joint with the situation in which he found himself. Time after time he concealed his person by making a shadowy application of Old Testament prophecies to himself (cf. Matt. 8:20);[48] and only later did the light fall on him who himself was the Light of the world. During his stay on earth there was no outburst of human opposition which, *as such, was outside the pale of forgiveness.* When the mystery of his messiahship was wrongly construed by his disciples and they inquired, "What is this that he says to us?" (John 16:17; cf. Luke 9:45, Mark 9:32), he replied that later they would understand (John 13:7), though *now* they could not bear to understand (John 16:12). In all of this we see a very deliberate concealing of his person and the hiding of the deepest revelation of his messiahship. Surely there was no excuse in that fact for his disciples and even less so for those who remained aloof from him. And yet the final *judgment of God* did not fall in this nimbus of uncertainties. There was a time when Jesus himself did not wish that men should come to a "full knowledge" (cf. Mark 9:31) and when the lack of understanding among his disciples was not *alone* the product of their own reluctance to receive him but *also* of Christ's own concealment.[49] This was the phase of the "revelation in the flesh" which lasted until the climax of the crucifixion; it was the phase in which God's response to the ignorance and unbelief and hardheartedness of men was not as severe as in the ensuing period. The warning was urgent but was *not yet definitive,* and only later was the messianic secret fully set forth.

We cannot contemplate the distinction between a sin "against the Son of man" and a sin "against the Holy Spirit" unless we

46. F. W. Grosheide, *Comm. Mattheus*, p. 242.
47. Cf. H. N. Ridderbos, *Mattheus*, I, 239.
48. Cf. Ridderbos, *Zelfopenbaring en Zelfvernedering*, 1946, p. 61.
49. *Ibid.*, p. 86.

first see the Son of man himself as a man who was humiliated.
We must see him as a wanderer on the earth, whose mystery
was only completely removed in the act of his messianic suffering and death. This distinction is evident when the Kingdom of
God and the power of the Spirit are revealed and are set in
contrast to the former hiddenness of Christ as Messiah. Demons
are then cast out and undeniable healings are manifest.[50] But
where this indisputability is *nonetheless disputed* and the evidence of Christ is *rejected,* precisely *there* we read this unique
warning concerning the sin against the Spirit.[51] This is no
reprimand concerning the deliberateness of sin in general or its
willfulness and wantonness. Yet it is a warning against the conscious disputing of the indisputable which is *here made evident.*
The admonition is not concerned with a general antagonism
of men against Christ or with Israel's daily rejection, but rather
with the circumstance in which the Holy Spirit is obviously
present, in this act of the humble Lord, and yet the credit is
given to Beelzebul. Once having spoken this warning, Christ
proceeded on his way to the cross. There too a blasphemy was
spoken against him, as those who passed by laughed at him and
wagged their heads (Matt. 27:39; Mark 15:29), and those who
guarded him mocked him and beat him (Luke 22:64), and
one of the murderers on the cross railed at him (Luke 23:39).
But all this, dreadful as it was, did not ring down the definitive
refusal of God to forgive. Thus the people of Israel were called
to repentance at Pentecost and were still invited to experience
God's pardon.

We see in this light that the sin against the Spirit cannot be
featured in terms of deliberateness, or stubbornness, or blasphemy *per se.* Only when we look at the incontestable evidence
of Christ which is nevertheless contested can we possibly under-

---

50. We recall the "apology" of Jesus, which also implied a holy offensive.
The answer of the Pharisees was *impossible,* since "every kingdom divided against itself is laid waste" (Matt. 12:25). This analogy was no
purely rational argument, but was rather the reference to the *evidence*
of what Christ did. Because that evidence was so plain, the warning
against *wanton sin* was also severe.

51. Frequently the question is discussed if the Pharisees *did,* in fact, commit this sin. Schilder once answered in the affirmative (*Om Woord en
Kerk,* I, 214), as also did Kuyper; Bavinck and Geesink preferred to
make no judgment here. Schilder, it seems, later modified his view
(*Heid. Cat.,* I, 465) and made no inquiry into the Pharisees' actual
psychological frame (466).

stand the warning which Christ gives. The Pharisees exemplified the abysmal apostasy of man's heart and necessitated this stern rebuke. Hence the distinction between blasphemies against Christ and blasphemies against the Spirit. Hence, too, we understand why, in the rest of the New Testament, where the burden is to see Christ crucified and risen, we *never once come upon this distinction between Christ and the Spirit.* This later revelation is no longer concerned about the concealment of Christ's messianic secret. For the mystery has now been revealed in the *proclamation of the full light of Christ.*

From that standpoint it is plain why Hebrews points us to a deliberate and willful sinning as the conscious rejection of what *has occurred* and *is now manifest.* There is now a flagrant and purposeful outraging of the Son of God, a crucifying of him anew, and a deliberate despising of his blood. Against the curtain of what has happened, it is now evident why this distinction between the christological and pneumatological falls away. That which men now commit against the Son of God is sewed up with blasphemy against the Spirit of *grace.* Everything *now* is concentrated on the resistance or antipathy in which evil men respond to this decisive act in Christ. There are many who blasphemed the crucified Lord and despised him in his deepest humiliation; yet for all of these there is still forgiveness. "Father, forgive them; for they know not what they do" (Luke 23:34; cf. I Cor. 2:8). But when the sun arose on Easter morning and the message of the cross was preached abroad and confirmed by the Spirit in the resurrection of Christ and Pentecost, a *new era* was given birth and men no longer could differentiate their sinning against Christ from their sinning against the Spirit. Sin was now qualified for all time as the renunciation of salvation in Christ and the light which shines in darkness (I John 2:8). Therefore the whole counsel of God must now be proclaimed (cf. Acts 20:27; I Cor. 2:2), and men must be adjured to come to faith and repentance. From this time forth (as we read in Hebrews) any despising of Christ's blood is the very same thing as a blaspheming of the Spirit of *grace.*[52]

Therefore, there is every good reason to see lines of con-

---

52. Cf. Acts 17:30. For this reason Bavinck says correctly that the sin against the Spirit is not "a sin against the law alone, but certainly also against the Gospel; moreover, against the Gospel in its clearest revelation" (*op. cit.,* III, 137). Bavinck comments that the devils do not commit this sin, "since God's grace has not appeared to them" (138).

nection between the Gospel accounts which we have cited above
and the rest of the New Testament, especially the book of Hebrews. But the relation is not a relation of a simple identification; nor is there a formal concept of a willful sinning which
brings these various passages together. The adjective *deliberate*
holds equally as well for sins of the Old Testament as for those
of the New. *This,* in other words, cannot be the key for opening up Hebrews 10 or for seeing that passage in the light of
the Gospels. Our theological intuition might tone down the distinction between a sinning against Christ and a sinning against
the Spirit; at the same time, we can never say *why this is the
case* until we have seen the proper relation of the Gospels and
Hebrews. We must note the relation between the veiled and
humiliated Christ in the Gospels and the fully manifest Christ
in Hebrews. Only then can we appreciate that the sin against
the Spirit is a despising of the Christ and the grace of the
Gospel and *therefore* of the Holy Spirit as well.[53]

Heinrich Heppe has summarized this thinking of Reformed
theology as follows. The sin against the Spirit is not an acting
against one's better conscience or a persecuting of the Church
of Christ, but an apostatizing from Christ and his Kingdom
even though one already has the knowledge of Christ through
the Spirit. Therefore it is a falling away in a very conscious
rebellion against the Kingdom of God's grace. It is *this* kind
of willfulness which is manifest in this sin. Reformed theology
has intuitively recoiled from any explanation of this willfulness
in simple psychological terms.[54] She has seen (though inad-
equately) that the standpoint of salvation-history discloses the

---

53. Cf. the *Synopsis Purioris Theologiae,* ed. Bavinck, p. 143: "Definimus
    autem *peccatum in Spiritum Sanctum,* contemptum et oppugnationem
    malitiosam *Christi* et *gratiae evangelicae* per externum verbi auditum
    cognitae *et per Spiritum Sanctum* intus persuasae."
54. A. M. Landgraf (*Dogmengeschichte der Früh-Scholastik,* IV, 1, 1955,
    13-69) gives an extensive analysis of this problem in the period of early
    Scholasticism. The notion of "against one's better knowledge" played
    an important role (14); also the ideas of *obduratio* (16), *ex industria
    peccare* (22), and *obstinatio* (66). Along with these concepts, impeni-
    tence was seen as the heart of the sin against the Spirit (61f.); and the
    effort was made to distinguish *impoenitentia* from *obstinatio.* Still, it
    appears that the early Scholastics were concerned to *fill out* the *ob-
    stinatio-*concept by relating this to the Spirit of *grace;* thus the sin
    against the Spirit was the sin against *the goodness of God.* At the same
    time, we notice a certain confusion in the distinction between the sin
    against the Son of man and the sin against the Spirit. The position of

fullest reason to warn against the irreversible consequences of sin. In the working out of God's salvation plan and its definitive revelation this *mysterium iniquitatis,* this sin against the Spirit, is made known as both christological and pneumatological. When we observe that fact we do not diminish the deathly gravity of this sin, but we do deny its special intrigue and its special quality of "strangeness." Too often the Church has been stymied by the "mystery" of this sin, and its very mystery has been a threat in the lives of believers. An anxious dread has taken hold of those who have thought that they succumbed.

The Christian pastorate gives advice where the Gospel itself directs. But how can the minister give advice when this sin is seen as "mysterious" and "unknown"? It stands to reason that the pastorate tries constantly to show that any real dread is only a sure index that one has *not* committed this sin. Perhaps this is the most common pastoral approach. But it is also commonly frustrated and is sometimes foiled by the stubborn resistance of those whom the pastor would desire most to console. The impotence of such a comfort has everything to do with the *"grande secretum"* of this sin. What comfort is there, after all, in dread? And yet it holds for this sin as well as any other that "perfect love casts out fear" (I John 4:17).

It is important, therefore, to eliminate all grounds for calling this sin "mysterious." We must underscore the deep seriousness of the biblical warning against apostasy "after enlightenment" and "after the knowledge of the truth." This is the apostasy which reviles the Spirit of grace and despises the Son of God and crucifies the Man of Sorrows anew. But since it is the apostasy of sin against the *obviousness of salvation,* there is nothing "mysterious" here at all. The sin against the Spirit is not a particular sin and has no special reference to one of the commandments of God; nor can it be localized in a spec-

Abelard is illustrative here (Landgraf, 18-19): "The question of Heloise, which gives him the occasion for this problem, is simply whether a man is able to sin against the Son of God and not against the Holy Spirit. For the one cannot be offended apart from the other; and the offense against the one necessarily affects both, since the one cannot be favorably disposed toward that which is committed against the other." Therefore Abelard denies that this sin consists in doubting God's pardon. "Sed, si hoc dicimus peccare vel blasphemare in Spiritum, quid dicemus peccare in Filium hominis?" (20).

tacular form or designated "the great sin." We see the contours of this sin in a radical and total, blatant and willful apostasy; therefore the Scripture warns us that we must flee from this sin with our lives. When once we set aside this element of "mystery" the warning against apostasy looms all the larger and is even more cogent in the context of every Christian's experience. For it is exactly the *Christian's* living that is threatened by apostasy. The witness of Scripture has not been given for speculation or a simple judgment on others. It has been given for ourselves, as well as for others, who are tested by the touchstone of the Gospel. Warning and Gospel, the blood of the covenant and the Spirit of grace, are tied up together. Certainly one can speak of a "border concept" or a "terminal sin" when we reflect on this sin against the Spirit: for here we stand at the *extreme limit and final danger at the border of the promised land.* But how can we pass judgment on someone else? When the author of Hebrews noted these things he added immediately: "Though we speak thus, yet in your case, beloved, we feel sure of better things that belong to salvation" (Heb. 6:9).

Why did he write those words? Surely not to anesthetize the hearts of believers or to set them at ease in the vain expectation of no further dangers awaiting them. The most urgent *warning* (vv. 4-8) is here tied up with a very fervent *comfort* (v. 9) as well as a commendation of the works and love of the readers (v. 10). If anywhere in Scripture, certainly here we find a strong antidote to the devaluation of good works performed in the spirit of love. Indeed, these works are even seen as a kind of "counter-evidence" that believers have not overstepped this "final border." The author of Hebrews assures his readers that "God is not so unjust as to overlook your work and the love which you showed for his sake in serving the saints" (6:10). But he also continues to warn: "We desire each of you to show the same earnestness in realizing the full assurance of hope until the end" (6:11). Christians must persevere in that way which is good for themselves and others, and in which they realize their hope. Yet a peril awaits them, and they must not be "sluggish" (6:12). Therefore the Church, in Hebrews 10, is enjoined to "stir up one another to love and good works, ... encouraging one another, and all the more as you see the Day drawing near" (10:24-25). Precisely *this* is the context of this *"final sin."* The sin against the Spirit is not an isolated "riddle" to be solved but is rather a real menace to be guarded against in the concreteness of our living before the gracious face of God and the critical gaze of our fellows.

For that reason it is completely wrong to see this sin as a "mystery" or a single and very special vice. False preaching on this score can lead to serious traumatic disturbances. The Christian pastor must deliver the only message of comfort which can possibly bring relief to those who need it most: the glad tidings of the Gospel. The Gospel must be preached in all its fullness. The rationalistic idea that anxiety itself brings comfort to those who are discomforted will never suffice.[55] The preaching of the Gospel will show us that only in the *rejection of God's good invitation* can we possibly see that "border" from which we are constantly called forth, no matter what our offense, back into the promised land.

We pause briefly to consider the tragic figure of Fritz Spiera. A contemporary of Luther and Calvin, Spiera has always been regarded as a notorious example of a "sinner against the Holy Ghost." Richard Schmitz has recently written a biography in that vein, and begins with these words: "A striking instance of insulting the Holy Spirit, with staggering results, took place at the time of the Reformation."[56] Spiera was impressed by the Reformation revival and dedicated himself to the study of Scripture. He invited others to share in his newly found joy. But at that same time a charge was levelled against him, from within the Catholic Church, where Spiera still retained his membership. He was accused of undermining the ecclesiastical dogma and the authority of the pope. Faced with the choice of withdrawing his statements or dying at the stake,[57] Spiera, in a moment of doubt and frustration, recanted. For five years his

---

55. It is not our purpose here to minimize the so-called "syllogismus practicus." Indeed, we should see that this is inextricably bound up with the conquering of our fears (cf. HC, Lord's Day 32). Note the accent on sanctification in Heb. 10; also, see my chapter on the "syllogismus practicus" in *Divine Election* (Chap. 9, "Election and the Certainty of Salvation"). Yet it should certainly be said that this is a very unclear term.

56. R. Schmitz, *Die Sünde wider den Heiligen Geist. Das Lebensende des Franz Spiera, mit einem Anhang: Judas Ischarioth*, 1957, p. 89. Schmitz opens his book with a discussion of several scriptural references. Cf. *P.R.E.*, *s.v.* "Spiera." Spiera lived c. 1500-1548.

57. Schmitz, *op. cit.*, p. 96.

conscience tormented him and he finally concluded that there was no hope for someone like him. He had committed the sin against the Spirit.[58] No efforts to console him could possibly succeed. Schmitz comes to the conclusion that seldom in the Church's history has such a clear case of apostasy been open to view;[59] we do wrong, he suggests, if we speak of a "religious insanity."[60] Spiera himself rejected that diagnosis and knew full well what he was doing. Therefore Schmitz has no qualms whatever in comparing the sorrow of Spiera to that of Judas Iscariot. In both cases we observe an example of denying the Christ and of blaspheming the Spirit.[61]

But why is it that Schmitz leaves us so cold, and with such an utterly simplistic impression? Why does he even irritate his readers? Certainly *not* because he deals so seriously with a biblical warning or pictures a real threat. The reason lies in his supercilious attitude in condemning these real struggles of Spiera. We cannot use Spiera's own statements to verify the judgment which Schmitz makes on this act of recanting. We can only listen to the biblical warnings which enjoin us to constant self-examination in the light of the Gospel. The case of Spiera was a noted incident in the time of the Protestant Reformation, and many tried to help him in his need.[62] Calvin himself, while criticizing his retraction, admonished the Italians, French, and Germans against any superficial prejudice. He called upon the English to learn "with what awe and how zealously" we must always receive the Christ when once he has revealed himself to us.[63]

Obviously, this situation of Spiera is very complicated. But why should we tarry at this point when the warning is so urgent for our lives? It is in everyday living that the admonition against apostasy takes place. In the midst of living we

58. *Ibid.,* p. 111.
59. *Ibid.,* p. 133.
60. *Ibid.,* p. 135.
61. *Ibid.,* p. 141.
62. *P.R.E.,* XVIII, p. 648.
63. *Ibid.,* p. 649, where a reference is also made to the *Corpus Reformatorum,* 37, 855f. Benrath comments that the *casus Spierae* quite naturally had an interest for Rome, the more so because Spiera saw and experienced his recantation as the sin against the Spirit. Further measures, however, were not taken. There was tacit agreement in the judgment of the priest who thought that Spiera was no longer rationally responsible.

are set before the danger of refusing to believe the *Son*, and
thus sinning against the *Spirit*. For the *Witness* of Christ in our
world is the One who convicts the world of sin when men
refuse to believe the *Son*.

On the one hand this sin is called "unpardonable," for the
one who commits it "never has forgiveness, but is guilty of an
eternal sin" (Mark 3:29). On the other hand it is also impossible for a sinner to repent, for it is "impossible to restore
again to repentance those who have once been enlightened"
(Heb. 6:4). This latter fact has led many to conclude that
the ground of unpardonableness is not so much the magnitude
of one's sin as the subjective disposition of one's heart. The
heart of man excludes the final possibility of renewal, and
therefore there is no forgiveness. St. Augustine already gave the
classic expression to this idea when he defined the sin against
the Spirit as *impoenitentia finalis*.[64]

Here the idea is not to designate this sin by its objective
structure but rather by the subjective stance of the sinner.
In so doing, however, we stand face to face with the problem
of the knowledge of this sin. The words *objective* and *subjective*,
it seems to us, shed very little light. Any sin, in its objectivity,
is performed by the subject, man; and certainly this "border
sin" is no exception. Furthermore, we cannot given an accurate
picture of the finality of this sin by appealing to the term
impoenitentia. Why should we call *this* sin of impenitence the
"final" sin when *all* of sin takes root in the adamantine hearts
of men? Moreover, if we call all sin the sin of impenitence, then
all our sins can be classified as "final."[65] Therefore Calvin was
not happy with this definition of Augustine. He first defined
the way of salvation as the way of repentance (*Inst.*, III, 3, 21)[66]
and then made a further comment on Augustine's view of the
unpardonable sin. This he denied as a "persistent stubbornness
even to death, with distrust of pardon" (III, 3, 22).[67] His objection here is not entirely clear. For in Calvin's own discussion
of the sin against the Spirit he too was concerned largely with

64. Cf. Heppe, *Dogmatik*, p. 260.
65. Ursinus (see *ibid.*) states that the sin against the Spirit is not the
"perseverantia finalis in quocunque peccato."
66. However, "not that repentance, properly speaking, is the cause of salvation, but because it is already seen to be inseparable from faith and
from God's mercy" (*Inst.*, III, 3, 21).
67. "... Obstinata ad mortem usque pervicaciam cum veniae diffidentia."

impenitence.[68] He defined this sin as a resistance in one's heart against the truth of God, even though one is touched with the glory of that truth and cannot plead ignorance (*ibid.*). Therefore this sin is seen as a bitter and hardhearted resistance. "Such resistance alone constitutes this sin" (*ibid.*).

Obviously Calvin was very concerned about the matter of impenitence, but only with the impenitence that plays the dominant role in the Hebrews passages. He was not interested in the intrinsic subjectivity of impenitence but only in subjectivity as the correlate of the salvation which has now appeared, and the knowledge of this which man now has. He distinguished between those who "stumble" (not knowing the truth and blaspheming the Christ in ignorance) and those who bitterly "revile" and refuse the living Word, knowing in their hearts that this Word is *God's*. The former, according to Calvin, sin against the Father and the Son, but the latter sin against the Spirit, for they "strive against the illumination that is the work of the Holy Spirit" (*ibid.*).[69] "Such were certain of the Jews, who, even though they could not withstand the Spirit speaking through Stephen, yet strove to resist" (*ibid.;* Acts 6:10). It is clear, according to Calvin, that many Jews were motivated by a zealous desire for the law, but others "raged against God himself with malicious impiety; that is to say, against the doctrine that they well knew came from God" (*ibid.*). In this line Calvin sees the Pharisees who, "in order to enfeeble the power of the Holy Spirit," slandered Christ by attributing his works to Beelzebul.[70]

Thus Calvin wrestled, on the one hand, with a malicious impenitence; on the other hand, he saw a certain illumination, with its knowledge. But when he presses his distinction between the Jews who were "zealous" for the law and those who were only "obstinate," he adds very little to our knowledge of this sin against the Spirit. We cannot come to clarity in this way. Exactly in this zeal for the law the antagonism against the grace of God is manifest; and here we see the resistance against the Messiah and his Spirit. Stubbornness in this sin is more than a simple recalcitrance and a dogged obstinacy, and is bound up with the salvation which has appeared in Christ. It

68. Apparently Calvin's objection was to the words "even to death."
69. "...Adversus illuminationem, quae opus est Spiritus sancti."
70. Calvin points here to Paul's ignorance. If with unbelief there is *also knowledge,* there is no room for pardon.

is *therefore* a brazen obduracy and contemptible stiffheadedness. Calvin, however, was not blind to seeing impenitence in *this setting*. He spoke of the sin of "ungratefulness" (III, 3, 24) and denied that serious admonition detracts at all from the full goodness of God, "for the author of Hebrews does not say that pardon is refused if they turn to the Lord" *(ibid.)*.[71] The correlation between penance and repentance is not violated in Calvin, and he carefully notes that "otherwise God, who by the prophet proclaims he will be merciful as soon as the sinner repents, would be at war with himself" *(ibid.;* cf. Ezek. 18:21-22).

Everything is here oriented to the theme of repentance; and the warning concerning the sin against the Spirit is a warning that sounds in the midst of man's living. The door is left ajar for those who repent. God's "promise to those who call upon him will never deceive" *(Inst.,* III, 3, 24).[72] It is obvious that Calvin, in discussing this sin, takes issue with the ancient Novatian understanding of Hebrews 10. He is very concerned about the openness of the Church in accepting back into her fellowship the sinner who repents. This was also the problem that animated Tertullian in his Montanist writings, as he fulminated against the "lax practices" of the Church and wished to raise the price for a sinner's forgiveness.[73] In these views he severed the real correlation of penance and pardon and appealed unjustly to the admonitions of the New Testament.[74] The way

71. *Inst.*, III, 3, 24: *"Non* enim denegari veniam dicit si ad Dominum se converterint."
72. *Ibid.*: "De invocatione etiam nunquam fallet promissio."
73. Note especially, in this connection, Tertullian's *De Pudicitia*, where he begins his protest against the edict of the "bishop of bishops." The edict opened a back door for those who had committed fornication and adultery *(De Pudic.,* 1). Tertullian appealed to I John 5:16 (2). The parable of the lost sheep, he contended, applies only to the heathen (7); so too the parable of the lost coin. It is remarkable that Tertullian's standpoint is motivated by a *heilshistorisch* consideration: he is interested in ecclesiastical discipline *since Christ* (6). Everything has *now been changed;* therefore it is wrong, in Tertullian's view, to appeal to earlier examples of forgiveness for fornication and adultery. A temporal boundary is apparent in Christ (6).
74. See the excellent study of H. F. von Campenhausen, *Kirchliches Amt und geistliche Vollmacht in den ersten drei Jahrhunderten*, 1953; especially Chap. 9 ("Der Kampf um die Busze im Abendland"). Von Campenhausen correctly points out that the texts concerning *the* sin against the Spirit do not answer the "concrete question of the later penance discipline: whether, and in which cases, absolution might also be denied to those sorrowing sinners who desire penance" (p. 244). For

was then opened for a quantitative measuring of sin, instead of the New Testament accent on the *gravity of all sin*. No justice was done to the *impenitence* of men in view of the salvation which now has come in Christ.

Luther, along with Calvin, was also concerned about the nature of this sin against the Spirit. Like Calvin, he rooted his argument in God's grace. The sin of the publican was very great; yet greater still was the sin of the Pharisees who denounced the Gospel of God's grace. Von Loewenich has summarized Luther's view in the following sentence: "Resistance against the mercy of God is the only unpardonable sin."[75] This was not a grave "secular" sin but a sin against the holy and the spiritual. Here Luther was not willing to localize this sin in Pharisaism: he was not interested in stubbornness *per se* but in the essence of the Pharisees' resistance. As in the case of Calvin, he centered attention on animosity or enmity against the grace of God.[76] He saw the relation of this sin to the "proper office of the Holy Spirit."[77] Therefore it is obvious why this sin is both christologically and pneumatologically defined, and why the Church is warned against resisting the Holy Spirit — that is to say, the Spirit of *Christ* and the Spirit of *God's grace*.

In this same perspective it is possible to escape the notion that this sin is a *grande secretum* or a "mystery" whose inner nature eludes us. The urgent warning against this extreme peril should be enough to eliminate that thought. We cannot isolate this sin or pretend that it stands apart from other sins of resistance against the Spirit. Think only of the case of Ananias and Sapphira. There the words of Peter are significant: "Why has Satan filled your heart to lie to the Holy Spirit?" (Acts 5:3; cf. v. 4). The account of this sin and God's reaction were not written to give an answer to the query: Was the "border" overstepped or not?[78] Suffice it to say that the early Church

these texts simply do not take account of contrition. See also the discussion of New Testament texts in B. Poschmann, *Handbuch der Dogmengeschichte*, IV, 3, 1951 ("Busze und Letzte Ölung," 3-10). For the earlier standpoint of Tertullian, cf. *De Poenitentia*. Tertullian distantiated himself from this in his *De Pudicitia*.

75. W. von Loewenich, *Luther als Ausleger der Synoptiker*, 1954, pp. 144-145.

76. Luther also speaks of the "impugnatio veritatis agnitae" (*ibid.*, p. 145).

77. Heppe, *Dogmatik*, p. 259: the "proprium officium Spiritus Sancti." Cf. Cocceius' reference to Hebrews 6; *ibid.*, p. 261.

78. Therefore this question does not come to the fore in Grosheide. Cf.

was very impressed by the seriousness of what happened. How can deceiving and lying find place in the domicile of the Holy Spirit or the living Church of Jesus Christ? The death of Ananias was seen as an omen of the Spirit himself — "and great fear came upon all who heard of it" (5:5). Now that the Spirit had come as the Great Witness of the resurrected Lord, the stern warning was broadcast for those who resist the Christ. This explains the severity of the words of Stephen ("full of the Holy Spirit"; Acts 7:55) as he called for repentance.[79]

The New Testament does not point to a single final sin but focuses attention on a certain resistance or antagonism. Of this it *warns the Church*. Therefore the Church is cautioned not to "grieve the Holy Spirit of God, in whom you were sealed for the day of redemption" (Eph. 4:30). Why is it that many who discuss this sin against the Spirit make only a passing reference to this text and seldom take note of that other passage: "Do not quench the Spirit" (I Thess. 5:19)? Possibly this kind of "isolation," or "bracketing," explains more than anything else exactly why people have insisted on calling the sin against the Spirit a *grande secretum*. The final gravity of Paul's words is only obvious in the context of warning: "Let all bitterness and wrath and anger and clamor and slander be put away from you, with all malice" (Eph. 4:31). This is another way of saying: Do not grieve and do not quench the Spirit.[80]

Some have seen these words on grieving the Spirit as a prime example that the New Testament never gets beyond the "anthropomorphism" of the Old. But certainly these words demonstrate (as well as their Old Testament counterparts) the grave possibility of "grieving the Spirit." The Old Testament already speaks of this "grieving" in very urgent tones: "but they rebelled and grieved his holy Spirit" (Isa. 63:10). Was Paul thinking of Isaiah when he wrote his own words? Schlier doubts that this was the case,[81] though Ewald thinks it was.[82] In any event, the repugnance of "grieving the Spirit" is underscored in the words that Paul then adds: "... in whom

K.V., I, 77, on the possibility of Ananias' repentance. Grosheide (159) points out that Ananias wanted to be "praised like a Barnabas."

79. *Ibid.*, 115.

80. Cf. I Thess. 5:20: "Do not despise prophesying" (*exouthenein*: regard it as nothing, despise it utterly; treat it with contempt).

81. H. Schlier, *Der Brief an die Epheser*, 1958, p. 227.

82. Zahn, *Komm.*, *ad loc.*

you were sealed for the day of redemption" (Eph. 4:30) .[83] Paul
never gave warning apart from comfort, nor comfort apart from
warning. He implored *believers* to have nothing to do with
the children of disobedience, on whom the wrath of God was
poured (Eph. 5:6). *Believers* were not to fall back again to
heathendom (5:7-10) .[84] "For once you were darkness, but now
you are light in the Lord; walk as children of light" (5:8).
Believers must not grieve the Spirit or close the "eyes of their
hearts," but must look constantly on Christ's glory.[85]

The admonitions not to "resist the Spirit" are set forth
within the full fabric of the *Gospel*. Therefore this "final sin"
must be seen in the closest relation to the entire preaching of
the Spirit of Christ, who lives within the Church (cf. I Cor.
6:19) .[86] Anyone who refuses to take this "final sin" very seriously, or dismisses it because it is difficult to square with the
perseverance of the saints, has made a caricature of its confession.[87] At the same time, every warning against resistance must
be seen as a reference to that border which is never pointed
to in order to disquiet us but rather to call us back again to
that *"promised land" which we already possess.*[88]

---

83. Bultmann understands *lypeín* in Eph. 4:30 in the sense of "to wound,"
"to insult"; see *TWNT*, IV, *s.v. lýpē*. In the commentaries a frequent
reference is made to the Pastor of Hermas, with its "far-reaching
speculations" ("ausführliche Speculationen"; Schlier, 227). Bultmann
further points to the admonition which appears as the "word of the
Lord" in Pseudo-Cyprian and reminds us of a combination of Eph.
4:30 and I Thess. 5:19: "nolite *contristare* spiritum sanctum qui in
vobis est, et nolite *exstinguere* lumen quod in vobis effulsit" (*TWNT*,
loc. cit.).

84. The new situation was this: the heathen were now fellow-sharers, or
joint-partakers in God's promise *(symmétochoi tēs epangelías)*. But
therefore: "Take no part *(mē synkoinōneite)* in the unfruitful works
of darkness, but instead expose them" (Eph. 5:11).

85. Cf. the "enlightened eyes of your hearts" — enlightened to see what is
now accomplished in Christ (Eph. 1:18, 20); also the "spirit of wisdom
and of revelation in the knowledge of him" (v. 17).

86. Cf. Christ who lives within the heart, Eph. 3:17.

87. Cf. my *Faith and Perseverance*, 1958; also M. Barth, *The Broken Wall*,
1959, pp. 160ff.

88. The "quenching" of the Spirit is usually related to extraordinary
charismatic gifts of the Holy Spirit. Cf. B. Rigaux, *Les épîtres aux
Thessaloniciëns*, p. 591. This, however, does not mitigate the seriousness
of the warning; cf. I Thess. 5:19-24. When Van Leeuwen writes
(Komm., p. 392) that the issue is not the regenerating and sanctifying
work of the Spirit, "who is irresistible," but the revelation and work

Why then should we call this sin a *grande secretum?* We can appreciate what Augustine had in mind when he utilized that term. The specifically pneumatological accent in the Gospels has always stirred a whirlpool of debate. Furthermore, who can substitute for the "mysteriousness" of this sin a lucid explanation which can make it "rational"? The gravity of this sin lies precisely in its enigmatic character against the background of God's grace. But that enigma of guilt is a far cry from the "mysteriousness" which men have commonly attached to this sin against the Spirit. When we call this sin a "mystery" we only break down our defenses against it. On the other hand, the armor of Ephesians 6 has no weak links and does not fail us when we put it on (cf. Eph. 6:13).[89] It repels the most violent enemy. And could that be any different for the man who wields the "sword of the Spirit" (6:17)?

When someone calls this sin the "sin of our century" (as G. Wisse has done)[90] we sense immediately the peril of a temporal limitation and the strictures of applying a model of time. The man who refuses to accept that model does not violate the seriousness of this sin.[91] The real gravity of the sin against the Spirit is evident in the unbroken harmony of comfort and warning. This is a theme that is constantly underscored in the preaching of the New Testament. Here, then, is a message for these "last days." For the "mystery which was kept secret for long ages" has now been revealed in Jesus Christ (Rom. 16:25), and the "final sin" is more apparent now than ever before. But we need not be indifferent, on the one hand, or try to persecute ourselves, on the other. "The blood of Jesus... cleanses us from all sin. ... If we confess our sins, he is faithful and just, and will forgive our sins and cleanse us from all unrighteousness" (I John 1:7, 9).

---

of the Spirit in special charismata, the presupposition seems to be that resisting the Spirit is only possible in charismatic situations.

89. Cf. in this connection HC, Q. 103: *"let the Lord work in me"* by his Holy Spirit."

90. Wisse, *op. cit.*, p. 12. Cf. footnote 9, above.

91. Note the many qualifications in Wisse himself; *ibid.*, pp. 12-16.

CHAPTER ELEVEN

SIN, WRATH, AND FORGIVENESS

THE MAN WHO listens to the biblical indictment of sin as enmity and rebellion against God — as transgression, pride and apostasy — can only take seriously what Scripture says concerning the wrath of God. But we must not forget that this subject has been the occasion for an animated and even emotional debate. Is there any reason to speak of God's *wrath;* or does this very subject do violence to the concept of *God?* Should we set the Old Testament against the New and find in the Old the traits of a "wrathful God" while preserving for the New the "God of love"? This approach has quite frequently been made. Men have discovered the reality of God's wrath by pointing to Jesus Christ as the *revelation of his love.* The purpose of the advent is then seen as the elimination of all human misconceptions concerning the reality of God's wrath and the disclosure of the love of God as diffused among all men. Thus the wrath of God is pre-empted by his love. The strongest "proof" of this idea is found in the first letter of John: *"God is love"* (4:9, 16).

Now it is striking how many difficulties and problems remain when we go in this direction. All of these are tied together with the fact that the biblical witness warns us so emphatically of God's wrath. In the Old Testament, but also in the New, we find this unassailable accent. If we look at the very heart of the Gospel (the Gospel of *joy!*) and the very context of an invitation to faith, we already hear the piercing ring of Christ's words: "He who believes in the Son has eternal life; he who does not obey the Son shall not see life, but the wrath of God rests upon him" (John 3:36). Here the Gospel does not shift its course and flow in a different direction. John the Baptist already, pointing to the Lamb of God, specifically mentioned in his preaching of the Kingdom the reality of *wrath.* When he saw the Pharisees with their tainted motives

354

presenting themselves for baptism he reprimanded them: "You brood of vipers! Who warned you to flee from the wrath to come?" (Matt. 3:7).[1] He who refuses to reckon with God's wrath must find the New Testament completely incomprehensible. But more than that; for the scriptural injunctions on God's wrath do not suggest an original or primitive conception which may soon be overcome. They indicate, instead, the relation between the sin of man and the wrath of God. Man, in his intransigence and impenitence, "stores up wrath" for the "day of wrath" and the final revelation of the righteous judgment of God (Rom. 2:5; cf. II Pet. 3:7). Yet there is also the sound of jubilee: Jesus "delivers us from the wrath to come" (I Thess. 1:10). The Gospel neither eliminates our human "ignorance" nor takes away our human "misunderstanding"; at the same time, our broken communion is restored and our lostness is reversed in a new and surprising "being found." Divine forgiveness is never, in Scripture, an indifferent love or a matter of God's *being blind*. It is rather a turning from real *wrath* to real *grace*.

We need not wonder that this theme of God's wrath has called forth such frequent and embittered controversy.[2] That fact has everything to do with the Bible's message of jubilee and forgiveness — a message which is tied together in a single package with the knowledge of the wrath of God against man's sin. It is reasonable that a softening down or denying of God's wrath has frequently gone with a relativizing of man's guilt. Indeed, an optimistic vision of man's plight has always implied an emptying of God's wrath.[3] Those who hold to this

---

1. Cf. F. W. Grosheide, *Comm. Matt.*, pp. 44-45.
2. We cite the following from the literature. From the ancient Church: Lactantius, *De Ira Dei*. From later times: A. Ritschl, *Rechtfertigung und Versöhnung*, II[4], 1900, 119-156; III, 300 (already in 1859, *De Ira Dei*); M. Pohlenz, *Vom Zorne Gottes. Eine Studie über den Einflusz der Griech. Philosophie auf das alte Christentum*, 1909; L. Pinomaa, "Der Zorn Gottes," *Z.S.Th.*, 1940; *idem, Der Zorn Gottes in der Theologie Luthers*, 1938; E. Brunner, "Der Zorn Gottes und die Versöhnung durch Christus," *Zw.d.Z.*, 1927; K. Barth, *K.D.*, II/1, 410ff. (ET, 365ff.); R. V. G. Tasker, *The Biblical Doctrine of the Wrath of God*, 1951; A. T. Hanson, *The Wrath of the Lamb*, 1957; *TWNT, s.v. orgḗ*; A. Rüegg, "Zorn Gottes," in *P.R.E.*, XXI, 719-729.
3. This point is referred to in the *P.R.E.* article on God's wrath ("Zorn Gottes"). Here a witness is also cited from the time of the Enlightenment (Wegscheider). The scriptural passages on the wrath of God were seen, at that time, as "merely the cross anthropopathisms of a backward age,

optimism have levelled their charges against this "unbiblical theologoumenon"; at the same time, an unbiased study of Scripture can only impress upon us the number and frequency of the biblical allusions to God's wrath. Obviously, it is futile merely to wish these away. Their undeniability has led Otto, for example, in the face of the rationalizing and humanizing tendencies of his day, to put stress on the *"mysterium tremendum"* of God's holiness and majesty. Otto saw that the Old Testament wrath of Jahwe emerges again in the New Testament;[4] he contended that we Christians must learn to know the reality of God's wrath. He took a position opposed to Schleiermacher and Ritschl.[5] Brunner, too, has crossed swords with Schleiermacher and Ritschl and has tried to avoid all negative reflections on God's wrath. He has spoken of the indissoluble unity (the *"unauflösliche Einheit"*) of the entire Christian message and the reality of God's wrath.[6] Karl Barth has accused Ritschl of an "exegetical violence" (*"exegetische Gewalttat"*) which could only eliminate grace as well as wrath.[7]

Now surely the differences between Ritschl and those who less quickly deny the reality of God's wrath, in our own day, are very apparent. These latter are very sensitive, at times, to the biblical witness.[8] But the crescendo of opposition against Ritschl is clearly indicative of the unmistakable clarity of Scripture. In our own century it is no longer out of fashion to be concerned about the reality of God's wrath.[9]

which pictured the divine justice according to human emotions" (p. 719).

4. R. Otto, *Das Heilige*, 1925[13], p. 18.
5. *Ibid.*, p. 19.
6. E. Brunner, *op. cit.*, p. 94.
7. K. Barth, *op. cit.*, 411 (ET, 366). Especially Ritschl's name comes up for discussion in all these treatments of God's wrath. In his judgment "the conception of a wrathful emotion in God is of no religious value for Christians, but is rather an alien as well as a worthless theologoumenon" (Ritschl, *op. cit.*, II, 154).
8. Cf. Barth's criticism of Otto (*K.D.*, II/1, 405; ET, 360-361). Barth refers to "the Holy One of Israel" in contrast to "the Holy" ("das Heilige"). For Otto's view of the irrational, and the "ideogram" of God's wrath as an aspect of feeling in religious experience, cf. *Das Heilige*, p. 19.
9. We cite, e.g., P. Althaus, *Die christliche Wahrheit*, II, 1948, 162ff.; H. Vogel, *Gott in Christo*, 1952, pp. 507ff.; R. Prenter, *Schöpfung und Erlösung*, I, 1958, 208f., 211f. On the influence of Ritschl, and of Harnack's *Das Wesen des Christentums*, see W. Robinson, "The Judgment of God," in *Scottish Journal of Theology*, 1951, pp. 137ff.

Many have denied the reality of that wrath with the argument that such talk in Scripture is really anthropomorphic. Therefore the references to this "affection" should not be taken as literal. Wrath is then seen in distinctly human terms and is surrounded by reservations and warnings. Paul's admonition to the Christian community sets wrath on a par with bitterness, clamor, and revenge; thus Paul sees wrath alongside those things which are contraband in the Christian Church and stand opposed to the new man "created after the likeness of God in true righteousness and holiness" (Eph. 4:24). Anger and quarrelling are seen in contrast to prayer (I Tim. 2:8), and a warning is sounded against "every one who is angry with his brother" (Matt. 5:22). The bishop must be blameless, and no drunkard, and he may not be "arrogant or quick-tempered" (Tit. 1:7); for anger brings forth no righteousness (James 1:19-20; cf. Eph. 6:4). When we reflect on these things, we can certainly understand why some people have regarded the idea of God's wrath as a very clear case of biblical anthropomorphism.

But it is remarkable that we read of an anger in Scripture which is *not blameworthy*. The Apostle Paul, though he condemned man's anger (Eph. 4:31), could write in the very same context: "Be angry but do not sin; do not let the sun go down on your anger" (4:26). Quite obviously, anger is not incompatible with "new life"; and this fact remains despite all the warnings and qualifications which Paul gives. There may not be and there cannot be a protracted anger. Furthermore, the seriousness of this injunction is plain from the words which follow: "give no opportunity to the devil" (4:27). The Power of Darkness finds room, in the *prolonging* of man's wrath, for its own pernicious and nefarious work. Some have seen in this reference to a ceasing of wrath a certain kinship to the older moralists (for example, the Pythagoreans) who argued that all controversy must end before the sun goes down below the earth's horizon. But in Paul there is no such moralizing strain; there is only the injunction to "put on the new man." Anger is not necessarily a sinful impulse, but may only be temporary and may not be prolonged. There are powers (like Satan himself) who are unimpeded by the passing of day to night and who know no boundaries. Therefore Satan is described as the "accuser of our brethren ... *day and night*" (Rev. 12:10). But the "new man," in contrast, does know of the temporality of wrath. He knows that we may not eternalize or absolutize the anger of a *man*. Sinful men who extend their anger beyond the setting of the sun prefer to do what is no longer human: they make no transition from wrath to forgiveness, and thus leave room for the devil. In the biblical perspective the opportunity must be real for a return to him against whom we are righteously angry. Therefore Paul places prolonged anger, with all of its perils, among those fearful acts which he mentions in Ephesians 4. To understand what he means we must take account of this ambivalent use of the concept of *anger*. We must also see the persistent warnings on the proximity of the devil.

These statements on the danger of human anger must not be taken as an argument against the reality of *God's wrath*.[10] Rather, a sharpened insight into the perils of man's anger will actually enhance our appreciation for the scriptural language concerning the wrath of God. In the face of human perils Christians in the Church are enjoined to take no revenge; yet they are asked to "leave room" for wrath (Rom. 12:19). Obviously, the wrath referred to here is the wrath of *God*. For the statement then follows: "Vengeance is mine, I will repay, says the Lord" (cf. Deut. 32:35). The man who avenges himself in wrath does not leave room for the wrath of God; instead he takes punishment into his own hands. In such an activity the problems of injustice and enmity are *not* resolved but are only confused and are rendered insoluble.[11] What the believer must do is this: "if your enemy is hungry, feed him; if he is thirsty, give him to drink.... Do not be overcome by evil, but overcome evil with good" (Rom. 12:20-21). Here we can certainly speak of an "overcoming" or a "victory"; but the victory is not the victory of man's anger but the victory of God. The weapons of vengeance are now thrown aside, and everything is surrendered into the hands of him who is perfect and righteous, with a pure and holy wrath against all injustice. For

10. Paul asks, in Romans 3:5, if "God is unjust to inflict wrath on us," but he also adds, "I speak in a human way." Yet this latter statement does not imply an anthropomorphism in the image of God's wrath; it refers instead to the boldness of asking this question, Is God unjust? This fact appears more clearly in the Greek text: *mē ádikos ho theós ho epiphérōn tēn orgēn; katá ánthrōpon légō.* Cf. Michel, *Komm.*, p. 82, in reference to this "apology"; also H. N. Ridderbos, *Comm.*, p. 73.

11. Cf. K. Barth, *Der Römerbrief*, 1923², pp. 455f.

he is "of purer eyes than to behold evil and cannot look on wrong" (Hab. 1:13).

When we study the biblical witness we soon discover that this wrath of God is not an irrational or an incomprehensible kind. It is not a capricious vehemence which falls upon us and before which we are simply powerless. Nor is it an enigma in terms of which we see no sense at all. The wrath of God is pictured in Scripture as a divine reaction, or as the answer to that which has happened and continues to happen on "man's side." Therefore we can speak of the *comprehensibility* of God's wrath. Certainly it is not "comprehensible" in the sense of a naive and automatic activity but rather in the sense of a divine and dynamic "re-activity" in the lives of men. In that light we may speak of a God who "has indignation every day" (Ps. 7:11) and whose indignation is by no means an irrational affection of which he unburdens himself. God's anger is the indignation of a God who has "bent and strung his bow" for the eventuality that man does *not repent* (7:12). Here, then, we are touching on an important point concerning the wrath of God. His wrath is the reaction to apostasy and unchastity and other evils which rightly deserve death (Rom. 1:32). And no man can find an excuse (cf. 1:20).

Therefore, the wrath of God is the answer to ungodliness and wickedness (cf. Rom. 1:18) and is roused by the sins of men and the forsaking of his ways. God appears as the "enemy" of his people; yet his wrath is by no means arbitrary or strange. "Antagonism" is viewed as the divine answer to men's obduracy. "They rebelled and grieved his holy Spirit; *therefore* he turned to be their enemy" (Isa. 63:10). Against the "crooked" God has shown himself an adversary (Ps. 18:26).[12] His fire "was kindled against Jacob, his anger mounted against Israel; *because* they had no faith in God, and did not trust his saving power" (Ps. 78:21-22). *Therefore* "he made their days vanish like a breath, and their years in terror" (78:33).[13] Thus it is entirely reasonable to speak of a *motive* for God's wrath. Nonetheless J. Fichtner has asserted that alongside this Old Testament motive there are other elements of something *irrational*.[14] To

---

12. Cf. my *Faith and Perseverance*, 1958, pp. 181ff.
13. The whole of Psalm 78 is full of the fierce anger of the Lord, in opposition to a lack of appreciation. Cf. also Ps. 106:32, 40.
14. *TWNT*, V, *s.v. orgē*, B. III. 4. Fichtner refers to Job and various psalms.

be sure, it is conceivable that man's subjective experience could eclipse or entirely lose sight of the transparency of God's wrath; yet the clarity and the meaning of that wrath against man's sin are increasingly evident in Scripture. Fichtner himself acknowledges that "Increasingly, of course, Yahweh's dealings are lifted out of the sphere of the incalculable, and there is closer investigation of the reasons for His wrath. This is seen to be a reaction to the acts or failures of men."[15]

Here it is remarkable that we read of God's wrath not only against the nations of the world, in their iniquity and their attacks on God's people,[16] but also against the people of God themselves. There especially the motive of anger is very sharply defined. Frequently, in reference to Judah's and Israel's sin, we hear the words *because* and *therefore* (cf. Amos 2:4-16). When God's judgment impinges upon his own people, the question of the foreigner and the following generation and "all the nations" is *why*: "Why has the Lord done thus to this land? What means the heat of this great anger?" (Deut. 29:22, 24). It is then that the answer is given: "It is *because* they forsook the covenant of the Lord, the God of their fathers, which he made with them when he brought them out of the land of Egypt, and went and served other gods and worshipped them . . . ; *therefore* the anger of the Lord was kindled against this land" (Deut. 29:25, 26).[17] In this *wherefore/therefore* the real motive and the clarity of God's wrath are very evident.

One finds, in the Scripture, a great variety of stirring expressions and descriptions for the wrath of God. We read, for example, of the "fire of his anger," his "burning wrath," and the God who has "indignation every day." Yet this wrath is constantly set forth as the opposite of any disinterest toward

Yet exactly in these the disjunction between arbitrariness and God's anger is constantly evident.

15. *Ibid.* Cf. W. Eichrodt, *Theologie des Alten Testaments*, I, 1939², 132ff.
16. Cf. the examples in *TWNT*, *loc. cit.*, and the repeated "because" as motivation of God's wrathful activity in Amos 1:3-23; also Gen. 19, and Mic. 5:15: "And in anger and wrath I will execute vengeance upon the nations that did not obey." Cf. Tasker, *op. cit.*, pp. 11f.
17. Note the compelling force of this "because," and the clear "causality" in God's judgment, in such a passage as Micah 2:3, 5 ("therefore"!). When this judgment is regarded as impossible and the appeal is made to God's *patience* ("Is the Spirit of the Lord impatient?" 2:7), the answer is a reference to the rising of God's people as *enemy* (2:8). Note the strong words in Zeph. 1:14-18.

that which takes place before God's holy eyes. The man who savors these expressions is rightly impressed at the great distance here from any notion of God's "apathy," or any similar concept which stresses the "immutable, impassive" being of God.[18] We can never understand the biblical message of God's wrath by following this line; in fact, when once we accept a divine "apathy" it is impossible to warn against a dualism. In the wrath of God we are not gazing at the shadow side of God's being, or some dark and dreary attribute; for "God is light and in him is no darkness at all" (I John 1:5). Much rather, we are looking at the wrath of the *living God;* and whenever we hear of his wrath we also hear of his mercy.

All of this is implied in the fact that in God's election of Israel (that is to say, in the covenant) the possiblity of his being a wrathful God is by no means precluded. His wrath is ignited and burns precisely there where election is misapprehended and the covenant is forsaken. *Because* God elected *Israel* from all the nations of the earth, he also punishes her for all her iniquities (Amos 3:2; cf. Zeph. 1:12). The wrath of Jahwe is directed against the revolt against his holy will and the apostasy of Israel;[19] thus it is completely consistent with his own accusation. No wonder that the heavens are entreated to "be appalled . . ., be shocked, be utterly desolate," for God's people have forsaken the "fountain of living waters" (Jer. 2:12-13) and have done what no other nation has done, forsaking Jahwe for other gods (2:10-11). For that reason Jahwe entered into a controversy with his people (Mic. 6:3), the nature of which is of very great importance for understanding the nature of his wrath. The controversy begins with this disconcerting question: *"O my people,* what have I done to you? In what have I wearied you? Answer me. For I brought you up from the land of Egypt, and *redeemed* you from the house of bondage" (6:3-4). God's indictment is set forth in the form of a profound accusation. The question asked in no way detracts from his anger but points to the nature of his wrath against the background of his gracious and redeeming activity.[20]

---

18. The strange results of this kind of thinking are apparent in such an analysis as that of M. Pohlenz, *op. cit.* On the consequences of these ideas in the christological controversy, cf. pp. 66f.

19. *TWNT, loc. cit.*

20. Cf. Jer. 2:5: "What wrong did your fathers find in me that *they went far from me . . .?" "Therefore* I still contend with you" (2:9). "Why do

In that same vein we should read the repeated "woes" in Isaiah 5. That chapter is prefaced by the "song of the vineyard" in which Jahwe is portrayed as doing all there was to do (5:8, 11, 18, 20-22). We read of an *expectation* which was unfulfilled (5:2, 4), and therefore of a divine disappointment. The emotional element in God's answer is the reaction of his wrath to this unfulfilled desire. God's vineyard, instead of bearing good grapes, produced only wild ones; and the result was this clearly-motivated judgment of his wrath. "I will also command the clouds that they rain no rain upon it" (5:6). Thus a somewhat different situation arises from that of the judge who condemns a man for breaking a law. For the situation here is the situation of a *lack of appreciation:* it is the situation of man's ignoring God and grieving his Spirit. In short, it is the situation of man's recalcitrance (Isa. 63:10). The wrath of God, as pictured in the prophets, has everything to do with the mystery of this *unrequited love* and of man's own breaking of the covenant. Thus we see the wrath of God in its clearest focus: as motivated by the sins of men.[21]

It should not surprise us that the New Testament also makes mention of God's wrath. Some, as we have seen, have denied this by appealing to the mutual "exclusiveness" of wrath and love, or by viewing the Old and New Testaments in opposition. But the reasons why this "exclusiveness" is lacking in the Old Testament are the *very reasons why it is also lacking in the New.* We must not detract from the revelation of Christ as the One who was sent by the Father's love (cf. I John 4:9; John 3:16); yet, in the name of that love, we must not oppose the reality of God's wrath. Already in the preaching of the herald, John the Baptist, we find a clear reference to the wrath of God: the "axe is laid to the root of the trees" and the "winnowing

you complain against me?" (2:29). "Have I been a wilderness to Israel, or a land of thick darkness?" (2:31). Cf. the "why" in Jer. 2:14.

21. One might also think of the zeal or jealousy of Jahwe: "I the Lord your God am a jealous God" (LXX: *zēlōtḗs*). Cf. Deut. 29:26ff.: no forgiveness because of the wrath and jealousy of the Lord. This jealousy was aroused because of strange gods, apostasy, and infidelity. Cf. *TWNT*, II, *s.v. zḗlos;* and Jean Daniélou, "La jalousie de Dieu," *Dieu vivant. 16. Perspectives religieuses et philosophiques,* pp. 63f., who rightly opposes the criticism of this "affect." This zeal or jealousy is indissolubly tied together with what Jahwe has wished to be and to remain, in his love, for his people (cf. Ex. 20:5).

fork" is in God's hand (Matt. 3:10, 12). On hearing this we might think of an antithesis between the wrath and love of God, especially when we remember that this same John had second thoughts regarding the messiahship of Jesus. "Are you he who is to come, or shall we look for another?" (Matt. 11:3). The answer is very instructive. John is reminded of the joyful deeds of which he himself was the witness, even though these deeds were also the occasion for his present doubts. He is reminded of the *joy* of the new messianic era for the blind and the lame, for lepers and the deaf, for those who had already died, as well as for the poor who had received the Good News (11:5-6). John, by looking at these signs, would be reconvinced of the fact that Christ was truly the One who was to come. No one else was to be expected. Here was the Messiah who now preaches the advent of the "acceptable year of the Lord" (Luke 4:19).[22] This was the year which was now made manifest in the joyful *signs of restoration and liberty*.

This being the case, we are faced with the question of whether there is any room for wrath in the life and ministry of Jesus. It is very remarkable that whenever we hear of wrath in the Gospels it is *not a restriction of the Good News* but is rather a reference to the antagonism against the Kingdom as now revealed, or salvation as now proclaimed. The preaching of God's salvation is the burning issue and the real content of the messianic era.[23] But this content is not incompatible with

22. Cf. Isa. 61:1-2: "the year of the Lord's favor." The prophecy of Isaiah is fulfilled "today" (Luke 4:21). Cf. the reference to Isa. 49:8 and II Cor. 6:2.

23. J. Jeremias, in his *Jesu Verheissung für die Völker,* 1956, has noted that Jesus breaks off his quotation of Isaiah 61 at the point at which Isaiah himself continues: "and the day of vengeance of our God" (61:2). From this fact Jeremias explains the reaction of Jesus' listeners, not only in Luke 4:28f. (wrath, rejection) but also earlier — their "wondering" at the "words of *grace*" which came from his mouth (4:22). Jeremias sees in the words *emartýroun autō* not a witness *to* but a witness *against* Jesus, because of his "words of *grace*." "Jesus omits the day of vengeance." K. Bornhäuser, as Jeremias has noted, has also given this same interpretation. Already in 4:22, according to this view, we find an indignation ("Entrüstung") because of this abridgment of Scripture; and therefore there is no "change of mood" as we compare 4:28f. and 4:22. The *thaumázein* here is an astonishment which later turned into a protest and action — after the recollection of the healing of Naaman (v. 27). Cf. also Jeremias' comments on Isaiah 35 and Matthew 11:5f. (parallel to Luke 7:22f.). The references to "vengeance" and "recompense" (Isa. 35:4) are missing in the New

the words of the Gospel concerning the anger of the Lord, or
with Christ's own pointing to the wrath of God. Precisely *in*
these relations it is evident how intimately wrath is tied up
with the rejection of salvation. God's wrath is proclaimed as
abiding on him who "does not obey the Son" (John 3:36). For
that reason Christ was angered at the profanation of the temple,
for the temple is the *gracious presence of God* (John 2:13ff.). He
was also vexed at the hardening of men's hearts,[24] and he
warned them concerning the judgment of those who refuse to
repent despite the powers and signs which were now available.

Yet, this accusation and warning and wrath are not in conflict with Christ's own coming to save the world and not to
condemn (John 3:17; 12:47). In fact, they are inextricably
conjoined with the purpose of his coming. Exactly because of
his coming he marvelled at unbelief (Mark 6:6) and was
angered at the power of death in the case of Lazarus (John
11:33, 38); he directed his "zeal" against all that stood in the
way of his purpose and advent (John 2:17). Therefore he
issued his "woes" against the Pharisees who violated and misinterpreted the mystery of God's grace (cf. Matt. 21:13). When
seen in the context of this revelation of salvation, the wrath of
God is not incompatible with the Gospel but is tied up with
the Gospel; and precisely that fact is especially evident in the
warnings of Christ's parables concerning the Kingdom.[25] There,
too, his word of judgment was set against the background of his
unceasing concern for salvation: "How often would I have
gathered your children together as a hen gathers her brood

Testament quotation. Also Greijdanus (contra Bornhäuser), in *Komm.*
Lukas, I, 212.

24. One thinks of his looking upon his opponents "with anger" *(met'*
orgēs), as mentioned, e.g., in Mark 3:5. But this anger was not an
uncontrolled emotion; for it was coupled with "grief" *(syllypoúmenos)*
at the hardness of their hearts, and was bound up with the act of
healing as the sign of the Kingdom (Mark 3:5). In connection with the
variant readings of Mark 1:41 ("moved with pity," or *orgistheis),*
cf. Tasker, *op. cit.,* p. 30; Hanson, *op. cit.,* p. 114; and M. H. Bolkestein, *Het Verborgen Rijk,* 1954, p. 51 (angered with "divine anger at
the misery of this world").

25. Cf. Mark 12:9; Matt. 25:31-46; 21:28-32. The words of judgment are
sharply set forth in the parable of the fig tree (Luke 13:6-9; parallel
to Isa. 5, song of the vineyard), where even an ultimatum and a whole
year of meticulous husbandry produce no fruit (13:8-9). Cf. Matt.
21:18-22; also the parable of the marriage feast (22:1-14), where the
word of judgment is tied to an urgent invitation.

under her wings, and you would not" (Luke 13:34; Matt. 23:37).
Therefore the verdict which follows: "Behold, your house is
forsaken."[26] In the revelation of Christ the wrath of *God* is
reflected when the lost are sought and do *not want to be found.*

In that light, there is no contradiction between God's love
and wrath in the New Testament. These are not incongruent
but are mutually related in historical and dynamical terms.
They are interrelated in the preaching of salvation and man's
lack of appreciation and response.[27] Surely this wrath of God
played the same role in the preaching of the apostles; for
there too it cannot be seen as an inhibition of salvation but
as an urgent invitation to accept the Good News of God. All
of this received especially poignant articulation in the concept of the "coming wrath" (cf. I Thess. 1:10). We hear of the
song of praise to Jesus who delivers from the "coming wrath";
but we also hear of the "storing up of wrath" in impenitence,
as we wait for the "day of wrath" (Rom. 2:5).[28] The "power
of wrath" which men confront in the way of infidelity and injustice is not an impersonal force[29] but is rather a "coming
wrath" which stands in an indissoluble relation to the revelation
of God in Jesus Christ (cf. Col. 3:6; Eph. 5:6). "Since he came
into the world there takes place the eschatological judgment of
the world, both pardon (justification) and the sentence of
wrath."[30]

The question, then, is this: "How shall we escape if we
neglect such a great salvation," which was declared to us "at
first by the Lord" (Heb. 2:3)?[31] In the preaching of the com-

---

26. Cf. Grosheide, *Comm.*, p. 355; pain and judgment ("smart en oordeel").
    Your house is "left over to you: it becomes *their* house and will no
    longer be God's house."
27. Cf. *TWNT, art. cit.*, E. II. 2.
28. Cf. *ibid.*, E. II. 3.
29. Contra Hanson, *op. cit.*, who derives the impersonal character of wrath
    from the fact, e.g., that Scripture frequently speaks of "wrath" instead
    of the "wrath of God." Cf. further P. A. van Stempvoort, "Het Oordeel
    in het Nieuwe Testament," *Vox Theologica,* 1953, pp. 157ff.
30. *TWNT, loc. cit.*, and cf. E. II. 7.
31. Cf. Rom. 2:5, where reference to the coming wrath ("the day of
    wrath") is clearly in the context of warning against despising the riches
    of God's kindness (2:4). Rüegg has rightly remarked (*P.R.E.*, 722) that
    it is incorrect to see wrath as merely a means to an end, or as merely
    pedagogical, since wrath is thereby turned to love. Such a view renders
    wrath a mere appearance, or a pretension of God ("Verstellung
    Gottes"). But the preaching of the reality of God's coming wrath does
    point us to the way of repentance.

ing wrath there is also an avenue of escape in the way of repentance. It has sometimes been said that Paul, especially in I
Thessalonians 2:15-16, speaks in terms of the "exclusive"
character of God's wrath. We are referred to the Jews who
"killed both the Lord Jesus and the prophets, and drove us out
and displease God and oppose all men," and who now are
hindering the apostles "from speaking to the Gentiles that they
may be saved — so as always to fill up the measure of their sins"
(cf. Gen. 15:16). After that sharp indictment we read: "God's
wrath has come upon them *at last.*" The words here could
also be translated "unto the end" or "forever." But what does
Paul mean by these words?[32] Do we find a situation here in
which God's "not contending forever" or "not being angry always" is no longer possible (cf. Isa. 57:16; Ps. 103:9)? Is
Paul merely venting his spleen against the Jewish people because of their opposition to the preaching of the Gospel among
the heathen? Some have emphasized this passionate element
and have called to mind the pointed words: "they displease
God and oppose all men" (I Thess. 2:15). Such persons have
asked if Paul's purpose here is not to indicate the irreversible
and complete wrath of God ("unto the end") because of the
Jews' own "fullness of sinning" in a persistent and continued
resistance. Is Paul merely exposing his emotions here when he
charges that the Jews opposed both Jesus and the prophets
and "us"?

Recall, at this point, that Jesus also spoke of a certain
"fullness" on the part of the Pharisees: "Fill up, then, the
measure of your fathers" (Matt. 23:32). The context of his
statement points us in the same direction as Paul's words. But
in the case of Christ the reference is to the blood of the prophets
which was shed by those whose children he now addressed
(23:31). In that connection he spoke of the "measure" of their
fathers. The "fathers" therefore are still in view in Christ's
statement (and the Pharisees follow in their line), whereas Paul
concerns himself with an actual reality in the *present time.*
The Jews that Paul had in mind showed a continuity in their
accumulated antagonism ("Christ, the prophets, and we"), and
exactly *this* was the "fullness" of their sin.

Paul's words have given rise to a number of varying inter-

---

32. Greek: *éphthasen dé ep' autoús hē orgē̂ eis télos.* Besides the commentaries on this text, see A. Ritschl, *op. cit.,* II, 142. Cf. *TWNT,* art.
cit., E. II. 3.

pretations. We remember his statement in Romans 11, where he asserts that God by no means has rejected his own people (v. 1). But it is obvious that we cannot be done with the problems in I Thessalonians 2 by merely asserting that Paul, in this passage, did not reflect on his own pronouncements in Romans 11.[33] Some persons have thought to find a shift in Paul's thinking in reference to the Jews. Stauffer, for example, has seen such a development in Paul. In Romans, he contends, the Spirit of Jesus triumphs "over the spirit of antisemitism and the persecution-polemic of I Thessalonians 2."[34] Therefore the level of discussion in I Thessalonians, according to Stauffer, is surpassed by the idea of the ministry of the apostles to all nations and the importance of that ministry for the future of Israel.

But such a thesis of a Pauline "antisemitism" is rejected by a good many other scholars. So too is the notion of a shift of thinking at this point.[35] Paul was not trying, in Thessalonians, to express his attitude on the Jewish position before the eyes of God; his sentiments on this score are clear enough in Romans. But his interest, in Thessalonians, is the reality of God's wrath on Judaism. Paul saw the Jews, because of their own resistance, as undergoing the wrath of God which *now has come*. In Romans he is concerned about the divine economy of salvation, but in I Thessalonians his interest is clearly in the present, concrete antagonism against his own apostolic calling. Paul had an open eye for the wrath of God; but he did not isolate that wrath, as an absolute reality, from the salvation-activity of God. Precisely in that activity the invitation to salvation was still extended to the Jewish people.[36] Here we should not tone down the seriousness in which Paul wrote. And yet his words do not

33. Zahn, *ad loc.*
34. E. Stauffer, *Theologie des N.T.*, 1948, pp. 168-171. Cf. p. 171 on "the polemical thesis of the futurelessness of Israel" in I Thess. 2. As for Romans: "All antisemitism is lacking" (170).
35. Stählin speaks of "this 'antisemitic' paragraph" ("dieser 'antisemitische' Abschnitt"); but the quotation marks indicate that he does not mean the same as Stauffer. *TWNT*, V, 436 (German ed.).
36. On I Thess. 2:16, cf. especially B. Rigaux, *Saint Paul. Les épitres aux Thessaloniciëns*, 1956, pp. 451ff. "We do not have an exposition on the whole of the problem" (455). Ritschl had difficulty with this text, since his conception of wrath as *exclusively eschatological* could hardly find support at this point; moreover, the "coming" of God's wrath is clearly assigned to the present. Cf. further E. Bammel, "Judenverfolgung und Naherwartung. Zur Eschatologie des ersten Thess.-briefs," *Z.Th.K.*, 1959.

imply that this wrath is abstracted from the context in which it everywhere is consistently preached: the wrath of God *unto repentance*. There is no final pronouncement on "the Jews" in their relationship to Jesus Christ.[37]

We pause here to note the lines of connection between this salvation which has come and the Gospel which is preached, especially as that connection is apparent in the phrase, "the wrath of the Lamb." That phrase has always been very intriguing. It seems to combine the alien ideas of "wrath" and "lamb." But notice that the concept of *wrath* is defined in a very peculiar fashion, as proceeding from him who is the Lamb of God, or the "lamb without blemish or spot" (I Pet. 1:19). He is the One who *takes* away the sin of the world (John 1:29) but is also *led* away to slaughter (Isa. 53:7; Acts 8:32). In the book of Revelation especially we read of this "wrath of the Lamb." Yet we find this in only a single place (6:16), while there are several references to the wrath of *God* (11:18; 14:10, 19; 15:7; 16:1, 19; 19:15). In this single reference the context is the context of judgment. The kings of the earth, the great men and generals, the rich men and strong, and every man, both slave and free, hide themselves in the caverns and rocks of the mountains and say to the hills and the stones: "Fall on us and hide us from the face of him who is seated on the throne, and from the *wrath of the Lamb;* for the great day of their wrath has come, and who can stand before it?" (Rev. 6:15-17).[38]

Too little attention has been given to these words in reference to the wrath of God.[39] Yet there is every reason to see in this phrase, "the wrath of the Lamb," an important qualification which sets the wrath of God in focus. A. T. Hanson has found in this phrase "a doctrine of the wrath of God which is profoundly modified by the revelation of the love of God in Jesus Christ, and is at certain points essentially related to the Cross of Christ."[40] He does not mean that John's Revelation introduces a qualitatively different element from the other New Testament concepts of God's wrath, but he does judge that

---

37. For the relation of Paul and the Jews, cf. J. Munck, *Paulus und die Heilsgeschichte,* 1959, pp. 101, 112, 124.
38. There is a textual critical problem in Rev. 6:17 — *autŏn* or *autoú:* "their wrath" or "his wrath." Greijdanus chooses for the singular: the wrath of the Lamb.
39. For example, in the commentary of Zahn.
40. Hanson, *op. cit.,* p. x.

the doctrine of God's wrath "finds its climax and deepest expression in the Book of Revelation."[41] This statement is in harmony with the central place of Jesus Christ in the last book of the Bible. Christ is the main pivot, in his entire life and work. He is the Lamb of God who is introduced in the context of this stupendous fight: the Lamb who opens the seven seals and discloses thereby the meaning of history (Rev. 5:1ff.). We know, of course, that he who alone was worthy to open the scroll and to read its contents is also called the "Lion of the tribe of Judah" (5:5). But in the midst of the throne he is now envisioned as "a Lamb standing, as though it had been slain" (5:6). We hear of a bitter battle against the Lamb (17:14), but a battle in which he alone is victorious; for he alone is "Lord of lords and King of kings."

This is a great cosmic struggle; yet it is also a struggle that cannot be described in the conventional terms of a lust for "power." The real power here is the power that rises from Christ's own being the Lamb. Therefore it is the power of the *Lamb* which triumphs. Therefore, too, it is apparent that in this "wrath of the Lamb" we are not confronted by *another* wrath alongside the wrath of God; nor are we concerned about the wrath of a *deus absconditus* in contrast to the *deus revelatus*. The Lamb plays the crucial role in this battle, and the battle itself can only be seen in the focus of the Lamb that was slain. The opponents of the Lamb are those who oppose the event which has occurred, and their opposition can only be seen in the light of that event. So, too, the wrath of the Lamb is directed against their lack of appreciation and their scorn for that which has been done.[42] Therefore, we speak of the "wrath of the Lamb."

The proclamation of Christ is the announcement of the time of salvation. Thus, when we hear of the *wrath* of the Lamb we should see this term in the perspective of the salvation of him who was worthy to unravel the scroll of history and to break open the seals (Rev. 9:9; 6:1). The wrath of the Lamb is mentioned in terms of utmost gravity as the sixth seal is opened. We hear, at that time, of a "hiding" from the eschatological

41. *Ibid.* Cf. p. 169: "the deepest insight concerning the doctrine of the wrath of God."
42. Cf. Greijdanus, *Komm. op Openbaring* (6:16): "against those who have despised the compassion of God in him and the redemption through his blood" (p. 160).

judgment and a fleeing from the wrath of the Lamb (6:16).
This is the same "hiding" as we encounter already in Luke
23:30, where Christ remonstrates with the daughters of Jerusalem and depicts the eschatological judgment in terms of
fleeing from the wrath to come. We might compare, at this
point, the reference in Hosea 10:8 concerning the judgment on
Israel's sin. In the light of this warning we should read of
Israel's rejection of her Messiah, though the day of wrath is
still "to come." The meaning of that warning is clear; for the
wrath "to come" is the wrath of *the Lamb*.

Scripture speaks repeatedly, and in somber tones, concerning the reality of this wrath of God. It sets it in direct connection with the "mystery now revealed" and accentuates that
Jesus alone can save us from the "wrath which is to come." The
riches of the Messiah's salvation are set against the background
of man's guilt. In this perspective of preaching the wrath of
God, every relativizing of sin is undercut and the motive of
God's wrath is seen in its greatest clarity. We find no stronger
expression for this than the biblical description of man's "lostness." We read in John 3:36 of a "remaining" of God's wrath
for those who disobey the Son; so too we are also impressed by
the repeated warnings against remaining in that lostness. Over
and over again, the Scripture refers us to this state of being
"lost"; and especially is that the case where the heart of the
Gospel is at stake. Christ has come to seek "the lost" (cf. Luke
19:11; Matt. 15:24; 10:6; Ezek. 34:16; Ps. 119:176). There is
great joy in heaven at the *finding* of that which was *lost*.

It is no small peril that through a onesided fixation on this
"lostness" in terms of the future our vision is blurred for our
"being lost" *right now*. The Church has spoken of this "being
lost" in combatting the various forms of humanism and Pelagianism. She has made her confession of the total depravity of
man. Man is *dead,* as Paul once put it, in trespasses and sins
(Eph. 2:1; cf. 2:5). Yet the danger is real that we see this
category in too exclusively eschatological terms and ignore the
reality of our "being lost" today. As we look on our lostness we
find ourselves at the very heart of the Gospel. For the reality
of "lostness" is clarified in Scripture as an "open" situation.
It is not that insofar as our lostness in itself is concerned; but
it is that in terms of Jesus Christ, who searches for that which
was *lost*. He searches for the lost sheep, the lost penny, the lost
son. The light of the Gospel shines brilliantly in the word of

the Father: "Let us eat and make merry; for this my son was *dead*, and is alive again; he was *lost*, and is found" (Luke 15: 23-24; cf. v. 32).

All this is very different from what Rudolf Otto once wrote: "Lostness is the natural profanity of creaturehood in general."[43] Those who take that tack may end up in a rather "modern" reinterpretation of life; but the parable of the *lost son* with his *servum arbitrium* and his alienation from his father's house has nothing to do with such a notion. The word *lost*, in the New Testament, has all the earmarks of a very dire calamity. It suggests the situation of an utter fallenness in which no possibility is left for man to relativize or to water down his need.[44] Therefore, every softening of that concept can only fail when we recognize that "being found" is the *marvel of God's grace*. The lost son's "being alive from the *dead*" is the real and compelling reason for the father to celebrate (Luke 15:32). Sinful man is seen in the New Testament as *lost*, and apart from any recourse or escape. Yet the wonder of the Gospel is that even that lostness is not definitive. It is *God* who makes the dead to be alive (Rom. 4:17). But only when we acknowledge the complete *reasonableness of his wrath* do we see the Gospel as a *total surprise*.

Thus we cannot contemplate the wrath of God as exclusively the predication of the Old Testament or set his wrath in opposition to the New Testament accent on love.[45] Yet the question remains: Does the Scripture instruct us in the *modus of this judgment,* or the manner in which the wrath of God is manifest upon man's sin? The answer is sometimes given that there is no independent activity of God's wrath and judgment; thus we can only speak of the anger of God in the consequences and results of sin, or as wrath becomes apparent in the "ways of man's sin." The purpose of this assertion is to point out

43. Quoted from his chapter on "Verlorenheit," *Sünde und Urschuld,* 1929, p. 206. This, however, is by no means the whole of Otto's conception; cf. pp. 198-207.
44. It is a total misunderstanding, e.g., if we relativize the lostness of the son with an eye to his factual return! The statement of the father sufficiently refutes this notion.
45. When it is stated in *P.R.E.* (724) that "the anthropopathic picture of the wrath of God as pathos, or passionate irritability with somatic emotions, is lacking in the New Testament," it is obvious that nothing is said as yet concerning the reality of wrath.

the so-called immanent "dynamic of sin." On that issue the argument most frequently hinges. Here we are touching on what has sometimes been called the antithesis between God's immanent and transcendent judgment.[46] The dilemma is then posed as follows: Does God bring down upon the sinner, in a transcendent manner, a new and contingent, and even an un-anticipated stroke of his vengeance? Does he lead the sinner on darkened paths, or does he rather confront the sinner within and through the "dynamic" and results and consequences of man's sin? We are concerned, in this question, with the nature of God's *activity,* and of God *himself,* in his immediate dealings with men.

G. Koch has tried to throw some light on this problem by asserting that the Old Testament has no dogma of a "divine ret-ribution." He illustrates his thesis by pointing to the book of Proverbs. There we certainly read extensively of the context and the inner dynamic of sin; yet, in Koch's view, there is "no single tenable reference to a belief in retribution" in the entire book of Proverbs.[47] The issue at stake is the results and conse-quences of man's sin; it is the curse of his evil deeds, which in-evitably bring new evils in their train. *Within* man's sinning we find a "fatal working sphere of activity" (a *"schicksalwirkende Tatsphäre"*).[48] There is always a "fatal working human act,"[49] or an "empowering" of man's own deed.[50] Throughout the Old Testament we observe this remarkable alliance of piety and felicity, sin and misery. Therefore we get the impression that an evil deed "has distressful consequences as its inevitable result."[51] As a case in point, Koch cites the words of Proverbs 28:6: "An evil man is ensnared in his transgression." A good deed produces that which is good; an evil deed produces that which is evil. The Old Testament is not concerned with a "tran-scendent" rewarding and punishing, which is contingent on man's own act and is meted out according to pre-established norms.

46. In terms of this dilemma (unacceptable, as we shall see), we might assign the manifold impingements of God in the history of the nations and Israel to God's "transcendent" acts of judgment; also the New Testament deaths of Ananias (Acts 5:5) and Herod (slain by an angel of the Lord, "because he did not give God the glory," 12:23).
47. Koch, "Gibt es ein Vergeltungsdogma im A.T.?" *Z.Th.K.,* 1955, p. 9.
48. *Ibid.,* pp. 26, 29, 32, 33.
49. *Ibid.,* p. 9.
50. *Ibid.,* p. 19.
51. *Ibid.,* p. 3. Koch speaks of a necessity comparable to natural law.

Rather, it is concerned with the agent of that act who is "drawn into" his own activity. "He who digs a pit will fall into it" (Prov. 26:27); "he who misleads the upright into an evil way will fall into his own pit; but the blameless will have a goodly inheritance" (28:10).[52] Within the evil act we find enacted the "law of sowing and reaping." Thus, "he who pursues evil will die" (11:19). Koch does not suggest, according to the Old Testament, that God stands entirely outside this process; but where Jahwe is specifically mentioned his activity is a "setting in motion and completing this relationship of sin and misery."[53] With all of that, the accent remains on man's own causality. "Jahwe enforces what man has already done." There is no transcendent and unexpected judgment, but only a judgment that coinheres, indissolubly, in this one act of man.[54]

That same dynamic and its relations are apparent, according to Koch, in the Old Testament prophets. This fact is evident in the attention they give to the acts of men. The deeds of men "do not permit them to return to their God" (Hos. 5:4); and in sin there is an "unconditional imprisoning of men within their own history."[55] Therefore the deeds of men "encompass" them (Hos. 7:1ff.). In Hosea there is no suggestion of a requiting activity of God but only of a "fate-working activity of men";[56] it is not the transcendent but the immanent character of judgment that is clearly in the foreground. Sin is an "immanent captivity,"[57] and Jahwe brings men to see the power of their own deeds while he himself stands, as it were, on the sidelines, apart from the dynamic of man's sin.[58]

Yet this evidence concerning the "causal" power of good and evil acts, as experienced by men, is not equally apparent in

52. Cf. W. H. Gispen, *Spreuken*, II, 298, on Prov. 29:6 — the reference to sin as its "own snare" ("zijn eigen valstrik").
53. Koch, *op. cit.*, p. 7.
54. *Ibid*. In line with this view is that of Ratschow, "Vom Sinn der Strafe," in H. Dombois, *Die weltliche Strafe in der evangelischen Theologie*, 1959, pp. 105f.
55. Koch, *op. cit.*, p. 11.
56. *Ibid.*, p. 12.
57. *Ibid.*, p. 19.
58. Koch finds this "helplessness" of Jahwe (the "Ratlosigkeit Jahwes"), e.g., in Hos. 7:1: "When I would heal Israel, the corruption of Ephraim is revealed, and the wicked deeds of Samaria; for they deal falsely..." (*ibid.*, p. 12). He speaks of the acts of the people so encompassing them that even Jahwe himself must look on helplessly ("so dasz selbst Jahwe hilflos zusehen musz").

all parts of the Old Testament. Koch finds certain skeptical elements in the book of Ecclesiastes, where the Preacher "can no longer believe in a consequence that corresponds to the act."[59] Also the book of Job "shows a still more profound shaking of the idea of a fate-working sphere of activity."[60] It is wrong to speak, in Koch's judgment, of an essential revision of Old Testament thinking in this regard;[61] indeed, the ancient, original and immanent conception is still very evident in Paul, who conceived of death as "included within" man's sin (Rom. 5:21). Paul writes that we "must all appear before the judgment seat of Christ, so that each one may receive good or evil, according to what he has done in the body" (II Cor. 5:10). That same Old Testament motive of "sowing and reaping" appears explicitly in Galatians: "For he who sows to his own flesh will from the flesh reap corruption; but he who sows to the Spirit will from the Spirit reap eternal life" (6:8). Thus there is an unbreakable unity of cause and effect, and these words are even introduced by the familiar statement: "Do not be deceived; God is not mocked, for whatever a man sows, that he will also reap" (6:7).[62]

All these observations of Koch are designed as a polemic against the idea of a divine retribution.[63] Koch sees the common notion of a punitive judgment as a misinterpretation. The cause of this, he suggests, can be traced back to the Septuagint, where the concept of a "fate-deciding sphere of activity" is nowhere in view.[64] There is, of course, a good reason for Koch's directing our attention to the dynamic of sin and for seeing sin as no isolated or isolable activity. There is a good reason for his discerning in sin a power which holds a man captive in the quagmire of his own personal guilt, and for finding in sin a bondage or a compulsive force which cannot be broken. In many places in the Scripture we are cautioned against sin because of its irrevocable effects, not only for others but especially for our-

59. *Ibid.*, p. 33.
60. *Ibid.*, p. 34.
61. *Ibid.*, p. 36.
62. With a view to Büchsel's characterization of retribution in the New Testament as belonging "essentially to the future world rather than to the present" (*TWNT*, II, *s.v. apodidōmi*), we might say that in Koch's conception the immanent judgment is both this-worldly and other-worldly.
63. Koch, *op. cit.*, p. 37.
64. *Ibid.*, p. 39.

selves.[65] Yet what is totally inadequate in Koch's view is his posing of a dilemma: either reprisal *or* an immanent dynamic, transcendent *or* immanent. It is simply impossible to set the dynamic activity of sin *and* God's judicial activity alongside each other in an attitude of competition. Koch acknowledges that the dynamic of sin is not something that "happens" alongside God; yet he speaks of God's activity with a curious hesitation, and he finds an "explanation" in God's "keeping watch" over the relation between an act and fate. God sets that relation in motion when it is necessary; he accelerates it and even brings it to its end.[66] But Koch, very typically, refers to the "helplessness" of Jahwe in facing up to the dynamic of man's sin. In speaking of this *"Ratlosigkeit Jahwes"* his purpose is to underscore the tragic results of sin. At the same time he and others who use that language would do well to listen to the strong words of judgment in Scripture concerning God's "laughing" and "mocking" when panic comes (Prov. 1:26). Those words expose the gravity of sin but also emphasize the everlasting presence of that Wisdom which "cries aloud in the street" (1:20).

There is no trace of a dilemma at this point. Even when a man realizes the dynamic of his sin and the bondage of his guilt, and the power and activity of his evil, as well as his own increasing lostness and stubbornness, he cannot possibly embrace the "dilemma" of an immanent *versus* a transcendent. It is evident from what we have said that the Old Testament knows of no such thing as a systematizing or a demonstrable relation between man's sin and misery, or his piety and salvation. Were there such an ironclad "system" the friends of Job would certainly have been right in their simplistic notions of reprisal. From Job's great misery they could only conclude that he had committed some "secret sins." Therefore Zophar tried to arouse in him a true humility (Job 11:13ff.). But Job's reaction was entirely right: he denied that any such conclusions were valid. Surely we can speak of an immanent dynamic in man's sin and estrangement from God, but no dynamic which results

---

65. This is clear in Proverbs, e.g., 1:29-31: because they "did not choose the fear of the Lord . . . , therefore they shall eat the fruit of their way and be sated with their own devices. For the simple are killed by their turning away, and the complacence of fools destroys them." Cf. Gispen, *Spreuken*, I, 38, on the outcome or result of their conduct; also on several other texts in Proverbs with this same tendency.

66. Koch, *op. cit.*, p. 9.

automatically in man's misery and dismay. Psalm 73, in fact, disputes that view at a very essential point. The concern is with Asaph's own temptations and struggles. The psalm takes its point of departure in the factual prosperity of the wicked; but when Asaph entered into the "sanctuary of God" he was able to see, *even in that prosperity,* the sign of God's judgment (73: 17ff.).

What we have here is not a "crisis" in belief, or a reflection of the inner dynamic of sin, but a statement on the obvious inequities of men in time and history, combined with a vision of God's righteous judgment in the *future.* Even when we observe the dynamic of sin we can see that the concept of *dilemma* is untenable. This appears in what Paul says about sinners who are *"given over"* by God, *in the way of sin,* to impurity and a reprobate mind (Rom. 1:24, 26, 28).[67] Any suggestion of a deistic judgment or a vague transcendence is here completely excluded. For man's own recalcitrance (inextricably tied to the dynamic of his sin) is the manifestation of God's judgment; and that judgment is not an arbitrary sentence but comes in the way of *man's own sin.* Therefore we must get beyond the dilemma of Koch. Our purpose is not to take lightly the dynamic of sin but to see how very serious man's sin is. We must regard our sin within the theater of God's justice, or that theater in which the living God reacts *within our guilt.*

In this sense we may speak of the law of "sowing and reaping"; and in this sense the Old and the New Testaments are one.[68] We may also understand why the New Testament uses

---

67. Cf. Acts 7:42: "But God turned and gave them over to worship the hosts of heaven." The untenability of the dilemma is evident in the fact that the New Testament speaks of God's "giving over" and — at the same time — of man's giving himself over to sin (*parédōkan tē aselgeía,* Eph. 4:19). In Amos 5:27 (cf. Acts 7:42) we read the announcement of the judgment of captivity. That judgment can certainly be viewed as the "harvest" of sowing in unrighteousness, but cannot be understood *immanently,* in terms of the sinful acts themselves. The captivity was God's act, or his new "involvement" in the ways of guilt.

68. Cf. Prov. 22:8: "He who sows injustice will reap calamity"; and Gal. 6; also Hos. 10:13: "You have ploughed iniquity, you have reaped injustice, you have eaten the fruit of lies." The fact that the issue comes down to a proper interpretation of the law of "sowing and reaping" appears from the manipulation of this law by Eliphaz: "As I have seen, those who plough iniquity and sow trouble reap the same" (Job 4:8).

such strongly eschatological language concerning the decisive significance of human acts and the urgency of all that happens on earth.[69] There are those "fields" in which it is evident if a man sows according to the flesh or according to the Spirit (Gal. 6:7-8). This, then, is the motive in the admonition for our activity on earth: ". . . let us not grow weary in well-doing, for in due season we shall reap, if we do not lose heart" (Gal. 6:9). Nowhere does that admonition lead us to a "systematic" or "statistical" view of the divine activity in judgment. It is not punishment, for example, but comfort which arises as a motive in persecution. The revelation of the eschaton forewarns us against all premature conclusions at this point. Though we wish to do justice to the dynamic of sin, there is no reason at all to deny the concept of retribution. Therefore Büchsel, with an open eye for God's punishment, *even in history,* has spoken of the "secret of his majesty."[70]

Even that man who accentuates the elements of warning and judgment on sin in the "sphere of one's own activity"[71] can hardly profess that God merely "supervises" this process or "sets it in motion." For God is a living and a present God who meets his people in their own estrangement and sins. His meeting is sometimes apparent in spectacular and concrete acts, and at other times in prophetic words of judgment; it is even apparent in moments of prosperity and indifferentness. But in all of these various *modi* of God's judgment we hear constantly the call to repentance. Therefore the judgment is all the stronger and unavoidable when the invitation is not obeyed.[72] The divine indictment is most severe where judgment is not fathomed in its fullest meaning and intent. Because of what Jahwe had done in his good judgment (providing for the most elementary needs of Israel) we hear this recurring refrain and indictment: "Yet you did not return to me. . . . Therefore thus I will do to you, O Israel; because I will do this to you, prepare to meet your God, O Israel" (Amos 4:6, 8, 9, 10, 11, 12). Moreover, the New Testament warns us, in its pericope on

---

69. Cf. Eccl. 12:14 and Matt. 25:31-46; also the "harvest of the earth" in Rev. 14:15f.

70. *TWNT, loc. cit.*

71. "God permits men to manage their own destinies in their own activities." H. Schlier, *Gal.-brief,* p. 204.

72. On the thought of retribution in the O.T., cf. (besides Koch) the article of Würthwein, in *TWNT,* IV, *s.v. misthós.*

sowing and reaping, that God is not to be *mocked*. Here the same unbreakable union of sin and judgment is very evident.[73]

There is no reason, therefore, to follow A. T. Hanson, at this point, and to speak of an "impersonal wrath."[74] Hanson builds his case on a medley of scriptural data and appeals especially to Paul. Essentially he means the same thing as Koch, and that fact is very evident when he regards God's wrath as "a process which sinners bring upon themselves."[75] The lines of a "dilemma" are even stronger here than we have already seen in Koch; and man is now viewed as totally responsible. "God allows the wrath; he does not inflict it."[76] Wrath is not an attribute of God but "a condition of sin."[77] In that way, according to Hanson, Paul can harmonize the wrath and the love of God. "The wrath was not an emotion or attitude of God, it was simply a word for what happened to those who had broken God's moral laws."[78] Wrath is an historical process; and even in its eschatological aspect, it is "as much a revealing as an execution."[79] Wrath is an automatic and a self-working process of history.

Thus we can rightly speak of a depersonalizing of God's wrath in its reference to "the consequences of men's sins worked out in history and consummated in the parousia."[80] Hanson concedes that there are scriptural passages where wrath is presented as an activity of judgment,[81] but the "main New Testament tradition,"[82] he feels, is that wrath refers to "a condition of men."[83] At this point we see the transition to an impersonal

---

73. Koch has written concerning the shift of accent in the Septuagint, and the alleged result that the dynamic of sin itself could not stand out in clear relief (*op. cit.*, pp. 37-39). But there is no basis for Koch's dilemma here, since he interprets every element of retribution in the Septuagint as an understanding of religion in legal concepts (p. 39).

74. Hanson, *op. cit.*, pp. 69, 85.

75. *Ibid.*

76. *Ibid.*, p. 85.

77. *Ibid.*, p. 89.

78. *Ibid.*, p. 109.

79. *Ibid.*, p. 110.

80. *Ibid.*, p. 178.

81. E.g., I Cor. 10. Here Paul, according to Hanson, is "not at his most profound with respect to the wrath" (*ibid.*, p. 78; cf. p. 180). This same kind of reasoning is applied to I Cor. 11:30 (*ibid.*, p. 168).

82. *Ibid.*, p. 179.

83. *Ibid.*, p. 110.

wrath, or a view in which the reality of wrath (qua wrath of *God*) is denied, and a concept of wrath as historical process of sin is set in its place. The presupposition of this argument is that a real wrath of God cannot be harmonized with his love. Hanson gives the following explanation of the scriptural allusions to God's wrath: "That sin should bring its own retribution to infinite consequence is a law of the universe created by God; so the wrath is the wrath of God."[84] But all our speaking of God's wrath — if we really accept this analysis — is a dangerous anthropomorphism. That peril is also acute in the New Testament. On the other hand, we should not refer to the wrath of God, according to Hanson, as a mere "moral retribution,"[85] for in that purely impersonal view we could easily come to the karma-doctrine of Hinduism.[86] Thus, while continuing to speak of the wrath of God, Hanson does not conceive of this wrath as an emotion in God or an attitude of God. The Old Testament thought of the love and the wrath of God in a kind of harmony, but this construction is untenable for us. For the personal love of God precludes the possibility of his personal wrath.

It is a very strange thing, in all of this, that we begin by demanding attention for the gravity and dynamic of sin (the dire consequences) and return to a view that reminds us, at important junctures, of Ritschl. This is especially clear in the case of Hanson. In that way the real profit of investigating the scriptural bond of God's judgment and grace is set in a very dubious light. Instead of increasing our appreciation for the seriousness of sin, we confuse the reality of the message con-

---

84. *Ibid.*, p. 195.
85. *Ibid.*, p. 196.
86. *Ibid.* Hanson speaks of a "remarkable parallel" between his description of wrath and the karma-idea (p. 215). Others too have referred to the relation between karma and such passages as Gal. 6 and II Cor. 5:10 (p. 216). But it is remarkable that Hanson then points to differences (individualism and soul-migration in Hinduism) which have nothing to do with the essential structure of karma. He contends that karma itself "has no necessary relation to God at all" (p. 217). In that case, however, *the problem* stands before us anew and entirely unresolved. The heart of the difficulty is Hanson's own *depersonalizing of the wrath of God.* On "impersonal law" in Hinduism, cf. W. Stewart, "Preaching Forgiveness to the Hindu," *Scottish Journal of Theology*, 1949, p. 197; and J. H. Bavinck, *Chr. Encyclopaedie*, IV, 1959, *s.v.* "karma," concerning the opposition between "automatic" and "personal." Cf. also *idem, s.v.* "Bhakti."

cerning God's acts of judgment and coming wrath. The message
itself is meant to lead us to repentance. Therefore all kinds of
false arguments, on the reality of God's wrath, may easily return.
It is not the love but the wrath of God which is now regarded
as anthropomorphic and anthropopathic. Thus we are far removed from the preaching of Scripture. We cannot solve the
problems of an anthropomorphism or an anthropopathism in
this way;[87] furthermore, this process of "purifying" our God-
concept can only lead us to fogginess when we draw the antithesis between the wrath and love of God. We can only end
up by doing violence to the proclamation of God's wrath. We
then fail to see the real anger of the Lord, which is kindled in
vengeance and *jealousy* and *passion,* in the *fire of his wrath,*
for those who depart from his ways. In those ways he desires
that men should walk (cf. Isa. 5:25; 66:16; Ps. 2:12; 18:8-9;
Ezek. 35:11).[88]

These terms which we have just cited impress upon us the
reality of God's wrath. Therefore in our analysis of the scriptural data, we have no right to choose for *either* the love *or*
the wrath of God. We cannot stack the one characteristic against
the other. Our discussions of God's wrath often betray this *a
priori* prejudice; but Scripture is concerned to draw relations
so clearly that anyone who ignores the one must certainly lose
his sensitivity for the other. We cannot deny that the reality
of God's wrath is the background for the jubilee which we experience in redemption, and the unexpected salvation and new
reception of our sonship, which has left behind us our former
status of being "children of God's wrath." In the light of that
scriptural perspective it is possible to speak of the wrath of
God, *even for believers,* but it is not possible to make a bizarre

---

87. Those who have operated with an antithesis between the Old and New
Testaments have always found it difficult to place such a text as Heb.
12:28-29, where an appeal is made for greater responsibility on the
basis of the motive: "for our God is a consuming fire." The christological context of this reference, in Heb. 12, is clear beyond dispute
(cf. 12:24, 25, 28). Cf. Zahn (Riggenbach), *Comm.,* p. 425. Note the
accent, in v. 28, on an unshakable kingdom and thankfulness. The text
here is a quotation of Deut. 4:24, where the wrath and jealousy of
Jahwe are depicted against the background of forgetting God's covenant
(4:21, 23). The exegesis of H. van Oyen, *Christus de Hogepriester,* 1939,
pp. 267f., would seem to lie on a different level from what Van Oyen
has written in his article, "Liefde, Gerechtigheid en Recht," *N.T.T.,*
1947, pp. 27f.
88. On the "cup of God's wrath," see Hanson, *op. cit.,* pp. 27f.

"analysis" of God's "attributes." We must understand and translate into human language the witness of him whose wrath, in the language of Scripture, can also be "turned aside."

When we reflect on that "turning aside," and purge ourselves of *a priori* notions, we are struck by the fact that we read of a "time limit" on God's wrath. To be sure, there is no temporal limitation on God's wrath in the sense that we read of a temporal limitation on man's. Nor does Scripture speak of a "border," as in the case of man, beyond which one can only proceed at his own risk. Instead, the limit of which we are speaking is evident as the revelation of God's *grace*. "For his anger is but for a moment, and his favor is for a lifetime. Weeping may tarry for the night, but joy comes with the morning" (Ps. 30:5). "For a brief moment I forsook you, but with great compassion I will gather you. In overflowing wrath for a moment I hid my face from you, but with everlasting love I will have compassion on you" (Isa. 54:7-8). These are the doxologies of the biblical writers who stood in fear before the God who hid his face (Ps. 30:7). They are the doxologies of those who saw the burst of light which followed on the darkness of his wrath. *In* the darkness of his wrath we hear of the swearing of his oath: "I have sworn that I will not be angry with you and will not rebuke you" (Isa. 54:9). *Here* is the biblical witness on the repeated "turning aside" of God's wrath in favor of the consolation of renewed fellowship. "He restrained his anger *often,* and did not stir up all his wrath" (Ps. 78:38). "I will give thanks to thee, O Lord, for though thou wast angry with me, thy anger turned away, and thou didst *comfort me*" (Isa. 12:1). As a divine light of revelation there falls on Israel's darkness the message that God "repents." His heart "recoils" within him (Hos. 11:8) as his mercy is fully aroused. "I will not execute my fierce anger, I will not again destroy Ephraim; for I am God and not man, the Holy One in your midst, and I will not come to destroy" (Hos. 11:9). "I will heal their faithlessness; I will love them freely, for my anger has turned from them" (14:1). God "does not retain his anger for ever because he delights in steadfast love" (Mic. 7:18).

In human language it is difficult to formulate this idea in other words than that God's love has set a limit on his wrath.[89] But whoever thinks of an antithesis in God, or a human kind

89. Cf. C. van Gelderen (and W. H. Gispen), *Hosea,* 1953, p. 390.

of "whimsicality," will certainly be amazed at the motivation for
this "turning aside" of wrath: "... *for I am God and not man*"
(Hos. 11). *This* is the God who is the *Holy One of Israel*.[90]
"Therein we see the essence of God in distinction from man:
for beyond all expectations and understanding he is motivated
by a love which is incomprehensible to men. For him the seriousness of judgment and a love which seeks and educates are
not incompatible, as they necessarily appear to be to man."[91]
When we observe that this "turning aside" from wrath is motivated by God's *being God,* we also see *how utterly foolish* all
criticism is which refuses to deal seriously with those references
which are commonly anthropomorphized and thus emptied of
their gravity. The old saw is that God's "repentance" cannot
be harmonized with the *immutabilitas Dei*.[92] But it is quite
unnecessary (even inappropriate) to make the Bible somewhat
"clearer" and more "real" than it is, or to think thereby that
we gain a purer insight into the "being of God." The idea
that God "turns aside" from wrath is not a hyper-humanized
notion with no relevance to God, but points us precisely to
that place where he differs from man: *"for* I am God and not
man."[93] There is, perhaps, no more revealing statement for
the entire discussion of anthropomorphism in Scripture than
this phrase. It is not in terms of a "human reason" but in terms

90. A. Weiser speaks of a "noteworthy foundation" ("beachtenswerte
   Begründung"; *Comm. Kleine Propheten,* 1949, p. 71); J. Ridderbos of a
   "remarkable" and "wonderful" expression of that which is "specifically
   divine" (*Het Godswoord der Profeten,* I, 1930, 217).
91. Weiser, *loc. cit.*
92. Some have wrongly said that Jonah objected to the concept of God's
   "changeableness," in reference to Nineveh. Rather, it is obvious that
   he fled to Tarshish because he knew who God was — a gracious God,
   merciful, slow to anger, abounding in steadfast love, and a God who
   repents of evil (Jon. 4:2). In 3:9 ("Who knows, God may yet repent
   and turn from his fierce anger") we find a parallel to Jonah's own view
   of God which makes him angry. But these pagan words, "who knows,"
   are answered by God's own act: "God repented of the evil which he
   had said he would do to them; and he did not do it" (3:10). Cf. the
   parallel "who knows" in Joel 2:14; the same context as we find in Jon.
   4:2.
93. J. Ridderbos speaks of a "change of direction in God's heart"; *op. cit.,*
   I, 217. The change is the revelation of his compassion and love, which
   reflects itself in the change of name in Hos. 1: *lo ammi* to *ammi, lo
   ruchama* to *ruchama* (vv. 8-12). The final motive is not the "will of
   annihilation, but rather of unfathomable love."

of the revelation of *this God* that the scriptural language, concerning God's repentance, is remarkably perspicuous.

The marvel is that God's mercies in no way detract from the profoundly serious nature of his wrath. In the prophets especially we see the wrath of God preached to Israel in all its severity. In that same book in which the transition from wrath to grace is seen as divine mercy, we also read of another "change" in God: the divine reaction against the sins of his people. "I will return again to my place until they acknowledge their guilt and seek my face" (Hos. 5:15). Listen to the harshness of God's judgment: "Shall I ransom them from the power of Sheol? Shall I redeem them from Death? . . . Compassion is hid from my eyes" (13:14). As a description of human affections, this would doubtless create the impression of a capriciousness and inconstancy; but in the context here we can only speak of the depths and stability of God ("for I am God and not man"). We can speak, at best, of the *appearance* of a certain tension and inconsistency — an appearance that results from the human language in which these thoughts are framed. This appearance suggests a "sudden effervescence in which love, though remaining in the background for a while, erupts anew and takes the initiative."[94] But that kind of description in human words, with an appeal to the tangible, is at least preferable to a statement that empties the reality of God's wrath or emasculates his mercies. There are no human words sufficient to express what really happens in this *divine compassion and concern*.

We have said that the wrath of God must not be minimized for the sake of doing justice to his mercy. Precisely in this wrath, God takes man seriously and does not leave him to his own fate. Indifference is the mark of man in his apathy, but the God of Israel is not of that sort. Certainly we hear the words of Paul on the Areopagus that God is not "served by human hands, as though he needed anything" (Acts 17:25). From such a statement as this we tend to deduce a kind of "self-containedness" in God. For that reason Haenchen has pointed to the Greek conception of the "needlessness" of God (the *"Bedürfnislosigkeit Gottes"*), though he finds this idea quite foreign to the Old Testament.[95] In all fairness he also

94. Ridderbos, *op. cit.,* 216.
95. E. Haenchen, *Die Apostelgeschichte,* 1956, p. 462.

adds that this God is the selfless Giver *("der selbstlose Geber")*. God's transcendence or "independence," in contrast to human conceptualization or imaginations, has nothing to do with an "apathy." Here is the God who made the world (as Paul once put it) that *men should "seek him,"* and he is "not far from each one of us" (Acts 17:27). Moreover, this proximity of God accentuates the *reality* of everything that comes to us from him, whether in love or in anger. The divine concern and interest are immeasurable in the categories of men. They stand opposed to every human indifference; and this too is a matter that is quite inconceivable to us. Even in wrath his involvement with men is evident. *In his wrath* he was occupied with the people of Israel, in dark and burdensome and sometimes in tedious ways of judgment. *In those ways* he was always the watchful and the waiting God. Only in this light can we understand why paeans of praise were raised in ancient Israel, not only when his wrath was "turned aside" but also *because of his wrath.*[96] Israel understood the "changeableness" of God *in concreto* and did not reflect on the "capriciousness" of this "inscrutable God." In the depths of her faith she experienced this God as the Unchangeable One precisely *in* his "turning aside" from wrath to mercy.[97]

Attempts to tone down the wrath of God are powerless in the face of the strong and frequent biblical words of threat and judgment. Only when we recognize this and proclaim the turning aside of God's wrath as an astounding and gracious reality are we able, the better, to listen to the central message of the Gospel: *the real forgiveness of our sins.* In these words, the "turning aside of wrath" is given its most concrete form. In these same words we meet up with one of the most familiar confessions in the Christian Church. This confession would seem to be initially clear. There would seem to be a general awareness of what "forgiveness" means, as well as an intuitive

96. J. Ridderbos, *Jesaja,* I (*K.V.*), *ad. loc.*
97. Obviously we do not deny that the way of God's wrath and judgment was frequently a temptation for Israel. It was that whenever the judgment of God was seen as an offensive "mutation." Thus it seemed that the Lord was no longer compassionate, that his clemency was ended, and his mercy was shut off. Cf. Ps. 77:6-10: "And I say, 'It is my grief that the right hand of the Most High has changed'" (v. 10). Note in this psalm, however, the twofold meditating in vv. 5 and 12; also the perspective on God's leading, in v. 20. Cf. also the "why" of Isa. 63:17 and the petition for God to "return." Cf. Ps. 85:5, 7; 88:14, 16.

"feeling" for the necessity and possibility of pardon. In short, there would seem to be a sensitivity in terms of which divine forgiveness makes "sense." But precisely here we must understand that in God's forgiveness we are not dealing with a "comprehensible" and "self-evident" matter. The words, *Dieu pardonnera, c'est son métier,* can rightly be called a blasphemy, but it is well to consider that a completely "comprehensible" view of God's forgiveness could only land us in that same peril. It is not our purpose to speak of the possibility of divine pardon before we consider its reality; for who could speak of that "possibility" except in terms of *that reality?* Yet it is also clear that we cannot discuss the forgiveness of sins in the mood of a human "forgiveness." When we do so we lose all feeling for the unexpected *surprise of God's pardon* and all sensitivity for his turning from *real* wrath to *real* grace.[98]

Men have frequently described this phenomenon of human forgiveness as the readiness of one man to release another from indebtedness and to hold him no longer accountable. We use those words that Scripture also employs in the case of divine forgiveness: "not reckoning," "pardoning," and "remembering no more." Yet we cannot say that this human analogy makes divine pardon a matter that is crystal clear, for there is still reason to inquire into the rightness and meaning, and the real foundation, of *human forgiveness. Is* there such a "right," which would make our forgiveness "praiseworthy" and in accordance with which we are also *commanded to forgive?* Commonly that question is set outside the purview of discussion, and it is simply assumed (in theory) that it is "necessary" to forgive. It is said, as a common human rule, that love does not take account of evil (cf. I Cor. 13:5). But it is *also possible* that this notion stems, in itself, from the failure to take evil seriously. It is instructive to observe, for example, that an ethical skepticism has no difficulty at all with the concept of forgiveness.[99]

Even the man who has no scruples with the biblical idea of the "mind of forgiveness" must recognize that this "natural" and "self-evident" concept implies a real danger. The danger

98. Cf. C. Stange, "Die Vergebung der Sünden," in *Studien zur Theologie Luthers,* 1928, pp. 134f.

99. For this entire chapter, cf. the important views of E. L. Smelik, *Vergelden en Vergeven. Een theol.-ethische Studie naar Aanleiding van Fr. Nietzsches Denkbeelden over Schuld en Straf,* 1943, pp. 162ff. and 190ff.

is that we forfeit the concept of *true forgiveness*. It is entirely possible to "take no account of evil" in a very superficial way, and scarcely to reflect on the gravity of the offense and its tragic influence. When we bear in mind the nature of our sinning against God and our neighbors there is every reason to inquire: On what basis does our human forgiving depend? That question is meaningful for the man who considers, in the light of Scripture, that God does not regard the guilty as guiltless. In fact he has sworn an oath not to forget a single sin for all eternity (Ex. 34:7; Num. 14:8; Amos 8:7). What, then, is the sense of our human pardon, and with what validity or legitimacy do we really forgive? Can forgiveness eradicate or exterminate the evil that is done?

Such questions are certainly not meaningless, and reflect the difficulties in speaking of the "necessity" or "naturalness" of human forgiveness. Even when we think of the punishment we mete out upon our peers it is obvious why we shall have to be reluctant to use this concept of a universal human "pardon." How could punishment make sense if the principle applies that all evil is simply decked over by the mantle of a "universal love"? This question of the right and meaning of our forgiveness, in essence, is the question of whether forgiveness is *more* than an overlooking or downgrading of evil. *Must* we forgive, and *may* we forgive, in *that way?* Do we pardon *everything* in a blasé universality of "forgiveness" and "not taking into account"? This was a compelling question in the period that followed the Second World War, when men were faced by the problem: How must we punish those who have committed the most ghastly of crimes? Surely, this was not the first time the question had been posed. Uncertainty is always present as we contemplate the horrible deeds which have been done. Do we have any power to recall the irrevocable? Are we inhibited in our activity and limited to the gestures of "forgiveness"? Is everything else beyond our control?[100]

We are not concerned, at this point, to bring the light of the Gospel to bear on these problems of human forgiveness.

---

100. One thinks of the complications and solutions in the monograph of K. Jaspers, *Die Schuldfrage. Ein Beitrag zur deutschen Frage,* 1946; especially the last chapter, "Unsere Reinigung." Also Hans Dombois, *Die weltliche Strafe in der evang. Theologie,* 1959; E. Brunner, *Gerechtigkeit,* 1943, pp. 262ff., on "Die gerechte Strafe"; G. Brillenburg Wurth, *De Straf. Haar ethisch en psychologisch Aspect,* 1956; and G. Stratenwerth, "Schuld und Sühne," *Ev.Theol.,* 1958, pp. 337ff.

But we do wish to touch on these questions in order to show
that a true forgiveness cannot build on an ethical skepticism
and finds no grain of support in the standard of indifference.
We must guard ourselves, necessarily, against the conclusion
of a natural "self-evidentness," as we seek to know what is meant
by "divine pardon." One can appreciate forgiveness, with its
biblical content, only when he takes his leave of the categories
of human "comprehensibility" and "self-evidentness." The key-
note of the biblical forgiveness is that it finds its place on a
totally different plane. It finds its place on the level of the
unsuspected and surprising. Any notion of an automatic forgiveness is out of tune with the biblical picture. Every *a priori*
conclusion on the manner in which God acts within man's guilt
is simply denied.

God's forgiveness cannot be understood by analyzing the
nature of human forgiveness. When Israel was invited to salvation in the way of repentance the promise of comfort was
added that God would have mercy and abundantly pardon (Isa.
55:6-7). But it was also stated that "my thoughts are not your
thoughts, neither are your ways my ways, says the Lord. For
as the heavens are higher than the earth, so are my ways higher
than your ways and my thoughts than your thoughts" (55:8-9).
Therefore the divine forgiveness could only be heard and accepted as the content of truly new and astonishing *tidings of
salvation.* In its novelty it is set forth in Scripture as "not taking account of sin" (II Cor. 5:19; cf. Ps. 103:3; 79:8), as "remembering no more" (Isa. 43:25), and as a "non-requiting"
(Ps. 103:10). God, we read, shall "tread our iniquities under
foot" and "cast all our sins into the depths of the sea" (Mic.
7:19); he shall sweep them away as a cloud and mist (Isa.
44:22) and cast them behind his back (38:17). In all of this,
as Israel's God, he cannot be *compared.* "Who is a God like
thee, pardoning iniquity...? He does not retain his anger
for ever" (Mic. 7:18).[101]
While an ethical *skepticism* has an easy time of this matter
of human forgiveness, an ethical *idealism* has great difficulty with
the matter of *divine forgiveness.* Idealists have found this "not
reckoning of evil" a violation of the moral code, and have
seen it as a profanation of the *moral* character of religion

itself. Were that the case we could understand the offense of the Pharisees at hearing the message of Jesus and observing his intercourse with publicans and sinners. This could only mean a weakening of the seriousness of the Torah-religion.[102] Furthermore, is there not something arbitrary in a God who "does not reckon sin"? Is there any "justice" in papering over a matter so deep and so catastrophic that it causes God's anger to "burn"? After all, the sin of which we are speaking is directed not only against our fellowman but also *against our God*. All of these are no problems at all for an ethical skepticism, but they certainly are for an ethical idealism which is just as deeply ingrained in the human spirit. The issue that compels our attention is this: Why has the Gospel so little sympathy for an ethical skepticism,[103] while the protests of the idealists would seem to be meaningless in the light of the divine act of forgiveness?

We have said that one of the most striking features of the biblical message is that forgiveness is not set in the context of watering down or relativizing man's sin. God's attitude does not share in the dubious qualities which we find in human forgiveness. But for that very reason the perennial question is asked: Is there some basis for God's forgiveness, or some motivation and occasion for his turning from burning wrath to loving grace and mercy? People have always sought for a clear connection or relation in terms of which it is evident that his "turning" in no way detracts from *either* God's holy antipathy against man's sin *or* the actuality of his pardon.

Some have sought for an essential bond between God's pardon and man's repentance, and have pointed to remorse as the real basis of forgiveness. G. J. Heering, in opposing the doctrine of satisfaction, has made an appeal to the parable of the lost son and the text in I Peter which reads: "God opposes the proud but gives grace to the humble" (5:5; cf. James 4:6, Prov. 3:34). In the human act of humiliation, according to Heering, we find the foundation of forgiveness. Thus the transition from God's wrath to grace answers to a transition in man himself. To be sure, Heering did not intend to say that man's contrition results automatically in God's forgiveness; he continued

---

102. Cf. Stange, *op. cit.*, pp. 138f.

103. We think of the seriousness with which God acted and spoke, already in the Old Testament, in regard to ethical skepticism. Cf., e.g., Mal. 3:13-18; the "book of remembrance written before him" (v. 16) and the distinction between the righteous and wicked (v. 18).

to call forgiveness the "free act of God."[104] He conceived of the Gospel as God's remission "on the basis of man's repentance and his grace."[105] But he continued to eye repentance as a conditional and even essential basis, and crossed swords with all those who held that remorse, as such, is quite inadequate.

No one denies that we have to do here with a very important question, namely the place and function, the meaning and significance of repentance in the economy of God's salvation. The history of the Christian Church shows a wide variety of interpretations on the significance of penance and remorse. Special attention has often been given to what might be called the psychological power of contrition. Especially Max Scheler has stressed this feature, and has drawn a distinction between a regret which stems from a fear of punishment and true remorse.[106] Scheler saw a number of qualities in this remorse, but especially the "disempowering of guilt" (the *"Entmächtigung der Schuld"*).[107] He did not presume that remorse is sufficient for erasing the results of a guilty activity. "It cannot do away with the external, natural reality of the act and its consequences, nor with the evil character which attaches to that act. All these remain in the world."[108] At the same time, a true repentance is able to wipe clean the guilt of man within the *soul of man himself*. Remorse creates a new beginning and is therefore the "mighty self-generating power of the moral world."[109]

Now all of this receives full significance for Scheler when we consider that abstract "evil" is not the important consideration but sin "in the eyes of God."[110] In that perspective he speaks of forgiveness as a "richly mysterious event" (*"geheimnisreicher Vorgang"*).[111] Thereby he passes over to a different level of discussion from his conception of repentance as not only regeneration but the "disempowering of guilt." He treats of guilt itself and inquires: "Who has removed our guilt from

104. G. J. Heering, *Geloof en Openbaring*, II, 1937, 161.
105. *Ibid.*
106. Scheler, "Reue und Wiedergeburt," in *Vom Ewigen im Menschen*, 1923, p. 32.
107. *Ibid.*, p. 39.
108. *Ibid.*, p. 41.
109. *Ibid.;* cf. p. 42: "the most revolutionary power of the moral world"; viz., regeneration.
110. *Ibid.*, p. 50.
111. *Ibid.*

us? Who or what is able to do that?"[112] The problematic here
flows forth from the fact that Scheler first analyzes the act of
repentance phenomenologically. He regards repentance as no
"specifically Christian thought,"[113] and is concerned for those
"natural functions of remorse" which are seen in full only
within the Christian Church.

In that way, of course, our problem is set in very clear
relief. For never shall we be able to deduce the divine forgiveness (as a taking away of guilt) from the mere phenomena
of penance and remorse. When Scheler lays accent on the
meaning of remorse as "psychic power" (*"seelische Kraft"*) he
already exhibits one of the most profound problems in the
Roman Catholic doctrine of penance. He seeks a synthesis between the "guilt-eradicating power of repentance" and the freedom of divine pardon. Yet it is clear that such a synthesis is
impossible. For repentance receives a function here which is
out of line with the *nature of repentance* and which relativizes
forgiveness as the act of God's mercy. Moreover, these problems
cannot be shaken off lightly. Men have always been concerned
about the relation of forgiveness and repentance, and their interest has been motivated by the real lines of connection which
the Scripture itself draws between these two.

Thus in Proverbs, for example, we read: "He who conceals his transgressions will not prosper, but he who confesses
and forsakes them will obtain mercy" (28:13). These words find
their New Testament parallel in I John: "If we confess our
sins, he is faithful and just, and will forgive our sins and cleanse
us from all unrighteousness" (1:9).[114] Therefore it would seem
that there is an essential relation between God's turning from
wrath and showing grace, on the one hand, and man's own
turning from pride and embracing humility, on the other.[115]
The words "if not" are used repeatedly in reference to penance
and remorse, and are certainly very significant (cf. Deut. 27:

112. *Ibid.,* p. 51.
113. *Ibid.,* p. 52.
114. Cf. Acts 19:18 on those who came to believe and confess their guilt;
     also the connection between *metánoia* and forgiveness (Luke 24:47).
     Cf. the baptism of John and confession of sins (Mark 1:5). Further:
     Acts 2:28; 5:31 (repentance and forgiveness); 8:22.
115. I Pet. 5:5: *tēn tapeinophrosýnēn enkombōsasthe* (*TWNT,* II, *s.v.*
     enkombóomai: "to make one's essential characteristic" — "zum wesen-
     haften Merkmal machen"). Cf. Col. 3:12 *(endýsasthe).* We recall Jesus'
     words on humbling ourselves and being exalted (Matt. 23:12; cf. Luke
     1:51. Also cf. I Sam. 2:7).

1-3; 30:2). One should not blunt those warnings and appeals for the sake of vindicating or guarding the freedom of God's pardon. At the same time, it is evident that there is no mention in Scripture of a causal dependence of forgiveness upon remorse. Nor is there any conception of remorse as the "foundation" of forgiveness. The man who converts this essentially correlative relation into a causal one would seem to draw a very logical conclusion from the "if" of Scripture; yet he prostitutes the very nature of repentance or remorse and robs it of its essence. When communion with God is restored in the way of repentance and sorrow, we understand that it does not occur in the way of man's own "guilt-removing" power of penance. Man's own "turning" is not the cause of God's. Rather, communion depends on God's own free and very gracious pardon, which is known and experienced in the *penitence of man*.[116] Here, then, is the mystery of this correlation and the marvel of the Spirit. The essentially correlative bond of penance and pardon does not exclude, by any means, the fact that remorse has an influence in man. But a causal relation between these two is in conflict with genuine sorrow. The man who experiences sorrow cannot regard his pardon as "explainable" and cannot "conclude" from remorse to forgiveness. In repentance itself the marvel of forgiveness is always maintained,[117] for the sin-

116. We should observe that the "analogue" of human forgiveness, in Scripture, is not seen except in that definite relation in which communion is restored. "If your brother sins, rebuke him, and *if he repents, forgive him*" (Luke 17:3). Forgiveness is necessary seven times if one's brother returns and says seven times, "I repent" (v. 4). Yet here too there is no suggestion of a *causal dependence*. Thus in the Heidelberg Catechism's explanation of the Lord's Prayer (the sixth petition), no *ground* is given as a *motivation* for forgiveness.

117. In a striking manner, we find a *correlative* but not a *causal* relation between forgiveness and penance in Ps. 32, especially vv. 3-5. After silence comes oppression, and after confession, forgiveness. At the same time, the *blessedness* of sin's being covered and forgiven is celebrated in v. 1; so too the "deliverance" of God in v. 7, and being found by him in v. 6. In contrast to any *causality* of remorse we should read such a text as Heb. 10:22 — the heart purified of an evil conscience. The context (sacrifice, priest, sprinkling) excludes any *fundamental function* of repentance. Cf. the word to Simon: "Repent therefore of this wickedness of yours, and pray to the Lord that, if possible, the intent of your heart may be forgiven you" (Acts 8:22). In Acts 5:31 we read that God exalted Jesus as Leader and Savior "to give repentance to Israel and forgiveness of sins." Cf. also V. Taylor, *Forgiveness and Reconciliation*, 1946, Chap. IV.

ner knows that forgiveness of sins does not depend on him.[118]

If our forgiveness does not depend on our sorrow (either causally or meritoriously) there is every reason to speak of the *astonishing* proclamation of God's pardon. This theme of astonishment is treated in Scripture in a very simple way. We hear very simple words with an inconceivably profound content. Thus, when Jesus proclaimed forgiveness of sins in the very simplest of terms ("Son, your sins are forgiven," Mark 2:5), there was also a scathing rebuke from the side of the scribes: "Why does this man speak thus? It is blasphemy!" (2:7). While not denying the possibility of forgiveness, the scribes assigned that right to God alone. Here Jesus vindicated his own power to forgive and tied it up with his own person: "the Son of man has authority . . . to forgive sins" (2:10).[119] As a sign of that authority he healed the paralytic man (2:11). Therefore, what was seen as blasphemy was really a legitimate forgiveness and was actualized in the Kingdom which had now drawn near. Christ was not only the Witness or the Preacher of forgiveness. Rather, he himself forgave and caused men to share in the treasures of his Kingdom.

When we reflect on this authority of Christ it is clear that his proclamation of pardon is made on an entirely different basis from the tolerance of an ethical skepticism. Granted, we encounter in the Gospel what can rightly be called a "preference" of Christ for sinners; yet this preference was not a "moral preference" or a weakening of the concept of evil. Exactly because of the abysmal lostness of sinners he "came to them" and "called" (Mark 2:17). Not the righteous but *lost sheep* were those whom he sought as the special objects of his coming (Luke 19:10; cf. Matt. 1:21). He defended that "preference" against every criticism which opposed his mercy to "moral maxims" or took offense at him. The legalists of his day could not understand why he ate with publicans and sinners, and the mystery of his forgiveness escaped them entirely. They did not perceive that this forgiveness is no compromise with human superficiality and impetuosity,[120] and was founded

---

118. This is also expressed in the Roman Catholic confessional, in the reference to the "unsurpassed mercy of the Lord"; cf. A. Snoeck, *Biecht en Pastoraal-psychologie*, 1958, p. 61.

119. Cf. O. Cullmann, *Die Christologie des N.T.*, 1957, p. 163 ("Jesu Selbstbewusstsein"), and H. N. Ridderbos, *De Komst van het Koninkrijk*, 1950, pp. 189ff.

120. Cf. Stange, *op. cit.*

on his being the Messiah.[121] In that capacity he called a halt to the irrevocability and the irresistibility of guilt. In his messianic reality he fulfilled those Old Testament words in which the mystery of forgiveness is brought to expression. He had that unique capacity as the Lamb of God who takes away the sins of the world (John 1:29). In the power of *that deed* the disciples went into the world to preach "repentance and forgiveness of sins" (Luke 24:47-48).

Therefore, in Christ's forgiveness the forgiveness of God is fully manifest. The Christian Church has seen a direct line of connection between the forgiveness of sins and Jesus Christ. We discover in him (with an intuitive certainty) the radical cancelling of any ethical skepticism or ethical idealism which men urge upon themselves in order to be "saved." The Messiah shows a broad mercy which wipes away all human moral measures, and a pardon which points to and reveals the profundity of man's guilt.[122]

Some people have said that the preaching of forgiveness in the apostolic writings is more complex than we find in the Gospels. They suggest that in the Gospels we have a simple view of pardon on the basis of penance, while in the apostles we find a complication of the possibility and reality of forgiveness. Yet it is striking that in the apostles the jubilee of forgiven sins is certainly not diminished. The depths and the riches of divine pardon are fully acknowledged and proclaimed. To be sure, the act of God's gracious forgiveness is very different from the simplism of men who forgive in their naiveté, without any reference to the gravity of guilt and restoration. When we talk about this "simplicity" of the New Testament forgiveness, we find ourselves at the center of a very ancient and still current debate on the nature of God's atonement.

Men have come to see, in the course of this debate, that it is impossible to oppose the "simple forgiveness" of the Gospels to the more "complicated forgiveness" of the apostolic

---

121. Ridderbos, *op. cit.*, pp. 207f.
122. With this we stand before the heart of biblical forgiveness. We are not finished, in the Gospel, when we merely note that we are covered by the mantle of love. When the garment of righteousness is granted to us, our own sin is disclosed and revealed. We recall that God said to David after his sin: "For you did it secretly; but I will do this thing before all Israel, and before the sun" (II Sam. 12:12). Cf. the forgiveness in v. 13.

letters. In the Gospels themselves we find the explosion of every simplistic and ethically indifferent conception of pardon. The coming and the mission of Jesus Christ are in contrast to any such conception. Surely the Gospels point to the radical nature of Christ's act of forgiveness and sacrifice; they emphasize the giving of his life for the "ransom of many" (Mark 10:45) and the shedding of his blood, which was "poured out for many for the forgiveness of sins" (Matt. 26:28). This "forgiveness of sins" is not a declaratory pronouncement from the depths of eternity but a real actuality in the midst of history. For that reason it is totally impossible to cast a wary eye on the apostles and to say that they "complicate" the message of forgiven sins.

This is also apparent in the letter to the Hebrews. There we are referred repeatedly to the sacrifices of the Old Testament and (by way of fulfillment) the reality of forgiveness. If anywhere a "simplism" of forgiveness is denied, it is certainly in the witness to Christ's sacrifice in the book of Hebrews. "Simplism," of course, is not the same thing as "uniqueness" or "simplicity." These latter thoughts are constantly found in this letter. We need not deny that in the Old Testament the lines of the atonement are commonly seen in the form of the various sacrifices; but this is hardly the point at issue now. God's turning from wrath to grace is pictured in what must *first happen* for the atonement and the taking away of guilt; at the same time, this does not imply that the Old Testament regards forgiveness as the effect of human religious and sacrificial achievements. God himself, as Vriezen has so rightly said, indicated the manner of the sacrifices in Old Testament times;[123] yet the way of the atonement was not complicated by God's forgiveness but by man's *own guilt*.[124] It was man's guilt that had to be abolished and absolved.

Certainly it is necessary for us to warn against the primitive idea of God's *Umstimmung*, or God's changing of his mind. But this fact must not detract from the important point which we are now trying to make. For here we see the key to Israel's sac-

---

123. Th. C. Vriezen, *De Theologie van het O.T.*, p. 299.
124. Therefore it would seem improper to interpret the elements of "satisfactio" and "placatio" as human achievement or "self-deliverance" ("Selbsterlösung; *ibid.*, p. 305), in order then to eliminate these as indecisive for the Old Testament materials on the biblical doctrine of the atonement.

rificial cultus. In the sacrifices we observe a turning from wrath to grace; nonetheless this "way of atonement" does not suggest a limitation of God's mercy but the reality of man's guilt. So too, when we hear in Hebrews of the fulfilling of "shadows" in the "true sacrifice" we are confronted again by the "way of atonement" as a way of a real *occurrence and event*. We hear that message which has always seemed to many the very example *par excellence* of the New Testament "complications": "without the shedding of blood there is no forgiveness of sins" (Heb. 9:22). There can be no doubt as to what the author really means. He is thinking of the "one high priest" who "appeared once for all at the end of the age to put away sin by the sacrifice of himself" (9:26). In this "putting away of sin," or the atoning act of the Lord, the reality of pardon is made known. There is something which must *first happen,* according to this letter, in order that sin may be atoned for; and that something has *now happened* in the *sacrifice of Christ.*

Cocceius, in his view of the relation of the Old and New Covenants, drew the conclusion that the Old Covenant forgiveness is only a *páresis* or an "overlooking" of man's sins.[125] He came to that conclusion on the basis of a wrong interpretation of Romans 3:25: "... in his divine forbearance he had passed over former sins." But Cocceius rightly saw that divine forgiveness cannot be regarded as an isolated divine disposition apart from what happens on earth within the reality of guilt. Therefore he gave attention to God's activity in and with man's guilt, and the capacity of the Messiah to take away man's sin on earth. Thus the Messiah accomplishes his messianic work. In this view Cocceius was in harmony with the book of Hebrews: the "singleness" and "once and for all," and the decisive and definitive happening at the end of the age. There is then forgiveness, and "where there is forgiveness . . . , there is no longer any offering for sin" (Heb. 10:18). Therefore, we cannot speak in Hebrews of a complication of forgiveness, or a violation of its uniqueness and singularity. A single jubilee is now sounded, and gives birth to that great "boldness" which flows forth from the divine forgiveness. No "problem" is now made of God's pardon. Rather, the depth and riches of forgiveness are underscored in contrast to the deep darkness of man's guilt. For man's guilt is now *taken away.*

125. Cf. my *The Work of Christ,* 1965, pp. 254ff.

It should not surprise us that an animated discussion has risen on this question of *Umstimmung*. Once we see that it was *God* who instituted the sacrificial rites and was present also in Christ, reconciling the world to himself (II Cor. 5:19),[126] we can certainly appreciate that the issue of the relations in which forgiveness is proclaimed takes on a new relevance. We cannot deny that in the New Testament the sacrifice of Christ is preached as the *cause* and the *source* of our salvation (Heb. 5:9). *Jesus* is the one who saves us from the wrath which is to come (I Thess. 1:10). *He* is the merciful high priest (Heb. 2:17) who charts a new and a living way to the sanctuary (Heb. 10:19-20). But is there an inconsistency here? When we read that "we have confidence to enter the sanctuary by the blood of Jesus" (10:19), it would seem, in the estimation of some, that we stand before an incontrovertible dilemma. Either we choose for a real *Umstimmung* or we conceive of the sacrificial act of Jesus as nothing but the disclosure of God's love, quite un-affected by his wrath. It is important to consider if that dilemma is avoidable. Time after time we observe, in the history of the Church, even in her most deficient formulations, an intuition that this dilemma can never do justice to the depths and the mystery of God's atonement.

Beyond all doubt, the sacrifice of Christ did not take place apart from God's initiative and purposes. Nor is there anything here in conflict with the reality of God's wrath. The idea of "God himself," in the act of the atonement, is clear enough in the whole of the Scripture. But whoever draws from this un-shakable truth a number of speculative conclusions is thwarted by the Scripture itself. Scripture refuses to speculate on this transition from wrath to grace. In such conclusions we might come to a static or an automatic concept of God's love, or a concept in which he merely covers his eyes and ignores man's sin. Therefore it is not by accident that in many views of God's initiative in the atonement there is no room for an authentic *taking away and atoning for guilt in history*. Sin is already forgiven and not-reckoned in the disposition of God to love — and of this disposition *Jesus Christ is the Revealer*. Thus the line of "forgiveness" is merely superimposed on history, despite the fact that history is replete with the murky and musty evi-dence of man's *guilt*. Therefore, too, it is completely unclear

126. This text is constantly referred to in literature in opposition to the *Umstimmung*. Cf. my *The Work of Christ*, pp. 258ff.

why Scripture calls attention to God's "burning wrath" and "holiness," or why it regards the guilty as *not unguilty* and sees God himself as causing the guilty man to walk in the ways of judgment. No longer is it evident, then, that God takes sin and the sinner very seriously and holds a man responsible for breaking communion with him and departing from the life which he, in his goodness, has given.

When we reflect on these things (on sin, wrath, and forgiveness) it is well to proceed with the greatest care and humility. Though we speak of the "mystery" of the atonement, we are taking no recourse in an *"asylum ignorantiae."* That could only be the case if we rationalized forgiveness and drew completely bizarre conclusions on the basis of that "mystery," or conclusions in the light of which we would then proceed to excuse ourselves. Nothing can be further from our intent. Scripture warns us against every effort to derive forgiveness from the conclusions of a certain "God"-concept, even if that concept is the concept of his *love*. Only in the *reality* of the atonement in Jesus Christ can we rightly contemplate (in a mood of praise and adoration) the wrathful and forgiving God.

In this light we must notice the proclamation of the forgiving God in mercy and grace. Already in the Old Testament God is called upon in his "great mercy" (Neh. 9:19, 27; Ps. 51:3ff.; 69:16), his "many mercies" (II Sam. 24:14; I Chron. 21:13; cf. Isa. 63:7), and his mercies that extend as high as "the heavens are above the earth" (Ps. 103:8, 11). In the New Testament we hear a doxology of praise for God's activity ("rich in mercy") in Jesus Christ (Eph. 2:4; cf. James 5:11). Some persons, in view of such passages as these, have made a distinction between God's "covenant-love" and "election love." They have based their argument on specific scriptural terminology.[127] Snaith, for example, sees God's covenant-love enunciated especially in the Hebrew word *chesed*. This is the primary expression for God's relation to Israel in covenant. Here the faithfulness of God is emphasized: his remaining true to the stipulations of his covenant. *Chesed,* in that sense, can also be used for either "party" in the covenant, and as such is differentiated, in Snaith's view, from *chen*. The latter term has no specifically "covenantal" flavor and has reference to God's unmerited and monopleuric grace. Snaith recognizes that this distinction is not so "neat" as to permit us to speak of a "separation"; for

127. N. H. Snaith, *The Distinctive Ideas of the O.T.,* 1947, pp. 98f., 128f.

the very nature of God's covenant as a *gracious covenant* suggests the essential bond of *chesed* and *chen,* or God's faithfulness and grace. Therefore, in Snaith's own judgment, these two words "actually approach each other."[128] The fact that God remains true to his covenant does not *exclude* but rather *includes* his grace. Though Israel was unfaithful, her infidelity did not eliminate God's faithfulness. Thus the mercy of God toward those who are guilty and unfaithful displays the fact that *chesed* is fully revealed in *chen.*[129]

The close intimacy of these thoughts is also apparent in the New Testament concept of *éleos.* Again, it is impossible to understand this term, in a purely *formal* sense, as the holding of oneself in faithfulness to a given promise. The term refers to a "remaining faithful in *mercy.*" It is mercy that is revealed in the incomprehensible act of a radical forgiveness and the restoration of communion with God. This is the wonder that Zacharias celebrated when he sang of the "knowledge of salvation to his people in the forgiveness of their sins, through the tender mercy of our God" (Luke 1:77-78). God's act of mercy is an act which wells up within him innerly, for he *is the Merciful One* (Luke 6:36). His mercy transforms the self-chosen end of the sinner into a new beginning. It can never be deduced from the nature of its object (cf. Rom. 9:15; Ex. 33:4). Precisely in this fact (that mercy is unmotivated!) we see the greatest reason for amazement and deep humility. In that which God *does* in his mercy it becomes apparent that his love is totally different from an indifferentness. This is evident in the biblical doxologizing of his mercy; it appears in his own self-designation and the light which he sheds on his name. "Lord, the Lord, a God merciful and gracious, slow to anger,

---

128. *Ibid.,* p. 128.
129. In the LXX *chesed* is commonly translated by *éleos* (*TWNT,* II, *s.v.*). Bultmann also sees *chesed* as resting upon the covenant, to which a believer can make his appeal. But there is no contradiction between faithfulness and "unmerited love," since "appeal" and "claim" are not the same. "In that man, because he was faithless, can make no claim upon God's *chesed,* the *chesed* for which he nonetheless hopes now gains the character of forgiving grace" (*ibid.,* 477). On *chesed* and *chen,* cf. further E. Jacob, *Théologie de l'Anc. Test.,* 1955, pp. 82f.: *chesed* as loyalty (p. 83), and *chen* and *rachamim* in a "unilateral sense that excludes reciprocity" (p. 85). Vriezen, *op. cit.,* p. 175, speaks of *chesed* as "firm commitment" ("vaste verbondenheid"), and *chen* as "favor" ("gunst"). Cf. his reference to Hos. 2:18: *chesed* and *rachamim* as faithfulness and pity ("trouw" and "ontferming").

and abounding in steadfast love and faithfulness, keeping steadfast love for thousands, forgiving iniquity and transgression and sin" (Ex. 34:6-7). But notice that this statement is immediately followed by these words: ". . . who will by no means clear the guilty."

Moses understood the meaning of that self-designation and prayed for forgiveness. He confessed the hardheartedness of his people (34:9). He knew that in this way of confession there is also hope; for God is the Merciful One. God is not capricious and never breaks his covenant.[130] But Moses also knew that God's mercy is not the same thing as a "tolerance," and his wrath leaves no room for an indecision or indifferentness. Israel also experienced this repeatedly. The relation of love and wrath did not present a "problem" for Israel but emphasized the *legitimacy of God's anger*.[131] The wrath of God was not conceived as an "attribute" that is shoved aside when he makes room for his love. That fact is apparent in the many Old Testament references to his turning from wrath to love or from love to wrath. In the wrath of God we are not confronted by the "dark side" in contrast to the "light side" of his love. His wrath is directed against that which frustrates the revelation of his love. It is directed against man's sin or the breaking of communion with him. Precisely therefore we cannot argue and we may not argue from the love of God to the unreality of his wrath. This fact is evident in the Old Testament, and it finds its fulfillment in the New Testament reality of the atonement.

The statement is often made, with an appeal to the Scripture, that both the justice and the mercy of God are summed up in the light of the cross of Calvary. We grant that that statement has not always been made in a proper way, but the statement itself is certainly on the right track. It reminds us that God's mercy does not imply a toleration of man's sin. Rather, in the act of God's mercy man's sin is utterly condemned and completely absolved, and sinful man is taken up into fellowship with God again.

This issue of God's justice and mercy, in their interrelationship, has often been the burning focal-point in theological debates. We can understand why that is the case when we see how difficult it is to escape the idea that justice and mercy join

130. Cf. Gispen, *ad loc.*
131. Jacob, *op. cit.*, p. 91.

hands in the cross, while nonetheless a certain tension still remains. The tendency is then to isolate these two virtues from each other and to bring them back again in a kind of artificial harmony or balance. The whole debate on the atonement is then seen as hanging together with this concept of "balancing." In the history of the Church and her theology the debate has commonly found its center in the conceptual framework of Anselm. He it is, as history has rightly judged, who deserves the title of the greatest advocate of God's *justitia distributiva*. He tried to demonstrate that the atoning work of Christ could only be seen within that structure. But ever since the time of Anselm, and even down to our own day, there has been opposition to those views which he espoused especially in his *Cur Deus Homo*.

The nature of the opposition has been very complex. Socinians have opposed not only Anselm's doctrine of the atonement but any notion of vicariousness. At the same time he has been opposed by those who have no criticism of his substitutionary views at all. In the latter case the objection is usually against the priority of justice over mercy. Can we ever accept that kind of priority, or have we already betrayed an unbiblical bias in our conception of God? Some people have challenged that this conception implies a God whose first task is to take care of his own honor; only after his justice has already been satisfied is there room to consider his love and his mercy. These issues are very relevant in contemporary discussions on God's wrath and the mystery of the atonement.

Paul's letter to the Romans is especially important here. What does Paul mean when he speaks of the "righteousness of God"? Does he refer us to the *justitia distributiva*? One answer is that there is no such concept in Scripture; the idea of a "retribution" has no essential place at all. But other persons have stressed the "distributive justice" of God, to such an extent that his mercy and justice are set at odds. In our own day it is said, from various sides, that both these views are prejudicial and obscure the true light of Scripture. It is seen that the justice of God is treated by Paul in the matrix of the *Gospel*. Precisely in the *Gospel* (as the power of God unto salvation) is the righteousness of God most evident (Rom. 1:17). Righteousness is revealed "apart from the law" (Rom. 3:21; cf. 9:30-31); and the law and the prophets bear witness of "the righteousness of God through faith in Jesus Christ" (3:22). Luther was prompted by this new insight on God's righteousness, as recorded by the Apostle Paul; thus he experienced a crisis in his life and came to his liberating view of the Gospel. At first he had seen the justice of God as a divine attribute: the *justitia* in which he is right and punishes the sinner. At that time, as Bavinck has put it, the term *justitia Dei* was "one of the bitterest words of Holy Scripture."[132] But this does not mean that Luther later denied the wrath of God; it means that he had no liberty[133] until he had seen that Paul did *not* view the *justitia distributiva* as a divine "attribute" but as righteousness "apart from the law." Here was a righteousness that was granted in the Gospel and was therefore connected with faith in Jesus Christ.[134] In the context of that faith the righteousness of God was seen as a joyful and inspiring reality. This is what we would expect it to be from the complete *gift-character* of this righteousness.[135] Here, then, is a righteousness that is diametrically opposed to all self-justification which men seek to attain by their own strength.[136]

It is sometimes concluded that there is no such thing as a *justitia distributiva;* that is to say, there is no such thing as a punishing and retributive righteousness. That being the case, some persons have tended to identify, for all practical purposes, God's justice and mercy. But this conception is different from a recognition of the unity and harmony of God's virtues, and

132. "Qua Deus est justus et peccatores injustos punit." Bavinck, *Geref. Dog.,* III, 515. Cf. O. Weber, *Grundlagen der Dogmatik,* I, 480.

133. Cf. E. Bizer, *Fides ex Auditu. Eine Untersuchung über die Entdeckung der Gerechtigkeit Gottes durch M. Luther,* 1958, pp. 23f., 151.

134. Cf. Luther on Ps. 71:2 ("*in thy righteousness* deliver me and rescue me"), and Ps. 31:1 ("*in thy righteousness* deliver me"); also Bizer, *op. cit.,* pp. 15, 20, and W. J. Kooiman, *Luther en de Bijbel,* pp. 35-36. On righteousness in the O.T. (e.g., Ps. 71:2): K. Hg. Fahlgren, *Sedaka. Nahestehende und entgegengesetzte Begriffe im A.T.,* 1932, pp. 103f.; O. Weber, *op. cit.,* I, 476f. Luther's problem has been restated by K. Holl as follows: "For him the difficulty consisted in conceiving in how far that which God does in righteousness might be called his own righteousness, and in how far this could be harmonized with the otherwise common meaning of 'righteousness.'" Cf. Holl, "Die justitia Dei in der vorlutherischen Bibelauslegung," *Gesammelte Aufsätze zur Kirchengeschichte,* III, 1928, 172. Cf. also, especially, J. T. Bakker, *Coram Deo. Bijdrage tot het Onderzoek naar de Structuur van Luthers Theologie,* 1956.

135. Cf. Ridderbos, *Comm.,* pp. 35f.

136. Cf. Phil. 3:9 *(tḗn ek theoú dikaiosýnē epí tḗ pistei),* and Rom. 10:3. The Jews were "ignorant of the righteousness that comes from God" and sought to "establish their own."

it cannot possibly explain why Scripture speaks of both God's mercy *and righteousness*.[137] In addition to this, there are those who see in Luther's view a strong denial of *justitia distributiva* and the cancelling out of God's wrath. Ritschl, for example, has pitted the love of God against the concept of distributive justice. By drawing speculative conclusions on God's love, he has come into conflict with Paul himself; for in Paul the opposition of love and righteousness does not exist. Paul was not concerned about this problem of how the Gospel is to be harmonized with God's justice. Much rather, God's justice, as he saw it, is manifest *in the Gospel*. At the same time, Paul spoke of the great salvation of God in the context of God's justice.

This Pauline accent is apparent in such a text as Romans 3:25-26. Quite understandably, that reference has always occasioned a good deal of debate. Paul points us to what God has done to demonstrate his justice. The Pauline interpretation of the Gospel leaves no room for a disposition on God's part in terms of which he simply grants his amnesty as a sudden and erratic decision, or a decision that is not open to further inquiry and that stands apart from what he has done in history. Paul is concerned about what has happened "at the present time." God willed to exhibit his righteousness in time. He willed to prove "that he himself is righteous and that he justifies him who has faith in Jesus" (3:26). There is no mere pronunciamento here. There is no mere command that echoes in the corridors of eternity. Rather there is something *visible in history*. In contrast to every simple identification of mercy and justice we must set the strongest possible accent on the biblical context in which the Gospel is now preached.

Let us look, first, at that word which the Revised Standard Version has translated "to show" (*éndeiksis*, v. 25). Some exegetes and translators have found in this a "demonstration" (see the NEB): "God meant by this to demonstrate his justice." But were that the case, of course, we might well assume that this word is opposed to all our doubts concerning God's justice in justifying the ungodly man by his grace. It would then seem that there is a contradiction to the Old Testament message that God does not hold the guilty to be guiltless (Ex. 34:9); rather he speaks his "woe to those who call evil good and good evil" and who also "acquit the guilty" (Isa. 5:20,

137. Cf. here the important work of H. Cremer, *Die christliche Lehre von den Eigenschaften Gottes,* 1917[2], pp. 47f.

23; cf. Prov. 17:15). Certainly the threefold reference to God's righteousness in these verses is very worthy of our note. But this does not imply that Paul had a "demonstration" or a "proof" in mind. It seems to us that the term *show* is preferable to the idea of *demonstrate*, and that *demonstrate* is only acceptable in the sense of *show*. In that sense, of course, it is quite commonly used. In any case, the point is clearly to "let one see" and to "set something out to be observed."

W. G. Kümmel has taken issue with the concept of a "demonstration." Such an idea presupposes, in his judgment, that God justifies a man in such a way that his justice is and remains unblemished; moreover this fact is also demonstrable to man.[138] The background of that act would then seem to lie in a "problem": namely the problem of the compatibility of forgiveness and God's justice in regard to man's sin. Does Paul really wish to solve that "problem"? The answer we give must depend on the further context.[139] God shows his righteousness in the fact that in "divine forbearance he had passed over former sins" (Rom. 3:25). Here the word *páresis* compels our attention, the more so because "forgiveness" in the New Testament is rendered by the term *áphesis*. In that distinction we see the issue that Cocceius appealed to in drawing his radical conclusions on forgiveness in the Old Covenant.[140]

The idea of a "passing over" is by no means clear in itself. "In his divine forbearance he had passed over former sins" (RSV). Superficially seen, the concept might imply an indifferentness on the part of God, though in the rest of the chapter there is no suggestion at all that that might be the case. Furthermore, the stress on "forbearance" should point us in an opposite direction. God's attitude toward sins previously committed is defined by his "forbearance"; and in that fact we see the strongest possible argument against an identification of *páresis*

138. Kümmel, "[*Páresis*] und [*éndeixeis*]. Ein Beitrag zum Verständnis der paulin. Rechtfertigungslehre," *Z.Th.K.*, 1955; cf. O. Michel, *Der Brief an die Römer,* who also opposes the idea of a "demonstration."

139. In my *The Person of Christ,* pp. 149-150, I made mention of the "leitmotif of Paul's argument," that "not a shadow falls upon the righteousness of God"; also I somewhat presupposed, *in essence,* the element of a "demonstration." I wish to correct that thought at this time, as well as the error in footnote 49, where *áphesis* and *páresis* are turned around.

140. Cf. my *The Work of Christ,* 1965, p. 302, and *The Person of Christ,* 1954, pp. 149ff.

and *áphesis*.[141] Any such identification could only obscure the sense of what Paul wanted to say.[142] For when Paul used the term *páresis*, in connection with forbearance, it is clear that he had a different meaning in mind from our notion of "tolerance." Any "overlooking" or "ignoring" of sin is not present here at all. In *that* sense there is *no "passing over" of man's sin*. The thought, instead, is an attitude or activity on the part of God in which his "forbearance" is manifest as the "holding in" or the "non-discharging of" his holy wrath.

The divine forbearance, longsuffering, and restraint *(anochḗ)* are apparent already in Old Testament times. "For a long time I have held my peace, I have kept still and restrained myself" (Isa. 42:14; LXX, *anéxomai*).[143] This "holding back" creates the space, so to speak, in which very much can still happen. Therefore one cannot infer or interpret the attitude of God in regard to sin on the basis of what he does at any *particular moment*. Amid the commotion and uproar of the peoples, or their seething as mighty waters, he "quietly looks from his dwelling" (cf. Isa. 18:4). But we cannot conclude from this "quietness" the deepest intentions of his heart.[144] Surely there is no minimizing of evil in these words: for everything depends on what God does *later*, and *why* he restrains himself *at this time*. Why does he "pass over" former sins? Obviously we find a recollection in Romans 3:25 of God's "forbearance"; but that *anochḗ* is by no means the *end of his ways*. It is rather an arrow that points us to the future and that underscores the situation of his "holding within himself" and "not causing to flare up" his definitive judgment on man's sin. In this "holding within"

141. Cf. also Kr. Strijd, *Structuur en Inhoud van Anselmus' 'Cur deus homo,'* 1958, p. 269 (the relation between *anochḗ* and *páresis*). Therefore Strijd regards it as incorrect to deny a punishing or retributive righteousness in Rom. 3:25, 26; *ibid.*

142. Cf. R. Bultmann *(TWNT,* I, *s.v. aphíēmi).* Bultmann hardly sees any distinction here. *Páresis,* he writes, as found only in Rom. 3:25, has the same meaning as *áphesis.* Thus *páresis,* for Bultmann, also means "forgiveness." Note further Kümmel, *op. cit.* ("erlassen, aufgeben"; *páresis* as "erlasz"). Kümmel does not exclude the idea of "passing by" (p. 158), but correctly contends that the context must decide. Cf. p. 163, where he does not read an "Übergehen" of sin but a punishment which does not destroy.

143. Cf. Rom. 3:25, *anochḗ;* Isa. 64:12: "Wilt thou restrain thyself at these things...?" (viz., when the "holy cities have become a wilderness," v. 10). LXX: *kai epi pási toútois anéschou.*

144. Cf. K. Schilder, *Licht in de Rook,* 1951³, pp. 69f. (on Isa. 18:4).

his purpose is very evident: salvation in Jesus Christ. For in Jesus Christ we see God's true attitude in regard to man's sin, and in him there is certainly no watering down and no shred of tolerance. The very opposite, in fact, is true. In that which now happens ("at the present time"; 3:26) the *end of God's forbearance is already evident*.[145] It is now that he shows his righteousness; and yet his ire is not completely unrestrained. The atonement occurs in the way of God's *cursing of man's sin*. Therefore Paul does not refute a fallacious idea of God's patience; instead he indicates that precisely in this way (the sufferings of Christ) he "shows" his righteousness. Thus his "restraining himself in his wrathful judgment"[146] can only be rightly regarded in the light of his actions "at the present time." In those actions he takes sin seriously as never before. He condemns and atones for man's sin in his *full wrath*.[147]

Therefore the *páresis* of this text can only be viewed as the forbearance of God in strongly teleological terms. It has reference to the "divine course of action which, in his forbearance, is not yet brought to completion."[148] When we conceive of the *páresis* in that light we may also conclude that Paul preached the full Gospel by pointing to the cross as the locus of God's

145. Schlier, *TWNT*, I, *s.v. anéchō*.
146. *Ibid*.
147. Cf. K. Barth, *K.D.*, IV/1, 308 (ET, 280), on *páresis* and the limit of Old Testament sacrifice. Also Bavinck has given an extensive discussion on Rom. 3:25-26 *(Geref. Dog.*, III, 353f., and IV, 166f.), in connection with the relation between righteousness and mercy. Bavinck has written (IV, 166) that it *was possible* for God, in the way of the *hilastérion*, "with the retention of, and indeed in agreement with, his righteousness, to justify him who has faith in Jesus (Rom. 3:25, 26)." Thus Bavinck himself rightly corrects his own statement, "with the retention of" ("met behoud van"). Strijd has said (*op. cit.*, p. 271) that Bavinck denied that Rom. 3:25-26 is concerned with the punitive righteousness of God; he finds this the more remarkable because this note is sounded within those quarters in which men are wont to place too strong an accent on God's punitive justice. Surely Bavinck interpreted Rom. 3 according to Rom. 1:17 (the righteousness of the Gospel; emancipation; cf. III, 355); and here the full light of Rom. 3:25-26 is not entirely evident (cf. the *páresis*, IV, 166). Yet it is obvious that this does not inhibit Bavinck, in any substantial way, from citing the Reformed formulary for the Lord's Supper ("rather than to leave it unpunished . . ."), or from mentioning, in this connection, Rom. 3:24-26 (III, 362; cf. 353).
148. H. N. Ridderbos, *Comm.*, p. 86; cf. E. Gaugler, *Römerbrief*, I, 91, on the purpose of God's ambiguous "holding within himself" ("mehrdeutige Ansichhalten Gottes").

judgment.[149] It is remarkable that precisely the Gospel shows us how seriously God takes sin and is angered because of man's sin. Therefore it is clear that there is no independent "order" of justice to which we assign a priority to the "order" of mercy. There is no tension between these two "realms" which we, by our puny reasons, may overcome. Certainly it is not in this way that we preserve the notion of "simplicity."

Even in the Old Testament era God's wrath was not incompatible with his love and mercy. It was levelled against the leaving of his ways, or the despising of that goodness and that love by which he desired to be truly God *for men*. His turning from real wrath to real grace was never an "indifference" or "no longer taking sin so seriously." It was the revelation of his holiness and righteousness not only against "sin in general" but also against each particular sin and the sinfulness in every sin. Therefore we find nothing of a "balance" or a mutual delimitation of righteousness and mercy; indeed, we find only a profound harmony as sin is atoned for and is taken away in reconciliation. In the atonement it is evident how much God has loved our world and in what manner he hates our sin. He is completely intolerant of the sinner's walking in his own ways apart from the Father's house. Thus the mystery of the *páresis* is revealed. God's forbearance cannot be explained by human analogies but is manifest in the intolerance of God's "being in Christ, reconciling the world to himself" (II Cor. 5:19). The marvel here becomes a reality in the manner in which Christ was "made to be sin" (5:21). Being moved by that judgment of God, the ambassadors of Christ went out into their world and bore the "word of the cross" (5:20). For that word was given its shape in this act in which God *delivers men from the shame of their own sin*.[150]

149. Here, it seems to me, is one of the crucial junctures in Strijd's dissertation on Anselm (*op. cit.*, pp. 269f.). Strijd recognizes that Rom. 3:25-26 has reference to the punitive and retributive righteousness of God, but he takes issue with those who set such stock in this that other words of the text are drowned out (p. 271). What this means, in essence, is that he points to the limitation of this aspect (Rom. 3:25-26, Gal. 3:13) and does not let Romans 3 govern the whole of Paul's expression on the atonement.

150. In the controversy of Rome and the Reformation, the Tridentine interpretation of the Reformation justification "sola imputatione" continues to play a role. Trent, in an incomprehensible manner, saw in the Reformation an externalization and no "renovatio," despite the fact that the "sola imputatione" certainly did *not have this externaliz-*

Kümmel has found no point of contact here which binds the thinking of Paul and St. Anselm together.[151] But when we study the *Cur Deus Homo* we are led to say that this verdict does insufficient justice to the grappling of Anselm as he struggled with the biblical concept of God's wrath. It is not our purpose to give an analysis of Anselm's thought; yet it is well to consider why he continues to sustain such an interest today. We live in an epoch in which the meaning and significance of God's justice are a subject of real concern. How is the justice of God related to his mercy? How can God forgive an immeasurable guilt against both God and man? Along with those other objections which are commonly lodged against St. Anselm, the following is frequently brought to the fore. St. Anselm, it is said, isolated the justice of God from the fullness of his virtues and assigned to it a certain priority; thus he assumed that God's mercy can only be viewed within that framework. Surely the issues that emerge here are very significant. They virtually define our thinking on the topic of *who God really is.*

Harnack has discussed the Socinian criticism of Anselm: that guilt is not infinite and that satisfaction and forgiveness are mutually exclusive. He has then added these words: "Faustus was not confuted by the orthodox, in so far as he demonstrated the worthlessness of the *juristic* thought-material with which they worked." In Harnack's judgment, orthodoxy fell back "upon the position that the qualities of righteousness and mercy exist in God with equal claims."[152] Certainly there is an element of truth in that criticism. The peril has always been real, in the orthodox tradition, that God's justice and mercy are set at loggerheads and are only "reconciled" in the cross. One can take the rough edges off such thoughts by saying that they were made with the best of intents. But it is more responsible to warn, with Korff, against presuming that "justice holds firmly for punishment as grace presses on for pardon," while all the while wisdom is interposed as the "solution" which satisfies them

---

ing tendency — any more than did the Reformation "extra nos." Cf. A. J. Venter, *Analities of Sinteties? 'n Analise van die Dilemma insake die Werkelijkheid van die Regverdiging,* 1959. Venter has made this point well, and has thereby contributed to a meaningful discussion with Hans Küng.

151. "The Anselmian satisfaction theory, therefore, has no point of contact in Paul"; Kümmel, *op. cit.,* p. 161.
152. Harnack, *History of Dogma,* VII, 158f.

both.[153] For this kind of reference to wisdom as a "mediator" is simply opposed to the biblical witness. One may recognize the genuine motive here (viz., to take sin seriously) and may also appreciate the stress on the reality of forgiveness. But the formulation is very deficient. The unity of God's entire activity is now threatened. The suggestion is made of a "reconciliation" in God himself, or a unity of opposites; yet such a view can never shed light on the nature of God's atonement. The foundation of this thinking is the concept of a mutual "delimitation" of God's attributes with "wisdom" functioning as an "arbiter."[154]

We find nothing of those complications in the Gospel. It is not the case that God's mercy is only apparent *after* and only *because* his justice has been met. It is simply not true that his mercy is only "possible" in that light. God's justice, in fact, in the Gospels, is seen as his *wrath* against man's sin, and his *condemnation* of man's sin, and his utter *intolerance* for man's sin. Exactly *in* that intolerance the act of his mercy is revealed. Therefore we celebrate God's justice *and* his mercy — and our celebration is but *one*.

Along with the theology of Anselm, the Heidelberg Catechism has given rise to a new interest in the relation of God's justice and mercy. Some have seen in Lord's Days 4 and 5 a strong resemblance to Anselm's line of thought. The real question, at this point, is not whether the Catechism tries to prove the atonement rationally. We can certainly point to the very first Lord's Day, where the reality of the atonement is already spoken of in strongly confessional terms. We can also refer to Question 19, where the knowledge of the atonement is grounded in the "holy Gospel." Again the answer is already presupposed in the question and sets its stamp on the very method of questioning. That same thing is apparent in the

---

153. F. W. A. Korff, *Christologie*, II, 193. On Luther, cf. Kooiman, *op. cit.*, p. 36: "He had learned to view the righteousness and mercy of God as two attributes that stand next to each other and are weighed off against each other."

154. One could never ground this delimitation in the word *epieikeia* (cf. II Cor. 10:1: "gentleness of Christ"; also Acts 24:4). This "forbearance" (Phil. 4:5; cf. Greijdanus, "billijkheid": fairness, equity, reasonableness) has nothing to do with an ethical skepticism, or with a delimitation of justice by mercy. Cf. Preisker in *TWNT*, II, *s.v.*, and K. Schilder, *Heidelbergsche Catechismus*, I, 512-514 (in the treatment of Q. 11 of the Catechism).

case of Question 18. We do not read, *"Is* there a Mediator?" but *"Who is he?"* Our answer predefines the way in which the question is put, and the rational problem of the atonement is already denied, in principle, within the question. The real nub of our problem lies, instead, in this question: Does the Catechism presuppose a priority of God's justice over his mercy? Does it presume those things which must *first happen* if the atonement, or our being received into God's favor again, is to be both possible and real?[155] In this connection we should notice especially Question 12: "God will have his *justice satisfied."*

In Question 11 the problem is set forth very clearly. We read of God's fearsome wrath, in Question 10, and the issue is now raised: "Is, then, God not also merciful?" The answer comes: "God is indeed merciful, but he is also just." Obviously the Catechism is concerned here about the relation of God's wrath and grace. In the light of the reality of God's wrath we are now directed to his mercy; but the reality of his mercy does not detract from the reality of his anger against man's sin. We think of Psalm 77, where the question is raised in reference to God's wrath and mercy: "Has God forgotten to be gracious? Has he in anger shut up his compassion?" (v. 9). Yet that reference does not form a real parallel to Lord's Day 4. In Psalm 77 the poet already knows of God's mercy, as a present experience, and he ruminates on the possibility of God's ceasing to be merciful. In that case the wrath of God would again win the upper hand. According to the Catechism, however, the reality of mercy is itself the issue at stake.

Some have said that this question ("Is God not merciful?") is a very strange way for the Church to be speaking, even if we grant the peculiar methodology of the Catechism. This criticism, however, can hold no water, since a question certainly can have the positive intention of setting forth an indubitable matter in the clearest possible focus. Rhetorical questions are replete in the Scripture. Consider the following statements of

155. K. Barth takes issue with the view of A. Lang that QQ. 12-18 belong to the weakest section of the Catechism. (Barth calls this "ein Fehlurteil.") Only a superficial impression, in Barth's opinion, could permit us to speak of an *a priori* deduction here. In reality, according to Barth, the Catechism follows Anselm and the letter to the Hebrews (2:17, 7:26) on what "had to be." Cf. Barth, *Die chr. Lehre nach dem Heidelb. Katech.,* 1948, p. 42. On Anselm's reasoning at this point, see Barth, *Fides quaerens intellectum. Anselms Beweis der Existenz Gottes,* 1931, pp. 55f.

Paul: "Is the law sin?" (Rom. 7:7); "Do we then overthrow
the law by this faith?" (3:31); "Is God unjust to inflict wrath
on us?" (3:5); "Is there injustice on God's part?" (9:14). All
of these receive the very same answer: "By no means!" "Are
we to continue in sin that grace may abound? By no means!"
(6:1-2). In this vein we should also see the question in the
Catechism.

Nevertheless, it is striking that Paul asks, "Is God not *righteous?*" whereas the Catechism asks, "Is God not *merciful?*" The
Catechism could have done better to continue in the line of
Question 1 (concerning the reality of God's mercy) and to indicate in its later questions and answers that this mercy in no
way excludes his justice. Had it done so, it would not have
followed an inferior method. For the sense of these questions
can only be grasped and made clear, and can only be seen as
comfort for the Church, when we emphasize that God's merciful pardon entails his *taking of sinners seriously.* He refuses
to be deceived when he looks at what the sinner is. If the
Catechism had worked more fully within that perspective it
might have avoided entirely the misunderstanding which has
linked it together with Anselm. Moreover, nothing would then
be lost from the original intent.[156]

As things are, the purpose of the Catechism is very clear,
despite our methodological objections. Our concern is that
the proper form be utilized. Criticism of the Catechism has
usually had reference to its strong and apparently *a priori*
accent on the prescriptive or punitive justice of God (see Questions 11, 12, and 16). It is at that juncture, particularly, that
some have thought to find the similarity to Anselm. They have
asked if we observe the same isolation of justice, or the order
of justice, which must always remain intact in the interest of
the honor and majesty of God. Certainly, if the questions of
the Catechism are viewed in that way they can only be regarded
as inappropriate, despite their obvious rhetorical intent. For
such a priority is never to be found in Scripture.[157]

156. Cf. H. Kakes, "Over Methode en Oorsprong van de Vragen 12-18 van
     de Heidelb. Catechismus," *G.T.T.*, 41, p. 168, in connection with the
     questions in Ursinus' *Catech. major.* E.g., "Quare necesse fuit Christum
     esse verum Deum et verum hominem?" In Ursinus the questions come
     in a different context — viz., under the second article of the Creed.
157. On the impossibility of this priority, in the light of the simplicity of
     God, see K. Schilder, *op. cit.*, I, 508f. It seems to me that Schilder does
     not work out this theme consistently in II, 7ff. (Par. 33, "De Eisch

Therefore it is important to consider the motives of the Catechism. Very obviously, its major concern is that God's forgiveness does not imply a tolerant attitude in regard to man's sin. We miss the direct echoes of Romans 3:25, to be sure; for Question 11 is oriented to other scriptural passages. But the Catechism very plainly disjoins a genuine atonement from an automatic conception of forgiveness which can find no place for the wrath of God. There is something existential about these Lord's Days, even when we criticize their peculiar methodology. The anger of the Lord is not seen in abstraction, but in reference to our actual guilt — to that guilt which increases "every day" (cf. QQ. 7, 8, 12, 13, 15). The way of escape is not open to man in himself, and man can find no reprieve by exercising his own potentialities (Q. 12).

Here the Catechism is in complete agreement with the biblical witness (including Romans 3:25) which indicates the purpose and the end of the *páresis* and exposes how *much* God is angered because of man's sin. God refuses to tolerate or to overlook man's guilt. One might challenge if the biblical citations in the Catechism are as rich and as obvious as they might have been if the full weight of Scripture had been brought to bear at this point. We might also wish that the scriptural accent on God's justice and mercy *in the cross* had been more pervasively worked out. Yet the answer to Question 11 ("God is indeed merciful, but he is *also* just") is clearly in line with the Catechism's motive. At the same time, that answer might raise the specter of a unity of opposites; moreover, the scriptural riches can never be compressed in this term *also*. In Answer 11 God's justice is viewed in relation to that sin "which is committed against the most high majesty of God"; in Answer 12 the allusion is made to Romans 8:4, ". . . in order that the just requirement of the law might be fulfilled in us, who walk not according to the flesh but according to the Spirit." Nevertheless, we get the impression, from this and the other texts cited, that the Catechism is especially concerned about the *beginning* of Romans 8:4: "that the just requirement of the law might be fulfilled." The stress is on the "full satisfaction" which we must make, "either by ourselves, or by another."

In other words, Paul's point in Romans 8:4 includes much

der Satisfactie gaat voorop"), the result being an abstract view of God's righteousness. This chapter also ends with a reference to Anselm's *Cur Deus Homo*, I, 12.

more than the Catechism brings to expression. Nowhere does he regard the "justice of God" as something *isolated*. He prefaces his comments with the significant statement that God, "sending his own Son in the likeness of sinful flesh and for sin, ... *condemned sin in the flesh*, in order that the just requirement of the law might be fulfilled in us" (8:3, 4*a*). This element of an actual "fleshly" condemnation of sin is entirely lacking in the Catechism;[158] furthermore, that fact is all the more regrettable in view of the Catechism's appeal to this very section of Scripture. In Romans 8:3-4 the *full* gravity of sin, as well as the corresponding judgment of God, is the subject at hand. We can speak biblically of the justice of God when we have seen the gravity of sin in this light. Surely sin is committed against the "most high majesty of God"; but what precisely that means is only evident in that way in which God has acted in regard to man's sin. God condemns man's sin and casts it from its position of power,[159] to the end that the demand of the law might be fulfilled *in us*.

Therefore, Romans 8:3-4 speaks more deeply and more seriously of sin than the Catechism does. It sees man's sin in the light of the act and reality of that justice of God in which man's sin is absolutely condemned. This is no contradiction of what the Catechism says concerning man's sinning "against the most high majesty of God"; at the same time, it sets in a clearer relief who God in his majesty *is*. In that focus it is evident that there is no antithesis between God's justice and mercy. Biblically speaking, there is no "mystery" in the unity and the harmony of what seems to us irreconcilable. This harmony is manifest in the historical reality of the cross. But how then, we may ask, could the merciful God *not* be righteous and *not* be wrathful against man's sin when sin itself is the *departure from his good ways* and the *breaking of communion with him?* God is merciful exactly in his denouncing of man's sin, or his justice and condemnation of man's sin as that way in which man *must not go*. For in that way the shadows of his judgment are *certain to fall*.[160] The man who ignores God's

<hr>

158. Besides Rom. 8:4, the following texts are cited: Ex. 34:6, 7 (God's naming of himself), where a main accent is certainly God's not holding the guilty to be guiltless (v. 7); Ps. 7:9; 5:5; and Nahum 1:2-3 (jealousy and vengeance).
159. Ridderbos, *Comm.*, ad loc.
160. Cf. K. J. Popma, *Levensbeschouwing. Opmerkingen naar Aanleiding van de Heidelb. Catechismus*, 1958, pp. 99, 116f. "What we do learn

justice and glories in his mercy must surely be instructed in the nature of the atonement and the fundamental principle of God's "new way" with man. We find that way expressed in Genesis 3:15. It is precisely in the establishment of *enmity* that God proclaims the depths of his *mercy*.

We may grant that the Catechism refers plainly to the wrath of God against man's sin. Yet the scriptural materials, as reflected in Lord's Day 1, should certainly have excluded, once and for all, the appearance of an antinomy or a contradiction in God's justice and mercy. The mercy of God loses its glow when we conceive of it as a form of "toleration" in the face of man's evil. For God is more merciful than that sort of "tolerance" could ever permit. He does not permit a man to wallow in his sin but condemns his sin in actuality. He covers and atones for man's sin before his holy face.

All of this is given proper articulation in Article 20 of the Belgic Confession. The caption there reads: "God has manifested his justice and mercy *in Christ.*" It is confessed, at the very outset, that God is "perfectly merciful and just" — but this appears in the modus of his activity in the cross. "God therefore manifested his justice against his Son when he laid our iniquities upon him, and poured forth his mercy and goodness on us, who were guilty and worthy of damnation, out of mere and perfect love, giving his Son unto death for us." There is no special difficulty at this point. The criticism we had of the Catechism is met by the reference to what God did "against his Son"; moreover, this too is seen in the light of his mercy and perfect love in the Gift of his love. That same accent is certainly intended in the Catechism. God's "giving his Son unto death for us" (BC, 20) agrees entirely with the Catechism's reference to God's "giving" (Q. 18). But the point is more clearly and explicitly made in the Belgic Confession. There we find a unified outlook on the mercy and the justice of God.

This same accent is found in Article 21 on Christ as "our only High Priest." Christ is the One who "has presented himself in our behalf before the Father, to appease his wrath by his full satisfaction, by offering himself on the tree of the cross." He is depicted in the concreteness of his suffering and his death, and reference is made to Isaiah 53, Psalm 69, and the "once and for all" of Hebrews. We read of the "appeasing" of the

in the Holy Scripture is that always, whenever we see God's righteousness, we also discover and experience his mercy."

Father's wrath; but we misconstrue that human expression when
we conceive of an order of justice which must first be met
before there is room for God's mercy. The purpose is rather
to articulate God's wrath and grace. Any other interpretation
forces the Confession to be in conflict with itself and infuses into
it a doctrine of God's *Umstimmung,* or his turning from an
original "non-mercy" to later "grace."[161]

One cannot understand a thing of God's turning from
wrath to grace so long as he refuses to see the reality of the
cross in the context of the Gospel. Yet, given that reality, it is
obvious that we cannot describe the atonement in terms that
hold together God's mercy and justice in an intellectual synthesis. Who can define the forsakenness of Christ on the cross
and comprehend the "why" of his distress? Who can give an
answer to this "why" in a lucid theological theory? The "why"
of Christ on the cross was an appeal to God, in the anguish
of God's judgment, at the very moment that the *Father's name*
was on Christ's lips. We are not suggesting that the proclamation of salvation, which came into our world at that moment,
is impenetrable, or unclear, or irrational. Indeed, that proclamation is attested in the plainest terms in Scripture and is even
"revealed unto babes." But we are saying that the deep source
from which the "waters of life" well forth cannot be "measured"
and can only be appreciated and experienced in the acceptance
of salvation. Here the fourth word from the cross ("My God,
my God, why hast thou forsaken me?") is rightly interpreted
in the Lord's Supper formulary of the Reformed Churches:
". . . that we might be accepted of God, and nevermore be
forsaken of him." In a similar line, the confession of Christ's
descent *into hell* is understood as a source of certainty in our
own temptation and anguish (HC, 44).

Who can possibly "explain" the God who is proclaimed

---

161. In his discussion of Art. 21 of the BC, Polman concludes *(Onze
Ned. Geloofsbelijdenis,* II, 341): "It is about time for once to evaluate
the Reformation confession on its own merits, and no longer to criticize
it on the basis of the Anselmian conceptions." Polman also remarks that
Calvin only cited Anselm a single time. Indeed, it is very clear that
the Belgic Confession is entirely defined by Calvin's accent on *misericordia.* Cf. Polman, *Woord en Belijdenis,* II, 31. In the case of the
Catechism, however, there is far less reason, both in regard to the
method and the definition of the relation of justice and mercy, to
weaken this connection with Anselm. Cf. Kakes, *op. cit.,* pp. 165f.

in this way? "God did not spare his own Son but gave him up for us all" (Rom. 8:32; cf. Gen. 22:16). It is hard to speak of "deep and less deep" words concerning Christ; but this statement of Paul belongs to the very deepest mystery of the atonement. No fears of a theopaschitism may inhibit our speaking here with an utmost amazement and reverence. The text is generally seen as a harking back to the Old Testament story of Abraham's sacrifice and God's response: "By myself I have sworn, says the Lord, because you have done this, and have not withheld your son, your only son, I will indeed bless you . . ." (Gen. 22:16). Men have fumbled for words to shed light on that passage. Ridderbos speaks of "the divine offer" brought nearer to mankind in Romans 8:32: "In the surrendering of his Son, God revealed himself as the Sacrifice, as the One who gives himself. He gives himself not in a parsimonious way of sparing himself but in forfeiting his only, beloved Son for man's lostness."[162] Michel concludes, with a reference to Abraham: "the pain of the Father's love reveals the magnitude of his sacrifice."[163] Althaus refers to the "magnificent sacrifice of the Father's love."[164] All of these point, in view of God's gift of his only-begotten Son,[165] to the conclusion of St. Paul: "will he not also give us all things with him?" (Rom. 8:32). The unity of the text is very evident. Since God has not refrained from giving us his Son (his *only* Son) he will also freely give us "all things." His act of giving his Son is the "down payment" for "all things," the assurance of the eschatological riches of salvation,[166] despite all "powers" and "heights and depths"

162. Ridderbos, *op. cit.*, p. 198.
163. Michel, *op. cit.*, p. 184.
164. P. Althaus, *Römerbrief, ad loc.* Greijdanus does not recall the Gen. 22 passage but does refer, in connection with the words "his own Son," to the "magnitude of God's gift of love" (*Komm.*, I, 392). On Rom. 8:32 and Gen. 22, cf. H. J. Schoeps, *Paulus. Die Theologie des Apostels im Lichte der jüdischen Religionsgeschichte,* 1959, p. 159 (cf. 145f.).
165. Though Paul does not name Abraham as a parallel, yet Rom. 8:32 has frequently played a role in this kind of typology. Cf. D. Lerch, *Isaaks Offerung, christlich gedeutet,* 1950, pp. 109, 134f. (Abraham and God; Isaac and Christ). The sacrifice of Abraham, who offered up his *only* son (Heb. 11:17, *tón monogenê;* Vulgate, *unigenitum*), has entered into the christological debates, especially in the case of the Socinians. Cf. Lerch, pp. 246f. In reference to Socinus, Lerch has written: "Isaac as a type of Christ became, for him, a witness for his adoptianist christology" (p. 249).
166. Michel, *op. cit.*, p. 185. Zahn sees a connection here with the promise to Abraham (the entire world), p. 422.

(8:38f.). Now a certainty beyond all doubt takes hold of our
beleaguered hearts. God has given his only-begotten Son (John
3:16). He has "given him up" (Rom. 8:32) [167] in a giving that is
also, at the same time, a surrendering to the "curse," and is
therefore the most inscrutable of judgments.[168] God entered into
the arena of man's guilt and refused to spare his only-begotten
Son. He "gave him up" upon the cross.

We can only speak, at one and the same time, of the wrath
and mercy of our God. Paul stresses that *God* has sent forth
Christ as an "expiation" (Rom. 3:25; cf. I John 2:2, 4:10).
But the word which he uses here *(hilastḗrion)* has always been
a subject of discussion. It is evident that the term participates
in all the unfathomableness of God's own being "against his
Son" (BC, 20). In the reality of "expiation" the seriousness of
sin and the riches of God's mercy are very evident. There is
no doubt that God himself is active in man's guilt, for guilt is
bared in all its ugliness precisely where guilt is both expiated
and condemned. The event of the cross does not consist of "two
parts"; instead it is grace and judgment, judgment and grace,
in one. Wrath and grace do not come together, in a dualistic
fashion, from "opposite sides." Indeed, when we read (as we
do in the Old Testament) of God's turning aside from wrath
to grace, or a limitation or conversion of his wrath, we must
see in those statements historical and concrete acts which con-
verge in a single instant. This is what we observe in the Old
Testament sacrifices. Those acts were *fused* in the very moment
in which even such words as "turning" and "transition" are
inadequate. So too, in the cross of Jesus Christ both righteousness and mercy are one. Sin is taken away in the act of God's
gracious judgment.

Therefore it is apparent, from these New Testament examples, that the Socinian criticism of the atonement through
the blood of the cross is an irreligious and a rationalistic hy-

---

167. This "giving up" does not exclude but rather includes Christ's giving
up of himself (cf. Tit. 2:14: *hós édōken heautón;* and Gal. 2:20:
paradóntos heautén).

168. The word *give up* (or *surrender*) is also found in Rom. 4:25: *hós
paredóthē diá tá paraptṓmata hēmṓn*. Barth writes, in regard to the
parédōken of Rom. 1:24, 26, 28: "Given away — given into the
shame of human sin and human death" (*Kurze Erklärung des Römer-
briefes,* 1956, p. 130).

pothesis. The mystery of the vicarious sacrifice is here vitiated,[169] and what God did centuries ago is declared (for lack of human analogies) impossible for today. There "could be" no place where God restores man and condemns that which hinders his fellowship with God. There "could be" no place where the compassionate God serves notice of how far he distantiates himself forever from man's sin.[170] But this Socinian view can never appreciate why it is that we are no longer anxious as we think of God's repugnance against our sins. For the cross is the *invitation — God's final invitation — to be saved.*

At the cross we hear the invocation of God's commandment which is holy and right and good, and which quickens men to life. When we observe the wrath of God we know how much we *may* and we *must* abide in his love. Therefore it is understandable that the God of love does not abandon man to his own fate. Having reconciled him to himself he continues to look on him in favor and to discipline him in love. He disciplines him as a son (Heb. 12:6). "For the Lord disciplines him whom he loves" (cf. Prov. 3:12) .[171] Far from being incompatible with love, this discipline is the consequence and the manifestation of his love. "God is treating you as sons" (Heb. 12:7). Not on the basis of but only in the context of sanctification can the atonement be understood. Therefore every form of antinomianism is not only a contradiction of the law but also of the obvious sense of the *atonement.*

F. W. Korff has discussed the doctrine of the atonement and the cogency of God's pardon, and has drawn a comparison between God's forgiveness and our own. "So then," he concludes, "it is demanded of us that we give without receiving in return."[172] Korff expresses his approval of a statement of Harnack which refers to "the dreadful prerogative of God, not being able

169. Cf. W. B. van Wijk, *Die Versoeningsleer in die Rakouwer Kategismus,* 1958, pp. 96f.; Polman, *op. cit.,* II, 323f., on Calvin's answer.

170. We recall how Harnack, with all his sympathy for Abelard in preference to Anselm, recognized that Abelard did not see clearly enough that the love of Christ, "at the same time, reveals the magnitude of guilt" (*op. cit.,* VI, 79).

171. In I Pet. 4:17 we read that the judgment begins "with the household of God." The *usus legis* in the lives of believers is certainly not only a *usus didacticus* but also, at the same time, a *usus elenchticus.* Cf. my discussion above, pp. 156ff.

172. Korff, *Christologie,* II, 197.

to forgive from love."[173] It ought to be clear, of course, that any such protest against a notion of forgiveness unmotivated by love is a protest against a very obvious blasphemy. But if we look again we find that Korff gives us nothing but a caricature; moreover, he gives us a caricature which can hardly avoid the pitfalls of Socinianism. His analogy between a divine and human forgiveness is really very inadequate, since even *our* forgiveness is distinguished from an ethical skepticism. Furthermore, Harnack's impassioned criticism lacks appreciation for the real sense of the Church's confession, to say nothing of Anselm's intent. Surely the statements of Anselm are not always felicitous, but his purpose was very clear: it makes a vital difference to God, he said, if a man sins or if he does not. Anselm was concerned about the reality of that wrath of God which cannot be assuaged by a minimizing of man's sin (see his *Cur Deus Homo*, I, 12). Therefore he rejected the analogy of a human forgiveness. In this attitude he was certainly on the right track, though unfortunately, in working out that motive, he did not allow the full Gospel to be heard. He contended that although *we* are not permitted to demand a retribution, yet nevertheless *God is*. For God is Lord of all, and his honor is violated if sin is left unpunished. At that juncture Anselm introduced his own conception of the honor of God: "Therefore God maintains nothing with more justice than the honor of his dignity" (I, 12). He rightly spoke of the wrath of God, but he spoke too abstractly of God's honor. His method gave little scope to the concrete witness of Scripture. Therefore the full perspective of God's honor was confused and was limited almost entirely to God's "dignity" or "self-vindication" in reaction to man's sin.

In this argument, of course, Anselm touched on one of the most central concepts of Scripture: God is and will always be himself. But the implication of this statement, in its biblical setting, can only be that God is the complete antithesis of egocentric man. In a scathing reaction to the notion of God's self-vindication, H. van Oyen has asked: "Or shall we preach in the Church (alas!) that not only the world is the arena of inner

---

173. We find the exact reference in Harnack (*op. cit.*, VI, 77): "the dreadful thought that God is superior to man, as having the prerogative of not being able to forgive from love, a payment always being needed by Him." Harnack is here concerned with Anselm's *Cur Deus Homo*, I, 12.

struggle and of maintaining myself, or the failure to uphold my own ego, but that all of this is the faint adumbration of what happens around the cross? Shall we suggest that, as in Heraclitus, so too the Father of Jesus is a God of 'struggle'?"[174] Certainly this statement is a strident protest against any notion of a perverse or egocentric maintaining of oneself. Yet it implies an unreal antithesis. There *is* a divine self-maintenance which has nothing at all to do with human egocentricity. The fact that God is the "same" was seen as a comfort in ancient Israel: *"For my name's sake* I defer my anger, for the sake of my praise I restrain it for you, that I may not cut you off" (Isa. 48:9; cf. Ezek. 36:22ff.). We should see in this text how circumspect we must be in presuming antitheses to God, or in drawing parallels to sinful man. For the divine witness transcends *infinitely* any such models as this. It was certainly this picture of God's "remaining himself" that Anselm had in mind; and for that reason the criticism of Harnack is very unfair. Yet the manner in which Anselm formulated that biblical intuition has laid him open to the misunderstanding and the flood of criticism which has always come his way. Anselm exposed himself to the charge of a purely formal concept of God's "self-vindication."

This entire train of thought might have been altered if Anselm had remembered the angelic "Glory to God" in the evening that Christ was born. Then too the honor of God was made public: but precisely in *this way of humility* he came to his glory. In the manger scene we see, with an unmistakable clarity, how far God's honor is set apart and radically removed from an exclusive "self-interest." Preoccupation with himself could only preclude God's interest in man, and could only eliminate his love and his mercy. Anselm regarded the honor of God in too academic terms. He saw it in terms that compel an interest in themselves. Therefore he was not able to give full weight to the biblical doctrine of God's justice. In reading him we get the impression of a neatly-woven system of "checks and balances," or a system in which God's honor is first maintained and only thereafter (because of that) is there room for his mercy.[175] Thus the glory of God's justice is obscured. The

---

174. Van Oyen, "Liefde, Gerechtigheid en Recht," *N.T.T.*, I, 40.
175. There is certainly an unmistakable element of truth in K. Holl's remark on Anselm: "Justice holds for him as that which stands firm — as the indubitable — while mercy is that which must be explained" (*op. cit.*, p. 179).

justice of God is his burning and punishing justice, but it is always his justice for his own "name's sake" and for "our sakes." God's justice is in opposition to that sin of man which stands in the way of communion, or that sin against which he has "indignation every day" (Ps. 7:11).

He who sees this living justice of God can only turn aside from every fictitious "balance," and can only regard such a view as a contradiction of what is truly *one* in God and is manifest forever in the cross. If we speak of a "tension" at all, we can do so in the reality of the Man of Sorrows, and there alone. The Church's message concerning him makes sense only if it detracts in no way from the justice or the grace of God. In the cross we observe that God's pardon is no gesture of mere tolerance; certainly it is no Midas-touch of his scepter. It is the incontestable act of his non-capriciousness.[176] In the case of man an ethical skepticism (or a lack of real interest in someone else) may still dominate our conception of forgiveness; but in the case of God there is nothing of this at all. Furthermore, we do not come to this conclusion by an *a priori* rationalizing of God's virtues but by the biblical preaching of the cross.

---

176. Here, it seems to me, is the problem in A. A. van Ruler's article on "God en de Chaos" *(Wending,* 1959, pp. 336ff.). Beyond God's "chaoticizing" of things in the divine judgment, there is also a reference to God's *creation* of the chaotic (337), as well as to his divine "play" ("spel"). Obviously this "play" is different, for Van Ruler, from the lack of seriousness which I have rejected here. A number of factors play a role in this "play"-concept: play as a gracious coercion, as compulsion of the chaotic (339), as compulsion in the figure of "play," as not being frightened by chaos (*ibid.*). Yet Van Ruler wants to say more than this. We may not deduce this chaos from the sin of man (344), though man's sin is an "enormously important factor." I should like to read this "playful" article in the light of the incontestable statement: "On the other hand, that same cross creates, in this most dire of all chaos, an order: the only order, the order of the atonement. The cross of Golgotha is the establishment of the rule of God in the chaos of sin and is thereby the reality of love" (347). But I cannot square this with the statement that the Gospel of the cross teaches us "that we do not flee, at any moment, or even distantiate ourselves innerly from chaos," since Jesus (Gethsemane, Golgotha) says "yes" to the judgments of God and *therefore to chaos* (348). I should judge that precisely for that reason we should be all the more prepared *not* to enter chaos in an increasingly deeper way (*ibid.*). The fact that Van Ruler immediately veers toward "a growth in the knowledge of misery, or a permanent penalty," indicates, I think, that his vision of "God and the chaos" is not, in all respects, lucid.

K. Strijd's criticism of Anselm has set this whole discussion in a very sharp focus. Especially is that the case in reference to the *sola misericordia*. In the *Cur Deus Homo* Anselm posed the question of whether it is proper for God to "put away sins by compassion alone, without any payment of debt" (". . . *utrum sola misericordia sine omni debiti solutione deceat deum peccata dimittere,*" I, 12). Anselm denied this after Boso had first ventured the opinion: "I do not see why it is improper." Strijd now takes up the cudgels against Anselm and defends the *sola misericordia*.[177] It would seem that he has right on his side, insofar as the terminology is concerned. For Anselm's false dilemma can only breed a confusion.[178] Yet Strijd proceeds to interpret the *sola misericordia* as a "stopgap" against any notion of reprisal. He even cites the statement of Nietzsche: "Great love will neither retribute nor repay — reprisal is drowned in the sea of much love."[179] At the same time, he dissociates the *sola misericordia* of "true forgiveness" from any ignoring of sin on the part of God. True forgiveness both sees and does away with sin.

Precisely at this point, if we take Strijd seriously, we find ourselves in the neighborhood of Romans 3:25-26 and Galatians 3:13. It is not clear, in Strijd's case, if *sola misericordia* is any different from the "naked forgiveness" (the *"blosze Vergebung"*) which Brunner has so rightly contested. Brunner has seen in this notion a peril for our moral obligations. *Sola misericordia,* as a term, is solidly biblical; yet the *"sola"* in no way implies an antithesis to God's justice. The man who knows that God is angry when we depart from his ways is also the man who takes these words *sola misericordia* with utmost seriousness on his lips. For here the justice of God is not threatened but is only confirmed.[180]

---

177. Strijd, *op. cit.,* pp. 288f.
178. Cf. the critical questions of Barth, *K.D.,* IV/1, 541f. (ET, 486f.).
179. Strijd, *op. cit.,* p. 289.
180. Barth, in a sharp rejection of Ritschl, has laid a strong accent on this point; *K.D.,* II/1, 410f. (ET, 365f.). In this same perspective he has assigned a significance to the justice of God as *justitia distributiva* (439; ET, 391); cf. the justice of God as *condemning* and *punitive*. It is a central problem in Barth's theology, it seems to me, that although he distinguishes mercy and justice, yet, for the sake of unity and harmony, he depicts the relations between these in such concepts as "reverse side," "effecting," "alien form" ("Fremdgestalt"), etc. For that reason, I believe, he does not come to the full truth of his own exegesis of Rom. 3:25-26 concerning the reality of wrath and the cross of Christ.

The cross of Jesus Christ is not the symbol of God's "naked forgiveness." It is the emblem of his *sola misericordia.* Thus when the wrath of God is not pre-empted by his love, the cross is taken up into the fullness of the message of salvation. Therefore the "word of the cross" is the word which we preach to the entire world. The cross, and the cross alone, is the locus of God's ultimate judgment. There we hear God's final and deepest reproach. Yet the wrath of the *Lamb* is still experienced as the consolation of the Church.

With this we end our discussion of sin, wrath and forgiveness. We have taken notice of the relations of sin and wrath, and of wrath and forgiveness. We have said that we cannot reconstruct the biblical lines and accents in a completely lucid theological theory. It is not possible, in that way, to lead a man to believe in the reality of God's pardon. The essence of the biblical message is that forgiveness can only be understood and embraced in the way of faith. Yet it is also clear in the preaching of the Word that sin is an astonishing reality which God, "rather than to leave it unpunished, has punished ... in his beloved Son, Jesus Christ, with the bitter and shameful death of the cross." These words are taken from the Lord's Supper formulary. They remind us that no conclusion is possible from an analysis of God's virtues *remoto Christo.* We can only proceed from the reality of the cross.

But when we do start at that point we see how antithetical this view is to any conception of mere "tolerance." The total intention here is our sanctification and the full communion with God: our sonship under his scepter, the blamelessness of those who follow the Lamb (Rev. 14:5),[181] and the dwelling of God with his people (Rev. 21:3). In the light of God's forgiveness we understand that no one shall see the Lord without holiness (Heb. 13:14). Thus it is impossible that faith, in looking forward to the eschaton, can still be "moralized." Quite to the contrary. For only now do we appreciate how deep and

---

Cf. my *The Triumph of Grace in the Theology of Karl Barth,* 1956, pp. 235-236.

181. "And in their mouth no lie was found, for they are spotless." Cf. the "blamelessness" *(ámemptos)* in holiness "before our God and Father, at the coming of our Lord Jesus with all his saints" (I Thess. 3:13). Cf. I Thess. 2:10: "righteous and blameless." *This* blamelessness stands over against that of Phil. 3:6 *(dikaiosýnē* and *ámemptos),* which Paul "counted as loss for the sake of Christ" (v. 7).

how far the reality of our forgiveness extends. The final meaning of human life is now completely evident. In this vision of the Lord the final illusion of sin is shattered and faith is turned to sight. God once gave rest and peace to Moses by going forth despite the fact that Israel had sinned (Ex. 33:12-16). So too *he himself* shall wipe away all tears from the eyes of his people in that day when "former things have passed away" (Rev. 21:4).

CHAPTER TWELVE

THE PROBLEM OF AN ALIÈN GUILT

W E NOW ENTER an area in which a strenuous and emotional debate has been constantly waged throughout the entire history of the Church and her theology. The debate is still going strong in our own day. We enter with a certain sense of trepidation, aware that the issues here have always had a profound bearing on the ways in which we conceive the nature and the gravity of our guilt. We are referring to the Church's confession of the doctrine of original sin. In that doctrine we meet up with an issue that has always compelled attention both inside and outside the Christian community. Indeed, we can say that especially two dogmas of the Church have constantly borne the brunt of attack from those on the outside. These are *divine election* and *original sin*. Apart from the other criticism levelled, it has always seemed to some that these two teachings especially demonstrate, with a unique cogency, the irrationality of Christian faith.

Both of these doctrines have been called harsh and entirely arbitrary. Though the purpose of the original sin dogma is obviously very different from that of election, there would seem to be a kind of *trait d'union* which binds these two together. Critics have been quick to see a divine capriciousness in both. In the case of original sin this is evident, they say, in God's assigning to man a guilt, in an entirely arbitrary manner, for which man himself is not responsible. Similarly, in the case of divine election we find an "ironclad determinism" in complete detachment from man's own willing and doing. Thus we observe a kind of "fatalism" which emasculates man's responsibility of all real meaning and sense.[1] The critics have then concluded that the original sin dogma presupposes this same kind of "fatality."[2]

1. Cf. my *Divine Election*, 1960, Chap. 3.
2. We have already recalled the impression that the doctrine of original sin

424

Now in the course of our discussion above we have touched on this question of whether the Church herself, in her speaking and acting, has actually occasioned a misunderstanding of original sin as an inescapable or an ineluctable "fatality." We have not, as yet, given an answer. It is impossible merely to brush that question aside and to speak, in a shallow fashion, of an unfortunate "misunderstanding." For we stand face to face with the very hard fact that a number of questions, and doubts, and criticisms are heard not only *outside* but also *inside* the Christian Church herself. Furthermore, these are heard even when Jesus is sincerely preached as Redeemer of the world and Savior from sin. Therefore it is important to look more closely at these issues. Here, if anywhere, as we consider the nature and gravity of *guilt,* we must do away with every possible misconception.

The question, then, is this: In confessing the doctrine of original sin are we really obliged to adopt a view of "arbitrariness" or a concept in which the guilt of one man is merely "imputed" to another? Is it the meaning or the thrust of this doctrine to give us a causal explanation for the existential plight of the human race by pointing to the guilt of "someone else"? Are the results of that guilt with us today in a very uncanny manner, and to such an extent that they are really considered *our guilt?* All the objections to this doctrine center in this "great presupposition" which its critics say must underlie its confession: the concept of an *alien guilt* or a *peccatum alienum.*

In this light we can understand why Bavinck has called this doctrine "one of the most difficult subjects of dogmatics."[3] He cites a statement of Pascal which sets in relief, he feels, the depth and gravity of the problem. Pascal referred to this as the "mystery the farthest removed from our understanding." There is nothing "that offends our reason more than to say that the sin of the first man has made other men guilty, namely those men who are so far removed from this source that they would seem to be incapable of participating within it."[4] This kind of spatialized concept ("so far removed") is intended to articulate the reality of Adam's guilt and our own participation within

made on such figures as Marsman and Vestdijk. See above, p. 147, footnote 45.
3. Bavinck, *Geref. Dog.,* III, 78.
4. *Ibid.,* 79.

that guilt today. Bavinck's difficulty does not find root in the efforts of man to hide himself from his own responsibility; rather it rises in a very legitimate need to regard our guilt as that which is *concrete*. Only in the concreteness of guilt, concretely confessed, can the jubilee of *forgiven sins be sung*.

Some theologians have tried to free themselves from this problem by pointing to the obvious fact of the solidarity of the human race. But surely that argument can give us no solution, for the simple reason that the doctrine of original sin is not an example of a generally recognized "solidarity." It goes beyond all mere solidarity and cannot be explained in terms of "solidarity" alone. In this doctrine, as confessed by the Church, we are not concerned about our "common lot" or the truism that no man stands alone. We *are* concerned about the sin and guilt which *we ourselves must always confess*. Precisely therefore the questions concerning the nature of this sin have always been very perplexing. No wonder that critics find it astonishing, to say the least, that we continue to speak of sin in terms of "original sin." *My sin,* they insist, is a matter of *myself* and my own *personal guilt;* and therefore if we speak of a collective "culpability" we can never exclude our own responsibility and participation *in guilt*. Guilt, by very definition, is that which concerns ourselves. Therefore *we* must make *our confession*. Certainly it is one of the most elementary of legal maxims that we can never assign to a person a guilt for which he is not responsible. Do we throw out that maxim when we confess the doctrine of "original sin"?

We cannot sidestep these questions by recalling the universal human experience that the deeds of one man have far-reaching consequences for other men and sometimes for a host of other men. This argument cannot put to silence the criticism of the critics. For the doctrine of original sin does not make the pretension of diagnosing the results of the acts of single men; nor is it concerned about a "prince," so to speak, who has little sensitivity for his calling and who casts his entire people into endless suffering. Were that the case we could rise up, despite the disasters that beset us, and register our very legitimate complaint in a spirit of open rebellion. But the confession of original sin precludes *our* rising up and bringing *our charge*. It presupposes that *we are charged*. Therefore it is wrong to slough aside the valid questions which we have already observed at this point. We cannot ignore the questions which rise within the Church herself, or explain them away on the basis of an irresponsible or an insensitive *individualism*. We cannot deny that the reality of guilt is often apparent on individualistic lines. But the Scripture demands our attention for a guilt which is *uniquely and personally our own*. This is the case when Ezekiel, for example, reprimands the people for an unwarranted reference to the guilt of their fathers and reaffirms the justice of God. "The soul that *sins shall die*" (18:4). "The wickedness of the wicked shall be upon himself" (18:20). Therefore if we reject an illicit individualism, we must still have an open eye for that which is peculiarly personal or individual, and which always must *remain* so in every relation of solidarity and collectivity.[5]

In making this passing reference to Ezekiel, we are not intending to give a premature answer to our problems. Bavinck and others have spoken of a "difficulty" here. It is well to reflect, therefore, on the matter of individualism. This is all the more so when we realize that Ezekiel's prophecy is concerned precisely with this topic of the arbitrariness of God: "Yet you say, 'The way of the Lord is not just'" (18:25). Against this false charge the answer is very clear and adequate: "Hear now, O house of Israel: Is *my* way not just? Is it not *your* ways that are not just? When a righteous man turns away from his righteousness and commits iniquity, he shall die for it; for the iniquity which he has committed he shall die" (18: 25-26). The non-arbitrariness of God's activity is thus underscored, and every stress is laid on the demonstrable relation between God's judgment and Israel's own personal guilt.[6] There is no inconsistency between man's individual and collective culpability. Nor is there any reason to minimize the uniquely personal character of man's guilt. This fact has nothing to do with an "arid rationalism." It suggests the only way in which *true confession* of guilt is possible without falling into the temptation of hiding behind the "collectivity" of man and

---

5. We remember the New Testament words in Gal. 6:5, spoken in the context of bearing one another's burdens: "For each man will have to bear his own load." This is by no means in contradiction to Gal. 6:2. Cf. Schlier and Greijdanus in their commentaries. Cf. also II Cor. 5:10, on the judgment of each man, and Rom. 14:12: "So each of us shall give account of himself to God" (*hékastos . . . perì heautoû*).

6. In Chap. 16 we shall return to Ezek. 18.

avoiding the divine indictment: *"You are the man"* (II Sam. 12:7).

Herman Bavinck has discussed the weakening and eventual overthrow of the original sin dogma and the revival of Pelagius in Christian theology. At the same time, he has pointed to a later modification of this superficial attitude in regard to man's guilt. "The philosophy of Kant, Schelling, Schopenhauer, etc., and the doctrine of heredity and solidarity, along with historical and sociological studies, have all contributed to an unexpected and important support for the dogma of original sin. When theology rejected it, philosophy brought it back again."[7] Obviously, what we have here is an apologetic statement at a time in which men were inclined to spurn every form of individualism and to reaffirm communal bonds. Nevertheless, it is strange to hear that it was Schopenhauer, among others, who lent his "important" support to the dogma of original sin.[8] Bavinck's apologetic was clearly meant in only a relative sense; witness his statement that "original sin is something quite different from what we today understand by heredity."[9] When we look at the cohesiveness of the human race, said Bavinck, all individualism can only be seen as unsatisfactory;[10] yet the man who says only that much has not begun to deal with the problems of *original sin,* to say nothing of "solving" them. Bavinck called special attention to a single aspect of these problems — namely the difficulty in "the propagation of original sin."[11] In the same connection he broached the really important issue and spoke of an unmerited reception of blessings, to which no one objects, though a spirit of rebellion takes over in all of us as soon as we apply this same "law" of non-merit to the topic of *evil.*[12]

This spirit of rebellion may find its expression in the very questions we ask concerning the doctrine of original sin. It may come to light in our failure to acknowledge our own personal guilt in "hereditary sin." This is clearly the problem that Otto Weber set down in the following words: "The objections to the Church's dogma of original sin are, when taken as a

---

7. Bavinck, *op. cit.,* III, 78.
8. On Kant's doctrine of the radical nature of evil, cf. my *Man: the Image of God,* 1962, pp. 122ff.
9. Bavinck, *op. cit.,* III, 96. See also Chap. 16 below.
10. *Ibid.*
11. *Ibid.,* 97.
12. *Ibid.,* 83.

whole, the expression of a self-understanding which centers in the concepts of *freedom, responsibility* and *person*. How can sin be regarded as a responsible and personal decision when the 'primal sin' (Luther) is precisely *not that* but discloses a situation for which I am charged in a completely heteronomous way?"[13] Whatever else we may say about this question, it is clear that a right understanding of what the Church has meant by this doctrine of original sin is very important. How has the Church conceived of the relations between *guilt and responsibility,* or *guilt and confession,* or *guilt and the wrath of God?* Critics have said that those who hold this doctrine can respond to the accusation of guilt by pointing at someone else. But is this what we mean by *original sin?* Are we saying anything different, then, from what Adam and Eve already said in Paradise?

The question that urges itself upon us, in all of this, may be formulated as follows: Do all these criticisms imply a valid interpretation of the doctrine of the Church? Has the Church spoken of an "alien guilt," or the guilt of "someone else," as a solution to the problem of *my guilt?* Does original sin suggest an "alien guilt" to which *my guilt is added?* These are the pressing issues in the entire history of this doctrine. But a very wrong answer is given if we conceive of God as *arbitrary* in the imputation of man's guilt.[14]

Before we look at these questions more fully, and listen to the various solutions proposed, we should observe that almost the entire history of this doctrine has been influenced, positively or negatively, by its great opponent: Pelagius. Bavinck has

13. Weber, *Grundlagen der Dogmatik,* I, 668.
14. As examples of this charge of "arbitrariness" we refer to Schleiermacher, *Der christliche Glaube,* I, 1884, 385 ("auf eine höchst willkürliche Weise"); A. Ritschl, *Rechtfertigung und Versöhnung,* III, 1883, in the paragraph on "Das Reich der Sünde," pp. 311ff.; and Th. Haering, *Der christliche Glaube,* 1912, p. 358: "But no theory concerning Adam, either as physical head or as representative of the human race, is able to put to silence the question of how — if that monstrous consequence of the first sin is the only cause of all sin, and even of *sin affirmed as guilt;* of which we are all guilty for the sake of Adam and are made subject to God's hate — this could possibly be squared with the just and wise love of God" (italics ours). Also H. Stephan, *Glaubenslehre,* 1928, p. 155, on "the inadequacy of the *inheritance*-concept," and on imputation as the "distortion" of guilt. On the inner "untruthfulness" of this doctrine, see *ibid.,* p. 147.

pointed out that in the Seventeenth and Eighteenth Centuries Pelagianism again became a popular option in the original sin debates.[15] He has seen that the general triumph of that spirit was a return to the notion of the essential goodness of man. Here it is clear that a number of motives have played a role in the history of this doctrine and have sometimes appeared together as strange bedfellows. Thus, for example, Cassirer, in his description of the great difference between humanism and the Reformation, can fasten attention on the fact that humanism, too, did not disavow (at least not openly) the doctrine of the Fall. Rather it sought to "loosen up that dogma to a certain extent and to weaken its authority."[16] We must have open eyes for these considerations and must also examine carefully the real reasons why Pelagius rejected the dogma of original sin. Certainly he advanced too rapidly from questions to answers, and his position has therefore been regarded, by many, as very unsatisfactory. Yet, within the discussions of the later centuries, Pelagianism has always exerted a profound and a very lasting influence.

Pelagian theology has frequently been seen as very shallow. Indeed, Pelagius himself took his point of departure in a naive interpretation of man's freedom, which he assumed to belong to every man's essence. Therefore freedom could not be lost without man's *ceasing to be man*. The choice between good and evil is and remains a choice of man's own will, and every act is a manifestation of his freedom. For that reason a performance of perpetually good deeds cannot be seen as *a priori* impossible. Man's will is not inclined, in itself, in a depraved direction, and certainly it is not in the sense that all the acts of men are "predetermined" by his sinful *nature*. Thus, on the basis of these thoughts, Pelagius became the great antagonist of the doctrine of original sin. He saw that doctrine as a flagrant contradiction to the essence of a free man, who was created by God as a good creature. He regarded it as the denial of the character of man's own sin, as concrete and actual disobedience, committed in *responsibility*.

The problem of the universality of sin is a problem that

15. Bavinck, *op. cit.*, III, 78.
16. E. Cassirer, *Die Philosophie der Aufklärung*, 1932, p. 185, in his chapter on "The Dogma of Original Sin and the Problem of Theodicy" (ET, p. 139). Note Cassirer's statement: "The influence of Pelagianism in the religious position of humanism becomes increasingly evident."

looms large in Pelagius' theology. He answered that problem by pointing to the general phenomenon of *imitatio*. Here he saw the way in which sin is habitually repeated by most men. In Pelagius, therefore, the problem of the origin of sin is made acute, and is even intensified, for every single member of the race. Thus he seized on the empirical fact of universality to clarify why it is that a *good nature* does not habitually lead to *good decisions*. The fact that he did not surrender that bogus argument, despite the refutations of Augustine and the anathemas of the Church,[17] has everything to do with his fundamental outlook on man's nature. In any view other than *imitatio*, he contended, a man is wrongly conceived as corrupt. Here the influence of Manichaeanism is very apparent. Such thinking implies, according to Pelagius, an all-too-simple dualism and a location of evil in man's own *nature*. Therefore Pelagius wished to accentuate the *responsibility* of man in his sinful activity; he wanted to eliminate the possibility that man might escape responsibility by pointing to his own sinful character.[18] Sin is visible and real in the concrete acts of man's *own will*. It is neither deducible from man's nature nor derivable from a further "act" which precedes the act of man. There is no such *ante actionem* to which a man can legitimately make an appeal.[19]

Judging on the basis of these thoughts, a good many of Pelagius' opponents have found his theology a mere form of moralism or religious humanism. They have pointed to the anomaly of "sovereign grace" in such a theology as this. Others, however, have suggested that there are no shades of humanism in Pelagius since he certainly wished to assign a significant place to God's grace. All the same, there is little essential disagreement on the structure of Pelagius' doctrine of sin. The denial of original sin is evident in the denial of any *ante* whatever.[20] Man must be viewed and judged in the concreteness of

17. For the condemnations of Carthage, 418, see Denz., 101-108.
18. Cf. Torgny Bohlin, *Die Theologie des Pelagius und ihre Genesis*, 1957, p. 15. According to Pelagius man's nature is given "an entirely good and divine meaning and therefore cannot serve as an explanation for sin."
19. It is "characteristic of Pelagius' manner of thought that he divorces the factual activity of the will from the will *ante actionem*" (*ibid.*, p. 16).
20. While recognizing certain positive motives in the Pelagians (e.g., their repudiation of Manichaeanism), Harnack nonetheless passes the strong judgment that their doctrine at its deepest level "fails to recognize the

his act.[21] In Pelagius, this unwavering conviction goes hand in
hand with an ascetic view of life, in terms of which he combatted all self-excuse as reprehensible and denied that man can
appeal to an already-present guilt and corruption. In short,
man cannot make an alibi for pursuing the highest ideal of
holiness. Thus we see in Pelagius an "actualistic" view of man's
sin which was easily combined with a similar view of God's
grace. The grace of God must always refer to man's real sin.[22]

No matter how he tried to combine these motives of sin
and grace, the point of departure in Pelagius is always the
same. Sin is constantly seen as the free act of man himself
within his own responsibility. Augustine opposed that thesis by
saying that sin should not be viewed as the new and "actual"
deed of one's own will but as tied together, *in* its actuality, with
one's perverse and apostate nature. He added that this nature
must be regarded in the light of man's *peccatum originale.* Thus
the stage was set for the great discussions of later times. We
must see that one basic question kept thrusting itself to the
foreground in those later disputes: What is the relation between the *"alienum"* and the *"proprium" peccatum?* To be sure,
that question assumed a variety of forms, but it was always
regarded as a matter of the greatest importance. All the more
so when the attempts were made to demonstrate that the
Church's dogma of original sin does not imply an *asylum ignorantiae* or a doctrine in which man's guilt could no longer
be truly confessed. When she gave an answer to Pelagius the

misery of sin and evil, that in its deepest roots it is godless, that it
knows, and seeks to know, nothing of redemption" (*op. cit.,* V, 203).
Cf. A. Ritschl's criticism, *Rechtfertigung und Versöhnung,* III, 312.

21. "Insaniunt, qui de Adam per traducem asserunt ad nos venire peccatum" (F. Loofs, *P.R.E.,* XV, 751, *s.v.* "Pelagius").
22. On this the *Theologisch Woordenboek* (Brink), III, *s.v.* "Pelagius,"
   3819, speaks in the following severe terms. "Logically this leads, in the
   final analysis, to a failure to appreciate our redemption in Christ, since
   in the thought process of Pelagius this is ultimately superfluous." Note
   the further comment: "in this system there is *no place left for divine
   mercy."* Bohlin gives a different interpretation when he says that
   Pelagius still regarded the atonement as necessary, since men, by their
   sinful acts, have still become the enemies of God (*op. cit.,* p. 31). Cf.
   Loofs on the "sola fide" in Pelagius: "the 'sola fide,' before Luther's
   time, had no such energetic representative as Pelagius" (*op. cit.,* 753).
   This statement has everything to do with Pelagius' view that in the
   way of imitation sin becomes a power ("consuetudo") which involves a
   man in death (*ibid.,* 752). On Pelagius' conception of grace, see also
   Augustine, *De Gratia et Libero Arbitrio,* X, 22, 23, 25.

Church not only intended to refute his doctrine of the "natural goodness" of man. She also desired to address herself to one of the most basic motives in Pelagius' theology: the simplicity of the individual *peccatum proprium*.

The Church in general has followed Augustine in rejecting the Pelagian doctrine. The Council of Carthage already, in 418, renounced the standpoint of those who say that children are not baptized "unto forgiveness of sin" and receive nothing of the sin of Adam.[23] On the basis of Romans 5 *("in quo omnes peccaverunt")* the universal character of sin was referred back to the sin of Adam, in which even children participate. Though children do not overtly sin, they are nonetheless baptized unto the forgiveness of their sins.[24] Carthage refused to isolate a man in his constantly "new" activities. She taught emphatically that the corruption received in generation must be extinguished and purged in *regeneration*.[25]

One cannot say that the Council of Carthage gave a convincing answer to the most urgent question of Pelagius. In the decretal *In generatione* there is a reference to the biblical data,[26] but the stubborn question of what precisely is meant by these words continued long after the fracas of Pelagius and Augustine. It also lured the Church into discussions which are far from noteworthy for their clarity. Yet it is doubtful if we could have expected more from the Council of Carthage. In any case, we find there the *terminus a quo* for the Church's new reflection on the untenability of Pelagian teaching as well as the necessity

23. "... Nihil ex Adam trahere originalis peccati" (Denz., 102).
24. In "De Peccato Originali et Gratia" *(ibid.)*, it is stated that on Pelagian grounds the baptismal formula is utilized "non vera, sed falsa" (viz., "in remissionem peccatorum"). As is well known, Pelagius did not dispute infant baptism. "Pelagius had no occasion to give a negative answer to the question of whether children also ought to be baptized; but when he did have occasion, in his commentary, to speak of a baptism of children *in remissionem peccatorum*, he could not regard this practice as correct" (Loofs, *op. cit.*, 754). Cf. Harnack, *op. cit.*, V, 202.
25. "... Ut in eis regeneratione mundetur, quod in generatione traxerunt" (Denz., 102). We recall the words of Augustine's criticism against the Pelagians, in his "third point" of the Church's defense: "obnoxium et vinculo damnationis obstrictum nisi reatus, *qui generatione contrahitur regeneratione solvatur*" (De Dono Perseverantiae, II, 4). Italics added.
26. Rom. 5:12 (Denz., 102); John 15:5 (104); I John 1:8-9 (106); Matt. 6:12 (107). These references to the sins of men did not form a witness in which Pelagius heard a valid answer.

of shedding light on the meaning of these words: *"in generatione."* Augustine himself labored on that problem and never
came to clarity, not even for his own thinking. After him questions arose of special relevance for the propagation and the
corruptive influence of sin. Men felt increasingly the urge to tie
up the contaminating powers of sin and the act of physical generation. But in that way the problem of the *proprium peccatum*
and the *peccatum alienum* could only confront the Church with
a new urgency.

Therefore the criticism of Pelagius, by the Church and her
theology, is a very stirring and important episode in the history
of doctrine. Pelagius laid stress on the *proprium peccatum* and
viewed it as a new, and actual, and personal sin. He saw it as
a sin for which man himself is only and entirely responsible.
He put an accent on man's "uncontaminated nature" and maintained as his dominant theme (as Loofs has correctly seen) the
"freedom of man's will."[27] This detachment of "actual sins"
from man's total inclination to sin could only be viewed, from
the Reformation standpoint, as the fruit of a very shallow
analysis. It was a flagrant contradiction of the divine indictment
and the preaching of God's salvation in the midst of *man's
lostness.* Yet, when we bear in mind the scandal of the cross
and the opposition which always roots in the concept of man's
"relative goodness," we can appreciate why Pelagianism, despite
the repeated anathemas of the Church, has always raised its
head anew.

This influence of Pelagianism cannot be explained in terms
of a humanizing soteriology alone. More often than in Pelagius
himself the tendencies in later disputes were bound up with a
choice in favor of *peccatum proprium* and in opposition to
peccatum alienum. Pelagius, to be sure, inclined in that same
direction. He could do nothing else in view of his peculiar
concept of man's nature.[28] Yet the antithesis of *proprium/
alienum* received, in later times, a stronger accent as attention
was concentrated on the problems of God's imputing or "taking account" of man's sin. The stubborn obstinacy of Pelagianism

---

27. "The words 'ne tollatur libertas arbitrii" are commonly, for him, a
    definitive argument" (Loofs, *op. cit.,* 751f.).
28. Cf. A. Souter, *Pelagius' Expositions of Thirteen Epistles of St. Paul,* II,
    1926, 46f. Pelagius could cite with approval those who say: "nulla
    ratione concedi ut deus, qui propria peccata remisit, imputet aliena."
    Cf. also Harnack, *op. cit.,* V, 198.

is apparent in its frequent criticisms of what has often been seen as an immanent tension in the Church's tradition — namely the very concept of a *peccatum "alienum."* Therefore the most common appeal in the later debates has not been to such issues as the relative goodness of man, or the freedom of his will, but to man's *own guilt and responsibility.*

The Church, and especially the Reformation, has combatted this Pelagian denial of the *corruptio totalis.* She has firmly held to the vision of the sovereignty and the gratuity of grace. Yet the shadows of an *alienum peccatum* have constantly loomed large in the background of these soteriological struggles. One can say that the Church had an easier time resisting the Pelagian soteriology than meeting the criticisms of the original sin doctrine. By contending for the correlation of sin and grace, the Reformation especially addressed herself, clearly and urgently, to this problem.[29] She did not hesitate to take issue with the critics of original sin. At the same time we observe in the Reformation and the entire tradition of the Church a certain wholesome reserve in regard to the particular formulations that are used. This explains why Bavinck has spoken of a "difficulty." Nevertheless, in the face of that difficulty a single *a priori* is constantly at work and is also applied with the greatest of conviction. This is the principle that our confession of original sin may not function and cannot function as a means of *excusing ourselves* or of *hiding behind another man's guilt.*

29. As a first criticism of the Pelagians Augustine summarized the argument of the Church as follows: "gratiam Dei non secundum merita nostra dari, quoniam Dei dona sunt et Dei gratia conferuntur etiam merita universa justorum" *(De Dono Perseverantiae,* II, 4).

CHAPTER THIRTEEN

REALISM

A S WE HAVE seen, the central problem in the doctrine of original sin is the problem of a *peccatum alienum* or alien guilt. When we observe the frequency with which that issue crops up in the history of this dogma, we are not surprised that frequent attempts are made to demonstrate that an alien guilt is by no means necessarily implied. One does well to keep his ears attuned to the religious motives in those attempts. The idea has most frequently been to remove from the sinner every avenue of self-excuse. For the man who fastens onto the guilt of someone else is always ready and able to make an alibi, even if he himself is involved in that same guilt. Therefore we find these attempts, of which we are now speaking, *to expose and to eliminate the alibi*. The purpose here has usually been to fashion a doctrine of original sin in which it is obvious that the guilt of sin is our *own guilt*. The guilt in which we are involved is always *peccatum proprium* or *peccatum nostrum*.

Those who have talked this way have wished to emphasize that original sin does not presume a dismal or a fatal lot which hangs upon us as an inexorable or enigmatic fate. They have accented that human life is not caught in a "spell" which is now upon us, once and for all, and in the face of which we can only resign. Rather, the guilt of all men is a guilt in which every man participates and for which no man can make an excuse. This fundamental problem, so the argument continues, is not sufficiently defined when we merely refer to the *results of man's sin,* or *Adam's sin*. It is only rightly set forth when we focus attention on the actual relation of Adam's sin and our own lives. In that perspective it is at least understandable that the dominant motive in the original sin dogma has always been *our guilt*.

But the man who inquires into the nature of this "actual relation" is confronted by a number of tentative and very grop-

ing formulas. Bavinck has spoken of "a certain relation" between Adam's sin and that of the human race.[1] He has referred
to Adam's sin "in a certain sense" as our own deed.[2] Therefore
we too, in some manner or other, are guilty *in Adam*.[3] The
nature of that relation is described in such terms as *virtualiter,
potentialiter,* and *seminaliter*.[4] Thus it is described in terms
which suggest that the problem is *seen* but is far from *solved.*
The heart of the matter is what it means, *in concreto,* when
Bavinck calls Adam's sin "in a certain sense" *our act.* When we
proceed in that direction and cancel out the alibi ("to a certain extent") do we do any more than make a subtle overture
to reintroduce an explanation for our guilt? Yet, if that be the
case, with what compelling right can we stand up to those who
continue to invoke the alibi and to regard it as historically
valid? They, of course, have no reason to use this modest phrase,
"in a certain sense." When we bear in mind the important
function of the concept of *alibi* in criminal law, we can understand why we find ourselves now at the vortex of discussion
and criticism concerning the original sin dogma.

Only a single general theory, in the history of doctrine, has
proposed to get beyond the words of Bavinck, "in a certain
sense." That theory has attempted to lay bare the alibi in a
very emphatic way. It has tried to eliminate any basis of excuse
in the *peccatum alienum.* Here we are referring to the so-called
doctrine of *realism.* The realists have wanted to do away with
any concept of alibi and to point to the naked facts of man's
own guilt.

Realism came to be known in America especially in the writings of W. G. J. Shedd. On the Dutch scene the realism of
Shedd was enthusiastically endorsed by S. Greijdanus, whose
own theology was followed in turn by K. Schilder. Little attention has been given, in general, to the realist position. This is
certainly owing to the fact that realism, in its fundamental
posture, makes a very strange and *unreal* impression. Yet there
is good reason for us to examine the realistic arguments; for
here, if anywhere, we find an answer to the recurring criticism
that we cannot be held responsible for the sins which we "in-

1. H. Bavinck, *Geref. Dog.,* III, 67.
2. *Ibid.,* 72; cf. p. 80.
3. *Ibid.,* 89.
4. *Ibid.,* 81.

herit." For that reason already it is very necessary to consider this hypothesis.[5]

The hallmark of realism is the conviction that all men are *"co-sinners" with Adam* in the fullest meaning of that word. This conception finds a clear articulation in the theology of Greijdanus. Refusing to throw out the traditional term of *imputatio,* Greijdanus contended that this does not eliminate man's own being responsible for the "imputation" of God.[6] Imputation can mean a "bringing into account." Thus, when we speak of "charging Adam's sin *to us"* we can only mean that Adam's sin was truly *our own* and was therefore put on our account. Only in that way is the term *imputatio* valid. Only as such can Greijdanus find a solution to the difficulties which have commonly plagued this doctrine. Greijdanus was concerned about an actual sinning of all men *in and with Adam.* He spoke of all men "in Adam's transgression, which was also their sin."[7] Therefore he refused to regard imputation in the sense of "as if." There is no such thing as God's acting "as if" we were partners in sin without that being, in fact, *the case.*[8] It is a matter of *fact* that we are co-sinners with Adam in a uniquely personal and individual way.

Before we inquire what this co-sinning really means, we do well to honor the fact that Greijdanus' realism takes root in a thoroughly biblical idea. God's judgment does answer to man's own guilt. There is a divine "rule of justice" which we find expressed in such a passage as Ezekiel 18. A man must die

---

5. On realism see especially Shedd, *Dogmatic Theology,* II, Chap. 5 ("Original Sin"); Greijdanus, *De Toerekeningsgrond van het Peccatum Originans,* 1906; and *ibid., Komm. op Romeinen,* Chap. 5. Already in his dissertation *(Menschwording en Vernedering. Hist. crit. Studie,* 1903), Greijdanus advanced certain propositions (10, 11, 12) having reference to the doctrine of original sin. Also see K. Schilder, *De Heidelbergsche Catechismus,* I, 331ff., and C. Vonk, *De Voorzeide Leer,* III, 325f., on Lord's Day 4. Much critical attention has been given to the doctrine of realism by Charles Hodge, in his *Systematic Theology,* II, 1880, 216ff., where he especially discusses Jonathan Edwards. On the standpoint of Edwards there is considerable disagreement, particularly on his *The Great Christian Doctrine of Original Sin Defended* (in *The Works of President Edwards,* II, 1817, 81-387). Cf. J. Ridderbos, *De Theologie van Jonathan Edwards,* 1907, pp. 150ff., and J. Murray, "The Imputation of Adam's Sin," *Westminster Theological Journal,* XIX, pp. 151-163.
6. Greijdanus, *Toerekeningsgrond,* pp. 57-58.
7. Greijdanus, *Komm. op Romeinen,* I, 280.
8. *Toerekeningsgrond,* pp. 41-42. Cf. Schilder, *op. cit.,* I, 334, in opposition to an "as if"-theology.

because of his *own sin*.[9] Greijdanus sees in this a far-reaching principle which corresponds to our own consciences and finds a certain resonance in legal processes. In the case of the imputation of Christ's righteousness we know that we ourselves did not do what was done for us;[10] in the case of original sin, however, we know just as well that we are *not guiltless*. Our guilt is only our own guilt and our own activity, with no pretensions whatever. There can be no "as if's."

That same note is heard in Schilder. We are reminded that in so-called "federalism" the sin of Adam is imputed to us because he merely "represents" us as our covenantal head.[11] Therefore the federal imputation of guilt runs parallel to the imputation of Christ's righteousness. In both cases — that of Christ and Adam — we do nothing for ourselves, for either our weal or our woe, and whatever happens is merely "imputed" to us. In contrast to that view, Schilder sets forth his own realistic conception. We have all *really sinned with Adam*.[12] We cannot say precisely how that is, but there *is* and there *must be* a certain cooperation as the basis of God's imputation.[13] If we were merely concerned with an imputation of guilt as something apart from ourselves, and if God were to lay that guilt on our account by his sovereign good pleasure, our sensitivity for what is right could only be impaired.[14] An alibi would then be inescapable, and we would still be left with an "explanation" for our guilt. In recognizing that peril, the realists have spoken of guilt as an *actual and real co-sinning*. Therefore all men are subject to the wrath and the curse of God. "We have all done our share, though we cannot say how."[15]

9. Greijdanus, *op. cit.*, p. 45.
10. According to Greijdanus, there is therefore a clear distinction between the ground for imputation in the case of Christ's righteousness and the ground in the case of Adam's sin. This same essential thought is found in Shedd.
11. K. Schilder, *op. cit.*, 336.
12. *Ibid.*, 338.
13. *Ibid.*, 339.
14. *Ibid.*
15. *Ibid.*, 357. Therefore both Shedd and Greijdanus, as well as Schilder, reject the doctrine of Placaeus, who only spoke of guilt in the wake of pollution and defilement. They saw *guilt (our guilt)* as preceding the corruption of sin that followed (*ibid.*, 353). In clear contrast to this interpretation of imputation, which he wished to deny, Shedd contended that imputation takes place "upon the same principle upon which all sin is deservedly and justly imputed: namely, that it was committed by those to whom it is imputed" (*op. cit.*, II, 186).

We can only do justice to realism, however, when we inquire exactly what is meant by this "co-sinning." In what biblical categories can this conception be set forth? It is very striking that when we ask that perfectly legitimate question, we receive no clear answer. Surely it is not ridiculous, or a mere game of logical consistency, when we try to make sense of the realistic claims and inquire if they entail an actual "pre-existence" of all men in Adam. That question cannot be thrust aside as too "subtle" or "captious." For whenever we make an effort to unmask the alibi and to speak of an authentic "co-sinning," the ghost of a "pre-existence" enters our picture anew as the reverse side of the alibi which we sought to exorcise. We meet up with that thought in the words of Shedd: "the posterity were *existent* and *present* in the progenitors by natural and substantial union."[16] Such a statement underscores the point of Shedd's criticism, and that of others, concerning the concept of Adam as the "representative" of us all. For men do not need to be "represented" if they are already "present" in Adam.[17]

Moreover, it is impossible for the proponents of realism to justify their thinking on the basis of "not knowing how." They cannot find a recourse in the unintelligibility of an actual "co-sinning." The realistic thesis is far too positive in its implications to permit this, and the realists themselves are too definite in their very sweeping expressions. We hear, for example, that the descendants of Adam are "apostates"; furthermore they are that "not only as a manner of speaking but in reality, for all ages."[18] When we read such a statement we are obliged to take the realistic position very seriously and not to play down its significance. We are not to say that this "co-sinning" is only real "in a certain sense." Obviously, the realists themselves have shrunk back, on occasion, from the consequences of their

16. *Ibid.*, I, 38.
17. *Ibid.* Cf. the comment: "natural union logically excludes representation." Here Shedd differs, at least terminologically, from Schilder, who sought to combine his realism with the idea of representation. According to Shedd, these two themes have been wrongly combined since the time of Turretin. Only in a *natural* union are arbitrariness and an "as if"-conception excluded, while no disjunction is made between *poena* and *culpa* (p. 51). "Men must sin in Adam, in order to be justly punished for Adam's sin. And participation requires union with Adam" (p. 187).
18. Schilder, *op. cit.*, 358. Schilder speaks of the doctrinal *datum* ("het leergegeven") of our sinning in Adam.

own view and have shown a healthy diffidence in the face of the problems and the implications of their own conception.[19] But their purpose of excluding the alibi has always been very dominant. Therefore they have not hesitated in using very strong terms.

When we consider the main proposals of realism we find ourselves before an implied "pre-existence"[20] and the problem of the function of the realistic view of man's own guilt. Yet we also meet up with a definite scriptural argument. Not only the rule of Ezekiel (referred to above) has played a role in this hypothesis, but other passages as well would seem to indicate a real or a natural "homogeneity" in the human race. These passages are the final basis on which the realistic thesis is built. A special appeal is frequently made to such expressions as we find, for example, in Hebrews 7:5, 10: "out of the loins of Abraham" and "in the loins of his father." These ideas are important in Greijdanus and especially in Schilder. By leaning hard on the earlier work of Rivetus, Schilder has cited a number of Reformed authorities who likewise appealed to these texts in defending the doctrine of original sin.

It is true that the Hebrews 7 pericope is not concerned with the doctrine of original sin *per se*. At the same time, realists and others have thought to find in this passage a general "law" which holds in the case of Adam and his posterity. The theme of the chapter is the meeting of Abraham and Melchizedek, or the story of Abraham's giving to Melchizedek a tenth of all he had (cf. Gen. 14). For the writer of Hebrews it is remarkable that Melchizedek did not belong to those who had a peculiar right to receive tithes. His situation was different from the later tribe of Levi. Moreover, it is precisely in that fact that we see the uniqueness of Melchizedek. The event set forth in this chapter signifies that Levi himself, to whom the later tithes were given, was himself subject to the *payment of tithes*. For

19. Thus Schilder says that the "co-sinning" with Adam was "in God's eyes." This is a strange and an unclear expression for realism. In consonance with the realist thesis, we could better read: "before the eyes of God." *Op. cit.*, 350.

20. We recall that Greijdanus, in his dissertation, *Menschwording en Vernedering*, 1903, already proposed this same thought for discussion (Proposition 9): "Original sin is the standing guilty of Adam's (natural) descendants in his very first transgression of the commandment in Paradise."

he was still, we read, "in Abraham" (Heb. 7:9). Here the author sees the temporal chasm between Abraham and Levi as truly bridged. He regards Levi already "in Abraham" though only later did Levi proceed "from the loins of Abraham" (7:5).

The "implicit" or "inclusive" presence of Levi in Abraham is now used by realists to demonstrate that we "could make ourselves co-responsible and could even genuinely sin in Adam's loins."[21] Therefore we find in this passage an "anthropological" suggestion of our actual sinning in Adam. The whole subject of this chapter, or the view of generations and the relation of the priesthoods of Levi and Melchizedek, is seen as an important aid for explaining the doctrine of original sin. That approach is very evident in Schilder. He draws the conclusion that "God once and for all has been pleased to create in Adam no individual who merely stands by himself but a man who included others in his loins."[22] It was *really* Levi ("genuinely and truly")[23] who bowed before Melchizedek. Nor is this an idle notion. For the words "so to speak" in verse 9 ("one might even say": RSV) do not imply the thought of a make-believe or "as if." They imply the conception of "if we consider this matter well."[24] Therefore, according to Schilder, we read of an actual and a physical reality, or a reality that was *genuinely present.*

Now it is true, of course, that Hebrews 7, in the creeds, is mentioned frequently in connection with the unity of the human race. It is so used in one of the main confessional writings: the Formula Consensus.[25] But when we ask if this passage can be consciously or consistently used in a way that resembles the realistic hypothesis, we can only answer in the negative. The usual manner of dealing with this passage has been in Bavinck's rather halting words: "in a certain sense." It has

21. Greijdanus, *Toerekeningsgrond,* p. 50.
22. Schilder, *op. cit.,* 343.
23. *Ibid.,* 345.
24. Greek: *hōs épos eipein.* Schilder's translation is that of F. W. Grosheide *(Comm. op Hebreeën, ad loc.),* to whom he makes an appeal. Yet it is clear that Grosheide did not mean these words "realistically." Cf. his *K.V.,* p. 82: "Whoever says 'Abraham' says 'Abraham's generation,' the people of Israel, to whom also Levi belongs."
25. Man is guilty "ob [*paráptōma*] et inoboedientiam, quam *in Adami lumbis* commisit" (Müller, *Bekenntnisschriften,* p. 865). Cf. the further comments: "in lumbis existentes"; "in eius lumbis"; "nos in Adamo peccavimus et legem transgressi sumus"; etc. We shall return later to this confession, as formulated against Placaeus.

not been in the manner of consistent realism. Surely we cannot deny that in the explanatory comments of Hebrews 7 there is a definite reference to the continuity and perspective in which we should see the relation of Abraham and Levi. As a matter of fact, the argument loses all meaning if these figures are merely viewed as isolated individuals, each having his own separate identity in history. Van Oyen has spoken of the "togetherness" or coherence of the generations as an essential feature of the Jewish spirit.[26] He finds in Hebrews 7 a conclusion from this "togetherness" which illumines our perspective concerning the history of salvation. Yet there is no suggestion in this pericope of a "contemporaneity" or "consequence" which the realistic thesis must certainly demand. When we read that the Levites "came forth" from the loins of Abraham[27] there is no reason to find in that perspective on the generations an anthropological thesis which can hardly be distinguished from the idea of a pre-existence.

Obviously the writer does not suggest the idea of "as if." He *did* wish to say: "If we consider this matter well."[28] But that fact does not imply an endorsement of realism. Nor does the coherence of the race, in its orderly advance, support this argument.[29] One would have to stand already on the anthropological *principia* of realism to find in Hebrews 7 an argument for the realistic concept of original sin.[30]

Therefore the appeal to Hebrews 7 cannot be regarded as the main reason for adopting a realistic conception. Another chapter, however, viz. Romans 5, has always been in the limelight of the original sin debates. Later we shall give a fuller discussion to that chapter, but for now we should see that it has always been a favorite "prooftext" of realists. Greijdanus has considered the traditional explanation of Romans 5:12

26. H. van Oyen, *Christus de Hogepriester*, p. 123.
27. Heb. 7:5 *(exelēlythótas ek tēs osphýos Abraam)*. Cf. also Acts 2:30: "one of the fruit of his loins."
28. Cf. C. Spicq, *L'épître aux Hébreux*, II, 1953, 187: "pour parler exactement."
29. Cf. *TWNT*, V, *s.v. osphýs*, which further points to Gen. 35:11 and II Chron. 6:9 ("comes forth from your loins").
30. Calvin does not draw this realist conclusion: "Abraham qui omnium pater est" (Comm. on Hebrews, *ad loc.*). To be sure, the writer of Hebrews has uncovered an event "that reaches out beyond the borders of personal existence" (Michel, *Der Brief an die Hebräer*, p. 168).

("because all men sinned") and has rejected its theory of "imputation" in favor of realism. He concedes that the Vulgate translation *("in quo")* is inaccurate, but he sees in this a fact of very little significance.[31] The burden of the chapter, in his judgment, is not an imputation of guilt to all men though not all have actually or personally sinned. It is rather the physical coherence of all men. The words "because all men sinned" can only get their full significance when we recognize that "basic to all death, also spiritual, is a personal or individual sinning along with Adam's sin."[32] Thus the assertion that "all men sinned" can only be understood in a realistic sense. Surely Paul did not express "in what manner we must think of this,"[33] but it remains the case that Adam's sin was the sin of all men in a uniquely personal, proper, and individual way.[34] Therefore Paul emerges, in Greijdanus' theology, as the crowning witness of realism.[35]

Greijdanus defended this realism against its various critics. Anyone who thinks that in realism, with its anthropological bias, we are co-responsible for not only the first sin of Adam but for all his later sins as well, to say nothing of Noah and others,[36] must see how very seriously Greijdanus takes his realism. He does not point to the uniqueness of Adam (as a federalist would) but asks the following question: "Who is able to say ... what has transpired in the hidden life of men's souls even before their own birth? Only in the day of reckoning will all be brought to light."[37] In that statement we are warned against reducing realism to a merely "corporative" idea. For in such a concept realism is weakened and robbed of its virility.[38] The

---

31. "If now one translates [*eph' hŏ*] by *in quo* or by *propterea quod,* this makes no difference to us at present" *(Toerekeningsgrond,* p. 41). Cf. his commentary (p. 278): "the conception of [*eph' hŏ*] is of subordinate importance."
32. *Toerekeningsgrond,* pp. 41-42.
33. *Komm.,* I, 278.
34. *Ibid.,* 280.
35. Cf. also Shedd on Rom. 5:12; *op. cit.,* II, 182f. The term *hĕmarton,* he asserts, must be understood *actively* and cannot mean "were regarded as sinful" (183). The issue at stake is the act of *men,* and is not God's imputation (184).
36. This argument appears in Bavinck.
37. *Toerekeningsgrond,* p. 50.
38. Cf. also Shedd, *op. cit.,* 189: "No man remembers the time he was innocent and the particular first act by which he became guilty before God." This is a worthwhile comment within the defense of realism.

unmasking of the alibi, in Greijdanus' theology, is a matter that is very serious and very real. Thus he presses that theme despite the anthropological consequences which cannot be avoided. There is, indeed, an "imputation," but it is only of a *real and proper guilt*. When we read in Romans 5:19 that "many were made sinners," it means, for Greijdanus, a juridical declaration; nevertheless, this declaration has reference only to a *proper, human guilt*. When we compare this to the dilemma of "analytic or synthetic," in the doctrine of justification, we can say that realism has an *analytic* concept of the imputation of guilt while the imputation of Christ's righteousness is *synthetic* in character. There is no punishment apart from an actual guilt.[39] Therefore the realistic conception, of all the options in the original sin dogma, does the fullest justice to the righteousness of God.[40]

This motive of God's justice is the dominant and decisive theme in realistic theology. Realists have admitted that many questions are unanswered in their theory. Solutions to many problems are very far from obvious.[41] Yet all of this is of no great significance for a realist. What is important is that God's justice is preserved, even though our insights are unclear.[42] A jealousy for the justice of God controls this theory to such an extent that little appreciation is left over for the internal problems and the exegetical deficiencies. Realists, however, cannot eliminate those problems. Their denial of the alibi has a very definite content, and man is seen as guilty *within his own place*. Therefore we must reach beyond the category of "mystery," for in such a category we are unable to shed light on the concept of man's *guilt*.

39. Greijdanus, *op. cit.*, p. 46.
40. In Greijdanus' doctrine of original sin this is illustrated in his plea for a necessary modification in the concept of creationism (*op. cit.*, p. 48; cf. my *Man: the Image of God*, 1958, Chap. 8). Creationism, in his judgment, is not adequate to laying bare the basis for imputation in the *peccatum originans*, though traducianism is likewise not in a position to do this. In the case of Shedd, traducianism is consciously embraced as the consequence of his realism. There is no escaping that conclusion, he feels, when we take seriously "the Adamic connection" (Shedd, *op. cit.*, 17). Three grounds are adduced for this argument: Scripture, systematic theology, and physiology (*ibid.*, 19).
41. Co-sinning occurs, according to Greijdanus, in a "manner still presently, in many ways, incomprehensible and unexplainable for us." *Op. cit.*, p. 55.
42. *Ibid.*

The only way in which realists have tried to get beyond this category is apparent in Shedd's theology. Shedd, to his credit, endeavored to work out the implications of his view from an anthropological point of view. It is obvious, he said, that Adam's progeny could not have shared in Adam's sin "in the form of individuals, and hence they must have participated . . . in the form of a race."[43] Therefore the concept of *race* or *humanity* is imported to aid us in resolving the internal problematic of a real co-sinning. The priority of race to individual is presumed to make clear that man is a "co-sinner" in this particular mode of his existence, namely in his "race."[44] Nevertheless, the basic structure of realism would seem to demand a greater accentuation than this on *individual man himself* and his own being guilty, personally, and by means of his own activity.

Greijdanus did not follow Shedd in this kind of explanation. He proposed a rather naive and finally an unintelligible realism. Yet he too stood before an insoluble difficulty, especially in his exegesis of Romans 5:14. There Paul refers to those "whose sins were not like the transgression of Adam." In the course of Paul's argument this clause is very clear. For Paul was considering a different *modus* of sinning, in view of the absence of the law, in the period between Adam and Moses (5:14). But this distinction is very difficult to maintain in the structures of realism. This is because realism can only opt for a definite and positive command which was broken by *all men* in the very *beginning*. All men, in Adam, have sinned. Greijdanus held to both Romans 5:14 and the realist hypothesis, and he merely set these two alongside each other, unreconciled and unresolved.[45]

43. Shedd, *op. cit.*, 29.
44. "This supposes that the race-form is prior to the individual form; that man first exists as a race or species and in this mode of existence commits a single and common sin" (*ibid.*). Shedd speaks of "mankind," i.e., "the human nature *before it was individualized by propagation*. This nature sinned. Human nature existing primarily as a unity in Adam and Eve and this same nature as subsequently *distributed and metamorphosed* into the millions of individual men, are two modes of the same thing. . . ." *Ibid.*
45. Cf. Greijdanus' tenth proposition in his dissertation: "This standing guilty is not a being 'reckoned' as guilty, as though the persons thus 'reckoned' had not themselves committed that sin (cf. Ezek. 18:4, 20); rather, it is a being regarded and treated as guilty on the ground that Adam's (natural) descendants themselves have committed this sin, *be it that they did this in a different manner from him* (cf. Rom. 5:14)." Italics mine.

On the basis of what we have said, we can certainly understand why the objections against realism have always been very
strong. Yet the critics are frequently aware of facing the very
same problems themselves. As Bavinck has written, Scripture
and history point us to an original and a common guilt on
the part of all mankind.[46] Bavinck regarded that guilt as an
established fact "apart from whether we can make it at all intelligible."[47] In this starting point he had no argument against
realism, and he further joined hands in suggesting that we can
say something about this manner of God's activity. Though we
cannot explain it, we can certainly remove from it the appearance of an arbitrariness.[48] With that in mind, Bavinck pointed
to the organic unity of the human race. In a "certain sense,"
he suggested, we can say that "we all were that one man."
Therefore, "what he did was done by all."[49] Yet no matter how
close Bavinck seemed to come to realism, he always regarded
that view as inadequate. He referred to the unity of the human
race but refused to surrender the independence of man's own
personality. He affirmed that man is more than a mere formal
appearance of "human nature."[50] Therefore he adopted what is
commonly called the "federal" or the "representative" conception of original sin. We shall look at that conception in our
next chapter.

One may get the impression as we examine this controversy
and the radical implications of realism that we are bogged down
here at a rather strange and unprofitable juncture. At the same
time, when we examine the motives at work, which emerge in
the course of the arguments, we are convinced again of the
sense of this topic. Certainly we must not lose sight of the
religious motive in realism. It is remarkable that not more attention is given that matter by realists themselves, especially
when we recognize that realism has waged a perpetual battle
against the concept of an "alien guilt." Realism has fashioned
its own peculiar concept of *imputatio* in contrast to more
traditional thought. It wants an *imputatio* in which we are
held responsible for what we have actually *done*. Only in that
way can God be seen as non-arbitrary and completely right.

46. Bavinck, *op. cit.*, III, 79.
47. *Ibid.*, 80.
48. *Ibid.*
49. *Ibid.* "Nos omnes ille unus homo fuimus."
50. *Ibid.*

Thus realism gives an answer in which every human alibi is radically cancelled and the connection between man's guilt and punishment is fully acknowledged. This connection would seem to be an intrinsic feature in any real act of conscience.

The fact that realism is unable to impress upon us the full weight of its charge ("You are the man!") is understandable and inevitable in terms of its own internal structure. Yet the religious motive in realism is very valid. We must see the *reality of God's indictment*. We must ask now if federalism can show us a better way to hear that indictment. Can it provide us with a more proper response in the confession of our guilt?

CHAPTER FOURTEEN

FEDERALISM

W E HAVE touched on federalism above and have noted that Bavinck tried to make an approach to the original sin dogma at a point beyond the physical unity of the race. Along with the physical unity he spoke of a *federal unity,* which he also regarded as "moral" in character.[1] In that federal unity he saw the real relevance of the statement that "all members of this kind of body can be either a blessing or a curse to each other."[2] He contended that a certain "coherence" is visible in both the good and evil that men do. Yet, while the influence for good arouses no opposition among men, the influence for evil does.[3] In all of this the main concern of Bavinck was what men have commonly called the "solidarity" of the race, or the results of the acts of one man upon the lives of others.

It is evident that Bavinck did not give an answer to the pressing problems of realism. Nor was that his intent. Exactly in this regard he referred to the words of Shedd, who also conceded that the solidarity of the race in no way explains the imputation of Adam's sin to his posterity.[4] At the same time, in Bavinck's opinion a recognition of this solidarity puts to rest the argument that God acted unjustly "when he caused the entire human race to share in Adam's punishment."[5] For God acts at every moment in this "federal" way (in blessing and in curse), and such acts are not in conflict with his justice. Therefore we cannot speak of an injustice in regard to the impu-

1. Bavinck, *Geref. Dog.,* III, 82.
2. *Ibid.* Bavinck speaks of the influence of those persons who have an important place in an organic whole.
3. *Ibid.,* 83.
4. Cf. Shedd, *Dogmatic Theology,* II, 187: "to suffer in consequence of the sin of another is not the same as to be punished for it." Bavinck adds to this: "and thus also to be viewed as oneself the doer of that sin" (*loc. cit.*).
5. *Ibid.*

tation of Adam's sin.[6] Yet we have seen that realism raises its
complaint at precisely this juncture and finds the evidences
of an arbitrariness in this concept. Realism takes exception to
a view which imputes to all men a guilt for which *they are not
responsible*. Therefore, by alluding to the solidarity of the race
and the freedom and sovereignty of God, the federalists cannot
answer the challenges of realism.

In our present chapter we are not concerned with a complete description of the federal view. We do, however, wish to
consider if federalism can offer a meaningful and a biblical
answer to the problematic which realism has set before us. This
problematic centers attention on the matter of God's justice.
Thus we are interested in the real meaning of *imputation* in
the federal conception.

The difficulties in the relation of realism and federalism are
made clear when we see that Bavinck himself plays down the
motive of "solidarity" in the original sin doctrine. He contends
that the "law" of solidarity cannot apply entirely in the case
of Adam and his posterity. Though all solidarity is "defined"
in some way or other, the original sin dogma is concerned with
the significance of Adam's sin for the *entire human race*. Here
we stand at the very heart of our problem. There are only two
men, Adam and Christ, whose lives and works have a universal
importance until the end of the world.[7] This means, however,
that the issue is not a general "law" of solidarity which illumines
the dogma of original sin. The issue is the *unique significance*
of Adam and Christ for all humanity.[8]

These two men, says Bavinck, were appointed by the special
ordinance of God. As it goes with them, so it goes with the
entire human race.[9] In line with that specific ordinance, Bavinck proposes the following definition of original sin. God
"pronounces all men guilty in one man, and therefore humanity
is unclean and subject to death in Adam." *All men* are now

6. *Ibid.,* 84.
7. *Ibid.*
8. We do not forget, in this statement, that Bavinck laid strong emphasis
   on solidarity. He even came to the point of saying that the philosophy
   of Kant, Schelling, Schopenhauer, *et al.*, and the doctrines of heredity and
   solidarity, have given us unexpected and important support for the
   dogma of original sin.
9. "If Adam fell, humanity fell; if Christ stood firm, humanity would stand
   erect in him" *(ibid.,* 85).

regarded as sinners, or assumed to be sinners, on the basis of *God's ordination in Adam.* Therefore we stand before an entirely different conception of original sin than we find in the doctrine of realism. For in realism we have an actual co-sinning; but here the sin of Adam is imputed and assigned to all his progeny. Because of Adam's position as the head of the covenant, we refer to this view as the "federal" conception.[10]

We have already observed that realism opposes this conception of imputation and casts a wary eye on any notion of a "representation" in the covenant.[11] Though the federalists speak of *God's* imputation of guilt, the realists are by no means satisfied. They point out that Scripture itself regards a "divine imputation" of guilt on originally guiltless men as nothing more or less than an arbitrary fiction. One can only speak of imputation in regard to what a man *himself has done;* and man's own guilt can only be written on his *own account.* Realists agree that God is free and sovereign — but this does not imply that he is capricious in his acts. When God affirms man's guilt, according to Scripture, he is concerned with the man who is really guilty of forsaking his ways.[12]

Now obviously we are dealing here with the fundamental issue at stake in the relations of realism and federalism. For if imputation is assigned to all men and all are therefore born in sin and wrath, and if our "original corruption" is the product

10. Cf. A. de Bondt, *Het Dogma der Kerk,* 1949, p. 273: "God created humanity as one whole. He contracted a covenant with humanity in its head, Adam. The decision of Adam is our decision." Cf. p. 274: "the guilt of Adam imputed to us," and the "division" of original sin in inherited *guilt* and inherited *corruption.*

11. Bavinck sees no contradiction in realism and federalism and recognizes the truth of realism (II, 82). By this he means the "unitas naturae." Cf. also A. G. Honig, *Handboek van de Gereformeerde Dogmatiek,* 1938, p. 413, who contends in his discussion of realism that the "physical unity" is of great importance, but is inadequate as an explanation of original sin. But the characteristic feature of realism is the manner in which the unity of nature is seen. It seems to me that the case is as Shedd has so vigorously defended: Consistent realism cannot be allied with federalism.

12. Honig has written, in connection with original sin: "Here much remains unexplained to our understanding. But in childlike faith we confess that original guilt is not opposed to the virtues of a completely beatific God" (*ibid.*). We must say, in response, that on this level no decision is possible. For realism also desires to live in this childlike faith; and in the light of that faith it proposes the *meaning* of imputation.

of that imputed guilt of Adam,[13] then realism would seem to be right in saying that something else is meant here than man's "own guilt." Recall that realism wants to do away with the human alibi and to underscore the relations between accusation and guilt, and the guilt of man and the confession of his own sin. Realism sees all this as the necessary corrective of the traditional doctrine of original sin. Our purpose, at this point, is to ascertain if and to what extent a federal view is a meaningful answer to the realistic conception.

It is important to see that the Church has used the concept of *imputatio* not only in regard to original sin but especially in regard to the righteousness of Christ. Here we stand at the very heart of the salvation of God: his unspeakable Gift of completely unmerited grace. The Church, in her confessions, has spoken of this imputation of Christ's righteousness in a very bold way. She has recognized, at this point, the reverse side of what Scripture calls the *non-imputation of man's sin* (cf. II Cor. 5:19; Ps. 32:1-2). Though objections have been brought against this idea (by Socinians especially, who regard it as an unrighteous "fiat" in conflict with the character of God's activity), the Church has not bowed before her critics and has continued to speak of imputation as the "mystery of the atonement."

It is very remarkable that there is no difference in insight, at this juncture, in the realist and the federalist views. Both endorse wholeheartedly the Reformation confession that God, "without any merit of mine, of mere grace, grants and imputes to me the perfect satisfaction, righteousness, and holiness of Christ" (HC, 60).[14] To that confession the words are then added: "... as if I had never had nor committed any sin." That same line of thought is found in the Lord's Supper formulary. There we read that the person who rightly celebrates the supper should believe "that the complete righteousness of Christ

13. Cf. Honig (*ibid.*), who calls original sin "indispensable" as an explanation for sin's coming into the world (God's declaration of guilt). Also Bavinck, *op. cit.*, 107: original sin is "nothing else but the sin of Adam, imputed to all his descendants, and ... thus results in their all being born with the same guilt, the same uncleanness, and the same perniciousness as befell Adam immediately after his transgression of God's command."

14. Cf. the heading of Article 23, Belgic Confession: "the imputation of Christ's righteousness."

is imputed and freely given him as his own — yea, so completely *as if* he himself, in his own person, had satisfied for all his sins and fulfilled all righteousness." It is plain that nowhere in Reformed theology is there a burning issue regarding the possibility of combining *imputatio* and the righteousness of God. The thought of "as if" (which plays a dominant role in these statements) is not open to serious dispute. Nevertheless, the combination of *imputation and Gift* has proven to be an important barrier to any abstract Socinian criticism. That criticism can only regard this notion as "impossible." The concept of *"aliena" justitia* has not led to real difficulties in Reformed theology. For the purpose of this term is only to underscore the real marvel of the vicarious atonement. The idea of "as if," in the Reformed confessions and formularies, accentuates the sufficiency of God's Gift. Thus the *aliena* restrains a man from making any claims of his own merit. Furthermore, the "as if" and the *aliena* are experienced as the opposite of arbitrariness; and the evidence of God's providing his own salvation "for nothing."[15]

Precisely in this light the realists have strongly denied that the imputations of Adam and Christ are parallel. They have taken issue with the idea that an identical concept of "imputation" applies in the cases of our condemnation and salvation. We cannot speak of a "similarity" between the *imputatio primi peccati* and the *imputatio justitiae Christi*. The "as if," in the case of salvation, is a thankful confession of faith and *aliena justitia;* but there is no similar "as if" or *alienum* in the situation of our guilt. In making this point the realists do not reject the "as if" of the confessions but the "as if" of federal theology.

Now it stands to reason that this whole discussion has centered so largely in the exegetical problems of Romans 5. There

15. The sense of the "imputatio justitiae Christi" is introduced in Lutheran theology especially in connection with its meaning in Luther and the *Apology* of Melanchthon. When H. E. Weber sees a shift in the direction of an objectifying of imputation (in abstraction from sanctification), and a "purely imputative" conception in orthodoxy, he recognizes that the "original concern" of the Reformation's speaking of "imputation" lay in the "imputatio gratuita" as the reverse side of the "sola fide." It is *this* imputation-concept that we have in mind here; and in this concept there is no problematic strain of arbitrariness. Cf. Weber, *Reformation, Orthodoxie und Rationalismus*, I, 1, 1937, 96f.

Adam and Christ are set in tandem, as it were, in a very special
way. Later we shall look more fully at this chapter, but for
now we are especially concerned about the dogmatic answer
which the federalists have given to the religious objection of
realism. With that in mind, it is important to observe the battle
which once revolved around the famous figure of Placaeus in
the French School of Saumur. Especially in that struggle the
meaning of *imputatio* was the issue at stake. This is very apparent from the distinction Placaeus drew between *mediate
and immediate imputation.* Adam's sin, said Placaeus, was imputed to all men, but it was also imputed in a "mediated" way.
Thus Placaeus wished to do away with any concept of arbitrariness. He pointed to man's factual defilement from Adam
and saw in this the real basis of *imputatio.*[16]

Bavinck has discussed this view and has mentioned the wave
of resistance which followed upon it and the influence which
it exerted. "The time seemed past for the Reformation doctrine
of original sin. Placaeus found acceptance everywhere."[17] The
widespread influence can be explained by various factors, but
not the least of these is the fact that Placaeus seemed to eliminate
all arbitrariness and to fasten imputation to an already-present
depravity. A certain gap was still present between Placaeus and
realism; nonetheless a point of contact was clearly apparent.
Both of these views rooted *imputatio* in actual sin and desired
to purge that concept of any arbitrariness. The difference between them is that realism takes its point of departure in the
concept of "co-sinning" and Placaeus ties his *imputatio* to the
defilements which come from Adam.[18] In both cases, however,

---

16. On Placaeus, cf. especially Bavinck, *op. cit.,* 77ff.; *P.R.E., s.v.* "Placaeus";
    Greijdanus, *Toerekeningsgrond,* p. 23; J. Murray, "The Imputation of
    Adam's Sin," *Westminster Theological Journal,* Vol. XIX, 1957, pp.
    141ff.

17. Bavinck, *op. cit.,* 79. In the same context Bavinck states that Pelagian-
    ism found an entrance on every hand. Many were won over by the idea
    of *imputatio mediata;* in Bavinck's judgment, also Jonathan Edwards'.
    In opposition to Charles Hodge and W. Cunningham, who held to this
    same view, J. Murray has contended (following B. Warfield) that this
    rests on a fallacious interpretation of Edwards' doctrine of original sin
    (*op. cit.,* 152f.). So too Shedd, *op. cit.,* 171.

18. Greijdanus (*op. cit.,* p. 14) takes issue with the *imputatio mediata* be-
    cause our sense of justice remains equally unsatisfied in that view. For
    what is then the *basis* of degeneration? Furthermore, he sees the course
    of development in such a way that the contention of Placaeus provided
    the occasion for accentuating the non-realistic imputation even more

it is simply wrong to speak of an imputation where there is no personal or actual guilt.

Can a biblical answer be given to these objections? Very important here is the condemnation of Placaeus' doctrine at the Synod of Charenton in 1644. There the charge was made that he actually denied the imputation of Adam's sin.[19] By putting all his stress on man's factual corruption (*imputatio mediata, consequens,* instead of *immediata, antecedens*), he did away with any real notion of imputation at all. Why should the effect and not the cause be imputed to all men? That question proved to be an embarrassment from Placaeus' own standpoint. Because of that inadequacy his opponents put an even greater stress on the *imputatio immediata et antecedens.*

But in how far is a meaningful answer given here to a question which has certainly vexed the minds of men on every hand? Is there, or is there not, an arbitrariness in God? In Placaeus and realism, but also in Bavinck, this question is always in the foreground of debate. It demands our attention whenever we reflect on the meaning of *imputatio.* Federalism has gone to great lengths to clarify that in *imputatio immediata et antecedens* we are not involved in a divine caprice and that something very different is implied from our human habit of merely shifting the blame. Realism, however, knew what it was doing when it renounced all arbitrariness and rejected any notion of the alibi. In the original sin dogma, according to the realists, we have need of the most realistic concept of *peccatum proprium.* The federalists, on the other hand, could make no such appeal and found themselves in the very difficult position of saying *how* a federal conception does *not* involve us in caprice.

Many have tried their hands at answering that question. The difficulties here arise especially in the efforts to demonstrate that immediate imputation does not entail a parallel to the human and illegitimate imputation of one man's guilt to an-

---

strongly and clearly. Cf. also Shedd's criticism: "Why should the effect be imputed and not the cause? Such a kind of imputation looks unreasonable" (*op. cit.,* 193).

19. The synod mentioned no names but opposed the contention "that the whole nature of original sin consists solely in the corruption that is hereditary in all the posterity of Adam, or that with which all men are born, and in which it is denied that the first sin of Adam has been imputed unto us." J. Aymon, *Tous les synodes nationaux des églises réformées de France,* II, 1710, 680.

other man who is not responsible. In all such efforts the tendency is to speak of imputation in the sense of a "bond" which merely joins together Adam and his posterity. In line with the rejection of realism, this "bond" is then described as "federal" in character; and in terms of that federal relation the descendants of Adam are said to be *implicated in Adam's sin*. We have commented already on Bavinck's cautious reference to the sin of all men in Adam "in a certain sense." By using such qualified terms as these the federalists have tried to unloosen themselves from the onus of an arbitrariness. Therefore, although the unity of the race cannot be seen in realistic terms, the concept of "all men" does not stand apart from Adam and his sin. The sin of Adam is not "imputed" to all men in the sense of a "human whimsicality" but only because of the bond of community which exists by *God's own ordinance*. For that reason the federalists opposed Placaeus for seeing the proper ground of imputation in the corruption of Adam's descendants. They preferred to conceive of imputation in the light of the federal union of Adam and his posterity. They saw that union in such a way that God looks down upon the human race as one in Adam and accounts the sin of *Adam* as the sin of *all men*. Here the question rises if such an answer does not display a certain kinship with realism, which likewise speaks of an imputation of *our guilt in Adam's own sin*. Since the federalists honor that relation to Adam, they end up with the same sorts of expressions as realists. God does not impute an alien guilt but treats all men as partners in Adam.

J. Ridderbos has made a study of Edwards' theory of identity, where the descendants of Adam are seen as one with him. Such a view, says Ridderbos, does not stress an imputation *per se* but "the result of the unity, which consists by God's decree, between Adam and his posterity."[20] In this view "the first sin is the sin of ourselves, not only because God imputes it to us but because it *really* and *truly* is our own and is imputed to us therefore."[21] This, we might say, is the real basis of realism. Nevertheless, it is debatable if Edwards was a realist in the later sense of Shedd, Greijdanus and Schilder.[22] Apart from all that,

20. Ridderbos, *De Theologie van Jonathan Edwards*, 1907, p. 163.
21. *Ibid.*, p. 164.
22. The answer to this question is of one piece with the peculiar conception of identity in Edwards (Ridderbos, pp. 165f.). This conception is not of importance for us at this time.

we have to notice that federalism too — though in a different sense — regards the sin of Adam as *our own*. To *that* extent it approaches the realist conception of *imputatio*. Hence the impassioned rebuttal of federalism to the realist charge of arbitrariness. The real difference in these two views does not consist in the antithesis of real and unreal *imputatio*. As a matter of fact, both realism and federalism wish only to speak of a *real* imputation of man's guilt.

The difference can better be seen in the following way. Realism says that imputation is only thinkable when all posterity are "actually and really co-sinners," while federalism clings to the phrase "in a certain sense" and contends that God regards and treats, and therefore *declares all men as guilty in Adam*.[23] Here, however, it is clear that our problem is no less real. Both parties agree that there is an actual "imputation" of guilt and not a merely external act; yet they cannot come to terms at the deeper level as long as the religious charge of realism has any ring of validity. The charge is that the federalist "declaration of guilt" is nothing but an act of God's caprice. According to the realists, it cannot be more than that as long as the federalists refuse to accept the premise that Adam's sin is the *sin of all men* in the fullest and most realistic sense of those words. Therefore the question of the meaning of *imputatio* returns as the question of God's *ordinatio*. This, then, is the concept which the federalists have used as the basis for the imputation of Adam's guilt to *all*.[24]

In the Formula Consensus Helvetica of 1675 the concept of mediate imputation was rejected and that of immediate imputation was upheld. We hear that Adam's sin was imputed to his posterity by a *hidden and righteous judgment*.[25] By appealing to the *in Adamo omnes peccasse* it is said to be im-

---

23. Bavinck, *op. cit.*
24. One might compare the realist criticism of tradition with Karl Barth's statement in *K.D.*, IV/1, 570 (ET, 511): "The question still remains what is meant by this *imputatio* and what basis there is for the idea." Polanus answered that the "ratio huius veritatis nulla est praeterquam voluntas creatoris," and Barth interprets this by saying: "This obviously means that it is the truth which God himself tells us, which is therefore indisputable, which we have to accept, however strange and bitter it may be." In such a statement we stand before the same questions as in the realistic criticism of the "mera imputatio."
25. "Peccatum Adami omnibus eius posteris judicio Dei arcano et justo imputari" (Art. X); Müller, *Bekenntnisschriften,* p. 864.

possible to see how the corruption of the human race could fall
under God's righteous judgment if no fault at all *("delictum
aliquod")* had preceded that corruption. A righteous God does
not punish a man who is guiltless.[26] Therefore in these words
the realistic motive of God's justice is expressed in a federalist
statement which shows a certain sensitivity for the perils of an
arbitrariness. To avoid the pitfall of an arbitrary God[27] a
twofold concept of guilt is now introduced. There is guilt on
the basis of Adam's disobedience and guilt on the basis of
man's own factual corruption. What we see, in other words, is
really a notion of inherited guilt and hereditary depravity.[28]
Having affirmed this twofold or double guilt, a disagreement
is now registered for all those who refuse to admit this "first
guilt": viz., that of immediate imputation.[29] Instead of the peril
of doing away with the *imputatio,* we find in this formula a
proposed solution in the concept of duality. There is a "twoness" in our sinning in Adam and the corruption which then
follows.

When we ask what light this sheds on the doctrine of imputation, we should examine the concepts used both here and
elsewhere: "sinning in Adam," "representation," "immediate
imputation," and God's "regarding and treating us as guilty,"
or his "declaration" that we *are such.* We hear of the "hidden
and righteous judgments of God." Especially in this latter
phrase we see an effort to escape the opprobrium of an arbitrariness within the structures of federalism. Yet all this falls
short of giving an answer to the objections which realists and
others have posed. The question of the *justice of God* comes up
again and again in the concepts of "declaring," "judging," and

26. "Cum Deus justissimus totius terrae judex nonnisi sontem punit" *(ibid.,*
    p. 865).
27. Cf. Bavinck, *op. cit.,* 84.
28. *"Primum* quidem ob *[paráptōma]* et inobedientiam, quam in Adami
    lumbis commisit; *deinde* ob consequentem in ipso conceptu haeredi-
    tariam corruptionem insitam" (Müller, *loc cit.).*
29. Article XII: "qui Adamum posteros suos *ex instituto* Dei repraesentasse
    ac proinde eiusdem peccatum posteris eius *[amésōs]* imputari negant."
    Here it is further stated that in this way one also brings into peril the
    "haereditaria corruptio" — an accusation which was frequently expressed
    against Placaeus but which he always disputed. Compare: "Sub imputa-
    tionis mediatae et consequentis nomine non imputationem duntaxat
    primi peccati tollunt, sed haereditaria etiam corruptionis assertionem
    gravi periculo objiciunt" *(ibid.).*

"regarding" man as guilty. On the one hand, federalism has pointed to a real guilt and to sin as *peccatum proprium;* on the other hand, it speaks of a declaration of guilt on the basis of God's ordinance. Thus we are left with a different doctrine of *imputatio* from when man is held responsible for an act which he himself commits. No matter how the federalists try to combine *peccatum proprium* and *peccatum alienum,* the relativizing that is implicit in the words "in a certain sense" compels them to understand "imputation" as a forensic judgment of God. Therefore the federalists have been challenged to show how *such* an imputation is in harmony with Scripture. How can we speak of an "imputation" when we do not mean *an active and a personal sinning* in the fullest sense of those words?[30]

The federalists, when they refer to the hidden justice of God, have intended to speak of God with great reverence and to reject, *a priori,* an arbitrariness in his activity. But that intention is also found in others in no less *a priori* a fashion. In fact, the justice of God is the point of departure in the realism of Shedd and Greijdanus. Therefore, the introduction of such terms as *justum, arcanum,* etc., cannot afford us a solution to this problem of *imputatio.* The fact that Placaeus' criticism was met by a simple allusion to these terms could only inspire his followers to reject all the more the concept of *imputatio immediata.* In that reaction, however, they frequently overlooked the tenuousness of their own conception of *imputatio "mediata."*[31] All accent was now placed on the *a priori,* biblical motive

30. This challenge is all the more urgent because nowhere in Scripture is there any reference to the "imputation" of Adam's sin upon all men, though federalists have certainly thought that this is materially implied in the scriptural witness. Murray, who defends the *imputatio immediata,* writes: "it is admitted that nowhere in Scripture is our relation to the trespass of Adam explicitly denied in terms of imputation" (*op. cit.,* Vol. XX, p. 1). On the biblical *logizesthai,* as an act of God's salvation, see *TWNT,* IV, *s.v. logizomai,* B. 4. b. On the non-imputation of sin, see Ps. 32:2 (also Rom. 4:7) and II Cor. 5:19. Concerning that text on which imputation is *essentially* based (Rom. 5:19), see Chap. 17, below.

31. O. Kirn (*P.R.E., s.v.* "Sünde," XIX, 141) calls this doctrine of *imputatio mediata* a "moderation" ("Milderung"), or a "weakened form of the dogma" — an "auxiliary construction" ("Hilfskonstruktion"). When Bavinck writes that "Placaeus found acceptance everywhere" (*op. cit.,* 78), he sees in this only a deterioration in connection with the influence of Pelagianism. But this judgment (as well as that concerning Edwards) is too little aware of important nuances; for the entry of Placaeus was also dependent on questions that had remained unanswered.

of contradicting the arbitrariness of God. No wonder that the frequent immanent criticism of this doctrine of "mediate imputation" has never succeeded in convincing its defenders. How could it as long as their own criticism failed to receive an adequate answer? How should we speak of that which God has "once and for all ordained"? All the arguments against federalism (whether of Placaeus or realism) come down to a single main issue. Therefore Greijdanus has quite rightly asked for a "further, somewhat modified development in regard to the problem of *imputatio*."[32]

In all of these historical aspects of our problem the main issue is very clear. Realism has done us the service of sharpening our insights concerning the meaning of *imputatio*. It has tried to answer the question of whether God imputes to men an "alien guilt." Is the concept of *imputatio* at odds with the very nature of his justice? Does it contradict the statement of Ezekiel concerning the activity of God? Surely the "rule of Ezekiel" underscores the correlation of guilt and punishment in a very unambiguous way. Furthermore, as we have already seen, federalism is unable to answer these questions in a satisfactory manner. This is obvious when it forges a synthesis with "realistic" elements and tries to hold to the concept of *peccatum proprium*.

It is a symptom of these problems and tensions when the Formula Consensus Helvetica proposes a twofold guilt and when Edwards seeks later to avoid this very "twofoldedness." Edwards, of course, did not deny the doctrine of original sin; at the same time he tried to eliminate the appearance of an arbitrariness which might possibly lurk in the causal relation of inherited guilt and hereditary corruption. His aim was thoroughly religious. "Therefore I am humbly of the opinion," he wrote, "that if any have supposed the children of Adam to come into the world with a *double* guilt, one the guilt of Adam's sin, another the guilt arising from their having a corrupt heart, they have not well conceived of the matter."[33] The guilt of man is singular. It is both "one and simple."

Therefore we see the attempt to conceive of original sin as *peccatum proprium*. We agree with Murray that Edwards does not stand in line with Placaeus; at the same time, it is very

32. Greijdanus, *op. cit.*, p. 53. Note that Greijdanus also speaks here of a "merely formal construction" which cannot uphold God's justice.
33. Edwards, *The Works of President Edwards*, 1817, Vol. II (*The Great Christian Doctrine of Original Sin Defended*), 342ff.

unclear, also in Edwards, *why* it is wrong to speak of a "twofold guilt." Why *should* it be wrong when we take our point of departure in the *imputatio immediata?* It is obvious that Edwards' protest against a "double guilt" was prompted by his desire to do away with fatalism or determinism, or the *alienum peccatum,* in the original sin doctrine. He wanted to see and confess man's guilt as existentially *his own.* Yet the impression lingers that federalism cannot defend on what grounds the idea of a "double guilt" is biblically tenable.[34] For that reason the meaning of an "imputation of *guilt*" has remained, for many, a very real question. It has led to inner uncertainties as men have faced the radical criticisms of the original sin doctrine. This is especially the case in regard to the question: Are we speaking of a fatalism here? Obviously, these problems are not removed when we merely refer to the *"judicium arcanum* of God."[35]

The deepest and truest motive in these discussions is the urge to speak of God's activity in a responsible and biblical way. We are struck by the fact that these questions are really at bottom one: namely, the manner of the *imputatio.* They are questions of concern to both Catholics and Protestants. Here our purpose is not to give a complete picture; nevertheless it

34. Especially Murray has gone deeply into the meaning of the imputation (particularly in *op. cit.,* Vol. XX, pp. 1-25). He rejects the idea of a pre-existence (p. 20), and wants to hold firmly to the "peccatum alienum et proprium" (p. 16). With that in mind he suggests as a solution — somewhat in line with Edwards, it seems to me — that it is not "depravity" that forms the punishment upon imputed sin (the traditional federalist idea); rather, "the infliction with depravity is *involved* in the imputation of Adam's sin" (p. 23). In my judgment Murray is no more successful than Edwards in making this distinction clear. Yet in both attempts the existential motive in regard to *our guilt* is strongly evident.

35. It is striking that the realistic criticism of the federalist original sin dogma shows a number of *formal parallels* to the non-Christian criticism which speaks (in simplistic terms) of a guilt with which we have nothing to do but is nonetheless imputed unto us. See Marsman and Vestdijk. The realists, of course, have desired to eliminate all misunderstanding in their criticism of the *alienum peccatum.* This criticism of federalism is expressed in the most remarkable terms by Greijdanus: "with his grace God may do, in his sovereignty, what he desires. It is only his — but the guilt is not from him. Therefore, in his sovereignty, he takes his stance in a different way in regard to guilt than in regard to grace" (*op. cit.,* p. 55). It is unfortunate that Greijdanus saw no other possibility here than realism.

is well to consider the "ecumenical" aspect of this problem.[36]
For Catholics too, with Bavinck, have pointed to the special
"difficulties" in the original sin dogma.[37] They have pondered
these difficulties and have recognized that our problems do not
stem from an idle speculation alone. Is it not true that our
being guilty (or "inherited guilt") can best be expressed in
terms of a *confession of our guilt?* But how can the sin of Adam
be *our own?* This is a question which both Catholics and Protestants have asked.

The Catholics have taken their point of departure in the
decree of Trent in which it is denied that Adam's disobedience
brought only death and physical punishment to the human
race, *but not sin.*[38] Van Hove, on the basis of that statement,
has called it inadmissible to speak of only an external imputation of Adam's sin. This latter view was endorsed by such
Catholic theologians as Ambrosius Catharinus and Albertus
Pighius. Both of these saw the sinful plight of mankind as a
punishment for Adam's transgression. But that position, according to Van Hove, is in conflict with the Council of Trent, for
original sin is not then construed as a true or proper sin but
as only the *first sin* imputed to all mankind.[39] In Van Hove's
judgment, the Protestants also follow this same line of reasoning and proclaim an *external imputation,* despite the fact that
this view is insufficient for maintaining the full justice of God.[40]

36. For the Roman Catholic doctrine of original sin we cite the following:
A. van Hove, *De Erfzonde,* 1936; G. Feuerer, *Adam und Christus als
Gestaltkräfte und ihr Vermächtnis an die Menschheit. Zur christliche
Erbsündenlehre,* 1939; H. Volk, *Das christliche Verständnis des Todes,*
1957; K. Rahner, *Zur Theologie des Todes (Quaestiones Disputatae 2,
1958); ibid., Zum theologischen Begriff der Konkupiszenz (Schriften zur
Theologie,* I, 1954, 377-414); *ibid., Theologisches zum Monogenismus
(Schr.z.Theol.,* I, 253-322); P. Schoonenberg, *Het Geloof van ons Doopsel,*
I, 1955, 231-264; M. M. Labourdette, *De Erfzonde en de Oorsprong van
de Mens,* 1956.
37. Cf. Van Hove, *op. cit.,* p. 125.
38. "Aut inquinatum illum per oboedientiae peccatum mortem et poenas
corporis tantum in omne genus humanum transfundere, non autem et
peccatum ..." (Denz., 789).
39. Van Hove, *op. cit.,* p. 136.
40. Van Hove contends that Anselm already took issue with this idea of
imputation: "Quapropter cum damnatur infans pro peccato originali,
damnatur non pro peccato Adae, sed pro suo." So too Thomas: "cum
aliquis punitur, pro peccato primi parentis, *non punitur pro peccato
alterius,* sed pro peccato suo" *(loc. cit.).* At the Council of Sens, 1140,

We must see in this criticism a Roman parallel to the main impulse of realism. Original sin is *peccatum proprium* and cannot be imputed to us as an *alienum peccatum* or a merely "external sin."[41]

Yet if, according to Rome, the real issue is not the *consequence* of sin but *sin itself,* we shall have to come to a clearer explanation than Van Hove has given. When men have seen original sin as a "consequence" they have been able to fence off the element of arbitrariness and to point especially to the sinful *status* of mankind. But when they have seen that the classic concept of *sin* is insufficiently guarded in that way[42] they have felt constrained to say that the free will of man itself belongs to his real sin. That is to say: original sin *belongs to man freely.*[43] This was the verdict of Rome in the case of Baius, who taught that sin's "being willed" does not belong to the very essence of man's sin.[44] Rome contended that only a single conclusion is possible in regard to this conception. Some sort of connection must now be established between the will of Adam and our will.[45]

Therefore, at this point similar questions arise in both Catholic and Protestant theologies. In both there is a tendency to speculate on a possible "inclusion" of our will in the will of Adam. Nevertheless that proposal raises the problem of how this is possible, or how we conceive of that possibility in very concrete terms.[46] Here there is a kind of Catholic "federalism" which runs parallel to its Protestant counterpart and shows a similar interest in the divine *decree* and *ordinance,* as well as in Adam's position as the *juridical head of the human race.* Again, the same sorts of problems are very apparent. No "ordination" of God can *make* us "sinners" if we *are not.*[47]

In view of these alternatives Van Hove has adopted a posi-

the idea of Abelard was already condemned "quod non contraximus culpam ex Adam sed poenam tantum" (Denz., 376).
41. Cf. the formulation of Trent concerning "Adae peccatum, quod origine unum est et propagatione, non imitatione transfusum, *omnibus inest unicuique proprium*" (Denz., 790).
42. Van Hove, *op. cit.,* p. 176.
43. *Ibid.,* p. 177.
44. "Ad rationem et definitionem peccati non pertinet voluntarium . . ." (Denz., 1046).
45. Van Hove, *op. cit.,* p. 180.
46. *Ibid.,* p. 185.
47. *Ibid.,* p. 186.

tion which shows a clear relation to realism. In Adam, he says, man's *nature* was present. (Recall the concepts of *race* and *mankind* in Shedd.) Thus the sin of Adam was the sin of *ourselves* or the sin of *our own nature*. The goal of creation was the elevation of Adam to the supernatural order, or the elevation of all of man's *nature in him*. When we see things in that way, says Van Hove, it makes sense that only the *first* sin of Adam was the sin of us all.[48] For in Adam's unique position the *nature of man sinned*. Furthermore, it is now explainable that we have no personal or nostalgic regrets for our own original sin, or that Rome once chided the Jansenists for saying that we *must have*.[49] Certainly we participate in the sin of Adam,[50] and in this we find an "impenetrable mystery." But the very same "mystery" holds for the counterpart in Christ's work of redemption.

Thus, the objective foundation of original sin, *as true sin,* is found in the character of original sin as a sin of *nature*. Van Hove has anticipated the criticism and has also defended himself against the objection that the term *nature* is "merely abstract."[51] There can be a sin which a man does not personally commit but has nonetheless received by a direct line from the first sinner, the father of the human race. All of us participate in that sin. In this way Van Hove has tried to do justice to the Tridentine statement that Adam's sin is one in origin and is yet, in the process of propagation, peculiar to every man's sinning.[52]

It is understandable that in Catholic ranks themselves there is a certain awareness of the internal problems in this solution. There is always a persistent uneasiness in the assumption that original sin is a "sin of nature." Quite recently the question has been asked in how far this position does real justice to the "veridical" nature of man's "original sin."[53] That question highlights, of course, that Catholics are concerned at this point with the very same problems as Protestants. Furthermore, when we

---

48. *Ibid.,* pp. 202, 204. Cf. Labourdette, *op. cit.,* pp. 88f.
49. "Homo debet agere tota vita paenitentiam pro peccato originali" (Denz., 1309).
50. Van Hove, *op. cit.,* p. 221.
51. *Ibid.,* p. 200.
52. Denz., 790.
53. *Theologisch Woordenboek* (Brink), I, 1952, 1391. In this context the question is further asked "if we must accept any part in Adam's sinful act."

see how often the "mystery" of original sin is discussed, and
with what reservations it is also hemmed in, we are all the
more convinced of the value of speaking of an "ecumenical"
problem.[54] There is a profound appreciation, in Catholic theology, for the real peril that an "explanation" may open the
way for a self-excuse and for pointing to the *"alienum" peccatum*.

In Chapter 13 we discussed the doctrine of realism and its
efforts to unmask the human alibi. In the present chapter we
have concentrated on the doctrine of federalism, with its greater
stress on the themes of imputation and representation. Both
of those views, of course, have spoken of "imputation." And yet
there remains a different insight on the nature of that concept.
Realism maintains an actual charging of responsibility for a
sin committed by all men in Adam, while federalism relates
that concept to God's ordinance, on the basis of which the sin
of Adam (as head of the race) is assigned to all men. The federalists admit that not all men are *personally responsible* for
the sin which Adam has committed.

It is only natural to inquire if and to what extent the
Church's confessions have run parallel to, or have actually reflected, these theological debates. As we have seen, Trent did
not enter into those debates. Nevertheless she attempted to give
a definition and to emphasize the *sin-character of original sin*.
To what extent, then, do the Protestant confessions proceed
to give us a "solution"? What have they thought was necessary
to confess in the original sin doctrine? In the chapter which
follows we shall limit ourselves to an examination of the Lutheran and Reformed symbols. We shall notice, in both cases,
the obvious concern for the depth and gravity of "original sins."
We can only do justice to that depth and gravity when we
entitle our chapter with the words which these confessions have
very clearly had in mind. For the doctrine of original sin is
first of all a *confession of our guilt*.

54. We also recall the questions in the Greek Church, in which the thought
    of an *inherited punishment* — more than an inherited guilt — has come
    to the foreground. Cf. *Theol. Woordenboek*, I, 1377f.

CHAPTER FIFTEEN

THE CONFESSION OF GUILT

O UR PURPOSE in this chapter is to listen to the manner
in which the Reformation confessions have spoken of
original sin. It is only right that we call this chapter "the confession of guilt" since our interest is not in theoretical abstractions and guilt-phenomena which need to be analyzed but is
rather in "my confession of my guilt." This practical and existential note is a striking feature in both the Lutheran and Reformed confessions. We find nothing in these of a faithless
objectifying of guilt or the casual attitude of a disinterested
spectator. Rather, the element of a personal confession is inescapably present. We are constantly reminded of the strong
and healthy words of Nathan: "You are the man" (II Sam.
12:7) .[1]

There is every reason for us to listen carefully to this confession of our guilt. For we cannot assume that what the symbols say on original sin reflects, in a material way, what the
theologians have said on that same doctrine. Consider, for example, the earlier Reformed confessions. In these we cannot find

---

1. Here we are touching on a very significant problem in regard to the
symbols and the nature of confession. In the Nicaenum we read "I
believe" and "I *acknowledge*" (viz., "one baptism for the remission of
sins"), and "I *look for*" (viz., "the resurrection of the dead and the life
of the world to come"). The Athanasianum states what "the *catholic*
faith" is, having first expressed the necessity of this faith in order to be
saved (1, 2, 44). Schlink speaks of a shift in "the structure of dogma, from
confession to doctrine," which is apparent, among other places, in the
disappearance of the doxological aspect. In regard to the Confessio Augustana, he suggests that this was drawn up, not *coram Deo*, but for the
king and, "therefore, for fellowmen." It seems to me that with all this
development and crystallization it cannot be denied that both the doxological aspect and the confession of guilt as well are implied in the
"doctrine," and that these even get an explicit expression. Therefore we
can speak of a confession of guilt *within* the confessional writings. Cf.
E. Schlink, "Die Struktur der dogmatischen Aussage als oekumenisches
Problem," *K.u.D.*, III, 1957, pp. 251ff.

an explicit distinction between hereditary guilt and inherited corruption, even though that same distinction played an important role in theology. Or reflect on the example which Polman has recently called to our attention. He has observed that Article 15 of the Belgic Confession does not make a choice between a realist and a federalist conception. Furthermore, the relation between original guilt and hereditary corruption is not even mentioned.[2] We shall have to return to that fact at a later time, but for now we remind ourselves of how very necessary it is to judge the speaking and confessing of the Church on their own merits. The argument cannot be lightly dismissed that the difference between a confession and a dogmatical treatise is not a matter of "size" alone. Indeed, it could be that the more concentrated confession is more sober and circumspect than the larger dogmatical analysis would tend to be. Therefore it is wrong to suggest that a confession which is silent on problems treated at length in dogmatics must also display, by that token, a certain poverty. If the scarcity of words in confessions has anything to do with Ecclesiastes 5:1 ("God is in heaven, and you upon earth; therefore let your words be few"), it is very feasible that a symbol states what is proper and essential and sounds a warning against a dogmatician's overstepping his boundaries.[3]

We shall look first of all at the Lutheran confessions. In doing so, we are struck by the strong accent they lay on the total and radical character of original sin. The Augsburg Confession states that after the fall of Adam all men were both conceived and born in sin. They were born with "fleshly appetite" and without the fear of God and faith in him. This state of sin is called "truly sin" and is entirely hopeless from the point of view of man.[4] It is very clear that this confession of guilt is by no means individualistic, for it refers us to more

2. A. D. R. Polman, *Woord en Belijdenis*, I, 271.
3. With this statement we intend no antithesis between confession and dogmatics. This could never do justice to the state of affairs in the Reformation churches and the formulation of their confessions. But we do wish to warn against a dogmatizing of those confessions.
4. "Quodque hic mormus seu vitium originis vere sit peccatum" (Art. II); J. T. Müller, *Die symbolischen Bücher der evangelisch-lutherischen Kirche*, 1928, p. 38. In the Latin text we read the words "nunc quoque" in connection with being condemned by this sin. Cf. E. Kinder, *Die Erbsünde*, 1959, p. 61.

than one's own guilt alone. "All men" are involved. And yet
within that universality the confession of personal guilt is very
obvious. Man's guilt, however, is seen in the context of God's
salvation. This means that whoever speaks lightly of guilt, in
any way, must necessarily cast a haze upon the glory and merits
of Christ.

This subject of original sin is given a broader treatment in
the Apology. It is there denied that original sin is only a defect
or a burden which men bear as the consequence of Adam's sin.
Original sin is not the result of the transgression of someone
else.[5] A very special warning is sounded against any relativizing
of man's original sin. The Scholastic description of this as
carentia justitiae originalis is seen as very revealing, but especially if *original justice* and *carentia* are given their full due.[6]
Thus, original sin is a power of corruption and a deeply profound reality. The same conviction is apparent in the Apology's
defense of Luther's statement that this sin remains *even after
baptism*. In that statement Luther refers back to the earlier
view of Augustine that the sin of man is forgiven not because
it *is no more* but because it *is no more imputed.*[7]

What we have here is a certain perspective on the situation
after forgiveness and baptism. *Concupiscentia* is explicitly mentioned, and is also contrasted, from the Lutheran standpoint,
with the Roman doctrine as later formulated by Trent. At the
time of the Apology the mood of the Tridentine statement had
already won a kind of universal appeal in Catholic theology.
This Catholic view presupposed that concupiscence, or covetousness, is no longer a sin after baptism.[8] Now obviously, our
present concern is not with this conception of the Lutheran

5. "Sine aliquo proprio vitio praeter alienum peccatum" (Müller, *op. cit.*,
   p. 78). Kinder correctly sees as the main burden of this confession
   ("Hauptskopus") the "full guilt-character of original sin" *(loc. cit.).*
6. Müller, *op. cit.*, p. 80.
7. "Peccatum in baptismo remittitur non ut non sit, sed ut non imputetur."
   "Thus Augustine confesses openly that sin remains in him, though it
   is not imputed unto us."
8. In the decree on original sin it was contested that sin "tantum radi aut
   non imputari." For, "in renatis enim nihil odit Deus, quia..." — and
   here follows a reference to Rom. 8:1 (Denz., 792). To be sure, *concupiscentia* remains in the man who is baptized. It is "ad agonem relicta," but
   "hanc concupiscentiam, quam aliquando apostolus peccatum appellat
   (Rom. 6:12) sancta synodus declarat, Ecclesiam catholicam nunquam
   intellexisse, peccatum appellari, quod vere et proprie in renatis peccatum
   est, sed quia peccatum est et ad peccatum inclinat" *(ibid.).*

confessions on the state of sin in believers; at the same time, it is significant that here too, in regard to our original sin, the focus is on the *factual depravity of man.* The depth of corruption was the matter of central importance in the confession of man's guilt. Thus original sin was described as *"Hauptsünde"*[9] or *corruptio naturae.* Neither of these terms, however, had any room for a notion in which the powers for doing good (or "free will") are still assigned to fallen man.[10]

In the "Epitome" of the Formula of Concord there is a further reference to the corruption and sinful state of man. It is now denied that original sin is only *reatus* or guilt *ex alieno peccato.*[11] Once again, *concupiscence* is the subject of concern, and is introduced to show how deeply and how far corruption extends.[12] Neither here nor elsewhere in the Lutheran confessions is the relation to Adam's own guilt in any way obscured;[13] nevertheless the dominant accent is on original sin as "a deep, malicious, heinous, unfounded, inscrutable and unspeakable corruption of all of nature and of all our faculties."[14] We shall have to agree with Kinder that these confessions are concerned with the real "depth dimension" of sin.[15]

The confessions have no interest in isolated sinful acts, which are enumerated and set next to each other. They are interested in the sinfulness or the sinful state of man's entire being. Sinful existence is not seen *as* man's creaturely existence but finds its place *within* the creaturehood which was the good and gracious gift of God.[16] Therefore sin is regarded as "personal sin" *("Person-sünde")*. Sin wells up from the heart of man, and man performs sin because he is a *sinner before the face of God.* There is no possibility of escaping to some place or part of himself

9. Art. Smalc. (Müller, *op. cit.*, p. 310); Latin text: "originale, hereditarium, principale et capitale peccatum."
10. *Ibid.*, p. 311. Here too is the correlation between sin and salvation: otherwise Christ has died in vain. We meet up with this correlation in the entire Lutheran dogmatics. Cf. *Hutterus Redivivus* (published by K. Hase, 1883[12]), p. 176.
11. "...Absque ulla naturae nostrae corruptione, in nos derivata" (Müller, *op. cit.*, p. 521).
12. *Ibid.*, pp. 520-522.
13. E.g., "propter inoboedientiam Adae et Hevae"; *ibid.*, p. 576. Cf. Art. Smalc., *ibid.*, p. 310, where a reference is made to Rom. 5.
14. *Ibid.*, p. 576.
15. Kinder, *op. cit.*, p. 37.
16. Cf. my *Man: the Image of God*, 1962, Chap. 4.

removed from the power and reality of corruption.[17] There is a slavery and "inevitability" in all of man's sinning;[18] nevertheless we cannot speak of "fatalism" and we cannot make an excuse. As a matter of fact there *is* a sinful necessity in fallen man, but it is not the necessity of an external compulsion. What we see is the necessity *in* and *from* one's own guilt and corruption. Only the glow of God's *grace* can penetrate this gloom.[19]

In view of these thoughts, we must certainly speak of a *confession* of our guilt. Original sin is set within its historical matrix: but nothing is said about an "explanation" in terms of the *alienum peccatum*. Every shred of self-excuse, or every appeal to causal relations, is now set aside. There is a constant reminder of our corruption and a repeated warning against the making of alibis. Thus we can only say "no" to the question of whether there is an "imputation" in these confessions as we find in the later history of theology. The Lutheran interest in "imputation" comes later. As H. Schmid has quite rightly observed: ". . . we note that the doctrine of the *imputatio culpae et poenae primorum parentum* is only developed in the later dogmatics, in the time of Calov."[20] In the confessions, however,

17. Kinder, *op. cit.*, p. 53. On Luther himself, cf. W. Braun, *Die Bedeutung der Concupiscenz im Luthers Leben und Lehre*, 1908, p. 171: "something real, factual and actual" ("etwas Reales, Tatsächliches und Wirkliches").

18. Kinder, *op. cit.*, p. 49; an "Unentrinnbarkeit."

19. H. J. Iwand has laid special emphasis on the statement of Luther in his commentary on Rom. 5:12: "Actualia enim omnia in mundum per diabolum intrant et intraverunt sed originale per hominem unum" ("Sed originale per hominem unum," *Ev.Theol.*, 1946, pp. 26f.). Cf. E. Ellwein, *M. Luther, Vorlesung über den Römerbrief, 1515-1516*, 1928, p. 211, where Luther leans on Augustine for support. Iwand sees Luther's statement as suggesting that sin can only be undertood *in and from sin itself:* "the origin of sinful activity is sin itself. Thus sin remains something, in the strongest sense, irreducible and inexplicable." It cannot be "explained" by demonic temptation. It is not clear to me why Iwand makes the statement that Luther here "has gone beyond Paul, with the precedent of Augustine" — though he adds to this: "but is this not a right interpretation?" (*op. cit.*, p. 34).

20. H. Schmid, *Dogmatik der evangelisch-lutherischen Kirche*, 1893[7], p. 172. Schmid finds an "intimation" of this in the Formula Concordiae, and refers, for his substantiation, to *Solida Declar.*, I, 9. There we read: "quod hoc haereditarium malum sit culpa seu reatus, quo fit, ut omnes propter inobedientiam Adae et Hevae in odio apud Deum et natura filii irae simus, ut apostolus testatur" (Rom. 5:12ff.; Eph. 2:3); Müller,

the corruption of human nature is affirmed and man is seen as spiritually dead.[21] Only later did men begin to ask if the *alienum peccatum* is a practical result of the original sin dogma. Lutheran theology, therefore, proceeded from the indication of man's corruption to the more "subtle" question of the manner of God's imputing the sins of our ancestors to us.[22]

The common way of answering that question was to say that the fact *that* God does this is sufficient for our needs. The *how* is entirely unknown.[23] Those who insist on a formula here have sometimes spoken of "Adam and Eve"[24] and sometimes of "Adam" alone. Yet Adam is not a private person and is always seen as the head of the human race. The "imprecision" of the Lutheran confessions, on this score, is owing to the fact that the accent remains on *our guilt* and *our corruption*. We cannot say that the later Lutheran dogmaticians added essential or even fruitful elements to that earlier confession of man's guilt.[25]

Here the Reformed confessions agree, in general, with the Lutheran. Thus, in the Heidelberg Catechism the corruption of "our nature" is confessed and we are said to be "conceived and born in sin" (Q. 7). Man has deprived himself and all his posterity of those gifts which were given him by God (Q. 9). In this connection the Catechism speaks of God's punishment for both "our original as well as actual sins" (Q. 10). This latter statement, of course, is not clear, since in the final analysis the Catechism also regards our "original" sins as "actual." Nevertheless, the intention is very obvious. There is

op. cit., p. 576. It seems to me that the expression "propter" here does not go beyond the earlier terminology.

21. Cf. the Formula Concordiae, *Solida Declar.*, II; Müller, *op. cit.*, p. 586. So deep does this corruption extend that "through original sin man is truly, before the eyes of God, spiritually dead, and has died, with all his powers, to the good."

22. In Schmid, p. 170: "quomodo Deus lapsum protoplastorum posteris ipsorum, *nondum existentibus,* ita imputare potuerit, ut propterea etiam ipsos justitia originali destitutos et peccatores nasci oportet?"

23. "Non opus est, nec fortasse consultum. Sufficit enim [*tó hóti*] esse revelatum, etsi [*tó pós*] ignoscatur" *(ibid.).*

24. *Ibid.,* p. 173.

25. Often we find in them a combination of realist and federalist motives; e.g., in Gerhard, *Loci Theologica,* II, Locus IX: "Peccatum ergo illud non est modis omnibus a nobis alienum, quia Adam non ut privatus homo, sed ut caput totius humani generis peccavit." In the same context a discussion is given to the "in lumbis Adae" (p. 153).

no effort to regard man's sins as a series of human acts but
only to see behind and in those sins the sinful man himself.
Clearly, the Catechism envisions a definite relation between the
sin that came into the world in Paradise and the sin of *all men.*
Furthermore, it is striking that reference is made not only
to Adam but to "Adam and Eve," our "first parents" (Q. 7).
Thus we find the same accent as we have already seen in Lutheran theology. We read of generic "man" (QQ. 6, 7, 9, 14)
and of "human nature which has sinned" (Q. 16), and in all
these expressions we sense the strong accent on the results of
that first sin. Yet there is no further indication of how we
came to those results. "Our" nature is corrupt, and "man" is
conceived and born in sin. But the man referred to is the man
who confesses: "*I* am prone by nature to hate God and my
neighbor" (Q. 5). Thus, within the boundaries of confession
we hear constantly the acknowledgment of corruption. We hear
of *"our* sinful nature" (Q. 115; cf. 26) and "the evil which
always cleaves to us" (Q. 126).

These same accents are found in the Canons of Dort. *Man*
has forfeited the gifts of God, and a certain coherence is indicated within the human race. "Man after the fall begat children in his own likeness. A corrupt stock produced a corrupt offspring." But this statement does not point us to a
natural inevitability in the process of procreation; for we also
read that corruption has passed from Adam to all his posterity,
according to God's just judgment, and that this occurs by the
propagation of man's nature (III-IV, 2).[26] Therefore the Canons
are not content to refer us to the consequences and pervasive
powers of evil. As in the later theology of original sin, they stress
the theme of the *justice of God.* Yet they do not "explain"
this theme of God's just judgment.

In turning to the Belgic Confession, we find a lucid and
explicit statement on original sin. Article 14 considers the fall
of man and his willful subjection of himself to sin. Man has
"corrupted his whole nature" and has made himself "liable to
corporal and spiritual death." But especially Article 15 relates
to the doctrine of original sin. As in the case of the Catechism,
so here the strongest accent is laid on the consequences of what
once happened. ". . . Through the disobedience of Adam origi-

26. "Corruptione ab Adamo in omnes posteros solo Christo excepto, non
    per imitationem (quod Pelagiani olim voluerunt) sed per vitiosae
    naturae propagationem justo Dei judicio derivata."

nal sin is extended to all mankind." This assertion is added to a description of original sin as "a corruption of the whole nature and a hereditary disease, wherewith even infants in their mother's womb are infected." The corruption of man's nature "produces in man all sorts of sin." Then we read, in this same article, the crucial statement that original sin or corruption "is so vile and abominable in the sight of God that it is sufficient to condemn all mankind."

Therefore God's judgment and wrath are tied up closely with the corruption of man's own nature. It is very remarkable that we find no solitary hint in this article of what is commonly called the "doctrine of imputation" in theology. The Belgic Confession follows the pattern which we have already observed in the Catechism. The gist of the discussion is man's *original sin as his own corruption* or as that corruption upon which God has now poured out his wrath. This theme is more evident when we read that original sin is not "altogether abolished or wholly eradicated even by baptism," notwithstanding the fact that it is certainly *forgiven* by God's grace and mercy. In other words, the correlation between original sin and forgiveness is very closely maintained. So is the correlation between original sin and a consciousness of guilt. Therefore we are reminded that "a sense of this corruption should make believers often to sigh, desiring to be delivered from this body of death." The same theme is continued under the heading of election (Article 16), where again we are referred to the corruption of the human race which has "fallen into perdition and ruin by the sin of our first parents."

The thrust of the Belgic Confession on original sin as corruption has brought a critical comment from the pen of A. D. R. Polman. Polman reminds us that Article 15 does not examine the basis for the imputation of original sin.[27] Nor does it choose for realism or federalism, and it leaves untouched the relation of original guilt and original corruption. Therefore the Confession gives rise to the impression that "corruption really precedes guilt." "For original sin is described as a moral depravity, or hereditary deficiency, which is fit for condemnation." Polman can only conclude that "here the formulation is doubtlessly deficient."[28] Very obviously he misses something essential in Article 15, and something which Scripture, in his judgment,

27. Polman, *op. cit.*, I, 271.
28. *Ibid.*

very clearly teaches.[29] That something is described as an "objective transfer of sin and guilt."[30] The thought, says Polman, is "clearly and unmistakably" set forth in Romans 5:12-21 and I Corinthians 15:21-22. As an explanation for the "deficient formulation," he suggests that the Belgic Confession is concerned to make especially two points in this particular article: the radicalness of original sin in the "whole" of man's nature and the participation of even children in this "hereditary disease."

Yet it is a real "deficiency," according to Polman, when the Confession "makes no clear choice for the federal explanation in which Adam is acknowledged as the covenantal head of the entire human race."[31] Here, of course, the verdict of "doubtlessly deficient" is very radical, also from a material point of view. It covers considerably more than the "formulation" of the article and is concerned with the ignoring of something that is really *essential*: the objective "transfer" of sin and guilt from Adam. Therefore this article might give rise to a misunderstanding, for we can easily conclude that hereditary corruption is the real foundation of our original guilt. In thinking that way, we could end up with the thought of an *imputatio mediata*, as taught by Placaeus. That suggestion is plausible when we see that the Synod of Charenton, while rebuking Placaeus, spoke of an "omission" at exactly this point. It took issue with those who limited original sin to hereditary corruption and stated, in contrast, that the Protestant churches have always acknowledged, *besides this corruption,* the imputation of Adam's first sin upon his posterity.[32] Thus original sin, as corruption, was not denied, but beyond that corruption *("outre cette corruption")* it was necessary to speak of something else: namely *imputatio.*

In view of these criticisms we stand before a remarkable

---

29. Polman refers to Rom. 5:16, 18.
30. *Ibid.,* p. 270.
31. *Ibid.,* p. 271.
32. In contrast to the view, namely, that "would restrict the nature of original sin to the hereditary corruption of Adam's posterity alone, though not imputing to his posterity the first sin by which Adam fell, and would defend this under penalty of hearing the censures of the Church; thus departing from the common opinion received in the Protestant churches that *besides* this corruption all have experienced the imputation of the first sin of Adam upon his posterity." J. Aymon, *Tous les synodes nationaux des églises réformées de France,* II, 1710, 680.

situation. We must bear in mind that the Church is confessing her original sin. Notice the introductory words, "we believe." In that regard it is hard to imagine that an essential element (viz., imputation) has been either forgotten or ignored. Therefore it is important if we can rightly substantiate this criticism of Article 15. Has something been omitted, or can we make this confession our own without any "supplementation" for the sake of completeness and purity? As we look at Polman's criticism, we can summarize the problem as follows: Is original sin really concerned with a "twofold guilt"? Is the guilt here a guilt that is analyzed and confessed in terms of two separable factors of "hereditary corruption" and "inherited sin"? If it is, then Article 15 is subject to our legitimate complaint. For in that case this article cannot point to the fullness of man's guilt. In a confession of guilt that lack would be very serious. If, however, this is not the case, then Article 15 is not open to the criticisms of Polman. As we shall observe, our decision here can only be made when we have rightly looked at the problem of "twofold guilt."

This whole issue takes on a greater significance when we compare Article 15 of the Belgic Confession with the Gallican Confession. There the idea of "infection" or "contagion" of original sin is strongly emphasized, and this is seen as an "hereditary evil."[33] But the element that Polman finds lacking in Article 15 of the Belgica is also lacking in Article 10 of the Gallicana. The reason is now apparent, however, when we notice the words which are added: "... We do not think that it is necessary to inquire how sin was passed down from one man to another, for what God gave to [Adam] was not for him alone but for all his posterity." Therefore the problem of the manner of the "transfer" is very deliberately left outside our purview. It is merely stated, in conclusion, that we "in his person ... have fallen ... into a state of sin and misery." This, then, is the question before us: Is Article 10 of the Gallican Confession also "deficient"? Does it lack something "essential" for the confession of our guilt?

That question is all the more important when we see that the Belgic Confession (as Polman has himself written) is a copy, though not a slavish one, of the Gallican Confession.

33. "We believe that the entire posterity of Adam is in bondage to original sin, which is an hereditary evil" ("... est infectée de telle contagion, qui est le péché originel, et un vice héréditaire"). Art. 10.

Furthermore, the Gallican Confession is "largely in line with the plan of Calvin."[34] Therefore we ask: Is the criticism of Article 15 really legitimate? Polman, in his very excellent book, discusses Article 15 in the context of St. Augustine. He argues that the "main concern" of this statement is *not* the complicated picture that taxed Augustine for all of his life. It is not the problem of the "inheritance" of original sin. It is rather the fact that the entire race is corrupted by the sin of Adam.[35] Later, however, Polman makes an about-face and informs us that Article 15 does display a "complete acceptance of the Augustinian heritage." Guido de Brès was in total agreement with Augustine's confession of original sin and the horrible consequences of that act.

We have looked at this criticism of Polman at some length. The reason for that is obvious for anyone who sees that from the standpoint of confession we are now touching on one of the deepest problems in the original sin dogma. Polman vacillates between a positive attitude, which he bases on Romans 5, and a negative reluctance, which explains why he hedges on the "main concern." But that kind of reluctance or hedging has everything to do with the nature of our problem. This fact is apparent in the case of the Belgic Confession, Article 15, and the Gallican Confession, Article 10.[36]

What about the rest of the Reformed confessional writings? Do they shed any light on the problems which have occupied us here? In the remaining symbols of the Sixteenth Century there are no elements other than those which we have already noted. There is a constant reference to the fall and corruption of the human race, and the devastation which is everywhere manifest. Furthermore, this is seen as the very context in which our *peccata actualia* spring forth.[37] Yet in the later confessions

---

34. Polman, *Onze Ned. Geloofsbelijdenis*, I, 108.
35. *Ibid.*, II, 155.
36. C. Vonk comments on the fact that BC, 15, does not use the terms *inherited guilt* and *hereditary corruption* but only speaks essentially of inherited guilt. He adds that there is no reason to depart from this terminology, which Calvin also employed in *Inst.*, II, 1.
37. We cite here the Basler Bekenntnis, 1534 (Art. 2): the wanton fall by which the entire human race is corrupted; our nature has become weakened and inclined toward sin; also the Confessio Helvetica Prior, 1536 (Art. 8): man, through his fall, has dragged with him the entire human race in that fall, and the "inherited disease" ("Erbsucht") has

we encounter a wider range of reflection, and the concept of *imputation* is now explicitly discussed. This is obvious in the Westminster Confession, in the section on the fall of our first parents. "They being the root of all mankind, the guilt of this sin was imputed, and the same death in sin and corrupted nature conveyed to all their posterity descending from them by ordinary generation."[38]

Shedd has said that in this confession there is no room for the idea of a "representation," since the concept of "the *root* of all mankind"[39] must point us in a different direction. It must point us to the thought of a "natural union."[40] Yet, though the confession does not give a clear "solution" to that problem, it is difficult to accept an interpretation (as Shedd's) which does not and cannot give full weight to the term *imputed*. Furthermore, it is important to see that the Catechism of the Westminster Assembly does give a closer "analysis" of our relation to Adam. It asks if the entire human race has fallen *in* his first transgression,[41] and its answer shows a definite federal or representative bent. We are pointed to the *covenant* that was made with Adam as a public figure. In that light the conclusion is drawn that the human race sinned "in him"[42] and fell "with him" in his own transgression.

Therefore the sinfulness of man consists in the guilt of the first man *to which is added* the corruption of man's nature.[43] In the Shorter Catechism the question is asked: "Did all mankind fall in Adam's first transgression?"[44] The answer then follows: "The covenant being made with Adam, not only for himself, but for his posterity, all mankind ... sinned in him, and fell with him, in his first transgression." Thus the sinfulness

so permeated the race that it is "ruined" and "poisoned"; and the Confessio Helvetica Posterior, 1562: sin is the corruption "ex primis illis nostris parentibus in nos omnes derivata vel propagata" (Müller, *op. cit.*, p. 178).

38. *Ibid.*, p. 557. (Transl., P. Schaff, *Creeds of Christendom*, III, 615.)
39. "Radix totius humani generis."
40. "A representative is not the root of his constituents" (Shedd, *Dogmatic Theology*, 45). The term *representation* does not appear in the Westminster Confession. "A root buried in the ground does not stand for an absent tree and still less for a non-existent one" (48).
41. "Totumne genus humanum lapsum est in prima illa transgressione?" (Müller, *op. cit.*, p. 614).
42. "In ipso peccavit" (*ibid.*).
43. *Ibid.*, p. 615 (Schaff, 679).
44. Müller, p. 644.

of the human state is described as "the guilt of Adam's first
sin," *plus* "the corruption of his whole nature,"[45] together with
"all actual transgressions which proceed from it." Shedd's realistic
interpretation of the Westminster forms can be appreciated
when we see this "twofoldedness" in the expressions that are
used. But we cannot ignore the rather obvious fact that federal
or representative ideas still play the dominant role.[46]

Is there a shift of accent in the original sin dogma as
reflected in the Reformed confessions of guilt? Is there a "problem" in regard to the *peccatum proprium?* Do the later creeds
show a marked departure from the earlier confessions? Greijdanus makes the judgment that they do and that furthermore,
owing to their rejection of traducianism, there is, as a matter
of fact, an increasing stress on the *federal* character of this relation of Adam and his posterity.[47] That tendency, says Greijdanus,
was enhanced by the polemic against Placaeus.[48] As a corollary
development, an increasingly consistent parallel was drawn
between Adam and Christ, even in regard to the basis of *imputatio.* Therefore Greijdanus concludes that "Reformed theology has made no progress in this matter."[49]

Even those who cannot accept Greijdanus' realism will have
to admit that a number of difficulties are introduced in the
later developments. It is not always clear how references to
federal, representative, and imputational theories can be squared
with the earlier confessions of guilt. It is very difficult to say
why we are *not led* to a so-called "as if"-theology. No wonder
that the specter of a vague "imputation" has brought later realists
to renounce federalism as a theological mirage. They have rightly said that an "as if"-theology cannot be upheld. Therefore
they reject an imputation that is more (or less) than an assign-
ment of an actual or personal guilt.

Granted, the realistic position is itself bizarre in many of
its implications. Yet that view has served a worthwhile function in the history of the original sin debates. It serves that
function today. It defines the issue of *peccatum proprium* in
such a way that the cutting edge of controversy is seen in our

45. Followed by: "which is commonly called original sin."
46. Cf. A. A. Hodge, *A Commentary on the Confession of Faith,* 1870, pp.
    111f.
47. Greijdanus, *Toerekeningsgrond,* pp. 26f.
48. *Ibid.,* p. 28.
49. *Ibid.,* p. 29.

reflection on the parallel of Adam and Christ.[50] Realists have said with joy that the imputation of Christ's righteousness is the free gift of God and by no means an example of arbitrariness. But we cannot remove the picture of an arbitrary God as long as we conceive of a Deity who merely *"assigns" to us the guilt of "someone else."*

We shall close this chapter by looking at the theme of confession in Calvin. Our purpose now is to ask if Calvin's thought sheds any light at all on the later shift of accent in Lutheran and Reformed theology. Theologians never ignored the relation of man to Adam, but the shift can be seen as a moving away from an almost exclusive accent on *peccatum proprium* to a later stress on *peccatum alienum* and *imputatio*. It makes good sense to look at Calvin since the various principals in later debates appealed to him so consistently. This holds for the federalists and Placaeus as well as for others.[51] It is a tribute to the sober and careful way in which Calvin addressed himself to this topic.

Calvin took his starting-point in the corruption of man's nature. Adam, by his apostasy, brought ruin to the human race and consigned it to misery *(Inst.*, II, 1, 5). "This is the inherited corruption, which the church fathers term 'original sin,' meaning by the word 'sin' the depravation of a nature previously good and pure." Against that background Calvin discussed a problem which apparently wells up in man's universal sensitivities. ". . . Nothing is farther from the usual view than for all to be made guilty by the guilt of one, and thus for sin to be made common" *(ibid.).*

The ancient doctors of the Church regarded this matter obscurely, said Calvin, and confessed it with less clarity than the issue really demands. In opposing Pelagius, he denied that the first sin was passed on to all men by imitation, for we bring our corruption into the world with us. Here Calvin leaned hard on Psalm 51:5 and the statement in Job 14:4 that we are

50. In *Het Werk van de Heilige Geest*, 1927[2], A. Kuyper gives an extensive view of imputation (pp. 453ff.). He approaches original guilt from the perspective of the divine righteousness which accounts us to be, in Christ, *what we are not in ourselves*. If God passes a guilty verdict on us in Adam, and regards us as fallen in Adam, "then we are also guilty, fallen" (p. 458). Cf. p. 459: God has the right "as Sovereign to determine someone's state."

51. Cf. *P.R.E.*, *s.v.*, p. 471.

all born of impure seed. Adam was the "root of human nature" and has cast our nature into misery by means of his own sin (II, 1, 6). Therefore we are infected with the sinfulness into which Adam himself fell. God *"entrusted* to Adam those gifts which he willed to be conferred upon human nature" (II, 1, 7) ; and when Adam lost those gifts he lost them for himself and all men. Nevertheless, Calvin does not mean that corruption finds its origin in the substance of our flesh or soul. God has so ordained that the first man *received* these gifts for himself and his posterity; therefore he also *lost* them for himself and his posterity *(ibid.).* Thus Calvin saw original sin as an hereditary depravity of our nature, diffused into all parts of the soul (II, 1, 8). *"By this great corruption we stand justly condemned and convicted before God" (ibid.).*[52] Furthermore, this punishment is not a liability for another man's crime *("obligatio alieni peccati"),* as though we, "guiltless and undeserving, bore the guilt of his offense." Rather, "since we through his transgression have become entangled in the curse, he is said to have made us guilty."

Obviously Calvin was concerned about the central issue in the original sin debate and the main cause of stumbling for those who take offense. He saw this as the *problem of an alien guilt.*[53] He pointed to the *alienum peccatum* of Augustine, but he also recalled the assertion of Augustine that sin is *our own.* Man does not bear an "alien sin." In fact, as Paul has written in Romans 5:12, *all men must die* since *all men have sinned.* We are not concerned, at this point, with the problem of whether Calvin rightly understood this Pauline reference. We are interested in the way in which he used that text to clarify the question of original sin. Paul means, in his judgment, that all men, and even children, "have been enveloped in original sin and defiled by its stains" (II, 1, 8; cf. BC, 15). There is no basis for accusation apart from an actual guilt.[54] Therefore, when Calvin spoke of man's guilty depravity he referred to Romans 3, where the factual and concrete pollution of man is seen as "nothing but a description of original sin" (II, 1, 9).

52. "Ob talem duntaxat corruptionem damnati *merito* convictique coram Deo tenemur."
53. Cf. his commentary on Rom. 5:12 (polemical) and Rom. 5:17: we bear his punishment "because we also have part in the guilt, seeing that our nature, since it is corrupted in him, is also placed by God under the penalty of the guilt of unrighteousness."
54. "Quia non esset reatus absque culpa" (II, 1, 8).

Ever since that day that Adam subjected himself to it, the tyranny of sin has wrought havoc in the entire human race (II, 1, 11). We have seen already that Calvin was strongly influenced by Psalm 51:5. As a matter of fact, that text could be called the quintessence of his original sin doctrine. He referred to it as the *"illustre testimonium"* of original sin,[55] in the light of which we arrive at a *"recta definitio."* When David said that he was "born in iniquity, and in sin did his mother conceive him," he really meant that there is no excuse and no possibility of pointing his finger at the unrighteousness of someone else. He experienced that he himself was standing before God's judgment-seat *("se ad tribunal Dei sistens").*[56] Therefore the concern of Calvin was to underscore the totality and unlimited character of sin *("nulla pars eximens").*

We may ask in what way sin is "transferred" from parents to children,[57] but Calvin refused to go into that "labyrinth."[58] He was satisfied to know that Adam was deprived of all his gifts and that God did not adorn him privately *("privatim")* with all the treasures of his Spirit. He encompassed in him what he wished to be shared with the entire human race.[59] Thus, it was not the "way in which" that occupied Calvin but the idea of the totality and universality of corruption. He was very similar to the Confessio Gallicana. Repeatedly he returned to the concept of the "trusteeship" of Adam.[60] When Adam was deprived of his gifts he was deprived for *himself* and for all those who were *his*.

Thus Calvin was forced to face up to the problem of *peccatum alienum.* Though the concepts of "inherited guilt" and "hereditary corruption" are absent in his theology, he was obliged to wrestle with the problems involved in that later distinction. He waged warfare against those who say that we are not lost by a guilt of our own but because Adam, as it were, "sinned

---

55. "Ceterum hoc est illustre testimonium de peccato originali quo Adam totum humanum genus implicuit." Comm. on Psalms, *ad loc.*
56. *Ibid.*
57. ". . . Quo modo a parentibus peccatum transfertur in filios."
58. "Sed ne istos labyrinthos ingredi necesse est" (Comm. on Ps. 51:7).
59. *Ibid.:* "sed in eius personam *contulerat* quod volebat *commune* esse toti humano generi."
60. "Apud Adamum posuisse" *(Inst.,* II, 1, 7). Cf. his Comm. on Gen. 3:6: "quidquid donarum nobis in Adae persona contulerat Deus." "Id potius ex Dei ordinatione pendet qui secuti totam humani generis naturam in uno homine ornaverat praestantissimis dotibus, ita in eodem ipsam nudavit." Cf. also on Ezek. 11:19-20.

for us."[61] *All men* have sinned; *therefore* the entire posterity of
Adam is subject to the tyranny of death.[62] This term *therefore*
implied, for Calvin, that we too are vicious and corrupt;[63]
furthermore it is our viciousness and corruption that are meant
by "original sin." Therefore Calvin combined the consequences
of Adam's being deprived of his gifts and our own defilement
in natural corruption. Adam's fall leads us to perdition. Yet
"we do not perish by his guilt in such a manner as though we
were outside his guilt: but because his sin is the cause of *ours,*
therefore Paul ascribes our destruction to him."[64]

It is very important to see that Calvin drew a distinction, at
this point, between the figures of Adam and Christ. ". . . We are
not condemned by mere imputation in the sin of Adam, as
though the penalty of another man's sin were exacted of us;
rather we sustain his penalty because we too are accounted
as guilty."[65] This is not the case in regard to the imputation
of Christ's righteousness. For the righteousness of Christ is imputed not because it already is ours but "because we possess
Christ himself and all his treasures, who is given to us by the
tender favor of the Father." Thus the accent on our own personal guilt is further emphasized in this vision of Adam and
Christ in relation to what is properly our own.[66]

This is a matter which Calvin treats in his commentary
on the most frequently cited of imputation texts: Romans 5:19.
Paul, in that passage, refers to the many men who were "made
sinners" by the one sin of Adam.[67] However, says Calvin, this
is no repetition of what had gone before but a new description

61. "Ac si nulla nostra culpa periremus, ideo tantum quasi ille nobis pec-
    casset" (Comm. on Rom. 5:12).
62. The *ratio* lies in the "quoniam omnes peccavimus."
63. "Corruptos esse et vitiatos" (Comm. on Rom. 5:12).
64. "Neque enim sic perimus eius culpa quasi extra culpam ipsi sumus: sed
    quia eius peccatum nostri causa est, exitium nostrum illi Paulus
    ascribit" (Comm. on Rom. 5:15).
65. "Quod peccato Adae non per solam imputitionem damnamur, acsi alieni
    peccati exigeretur a nobis poena sed ideo poena eius sustinemus, quia
    et culpae sumus rei" (Comm. on Rom. 5:17).
66. Greijdanus, it seems to me, has correctly appealed to Calvin in connec-
    tion with the Adam-Christ parallel (*op. cit.,* p. 39). "But the question
    is whether Adam and Christ are *also* in parallel in regard to the *basis*
    of imputation, so that in that respect too they form the thesis and antith-
    esis of each other. Calvin denies this."
67. For the exegesis, see the following chapter. Our concern at this point
    is with *Calvin*.

of *our guilt*. Paul had already made mention of condemnation, but he now removes any notion of innocence and contends that each man is condemned for one reason alone: because he is *personally a sinner*.[68]

Therefore Calvin's discussion of this topic comes down to a single, sustained confession of our guilt. He is concerned about *our* guilt, *our* sin, or *peccatum proprium*. We find a sharp vigilance in Calvin against the dangers of possible excuse. The echo of that insight is found in his commentary on Ezekiel 18. There he writes that no man can plead for God's mercy because his own innocence was lost as a result of another man's sin.[69] *We* are not blameless; and yet *we* are condemned *in Adam*. Through Adam's sin *we too* are now depraved.[70]

From the discussion above we may draw the conclusion that Calvin was no realist in the sense of Shedd and Greijdanus. He could easily use the utterly unrealistic expression that sin took place "outside us." He was more concerned about the *results* of Adam's transgression than the realistic "in Adam"-theme. When he spoke of these *results* he disavowed any self-excuse that could possibly lurk in that concept. For the results of sin are manifest in *guilt*. Once we see this guilt we may not extrapolate or speculate or presume that outside our guilt there are "causal relations." It is not by chance that we never find in Calvin the later rigid distinction of "inherited guilt" and "hereditary corruption." Certainly there is a more adequate reason for this than that Calvin did not reflect "deeply enough." That reason can be found in his consistent repudiation of every appeal to the *alienum peccatum*.[71] In this attitude Calvin was on the heels of an important and even decisive thought in the confession of original sin. The *confession of guilt* was very strong in his theology.

68. Comm. on Rom. 5:19.
69. Comm. on Ezek. 18:1-4.
70. *Ibid.*
71. We are also reminded of Paul's statement in Eph. 2:3 ("by nature children of wrath"). Calvin contended that this is no effort "justificare homines coram Deo." Cf., further, his reflections on Job 14:4, where he lays all emphasis (against the Pelagians and the watering down of corruption by the "Papistae") on the reality of guilt — his purpose being to refute those who take original sin lightly. In this same context he refers again to Ps. 51:7: "non accusat patrem nec matrem, sed seipsum condemnat." So too Job's statement is no "subterfugium, ut elevet condemnationem, cui omnes homines sunt obnoxii."

The man who misses a "sophisticated" argument in Calvin, as we find in the later dogmatics, should inquire why this is so before accusing him of an incompleteness in his confession of man's guilt. Since this accent forms a background for the Gallican and Belgic Confessions, it is possible that motives are at work here which reach far beyond the historical dilemma of "realism or federalism." With an eye to Calvin, it is certainly questionable if Article 15 of the Belgica is so "doubtlessly deficient." Possibly the formulation of that article is the index of a very *profound discernment of our guilt*. We should judge that it is.[72]

Certainly in saying this we are not implying that all subsections of Calvin's doctrine are equally perspicuous. Calvin himself was aware of the impossibility of seeing this dogma in a way that makes clear the reality of our guilt. It seems that his conception of Adam as the "trustee" of human nature and the one who lost the gifts of God, for himself and others, betrays an affinity with the Catholic view of original sin as a "sin of nature." We might challenge if his exegesis of Romans 5:12 has rightly weighed the context in which Paul spoke and thought. It seems likely that he merely used these words, "because *all* men sinned," as an argument for his own side.

But all of these qualifications should not deter us from seeing the consistency of Calvin's pointing to *peccatum proprium*. We must carefully observe his outlook on the confession of our guilt. For this, it is obvious, is the matter of greatest concern whenever the Church has concretely confessed the doctrine of original sin. And so it must be whenever a Christian discusses his sin in the bosom of the Church.[73]

72. Cf. W. A. Hauck, *Sünde und Erbsünde nach Calvin*, 1939², pp. 102ff.; and A. S. E. Talma, *De Anthropologie van Calvijn*, 1882, pp. 95ff.
73. John Murray (in "The Imputation of Adam's Sin," *Westminster Theological Journal*, 1955, pp. 158ff.) remarks that Calvin's exegesis of Rom. 5:12 "is similar to that of Rome," and proceeds to reject this (rightly, it seems to me; see the following chapter). Nonetheless he contends that "Calvin's view of original sin is thoroughly Pauline and biblical" (p. 159). Thus we stand before the very heart of the question of the essence of Calvin's doctrine and the idea of "imputation," as later developed also by Murray.

CHAPTER SIXTEEN

THE DIVINE INDICTMENT

THE WIDESPREAD disagreements in the Church's dogmatics might tempt us to abandon, or at least to water down, the Reformation teaching on the clarity of Scripture. This is surely the case when we look at the original sin debates. If we resist that urge, however, and examine the debates in a scriptural focus, we shall soon discover a remarkable consensus on the *common and universal character of sin*. The disagreements are apparent when the issue turns on the *seriousness and depth of sin*. They are apparent, for example, in the concept of total corruption and its implications for the original sin dogma.

Now obviously, we are not concerned at this point with two divorceable problems. The issue of the nature and reality of "original sin" is always of one piece with the question of the universality of sin. On every hand we find an awareness, in the Christian Church, that sin is not a haphazard phenomenon or a merely incidental occurrence which cannot be "generalized." There is a common agreement that Scripture and man's own experience both attest the universality of sin. One may grant immediately that our own experience is subject to a number of reservations and is difficult to maintain as an "indubitable" result of induction. But one cannot dispute that *Scripture* repeatedly relates the concept of sin to a very common and universal view of "man." It gives voice to a very *general* divine indictment and a truly *universal* testimony in which no man can find a legitimate excuse.

The words of Psalm 14:3 ("there is none that does good, no, not one," and all have "gone astray, they are all alike corrupt") may well be taken as a compendium of the whole witness of Scripture on the universal character of sin. In that witness there is no room for any exception. This text finds its place in a vision of God in which he "looks down from heaven upon the children of men" to see if there be *any* who act wisely and seek after God.[1] Certainly the primary focus of Psalm 14 is the Israel of long ago; furthermore, there is also a reference to the "generation of the righteous" (v. 5). Yet it is also obvious why this psalm has always been cited to emphasize the universality of sin.

There is no "flat generalization," in this regard, in the language of Scripture, but only a reference to the striking universality of man's *own sin*.[2] This is a point that is further clarified in the biblical reference to God's impending judgment in the flood. In that case again we read that God "saw that the wickedness of man was great in the earth, and that every imagination of the thoughts of his heart was only evil continually"; therefore "the Lord was sorry that he had made man upon the earth, and it grieved him to his heart" (Gen. 6:5, 6; cf. 8:21). There are other passages as well which point to this universality of sin as a matter that is indisputable. Thus, in connection with the concrete sins of Israel, we hear the statement in Solomon's prayer: "for there is *no man* who does not sin" (I Kings 8:46; II Chron. 6:36). Psalm 143 also "generalizes" in this thoroughly biblical way: "for *no man* living is righteous before thee" (v. 2).

We may find ourselves irritated, at times, by human generalizations which do insufficient justice to the uniqueness of man. But in Scripture we find a distinctive kind of indictment which roots in a generalization and permits of no exception or excuse. We read in Ecclesiastes: "Behold, this alone I found, that God made *man* upright, but *they* have sought out many devices" (7:29).[3] That same universality is presupposed throughout the entire New Testament. Time after time we hear that generic *man* is addressed in this divine indictment, and by way of invitation *they* are called to repent from their evil and apostate lives. Christ himself spoke a word of sharp criticism against the Pharisees, or the "healthy ones" who had no need of a physician. The purpose of his coming was to seek out the

---

1. Ps. 14:2-3. Cf. Paul's reference to Ps. 14 in Rom. 3:10-12, to confirm that "none is righteous" (3:10).
2. Cf. Rom. 3:18: "There is no fear of God before their eyes." This is manifest in many concrete sins (3:13-17).
3. Cf. v. 20: "Surely there is not a righteous man on earth who does good and never sins." Also Prov. 20:9: "*Who* can say, 'I have made my heart clean; I am pure from my sin'?" and 20:6: "a faithful man who can find?"

lost and the sinners of this world. Therefore the terms *no one* and *all* are deliberately chosen, in the New Testament, to indicate the bleak and dreary background of this salvation of God. In Christ's preaching we hear the universal indictment: "...if you, then, *who are evil*..." (Matt. 7:11). Therefore, too, when the Pharisees brought an adulterous woman ("caught in the very act"), they were met by this very telling rebuke: "Let him who is without sin among you be the first to throw a stone at her" (John 8:7). In the spirit of Psalm 14, we read in the Apostle Paul: "since *all* have sinned and fall short of the glory of God" (Rom. 3:23).[4]

The gist of these and other references is obviously not the product of a "neutral analysis" of human nature or the normal practices of living. One cannot speak of the universality of sin as the patent result of our own investigations on "sin as the fact of experience."[5] Such an analysis is much too weak a basis for this kind of universal indictment. The indictment permits of no excuse whatever. Furthermore, by going in this direction, we can only end up with an arid moralism. The scriptural concern is not an affirmation of a generally human, moral deficiency, but is rather the confirmation of what God observes from the "heavens above." This vision of God does not find an echo in the statistics and facts of human experience but only in the accusation of *man* (*all men*) as guilty before the *face of God*.

Thus Scripture speaks of "sinlessness" only in the case of the Lord himself. Of him alone we hear that he "knew no sin" (II Cor. 5:21) and "no guile was found on his lips" (I Pet. 2:22; cf. John 8:46). He is our only high priest — "holy, blameless, unstained, separated from sinners" (Heb. 7:26). He alone is the lamb "without blemish or spot" (I Pet. 1:19).

This generalization of sin, which is so frequently mentioned in Scripture, has given rise to the question: Can the universality of sin be *explained?* Is it the case that Scripture never reaches beyond the mere affirmation of this fact? Certainly, it cannot be denied that various texts would seem to suggest that an ex-

4. On the situation as it "once" was, cf. Eph. 2:3: "*we all* once lived in the passions of our flesh," and "we were by nature children of wrath, like the rest of mankind." There is no distinction here: "Therefore you have no excuse, O man, whoever you are..." (Rom. 2:1).

5. J. Müller, *Die christliche Lehre von der Sünde*, II, 1849, 309.

planation is not needed. Furthermore, could we really expect anything else from the fact that each child is born of sinful parents? Recall the statement of Job: "Who can bring a clean thing out of an unclean? There is not one" (Job 14:4). This text is sometimes referred to in order to "prove" the dogma of original sin and especially the so-called "hereditary corruption" or contamination of man's nature.

We do well, however, to remember that Job was far from making a confession at this point. He was only voicing his complaint in answer to the tirade of Zophar. He spoke of the brevity of life, and of unrest and shadow and the withering flower. In that mood he turned his face toward God and challenged: "And dost thou open thy eyes upon such a one and bring him into judgment with thee?" (14:3).[6] Job 14:4 expresses Job's awareness of what would seem to be a natural implication in the procession of generations. But in that procession he found no reason to be encouraged. He asks God to remove his gaze from him and to let him find some peace. In all this he had no consolation at all. There is nothing that awaits him after death. Therefore, why cannot God allow his transient creature some sleep? Job's remarks concerning man's universal corruption are a deploring of man's lowly estate, and are certainly no explanation for man's sin. They are the attempts of an anguished soul to excuse himself and are certainly no confession.[7] Furthermore, such words as we read in John 3:6 ("that which is born of the flesh is flesh, and that which is born of the Spirit is spirit") are only meant to point out the sinfulness of man within his powerlessness and the necessity of his new birth. They emphasize the inanity of all man's possibilities. They shed no light on the cause of this obvious helplessness and complete incompetence of man.[8]

A doctrine of original sin which says much more than this "universal sinfulness" of man can only be founded on isolated scriptural data of very incidental significance. We are commonly referred to those texts which exemplify the "coherences" in evil and the "solidarity" of all men, or their being "alike

6. Note the speech of Eliphaz, Job 4:17; also in his second speech, 15:14. In a very general sense: Bildad, Job 25:4.

7. Cf. *Bijbel met Kanttekeningen*, S. P. Dee, 1952, p. 36. "Job wishes to say that this general sinfulness . . . must move God to excuse him."

8. Cf. Calvin on John 3:6: "Probat a contrariis clausum nobis omnibus esse regnum Dei, nisi per palingenesiam ingressus nobis patefiat."

corrupt" (Ps. 14:3). This is what happens, too, when Protestant dogmatics takes as an illustration, and Catholic as a legitimate scriptural argument, those words in the apocryphal books where continuities and even causal relations in sinning are underscored. We think of the following statement in Jesus Sirach: "By a woman came the beginning of sin, and because of her we all die."[9] Obviously, the allusion is to *Eve,* who is now seen as the cause of the death of all mankind. We must certainly observe, however, the remarkable setting in which this text is found. It is found in an *invective against women.* All other plagues can be borne, but not the anger of a woman! A man could better live with a lion or a dragon! Consider, too, that *death* is the subject of real interest here, and that what we have is really a "testimony of painful reflections provoked by the thought of death."[10] Granted, this text reverts to the story of Genesis 3; yet it is quite impossible to find here an illumination of original sin.[11] Furthermore, this same comment holds for that other reference which is sometimes cited, which refers us not to woman but the *devil.* "For God created man for immortality and made him the image of his own eternity; but through the devil's envy death came into the world, and those who belong to his party experience it."[12] Here too the accent is on *death,* but not on *sin.*[13]

Those who consider the Old Testament materials have shown an almost exclusive interest in Psalm 51:5, where David envisions his own life and sin as woven together with his whole being, including his birth from his mother. Yet David refuses to step beyond a consciousness of this boundless sin to a *clarification of that relationship.*[14] Often it is asked why the Old Testament gives us so little light on this issue, while the same issue is so important in the later disputes. Certainly we hear of evil's reaching beyond itself and the spreading and bursting forth of sin against both God and man, to say nothing of the wickedness of

---

9. Sirach 25:24 (LXX): *apó gynaikós archē hamartías kaí di' autēn apothnēskomen pántes.*
10. Cf. A. M. Dubarle, *Le péché originel dans l'Écriture,* 1958, pp. 79f.
11. Cf. the statement in Jesus Sirach, 37:3: "O evil thought, from whence were you formed, to cover the earth with deceit?"
12. Wisdom 2:23-24 (Goodspeed transl.).
13. Cf. Dubarle, *op. cit.,* pp. 86f.; J. Freundörfer, *Erbsünde und Erbtod beim Apostel Paulus,* 1927, pp. 60f.
14. On Ps. 51:7, cf. Calvin, *ad loc.;* also on Job 14:4. Also cf. Part I, above, p. 19, and Ps. 48:8; 58:4.

man which is "great in the earth" (Gen. 6:5) and the earth's corruption and the fullness of violence in the sight of God (6:11, 13). But all these factors merely indicate the reality of sin and do not explain its causes from generation to generation. J. Freundörfer has attributed this remarkable Old Testament silence (even in Genesis 3) to the lack of any felt need, in pre-exilic times, for a speculative reflection on the content of faith.[15] Be that as it may, it still remains the case that when Hosea 6:7, for example, reaches back to the sin of Adam it does so not in order to "explain" this relation but to indicate the parallel between Adam's sin and the sin of Hosea's own day.[16]

In like manner, the New Testament points emphatically to sin, and the preaching of Jesus has sin as its constant assumption. Yet, while there are frequently allusions to what happened "in the beginning," there is no explanation for man's universal sinfulness.[17] Therefore it is understandable that only a few New Testament loci have played a decisive role in the later reflections on original sin. In terms of these men have sought to throw light on the guilt-relations in which the entire human race is enmeshed. Especially important here are Romans 5:12-21 and I Corinthians 15:22. These address themselves to the definite *relation of "all men" to Adam*.

Of these two texts the Romans 5 passage carries the greater weight, since in I Corinthians 15:22 the accent is exclusively on *death*. "For as by a man came death, by a man has come also the resurrection of the dead. For as in Adam all die, so also in Christ shall all be made alive" (I Cor. 15:21-22). Paul, in this context, sets the themes of death and life alongside each other and does not really mention the theme of sin at all. He speaks of a "dying with Adam." And yet this theme is easily combined with the statement in Romans 5 that death has come into the world *by sin*. In that way, therefore, the Romans 5 and I Corinthians 15 passages have come to be seen together as the

15. Freundörfer, *op. cit.,* p. 54.

16. "But like Adam they transgressed the covenant; there they dealt faithlessly with me." Cf. A. Kuyper, *Uit het Woord. De Leer der Verbonden,* 1885, p. 183, who derives much from this passage for the "covenant of works." Also C. van Gelderen, on the analogy to Paradise (*Komm., ad loc.*).

17. One thinks of Matt. 19:4-5, 8 in connection with divorce. In John 8, where the question of origin arises, the concern is not a causal explanation for an accusation against the Jews (8:44). Cf. above, Part I, pp. 101ff.

loci classici of the original sin doctrine. Theologians have seen I Corinthians 15:22 as the "prooftext" for a *dying in Adam* and Romans 5 as a "prooftext" for a *sinning in Adam*.

With no trace of exaggeration at all, we can say that the entire history of the original sin dogma is decisively defined by the question of what is meant by these words in Romans 5:21b: "because all men sinned." In both realism and federalism, as well as in Calvin, this phrase has had a profound importance. This significance is the more apparent when we bear in mind that it forms a peculiar witness, within its own pericope, which is very rarely seen in other scriptural passages. With a view to Psalm 51:5 and Romans 5, Emil Brunner has spoken of "the alleged *loci classici*" of the original sin dogma. He has contended that these texts do *not* say what theologians have made them say from the time of Augustine until our own day.[18] In contrast, we recall the opinion of Herman Bavinck, who maintained, with an eye to Genesis 3,[19] that the rest of the Old Testament does not conceive of the universality of sin in explicit relation to Adam's fall, and that only Paul, in I Corinthians and Romans, "clarifies" this universality in the perspective of Adam's disobedience. After discussing these two Pauline references, Bavinck concludes: "On these data of Scripture the original sin dogma has been constructed in the Christian Church."[20]

This latter fact, of course, has been generally acknowledged. But it is precisely for this reason that the question is all the more real: What is the significance of especially the Romans 5 pericope? This whole problem is intensified by the important question of translation in Romans 5:12. In the Vulgate the Greek words are rendered: *"in quo omnes peccaverunt."*[21] So long as that translation was regarded as accurate (and as virtually definitive in the history of the original sin dogma) the tendency

18. Brunner, *Dogmatik,* II, 119.
19. Even Genesis 3 does not deduce the universality of sin ("in so many words") from the fall of Adam (*Geref. Dog.,* III, 59). But according to Bavinck, this is certainly implied.
20. *Ibid.,* 62. Freundörfer even calls Romans 5 "the only document for the existence of a biblical doctrine of original sin" (*op. cit.,* p. 105). In regard to the *universality of sin* the Scripture gives a clear witness in "unambiguous and numerous expressions" (Bavinck, *Bijbelse en religieuze Psychologie,* p. 129).
21. Greek: *eph' hō pántes hēmarton.*

was to tie the *in quo* to the concept of *one man* and not to the thought of *death*. Therefore the text was read: "in whom (viz., Adam) all have sinned." Thus a parallel was drawn to "dying in Adam" in I Corinthians 15:22.

The fact is that this translation of *in quo* has now been abandoned on practically every hand.[22] This turn of events has given added impetus to asking if the change ("because all men sinned") has any direct relevance for a proper understanding of Romans 5 or the traditional dogma of original sin. The traditional view was largely built on the old translation of *in quo*.[23] It is exactly because this text has had such a crucial role in this centuries-long debate that our question now is of great significance. Is an essential difference implied when we change the translation from *in whom* to *because*? Or is there no difference at all?[24]

It is hard to find a clear answer to that question. Some have said that the explanatory concept of *because* makes very obvious that Paul was interested in the sinning of all men later. That is to say, he was interested in their own *personal and individual sins.* Pelagius was convinced that the reference here is to an actual sinning,[25] and Calvin regarded this text in a roughly similar manner. It is significant that Calvin defended the *personal* character of original sin on the basis of Romans 5:12: *all men have sinned.*[26] This view has found its adherents

---

22. Cf., e.g., Freundörfer, *op. cit.*, pp. 156f., who cites Jacques Lefèvre d'Etaples, and especially Erasmus, as those from whom, in his judgment, the "modern exegesis" should be dated (p. 159). In the Nineteenth Century the majority of Roman Catholic exegetes, according to Freundörfer, went along with Erasmus, though not wishing to endorse his "Pelagianism." They continued to hold "materially" to the Augustinian line. On Luther, Melanchthon, and Calvin, cf. p. 178.

23. Cf. the text of Trent, in the decree on original sin (Denz., 789).

24. Brunner, *op. cit.*, 120, writes: "All contemporary exegetes agree that this translation of the text is false." It should be remembered that Calvin already rejected the "in quo" (*Comm.*, Rom. 5), and exchanged for it "quia, quandoquidem." For our own century, cf. Kuyper, *Dictaten Dogmatiek*, III, 56; Bavinck, *Geref. Dog.*, III, 60; H. N. Ridderbos, *Comm. op Romeinen;* S. Greijdanus, *Toerekeningsgrond* and *Kommentaar*. Note that Ritschl, *Rechtfertigung und Versöhnung*, II2, 321, calls Augustine's exegesis wrong and says that Paul's intent "probably cannot be made clear at all."

25. Cf. A. Souter, *Pelagius' Expositions of Thirteen Epistles of St. Paul*, I, 1922, 45, and II, 1926, 45f. (on Rom. 5:12).

26. Note Calvin's Comm. on Rom. 5:12. In discussing Rom. 5:12*b* Calvin

in our own day.[27] Brunner, for example, has spoken in this same vein: "those who come later participate in death by doing their own sin."[28] The idea here is that the concept of *because* suggests an assertion that sin has come into our world by man, that through man's sin comes death, and that death has now passed on to all men, since all men are sinners, even though their sinning comes *later*. There is no reference here to a "sinning in Adam."

Yet such a view is opposed by the thinking of others who say that the context of Romans 5 must certainly lead us to very different conclusions. They maintain that even in the rejection of the terms *in whom* and the acceptance of *because* (that is, even in the revised translation of Romans 5:12) we still have a substantial reference to a "sinning in Adam." Thus these people do not wish to draw doctrinal conclusions from this revision. They suggest that the entire thrust of Paul's argument must point us in a certain direction. It is especially important, they say, to notice what Paul writes about the era between Adam and Moses. Sin was certainly in the world, according to Paul, in this "pre-law" period; yet because there was no law man's sin was not "imputed." At the same time, death continued to reign supreme in the lives of those who sinned, even though they sinned in a different way from Adam (Rom. 5:14).

In this description of the period from Adam to Moses the inference is now drawn that Romans 5:12 cannot possibly entail a later, personal sinning. Rather, the "regnancy" of death has everything to do with the sinning of *all men in one*. Therefore this text can rightly be paraphrased: "because all men sinned in Adam."[29] Thus Bavinck finds the inclusion of all

---

refers to 3:23 ("since all have sinned"), where he also finds this same thought. (Cf. our previous chapter.)

27. Freundörfer cites, among others, Bullinger and Peter Martyr (*op. cit.*, p. 179).

28. Brunner, *op. cit.*, 121. Barth remarks, in reference to Rom. 5:12, that grace comes in "where the work of sin, having been introduced into the human cosmos by one man, is therein both consummated and crowned; so that, as the one, so also all men factually sinned, and were thus likewise guilty and worthy of damnation" (*Christ und Adam nach Röm. 5*, 1952, p. 18). In other words, Barth has the same exegesis as Calvin. Cf. *ibid.*, p. 33, on Rom. 5:12: the reference to the "actual repetition of that in which Adam sinned." Cf. also O. Michel, *Der Brief an die Römer*, 1955, who sees in the statement that "all have sinned" the "close tie between fatalism and one's own guilt."

29. Freundörfer, *op. cit.*, p. 107.

men in Adam entirely apart from the translation of *in whom*.[30]
So too, Greijdanus asserts that the modified translation is no
real reason for a changed insight on the original sin dogma.[31]
Similarly, Murray refers to the *in quo* as "grammatically untenable" and "theologically true."[32] In the same line we find
such figures as Nygren and Ridderbos. It cannot be, according
to Nygren, that in Paul's conception the sin of Adam brought
death for Adam alone, or that death came only *later* to rest on
all mankind when they *too came to sin*.[33] Therefore Nygren
interprets Romans 5:12 in the spirit of Augustine, and Ridderbos regards this same argument (on the period between Adam
and Moses) as having a decisive cogency.[34] One might also
mention the name of J. A. C. van Leeuwen, who argues for a
return to the translation of *in whom,* and who does so with the
plea that the newer version ("because all men sinned") could
have the opposite meaning from what Paul obviously intended
in this passage.[35] The term *because,* according to Van Leeuwen,
can only imply a later, personal sinning. Thus Van Leeuwen
takes his position, in essence, with those who find in Romans
5:12 an actual *"sinning in Adam."*[36]

The fact is that many in our own day find no material
change implied in this conception of *because.* Paul's purpose
was to point to the involvement of *all men* in the sinning of the
one.[37] The general unanimity among those who argue in this

30. Bavinck, *op. cit.,* III, 60f.
31. *Komm.,* p. 278.
32. Article in *Westminster Theol. Journal,* 1955, p. 150.
33. A. Nygren, *Der Römerbrief,* pp. 158ff.
34. H. N. Ridderbos, *Comm.,* pp. 113-116.
35. J. A. C. van Leeuwen, *K.V.,* on Rom. 5:12, p. 112.
36. *Ibid.,* p. 113: "linguistically the translation 'in whom' is permissible.
    And in this context and train of argument, it recommends itself the
    most."
37. Along with the two explanations referred to here there is still a third,
    namely that of Zahn. This holds that the issue at stake is not an "in-
    clusiveness" in Adam, since this thought is untenable ("unvollziehbar")
    for anyone who does not believe in the pre-existence of souls in Adam
    (Zahn, *Komm.,* p. 265); moreover, the concept of *"all men* in Adam"
    imperils the image of "through *one man."* Therefore Zahn translates:
    "and on the basis of this (or, under these circumstances) all have
    sinned" (267). Through the sin of one man death has come upon all,
    and in such circumstances all have now sinned. Death was the founda-
    tion "on which the sinning of all the children of Adam has sprung
    forth." We recall also the conception of Stauffer (*Theologie des N.T.,*
    p. 248), who takes the *eph' hŏ* as referring back to *thánatos* (*epi*

way[38] must be seen in terms of the unexpected reference which Paul makes to the time between Adam and Moses. In the picture of antithesis between Adam and Christ we are pointed to the in-between position of Moses and the Mosaic law. This is a matter to which Paul returns in the course of this chapter (5:20). Paul spoke of a definite time at which the "law came in." In so doing he did not regard the period before the law as a "sinless epoch" but as qualitatively different from the period into which the law now "came." The remarkable point is that in this period before Moses men are not regarded as sinning in the same manner as Adam. It is obvious that Paul was not concerned about the problem of "heredity," for if he were he would not have pointed to the *very specific character* of this period from Adam to Moses. The Apostle is concerned about salvation-history. In the period of the law which followed Moses, man's sin is now imputed, and what happened *before this time* is not to be compared (or is not parallel) to what was manifest *since the coming of the law.*

Therefore, the peculiar feature of what came "with the law" does not lie merely in the fact that an explicit command was set alongside, as it were, the explicit commandment as given to Adam. Greijdanus and Ridderbos both lay stress on this emphatic or positive character of God's command.[39] In itself, of course, that accent is certainly correct. But what was really profoundly "new" in this "new situation" does not lie in a formal "positiveness" but rather in the positiveness of *this command.* That is to say, it lies in the command of the gracious and electing God for his people. *In that way* the new situation was set forth; and in contrast to this the sin *of Israel* was now manifest. Furthermore, that sin was *now imputed* because of the emphatic and positive nature of God's *grace* which came to Israel in *this command.* Thus we read of the increase of sin in the light of what has now occurred. Indeed, the law was introduced to this very end: that the trespass might increase (5:20). Now begins the history of the unfaithful people of the covenant; and it is now that we read of a clear registra-

thanátō), and reads, "in the direction of...." The reference here is "death, in which they fell man for man, through their sinning."
38. Cf. also E. Gaugler, *Der Brief an die Römer,* I, 1945, 129.
39. Greijdanus, *Komm.,* p. 280. Note the statement: "Their sins were not such transgressions of a command expressly given to them, with the threat of mortal punishment." Cf. Ridderbos, *op. cit.,* p. 117.

tion of sin, not merely because of the transgression of a "positive command" but because of the transgression of *this* command and *this* law.[40]

We must notice, of course, that when Paul refers to the period between Adam and Moses he sees even there (despite the non-imputation of sin) the "regnancy of death." Certainly this is a strong argument that Paul did not assign the power of death to the "new phase" of history alone or the sinning that occurs in that phase. He related that power to the concept of "all men in one." Yet, when we say that much, we stand again before the meaning of the Adam-and-Christ parallel and the real point of Paul's entire argument. Many have suggested that Romans 5:12ff. is an "excursion" in Paul's letter to the Romans, a kind of *Spaziergang* (as Luther once put it)[41] in which the thread of the argument is temporarily discontinued. But it is obvious that Paul does not drop off his discussion in Romans 1:1—5:11. He does this no more than he introduces the new and independent theme of predestination in chapters 9-11. The force of the argument in Romans 5:1-11, and the section following, is clearly the *glory of Christ's grace*. Paul does not demand attention for the new and unexpected "problem" of the origin of sin. He pictures the grace of him who died in his own time for the godless, and he draws a contrast between that grace and the dismal reign of death over every man in our world (5:14, 17*a*, 21). Death, as it were, finds its *porte d'entrée* in the sinning of one man. Yet in that *way* it comes

---

40. Ridderbos (*Comm.*, p. 117) writes that the concern here is with "the law as expressly legal demand and as the ground for the death penalty." Cf. his comments on Adam and the express command, and "Israel-after-the-giving-of-the-law"; also on "God's express command and threat of punishment" (*ibid.*). The manner in which the peculiar "newness" of the law is here indicated gives insufficient articulation to the fact that all of this has meaning and place only in terms of the structure of this law in God's covenant with his people. The resistance of his people was a resistance against the *grace* of God and the law which came with it. Also in his exegesis of Rom. 5:20, Ridderbos accentuates this law (which came with grace) as the law "with its demands and sanctions" (p. 123). But if sin is now revealed in all its "damnworthiness," this very damnworthiness is indissolubly qualified by *this* law which was given in *this* new situation. In this view, we do not eliminate the emphatic nature of the law, but we actually underscore it *in the framework of God's covenant and election*. When God turns himself to Israel in *this* way, sin is fully revealed *as sin*.

41. Cited in Nygren, *op. cit.*

to dominate all men. In contrast to this power of death, Paul now celebrates the new life which has come to light in Jesus Christ (5:17, 21).

Thus it is undeniable that in Romans 5 the power of *death* is accented and set in clear relief. At the same time, this is *all the more so* in the case of I Corinthians 15:21-22. There we read: "For as by a man came death, by a man has come also the resurrection of the dead. For as in Adam all die, so also in Christ shall all be made alive." There is no implication in this statement ("by a man came *death*") that the concept of *sin* is ignored; yet the absence of this term would seem to indicate the direction in which Paul wished to push his argument. Furthermore, that same accent is found in Romans 5, where the concept of sin is *explicitly mentioned*. Sin, we read, has come into our world (5:12), and through sin came death; and now sin reigns, as king, in death (5:21). But this does not alter the fact that Paul was concerned about the problem of "inheritance" or the "passing on" of sin. Ridderbos has rightly said that the entire context of Romans 5:12, "strictly speaking, does not concern original sin as a moral corruption but rather the immediate involvement in Adam's sin and Adam's death."[42] It is not the "inheritance" or the "way in which" sin is propagated in the human race, but the reign of sin and judgment which interested Paul. Death has now passed on to all men, and through the transgression of the *one* the *many* died (5:15). *All* are now subject to judgment (5:16, 19). What is more, Paul clearly states that through the disobedience of the one man the "many were *made sinners*" (5:19).

It is understandable that especially Romans 5:19 has played a major role in the original sin disputes. This is particularly the case in what dogmaticians have called the doctrine of "inherited guilt." Ridderbos has lent his support to some of the older translations which strongly affirm a forensic judgment of God.[43] The issue at stake, he feels, is God's judgment of men "by virtue of their inclusion in Adam." *In* the transgression of the *one man, Adam,* the judgment has passed on to *all men.* All are now reckoned or accounted as sinners, even as the "the many" are regarded as righteous through the obedience of "the One."

Yet is this the point that Paul really wants to make? Expositors in recent times have shown great difficulty in catching the

42. Ridderbos, *op. cit.,* p. 116.
43. *Ibid.,* p. 122.

meaning of these words. Ridderbos has suggested that the meaning of this "reckoning" or "imputing" is clarified when we call to mind the Old Testament reference in Deuteronomy 25:6. There the subject is the firstborn son who performs the "duty of a husband" in the case of a brother who has died. By the use of this parallel, Ridderbos states, we can appreciate that *imputatio* does not refer to what a man, as a matter of fact, *is*. It refers to his *"status before the law."*[44] Therefore Ridderbos takes issue with those modern translations which find in Romans 5:19 the idea of "becoming sinners" as a consequence or effect of Adam's first sin. He argues for a translation of "being reckoned" or "being accounted."

The way in which Ridderbos understands these words is evident in his polemic against Oepke,[45] who sees in Romans 5:19 the concept of "making someone something" or actually "putting him in a certain position or state." Oepke refuses the notion which finds in "imputation" something different from the factual situation of man. In that case we could only speak of a judgment of God in terms of his sovereign or inscrutable decree. But the situation of man, according to Oepke, is "always presupposed" as real. Therefore he finds little difference, in regard to Romans 5:19, between the thoughts of "being regarded as sinners" and actually "becoming sinners." Oepke rejects the exclusively forensic understanding of this text, which could only regard a man as being what he, as a matter of fact, *is not*. Thus he takes a position very different from Ridderbos' suggestion on the basis of Deuteronomy 25:6. In Oepke's conception the forensic judgment of God is concerned with a *reality*. So too is the forensic judgment of justification. Those who are justified in God's eyes are justified *in reality*.

Ridderbos objects that Oepke has confused the concepts of a "virtual" or habitual sinning and the real nature of man-as-sinner. In that way he has come to a wrong interpretation of Paul's specific intent. But we ask if Oepke, in such an appraisal, has really been given his due. Oepke specifically states that according to Paul "the many" are *not* condemned because of their own sin; nonetheless Paul is concerned about the *reality* of man's own being-a-sinner and the *reality* of God's judgment. God's viewing man as a sinner does not imply an "as if" but an actuality; therefore it does not involve the con-

44. *Ibid.*
45. *TWNT,* III, *s.v. kathistēmi.*

demnation of man for something he *is not*. Obviously, Oepke does not "resolve" the problems of Romans 5. Yet when Ridderbos points to the Deuteronomy passage and speaks of our "status" before the law, *in distinction from what we actually "are,"* it is just as obvious that he says little or nothing to clarify God's "forensic judgment." At the very most, he sets forth the problem here by utilizing the terminology from the doctrine of justification. For in the doctrine of justification the term *forensic* is only relatively perspicuous if it is used in concert with other equivalent terms. We think of such terms as *declaratory* and *imputative*. These terms then point to the gift and grace of God, and the imputation of Christ's righteousness. They emphasize that man's acquittal is a deeply meaningful and astonishing conversion from God's anger to his grace.

Thus when we utilize this term *forensic* in our explanation of Romans 5:19 we are suggesting a parallel to the doctrine of justification which can very easily lead us to confusions. This is because the main feature in forensic justification is *not* an impenetrable divine decree but the grace of God which is evident in the *taking away of guilt*. Forensic justification is not an inscrutable "declaration" that the sinner is a righteous man. It is not a calling of something "white" when really it is "black." Certainly it is the act of God's imputation, but only the imputation of Christ's righteousness. Certainly it is a great mystery, but only the mystery which is plain to faith in the light of Jesus Christ. The term *forensic,* in the dogma of justification, has nothing to do with an unreality or pretension. It is not a matter of "as if." Therefore the question is very relevant: What do we mean when we speak of a "forensic judgment" of God in Romans 5:19? What should we understand by this "being reckoned as" or "being regarded as" sinners? If we take the term *reckoned* in the light of Deuteronomy 25:6 we immediately beg the question of how this view is compatible with the words of Romans 5:12: *"because all men sinned."* As Greijdanus has rightly noted, we do *not read* "in whom all man are *reckoned to have sinned."*[46]

Obviously, we cannot ask what these words mean, in Romans 5:19, from a purely "dogmatological" point of view. We can only inquire into their meaning in terms of the text itself. But in the light of the text we may also seek to know the meaning

---

46. Greijdanus, *Toerekeningsgrond*, p. 41 (*eph' hó pántes hamartánein elogísthēsan*).

or intent of this dogmatical concept of *forensic*. Here we are concerned with a term that has always been misunderstood in the entire history of doctrine. It has been defended, nonetheless, from the side of the Reformation in the context of justification. Thus we have the background in the light of which very urgent questions emerge as we look at the meaning of Romans 5:19. Forensic justification is not a mere "reckoning" (as opposed to "reality") but is rather the reference to the reality of *justitia aliena*. It implies the declaration and imputation of man's real justification. But how, then, can we still use this word to speak of a "forensic judgment" on the analogy of Deuteronomy 25? Do we find a clarification in the commandment concerning a brother's wife? In our opinion, we do not. Furthermore, if we say that we *do* it is impossible to distinguish the concepts of *quasi* and *forensic, imputed* and *as if*.

This is not a criticism that stems from Socinian ideas. For the Socinians renounced the reality of any forensic imputation and could only see in this the earmarks of a *quasi-* or "as if"-theology. But the forensic judgment of "imputing" an unreal guilt to man (an alien sin) can only revive the questions which Greijdanus already asked in 1906. These questions have never received an adequate answer. At the same time, they are very real questions, and their biblical rootage can hardly be ignored. Does the biblical statement that the guilty are not guiltless find its opposite side in a divine "declaration" that the *guiltless are guilty?* That question has nothing to do at all with a "rationalism." It retains its biting edge apart from the context of an unacceptable realism. In short, it finds its basis in a biblical motive which cannot be cancelled out by an empty allusion to God's inscrutable "decree." For there is no such decree which holds a guiltless man to be "guilty."[47]

Here we must notice the explicit statement in Paul that all men have sinned. Surely Paul does *not* refer to a "forensic judgment" in contrast to what has *happened* in reality. Even those who have refused to understand this judgment in the sense of a "later individual sinning" (i.e., Nygren, Ridderbos, Gaugler, Greijdanus; *contra* Calvin, *et al.*) have acknowledged that a

---

47. Greijdanus once spoke of an "insult" to our legal sensitivity — but this is an unfortunate expression. Schilder has added that what was meant here, of course, was a sensitivity aroused and normed by Scripture (*Heidelbergsche Catechismus*, I, 339). The biblical motive in Greijdanus' statement cannot be ignored.

proper understanding of Romans 5:19 requires an appreciation for this genuinely Pauline accent. Oepke, it seems, was motivated by this very wholesome desire to avoid the *quasi*-character of God's indictment and to emphasize the true reality of guilt. Therefore he dealt so seriously with that reality. Precisely because God's judgment of men is never a *quasi*-judgment (even in forensic justification) [48] it is obvious why this element of "unreality" is lacking in the context of Romans 5.[49] The realistic criticism cannot be lightly shoved aside. For this criticism is essentially an appeal to the non-arbitrariness of God's activity. It is really a rejection of the proposal that God regards the *unguilty man as guilty*.

That kind of proposal (or that kind of *imputatio*) finds no grain of support in the entire argument of Romans 5:12-21. Furthermore, the problems in referring "imputation" to the Deuteronomy passage are so very real that they can only persist throughout all our reformulations. When Polman opposes the new translation of Romans 5:19 (that "many have become sinners") [50] he nonetheless supports that thought in principle and refers to its "legitimate expression."[51] At the same time, in setting forth the proposal of an "objective transfer of sin and guilt,"[52] he introduces a new category which can only give rise to a number of new questions. It is obvious that the only way

48. Here is a matter of life and death importance for the Reformation confession, as opposed to Rome's criticism of an "external imputation." Cf. my *Faith and Justification*, 1954, and A. Venter, *Analities of Sinteties? 'n Analise van die Dilemma insake de Werklikheid van die Regverdiging*, 1959, especially Chap. 5.

49. Oepke cites James 4:4 — and not without reason: "Therefore whoever wishes to be a friend of the world makes himself an enemy of God" (*kathistatai*). The point, he wishes to say, is the reality of being an enemy, and not an "imputation" or "regarding as," to which no reality belongs. Cf. Grosheide: "*is* an enemy of God." Though a man has the place and status of an enemy, he *is* that also. Cf. *Comm.*, p. 387: *kathistatai* has a meaning which is not very different from *is* (reference here is to James 3:6). Zahn, *Komm.*, p. 195, sees something more in this term: "who makes himself the enemy of God: i.e., who takes his place as God's enemy." He refers to Rom. 5:19 and II Pet. 1:8. Cf. also James 4:4*a*: "friendship with the world is enmity with God."

50. Dutch Nieuwe Vertaling: "zondaren geworden." A. D. R. Polman, *Woord en Belijdenis*, I, 269. Cf. Gaugler, *op. cit.*, I, 120.

51. Polman, *loc. cit.*

52. *Ibid.* Cf. also the article on original sin ("erfzonde") in *Christelijke Encyclopaedie*, II, 1957², 626: "an objective transfer of sin, guilt and death."

to "solve" these questions is to argue that God, once and for all, has *so decreed*. In that case, however, the concept of an objective "transfer" sheds preciously little light; moreover, the complications in which we find ourselves are all the more apparent. This is very evident in Polman's conclusion: "thus the doctrine of original sin is opened up in this section of Scripture with all the clarity which we desire." That "clarity" is found in the "transfer" which forms a parallel to the "transfer" of Christ's own righteousness and life.[53] On the one hand, therefore, we hear of a "representation" of men in Adam; on the other hand, we hear of an "imputation" and a "transfer."[54] Yet in all these formulae the very real problem is still squarely before us. At the most *crucial juncture* of the Adam-Christ parallel the notion of an objective "transfer" is entirely unsuitable.

Must we throw up our hands in despair and admit the obscurity of what Paul means?[55] It is much better to say that we are challenged at this point to a new understanding. We would seem to have an intuitive awareness of the need to grasp the meaning of this doxological pericope concerning the glory of Jesus Christ. Romans 5 calls us to a new appreciation of the Adam-Christ parallel; it also urges us to inquire into the meaning of thus juxtaposing Adam-and-Christ in the development of the original sin dogma. What about the similar parallel of *Eve and the Virgin Mary*, which we frequently meet up with, especially in Catholicism? In bringing up this matter now we are not concerned with a merely subordinate feature in the original sin dispute. As a matter of fact, a number of questions are very important here and impinge (at least indirectly) on a proper understanding of Romans 5.

Yet there is something strange about this Eve-and-Mary parallel when we draw it into the context of our present discussion. Romans 5 says nothing about either Mary or Eve. The fact remains that Rome assigns a critical importance to the Romans 5 passage and *alongside this* demands attention for the Eve-and-Mary parallel. On the one hand the stress is on the formal analogy or decisive significance of what both Eve and

53. *Ibid.*
54. Polman judges that the element of truth in realism must be supplemented by the federalist explanation *(ibid.)*.
55. Nygren: "ratlos," *op. cit.*, p. 22. Dahl speaks of "the bewildering multitude of answers" (N. A. Dahl, "Two Notes on Romans 5," *Studia Theologica*, 1952, p. 42).

Mary have done. This is also apparent in the parallel of Adam-and-Christ. On the other hand there is an emphasis on the antithesis of calamity and salvation. It is not true that Rome desires to supplant the Adam-and-Christ parallel by that of Eve-and-Mary. Much rather, she accepts a twofold parallel, which she sees as vitally important for understanding the nature of God's activity. Though this twofold parallel is far from clear, it is evident that the Eve-and-Mary analogy has risen in the light of the important place which Mary assumes in the divine economy of salvation. It is noteworthy, furthermore, that the antithesis is worked out with an appeal not only to tradition but also to the structure and terminology of Romans 5. This is especially apparent in the contraposition of Eve's disobedience and Mary's obedience.

In the Middle Ages the question was asked: Would the world have fallen if only Eve had sinned and not Adam? This, of course, is a highly speculative question; yet it is also a question that illustrates the complexity of the Eve-and-Mary parallel. We should notice that this parallel was not construed in the light of Eve but rather of *Mary*. As Paul, in Romans 5, sets forth the majesty of Christ against the background of a world of sin and death and judgment, so the figure of Mary is cast, in the Eve-and-Mary parallel, against the background of Eve's transgression. Someone might object that the specific accent on Eve is a very subordinate one in Scripture, or that Eve, in contrast to Mary, is not assigned an essential role in the biblical kerygma. But the Catholic answer is that the issue here is much more than an illustration of disobedience *versus* obedience, and is far more than a psychological or aesthetic commentary on the figure of Eve.[56] Only in the light of the *act of Mary* is Eve's important seen as very evident.

Therefore, although the Eve-and-Mary parallel does not find a place in Scripture, the Catholic form of that parallel is dependent on the structures of Romans 5 and I Corinthians 15. When we see in I Corinthians 15:45 that the first man, Adam, is set in opposition to the "last Adam,"[57] the pattern is already

---

56. We think of the breadth of material in Anthonie Donker's *Eva en de Dichters*, 1958, where considerable attention is given to Eve apart from the antithesis with Mary — often in the attempt to dechristianize the biblical-Christian motives. Cf. p. 115. Here the relation of Eve to Adam and Satan also plays an important role (pp. 68ff.).
57. The "second man," I Cor. 15:47.

established for the antithesis of Eve-and-Mary. Mary is viewed as the "new" or "second" Eve.[58] In this picture of antithesis ("first" and "second") our eyes are now focused on Eve as the one through whom despair and need have come into our world, and Mary is regarded (in a "mediatorial" fashion) as the one through whom our salvation is made known. Thus the accent is on Mary's position in the history of salvation, precisely as the accent is on Christ in the "masculine parallel" of Paul. Therefore Schmaus has spoken of "the salvation-historical significance of Mary."[59] He has referred to Eve and Mary as "type and antitype." Here again we have a clear reference to Romans 5; but we also see that such a formula is by no means an attempt to exchange the Adam-and-Christ parallel for that of Eve-and-Mary. Two individuals stand opposed to each other (Eve and Mary); but the figure of Eve cannot be divorced from that of Christ. Therefore the Eve-and-Mary parallel is not a depreciation, in Catholic theology, of the parallel of Adam-and-Christ. It is readily acknowledged that Paul, in Romans 5, points only to Christ and the superabundance of his grace, in contrast to the first act of disaster.[60] Therefore the Eve-and-Mary analogy is construed, as it were, *within that parallel.* "Though her 'yes' was grounded in God's eternal decision, yet God would not have come to men apart from the 'yes' which Mary spoke on behalf of mankind."[61]

And yet, while observing the subordinate role of Mary and the non-independence of the Eve-and-Mary parallel, we must not ignore the fact that the terminology of Romans 5 and I Corinthians 15 is very consistently employed in this new parallel of Rome. Consider the following quotation from Schmaus: "Eve became the basis of death, for death came into the world through her. But Mary is the ground of life, for through her our lives are born to us." In this very same context, in Schmaus, we find a reference to Romans 5:20: "where sin increased, grace abounded all the more."[62] Thus Eve is introduced as the typological antithesis of Mary. She is designated the "mother of sin" in contrast to the "mother of grace."[63] The parallel is made complete, at this

58. M. Schmaus, "Mariologie," *Kath. Dogmatik,* V, 1955, 263.
59. *Ibid.*
60. *Ibid.,* 301.
61. *Ibid.,* 357.
62. *Ibid.,* 266.
63. M. Scheeben, *Kath. Dogmatik,* V, 2, 1954, 487.

juncture, by pointing to Mary as the "antitype" or *"Gegenbild"* of Eve.[64]

We have said already that Paul, in Romans 5, does not refer to Eve. Yet we do well to remember, as we look at this "crucial and subordinate" parallel, that he does consider her importance in other passages.[65] He harks back to the Genesis account and relates that story to the subject of man's sin. He recalls the temptation of Eve by the craftiness of the serpent (II Cor. 11:3), but he does so in a chapter that is not at all concerned with the problem of the origin of sin. Indeed, his interest is in an entirely different matter. He refers to the temptation of Eve in connection with what he fears may again be a *threat for the Church*. He points to the peril of being drawn away from the thoughts of Jesus Christ. Thus the recollection of Eve's seduction is taken up into the theme of his own *vigilance on behalf of the Church*.

Furthermore, when we turn to the context of I Timothy 2:13, we find an even more striking reference to Eve and an even clearer example of how little Paul was concerned about the "origin of sin." His interest was in the moral behavior of women. What was expected of women was "silence with all submissiveness" (2:11), and as the motive for this we read: "For Adam was formed first, then Eve; and Adam was not deceived, but the woman was deceived and became a transgressor" (2:13-14).[66] Once again, the fact of Eve's transgression is utilized by Paul as an admonition for the Church. He built his entire argument on the temporal priority of Adam's creation and Eve's initial transgression. Though C. Bouma has commented that Paul remains, at this point, within the sphere of God's own words in Genesis 3:16,[67] it is not this issue that really concerns us here. The remarkable fact is this reference to *Eve's iniquity*. It was not Adam but Eve, according to Paul and Genesis 3, who first

64. *Ibid.*, 360.

65. Also in papal encyclicals we frequently encounter the term *the new Eve* as a designation of Mary. We merely cite "mystici corporis Christi" (*Eccl. Doc.*, 1943, p. 102): in her sacrifice of motherly privileges and motherly love the new Eve has borne Christ on Calvary to the Father, "for all children of Adam, who were stained by his unhappy fall." Here Mary stands, as the new Eve, in contrast to *Adam*. Cf. "Munificentissimus Deus," 1950, p. 49: "the new Eve, bound up with the new Adam, howbeit in a subservient fashion" ("etsi subjecta").

66. Here the same word is used for transgression as in Rom. 5: *parábasis*.

67. Bouma, *Komm.*, p. 125.

began to sin. This is the only "beginning" that really interested Paul (cf. I Cor. 11:7-8).

But how must we think of the relation between Eve's sin as "beginning" and the statement that Paul makes in Romans 5: through *"one man"* (*Adam*) our sin has come into the world (v. 12)? L. Hick has noted the peril that Paul very obviously wished to avoid, namely, the vanity and ostentatiousness of women. With this in mind Paul refers to the Genesis story and makes use of "that which was serviceable for him in his present purposes."[68] Paul pointed to "feminine guilt" in order to keep women humble. Hick suggests that he laid hold on the words of Jesus Sirach, and he also interprets Paul as contending that "the devil already knew by what manner he would make his approach to Eve. He was familiar with her peculiarity and took it into account, to attain more easily his purposes through her. In this he made no mistake." Thus, in these words a complete phenomenology of manhood and womanhood is assigned to the devil,[69] even though such a phenomenology can hardly be concluded from the sentiments of Paul. One may grant that Paul took his point of departure in the *beginning* of the temptation of the first human pair. Furthermore, we agree with Hick that his intention was not "to free man from every guilt."[70] But it remains the case that Paul, in Romans 5, speaks *only of Adam,* and that elsewhere he refers to *Eve in subjection to Adam.* Hick cannot "solve" that problem. On the one hand, he regards Adam as the one who brought "the great fate" (*"das grosse Verhängnis"*) upon the world; on the other hand, he sees Eve as "the 'representrix' of the feminine race" through whose "feminine weakness" catastrophic results have now followed.

We admit that Paul's reference, at this point, is certainly not clear. Nevertheless, it is evident that he did not relate the figure of Eve to the wider perspective of salvation-history or grace opposed to sin. He selected a single element in the Genesis account for its practical application. It is significant that in I Timothy he does speak of a "salvation" in contrast to lostness — but the "salvation" he has in mind is peculiar to a *woman in child-bearing.* "Yet woman will be saved through bearing children, if she continues in faith and love and holiness, with

---

68. L. Hick, *Die Stellung des hl. Paulus zur Frau im Rahmen seiner Zeit,* 1957, p. 192.

69. Cf. Bengel: "facilius decepta, facilius decipit" (in Zahn, 119).

70. Hick, *loc. cit.*

modesty" (I Tim. 2:15). Here there is no hint of a salvation-historical perspective as we find it in Romans, chapter 5. In the Romans passage Paul latches onto the great antithesis of Adam and Christ, and it is not his purpose (as elsewhere in regard to Eve) to warn us as he points to the tragic "example" of Adam. He underscores the *power of death* in our world which has filtered down to all men. Romans 5, therefore, is not a "remonstrative" or an "exemplary" chapter but points us, instead, to the salvation-historical antithesis of Christ in opposition to Adam.

In other words, it is totally in conflict with the New Testament when the Eve-and-Mary parallel is interwoven with and depicted in the categories of Romans 5. The "feminine parallel" can only get its status in the increasing accent which Rome has laid on the salvation-historical place of Mary, or the increasing devotion which she has bestowed upon the Virgin. But Paul, on the other hand, refused to see the figure of Eve in a salvation-historical perspective. When he mentioned Eve at all he was far from conceiving her as *causa peccati*.[71] In fact, he specifically refused to go in that direction. The great antithesis, for him, was not "Eve-and-Mary" but "Adam-and-Christ." Mary assumes a very modest place in the Pauline epistles (cf. Gal. 4). Moreover, it is worth our while to observe that at the crucial juncture of salvation it is *Christ,* in opposition to *Adam,* to whom the Apostle *exclusively refers.*

Men have asked, from various standpoints, how Paul ever came to this idea of an antithetical parallelism. Some have seen the background in rabbinical and others in hellenistic sources; in either case they have noted a certain "swerving away from the track of what is truly Pauline and biblical."[72] Nygren, on the other hand, has rightly said that Paul was not concerned about a speculation or an *"Adam redivivus."*[73] Instead, he "read

---

71. Cf. Schmaus' appeal to Irenaeus; *op. cit.,* 264.
72. Nygren, *op. cit.,* p. 154.
73. *Ibid.* Bultmann sees a Gnostic thought in Romans 5 (the Adam-Christ parallel), in which death is understood as "fate." Paul then gives the *heilshistorisch* meaning to this. "Thus the cosmological construction of myth becomes salvation-historical" ("Adam und Christus nach Röm. 5," *Z.N.T.W.,* 1959, pp. 155, 160). In all of this Bultmann finds a great "confusion," and he accuses Barth of failing to appreciate the mythological foundation of Paul's argument (165). Cf. also Bultmann, *Theologie des N.T.,* 1948, pp. 246f., where he likewise refers to a "lack of clarity," and calls Rom. 5:13 "completely unintelligible."

about Adam in the first pages of his Bible."[74] Therefore he
pointed to salvation in Christ in contrast to the world of sin
and death and guilt.

There is little room for a difference of opinion concerning
the purpose and direction of Paul's thought.[75] He wanted to
point to the glory of Christ's saving grace and the "much more"
of his righteousness and life in contrast to the regnancy of
death.[76] For that reason he did not make a simple analogy between Adam and Christ, as though Christ merely sets aright and
restores what once was "broken down" in Adam. Paul affirmed
emphatically that there is no real parallel between the "free
gift" and the "trespass of the one."[77] Furthermore, the in-
between period, from Adam to Moses, is not a merely incidental
feature in the Pauline argument concerning the regnancy of
death, which now has come on all. It forms an essential (if
subordinate) aspect of that argument, and it accentuates the
superabundance of God's grace. That superabundance is evident
in the face of the "many trespasses"[78] and the sin which
actually "increased" *by means of the law* (Rom. 5:13, 20).

We shall see that the relation between the "one" and the
"many" is very important in Paul's argument. But in the light
of that relation the "much more" cannot possibly be "explained."
The concept of "much more" has everything to do with the
revelation of Christ's grace in contrast to the increase of man's
sin. Through the law a new situation is created and sin is now
"reckoned." Within that situation grace is manifest in all its
superfluity. It is now apparent (in "many trespasses") how
much the sin of man puts all thing in crisis. For grace is not
merely the equivalent of Adam's sin but is something "even
more." Grace is *"abundant* grace towards those who were guilty

74. Nygren, *loc. cit.*
75. There is, of course, a good deal of speculation on the term *Adam*. One
thinks of the views expressed by E. Bock, under the influence of Rudolf
Steiner, in his *Urchristentum*, IV ("Paulus"), 1954, especially Chap.
XII ("Der alte und der neue Adam"), pp. 211-228. See further E. Bentz,
Adam. Der Mythus vom Urmenschen, 1955 (the "androgyne myth").
76. Jeremias treats of the origin of the typology Adam-Christ (e.g., in the
broad Jewish presupposition of the 'Ur-man' as ideal man); and he
points to Paul's use of this concept "to show the universality of grace"
(*TWNT*, I, *s.v. Adám*).
77. Rom. 5:15: *All' ouch hōs tó paráptōma, hoútōs kai tó chárisma.*
78. The gift of grace led from "many trespasses" to justification (Rom.
5:16).

both through Adam's sin and as transgressors of the law."[79] When Paul sees Adam and Christ next to each other, he does not have in mind a mere abstraction but rather an *heilshistorisch* perspective. Therefore the entrance of the law is not only found in verse 13 but returns at the climax and end of Paul's argument (v. 20). In that same light we see that sin is revealed most fully *as sin* in all its reality; furthermore, the fact that the "much more" has this reference is evident from Paul's addressing himself again to this "superabundance" in verse 20. "Where sin increased, grace abounded all the more." Grace, in other words, was "more than abundant."[80]

Thus Paul uses a concept that has a kind of "hyper-superlative" ring to it. "Abundant," in itself, is already immeasurable. Therefore the very term here is a demonstration of the depths of God's grace and ought to be seen as a doxology in one word.[81] "Whereas in earlier times sin increased through the Law, grace is superabundantly greater in Christ."[82] Here, then, is the "superfluity" of which Paul now speaks: the "superabundant fulness of the time of salvation,"[83] as opposed to the reality of increasing sin, or the sin against the law. The law which Paul had in mind is the historical law of Mt. Sinai, or the law of God's grace, in which God turned himself to Israel in election and salvation.

Within that context of the "superfluity of grace" Paul now speaks of Adam. He does not analyze the world of death and guilt in order to inquire, from that standpoint, concerning the "possibility" of salvation. He points to the reality of grace as opposed to the world of death. Therefore it is understandable that such men as Ridderbos and Barth have spoken of the parallel here as a parallel of *Christ-and-Adam*.[84] Certainly one could draw a number of radical conclusions from such a reversal of terms; he could even revamp the whole superstructure of dogmatical thinking. But these possibilities must not deter us from seeing that the reversal itself has nothing to do with a process of "de-historicizing" and only attempts to express what Paul most obviously wanted to say. Adam, according to Paul,

---

79. Dahl, *op. cit.*, p. 48.
80. Greek: *hypereperisseuen hē cháris.*
81. In II Cor. 7:4 Paul uses this term in connection with his own joy ("I am overjoyed"). Cf. Eph. 3:20: "far more abundantly."
82. *TWNT*, VI, s.v. *perisseúō.*
83. *Ibid.*, s.v. *perisseía;* cf. H. N. Ridderbos, *Comm.*, p. 123.
84. *Ibid.*, p. 111; Barth, *Christus und Adam nach Römer 5*, 1952, and *K.D.*, IV/1.

must stand in the *light of Jesus Christ*. Christ is the *theme* and the *starting-point* in this chapter. Thus, while Adam is seen as the darkness, Christ is the *Light which now has come*.

That being the case, it is not original sin but divine grace that forms the message and content of this pericope. Paul was not concerned about the *manner* in which the sin of one man is "transferred" to another, or the *manner* in which the pollution of one generation "becomes" that of another. We understand why, in this light, traditional dogmatics has made a distinction between "inherited guilt" and "hereditary corruption," and why Romans 5 has frequently been used to support the former and less frequently to support the latter. In that way the exegetical tendency has arisen to read this chapter in the light of *imputatio*. Yet, although we cannot deny that Christ's superabundant grace is the real message of this pericope,[85] it is apparent that Paul refers to this theme in an antithetical analogy.[86] Thus on the one hand we find a framework or parallel that is rooted in the words "through one man"; on the other hand, there is also a diametrically-opposed antithesis within that framework. The accent on the "one" or "many" (or "all") is repeated in this chapter with remarkable persistency;[87] at the same time we see a decisive antithesis in which two "men" are set against each other in their importance for the "all." Therefore we find those peculiar problems which we have already noted above in our discussion of the realist and federalist hypotheses. We do not get the impression, in Romans 5, that this problematic is a special concern of Paul. Nonetheless it all too often is for us.[88] Certainly Paul did not stop thinking at this point: and yet his outlook on the superabundance of grace was so central and intense (even when he thought of guilt and death) that nothing could separate him from the love of Jesus Christ. In Romans 5:12ff. we hear the continuation

---

85. This also holds — just as much — in the case of I Cor. 15:21-22. There the antithesis is mentioned to point to Christ's glory — in order to speak more extensively, in turn, of Christ (vv. 23f.).

86. Dahl, *op. cit.*, p. 42.

87. Cf. S. Hanson, *The Unity of the Church in the N.T.*, 1946, p. 66. Cf. Rom. 5:12, 15, 16-19.

88. Dahl makes the courageous comment: "The thought of Paul is not so complicated as the commentaries may make one think." His statement here is certainly not directed against "commentaries" *per se,* since he himself has proceeded very carefully in giving a detailed exegesis of this pericope.

of this paean which begins in verses 1-11. The paean is not interrupted by a tedious or a speculative argument.[89]

Here, it seems to us, we come to the heart and the deepest problem in Paul's entire discussion. Frequently we have difficulty in penetrating the real music of Paul's paeans. We find this, for example, in the case of Romans 11:33-36. Yet, although we may never say that the history of exegesis and dogmatics is the history of a "riddle," the purpose of a song of praise is obviously that we should sing along and not get bogged down in extraneous and speculative problems. For the man who is mired deeply in problems can only relativize and disharmonize his song of victory.[90]

On the other hand, none of this detracts from the necessity of considering the manner in which Paul himself regards the superabundance of light and life and righteousness. It is wrong to complicate the Pauline message, but it is just as wrong to oversimplify. Paul was not concerned to draw a picture of two isolated "men" but to see the contrast in this relation of the "one" and the "all."[91] Precisely *here* is the relation which has played the dominant role in every subsequent discussion of this topic. We have seen that fact in the realist hypothesis, which conceives of an organophysical unity of the "one" and the "all," at least in reference to Adam and his posterity. Thus the "all" are actually *in* the "one." But the same relation is also found in federalism, which conceives of the bond between the "all" and the "one" in a "representative" or a "federal" manner. The "all" are accounted within the "one" on the basis of the *ordinatio Dei* or divine decree.

This has been a topic of interest especially in our own

89. We recall the "therefore" (*did toúto*) in Rom. 5:12, which binds together our pericope with Rom. 5:1-11 (cf. Greijdanus, *Komm.*, and Ridderbos, *ad loc.*). This "therefore" has been seen by Lagrange, and after him by Feuillet, as a "simple literary conjunction of transition" (cf. A. Feuillet, "Le plan salvifique de Dieu d'après l'épître aux Romains," *Revue Biblique*, 1950, p. 358). That position was disputed by Dupont, who saw the pericope in 5:12-21 as "a demonstration of the thesis proposed in vv. 1-11" (J. Dupont, "Le problème de la structure littéraire de l'épître aux Romains," *Revue Biblique*, 1955, p. 381).
90. Gaugler, *op. cit.*, I, 121.
91. Rom. 5:12: "through *one* man"; "death spread to *all* men." Rom. 5:15: "*many* died through *one* man's trespass"; cf. "the grace of that *one* man Jesus Christ abounded for *many*." Rom. 5:18: "*one* man's act of righteousness leads to acquittal and life for *all* men."

century. Frequently men have proposed the concept of a "corporate personality." Lightly weighed, this would seem to be an abstract idea, or at least a term that communicates quite badly. We might think that the effort is made here, by way of modern terminology, to unravel the "mystery" of the Pauline pericope. But this is far from the intention of those who have proposed this thought. We have in mind here such a man as H. Wheeler Robinson and quite recently, in a more extended discussion, J. De Fraine.[92]

It is highly important to understand the significance of this idea for such a chapter as Romans 5. This is all the more the case because it is sometimes seen as an explanation, or illumination, of the original sin dogma. "One finds," according to De Fraine, "that the notion of a 'corporative personality' aids us, in our discussions, in 'expressing' the dogmatical truths of original sin and and redemption."[93] Robinson writes along these same lines. H. N. Ridderbos also employs the concept of "corporate personality" in his exegesis of Romans 5. "In this whole thought of 'all men through the one' (or 'in the one') it is not improper to refer to the Old Testament concept of a 'corporate personality.'"[94] Therefore Ridderbos speaks of understanding Romans 5:12 ("because all men sinned") in a "corporative sense."[95] Yet the question remains: What is the real meaning of this thought, and in how far does it contribute to an understanding of this pericope? That question is important because

---

92. The following are important here: H. Wheeler Robinson, "The Hebrew Conception of Corporate Personality," in *Werden und Wesen des A.T.*, 1936, pp. 49-62; idem, *Inspiration and Revelation in the O.T.*, 1946, pp. 70f., 81f., 169f. Robinson develops these thoughts already in his *The Christian Doctrine of Man*, 1913. In connection with Rom. 5, cf. further: S. Hanson, *The Unity of the Church in the N.T.*, 1946, pp. 11 and 67; J. A. T. Robinson, *The Body. A Study in Pauline Theology*, 1955, pp. 13f.; and the detailed study of De Fraine, *Adam et son lignage. Étude sur la notion de 'personnalité corporative' dans la Bible*, 1959.

93. *Ibid.*, p. 223.

94. "If there had been no doctrine of 'corporate personality,' there would have been no doctrine of original sin, according to which the sin of Adam has condemned to death the entire human race..." (*ibid.*, p. 127).

95. H. N. Ridderbos, *Comm.*, pp. 114, 116. Cf. also De Fraine, *De Bijbel en het Ontstaan van de Mens*, 1953, pp. 49f.; H. Reinckens, *Israëls Visie op het Verleden*, 1956, p. 201; Th. Delleman, *Wording van Mens en Wereld*, p. 68; A. Nygren, *Der Römerbrief*, 1951, p. 158 (without this term).

of the fundamental role of this chapter in the original sin disputes.

Very obviously, Robinson and De Fraine in no way intend this conception as a modern "viewpoint" which is superimposed on the Scripture *a posteriori*. They want to show that it represents a form of thought defined already by the Old Testament, as well as by the New, in a very decisive manner. This conception implies a peculiar relation between the individual and the group which is manifest in far-reaching consequences.[96] The very idea that the individual and the group are completely tied up with each other may strike us, in our individualistic age, as quite strange. At the same time, Robinson sees in this an important aspect of the Hebrew psychology and the echo of the Hebrew relation of God and man. He speaks of "the idea of a close relation, and for some purposes an identity, of the individual and the group to which he belongs."[97] The Old Testament covenant alliance is foreign to all individualism and atomism, and cuts across the whole of Israel's life and religion. Thus in her position before God her concern was not with a number of isolated individuals set loosely next to each other, but rather with a relation that was "throughout corporate."[98] Here we see an anti-individualistic appreciation of man's life in relation to God and "the primacy of the corporate idea over the individualistic."[99] So strong was "the union of the individual and community"[100] that the entire group could be regarded as acting in the single individual. In that way the individual took his place as the "representative" of the group. Furthermore, there is no trace at all, in this Hebrew view, of an abstract or "juridical" concept of "as if." The relation was not merely "fictional" or "by way of speaking";[101] as a matter of fact, what we see here is no "stylistic procedure" or merely "literary de-

---

96. Among other examples, reference is made especially to the account of Achan's sin (Josh. 7); cf. vv. 10-12, in particular — Joshua's "why?" (v. 7), and God's answer (v. 11) that "Israel has sinned." Cf. I Chron. 2:7: "Achar, the troubler of *Israel*." See also De Fraine, *op. cit.*, pp. 72f., and more extensively, on Achan: P. J. Verdam, 'On ne fera point mourir *les enfants pour les pères' en droit biblique* (Mélanges F. de Visscher, *Rev. internat. des droits de l'Antiquité*, 2-3), 1949, pp. 398f., 403f.

97. W. Robinson, *Inspiration and Revelation*, p. 70.

98. *Ibid.*, p. 71; cf. "the corporate emphasis" (p. 81).

99. *Ibid.*, p. 82.

100. De Fraine, *op. cit.*, p. 17.

101. *Ibid.*

vice."[102] Everything was concrete and very real. The group and the individual formed together "a single total reality";[103] and this was not merely a subjective category but "a realistic conception."[104] There are many biblical examples of the individual thus representing an entire group. In this light, according to De Fraine, it is possible to understand Paul's thinking on the topic of "original sin."[105]

Now the "transfer" from the individual to the collective Adam is no longer a difficult concern. For the group participates in what the individual Adam does.[106] One man represents the whole of humanity[107] — and therefore Paul can write that "all have sinned." *Corporatively* we see a "mysterious inclusion of humanity in Adam."[108] If Adam is guilty, then all men are guilty; if Adam dies, then all men die. What is more, this does not occur in a "later sinning." For "even in the absence of strictly individual sins, all the true 'sons of Adam' are sinners."[109] In *this sense* the entire human race is "there present and takes part in his destiny of sin and death."[110] Therefore, within this context, De Fraine takes note of the various New Testament data, including Romans 5. There the Adam-and-Christ parallel can only be seen, in his judgment, in the framework of a "corporative personality." When we look at both Adam and Christ we see the "transmission of the effects of an individual to a multitude."[111] Christ, by analogy to the representative Adam, represents the new humanity "which forms with him a body."[112] In short, the concept here is a concept of a "representation of an individual who includes within his person all those individuals of whom he is the representative."[113]

Surely, the questions that center in this idea of a "corporate personality" are very profound. One of the most important is

102. *Ibid.*, p. 129.
103. *Ibid.*, p. 26.
104. *Ibid.*, p. 18.
105. *Ibid.*, p. 128: "to elucidate the Pauline conception of original sin."
106. *Ibid.*
107. *Ibid.*, pp. 128-129: "he represents and incarnates the whole of humanity."
108. *Ibid.*, p. 128.
109. *Ibid.*, p. 129.
110. *Ibid.*, p. 208.
111. *Ibid.*
112. *Ibid.*, p. 209.
113. *Ibid.*, p. 211.

what we mean if we call this view a "realistic conception." Very clearly, the proponents have not meant a "realism" as we find in such figures as Shedd and Greijdanus. De Fraine, as a matter of fact, does cite the text in Hebrews 7 which speaks of the "loins of his ancestor" (v. 10) ;[114] yet what he seems to have in mind is something quite different from realism. He is concerned about the idea of a *representation* which also has a certain *reality*. This reality, however, is not the same as he finds in the so-called "mystical" interpretation, "in *whom* all men sinned." The latter conception of a sinning of "all men" in Adam must presuppose, according to De Fraine, a platonic notion of Adam. It must presuppose a view in which Adam is the "ideal" in which individual men "participate."[115] Having said that much, of course, the question of the *nature* of the representation, or the *reality intended,* is still very much with us.

"Realism" has spoken of an *immediate* relation to the sin of Adam, or a relation that is comprehended in him in a "realistic manner." Quite in contrast, the idea of a "corporate personality" speaks of a "representation," though it also continues to recognize the urgency in "realistic" problems. This is especially obvious in regard to the question of how we find "clarity," in the corporate idea, for the doctrine of original sin.[116] De Fraine, for example, points to the unity of the group and individual, and the sinning of "all men," and cites a text from the Apocalypse of Moses in which Eve complains that all sinners will curse her because she did not obey the commandment of the Lord and because all men must *therefore die.*[117] We must notice, however, that this is really a *complaint* and sheds no light at all on the significance of "corporate personality" for the original sin dogma. De Fraine takes a bow to the traditional doctrine and refuses to speak of the "one" and "all" as *merely* tied together in a "corporate unity." He affirms that in the *inclusion* of all in Adam there is also a certain *influence which Adam exerts on all.*[118]

But it seems to us that this idea of "causality" introduces a foreign element in the concept of a "corporate personality." For the presupposition in "corporateness" is an anti-individualistic

114. *Ibid.,* p. 130.
115. "A platonic view, which considers 'Adam' as a general idea, in which the individual men are the participation"; *ibid.,* p. 249.
116. "Elucidation" — *ibid.,* p. 128.
117. *Ibid.,* p. 130.
118. *Ibid.,* p. 250 ("a certain causality"); in contrast to Wheeler Robinson.

outlook on human living or a mysterious solidarity in all of
human relations. That very solidarity itself precludes an individual's isolating himself from his various relationships and
looking at himself "alone." If that be the case, however, it is
impossible to say how original sin is "explained." It seems obvious to us that Paul had a "corporate"-idea in mind when
he looked at both Adam and Christ; at the same time, that
very "corporativity" can never have the character of an *explanation*. The darkness of death and judgment on "all men" are
indicated in Paul, and we also hear of the "regnancy of death"
to which all men are now made subject. But Paul does not
explain the manner in which the sin of "one man" is transferred to "all men." Nowhere do we find the idea that the
universality of sin has something to do with the notion of procreation, or that procreation is the real *causa* of the spread of
man's sin. In such a view marriage and procreation are fused
together in a fallacious "causality" by means of the concept of
concupiscence. Paul, on the other hand, speaks of "all men"
as sinning in the *"one."* He sees the sovereignty of death in the
light of a relation that is *corporately defined;* moreover, in contrast to this sovereignty of death he speaks of the glory of
God's grace. No wonder, then, that Ridderbos frequently combines these ideas of *corporative* and *salvation-historical*.[119]

We have seen that Paul, in Romans 5, regards Christ as the
great initiator of "new humanity" in contrast to "Adamic
humanity." Now we must observe that he continues in that
same line in Romans 6 and considers the corporate "included-
ness" of the "many" in Christ. Salvation is described in corporate
terms as a "being crucified," in our old man, along with Christ
(6:6). Within the perspective of that reality Paul enjoins us
to be subject to Christ's kingly dominion (6:8, 9). No one
should think that his purpose, in these corporative expressions,
is merely "literary" or "stylistic." There is a *reality* that corresponds to this "being in Christ." Were this not the case there
could be no meaning in Paul's proclamation of "riches." As a
matter of fact, the power and reality of "corporateness" are
nowhere so evident as when he says that "one man has died for
all; therefore all have died" (II Cor. 5:14). Paul's insight here
has reference to the deep and unspeakable *reality of salvation*.
Therefore the "corporate" expressions do not betray a merely
subjective interpretation. There is no disjunction between our

119. Ridderbos, *Comm. op Romeinen*, pp. 125-131.

dying with Christ and Christ's own dying "for us."[120] So effective
and so real is Christ's dying "for us" that it naturally entails
a dying of ourselves "in him."[121]

It is clear that Paul's intention was not to "explain" the
universality of sin.[122] But it is also impossible to take Romans
5:12 ("because all men sinned") in the sense of Pelagius, Calvin,
and Brunner. For one finds nothing, in this text, of a later,
individual sinning. Obviously, Paul was quite aware of later,
personal sins; but he also saw the sin of "one man" as the sin
of "all." Within his corporative mode of thought it is entirely
impermissible to adopt the conclusions of *either realism or
federalism*. This is because realism converts the words of Paul
into an anthropological concept in which the corporative aspect
can only be cancelled out (speculatively) by an assumed "pre-
existence" in man's ur-reality. On the other hand, federalism
shows numerous similarities to the corporative idea but lies,
nonetheless, on a very different plane. That fact is evident
when the concept of "representation" is worked out (by means
of *imputatio*) in a concept of being "held responsible," in and
with Adam, for his first sin. In this being "held responsible"
(as a forensic judgment) the very idea of a "corporate reality"
is already rejected in principle. Moreover, this is surely the case
when we relate the *imputatio* to something which, as a matter
of fact, is *not real*.

Thus, with Ridderbos and others, we strongly accentuate
this corporative aspect. We cannot help saying that Paul had
in mind an undeniable connection and solidarity in death
and guilt. At the same time, he nowhere tries to *explain* this
solidarity in theoretical terms. Only in this light do we understand why there is nothing in Paul of that anxious problematic
which we find in the later discussions. We grant immediately
that there have always been those who have read this "problematic" back into Paul and have asked if we find in him a
fatum or a *Schicksal* which rests upon all men. Bultmann especially has found in him a "Gnostic" motive or the "consequence of a destiny (*Verhängnis*) for which mankind is not

120. Grosheide speaks (in reference to II Cor. 5:14) of "vicariousness" and
  "representation."
121. Christ's death, as it were, is a "juridical decision of God" which "impinges upon others and effectuates their death" (Wendland, *Comm.*,
  p. 177).
122. H. N. Ridderbos, *Comm.*

itself responsible."[123] But this is by no means the problem that really animated Paul.

The Apostle's attention was fastened on the triumphant and superabundant grace of God. For that reason there could be no fatalistic self-excuse. For that reason it is clear why constantly, on every hand, he renounces the idea of any self-excuse at all. With this statement, of course, we touch on the deepest heartstring of the biblical witness concerning the guilt of man. It is completely illegitimate, in any circumstances whatever, to excuse ourselves on the basis of a "causal" involvement in the relations or universality of guilt. Paul's persistent reference to "through one man" is not a gratuitous allusion which opens the possibilities of self-excuse. For the reality of the guilt of "all" is not erased in self-excuse but only in Jesus Christ. Paul's reference to the reign of death, in Romans 5:12, does not anticipate a later, individual sinning. It pictures the dark background against which the grace of God must always be seen. This background, however, does not permit us to "deduce" our sin from those "components" in terms of which we can also rationalize our guilt.

This brings us again to the well-known prophecy of Ezekiel. We could call the message of Ezekiel a rebuttal against the "causal" thinking of his contemporaries. In making this statement, of course, we are passing no judgment on the theme of "causality" *per se;* nor are we negating the interrelations in guilt or referring to these as non- or anti-causal. Ezekiel, however, takes issue with a certain kind of causal argument and repudiates it in a very telling manner. Both Ezekiel and Jeremiah renounce, in the most fervent terms, any attempt whatever to take recourse in near or distant relations between the generations. Both shed a religious light on the illegitimacy of this suggestion and apparently "logical" claim. Sometimes men have seen in these two prophets an individualizing tendency which presumably reared its head in Israel's later religion and even obscured the earlier "corporative" view of life. But others have rightly rejected this thought. Rowley, for example, has called it an exaggeration to refer to Jeremiah as the "father of individualism."[124]

---

123. Bultmann, *Theologie des N.T.,* p. 247; cf. *Z.N.T.W.,* 1959, p. 158.
124. "In no period of the life of Israel do we find extreme collectivism or extreme individualism, but a combination of both" (*The Faith of*

In Jeremiah we find an "individualistic" accent which is very far from one-sided. Witness the statement that "every one shall die for his own sin" (31:30) when combined with the assertion that God's judgment is visited from parents to sons and daughters (16:3ff.) .[125] The latter text reminds us of the second commandment. Yet in this same context of communal sin and judgment it is simply impossible to divest ourselves of all personal responsibilities. The people made the effort to do so and inquired, "Why has the Lord pronounced all this great evil against us? What is our iniquity? What is the sin that we have committed against the Lord our God?" (16:10) .[126] Jeremiah's answer was that their "fathers" had departed from the Lord. At the same time, it is added immediately: ". . . because *you* have done worse than *your fathers,* for behold, every one of you follows his stubborn evil will, refusing to listen to me" (16:12) . *Therefore* the judgment was coming and God would show no mercy (16:13) . Thus the real issue was the sin of Judah, engraved "with a point of diamond . . . on the tablet of *their heart"* and visible as a memoriam against *them* "beside every green tree, and on the high hills," and "on the mountains in the open country" (17:1-3) .[127]

Ezekiel criticized, as the spokesman of God, the illegitimate interpretation of God's judgments which were manifest in the interwovenness of sin and misery in successive generations.[128] Israel had completely misunderstood the proverb concerning "sour grapes" and the children's teeth that were "set on edge" (Ezek. 18:2) . She had failed to appreciate the validity of God's retributive justice. Therefore her confidence was shattered in what had formerly been an important element in her own religion. The ardor of a self-excuse now formed the real impulse in her criticism of God's activity. The slogan concerning "sour grapes" and the "children's teeth" was now transmogrified into a "derisive mockery which characterized in a curt and pithy

---

Israel, 1956, p. 99). Cf. also Vriezen, *Theologie van het O.T.,* 1954², p. 336.

125. On the punishment of Shemaiah and his descendants, cf. Jer. 29:32.
126. Cf. G. Ch. Aalders, *Jeremiah (K.V.),* I², 1953, p. 189, on the unconsciousness of any self-guilt.
127. The accentuation of the guilt of the people *now* is seen as all the more significant since Jeremiah both acknowledged in prayer the marvellous goodness of the Lord (32:17ff.) and yet spoke of the "guilt of fathers to their children after them" (32:18).
128. On Ezekiel, cf. P. J. Verdam, *op. cit.,* pp. 409f.

witticism the senselessness of putting confidence in God's justice."[129] Israel assumed that the reason for her plight was obvious: *the guilt of her fathers.* Therefore she concluded that her relation of friendship with Jahwe had come to an end. In earlier days it had seemed incontrovertible that God's judgments were manifest in successive generations; moreover, that fact had impressed upon "fathers" their tremendous responsibilities. This being the case, the judgment which cut across generations was no reason for Israel to cast a wary or suspicious eye on God's justice. Israel was constantly made aware of that "new way" in which God's grace is evident, even in the very passion of his judgment. For God's judgment on Israel was not a *fatum,* and Israel was not an "unwilling victim," innocent though impotent. Rather God's judgments were (as we see in the second commandment) a clear invitation to experience his ever-new promise which was constantly fulfilled for those who feared and loved the God of Israel.[130]

Thus it is not because of an "individualism" alone but because of a lost contact with Jahwe that Israel came to have an impersonal and fatalistic interpretation.[131] Therefore God's judgment, along the lines of the generations, was now conceived as an absurd and meaningless *fatum.* For that reason the contemptuous slogan which had seemed irrefutable, and had even won a kind of popular support, was forbidden by the decree of God himself (Ezek. 18:3). The way in which the people had used that proverb completely altered God's original intent. Moreover it did so to such an extent that the proverb itself was *false.* At the heart of that falsehood[132] was the attitude the people took toward this interrelatedness of guilt and judgment, which now was regarded in terms of a faithless "causality." Though Ezekiel inveighed against that attitude, he did not dismiss the lines of collective guilt. He reaffirmed the

---

129. W. Eichrodt, *Der Prophet Ezechiël,* I, 1959, 146.

130. Ex. 20:6; Deut. 5:9. One thinks of the "variated harmony" in God's self-designation, Ex. 34:6-7. Cf. also Num. 14:18. In line with that "harmony" the thrust of God's warning and promise is apparent in many ways. In Deut. 7:9-10 there is no word of judgment concerning the generations, but God "requites to their face those who hate him, by destroying them; he will not be slack with him who hates him, he will requite him to his face." Cf. Deut. 24:16, which is reverted back to in II Kings 14:5-6 (the acts of Amaziah).

131. Eichrodt, *op. cit.,* p. 147.

132. G. Ch. Aalders, *Ezechiël,* I, 1955, 296 ("volslagen onjuist").

familiar judgments of God. But he also recalled that those who reason causally at this juncture and naively "deduce" their misery from the sins of their "fathers" must hear anew the truth of this statement: "Every man shall die for his own unrighteousness."

Notice that Ezekiel, in answering this criticism of Israel, did not respond to the charge of God's "arbitrariness" by referring to his inscrutable "sovereignty." He exposed this appeal to what seemed to be very "true" in the light of the second commandment. Thereby he disclosed the propriety of God's judgment. The ways of God's righteousness were made very evident — therefore the man who is righteous "shall surely live" (18:9). If a son does not continue in the sins of his father he shall *not* die because of his father's unrighteousness (18:14-18).[133] Here, then, is Ezekiel's critique of the false notion of "causality" which Israel combined with her own allegedly "guiltless" state. In such a view the lines of connection were badly drawn. Therefore it is revealing that precisely in this chapter — and precisely *in* the ways of God's *judgment* — the purpose of God is now made manifest. "Have I any pleasure in the death of the wicked, says the Lord God, and not rather that he should turn from his way and live?" (18:23; cf. v. 32).

In the interlacement of guilt and judgment a new beginning is now made possible; furthermore, the judgment of God is related to that "new beginning."[134] Thus all fatalism is now eliminated. It is not by accident that the "individualism" of Ezekiel's prophecy does not exclude but rather *includes* (in a very pregnant sense) a vision of God's temple and the restoration of his people. Those who spoke in a faithless or a "causal"

133. This is very clearly set forth in Aalders, *loc. cit.*: "the solidarity of guilt finds its expression in the formula that innocent children are punished for the guilt of their sinful parents and forebears; but posterity is sucked along in the sin of the forefathers, and therefore they are *sinful children* on whom the sin of the fathers is visited."

134. It is obvious, time and again, that everything here depends on the manner in which God is seen in his acts of judgment. Entirely different from the "proverb" in the time of Jeremiah and Ezekiel is the experience of God's wrath "against us" because of the sins of the fathers, as expressed by Josiah (II Kings 22:13; II Chron. 34:21). Here the observance of God's judgment is bound up with the inquiry of God concerning the book of the law, which the fathers had not obeyed (II Kings 22:11-13). Cf. the relation between the guilt of the fathers and one's own guilt in Amos 2:4: "but their lies have led them astray, after which their fathers walked."

manner might well have convinced a number of people by using the proverb of Ezekiel 18. Yet they remained entrapped in the guilt of their old way. It was now made evident *how much* the teeth of the children were "set on edge." The very mode of God's judgment was a reminder of his summons to confess the sins of the fathers as well as one's own personal guilt.[135] Yet in that same judgment we hear the promise that — for those who do confess — he too will remember his covenant.[136]

As we have seen, the realism of Shedd and Greijdanus appealed to Ezekiel 18 to demonstrate that the accent in guilt is always, and *must ever be,* on man's own sin. Certainly, for our own part, we agree that Ezekiel's criticism is very important for any situation in which we reflect on man's responsibility and guilt. But realism concludes from the justice of God that "all men" participate in Adam's transgression in a very "real" and "physical" way. It is also assumed that it is only in this sense that the rule of Ezekiel 18 applies. Quite obviously, we cannot accept this definition. It is important that we never use the category of *causality* to cut ourselves free from guilt or to hide under the umbrella of "universal blame." We cannot escape our guilt: for universal guilt is manifest *in the modus of our guilt*. Furthermore, in this perspective of *our guilt* it is impossible to disparage the justice of God or to refer to his righteousness as caprice. This point, it seems to us, is the most crucial issue in any reflection on the guilt of *all mankind*.

There is a rather monotonous ring to the criticism of the original sin dogma throughout the course of the ages. The critics regard the question of guilt as an abstract problem, or a problem which (by means of the concept of *causality*) will introduce us to the "components" of our guilt. They then proceed to reject this "guilt" as falling outside the arena of our own

135. We recall the remarkable statement in Ps. 79:8: "Do not remember against us the iniquities of our forefathers; let thy compassion come speedily to meet us, for we are brought very low" — after which we read a prayer (v. 9) for the forgiveness of "our sins." (Cf. J. Ridderbos, *De Psalmen*, II, 1958, 306.)

136. Lev. 26:40: "But if they confess their iniquity and the iniquity of their fathers. . . ." Cf. v. 42. J. Scharbert ("Unsere Sünde und die Sünden unserer Väter," *Biblische Zeitschrift*, 1958, p. 23) also recalls Lam. 5:7, *"Our fathers* sinned, and are no more; and we bear their iniquities"; and 5:16, "The crown has fallen from our head; woe to us, for *we* have sinned." Also Ps. 106:6, and Neh. 9:2.

responsibility. But this sort of thinking should not be refuted by the argument that it is too individualistic; much rather, we should see that it takes place at a level at which we lose our moorings concerning the nature of man's guilt and revise our perspective into a "guilt-problem." Here, as we have already written, it is very obvious that every "explanation" of guilt, in the history of theology, must lead us to a self-excuse. In any explanation the components of sin are apparent; furthermore these are sufficient to make sin "rational." To understand all may not be to forgive all — but it is certainly to forgive very much.

This approach is not open to those who have heard the biblical indictment of man's guilt. We have seen that Calvin cautioned against an understanding of original sin which implies a punishment apart from man's *real sin*. In this same line we have observed the Gallican and Belgic Confessions, both of which refer to the reality of that corruption of man on which God's wrath is poured. But this is very different from an interpretation of Romans 5 which presupposes man's "later," individual sins. In any such view the Pauline conception of the "corporative" cannot be understood. Certainly it is evident that Paul, in using this idea, did not desire to "explain" man's original sin. He did not reiterate the false proverb of Ezekiel's own day. As a matter of fact, that proverb was now forbidden even for Paul. If Ezekiel's compatriots had known of Paul's words they could have lodged the same criticism against an "arbitrariness" as once they lodged. Only this time they could argue in terms of the Apostle Paul himself. In latching onto the concepts of "one" and "all," their ensuing problems could only be greater.

For this kind of causal reasoning has no place at all in the thinking of the Apostle. It is obvious that Paul was not concerned to give an analysis of the "components" of the world of sin and death. He pointed his finger at the "power" of death, but he also knew that that power was no *fatum*. His own preaching was motivated by the light of that "new way" which is paved by him whose grace is the theme of Romans 5 and of that entire book. Paul did not concern himself about the question of how sin is transferred from one person to another. At the same time, he knew of the "world of death" and the "sovereignty of death," and of being "in Adam" in contrast to being "in Christ."

Within the focus of that corporative and *heilshistorisch* antithesis, every concept of a "fatalism" is cut down. The criticisms of original sin show the very striking weakness of failing to recognize that *this confession* cannot be refuted on a merely theoretical basis. It cannot be touched apart from the arena of our faith. Therefore the doctrine has persisted, with renewed vibrancy, throughout the entire history of the Church. Only in the perspective of *Jesus Christ* is it understandable to *what extent* all fatalism is now excluded. As a matter of fact, if we start with a fictitiously "guiltless" situation we can only end up with an analysis of original sin which is rather similar to the proverb of Ezekiel's own day.

How should we answer the challenge that Romans 5 must lead us to a "realism"? We must notice, first, that metaphysical, anthropological and "realistic" ideas have always been wrongly deduced from a "corporative" mode of thought. On the surface, of course, there would seem to be a greater affinity between the "corporative" and "representative" ideas; also, this fact would seem to be apparent when we hear of a "representation" as a means of "clarifying" the relation between the "all" and the "one." Yet it remains the case that federalism, as well as realism, is lacking in the Reformed confessions. Furthermore, in federalism the idea of a "representation" is linked together with *imputatio* in a manner which leaves the impression that the unguilty are merely "declared" to be guilty. Thus the problem that concerned Calvin is very real: the chasm between the guilt of man and the punishment of God.

Some theologians have retreated, at this juncture, to the unfathomable justice of God. They have said that here we must hold our peace and make no further inquiry. Thus it would seem to be the case that inherited *guilt* is originally a *peccatum alienum* and that only thereafter, on the basis of this guilt, a *peccatum proprium* is added as the product of our own personal sins. But the fact that Greijdanus and others could not endorse this view is very understandable and says something important for our own present study. For when we go in that direction we cannot escape the thought of a twofold guilt or a dual causality.

One finds traces of that view in the Consensus of 1675. There an abstract and independent doctrine of imputation is proposed. The period of a "chasm" in the confession of guilt is very apparent. Thus the correlation of guilt and the confession of guilt is maintained in principle but can hardly be made clear. This same criticism holds for the Catholic view of original sin as a sin of nature and for every Protestant revision of that thought. Frequently the accent on the relation between guilt and punishment (or punishment and guilt) is not so obvious as we have already noted in Calvin. For that reason the danger of a merely theoretical knowledge of *peccatum alienum* casts its shadows on the depths of our confession of guilt. It continues to weaken our resistance against all fatalism.

We have said above that Paul did not open the floodgates of fatalism but closed them more tightly than ever before. Along with him, we can only appreciate that the gravity of guilt and apostasy from God, and the disruption of our fellowship with God, can never be "fathomed." Nor can the processes of man's universal guilt be completely laid bare. Romans 5 does not suggest the possibilities for that. At the same time, we must notice that Paul was not intrigued by the "problematic" which Bultmann and others have laid on his account. The fact that this is lacking in Paul is not owing, of course, to his impeccable analysis of human history; nor does it depend on some theory which discloses the "secret" of all of history. It depends on the certainty of salvation which now has come. Only *at this point* can we find the immeasurable powers which save a man from his own most grievous and most heinous and most ultimate sin. That is to say, it is only *here* that we can find salvation from our own *desires to excuse ourselves*.

These desires have always played a dominant role in the history of the original sin disputes. This is the case (whether implicitly or explicitly) from the time of Pelagius until our own day. In the Pelagian view the guiltlessness of man was simply assumed and was taken as the *a priori* starting-point. Great emphasis was laid on the guilt of those "actual sins" for which God's grace was necessary; at the same time, an "outlet" was provided in the thought of an uncontaminated nature. This thought recurs in other discussions concerning the nature of man throughout the centuries. Nevertheless, when we deduce the universality or spread of sin from man's sensual nature (or "created nature," in the manner of Schleiermacher), the element of a self-excuse is again apparent and the full gravity of sin is once again obscured. This is the case even if we accentuate,

in the strongest terms, the communal character of sin.[137] Ritschl
followed this pattern and exchanged the doctrine of original
sin for his own conception of the "sinful realm" (the *"Reich
der Sünde"*) .[138] Here he tried to go beyond Pelagius and spoke
of the "indescribable entanglement of sinful acts" in the "Kingdom of Sin."[139] Ritschl contended that this latter concept brings
to a proper expression everything "rightly envisioned in the
concept of original sin."[140] It is obvious, however, that this
psychological or sociological theory achieves as little as Pelagius'
own view in illuminating the communal character of guilt.[141]

In all these efforts the *contra*-character of sin, or the enigmatic contradiction of God's goodness and love, must lose its
very contrariety. The enigma of sin is lost in the relations of
human and rational psychology.[142] The attempt is now made
to throw light on the concepts of *causality* and its resultant *universality*. Yet, can there be an "explainable continuity"? In this
very question we are tempted to overstep the boundaries of our
faith and to put to nought the confession of our guilt.[143]

If this be the case, however, we can hardly avoid the ques-

137. Schleiermacher, *Der christliche Glaube*, I, 1846, 363: "the communal
act and the communal guilt of the human race." Cf.: "in each the
work of all and in all the work of each" (336).
138. Sharp criticism has been levelled against Schleiermacher's doctrine of
sin by E. Brunner, *Die Mystik und das Wort*, 1924 (Chap. 10, "Die
Sünde als Atavismus und als Schuld"; on original sin, especially pp.
238ff.). Brunner sees in this a naturalistic *explanation* of original sin
(239).
139. A. Ritschl, *Die christliche Lehre von der Rechtfertigung und Versöhnung*, II, 1883², 314.
140. *Ibid.*, p. 320.
141. Althaus, *Die christliche Wahrheit*, II, 1948, 131. Ritschl himself recognizes, to be sure, that we have "no complete and clear conception of
the extension of these effects."
142. Cf. Schleiermacher on the punishment of sin (*op. cit.*, I, 370-371).
143. In the nature of the case, no injustice is done in this way to acknowledging the influence of sins on others. Scripture points repeatedly to
the powerful influence of sin in human relations, as well as the influence of good and evil example. If Pelagius had only indicated this
much, he would have gone down in a different light in the history of
the Church. We recall the example of Jeroboam, who caused Israel to
commit sin (I Kings 15:26, 30), and Paul's statement: "Bad company
ruins good morals" (I Cor. 15:33). But this "influence" for evil does
not suggest an explanation of universality. It presupposes that universality instead, and sheds light on the tremendous dynamic *within*
the reality of sin.

tion: Is there really an adequate reason for speaking of an "original" sin or "hereditary" guilt? Can this terminology, unscriptural as it is, give a valid expression to the biblical indictment against man's sin? Is this a proper or even intelligible translation of the divine indictment against "all men"? Is there room for a response to that indictment in the confession of man's guilt? Can the term *original sin* give a reasonable resistance to our constant dilemma, in doctrine and confession, to fashion a causal and "biological" explanation for the universality of guilt? Especially in our own day the ineptitude of this term has often been a topic of concern. P. A. van Stempvoort, for one, has spoken of this "rather confusing term."[144] Otto Weber, for another, has remarked that the concept of *peccatum haereditarium* is really unintelligible.[145]

It simply will not do to construe these objections, in an *a priori* fashion, as the efforts to tone down or vitiate the Church's confession on the universality of guilt. The criticisms, very frequently, are not levelled because of a lack of appreciation for the full seriousness of sin. Much rather, there is an earnest desire to eliminate all needless misunderstanding. We too, in our discussions above, have warned against misunderstanding and have done so from various points of view. Thus it is futile to deny that the words *original sin* or *hereditary sin* have frequently led, and continue to lead, to a number of confusions. It is obvious why some people have concluded, as they think of "heredity," that we are really concerned about a biological "inheritance" of sin. This, then, becomes the "parallel" to a number of other attributes which parents "bestow" upon their children.

That concept is very strong in times in which scientific research investigates and discovers the various "laws of heredity." The peril is real to interpret the Church's confession as a specific form of that "inheritance." Bavinck, as a matter of fact, once saw the increasing knowledge of heredity as an unexpected support for the Church's doctrine of original sin; at the same time, we should observe his immediate and radical disqualification. "Heredity," he said, is something very different from "original" or "hereditary" sin.[146] Therefore Bavinck could speak of the "support" of science, which we gratefully acknowl-

144. Van Stempvoort, *De Mens en Ik*, 1959, p. 169.
145. Weber, *Grundlagen der Dogmatik*, I, 674.
146. Bavinck, *Geref. Dog.*, III, 96.

edge, since the study of heredity enables us to know mankind as a physical and ethical organism and removes an apparent inconsistency in the original sin doctrine. Nonetheless, heredity can never "explain" original sin. The propagation of sin is always a very "difficult problem," since sin is no substance which can be "passed on" by means of a generating act.[147]

If one approaches "original sin" in terms of "heredity" he may certainly presume a more or less rational phenomenon, observable or analyzable in terms of its various constituents. But it is obvious, in that case, that we find ourselves on a very different level of discussion from the confession of *our original sin.* Thus, when Iwand warns emphatically against this view, it is evident that he does not set up a straw man. One may conclude, in that way, that original sin can be known on empirical lines and by means of the natural light of reason. It is then impossible to escape the danger of a full or partial elimination of our guilt. The reality of guilt is then assigned a place alongside other "rational relations" in our lives. Certainly we can say that this is not the background or the content of the Church's confession of original sin. The doctrine is not concerned about a biological or sociological "causal nexus." In the words of Iwand, "We doubt that the origin or the meaning of our doctrine lies at that point."[148]

In other words, it is impossible to explain or illustrate the original sin dogma in the light of heredity. Sin (including original sin) is not a rationally analyzable phenomenon; it can only be known and confessed in relation to God. Therefore Bavinck has said that we must take our starting-point in the *fact* of original sin. Furthermore, that fact is the basis on which the concept of "hereditary" sin must rest and to which, in turn, it points.[149] Bavinck has added, to be sure, that the study of heredity brings us into contact with "all kinds of evil inclinations, bad habits, and qualities which display an hereditary character." Thus it refers us back again to the concept of original sin. In that case, our investigation corroborates the

---

147. *Ibid.,* 97. Besides in his Dogmatics (III, 89-97), Bavinck discusses heredity extensively in his *Bijbelse en religieuze Psychologie,* 1920, pp. 132ff. Here he emphasizes that original sin and the heredity of characteristics are by no means the same (p. 135). Cf. J. Waterink, *Erfelijkheid en Opvoeding,* 1935.

148. H. J. Iwand, "Sed originale per hominem unum," *Ev. Theol.,* 1946, pp. 26f.

149. Bavinck, *op. cit.,* p. 139.

reality of apostasy as it comes to expression in the course of each new generation. The connections that are evident in heredity themselves evince the depths and the breadth of man's own solidarity in guilt.

Emil Brunner, too, has spoken, in this connection, of "one of the manifestations of the solidarity of sin." He finds that manifestation in the "coherence of individuals through physical descent, which, inscrutable as it may be to us, is forced upon us by experience."[150] All of sin, qua sin, is known in relation to God alone and is seen as rebellion, disobedience, and apostasy. Sin is manifest in those disruptions of human life which are evident in the course of generations; yet original sin *cannot be clarified* in terms of that conception of heredity. The dismal path of sin, in the process of heredity, can never explain or excuse the sins of man; as a matter of fact, it can only be the symptom and the manifestation *of his sin*. Therefore, if we view heredity as a background for "original sin," or original sin as the "explanation" for the universality of guilt, we can only do an injustice to the deepest motive in the Church's confession.

This term *hereditary sin* came into our theological jargon at a time in which there was, as yet, no intensive examination of the laws of heredity. The purpose was to indicate the continuity of sin in the process of the generations. This was a continuity which Brunner has called the *"Dauer-revolution,"* or a "permanent revolution," or a revolution that is characterized by constancy.[151] We could argue over the question of whether these terms *original sin* (with the accent on "origin") and *hereditary sin* (with the accent on "heredity") do not land us *necessarily* in a misunderstanding and a causal-biological "explanation." But it is evident that these terms do not call forth the same sorts of emotional responses in all ages. Nevertheless, when men direct their attention increasingly to biological phenomena of heredity, the peril is real that we end up on an entirely wrong track in our analysis of "original" or "hereditary" sin. In that event, we miss the true heart of the Church's confession of her guilt.[152] Even if we take this reference to "inheritance" as an illustration of our "original sin," we cannot eliminate all mis-

---

150. Brunner, *Der Mensch im Widerspruch*, 1937, p. 138.
151. *Ibid.*, p. 146.
152. We find this already, it seems to me, in Kierkegaard's analysis of original sin, where he does insufficient justice to decisive motives in the time of the Reformation. Cf. his *The Concept of Dread*.

understanding. For the analogy of "inheritance" can still imply that "original sin" is fatal and can still exclude a view of our *own guilt*.[153] Once we go in that direction we will find it impossible to say that the confession of original sin is really an answer to God's indictment.

We admit, therefore, that the term *original sin* in itself (*hereditary sin*) is very far from clear. It is subject to a number of misunderstandings. Yet, the mere criticism of the term should not imply a lack of appreciation for the real depths of man's own sin. Furthermore, the fact of man's own guilt is very much in the center of discussion in a large number of original sin conceptions. Our guilt must not be relativized by an explanation of the "components" of *our guilt*. At the same time, it is manifest that the Church's confession has differed immensely from the notion of a fatal calamity or a natural and self-evident "inheritance" of evil. The doctrine of original sin has nothing to do with a "legacy" or a "heritage" which comes "upon us," willy-nilly, come what may. It is not isolated from our own action. Thus those of a critical bent have often misinterpreted this doctrine. Brunner, for example, has written that "the 'scandal' of the ecclesiastical doctrine . . . consists in this, that we are made responsible for a sin which another man has committed."[154]

One hears a very different note in the confession of his guilt. For in confession we refuse to take our flight in the *peccatum alienum*. Nevertheless, it is necessary to say that the terms *original sin* and *hereditary sin* do not do justice to the essence of what we confess concerning the nature of *our sin*. Instead of a sin "originally inherited" we should point to the *guilt-character of all sin*. When the Church spoke of "original" and "hereditary" she meant to lay bare the overpowering and the total character of sin. She meant to underscore the theme of man's own impotence. This could only imply the impossibility of man's escaping to some "area" untouched by his own guilt. In opposition to Pelagius, the Church maintained that there is no such "area" in human nature; that is to say, there is no such "area" which makes it possible for man to perform perpetually "good acts." Yet, the Church wished to avoid any hint of

153. Cf. H. Urs von Balthasar, *Die Gottesfrage des heutigen Menschen,* 1956, pp. 174f.
154. Brunner, *op. cit.,* p. 137.

fatalism or compulsion. For that reason she pointed to a bondage *in* one's guilt and a being guilty *in* one's bondage.

E. Kinder has tried to articulate this thought by introducing the words "*Schuld und Verhängnis*" (*guilt and fate*).[155] The crucial category, in his judgment, is certainly *guilt*. Therefore he has rightly added that a man is "guilty in his compulsory enchainment."[156] In our judgment, the words *compulsory* and *fate* can only lead us in a wrong direction; at the same time, the intention of Kinder is certainly proper and is very evident in his reference to the captivity of sin. ". . . Everyone who commits sin is a slave to sin" (John 8:34). Kinder has correctly written, in reference to this text, that "both the 'doing' and the 'being a slave' are simultaneous."[157] Thus the issue is the *guilt* of the *servum arbitrium*, which has nothing to do with a "fatalism." The distressing nature of the *servum arbitrium* is seen in *this slavery*, or the guilt of *this bondage*, or the *utter incapacity* of man to help himself and "do something else."[158] On the other hand, the astonishing liberty of Christ is only seen as the great light which now has come in the midst of this abysmal darkness.[159]

The connection (or identity) of guilt and bondage makes clear that the term *original sin*, in itself, is not adequate to give a full picture of the reality of guilt.[160] This does not mean a watering down of the gravity of guilt but an *accentuation* of guilt in the form of a confession. It is evident, we should judge, that this motive has played an important role in the discussions of the Church, especially where the relation between sin and punishment has rightly been conceived. That fact is seen repeatedly, throughout the history of the Church, wherever the orthodox doctrine has determined to hold firmly to the "*culpa-*

155. E. Kinder, *Die Erbsünde*, 1959, p. 69.
156. *Ibid.* On the "Zwangshaftigkeit der Sünde," cf. p. 68.
157. *Ibid.*
158. On this "incompacity," cf. my *Divine Election*, 1960, pp. 48ff., and the scriptural references cited there. Cf. especially Rom. 6:6. In this slavery man *loses* himself to sin, and therein he is guilty. Christ discloses this profound reality with the words "truly, truly" (John 8:34).
159. John 8:36. This liberation or freedom is also an omnipotent and therefore gracious redemption (*exagorázō*). Gal. 3:13.
160. Kinder recalls Luther's "Personsünde" and remarks that the expression "original sin" is "insufficient by itself alone." "No single concept is sufficient, by itself alone, to give full expression to the whole of this uncanny reality of 'sin'" (*loc. cit.*).

character of original sin."[161] Hence the accent on the impossibility of "clarifying" our guilt in the light of the *propagatio*-idea. Such an attempt is congenial to fatalism but never to man's *guilt*.

It was this motive of guilt that played an important role in the Reformation, in contrast to the Roman idea of original sin as a "sin of nature." At times it even influenced the exegesis of Romans 5:12. Thus men interpreted this text wrongly by pointing to later, individual sins as a means of eliminating entirely the *peccatum alienum*. We have said that such an exegesis is invalid; at the same time, its motive is very right. Furthermore, that motive is the only refutation for those who criticize the confession of original sin. Even in the concept of *imputatio* there has often been an effort to repudiate all fatalism in the Church's teaching.[162] Yet, because "imputation" implies an alien guilt, it has always been possible (via this detour) to come to that same old problem as we have already noted above. Furthermore, the problem is intensified by the parallel to forensic justification and its completely gratuitous "as if." Realism alone has rejected this implication consistently and entirely. *Imputatio*, however, is unable to give an answer to the obvious objection that not all are regarded as *sinners* though "*all have sinned.*"[163]

The term *corporative*, when seen in this light, cannot be taken as a magic formula or a panacea for solving the problems of "communal guilt." Yet this concept does lead us beyond the options of "realism" and "federalism." It points to the inescapability of universal guilt, which can only be contemplated in the focus of the cross and God's judgment upon man's sin. In that perspective man's sin is no longer seen as *peccatum alienum*. Rather, it is both known and confessed as *peccatum proprium*. That is to say, it is both known and confessed as *man's own*.

---

161. O. Weber, *op. cit.*, 667.

162. "Hence orthodoxy went in the direction of grounding the culpa-character of original sin in a kind of divine imputation" (O. Weber, *op. cit.*, 667). The complications that were sometimes apparent are evident in Joh. à Marck, *Het Merch der Chr. Godtgeleertheit*, 1705, pp. 437ff., who taught imputation but also called Adam's sin, at the same time, *our* sin (439); furthermore he tried to show that imputation is not unjust. Human laws also permit this in certain cases, according to à Marck, "notwithstanding the particular law in Deuteronomy 24:16" (438). Meanwhile, Ezekiel and Jeremiah are to be interpreted as "a gracious cessation or softening of God's most rigid justice" (439).

163. One of the main arguments of Greijdanus.

Therefore the confession of original sin is not a lamentation of a strange burden which we bear against our will. It does not imply an alien charge which is levelled against us because of our "heredity." It does not suggest that in the face of that charge we are only impotent. It does imply that we are delivered from the labyrinth of self-excuse. One can say, with no hesitance at all, that the Church has constantly groped for this acknowledgment of guilt and has constantly underscored this attitude as her only sure confession. As we see in her formularies, her intention has never been to "explain" man's actual or universal guilt. When faced with such an option (as in the case of Pelagius) [164] she has spoken of a lack of appreciation for the depth and gravity of sin. She has sought to refute the notion that sin is spread in the manner of *imitatio* and has proposed, instead, the idea of *propagatio*. That term, of course, has given rise to much discussion and misunderstanding. Yet it remains a fact that this answer is found not only in the Council of Trent but in such a document as the Canons of Dort.[165]

Thus we find two terms which can certainly be very misleading. One could conclude that a reaction to the one "explanation" (viz., *imitatio*) might lead us to another (viz., *propagatio*). In that way we could point to procreation itself as the source of man's infection. Here we remember the *transfusum* of Trent[166] but also the following expression in the Canons of Dort: "Man after the fall begat children in his own likeness. A corrupt stock produced a corrupt offspring."[167] None-

---

164. Kierkegaard typified Pelagianism in the following terms: "that every man plays his own small history on his own small stage without deriving anything from humanity" *(The Concept of Dread).*

165. Cf. Trent on the "peccatum Adae"—"quod origine unum est et *propagatione, non imitatione* transfusum omnibus inest unicuique proprium" (Denz., 790). Canons, III-IV, 2: the corruption of Adam has come upon all his posterity "not by imitation, as the Pelagians of old asserted, but by the propagation of a vicious nature" ("...non per *imitationem* sed per vitiosae naturae *propagationem* derivata").

166. Besides Denz., 790, see further the "transfudisse," 789, and the expressions in which the error is pointed up; viz. "nihil ex Adam *trahere* originalis peccati." Already in the year 418 this "nihil trahere" was repudiated (Denz., 102). Here *regeneration* was set over against *generation;* the baptism of children takes place "ut in eis regeneratione mundetur, quod generatione traxerunt" *(ibid.).* Cf. also Denz., 795: "homines...nisi ex semine Adae propagati nascerentur non nascerentur iniusti, cum ea propagatione per ipsum, dum concipiuntur propriam iniustitiam contrahant."

167. Canons, III-IV, 2. Terminologically, one should not force an essential

theless, it is clear that the purpose of this statement is to emphasize the continuity in guilt and to accentuate that deeper relations inhere in guilt than are possibly enunciated in Pelagius' *imitatio*-doctrine. Therefore the spotlight is turned on man himself and his *own sinful nature*. There is a reference to the advancement of generations as the manner in which the guilt of "all men" is made known. In the concept of *propagatio* the sphere is indicated within which the power of sin and death is manifest and experienced as inescapable reality. Yet, the "continuity" is not explained as an obvious or anthropologically lucid reality. Such an explanation is what Pelagius had in mind; therefore he spoke of an "undefiled nature." On the other hand, it is not what the advocates of the *propagatio* intended. One could get that impression and could even argue that the substitution of *propagatio* for *imitatio* can never bring us to a greater clarity. This is because *imitatio* in itself is conceived as an "explanation" for the universality of sin.[168] At the same time, in repeated contexts, it is evident that the Church's reference to *propagatio* was not a causal deduction of sin from the notion of progeneration as such. Therefore it was never proposed as the real *"causa"* of man's infection.

Even the Reformation used this idea of *propagatione, non imitatione*.[169] Ever since that time men have struggled to make clear that this concept does not entail a causal necessity.[170] The

difference between the "transfusum" of Trent and a good many Protestant formulas. Cf. K. J. Popma, *Levensbeschouwing*, 1958, p. 79: the fallen humanity and broken humanity of our first forebears has passed over to their posterity and has "flowed through and pervaded all their descendants." A fuller explanation of this thought is not given.

168. K. Rahner comments, in regard to Trent, that there were "rather unclear conceptions" on the issue of "why and how the *generatio, propagatio* transmits original sin" ("Theologisches zum Monogenismus," in *Schriften zur Theologie*, I, 1954, 270). The statements cited by Rahner are very telling: "propagatione et libidine in ordinata transfunditur, caro corrupta, contrahitur ex carne infecto." Rahner judges that most commentators have understood propagation "in the Augustinian sense of the corruption of the flesh through a libidinous generation, as the chief cause of the guilt-infection of the soul" (271). But he also regards this matter as by no means "defined." So also De Fraine, *De Bijbel en het Ontstaan van de Mens*, 1953, p. 82, who points out that the words "propagatione et libidine in ordinata transfunditur" were rejected (as a proposed formulation) in the case of Joannes de Salazar.

169. Calvin characterizes Pelagius, for example, in the following words: "per imitationem, non propaginem" (*Inst.*, II, 1, 5).

170. One might comment on the complicated explanations of A. Kuyper

intention in these words is to indicate the universality of man's being-a-sinner *within* his actual sinning. Therefore *propagatio* is seen as the way in which the unanimity and solidarity of guilt are manifest. In the Reformation these thoughts were not tied up with the notion of *concupiscentia* as the dreary background for the advancement of generations. There was, as a matter of fact, a rejection of any long shadows that fell on marriage itself as a divine institution. Anyone who combined (in a mysterious ambivalence) the glory of marriage and the bleakness of these shadows could only ignore the concept of an "ongoing guilt" and could only come automatically to a Gnostic reinterpretation of "infection" (*caro corrupta*). Thus he could only open the door to a final self-excuse.[171]

It is obvious, of course, that the Reformers did not wish to go in that direction.[172] But for that very reason it is necessary to understand the terminology of *propagatione, non imitatione* in its full polemical intent. In modern Catholic circles, in criticism of Augustine, we find this same sort of aversion to a causal

(*Loci Theologica*, III, "De Peccato," Par. 6). On the one hand there is a reference to the *arcanum* that can never be entirely fathomed (p. 87), and the impossibility of the propagation of sin through the body, or through the soul, or by means of the *actio conceptionis* (87). On the other hand there is a *sinful disposition* which is hereditary (89); and we also find a number of analogies which nevertheless purport to clarify the propagation of sin (92). Finally there is a discussion of *rebirth*, which creates no problem, in this connection, for the subject of propagation; for there is both a "natural" and a "supernatural" life, and children are conceived and born in the "natural" (93). So also Joh. à Marck, *op. cit.*, p. 440.

171. How much these questions have captivated thinking on the topic of original sin is apparent in the complicated view of Kierkegaard, in his *The Concept of Dread*, and the criticism of Bohlin (in J. M. Hasselaar, *Erfzonde en Vrijheid*, 1953, pp. 161ff.).

172. Olavi Lähteenmäki has recalled that Luther wrote, with a view to Ps. 51:7, that we do not read "mater mea peccavit, cum conciperet me," but "ego in peccatis conceptus sum." Marriage was a "magnus thesaurus," for Luther, though it was not exempt from the power of sin. See Lähteenmäki, *Sexus und Ehe bei Luther*, 1955, p. 49. Cf. Calvin's exegesis of Ps. 51:7, to which we have already referred: "neque enim parentes suos accusat David." In this connection Calvin takes issue with the notion that original sin can be limited "ad inferiorem animae partem et crassos appetitus"; and in reference to the *modus quo*, he warns against an entering into labyrinths. In this light we should also read those occasionally very strong expressions in the *Institutes* which run parallel to the Roman Catholic statements as noted above: "omnes ergo qui ab impuro semine descendimus" (*Inst.*, II, 1, 5).

explanation. One finds, for example, a commendation of virginity on other grounds from those which cast long shadows on marriage itself.[173]

One must always be on guard against depreciating, or devaluating, or perverting God's gifts. Therefore it is necessary to state that "original sin" is not a tragical lot or a curse which coincides with *propagatio*. A valid confession must point us to nothing but to sin itself in all its universality and tragic unanimity. Pelagius, when he looked at that unanimity,[174] could only lay hold on such concepts as "imitation," "environment," and the "influence of an evil example." Yet the unfathomable depths of sin, in the course of the generations, are not made known to us by empirical analysis but only by the strength of the divine indictment itself revealed in the *via dolorosa* of him on whom the "iniquities of all were laid" (Isa. 53:6).[175] There, and there alone, do we speak, and must we speak, of a *peccatum alienum*. There, and there alone, do we see the full reality of him who was "made to be sin" on our behalf (II Cor. 5:21).

In other words, it is not a flight from "demonstrable relations" but an insight into the full reality of guilt when we firmly confess that sin remains for us a riddle. Sin is a riddle in

173. This occurs also in line with official ecclesiastical pronouncements on virginity. The encyclical "Sacra virginitas" (1954) refers to the Council of Gangra which rejected the idea "that a virgin or someone who lives in abstinence renounces marriage as though it were objectionable (a matrimonio tamquam abominando), and not because of the beauty and sanctity of virginity (pulchritudo et sanctitas)." Cf. *Eccl. Doc.*, p. 19. See also P. Schoonenberg on the meaning of virginity, *Het Geloof van ons Doopsel*, III, 1958, 39f.; and *Theologisch Woordenboek* (Brink), II, *s.v.* "maagdelijkheid" — against all depreciation of marriage; p. 3046. Here the canonical statement on marriage also (contra: "statum conjugalem anteponendum esse statui virginitatis vel coelebatus"; Denz., 980) is said to have nothing to do with a devaluation. It seems to me that the "pulchritudo" and "sanctitas" are not entirely perspicuous, since there is not only a reference to the "ontic precedence of all this world" (Schoonenberg, III, 43, in regard to I Cor. 7), but also to a virginity within Mary's marriage to Joseph (42). It stands to reason that here the whole of Mariology is open for discussion. Schoonenberg, however, strongly accentuates the messianic or eschatological virginity. Cf. *Theol. Woordenboek*, II, 3047, on the "greater value" of virginity, as allegedly stated by Trent, in preference to marriage. (See, however, the canon cited.)

174. Cf. John. 7:48ff.: "Have *any* of the authorities or of the Pharisees believed in him?"

175. Cf. K. J. Popma, *op. cit.*, I, 82: it must always be repeated "that misery can only be visible from the gratitude of salvation."

all its universality. The riddle cannot be solved through rational explanations and speculative cognitions.[176] Here we must see that the real heart in every dispute on original sin is this question: Does God impute a *peccatum alienum?* Yet precisely *that* is the unfathomable *mystery of God's being "for us."* In the light of this mystery the guilt of all men is laid bare as a woeful and universal reality. We see that guilt as the riddle of man's sin, which can only remain a riddle when we observe the guilt of man in terms of the goodness and graciousness of God. For man's guilt is a measureless darkness in contrast to him in whom there is "no darkness at all."

This divine indictment against self-deceit and self-excuse is not an objective "pronouncement" in which a man can only acquiesce. It is not a mysterious "dictum" which cannot be understood. For precisely in and with the Gospel the indictment of God now comes to resound in the confession of man's guilt. Guilt is not preached to us as a foreign element or a distant reality but is underscored *within* the relations of our living. In the reality of guilt the disruption of our sin is obvious in our standing before God and our attitudes toward ourselves and our fellowmen. Guilt is made obvious in man's lostness *in his sin.* Therefore it is understandable, within this circle of sin, why Pelagius was intrigued by the notion of *imitatio* and Ritschl by the "Kingdom of Sin." Therefore, too, we can understand why men, in a number of ways, and a flurry of evidence, have always tried to explain the origin and spread of sin. No single area of life is left untouched by this universal and alienating power of sin. In every cranny of *reality* we experience that a docetic hamartiology is a radical depreciation of evil. Yet, within this universal scope of sin, we do not find a "fatalism" but only the power of the *servum arbitrium* and its disastrous effects.

Every effort to explain the unanimity of sin, in terms of its "components," can only demonstrate still further the nature of God's indictment.[177] This is always the case until our confession is heard and we appreciate how very serious the indictment is. We then see how desperately "all men" have need of salvation and healing. Confession does not ignore the solidarity of guilt

176. Iwand, *op. cit.,* p. 37.
177. There is an element of truth in R. Prenter's statement on original sin (*Schöpfung und Erlösung,* I, 1958, 267): "It expresses the impossibility of penetrating, by means of thought, the reality signified by this word. If this is not adhered to, sin, irresistibly, is either explained or denied."

but recognizes that precisely in this solidarity our sin is our *very own* and our need is for *God's pardon*. Unfortunately, in many discussions of original sin today the urgency of this point is no longer acknowledged. Original sin is seen as a factual "datum" or a situation which, once it arose, is now "with us." Therefore original sin is merely viewed as the "status" of the human race. In that way it is severed from the correlation of sin and forgiveness. All of this, moreover, is especially pertinent for those who speak of a "twofold guilt" and who give a separate treatment to each of these "parts." They can only tie forgiveness to one's "actual sins" and real perversity, in contrast to an "inherited guilt" which rests, out of reach, in our past.

We have said that the Belgic Confession speaks of *our* original sin in strongly confessional tones and regards our sin as subject to God's judgment. But it speaks of the *forgiveness of our sins* in exactly this same way. Article 15 affirms that even a life atoned for by Christ's death will continue to be in the throes of a conflict. Original sin is not "altogether abolished or wholly eradicated even by baptism." Much ado, of course, has been spent on these words, especially in regard to the power and the function of baptism. Yet, when we get bogged down at that point we too easily lose sight of the very lucid language concerning the forgiveness of *our original sin*. For *our* forgiveness is the forgiveness of God. It is the "casting away" of guilt by God's own "grace and mercy" and the "setting us apart" from the solidarity of "Adamic" and universal blame. Therefore the question of Otto Weber makes eminently good sense: "Is it, perhaps, the case that the ecclesiastical doctrine of original sin still takes too narrow a view of *God's grace?* . . . Is it not the case that we can only speak of *peccatum originale* as the sin from which we have 'come away' or on which, as it were, we ought to *look back* 'in Jesus Christ'?"[178]

One can only answer, of course, with "fear and trembling." Yet in the light of Article 15 he can only answer in the affirmative. He who conceives of an "area" where guilt remains (in an irreparable factuality) along with the forgiveness of "actual" or "concrete" sins, fails miserably to understand the jubilee of Romans 5 and the real nature of God's pardon. For *God* forgives despite that which *we* must see as irreparable in its factual reality. God forgives with a pardon which tramples our sins

178. Weber, *op. cit.*, 669.

under foot and which casts them into the sea. He remembers them no more and no longer assigns them to our account.[179] Therefore we cannot look back on our original sin as a "fatality." Nevertheless, this very impossibility is only apparent when we see that the divine indictment regards our sin as *peccatum proprium*.

When we take stock of the way on which we have come it is obvious that the burning issue in the original sin disputes has always been the so-called "scandal" of this doctrine. In most cases the scandal is viewed as a kind of fatality that is manifest in the imputation of an "alien guilt." The relations between communal guilt and "propagation" have cancelled out the reality of guilt in our own present time and our own personal living. Does not a guilt in the past (with its consequences in the present) exclude the full guilt-character of *my sinning today*? Is there a way to a genuine confession?[180] Very obviously, the answer to these questions is very important for the whole of Christian living. Determinism eliminates all comfort in the doctrine of election; so too it sweeps away all true confession in the doctrine of our sin. Life is then analyzed, apart from confession, in terms of a fatality.

Too often this happens not only in regard to our guilt and responsibility but also in regard to the sovereignty of death which now has passed to "all men." Thus people have tried to fashion theories which deal with this "inexorable sovereignty of death." At the same time, by so doing they have merely shown

179. The intent of BC, Art. 15, is obvious from the history of this text. After it was stated in the original text that baptism did not take away original sin, but that this sin is not imputed to the children of God, the words "not altogether (abolished)" were inserted in 1566. No crucial modification was here made; for the intention was to remove all misunderstanding concerning a "powerless" baptism — a misunderstanding which the original text might possibly have roused. Indeed, this whole view of forgiveness and non-imputation of original sin hangs together with the manner in which original sin is here confessed (cf. above, Chap. 15). But this in no way detracts from the importance of this doctrine.

180. One thinks of Augustine's term, "antiquum peccatum." "Inter omnia quae in hac vita possidentur, corpus homini gravissimum vinculum est, justissimis Dei legibus, *propter antiquum peccatum*, quo nihil est ad praedicandum notius, nihil ad intelligendum secretius" (*De moribus catholicae ecclesiae*, 22). Augustine is here discussing the virtues, and he speaks of "antiquum peccatum" in his treatment of fortitude.

how little feeling they have for the biblical injunction concerning "those who through fear of death were subject to lifelong bondage" (Heb. 2:15).[181] It is not at all strange that striking parallels are apparent between an "explanation" of sin and a kind of "mesmeric" or "tranquillizing" incorporation of *death* in the whole of human *living*. Men have pondered this sovereignty of death, in theoretical and practical terms, and have tried to find a "solution" which mitigates or even eliminates its horror. But these activities are spasmodic at best; furthermore, they clearly run counter to the biblical statements which exclude these very efforts.[182] Man's living is constantly cut short by the strange and disruptive power which has now passed on to "all men." While Paul did not refer to an "inheritance" of sin, he did refer to this universal "passing on" of the regnant, inescapable sovereignty of death (Rom. 5:12, 17). Therefore the question comes: Can this notion be distinguished from what we have commonly called "fatalism"? Is this power an inexorable force — or a *force majeure* — which strikes us with brutality? Can we only bow our heads, acquiesce, and die? Is this what we mean when we say that the devil has "authority" over death? Does he use his "power" as a sinister force and cast a spell upon the earth?

Certainly the concept of "authority" is not the same as "competence," or even "validity." Nonetheless it is "power."[183] It is very well possible to deny the *guilt* of man but not to deny his *death*. Yet the biblical witness sees sin and death as very closely tied up with each other. Sin is regarded as the dark background of death. Therefore when Paul writes of the reign of sin over Adamic humanity, he makes no mention of an inscrutable sovereignty or a fatal calamity but only of that death which has entered *by way of sin* (Rom. 5:12; cf. Gen. 2:17). Death is seen as the "wages" or "reward" of sin (Rom. 6:23; cf. II Pet. 2:15).

We can rightly speak of "wages" at this point. For those who

---

181. Cf. the antithesis in Rom. 8:15.

182. One might ponder the "shadow of death" (Luke 1:79; Matt. 4:16); minding the flesh (referred to as death, Rom. 8:6); being dead through trespasses and sins (Eph. 2:1); and the dying that is appointed for man, "and after that the judgment" (Heb. 9:27).

183. In Heb. 2:14 we read *krátos*. Van Oyen points to the difference between *exousía* and *krátos* (*Christus de Hogepriester*, p. 43). Cf. *TWNT*, III, *s.v. krátos*, on death as "a demonic force" ("eine dämonische Grösze").

do those things which are displeasing to God "deserve to die" (Rom. 1:32). No wonder, then, that death, in Scripture, appears as God's judgment. No wonder that God's warning is sounded in very sober terms. "Desire when it has conceived gives birth to sin; and sin when it is full-grown brings forth death" (James 1:15). "While we were living in the flesh, our sinful passions, aroused by the law, were at work in our members to bear fruit for death" (Rom. 7:5). In very many ways we are referred to this relation of sin and death. Man's death is proclaimed as God's judgment, or the encounter with the holy and the wrathful God. But such a God does not merely *end* man's sinful living in death. Rather, precisely *in* the act of his dying, he calls a man to be responsible.[184]

In recent times the question has been asked if creaturely living is limited by this "border" of death, apart from the influence and the power of man's sin. That is to say: Is man's death a general phenomenon or the natural concomitant of his creaturehood? The whole issue of a "biological death" is very important here. But that question has nothing to do with the "naturalizing" of human life expressed in the biblical phrase, "from death to death." L. Kuilman has answered this question in the affirmative and has added that we must not identify this death with the death which has come into our world by sin.[185] Karl Rahner, in particular, has made a very sharp distinction between "death as guilt and as natural phenomenon." He asserts that "obviously death cannot be the *mere outworking* of the senseless guilt of man."[186] But this does not suggest, for him, that death (as natural phenomenon) is the absolute terminal point of human, creaturely existence. It is the "actual completion of the entire man from within."[187] Rahner judges that the Catholic defense of this "natural" character of death, in addition to death's relation to sin, distinguishes Catholic thought from both Reformational and Jansenist theologies.[188] He is not concerned about the problem of whether a man after "death"

184. In connection with the judgment, as in the case of Sodom and Gomorrah, cf. Amos 4:12, "prepare to meet your God, O Israel!" and Heb. 9:27: "after that comes judgment."
185. Kuilman, *Christelijke Encyclopaedie*, II, 1957², 460.
186. Rahner, *Zur Theologie des Todes (Quaestiones Disputatae, 2)*, 1958, p. 33.
187. *Ibid.*
188. *Ibid.*, p. 34.

(as natural phenomenon) might still continue to exist.[189] Rather he is concerned about man's life in its *maturation and completion*. Rahner contends that natural death might well contain within itself the possibilities of either benignancy or malignancy. At the same time, it is only when death is a calamitous or malignant event that it can rightly be regarded as no "completion" but as rather a "thief in the night."[190] In that event man's death is not merely the "result" but is also the very acme of his sin.

The fact remains that Scripture is nowhere concerned about this matter of "natural mortality." Furthermore, these cogitations on life, sin, and death, and the fruitless question of "What if man had not?" have frequently led to a raft of vague hypotheses. This is the case in both Protestant and Catholic theologies. Very often the motive is a rather wholesome desire to understand better man's sin and death, and is not a compulsive speculation on "man's creaturely life under different possibilities." Nevertheless, we are bound to ask if Rahner and others have rightly conceived the nature of man's creaturely living when they speak of death as "completion" and "maturation." Do they overstep the very boundaries of a legitimate reflection?[191] Come what may, it is very clear that death, in Scripture, is the power of perdition and enmity and the "wages" of man's sin. As a matter of fact, the Scripture speaks of a very different "completion" when it speaks of man's "desire." "Then desire when it has conceived gives birth to sin; and sin when it is full-grown brings forth

189. *Ibid.*, p. 38.
190. *Ibid.*
191. By no one else in Protestant theology is this thought so strongly worked out as by Schilder, in his *Wat is de Hemel?*, 1935, pp. 124ff. (on "the acute change in its necessity"). Schilder speaks of a "border-setting change," in a moment of time (cf. I Cor. 15:52: "in a moment, in the twinkling of an eye" — an indivisible moment); and he takes this as a statement on Paradise (p. 66). He prefers the term "shock" to "catastrophe," since this latter concept causes us to think of something destructive (123). Cf. also his *Heidelbergsche Catechismus*, III, 1950, on the "transference" of man, "even if there had been no sin" (a transition to a higher form of existence, 447; a stepping out of the time-sphere, in Paradise, 449). In all of this Schilder does not wish to speak of "death." A noteworthy (formal) analogy to this "moment of time," as applied to creation, is found in P. J. van Leeuwen (in connection with natural *mortality*). Van Leeuwen interprets Heb. 9:27 in such a way that this "appointment" is included in the creational order (*Het christelijk Onsterfelijkheidsgeloof*, p. 310). On Van Leeuwen (and Barth), cf. further my *Man: the Image of God*, 1962, pp. 253ff.

death" (James 1:15). We shall have to agree with Bultmann that nowhere in Scripture is the effort made "to interpret death as a natural process."[192]

This whole relation of sin and death is set forth in a lucid way in Paul's description of sin as the "sting of death" (I Cor. 15:55-56). Once again, when Paul refers to the "power of death" he does not imply a "fatalism." The "sting" was that which makes death powerful or the venomous "bite" by which death "reigns." "The reality of its awful rule rests on the reality of sin."[193] In such terms as these — "awful rule," "grisly sovereignty," "ugly animosity" — the reign of sin is now made manifest. Yet there is nothing of a fatal power. As in Hebrews 2:14 so here, the preaching of death is in harmony with the omnipotence of grace. Therefore we read: "O death, where is thy sting?" That accent is the same as we have already seen in Romans 5; moreover, for the same reason there is no trace of a fatality. For Paul did not give a "neutral analysis" of the reality of sin and death. He did not interpret these concepts (with all their "inexorability") as fate. He did not regard them in terms of an alien guilt. As a matter of fact the real "enemy" (death) is now set forth in the full light of the Gospel. *Therefore* Paul could speak in defiant terms concerning that enemy. Sin has now been overcome and the atonement is *real*. This does not mean a depreciation of the "animosity" of death; nor does it suggest a strictly human conception. Indeed, Paul's interpretation is not really possible within the limits of mankind. It presupposes that the reality of our "enemy" is illumined by that "great light" which now has come.

Therefore the New Testament gives voice to what seems to be a contradiction. In the glow of the cross and resurrection we hear of him who *has robbed* death of its power and *has brought* "life and immortality to light" (II Tim. 1:10). We hear of the destruction of him who *had* the "power of death" (Heb. 2:14). Nevertheless, there is also a reference to the "last enemy" (viz., death) who *shall be deposed* (I Cor. 15:26). Thus it was not the "fatalism" of sin and death that occupied Paul; it was rather the twoness of "already" and "not yet." The disenthronement of death was described as a present reality;[194] at the same time, there was also an eschatological expectation. When "the mortal

192. *TWNT*, III, *s.v. thánatos.*
193. *Ibid.*, III, *s.v. kéntron.*
194. Cf. also the strong words in Col. 2:15: "disarming," "triumphing."

puts on immortality, *then* shall come to pass the saying that is written: 'Death is swallowed up in victory' " (I Cor. 15:54). In *that* context we hear of Paul's defiance of death. "O death, where is thy victory?" (15:55).

Obviously, we cannot play down the present reality or the eschatological perspective. Grace is apparent in the taking away of man's guilt; and guilt is seen as the "sting" or the venomous "instrument" of death. But the marvel of grace is preached so emphatically that it seems, at times, that our present reality is already a matter of the past and that sin and death (bound up together) are already put to nought in the death and resurrection of Jesus. Immediately, however, it appears that the history of sin and death goes on. Therefore that history must also be regarded in a very concrete manner. In this very twofoldedness we stand before the most important question in any eschatological expectation: What can be the meaning of the "time between" or the period between the reality of the atonement and the parousia? If the atonement is already preached as a "disarming" or "disenthronement," or a taking away of sin as the instrument or "sting" of death, then why do we need an eschatological perspective at all? Why do we need the "not yet" in addition to the "already now"? Do we weaken the "already" when we speak of "not yet"?[195]

The Church has wrestled with these questions throughout her long history. What must we say about the "power of death" or the "final enemy" whose disenthronement is still "to come"? Here the main issue has transcended the level of any fatality. The curse of an inconquerable death has already been broken; but precisely therefore men have asked, with amazement, why death is not totally or finally abolished. The Heidelberg Catechism has put the matter as follows (Q. 42) : "Since, then, Christ died for us, why must we also die?" We read of a "having to die," and yet we are introduced, in the answer, to a very new situation. Surely there is no false romanticism when we speak of the glorious light which breaks forth upon the graves of those who die in Jesus Christ. For "our death is not a satisfaction for

195. Especially in Rom. 8 (after the description of the riches of salvation and sonship), this perspective is very clear: the setting free of creation from the bondage of decay (*phthorá*, v. 21; cf. *mataiótēs*, v. 20). Cf. the *stenázō* of Rom. 8:22, 23; *synōdínein* (8:22); the "waiting" (8:19, 23, 25), and the hope (8:21, 24). On this pericope, cf. J. C. Schreuder, *De Overwinningsgedachte bij Johann Christoph Blumhardt*, 1957, pp. 86ff.

our sins, but only a dying to sins and entering into eternal life."
In other words, it is clear that this new qualification of death is
inextricably tied to the *atonement for our sins.* Therefore in
Question 42 we hear the echo of the words of Paul concerning
our sin as the "sting of death."

In this context a final question must be asked. One may
never underestimate the real "power" of death or the "animosity"
which lasts until the final disenthronement. Furthermore, any
view that waters down the inimical character of death can
only be described as empty and inane and even ridiculous in
view of the elementary facts of man's living. Yet an important
question frequently lurks behind this whole issue of the continuing character of death. What must we say about the *"continuing character" of sin?* Too often the answer given merely
points us to the "facticity" or the "indisputability" of that "continuance." It seems commonplace that there "must be" a continuation of sin in our present dispensation. Yet why need that
be so? We are not asking this question to give a systematic
"rounding off" of the doctrine of our sin. Rather, we are concerned about the real urgency of the question. The question itself is often assigned a merely secondary importance, at best, in
the problems of eschatology. But that only makes our problem
more serious. This whole issue literally cries out for an answer
on the part of those who are serious about confessing their
guilt and seeing the irresistible character of God's indictment.
Here we are speaking of the question of the *end of man's sin.*

CHAPTER SEVENTEEN

THE END OF SIN

WE HAVE called to mind the question of the possibility and meaning of the "not yet" and have seen that theme in the focus of what already is given to us in Jesus Christ. We have said that this question is frequently asked in regard to the continuing character of *death* and not so frequently in regard to the continuing character of *sin*. We must observe, however, that this abiding character of sin is a matter of primary concern in the biblical materials. The scriptural accent is not on some impersonal power in the future but is rather on *our living, our acting, and our destruction now.*

When we listen to the scriptural witness on *death* we should bear in mind the "new situation" in which Paul speaks. The new situation is rooted in the triumph of the Lord and provides the perspective in which our "final enemy" must be seen. Surely Paul could refer to a certain "strangeness" of death and the "destruction of our earthly tent"; yet he also knew of a "building from God" (II Cor. 5:1) and could look upon his own dying as "gain" (Phil. 1:21). In the face of animosity he had "good courage" which was not weakened by the thought of "not yet" (II Cor. 5:6). This courage was based on his outlook for the future: what is "mortal" will be "swallowed up by life" (5:4). There is no break in Paul's thinking between the "already" and "not yet." What *has* occurred and *has* been granted prepares him for the eschaton. Thus a bond of certainty is laid between the present and the future in the "guarantee" of the Holy Spirit (5:5). "For while we are still in this tent, we *sigh* with anxiety; not that we would be unclothed, but that we would be further clothed, so that what is mortal may be swallowed up by life" (5:4).

Behind all these problems of the "already" and "not yet" we must see the further question of a Christian's living *within the "time between."* This is the question of why it is possible

546

and even necessary, in view of what Christ *has done,* to use the
strong language of the confessions concerning the present state
of Christians. Even the "holiest of men," we are told, "while in
this life, have only a small beginning of . . . obedience" (HC,
114). Why must we still "sigh" for deliverance from "this body
of death" (BC, 15)? We may rest assured that there were good
reasons for these accents in the Reformation era. Time after
time we hear of the "continuance" of our sin and our abiding
"weakness" (HC, 127). We are told of the "evil which always
cleaves to us" (HC, 126), and are warned of our flesh as our
mortal enemy, in conjunction with the devil and this world
(HC, 127). The Church, in all these statements, is adjured to
fervent prayer for renewal, "till *after this life* we arrive at the
goal of perfection" (HC, 115). But this confession of continued
sinning is very striking when we read of our being "defended"
and "preserved" in the salvation *already obtained for us* (HC,
31). We are already "raised up" by Christ's power "to a new
life" (HC, 45). In the Belgic Confession we hear that true
faith regenerates a man and makes him a new creature, "causing
him to live a new life, and freeing him from the bondage of
sin" (BC, 24). Yet it seems frequently that our *certainty* of
deliverance and new life is covered by a deep shadow. In the
article on "freedom from the bondage of sin" (BC, 24) we
also read of that corruption which causes all our good works to
be depraved, except for the merits of the suffering and death
of Christ (BC, 24).

Is there a kind of tension in all of this? We are quite aware,
on the one hand, of the work of the Spirit who makes men
spiritually alive, and who heals them and corrects them and
"sweetly and powerfully bends" their will, so that "where carnal
rebellion and resistance formerly prevailed, a ready and sincere
spiritual obedience begins to reign" (CD, III-IV, 16).[1] But we
are informed, on the other hand, of a "not entirely" (CD, V, 1).[2]
Thus we hear of the "remains of indwelling sin" (CD, V, 3) and
even of the incurring of "deadly guilt," and of "grieving" the
Holy Spirit (CD, V, 5). How, then, can these ideas be reconciled?

1. Cf. also the making of man's will *alive* and *good,* where before it was
dead and evil (III-IV, 11).
2. ". . . Though in this life he does not deliver them altogether from the
body of sin and the infirmities of the flesh."

We get at the heart of this issue by pointing to the explicit statement in Lord's Day 44 that the end of sin coincides with "after this life." Particularly in this regard perfectionism has posed disturbing questions. Especially difficult has been the question of the end of this sad history of sin. We sometimes hear that perfectionism proposes the attainability of perfection already in *this life*, and that therefore it is the attempt to view in our present a foretaste of the eschaton; it is the desire to fill up, from the fullness of Christ, the entire "time between." Perfectionism "accelerates" our "dying to sins" (HC, 16) and relates that theme to our present reality. Yet, while this description is roughly accurate, it cannot suffice as a refutation of perfectionism. It is far too hastily and superficially conceived.[3] For obviously, this whole discussion depends on the manner in which we regard the "end of sin." Too often men have taken their polemical starting-point in the "self-evidentness" of those sins which continue in our present dispensation; thus they have tended to give to sin a certain legitimacy in the Christian life. So doing, they have actually inhibited a passion for "holiness, which can be attained in this world."[4]

It would seem that the important fact is that perfectionism has accentuated the *attainability of perfection in this life*. Here the controversy has most frequently turned.[5] But the real issue, in the "end of sin," does not lie on the level of perfection as an attainable reality in the present but on the concept of *perfection itself* or our *being already perfect*. In that issue we are not concerned with the more or less toilsome struggle of believers on their way to "perfection"; we are concerned about the definite moment of the end of sin *in Christ*. There have always been those who have tried to show that in Paul especially there is a definite point at which sin ends. They have said that this is what Paul means when he speaks of our old self as "crucified along with" Christ. Thus our "sinful body" is "destroyed" (Rom. 6:6).[6] Certainly it is meaningful to ask if this was not Paul's intention when he wrote that we are *no longer* "enslaved to sin."

3. On perfectionism, cf. my *Faith and Sanctification*, 1952 — the chapter on the "Militia Christiana."
4. R. Newton Flew, *The Idea of Perfection in Christian Theology*, 1934, p. xv.
5. Cf. H. Bavinck, *Geref. Dog.*, IV, 249: the doctrine of the "perfectibility" ("volmaakbaarheid") of the saints.
6. Cf. Col. 3:3: "For you have died."

For "he who has died is freed from sin" (6:6-7).[7] It would seem that the Church is already "alive to God in Christ Jesus," and is therefore "dead to sin" (6:11).[8]

Is it not a *reality* that Paul describes when he says that "those who belong to Christ Jesus have crucified the flesh with its passions and desires" (Gal. 5:24)? Is not this same reality referred to in the concept of "new creature"? "Therefore, if any one is in Christ, he is a new creation; the old has passed away, behold, the new has come" (II Cor. 5:17). Paul, it would seem, mounts up to this height in view of the reconciliation in him who was made to be sin that we might become the "righteousness of God" in him (5:18-21). Is any more radical transition imaginable than this stepping from death to life (cf. I John 3:14)? What then does the Catechism mean when it tells us that only *death itself* is the "dying to sins" (HC, 42)? How should we understand the statement that perfection is only attainable *"after this life"* (HC, 115)? In the focus of the New Testament we might think that this "dying" is an "end" that comes *too late;* moreover, it would seem to be an impoverishment of the Pauline phrase, "no longer" (Rom. 6:6). Here the problem is not an innate "perfection" of believers but their being *perfected by faith,* or their being genuinely *freed from sin, in Christ.*

The man who sees this "no longer" cannot speak of the "self-evidentness" of sin, or a sin that is "necessary" in our present dispensation. Indeed, if sin were "self-evident" and "inexorable" there would be no reason to "marvel" as we look at ourselves and others. At the same time, still deeper than the question of perfectionism, or its validity, is the question of why the Church has so frequently tied this "dying to sin" with our own death. Is that thought in conflict with the biblical conjoining of the end of sin and the *death of Jesus Christ?* We can only say that the Church did not intend to affirm a lasting "omnipotence" of sin; surely she did not endorse the idea that sin holds a man in its fatal clutches throughout our present dispensation. In her discussion of conversion she spoke of the "mortification of the old man" (HC, 88, 89). According to the Catechism, there is obviously a connection between the "now" and the "later":

7. Cf. H. N. Ridderbos, *Comm. op Romeinen,* p. 131, on sin which is no longer the sphere of power in which believers must still live.
8. Ridderbos, *ibid.,* p. 132: "no longer under its authority"; "escaped from its power."

between what has happened in the whole of life and the end of
sin in death. Furthermore, this "dying" in our present conversion is seen, repeatedly, in the closest relation to the death
of Jesus Christ. Being based upon the death of Christ, it refers
to his death in turn.[9]

The fact remains that the Church, in her confession, has
spoken of not only the future but of our present reality as well.
In that light we must see her expectation of the "abundance"
of grace and the marvellous "end" of sin. The Church has spoken
of the "freedom" from sin and of "no longer" being subject to
the tyranny of sin (Rom. 6). In her own judgment there is
no contradiction between the "end" of sin in Romans 6 and the
"dying to sins" in Lord's Day 16. Certainly this whole issue would
be very difficult if Paul, with an eye to the "end" of sin in Christ,
had taken no account of a further sinning in the lives of believers. In that case a further "ending" would be meaningless
for him. But to make such a claim as this we would have to
misconstrue entirely the relation between the indicative and
imperative moods in Paul. We recall that P. Wernle once
thought that Paul had in mind the total unshackling of sin in
our present; therefore he ascribed to Paul a view "which the
Protestant is accustomed to hope for only in the life beyond."[10]
But Wernle later revised his conception.[11] Precisely because a
believer is crucified "along with Christ," and because he has
freedom in Christ, Paul warned his readers as follows: "Let not
sin therefore reign in your mortal bodies" (Rom. 6:12), and
"do not yield your members to sin as instruments of wickedness" (6:13).

It is completely fallacious to see opposed to each other a
factual "sinlessness" and the "self-evidentness" of those sins
which remain. One could better say that the Christian life, in
the New Testament, is never depicted in such abstract and
sterile categories as these, but only in the living movement and
dynamic of promise and warning: that is to say, the "already"
and the implicit calling to live in the light of that reality. We

---

9. We recall what G. Oorthuys wrote on Lord's Day 33 (concerning the
   "too late" of this dying, in the light of Rom. 6); also his later correction. Cf. my *Geloof en Heiliging*, 1949, p. 98 (omitted in ET).
10. P. Wernle, *Der Christ und die Sünde bei Paulus*, 1897, p. 24. Cf. also
    pp. 89, 104. He saw in this the most remarkable difference. One thinks
    also of P. Althaus, *Paulus und Luther über den Menschen*, 1938 (see
    my *Faith and Sanctification*, 1952, pp. 54f.).
11. Althaus, *op. cit.*, p. 7; so also Bavinck, *op. cit.*, IV, 246.

find a repeated invocation to enter into the order of that "new life" which now has "already come." Therefore every invitation to sanctification is, in fact, a "remembering" or a "recollection." In this attitude of recollection of what *has happened,* and is already *given to us,* every moralism is cancelled by the divine invocation to salvation.

Therefore it is impossible to make a theory of the "inexorable character" of sins that remain, or the corresponding "incapacity" of man. We cannot regard our death as an "ending" or a sudden "breaking off" of our fatal impotence. Nothing which the Church has said on "sins that remain" can possibly be taken as an excuse for our own "powerlessness." Rather, in the light of the salvation which "has come," we can only see our remaining sins as a *riddle.* The apostles were *astonished* when they saw sin within the Church.[12] If anywhere, then certainly here, determinism is broken down[13] and we understand how *much* the "self-evidentness" of sin casts long shadows on the "novelty" of the life in Jesus Christ (II Cor. 5:17). Such a view can only fail to appreciate the apostolic injunction: "Yet I am writing you a new commandment, which is true *in him and in you,* because the darkness is passing away and the true light is already shining" (I John 2:8).

There is no *legitimate room* in the New Testament for the continuation of our sin.[14] There is only room for the power and

---

12. See Chap. 5, above, "The Riddle of Sin." One should read in this connection what Bavinck says about "the truth which may not be unappreciated" (IV, 246), in reference to the manner in which Scripture treats of the glory of believers. For this it "can scarcely find sufficient words."

13. Compare the important article of W. Joest ("Paulus und das luthersche *simul justus et peccator," K.u.D.,* I, 1955, p. 309), who points out that Paul does not speak of "the inevitability" of sin and its "invincibility" (see also pp. 317 and 319). From *this standpoint* he criticizes Luther's "simul justus et peccator." For Luther "extended the confession of factual sin into a dogmatic inevitability concerning sin" (319), so that the "actuality of remaining sin" was motivated by this consideration. (Cf. the statement on the "essential meaning" of remaining sin in the Christian, p. 320.)

14. One can say that the new exegesis of Rom. 7 (as well as chapter 8; e.g., H. N. Ridderbos) is essentially of one piece with this statement. The argument concerning this exegesis can only be rightly resolved if those who refuse to accept it do not proceed themselves from a relativizing of what Paul writes on freedom from the law of sin and death (Rom. 8:2). In reference to Rom. 7, see my *Faith and Sanctification,* 1952, pp. 55ff., and my questions in connection with Ridderbos' exegesis

the blessing of the indicative and imperative. Therefore we have all the more reason to inquire if the Protestant Churches have acted rightly in tying the "end of sin" so closely to our *death*. If we challenge the "self-evidentness" of that conclusion, we may also inquire if this whole concept of "sinning until death" is really quite arbitrary. Indeed, our sins must be confessed even after our reconciliation; our sins must always be confessed. But is there reason to assume that our sins are automatically "removed" in that moment of which the Scripture speaks: "it is appointed for men to die once, and after that comes *judgment*" (Heb. 9:27)? We are reminded of the harvest in which it is manifest in which fields we have sown (Gal. 6:8). We must all appear before the judgment seat of Christ and receive what we have done, whether it be good or ill (II Cor. 5:10). Thus there is an intimate connection between the present and the future. But in this same light, is there any basis for the great consolation and the joyful confession of the "end of our sin"?

The controversy of Rome and the Reformation had a bearing on more than such issues as Scripture and the Church, or papal primacy and the sacraments. It also extended to the most lonely and the most ultimate experience that a believer can undergo. We are aware of the deep rift in the Church on such matters as the Lord's Supper, or the "new covenant" of Christ; yet apart from an "egocentric" or an "individual" eschatology, there are similar radical differences in regard to man's *end*. These differences have had a great influence on both preaching and the work of the pastorate. Here we are referring especially to the Roman Catholic dogma of *purgatory*.

It may seem strange that shortly before the conclusion of our study we pause to examine this doctrine and the main question it poses. Many have judged that this doctrine is simply a bizarre and an individual-eschatological theory which scarcely warrants our serious consideration. But that kind of appraisal rests on a fallacious insight into the motives which have played a role in the formulation of this dogma. The mere fact that Augustine could not free himself from the thought of a *pur-*

in *Gereformeerd Weekblad*, XIV, 41-44 ("Een Nieuwe Commentaar op Romeinen"); also E. Ellwein, "Das Rätsel von Römer VII," *K.u.D.*, I, pp. 247ff.

gatorium[15] does not argue, in itself, for the truth of this doctrine; at the same time, it does caution us to a certain carefulness in our thinking. Bavinck himself has given a lengthy discussion to this matter and has even declared that the notion of "purgation," *on first hearing,* is a "rather attractive" idea.[16] In Catholic dogmatics this concept is brought into a close relation with the necessary process of purification from man's sins. That process begins in *this* life and must still be *ended later.* Therefore any rebuttal of purgatory must give an answer to precisely this motive. Significantly, the same motive has had an influence in certain Protestant theologies.[17] The motive itself accentuates the *gravity of man's sin.*

Now the thing that interests us here especially is that even in the Reformation confessions the sin of man is clearly set in an eschatological perspective. The depravity of man is confessed in Article 15 of the Belgic Confession, and we also hear of God's *forgiveness.* Yet it is stated that man is not permitted to "rest securely in sin," and that a "sense of this corruption should make believers to sigh, desiring to be delivered from this body of death." Guilt is acknowledged in the focus of sanctification and ultimate salvation, and the outlook is unmistakably on the *end of man's sin.* Therefore the controversy is very existential at this juncture and is clearly defined by the expectations which we have of *life after death.*

From the Roman side it is emphatically stated that the purpose of this doctrine is not to emasculate the power and the merits of our only Mediator, Jesus Christ. As a matter of fact

---

15. On Augustine (especially *Enchiridion,* 69), see A. Sizoo, G. C. Berkouwer, *Augustinus over het Credo,* pp. 46ff., particularly on the idea that a purging fire is not unworthy of belief, and the theme of a "slower" or "faster" rate of salvation. See the discussion of the relevant passages in Augustine by J. Gnilka, *Ist I Cor. 3:10-15 ein Schriftzeugnis für das Fegfeuer?,* 1955, pp. 78f.; and B. Bartmann, *Dogmatik,* II, 1932, 492.
16. Bavinck, *op. cit.,* 611.
17. Along with Schleiermacher, Althaus has named K. Hase and R. Seeberg. This influence goes together with the feeling of a "vacuum" between the still-sinful life of man, on his way to sanctification, and his later perfection (cf. P. Althaus, *Die letzten Dinge,* 1933[4], pp. 203f.). All sympathy for purgatory in Protestant theology is tied up with the opposition against a "magical" or sudden change in death. Thus R. Hoffmann contends, with Hase, that the evangelical protest is against the achievement-character of purgatory (masses for the souls of the dead and indulgences), but *not* against "the postulating of any circumstance of purification whatsoever after death" (*P.R.E., s.v.* "Fegfeuer").

the Roman Church was impelled to this idea of a "purifying fire" by the *incompleteness of the Christian's life on earth.* She came to this doctrine in appreciation of the theme of *death* which stalks about "as a thief in the night," even in the lives of those who are baptized, and have done their penance, and who still experience that their sinning is *real* in their own living. For those persons whose lives are already freed from sin there is a *possibility* that the dying of believers takes place "at once." These, then, "pass on" in death, with no delay, to the vision of the triune God.[18] But purgatory is for all those whose lives are not completely cleansed, and whose living shows deficiencies even after their baptism and the confession of their sins.[19] In opposition to the Greek Church, this doctrine was officially endorsed at the Council of Trent[20] and was taken up into the *Professio fidei tridentina.*[21]

Thus the Roman doctrine of purgatory is concerned about "remaining sins" in the lives of believers. It is obviously an attempt to come to a more "organic" or "gradual" conception, or a view in which the access to heaven is not so "sudden." This being the case, the confession of purgatory is not a "threat" of a possible or an ultimate "destruction." We are assured, on every hand, that the final purpose of purgatory is not suffering but cleansing. Furthermore, in this state of purgation a man is not deprived of all love and security.[22]

18. This was affirmed in the "Decretum pro Graecis" at the Council of Florence, 1439 (Denz., 693), in these words: "Illorum animas, qui post baptismam susceptum nullam omnino peccati maculam incurrerunt, illas etiam quae post contractum peccati maculam . . . sunt purgatae, *in coelum mox recipi et intueri clare ipsum Deum trinum et unum sicuti est.*" This statement (in connection with the controversy *ad hoc* between the Roman Catholic and Greek Catholic Church) appears in large part already in the "Professio fidei Michaelis Palaelogi" (*Concil. Lugdunense,* II, 1274; Denz., 464). On the controversy with the Greek Church, see *Theologisch Woordenboek* (Brink), III, 1958, *s.v.* "Uiterslee" (4643ff.), and the important study of Joseph Gill, *The Council of Florence,* 1959, especially pp. 117ff. (On the uncertainty of the Greek side, pp. 120 and 272.)

19. "Si vere poenitentes in Dei caritate decesserint, antequam dignis poenitentiae fructibus de commissis satisfecerunt et omissis, eorum animas *poenis purgatoriis post mortem purgari*" (Denz., 693). In connection with this: "prodesse eis fidelium vivorum suffragia." Cf. already Denz., 456.

20. Cf. Denz., 780, 840, 950, 983.

21. Cf. *ibid.*, 998: "constanter teneo purgatorium esse."

22. In the "Errores Martini Luther" (the bull, "Exsurge Domine," 1520;

Yet there is an open acknowledgment, in Catholic theology, of a "cleansing" through a temporary suffering. This is the case as we look at those sins for which believers have not yet repented, or on account of which they are still regarded as "imperfect." When we seek to know the foundation of that doctrine (and its tremendous importance for an eschatological view of life) we are usually told that we must not search for concrete scriptural passages where "purgatory" is explicitly mentioned.[23] The background of this doctrine lies in its presupposition of a *necessary repentance*. There is a need for repentance even after the guilt of sin is forgiven. Indeed, repentance can only reach its final goal in the *completion of our being one with Jesus Christ*.[24] Therefore the purification of. this life is continued after death,[25] and this entire process, according to Catholic theology, is nothing but the *benefit of God*. Meanwhile, the Church militant on earth participates in this same purification.[26]

Now clearly, it is a very serious matter to take issue with this kind of appeal to a necessary repentance. We could reject the motive of repentance in purgatory from a simplistic standpoint which conceives of an immediate "passing over" from this life to the glory of the *visio Dei* and the riches of God's immaculate presence. We could then continue to hold to God's "punishment" and the revelation of Christ's "judgment seat" and still do less than justice to the real gravity of these images. The antinomian

Denz., 778), the following thoughts are rejected as errors: "animae in purgatorio non sunt securae de earum salute"; also, "animae in purgatorio peccant sine intermissione" (Denz., 779). Bartmann, *op. cit.*, II, 496: "The comfort of the doctrine of purgatory is very great."

23. To the extent that scriptural references are given, Matt. 12:32 and I Cor. 3:10-15 are seen as especially important. On I Cor. 3, cf. Gnilka, *op. cit.*, where the proceedings at the Council of Florence are referred to in detail. In the *Theol. Woordenboek*, III, 4643, we read: "In the Holy Scripture we find no clear data on purgatory, but in the light of the tradition it is certainly possible to indicate certain scriptural lines." Cf. Bartmann, *op. cit.*, II, 493: the weight of the argument lies in *tradition*.

24. *Theol. Woordenboek*, III, 4647.

25. *Ibid.*

26. Besides the intercession in the Church triumphant we think here of the Catholic doctrine concerning the "missarum sacrificia, orationes et eleemosynas et alia pietatis officia" (Denz., 464, 693). Cf. Trent (Denz., 983): "animasque ibi detentas fidelium suffragiis, potissimum vero acceptabili altaris sacrificio iuvari."

has too easy a time of rejecting "final purification." But the Reformation, on the other hand, could not take that easy way out. In no sense did the Reformers want to underestimate the power of the havoc which sin has wreaked in the inner depths of man's living. They did not see this "passing over" from our present life to future glory as an "intelligible" or "self-evident" matter within the bounds of our sanctification. Therefore the Reformers were faced with the very same problems of the end of man's sin.

We see, then, that it is more than a facetious comment when Bavinck finds something "rather attractive" in the Catholic dogma, if only at first hearing.[27] We must not ignore the fact that the doctrine of purgatory is treated in connection with the *visio Dei*. According to the teaching of Jesus, the vision of God is only possible, before the resurrection, for those of a "pure heart."[28] Only they "see God" (Matt. 5:8).[29] Therefore this vision is impossible, as a sudden event, for those who are not entirely cleansed of their old defilements and have not yet entered into the new correlation of holiness and the *visio Dei*. How can a life in which perfection is not yet found be transported immediately to the vision of God? This process of "dying to sins" must first be completed in the man who is still "on his way" and has not yet reached his final goal.

We must observe the motive in the Reformers' rejection of purgatory, and the manner in which they conceived of this "passing" or real "ending" of man's sin. Were they insensitive to the "necessity" of this final benefit of God? How could that fit in with their doctrine of total depravity? What about the

27. Bavinck, *op. cit.*, IV, 611; cf. also K. Dijk, *Over de Laatste Dingen*, I, 1951, 24.
28. This thought was already articulated in 1274 (Denz., 462), in opposition to Pope John XXII, who ("as theologian," *Theol. Woordenboek*, III, 4643) denied this *visio* before the resurrection. Benedictus XII affirmed the doctrine of the Church in *De visione Dei beatifica et de novissimis*, and regarded this as a *visio* of the "divina essentia." "Nulla mediante creatura in ratione objecti visi se habente, sed divina essentia immediate se nude clare et aperte eis ostendente" (Denz., 530). John XXII later retracted (*Theol. Woordenboek*, II, 2571). See especially G. Hoffmann, *Der Streit über die selige Schau Gottes*, 1331-38, 1917, pp. 87f. Calvin took sharp issue with the view of John, who (in his judgment) "openly asserted that souls are mortal and die along with bodies, until the day of resurrection" (*Inst.*, IV, 7, 28). But this is certainly a faulty interpretation.
29. Cf. Ps. 11:7: "the upright shall behold his face." Also 17:15.

completion of this process begun on earth? The Christian life, it seems, is a pressing forward to the end or the *télos* or the summit of perfection. Paul himself could write as follows: "Let us cleanse ourselves from every defilement of body and spirit, and make holiness perfect in the fear of God" (II Cor. 7:1).

One could try to modify the Roman doctrine by assuming that God, and God alone, suddenly "draws a line," and that this process of "purifying ourselves" is suddenly broken off, as it were, before it has reached its fruition and full sanctification. But what can we make of the words of John: "And every one who thus hopes in him purifies himself as he is pure" (I John 3:3)? When we talk about "divine forgiveness" it is possible to drive a wedge, in an unbiblical manner, between our justification and sanctification, and to take little stock of the biblical admonitions to purity. But where then is our vocation to holiness precisely because of our forgiveness? What do we make of the urgent and concrete warning addressed to the Church: "Strive for peace with all men, and for the holiness without which no one will see the Lord" (Heb. 12:14)?

Calvin took exception to the dogma of purgatory and saw it as merely the attempt to speak of an atonement for sins apart from the blood of Jesus Christ. This "satisfaction" would have to be paid for, after death, by the souls of those who died.[30] But because of his prejudice at this point, and because he centered attention on the relations of purgatory, penance and satisfaction, Calvin could not give a sharp expression to the manner in which this "passing" from life to glory must be seen. He had an intuitive sense that the dogma of purgatory was not in tune with the *sola gratia et sola fide,* but he hardly considered the relation of holiness or purity and the *visio Dei.* It is only in recent times, after many a Catholic exposition, that Bavinck has given a fuller discussion to this topic. He sees this dogma entirely in the light of those who, after baptism and repentance, are still not cleansed and made perfect, and cannot be admitted immediately to the blessed vision of God. Bavinck correctly notes, according to Rome, that these persons come to the place of purification "not to earn new virtues and merits but to clear away the obstacles which prevent their entrance

30. *Inst.,* III, 5, 6. Cf. also Calvin's *Articles of the Faculty of Sacred Theology at Paris,* Art. 17, against the "alarming" defense of this article of purgatory.

to heaven."[31] Therefore purgatory is a place of "maturation"; it comes in lieu of a sudden transfer from continued sinfulness to the *visio Dei*. Bavinck's answer to this very "existential" doctrine was not merely that Scripture never speaks of a purgatorial fire.[32] He also criticized the implications for the justification of sinners.[33] He did not ignore the importance of sanctification but he pointed, in truly Johannine fashion, to the reality of eternal life and the *immediate portion* in heaven for those who believe.

God does not need to wait, according to Bavinck, for the increase of man's good works. Certainly he conceded that there is a certain modesty in the expression "O blessed purgatory"; yet Bavinck also saw that attitude as foreign to the biblical eschatological expectation.[34] It is far from clear, in the dogma of purgatory, in what manner the final cleansing must actually take place. Furthermore, it is unintelligible precisely why the remaining corruption in man (or the very reason for his purgation) is unable to bring him to new sins. Rome has always denied that possibility; but here the element of satisfaction enters again as an intrinsic factor in the dogma and practice of purgatory. It enters in such a way that we wonder if "purgatory" is really a *purgative fire* at all or a matter of *vindication*.[35]

Thus there are real problems in the dogma of purgatory as the "end of man's sin." In fact, we find a peculiar problematic at the very foundation of this concept. The "fire" is not merely the "blessing" and "benefit" of God, but there is also an enduring of suffering. Purgatory is "purgative" because it is also "punitive." For that reason it causes a man to repent of his sins. All of this is clarified when we see that in purgatory no further "merits" are gained.[36] If they were, then purgatory

31. Bavinck, *op. cit.*, IV, 586.
32. *Ibid.*, 611.
33. *Ibid.*, 613.
34. *Ibid.*, 614.
35. *Ibid.*, 615. Cf. K. Rahner, "Bemerkungen zur Theologie des Ablasses," *Schriften zur Theologie*, II, 1955, 207ff.
36. When Rahner (*ibid.*, 206ff.) sees this purgation as not so much juridical as a process of maturation, "through which gradually all the powers of human beings are slowly integrated in the fundamental decision of the free person," he adds immediately that this does not mean "that a man who has died is still capable of a supernatural meriting of a real increase in grace" (207).

would show an "organic" continuity with the dogma of the meritoriousness of works. But seeing that purgatory does not have this function, it receives a *new function* and is closely bound up with the petitions and penitential exercises of the Church for the souls of lost men. Even in Catholic theology we notice something of the strangeness of those problems in the doctrine of the end of man's sin. We find a recognition of tremendous difficulties,[37] especially in the *manner* of cleansing apart from man's own personal merit. Therefore we are far from surprised when the newer Catholic theology wrestles with the meaning of purgatory and all its implications and results.

We see that especially in the case of Hans Urs von Balthasar. In Von Balthasar's view the "fire" of the "Day of the Lord" (as we find in I Corinthians 3; note especially verse 13) should be seen in the context of meeting the Lord when he appears in his final judgment. Von Balthasar contends that, biblically speaking, we must not refer to two judgments but to only *one*. Purgatory is a "dimension of the judgment, as the encounter of sinners with the flaming countenance of Christ."[38] In that concept Von Balthasar finds an important point of reference for ecumenical dialogue. Moreover, it is striking that he speaks of a "reduction" here in regard to eschatology.[39] He pleads for an eschatology that renounces the rights of a closed system,[40] or an eschatology in which we no longer arrogate to ourselves "a knowledge concerning the outcome of judgment."[41] It is hard to see, however, in what way this "reduction" is compatible with the traditional dogma of purgatory.[42] For in the traditional

---

37. Cf. Pohle, *Dogmatik*, III, 614; and Bavinck, concerning Oswald (IV, 615). Gill reiterates (in translation) a comment of Cardinal Cesarini at the Council of Florence, in reference to the serious nature of the discussion. ". . . And because there seemed to be many difficulties, I almost despaired" (*op. cit.*, p. 285).

38. H. U. von Balthasar, "Eschatologie," in *Fragen der Theologie heute*, 1957, p. 411, where he refers to Rev. 1:14: "his eyes were like a flame of fire."

39. *Ibid.*, p. 406.

40. *Ibid.*, p. 414.

41. *Ibid.*

42. Von Balthasar himself in no way desires to deny purgatory. When he speaks of what belongs in eschatology "to the unshakable treasury of faith," which cannot be doubted, he also cites the "instantaneous entrance of the soul into the eternally blessed vision of God, after the expiation of all temporal punishments and venial sins in the place of purification" (*ibid.*, p. 405). Yet it seems to me that the "reduction" is

view this "knowledge" *is* presupposed and *does* function in a
very concrete way in the practice of the Church. This is apparent
in the basic distinction between the "saints" and those who are
"not yet fully purged." The unanimous confession of the Christian Church is that Jesus will come again to judge the living
and the dead; furthermore the reference to a "making known"
before the judgment seat of Christ is essential to the eschatological witness of the entire Christian community. But the dogma
of purgatory presupposes and systematizes that "knowledge"
in a way that goes far beyond this simple statement and far
beyond the opinions which Von Balthasar has expressed.

Recent Catholic theology has seen the last judgment as the
meeting with Christ and a single encounter. At the same time,
it makes a rapprochement to the official ecclesiastical dogma.
Purgatory is now drawn into a "dynamic relation to the final
judgment."[43] Within the strictures of the official dogma this
could hardly be conceived in any other way; yet the important
thing is that purgatory is still defended and the controversy
is still in force. One may grant that Von Balthasar is mainly
concerned about the eschatological meeting with Jesus Christ.
He rejects the concept of the "processes of judgment as a knowable object" and fastens attention on the coming Lord in his
holy judgment. But unfortunately, alongside that encounter and
its implied responsibilities, we also find the possibility and
reality of a necessary expiation. Therefore we also find a further
satisfaction for man's sin. Here the very core of sanctification is
at stake. Purgatory is still assigned a place within the structure
of the Catholic dogma of penance. Indeed, the dogma of purgatory is the strongest proof of Rome's definitive choice for an
analytic doctrine of justification. In such a doctrine, of course,
it is simply impossible to speak of a "purification" alone. No
wonder that Rome *also* speaks of penitential exercises, punishment, and a "satisfaction" for man's sins.

In opposing that idea the Reformation was concerned first
of all with the scriptural evidence. Since man's dying and "pass-

---

very important here — as also in his views of the *apokatástasis* (*ibid.*,
p. 413; cf. *Die Gottesfrage des heutigen Menschen,* 1956, p. 204). In this
latter conception he denies any *Umdeutung* in the content of faith,
though essentially he comes to an interpretation which strongly reminds
us of the "existential" interpretation of faith in P. Althaus (*Die letzten
Dinge,* pp. 180f.; *Die christliche Wahrheit,* II, 1948, 489f.).
43. Von Balthasar, *Fragen,* p. 411.

ing on" are outside our own experience, there can be no attempt to speculate here but only to speak in terms of the witness of Scripture. The Reformers denied that any scriptural support whatever can be offered for the dogma of purgatory. They regarded the appeal to I Corinthians 3:10-15 as a piece of dogmatical exegesis.[44] But they also emphasized, from Scripture itself, how much man's *earthly life* is referred to as the locus of his sanctification. In *this life* the grace of God is evident. Man's earthly living is the sphere in which believers are called forth to fight the good fight; it is precisely in living that they experience the power of God's grace, and name the name of Jesus, and resist all unrighteousness. Thus the "here and now" is set forth in Scripture, in all its decisive significance, and great seriousness, as the place of tremendous transition from "death to life." The gravity of man's sanctification and the "imperative" implied in the "indicative" must be seen as the "structure" of the New Testament admonition. Certainly the dogma of purgatory does not intend to soften down this feature of sanctification; moreover there *is* the "possibility" of an immediate transfer to the *visio Dei*. But the doctrine of purgatory *does weaken*, as a matter of fact, our calling to sanctification in earthly living. In the "purgatorial fire" there is still a final "cleansing" after death. Therefore there is a possibility which can easily lead to an ethical relativism.[45]

Protestant churches have boldly confessed the concept of an *immediate end of sin* (HC, 47, 115). They did not wish to deny their own sinfulness or to show a prideful optimism as they

44. Cf., e.g., Diekamp, *Katholische Dogmatik*, III, 447; also Bartmann, *Dogmatik*, II, 489. Pohle (III, 612) does not refer to this text. In our own time J. Gnilka is of the opinion that the I Corinthians passage does *not* refer to purgatory and that all efforts to combine this text with the fire of cleansing "take on an essentially false aspect and are therefore unjustified" (*op. cit.*, p. 118). The concern here is with the *dokimázein* of one's work (testing; "Prüfung"), and is not with "cleansing." But this exegesis has no influence on Gnilka's own conviction concerning purgatory. "The dogma of purgatory is raised above all doubt" (128). For the exegesis of I Cor. 3:10f., cf. Calvin, *Inst.*, III, 5, 9, and H. Bavinck, *Geref. Dog.*, IV, 612 (ignis revelatorius, probatorius), whose exegesis is quite similar to that of Gnilka.

45. Such a relativism played a role, as an argument, already in the opposition of Bessarion at the Council of Florence. Bessarion took issue with the doctrine of purgatory on the basis of its prompting a slovenliness or false desire for ease. Cf. C. Bovée, "De Eschatologie op het Concilie te Ferrara-Florence," *Studia Catholica*, 1949, XXIV, p. 179.

looked forward to the "harvest" of earthly living. But they
spoke of "immediate" in regard to the salvation in which we
are called to sanctification and the preservation of our inheritance. The Protestant churches pointed to the apostle Paul who
knew (not in pride but in trust) that his own dying would be
"gain." For he would *then be with Christ* (Phil. 1:21, 23; cf.
II Tim. 4:8). When we view perfection as a "precondition"
which must be met or realized in penance and punishment,
we set on end the order of God's salvation. Even in the course
of his own lifetime, Jesus Christ had communion with sinners
and publicans. Therefore the Pharisees criticized him severely
in terms of their own correlation of a legalistic obedience and
a communion with others. It is exactly the Pharisees who show
this "precondition" of a righteousness and holiness in all its
rigidity. But the scriptural perspective on the *visio Dei* is of a
very different sort. Surely we are called to sanctification, and
certainly this is the meaning and the consequence of forgiveness, or of being crucified and dead with Christ. Yet when the
godless man is justified and is challenged with that call there is
no more concern for an "expiation of his sins." There is only
concern for a *new living* in the strength of him who *takes our
sins away.*

Because of this "taking away," the Reformation celebrated
the gracious gift of God at the end of man's earthly pilgrimage.
It did not appeal to an anthropological analysis of the depths of
man's living in his transiency and struggle. It appealed, much
rather, to the firm conviction that after this life and the "crisis"
of man's death (Heb. 9:27) there can be no "penance" for
earthly inadequacies. Therefore the Reformation refused, with
an eye to man's death, to distinguish between those who are
saints already and those who are not yet "purified." In its
eschatology it riveted its attention on man's *earthly living* as a
preparation for his ultimate confrontation with God. The
Reformation churches confessed that this is the confrontation
with him who receives the judgment from his Father. Therefore
the conviction of an "immediate" end was not a boastful estimation of their own living. It was only a trusting dependence on
him who frees us from all condemnation (HC, 38). In this regard the very silence of Scripture, concerning this "final purification," was seen as a matter of the greatest significance and the
deepest consolation for the Church.

The struggle of faith is geared toward this end of sin and the expectation of God's activity in the "time of our departure."[46] Here we are not suggesting an evolutionary process of sanctification which man has in his own hands. The victory is already promised but is only realized in the struggle of faith and prayer for the power of the Holy Spirit. The power of the Spirit is necessary "that we may not succumb in this spiritual warfare but always offer strong resistance, till at last we obtain a complete victory" (HC, 127; *donec integram tandem victoriam obtineamus*). The attainment of that "victory" is not divorceable from the activity of God and is not the product of our effort. Therefore the Canons speak of a cleansing by the blood of Christ and a faithful *preservation* until the end. Christ, having preserved his saints, "even to the end," shall "at last bring them, from every spot and blemish, to the enjoyment of glory in his own presence — *coram se* — forever" (CD, II, 8).

"*Coram se.* . . ." In these words we find both the perspective and the *gravity* of our Christian living as we look forward to the "end of sin." *Also the gravity.* For the biblical expectation of glory is pictured in terms of a "making known" of our earthly existence.[47] When we read of the judgment seat of Christ we also read of this "revelation" or "making known." Each man will receive "according to what he has done in the body" (II Cor. 5:10).[48] In this eschatological focus, the good of man is now seen in contrast to his evil,[49] and the relation between his *life and judgment* is made clear. Paul sees a reward for walking in the ways of him whose judgment seat is now made manifest. Therefore our reaction against the meritoriousness of works should not entice us to play down the compelling force of this proclamation of reward.[50] Every antinomianism is excluded by the nature of *this reward*: for the reward is one and the same

46. Cf. II Tim. 4:6: *ho kairós tḗs analýseōs;* also Phil. 1:23 and II Pet. 1:14 (*apóthesis*). Also the directive — at this impending departure — for the congregation (v. 15).
47. Cf. the judgment according to works (see my *Faith and Justification*, 1954, pp. 103ff.).
48. Cf. F. W. Grosheide, *Comm. op 2 Corinthiërs*, p. 153; the idea of *appearance* ("verschijnen") does insufficient justice to the power of *phanerōthḗnai*.
49. Greek: *phaúlos* — the "less worthy" ("minderwaardige," Grosheide, *ibid.*).
50. Cf. my *Verdienste of Genade?*, 1958; and the answer of Walgrave, "Verdienste en Genade," *Studia Catholica*, 1959, and P. Kreling, "Verdienste als Genade," *Jaarboek Werkgenootschap van Kath. Theologen*, 1959, pp. 110ff.

as the manifestation of the judgment seat of Christ. That is to say, the reward is evident in the way of God's great *benefit* and calling to sanctification. This is also the way in which God's enmity against man's sin is consummated and is more and more apparent (even for believers) in its meaning and necessity.

In regard to this end of sin as a "dying to sin" there has always been a tension between a so-called "individual" and a so-called "cosmic" eschatology. The tension goes hand in hand with one's outlook on his individual end and his expectations for the parousia of the Lord. It is not possible here to discuss this important eschatological issue.[51] But it *is* possible to be duly warned against an idle curiosity, or any relativizing and minimizing of the parousia and the resurrection of the dead. We must continue to regard our "end" as a "dying unto sin." Therefore Calvin cautioned his readers against a vain inquisitiveness.[52] He stressed that "all things are held in suspense until Christ the Redeemer appear,"[53] and that "God postpones the crown of glory until that time."[54] Yet, while emphasizing the provisional character of our present living and the expectation of the full revelation of glory, he also spoke of the rest which we have already now in Christ.[55] In the light of the Gospel it is possible for believers to reflect on their individual "end" apart from a theoretical synthesis of an "individual" eschatology and the parousia. It is possible to reflect apart from an "egocentric

51. Cf. my *Man: the Image of God*, 1962, Chap. 7, and R. J. van der Meulen, *Het Vagevuur*, 1956, pp. 19ff.
52. See especially Calvin, *Inst.*, III, 25, 6: "porro de intermedio earum statu curiosius inquirere neque fas est." It is "stultum et temerarium de rebus incognitis altius inquirere quam Deus nobis scire permittat."
53. "Ita omnia teneri suspensa donec Christus appareat redemptor." Already in his *Psychopannychia* Calvin laid strong accent on this expectation of the great future.
54. "Et gloriae coronam eousque differat." *Inst., loc. cit.*
55. When Calvin in his *Psychopannychia* speaks of those who "expectant, quod nondum habent, nec finem suae felicitatis attigerunt," he also adds: "Cur *nihilominus* beati sunt? Quia et deum agnoscunt sibi propitium et futuram mercedem eminus vident et in certa expectatione beatae resurrectionis acquiescunt." Rest is here linked up with expectation. Cf. M. Schulze, *Meditatio futurae vitae*, 1901, p. 75, who speaks of a "meditatio futurae vitae post mortem"; also Quistorp, *Calvins Eschatologie*, 1940, p. 86. Calvin himself gives no "synthesis" but speaks, on the one hand, of an "enjoyment," and on the other of a "pax imperfecta." But, "cum certo expectent, quod desiderant, clarum et quietum esse desiderium." Cf. "*donec* impleta fuerit dei gloria" (*Psychopannychia;* in reference to Ps. 17:15).

individualism." In so doing we do not seek to escape from the "impotence" and "senselessness" of our earthly living but to realize the *end of our sin* and the *final resting in our joy.*

The peril is very real that a reference to this rest, and our eager expectation, could lead us to an individualistic or an egotistical anticipation of our "end." Here the Church's confession of the resurrection of the flesh and the second coming of the Lord has always been a necessary corrective. Without any onesidedness there is room — precisely because of our expectation of the great future — to be interested in our own personal living. We may still be concerned about our own salvation (Heb. 2:3; Phil. 2:12) and must still work for the completion of our struggle, through the gracious benefit of God. Thus every egocentrism is placed under the sharp criticism of the eschatological judgment; and that judgment extends all the way to the refusal of a glass of cold water to "one of the least of the brethren" (Matt. 25:40, 45). Beyond the shadow of a doubt, this transcending of onesidedness, as we look to the "end," is the marvel of the Holy Spirit. We can never make such a marvel psychologically "explicable." Indeed all of us are inclined toward "dilemmas," at this point, which well up from the inner structure and bent of our own sinful hearts.

Yet if our interest in the "end of sin" is legitimate, any thought of an expectation that is overshadowed by a post-mortal "fire of purification" can only be excluded. Once again, the silence of the Scripture speaks volumes. One could reject the idea of purgatory from a haughty pride or an optimistic concept of the "end" of man's sin. But there is another approach which avoids all superficial analyses. We think of that passage in I Corinthians 3 which is constantly appealed to by the supporters of the purgatory doctrine. If only we could have a meeting of minds on the meaning of such terms as "through fire" (v. 15) and the "Day" which will be "revealed with fire" (v. 13)![56] Perhaps then our thinking on the "end of sin" would lose its superficial ring! We would then be able to recall — in a vital sense — that our "testing" is made perfect in connection with, and only on the basis of, the foundation which *Christ himself has laid* (3:11).[57] The biblical accent on "the revealing fire"

56. Greek: *hōs diá pyrós* (v. 15); *hē gár hēméra dēlōsei hóti en pyrí apokalýptetai* (v. 13).
57. Cf. 3:13. The fire will "test" (*dokimásei*) what sort of work each one has done. Cf. *TWNT*, VI, s.v. *pyr*.

is seen in connection with the preaching of the *Gospel*. Yet we
hear, in these very words, a critical warning in the midst of
perils that surround our thinking concerning our *"testing"* in
the Day of judgment. In that day *everything, absolutely everything, will be revealed*.[58] Every possibility of escape, apart from
our own faith, will then be denied. There can be no room for
a pessimistic or an optimistic excuse.

Therefore we look forward to that "Day" in which all will
be made clear. Without any "individualism" at all we speak of
the "end of our sin" and our "dying unto sin." At the same
time, the legitimacy of that kind of talk is only obvious when
we return constantly to the death of another Man — namely,
the *death of Jesus Christ*. For the death of Jesus Christ is always,
and shall ever remain, the content of the Church's preaching and
her only sure *outlook for the future*.

It is at this point that we understand the real power of
Paul's "corporative" mode of thinking. In the same context in
which he speaks eschatologically of a "making known" before
the judgment seat of Christ (II Cor. 5:10), and a "fear of the
Lord" (v. 11), he also utters that remarkable insight that
"one has died for *all; therefore all have died"* (v. 14). We
need not wonder that the "all" no longer live for themselves
but for him who "died and was raised" for them (v. 15). In
that great reversal of life and death — death and life — our
outlook on the "end" receives its most decisive stamp. This is
the way to the *integra victoria,* or to being with God. This is the
way to the *visio Dei*.

But the injunction still remains (as we see in the great
Council of Florence)[59] that we must be "as he is" (cf. I John
3:2). The benefit of God will take way all misunderstanding
within the *visio Dei* when the "pure in heart" see *God*. For
God will then no longer *remember our sins*. We need not
speculate if there is room in the eschaton for a human "remembering" of this nightmare of sin which is now both "known" and
"driven away." This much we can say, that in the vision of the
Apocalypse the *ecclesia triumphans* brings glory to the *Lamb*
(Rev. 5:12). Beyond the least doubt, the "end of sin" is the
fulfillment of the prophecy that the *Lamb* shall be in the

---

58. Cf. Calvin, *Inst.,* III, 5, 9, on the presence of the Lord; especially — I
    Cor. 3 — "when his truth gleams forth" (preaching).
59. Denz., 693. "Sicuti est."

midst of God's throne (Rev. 7:17). "So Christ, having been offered once to bear the sins of many, will appear a second time, *not to deal with sin* but to save those who are eagerly waiting for him" (Heb. 9:29).

The "second appearance" of Christ ("not to deal with sin") is not a depreciation of the original, sinless advent.[60] Instead, we are referred to the *absolute end of our sin* in his "second coming." Thus the second appearing is "without a reference to sin,"[61] or without the burden of what had once been borne,[62] or without this original "connection."[63] Christ's second coming stands in the light of his first. Therefore it is a gracious and unfathomable manifestation of the end of sin in the *visio Christi*. This eschatological proclamation does not eliminate but only *enhances* our attention for our present earthly living. It impresses upon us the deepest meaning of sanctification. We cannot penetrate the reality of our "individual end" or the final parousia; yet *both of these* are infused with comfort by the overwhelming brightness of Christ's death. Here we find a comfort which manifests itself in every niche and cranny of our earthly living. It manifests itself till one day we experience a *new and full estrangement from the power of our sin*. To that end Jesus Christ once died, broken and alone, outside the gates of Jerusalem.

Such, then, is our expectation of him who will also be seen in the future *as he is*. For he is "of purer eyes than to behold evil" and is not able to "look on wrong" (Hab. 1:13). He is the One who shall open the fountain of cleansing in his boundless mercy, and "cut off the names of the idols from the land" (Zech. 13:1-2). He is the One who will give water to the thirsty *without price,* from the "fountain of the water of *life*" (Rev. 21:6).

60. Cf. Heb. 4:15 and 7:27, and almost all commentaries, unanimously.
61. O. Michel, *Komm.*, p. 216.
62. H. van Oyen, *Christus de Hogepriester,* p. 177.
63. F. W. Grosheide, *Comm.*, p. 223.

INDEX OF PERSONS

INDEX OF SCRIPTURES